Kiril Feferman

THE HOLOCAUST IN THE CRIMEA AND THE NORTH CAUCASUS

This publication has been supported by a grant from
The Conference on Jewish Material Claims Against Germany

This book is published with the support of the Jacob and Clara Egit
Foundation for Holocaust and Jewish Resistance Literature,
Toronto, Canada, through the Histadrut Assistance Fund.

This book is published with the aid of the Alexander D. Dushkin
Fund of the Institute of Contemporary Jewry,
The Hebrew University of Jerusalem.

Kiril Feferman

THE HOLOCAUST IN THE CRIMEA AND THE NORTH CAUCASUS

Yad Vashem ★ Jerusalem
The International Institute for Holocaust Research
The Moshe Mirilashvili Center for Research on the Holocaust
in the Soviet Union

Kiril Feferman

The Holocaust in the Crimea and the North Caucasus

Language Editor: Alana Holland
Production Editor: Leah Goldstein

P.O.B. 3477, Jerusalem 9103401, Israel
publications.marketing@yadvashem.org.il

ISBN 978-965-308-505-3

Typesetting: PageUp

Printed in Israel by Offset Natan Shlomo Press

To My Family

Table of Contents

Abbreviations

AOK – *Armeeoberkommando*
CSpSd – *Chef der Sicherheitspolizei und der SD*
CSPSS – Chief of Security Policy and Security Service
EM – *Ereignismeldung*
FG – *Feldgendarmerie*
FK – *Feldkommandatur*
HQ – Headquarters
HSSPF – High SS and Police Leader
KDRK – Committee for the Affairs of Religious Cults *(Komitet po delam religioznykh kul'tov)* under the USSR Council of Ministers
KTB – *Kriegstagebuch*
Korück – Kommandant des rückwärtigen Armeesgebietes
MbOg – Meldungen aus den besetzten Ostgebieten
NKVD – People's Commissariat of Interior (*Narodnyi komissariat vnutrennikh del*)
OK – *Ortskommandatur*
OSR – Operational Situation Report
PNTWC – Proceedings of the Nuremberg Trial of War Criminals
RMfdOg – *Reichsministerium für den besetzten Ostgebeiten*
RSFSR – Russian Soviet Federative Socialist Republic (*Rossiiskaia Sovetskaia Federativnaia Sotsialisticheskaia Respublika*)
SNK SSSR – Council of People's Commissars of the USSR (*Sovet Narodnykh Komissarov SSSR*)
TB – *Tätigkeitsbericht*
TsK VKP(b) – Central Committee of the All-Union Communist Party (Bolsheviks) (*Tsentral'nyi komitet Vsesoiuznoi kommunisticheskoi partii (bolshevikov)*)
VKP(b) – the All-Union Communist Party (Bolsheviks) (*Vsesoiuznaia kommunisticheskaia partiia (bolshevikov)*)

Acknowledgements

This book has long been in preparation. My first sally into the field was a Ph.D. thesis in Hebrew, on which I worked from 2000 to 2008. Over the next years, my thesis – reworked and rewritten in book format in English – took its final shape in the course of my interaction with Yad Vashem Publications.

This study could not have been written without the use of many archives and libraries in Israel and abroad. I would like to thank in particular the staff of the Yad Vashem Library and the Yad Vashem Archives, as well as the staff of the archives and libraries of the United States Holocaust Memorial Museum (USHMM). I benefited considerably from consulting the holdings of the Department of Oral History at the Institute of Contemporary Jewry in the Hebrew University of Jerusalem, the State Archive of the Russian Federation in Moscow, the Russian State Archive of Social and Political History in Moscow, the Russian State Military Archive in Moscow, the State Archive of the Autonomous Republic of the Crimea in Simferopol', the National Archives in Washington, and the Bundesarchiv in Berlin.

I have received encouragement, often far beyond the call of duty, from a very large number of people — including academic colleagues, librarians, archivists, editors, and secretaries — who have helped me along the long road to completing this book. I remember with feelings of deep gratitude the innumerable acts of goodwill and work well done. Unfortunately, I can only mention a small percentage here by name.

During my years at the Hebrew University, I was guided wisely by my mentors, Professor Mordechai Altshuler and the late Professor David Bankier (*z"l*). As for my time at Yad Vashem (roughly from 2002 to 2010), I am indebted to friends and colleagues at the International Institute for Holocaust Research, Professor Dan Michman (also from Bar Ilan University), Dr. Iael Nidam-Orvieto, Dr. Lea Prais, Dr. Leonid Rein, Dr. Arkady Zeltser, and Shlomit Shulchani for their comments and suggestions. At the marvelous archives of Yad Vashem I could always count on the unflagging support and advice of Masha Yonin, Mary Ginsburg, and Dr. Nataly Zeifman. I also owe much to Katya Gusarova and other staff members at the Department of the Righteous Among the Nations, as well as my colleagues at the Commission for the Designation of the Righteous Among the Nations. I would also like to acknowledge the professionalism of the staff at the Yad Vashem Publications Department, especially Yasmine Garval, as well as Leah Goldstein, who saw this book through to its happy conclusion.

At the USHMM, where I was a fellow in 2005, I was fortunate to have benefited from the close friendship and constant advice of Vadim Altskan, Dr. Michael Gelb, and Dr. Steven Sage. At the Russian Holocaust Center in Moscow, where I worked from 2010 to 2014, I was always been able to turn for professional advice to my friends, Chairman of the Center Professor Ilya Altman and the head of its archival department, Leonid Terushkin.

I would also like to thank Professor Zvi Gitelman from the University of Michigan at Ann Arbor, Professor Yaacov Ro'i from Tel Aviv University, Professor Dan Shapira from Bar Ilan University, Mikhail Tyaglyi from the Ukrainian Holocaust Center, and Dr. Mikhail Kizilov and for their invaluable encouragement, help, and advice.

A special word of thanks goes to my language editor Alana Holland, who patiently and meticulously edited this manuscript for publication.

I could not have completed my research without the following prizes, grants, and fellowships: the Egit Prize for Holocaust and Jewish Resistance Literature administered by the Israeli Trade-Union (2013); the Dushkin Prize for the publication of a book on the Holocaust in Eastern Europe from the Hebrew University of Jerusalem (2012); the Nevzlin Center Prize for outstanding doctoral dissertations on East European Jewish history (2008); the prize of the Ben Zvi Institute for the Study of Jewish Communities in the East (2006); the David Pritel Prize for outstanding research on Soviet Jewry from the Hebrew University of Jerusalem (2006); the Charles H. Revson Fellowship from the Center for Advanced Holocaust Studies at the USHMM (2005); the Danek Gertner Yad Vashem Ph.D. Scholarship (2004); the Ph.D. Prize of the World Sephardic Federation (2004); fellowships of the Institute of Contemporary Jewry, the Hebrew University of Jerusalem to an outstanding Ph.D. student (2004, 2007); and the Yad Vashem Studies Prize (2002 and 2004). The publication of this book was also made possible through the support of the Claims Conference.

A number of the chapters began life as public lectures that subsequently appeared in written form, in earlier and shorter versions upon which I have expanded, updated, and improved. Chapter One was originally a lecture delivered at the Mémorial de la Shoah in Paris (2007). Parts of Chapters Two and Four, which first appeared in the volume *Repression and Revival: The Jews of the Former Soviet Union* edited by Zvi Gitelman and Yaacov Ro'i (Lanham, MD, 2008), have been updated. Chapter Four A first appeared in *War in History* 15, no. 1 (January 2008). The part of Chapter Five dealing with Mountain Jews is an expanded and significantly revised version of lectures first given in Hebrew at conferences at the Ben Zvi Institute in Jerusalem in 2002 and at the Bar Ilan University in Tel Aviv in 2004. It was first published in *Holocaust and Genocide Studies* 21, no 1 (Spring 2007). The part of Chapter Five dealing with Karaites appeared in *Nationalities Papers* 39, no. 2 (March 2011).

Last, but not least, this study owes much to the personal background I inherited from my family. The family of my grandmother Fania (Feiga) (*z"l*) on mother's side lived in Ikor, one of the Jewish *kolkhozy* in the Crimea, in the 1920s and the 1930s. They survived the Holocaust by moving from the Crimea to Moscow in the late 1930s in pursuit of better employment opportunities. In the fall of 1941, when the Wehrmacht was rapidly advancing towards Moscow, they fled for Siberia. The other side of my family, consisting of my father Mark and grandmother Hanna (*z"l*), was fortunate to have been evacuated from besieged and starving Leningrad in the winter of 1942 and relocated to Siberia. Another important and randomly designated direction of evacuation from Leningrad was the North Caucasus, where thousands of unfortunate Jewish evacuees were killed by the Germans in the summer-fall of 1942. Both of my grandfathers, Avram (Abraham) (*z"l*) and Aron (Aharon) (*z"l*), fought against the Germans in the ranks of the Red Army and were wounded. The combination of two feelings shared by my family, near-escape and the fight for one's life, played an important role in my formation as individual and scholar and influenced my choice of this research subject.

Finally, I wish to thank my parents, Mark and Nellia, my grandmother Fania (*z"l*), and my wife Nastia who have followed the genesis and progress of this book with astonishing patience. It is dedicated to them. Last but certainly not least, I would like to dedicate this book to the memory of thousands of my brothers and sisters who were murdered during the Holocaust in the Crimea and the North Caucasus.

Introduction

The German invasion of the Soviet Union, code-named Operation Barbarossa, began on June 22, 1941 and was the largest German military operation of World War II.[1] Scholars are still divided on how to regard the German invasion. On the one hand, Hitler had always contemplated the overthrow of the Soviet regime. Anti-Bolshevism had remained his most profound emotional conviction, and he carefully began to plan the German invasion in mid-summer 1940.[2] On the other hand, the Soviet occupation of Bessarabia and northern Bukovina in June 1940, the consequent proximity of Soviet forces to the Romanian oil fields, on which Germany heavily depended, and the aggressive deployment of the Red Army were weighty factors in Hitler's decision to deliver a large-scale preemptive strike against the Soviet Union.[3] Yet, once this decision was made, the forthcoming strike transformed into a total war of annihilation against "Judeo-Bolshevism."[4]

1 On Operation Barbarossa, see Christian Hartmann, *Operation Barbarossa: Nazi Germany's War in the East, 1941–1945* (Oxford: Oxford University Press, 2013); and Ernst Klink, "The Conduct of Operations," in Horst Boog et al., *The Attack on the Soviet Union*, vol. 4 of *Germany and the Second World War* (Oxford: Oxford University Press, 1998), pp. 525-762.

2 Jürgen Förster, "Hitler's Decision in Favour of War against the Soviet Union," in Boog et al., *The Attack on the Soviet Union*, pp. 13-51.

3 Geoffrey Robert, "Stalin's Wartime Vision of Peace, 1939-1945," in Tymothy Snyder and Ray Brandon, eds., *Stalin and Europe: Imitation and Domination, 1928-1953* (Oxford; New York: Oxford University Press, 2014), pp. 233-263; David E. Murphy, *What Stalin Knew: The Enigma of Barbarossa* (New Haven, CT: Yale University Press, 2006).

4 Jürgen Förster, "The Relation between Operation Barbarossa as an Ideological

The German invasion caused deep population displacement within the territories still under Soviet control but endangered by the Germans. Hundreds of thousands of Soviet citizens, among them many Jews, left their houses in pursuit of safety.[5] Some were moved eastwards under the government-organized evacuation program,[6] whereas many others moved away on their own. The Crimea and the North Caucasus, the two regions investigated in this study,[7] were deeply affected by

War of Extermination and the Final Solution," in David Cesarani, ed., *The Final Solution: Origins and Implementation* (London: Routledge, 1994), pp. 85-102. On the connections between Jews and Bolshevism in the Nazi worldview, see Lorna Waddington, *Hitler's Crusade: Bolshevism, the Jews and the Myth of Conspiracy*, revised ed., (New York: I. B. Tauris, distributed by Palgrave Macmillan, 2012), especially pp. 173-208.

5 Solomon Schwarz, *Evrei v Sovetskom Soiuze s nachala Vtoroi mirovoi voiny (1939-1965)* (New York: American Jewish Working Committee, 1966), pp. 45-47.

6 After a short period of turmoil at the very beginning of the war, the central Soviet government made the decision to ensure the withdrawal of industrial, agricultural, and human resources from German reach. According to the directives, evacuation of populations was aimed first and foremost at: 1) safeguarding lives of the Party (Soviet and security agency functionaries of different levels and their families); 2) moving industrial (primarily of military character) and agricultural capacities and their employees; and 3) transferring all conscript-age men away from German reach. Decree of the Soviet Government (*Sovnarkom*, also SNK SSSR), "O poriadke vyvoza i raspredeleniia liudskikh rezervov i tsennogo imushestva," June 1941, Yad Vashem Archives (YVA), JM/24678. The evacuation of population was intended to be a highly centralized process. It was coordinated by the Council for Evacuation (*Sovet po evakuatsii*), which was created on June 24, 1941 in accordance with the joint decision of the Soviet Government and the Central Committee of the Communist Party. Attachment to the decision of the SNK SSSR, "Status i struktura Soveta po Evakuatsii," June 24, 1941, YVA, JM/24678.

7 The terms "Crimea," "Crimean peninsula," and "the peninsula" are used interchangeably throughout the paper. Unless stated otherwise, the terms "Caucasus" and "North Caucasus" are used interchangeably and denote for the purposes of this study: 1) Krasnodarskii *krai* (territory), including the autonomous *oblast'* (region) of Adygea; 2) a larger part of Ordzhonikidzevskii (renamed Stavropol'skii until 1935 and from 1943 onwards and referred to in this book as such) *krai* (territory), including the autonomous *oblast'* (region) of Karachaevo; 3) the Autonomous Republic of Kalmykiia; 4) the Autonomous Republic of Kabardino-Balkariia; and 5) a part of the Autonomous Republic of North Ossetiia, i. e. those areas that were occupied by the German army in the second part of 1942.

these developments, which changed the profile of the Jewish population there.

Despite increasingly fierce Red Army resistance, the Germans advanced deeply into Soviet territory. The Wehrmacht swept into the Crimean peninsula in the fall of 1941 and retained it (completely or partially) until the spring of 1944. The German army first penetrated the North Caucasus in the fall of 1941, conquering part of the Rostov district, including the city of Rostov-na-Donu, but were forced to retreat as a result of the Soviet counter-offensive. Yet, during the second offensive in the summer of 1942, the Wehrmacht occupied a considerable portion of the North Caucasus. The Germans finally lost control of this region in the winter of 1943.

Immediately after the German army occupied a certain area, special assignment forces (*Einsatzgruppen*) usually entered.[8] The

Generally speaking, contemporary Soviet names of territorial units (republic, *krai, oblast', raion*) are preserved in the study, unless specially stated. All of the chapters but one deal with the Ashkenazi Jews, unless specified otherwise, while the discussion of non-Ashkenazi groups and Karaites is relegated to a separate chapter. The terms "Russians" and "Slavs" refer basically to the same group of the local population, which included Russians, and to a lesser extent, Ukrainians. Other ethnic groups, usually Greeks, Armenians, and Bulgarians, were numerically negligible.

8 In March 1941, Hitler entrusted Himmler with the implementation of special tasks in the field of security within the framework of Operation Barbarossa. Richtlinien auf Sondergebieten zur Weisung 12 (Fall Barbarossa), March 3, 1941, IV Q, OKW/WFSt/Abt.L in Gerd R. Ueberschär and Wolfram Wetter, eds., *Der deutsche Überfall auf der Sowjetunion: "Unternehmen Barbarossa" 1941* (Frankfurt am Main: Fischer Taschenbuch, 1991), p. 247. In accordance with this decision, Himmler formed the special-duty squads of the Security Police and SD (*Einsatzgruppen*), which were solely authorized to deal with the elements alien to the German Reich in the Eastern territories, that is, in the occupied areas of the Soviet Union. As defined in the March 26, 1941 agreement between Himmler's deputy, SS-*Obergruppenführer* Reinhard Heydrich, and Army Quartermaster-General Eduard Wagner, the *Einsatzgruppen* would perform their tasks "on their own responsibility," but were "subordinated to the armies in relation to movement, supply, and accommodation." In addition, they had to notify "in a timely fashion" the respective army commander about their operations. Befehl des ObdH, Generalfeldmarschall von Brauchitsch betr. Regelung des Einsatzes der Sicherheitspolizei und des Heeres, April 28, 1941, OKH/Gen. St.d.H./Gen.Qu in ibid., p. 258. See also Klaus J. Arnold, *Die Wehrmacht und die Besatzungspolitik in den besetzten Gebieten der Sowjetunion: Kriegführung und Radikalisierung im*

main task of these units was to kill the all the Jews, alongside all others deemed hostile to the Reich. Other German forces, including the regular army, were also involved in murdering the Jews. Sometimes, the Germans employed local collaborators to persecute and exterminate the Jews. Both the Crimea and the North Caucasus were handled by the *Einsatzgruppe* D (EG D) In both of these regions the Jews went through similar treatment, which usually involved registration, forced labor, and, within a period of four-six weeks, killing operations. However, some Jewish doctors or members of mixed families were granted exemptions, usually limited in time. In addition, the Germans faced a special problem in the Crimea and the North Caucasus in dealing with those whom they regarded as racially non-Jewish but related to the Judaic religion.

I have selected these two specific regions as the primary focus of my study, as opposed to other more familiar regions of Eastern, Central, and Western Europe, because Western scholarship has hitherto failed to explore the unfolding of the Holocaust in the Crimea and the North Caucasus. In the instances in which Western scholarship has dealt with this region, it has overlooked those aspects which are analyzed in this book, such as evacuation, Jewish responses, and the attitudes of the local population and clergies. The components of Western scholarship regarding the Holocaust will be discussed in the following sections and chapters.

Although two distinct regions with separate character, culture, and history, I chose to incorporate them into the same thematic framework for this study. The Crimea and the North Caucasus have much in common. Historically, they are situated on what was and still remains Russia's ethnic frontier – hence, similarities in the composition of general (for example, the noticeable presence of

"Unternehmen Barbarossa" (Berlin: Dunker & Humboldt, 2004), pp. 124-140.

On the *Einsatzgruppen*, see Hilary Earl, *The Nuremberg SS-Einsatzgruppen Trial, 1945-1958* (Cambridge: Cambridge University Press, 2009), pp. 4-8; *Die Einsatzgruppen in der besetzten Sowjetunion 1941/42: Die Tätigkeits- und Lagerberichte des Chefs der Sicherpolizei und des SD*, Peter Klein, ed. (Berlin: Edition Hentrich, 1997) – in particular, Andrej Angrick, "Die Einsatzgruppe D," in ibid., pp. 88-110.

non-Slavs professing Islam) and Jewish (presence of non-Ashkenazi groups) populations. The fact that both regions are situated on the Russian ethnic frontier (and the similar population composition and Islamic presence that this entailed) proved to be a powerful common denominator, which alone suffices as reason to analyze the two regions in one study. Furthermore, during the war, the Crimea and the North Caucasus also had war-time specific similarities, such as the fact that they were both handled by the EG D. Perhaps most central to this study is my assertion that German policies regarding the Crimea and the North Caucasus were affected by two diametrically opposed trends, which I call "Southern" and "Eastern."[9] The "Southern" policy reflected German understanding of the complex character of the region and tended to consider local and international ramifications of the German population policies in the Crimea and the North Caucasus. In contrast, the "Eastern" policy orientation appeared to reflect their otherwise total neglect of local and international factors. In other words, this second "Eastern" policy appeared to exemplify tough Nazi racial and economic-based attitudes toward the local population. This proved the most decisive factor for combining the two regions into one research study.

At the same time, it should not be overlooked that the regions in question were subjected to different impulses prior to and during the Holocaust (for example, the presence of Cossacks in the Caucasus, the different timing of German entry into the regions, etc.). These similarities and dissimilarities will be enlarged upon further on in the book. Ultimately, I came to realize that a better understanding of the Holocaust in the Crimea and the North Caucasus is often best served by comparing those aspects of the Holocaust which seemed to me most compatible, such as evacuation, proximity to battlegrounds, heterogeneous Jewish and non-Jewish populations, and the presence of Islam. In other cases, I felt that direct comparison overlooks unique developments in

9 I expand upon these concepts in my article, "Looking East or Looking South? Nazi Ethnic Policies in the Crimea and the Caucasus," in Anton Weiss-Wendt, ed., *Eradicating Differences: The Treatment of Minorities in Nazi-Dominated Europe* (Newcastle: Cambridge Scholars Publishing, 2011), pp. 103-118.

the Crimea and the North Caucasus necessary for understanding the subject. In some instances I dealt with both regions separately, even if it involved unavoidable repetitions.

The Crimean peninsula and the North Caucasus were occupied as a result of different military campaigns. Of particular interest to the concern of this study are the intensity and length of warfare, involvement of Soviet partisans, and behavior of the local German command. This book analyzes how the singularity of warfare in every region affected the course of the Holocaust there, most specifically whether it accelerated it or not, and whether it triggered different Jewish responses. Furthermore, the smooth functioning of the killing machine would have been impossible had it not been for some sort of cooperation between the *Einsatzgruppe* and the German army. This study addresses the question of how this cooperation evolved, upon what it depended, and to what degree the relations between the Wehrmacht and the *Einsatzgruppe* affected the course of the Holocaust in the Crimea and the Caucasus.

The Germans occupied the Crimea in late 1941 and the Caucasus in mid-1942. The drive into the Crimea may be regarded as one of the last achievements of Blitzkrieg (lightening war) when swift German victory in the whole Eastern campaign still seemed possible. At this time, German attitude and policies toward many Soviet nations remained ruthless. In 1942, when all talk of a quick victory in the war was abandoned, the German policy toward the local population in the North Caucasus became more moderate. This study also explores whether and how the factor of time influenced the German *Judenpolitik* in the regions under review.

Alongside Ashkenazi Jews there were sizable communities of Karaites[10] and Krymchaks[11] in the Crimea, as well as Mountain

10 Karaites (Heb. *Qara'im, Benei Miqra, Ba'lei Miqra*; Ar. *Qarā'iyyūn*): Jewish sect that came into being during the middle of the ninth century. Its doctrine is characterized primarily by its denial of the Talmudic-rabbinic tradition. Daniel Lasker et al., "Karaites," in Michael Berenbaum and Fred Skolnik, eds., *Encyclopedia Judaica*, 2nd ed., vol. 11 (Detroit: Macmillian Reference USA, 2007), p. 785.

11 Krymchaks: Jewish ethnic and linguistic community. Before the Russian

Jews[12] in the Caucasus. For the purposes of the study these are henceforth collectively referred to as "special Jewish groups." During the Holocaust (specifically during the German occupation), local population authorities treated each of these groups in ways which often diverged from the policy applied toward Ashkenazi Jews. The factors that affected the German policies toward these groups were often singular, and differed from what influenced German policy in the "Jewish Question" as a whole. Consequently, what happened to "special Jewish groups" during the German occupation and the way in which those events unfolded turned out to be different from the Holocaust as the Ashkenazi Jews experienced it.

In terms of ethnic origin, these peoples emerged as a result of the northward migration of some Oriental Jewish communities from Ottoman Turkey, Persia, and the countries of the Mediterranean basin; the conversion of local people into Judaism; and, to a much smaller extent, the arrival of individual Ashkenazi Jews. In terms of religion, both Krymchaks and Mountain Jews practiced a full-fledged version of Rabbinical Judaism different than the Karaites' version of Judaism. The essential point is that these groups faced the danger of physical annihilation when the Germans occupied the southern part of the Soviet Union precisely because of their links to Jewry and Judaism.

invasion of 1783, they called themselves *Yehudi* (Jew) or *srel balalary* (sons of Israel). Only at a relatively late period, in late 19th-early 20th century – did they begin to call themselves Kirymchakh, from the Russian Krymchak. The name Krymchaks (Crimean Jews) first appeared in official Russian sources in 1859. Evidently, the term was coined to distinguish the Krymchak Jews in the Crimea from the Karaites who lived in the same region, and also from the Ashkenazi Jews who had moved there. Michael Zand, Dan Kharuv, and Shmuel Spektor, "Krymchaks" in ibid., vol. 12, p. 357. Prior to World War II, the Krymchaks lived mainly in the Crimean peninsula.

12 Mountain Jews: Jewish ethnic and linguistic group living mainly in Azerbaijan and Dagestan. The name "Mountain Jews" emerged in the first half of the 19th century, when the Russian Empire annexed those territories. It is believed that the name derives from "mountain of the Jews" (*Chufut* or *Dzuhud Dag* in the Tat language), an ancient name of Dagestan indicating its large Jewish population. Mordekhai Neishtat and Michael Zand, "Mountain Jews," in ibid., vol. 14, p. 579.

Another special Jewish group selected by the criteria of origin is refugees, i.e., those who came to the Crimea and the North Caucasus from other parts of the Soviet Union after the outbreak of the war. By the time of the German occupation, some Jews in the Crimea and most Jews in the North Caucasus were refugees. With respect to the Holocaust, they had particular concerns resulting from their pre-evacuation experience, their adaptation to a new setting, and, finally, their particular vulnerability during the Nazi assault. This study concerns itself with the development of German attitudes toward these Jewish refugee groups in the regions, the degree to which the future of these groups depended on the German policies toward similar groups elsewhere, and whether they were affected by the attitudes of the local population, as well as the Holocaust of the rest of the Jews.

The non-Jewish population in the Crimea and the Caucasus was made up of Slavs (including Cossacks[13]) and various Muslim and Christian peoples. There are several questions concerning their relationship with the Jews in the regions, including on what their attitude toward the Jews depended and the extent to which the different population segments were either loyal to or disappointed with the Soviet authorities (and the resulting repercussions it had on their behavior toward Jews). A further concern is the impact of the "German dimension" in their attitudes toward Jews, and whether that impact was of decisive importance or simply confirmed the arguably pre-existing local antisemitic tendencies. Finally, there is the question of how the religious factor, namely the stance of Christian and

13 Cossack: Russian *Kazak* (from Turkic *kazak* – "adventurer," or "free man"), member of a people dwelling in the northern hinterlands of the Black and Caspian Seas. They had a tradition of independence and eventually received privileges from the Russian government in return for military services. In the 19th and 20th centuries, the Russian Empire employed Cossacks extensively to suppress revolutionary activities. During the Russian Civil War (1918-1920), the Cossacks were divided. Those in southern Russia formed the core of the White armies there; about 30,000 fled Russia with the White armies. Under Soviet rule, Cossack communities ceased to function as administrative units. Serhii Plokhy, *The Cossack Myth: History and Nationhood in the Age of Empires* (Cambridge; New York: Cambridge University Press, 2012).

Muslim clerics and prominence of religious propaganda, affected the behavior of the lay people during the Holocaust. Thus, this study addresses the interplay of prewar conditions in the Crimea and the North Caucasus and the German occupation policy based on several factors.

Exploration of the Holocaust in the Crimea and the North Caucasus is a difficult task. Typically, only a few weeks passed after the arrival of the Germans before the killing operations began, and few (Jews and non-Jews alike) succeeded in fully grasping what transpired. As a result, researchers are confronted with a grave problem. That is, the German onslaught on the Crimean and the Caucasian Jews was too quick, and, therefore, the available testimonies and documents on the Holocaust in the Crimea and the Caucasus are scarce and terse.

Historiography

For many decades, Soviet exploration of what happened to the Jews in the Crimea and the North Caucasus confined itself to general notions of German victimization of all Soviet people.[14] Rich primary sources kept in the Soviet archives were inaccessible to researchers until the last days of the Soviet Union. At the same time, it should be emphasized that few Western scholars exhibited interest in the subject, and those that did made contributions focusing mostly on the fate of non-Ashkenazim and Karaites.[15]

14 Nikolai Maiorov, "Krasnodarskii protsess" in Mikhail Karyshev, ed., *Neotvratimoe vozmezdie: Po materialam sudebnykh protsessov nad izmennikami rodiny, fashistskimi palachami, i agentami imperialisticheskih razvedok*, 2nd enl. ed. (Moscow: Voenizdat, 1987), pp. 173-183; Khadzhi Ibragimbejli, "Krakh gitlerovskogo okkupatsionnogo rezhima na Kavkaze," in Aleksei Basov and Georgii Kumanev, eds., *Narodnyi podvig v bitve za Kavkaz: Sbornik statei* (Moscow: Nauka, 1981), pp. 265-285; Ivan Kondranov and A. Stepanova, eds., *Krym v period Velikoi Otechestvennoi voiny, 1941-1945: Sbornik dokumentov i materialov* (Simferopol': Tavriia, 1973).

15 Mordechai Altshuler, *Jews of the Eastern Caucasus: The History of the Mountain Jews from the Beginning of the Nineteenth Century* (Hebrew) (Jerusalem: Ben Zvi Institute for the Study of Jewish Communities in the East, Institute of Contemporary Jewry, the Hebrew University of Jerusalem, 1990); Idem., "Nazi

This is problematic because previous scholarship ignores the Holocaust of the majority of the Ashkenazi Jews, which was the largest Jewish group in the region. A growing interest in the research of the Holocaust in the Crimea and the Caucasus emerged only within the last fifteen years, which can be ascribed to the opening of previously closed Soviet archives.

Some recent studies exploring larger topics deal with various aspects of the Holocaust in the Crimea and the North Caucasus but because of their general nature do not zero in on specific regional developments. The most relevant research includes overarching studies by the German scholars Norbert Kunz and Andrej Angrick on the German occupational regime in the Crimea and the EG D, respectively.[16] Their studies provide important insight into the German policies toward the Jews in the Crimea and the North Caucasus. However, Angrick's study covers the activities of only one, albeit important, German agency involved in the extermination of the Jews (EG D), while Kunz's focuses on the most final stage of the annihilation of Jews. Also of note are the comprehensive researches by Dieter Pohl, Manfred Oldenburg, and, to a lesser extent, Klaus Arnold on the role of the Wehrmacht in the occupation of the Soviet territories.[17] Some

Attitudes towards the Jewishness of the 'Mountain Jews' and other Oriental Communities (Hebrew)," *Peamim* 27 (1986), pp. 5-17; Shmuel Spector, "The Karaites in Nazi-dominated Europe in the Light of German Documents (Hebrew)," *Peamim* 29 (1986), pp. 90-108; Idem., "The Holocaust of the Krymchak Jews during the Nazi Occupation (Hebrew)," *Peamim* 27 (1986), pp. 18-27.

16 Norbert Kunz, *Die Krim unter deutscher Herrschaft 1941-1944: Germanisierungsutopie und Besatzungsrealität* (Darmschtadt: Wissentschaftliche Buchgesellschaft, 2005), pp. 179-204; Andrej Angrick, *Besatzungspolitik und Massenmord: Die Einsatzgruppe D in der südlichen Sowjetunion 1941-1943* (Hamburg: Hamburger Edition, 2003), pp. 324-361.

17 Dieter Pohl, *Die Herrschaft der Wehrmacht: Deutsche Militärbesatzung und einheimische Bevölkerung in der Sowjetunion 1941-1944* (München: Oldenbourg, 2008); Manfred Oldenburg, *Ideologie und militärisches Kalkül: Die Besatzungspolitik der Wehrmacht in der Sowjetunion 1942* (Köln: Böhlau Verlag, 2005); Arnold, *Die Wehrmacht und die Besatzungspolitik*.
For studies focusing on specific regions, see, for example, Wade Beorn Waitman, *Marching into Darkness: The Wehrmacht and the Holocaust in Belarus* (Cambridge, MA: Harvard University Press, 2014). For studies focusing on

of their findings, most specifically those exploring the behavior of the Wehrmacht towards Jews and German food policy in the occupied territories, are of direct relevance to the central concern of current research.

Two additional comprehensive studies by Yitzhak Arad and Ilya Altman (Il'ia Al'tman) analyze the Holocaust of the entire Soviet Jewry.[18] Their books have been translated from their original Hebrew (Arad) and Russian (Altman) into English and German and recently published. Although extremely important to the study of the Holocaust in the Crimea and North Caucasus, Arad's and Altman's works do not focus on the specific local dimension of the regions under review.[19]

The rest of the studies are of a smaller scope and address geographically or thematically narrower topics.[20] Of special importance is the prolific work by local Crimean researchers in the last fifteen years. They have published collections of materials on the Holocaust in the region based on Crimean and German archives, as well as those of the United States Holocaust Memorial Museum (USHMM). Gitel' Gubenko made the first step in this direction, and her book based on local Crimean archival holdings dealing with the Holocaust in the Crimea was

specific Wehrmacht personalities, see, for example, Erik Grimmer-Solem, "'Selbständiges verantwortliches Handeln'. Generalleutnant Hans Graf von Sponeck (1888-1944) und das Schicksal der Juden in der Ukraine, Juni-Dezember 1941," *Militärgeschichtliche Zeitschrift* 72, no. 1 (2013): pp. 23-50.

18 Yitzhak Arad, *The History of the Holocaust: Soviet Union and the Annexed Territories* (Hebrew) (Jerusalem: Yad Vashem, 2004), pp. 373-389; Il'ia Al'tman, *Zhertvy nenavisti: Kholokost v SSSR, 1941-1945* (Moscow: Fond "Kovcheg," 2002), pp. 287-289.

19 Yitzhak Arad, *The Holocaust in the Soviet Union (Comprehensive History of the Holocaust)* (Jerusalem: Yad Vashem; Lincoln: University of Nebraska Press, 2009), pp. 202-212; 286-298; Ilya Altman (Il'ia Al'tman), *Opfer des Hasses: Der Holocaust in der UdSSR 1941-1945,* translated by Ellen Greifer (Gleichen: Muster-Schmidt, 2008), pp. 336-349.

20 Kunz, 2005; Norbert Kunz, "Die Feld- und Ortskommandaturen auf der Krim und der Judenmord 1941/1942," in Wolf Kaiser, ed., *Täter im Vernichtungskrieg; der Überfall auf der Sowjetunion und der Völkermord an den Juden* (Berlin: Propyläen, 2002), pp. 54-70; Mikhail Tiaglyi, "The Role of Antisemitic Doctrine in German Propaganda in the Crimea, 1941–1944," *Holocaust and Genocide Studies* 18, no. 3 (2004): pp. 421-459.

published in 1991.[21] The book has since been republished in English with important amendments.[22] Over the last five years, three more collections of documents on the Holocaust in the Crimea have been published in the region.[23] In 2005, a Russian scholar, Elena Voitenko, produced the first study of the Holocaust in the Caucasus, which remains the only dissertation written in the Russian Federation that deals exclusively with the topic of the Holocaust.[24] She made extensive use of the materials published under Russian scholarship but disregarded German and Jewish (Yiddish and Russian language) sources. In addition, her study only presents the German onslaught against the Jews and does not mention other weighty aspects, such as Jewish responses to it or the behavior of the local population. Another relevant study in Russian, a book by Sergei Linets, presents a detailed exploration of many aspects of the German occupation of the region, with the notable exception of the Holocaust.[25]

In Western historiography, the Holocaust in the North Caucasus has been overlooked and remains largely so today, with the exception of the aforementioned books by Angrick and Oldenburg dealing with EG D involvement in the Holocaust in the Caucasus[26] and the activities of the 17th Army in the region, respectively.[27] It is worth mentioning that all the articles on the

21 Gitel' Gubenko, *Kniga pechali* (Simferopol': Redotdel Krymskogo Upravleniia po pechati, 1991).

22 Idem., *The Book of Sorrows* (New York: GStanislav Company, Inc., 2003).

23 Boris Gel'man and Aleksandr Glubochanskii, eds., *Kholokost: Katastrofa v Krymu*, (Simferopol': Predstavitel'stvo "Soknut-Ukraina," 2004); Mikhail Tiaglyi, ed., *Kholokost v Krymu: Dokumentalnye svidetel'stva o genotsyde evreev Kryma v period natsistskoi okkupatsii Ukrainy (1941-1944)* (Simferopol': BETs "Khesed Shymon", 2002); Liubov' Kravtsova and Mikhail Tiaglyi, eds., *Peredaite det'iam nashim o nashei sud'be* (Simferopol': BETs "Khesed Shymon," 2001).

24 Elena Voitenko, "Kholokost na iuge Rossii v period Velikoi Otechestvennoi voiny (1941-1943)" (PhD diss., Stavropol'skii gosudarstvennyi universitet, 2005).

25 Sergei Linets, *Severnyi Kavkaz nakanune i v period nemetsko-fashistskoi okkupatsii: sostoianie i osobennosti razvitiia (iiul' 1942-oktiabr' 1943)* (Rostov-on-Don: Severo-Kavkazskii nauchnyi tsentr vysshei shkoly, 2003).

26 Angrick, *Besatzungspolitik und Massenmord*, pp. 545-670.

27 Oldenburg, *Ideologie und militärisches Kalkül*, pp. 297-306.

Holocaust in the region have been published by local authors. In this respect, Kamykiian researchers played a critical role in developing Holocaust study of the region by publishing the only specialized collection of analytical materials on the Holocaust in their area,[28] witness memoirs of the German occupation,[29] and collections of wartime Soviet documents from the Krasnodar and Stavropol' archives.[30] Of final and particular importance is the *Encyclopedia of the Holocaust on the Territory of the USSR* by the Russian Holocaust Research Center, edited by Ilya Altman (first edition published in 2009, second in 2011).[31] It contains a substantial amount of critical factual information on the Holocaust in various sites in the Crimea and the Caucasus emphasized in the current study.

Finally, it is worth mentioning Jonathan Littell's *The Kindly Ones*. Opinions are divided among critics about the literary merits of the book and whether the book, originally written in French[32] and later translated into English[33] and a host of other languages, is a great work of literary fiction. Despite the debates, the novel

28 L. B. Shaldanova, "Kholokost na territorii Kalmykii" in Kalmytskii institut gumanitarnykh issledovanii Rossiiskoi akademii nauk et al., eds., *Velikaia Otechestvennaia voina: sobytiia, liudi, istoriia* (Elista: Dzhangar, 2001), pp. 171-183; Svetlana Tavanets, "Chislennost' zhertv Kholokosta na territorii Kalmykii" in ibid., pp. 177-183.

29 Evgenii Krinko, *Zhizn' za liniei fronta: Kuban' v okkupatsii (1942-1943)* (Maikop: Adygeiskii gosudarstvennyi universitet, 2000); Totraz Balikoev, *Narody Severnogo Kavkaza v gody Velikoi Otechestvennoi voiny (1941-1945)* (Vladikavkaz: Severo-Osetinskii gosudarstvennyi universitet im. K. L. Khetagurova, 2000); German Belikov, *Okkupatsiia: Stavropol', Avgust 1942-ianvar' 1943* (Stavropol': Fond dukhovnogo prosveshcheniia, 1998).

30 Aleksandr Beliaev and Irina Bondar', eds., *Kuban' v gody Velikoi Otechestvennoi voiny, 1941-1945: Khronika sobytii*, vol. 1 (Krasnodar: Sov. Kuban, 2000); Valeriia Vodolazhskaia, Mariia Krivneva, and Nelli Melnik, eds., "Stravropol'e v period nemetsko-fashistskoi okkupatsyi (avgust 1942-ianvar' 1943)," *Dokumenty i materialy Komiteta po delam arkhivov Stavropol'skogo kraia, Gosudarstvennogo arkhiva Stavropol'skogo kraia, Tsentra dokumentatsii noveishei istorii Stavropol'skogo kraia* (Stavropol': Knizhnoe izdatel'stvo, 2000).

31 Il'ia Al'tman, ed., *Kholokost na territorii SSSR. Entsiklopediia* (Moscow: ROSSPEN, 2009).

32 Jonathan Littell, *Les bienveillantes: roman* (Paris: Gallimard, 2006).

33 Jonathan Littell, *The Kindly Ones: A Novel* (New York: Harper, 2009).

closely represents the atmosphere of the German occupation of the Crimea and especially in the North Caucasus. However, from the point of view of a historian of the Holocaust in these regions, the most important merit of *The Kindly Ones* is its lengthy fictional yet historically rather accurate depiction of the fate of the Mountain Jews in November-December 1942.

Source Base

German military and security formations active in the Crimea and the North Caucasus conducted diaries of military, security, and intelligence operations, which constitute the bulwark of the German documentation of which the present study makes use. These sources are characterized, however, by a serious imbalance. Numerically, German files relating to the Crimea far exceed those pertaining to the Caucasus. This stems from a noticeably shorter period of the German occupation of the Caucasus (four to five months), as compared to the Crimea (two-and-a-half years). Another reason accounting for this discrepancy is the fact that in the second half of 1942, the Germans were less willing to put concrete information concerning their anti-Jewish activity on paper.

With respect to German wartime documents, scholarship pertaining to other regions has already noted that they were occasionally distorted and not entirely trustworthy.[34] In many respects, such as attitudes of the local population toward German rule or German anti-Jewish measures, the sources seemed sometimes either too circumspect or, alternatively, full of delusional wishful thinking, such as how "the locals welcomed these steps." German reports rarely go into details of specific action and tend to consist of general appraisals and observations. Nevertheless, they represent valuable evidence concerning the Holocaust in the Crimea and the Caucasus. Literature produced

34 Hannes Heer, "The Logic of the War of Extermination: The Wehrmacht and the Anti-Partisan War," in Hannes Heer and Klaus Naumann, eds., *War of Extermination: The German Military in World War II, 1941-1944* (New York and Oxford: Berghahn Books, 2000), pp. 97-99.

by Nazi researchers and administrators prior to 1941 and during the German occupation of the Crimea and the North Caucasus is also often of relevance to current research.[35]

Trials and preliminary proceedings conducted in Western Germany against former Nazis after World War II constitute an important source of knowledge on the Holocaust in the Crimea and the North Caucasus. Many former officers of the Wehrmacht and members of the *Einsatzgruppe*, as well as of other agencies, were brought to testify. Quite predictably, overwhelming numbers of defendants and witnesses could not well recall their own deeds during the war. However, they offered occasionally valuable testimonies, as long as doing so did not compromise their position. In many cases, such testimonies constitute the only source on how the German killing machine operated.

Most of the information on the Holocaust can be retrieved from the proceedings of the voluminous investigation made during the war under the Soviet Extraordinary State Commission (ESC).[36] Its reports and investigations reflected the policies

35 See, for example, Alfred Eduard Frauenfeld, *Die Krim: Ein Handbuch* (Simferopol: Aufstab für den Generalbezirk Krim, 1942). Other books pertaining to this group are referred to in Chapter 5, "The Fate of Karaites and Krymchaks in the Crimea and Mountain Jews in the North Caucasus during the Holocaust."

36 The Red Army final victory in the Battle of Stalingrad in February 1943 signaled not only the turning point in the Soviet-German warfare, but also enabled the Soviet leadership to begin an all-out effort of examining the results of the German occupation of Soviet areas. The coordination of this task was assigned to the Extraordinary State Commission on Reporting and Investigating the Atrocities of the German Fascist Occupants and their Henchmen and the Damages Inflicted by them on Citizens, *Kolkhozy*, Public Organizations, State Enterprises (henceforth, ESC, or the Commission). On the ESC, see, for example, Niels Bo Poulsen, "War Crime Investigation *po-sovetski*? Evaluating material from the Extraordinary State Commission," *Kholocaust i suchasnost'* 1, no. 5 (2008): pp. 27-46; Idem, "The Soviet Extraordinary State Commission: An Analysis of the Commission's Investigative Work in War and Postwar Stalinist Society" (PhD diss., Copenhagen University, 2005); Marina Sorokina, "People and Procedures. Toward a History of the Investigation of Nazi Crimes in the USSR," *Kritika: Explorations in Russian and Eurasian History* 6, no. 4 (2005): pp. 797-831; Kiril Feferman, "Soviet Investigation of Nazi Crimes in the USSR: Documenting the Holocaust," *Journal of Genocide Research* 5, no. 4 (2003): pp. 587-602.

promoted by the Soviet authorities. They highlighted the role of local inhabitants in Jewish rescue, unless they belonged to some ethnic groups collectively designated in the Soviet Union as "the Germans' henchmen." In line with this standpoint, the collaboration with the German occupational regime was mostly attributed to underprivileged individuals under the Soviet regime, former criminals, and profiteers, etc. Soviet documents of this period did not contain any invocation of prewar antisemitism or any ethnically or religiously motivated tension which could have accounted for the behavior of an individual or a certain group during the Holocaust. In addition, it must be remembered that ESC testimonies were collected in the atmosphere of deportation of many peoples from the recaptured Soviet territories, in particular from the Crimea and the North Caucasus.[37]

Not only were these ethnicities simply not covered by the ESC investigations, it was also convenient for the Soviets to blame them *en masse* for siding with the Germans, including their alleged involvement in the persecution of Jews. The Commision's statistical findings were sometimes flawed.[38] Finally, the ESC was sometimes used as a tool to shift public attention from Soviet crimes to Nazi atrocities. Nevertheless, contemporary scholarship maintains that, despite many reservations, the ESC material can "be used to provide detailed and generally reliable information on Nazi crimes."[39]

Soviet investigations of anti-Jewish atrocities constitute

The Commission began its work following the March 5, 1943 decree of the Soviet Council of People's Commissars. Decree of the SNK, no. 299, YVA, M.37/156, pp. 15-16.

37 Upon having regained control of the territories occupied by the Wehrmacht in 1943-1945, the Soviet authorities exiled more than 2 million people, among them Crimean Tatars, Chechens, and Kalmyks, who were collectively accused of large-scale collaboration with the Germans. J. Otto Pohl, *Ethnic Cleansing in the USSR: 1937-1949* (London: Greenwood, 1999).

38 Sergei Stepanenko, *Deiatel'nost' Chrezvychainoi gosudarstvennoi komissii SSSR po vyiavleniiu voennykh prestuplenii fashystskoi Germanii na territorii Krasnodarskogo kraia* (PhD diss., Adygeiskii gosudarstvennyi universitet, 2010), p. 111.

39 Poulsen, "War Crime Investigation *po-sovetski?*, p. 28.

an additional but much smaller source on the Holocaust in the Crimea and the North Caucasus. Most of the findings referred to in this study occurred during two big open trials conducted in Krasnodar in 1943, the first open trial of this sort in the Soviet Union, and in Sevastopol' in 1947.[40] The deficiency of Soviet methods for extracting truth notwithstanding, these materials, particularly the preliminary interrogations, contain a great deal of important details concerning the Holocaust. In closed interrogations, Soviets did not hesitate to ask the defendants questions about the Holocaust that were usually avoided or subsumed in more public ESC investigations. Dr. Martin Dean from the USHMM, a leading authority in the field of "KGB files,"[41] evaluated the importance of these investigations as a source when they were presented during the proceedings conducted in the West against former Nazis and their collaborators. He found that the evidence, although occasionally containing inaccuracies, was largely regarded as an important and trustworthy source by Western prosecution and courts.[42]

40 On the Soviet public trials of war criminals, see Tanja Penter, "Collaborators on Trial: New Source Material on Soviet Postwar Trials against Collaborators," *Slavic Review* 64, no. 4 (2005): pp. 782-791; Manfred Zeidler, "Der Minsker Kriegsverbrechenerprozeß vom Januar 1946: Kritische Anmerkungen zu einem Sowjetischem Schauprozeß gegen Deutsche Kriegsgefangenen," *Vierteljahrshefte für Zeitgeschichte* 52, no. 2 (2004): pp. 211-244; Alexander V. Prusin, "Fascist Criminals to the Gallows!: The Holocaust and Soviet War Crimes Trials, December 1945–February 1946," *Holocaust and Genocide Studies* 17, no. 1 (2003): pp. 1-30.

41 The KGB security agency is no longer in existence. But it denotes a generally accepted reference to the archives of several security agencies, which are successors to the KGB.

42 I am grateful to Dr. Martin Dean from the United States Holocaust Memorial Museum for sharing with me his ideas presented in his unpublished (to the best of my knowledge) article "Examination of KGB Trial Files." See also Diana Dumitru, "An Analysis of Soviet Postwar Investigation and Trial Documents and Their Relevance for Holocaust Studies," in Michael David-Fox, Peter Holquist, and Alexander M. Martin, eds., *The Holocaust in the East: Local Perpetrators and Soviet Responses* (Pittsburg, PA: University of Pittsburgh Press, 2013), pp. 142-157; Martin Dean, "Crime and Comprehension, Punishment and Legal Attitudes: German and Local Perpetrators of the Holocaust in Domachevo, Belarus, in the Records of Soviet, Polish, German, and British War Crimes Investigations," in David Bankier and Dan Michman, eds., *Holocaust and*

Regrettably, most KGB files are still inaccessible to the research community. The situation is particularly grave regarding the North Caucasian files kept in Moscow's Central FSB Archive and its regional archives.[43] Their inaccessibility is likely due to increased sensitivity to opening "old wounds" that could further deteriorate the situation in this explosive area. In contrast, the Ukrainian counterpart of the Russian FSB, the SBU, transferred some of its Holocaust-related sources, primarily files of those accused of involvement in the murder of Jews in the Crimean peninsula, to the USHMM.[44]

Testimonies offered by Jewish Holocaust survivors and non-Jewish witnesses constitute one of the most important sources for the present study, many of which were collected by various Soviet authorities during the war. Their content may be defined as "Soviet oral history."[45] For example, they do not mention moderate Jewish responses frequently designated by the Hebrew term "*amida*", such as cultural activities, but instead emphasize life-and-death reactions, such as flight from ghettos and armed resistance. As such, more reliable information is gleaned from the testimonies submitted many years after the German occupation. The underlying problem with such sources, however, is that important details were possibly easily forgotten while others were highlighted.[46] In addition, the Soviet legacy had a deep and long-standing impact on the opinions of those Soviet Jews who left the Soviet Union, and even more so on those who

Justice; Representation and Historiography of the Holocaust in Post-War Trials (Jerusalem: Yad Vashem, 2010), pp. 265-280.

43 FSB - *Federal'naia Sluzhba Bezopasnosti* (The Federal Security Service) is the most powerful of the successors to the KGB and is in charge of internal security broadly defined in the Russian Federation.

44 SBU - *Sluzhba Bezpeki Ukraini* (Security Service of Ukraine).

45 On this source, see Jochen Hellbeck, *Revolution on My Mind: Writing a Diary under Stalin* (Cambridge, MA: Harvard University Press, 2006).

46 On the influence of time on testimonies given by Holocaust survivors, see, for example, Henry Greenspan, "'An Immediate and Violent Impulse:' Holocaust Survivor Testimony in the First Years after Liberation," in John K. Roth and Elizabeth Maxwell, eds., *Memory*, vol. 3 of *Remembering for the Future: The Holocaust in an Age of Genocide* (Houndmills and New York: Palgrave, 2001), pp. 108-116.

remained.[47] Regarding the testimonies offered after the collapse of the Soviet Union, one should take into consideration the fact that the witnesses frequently continued to live in the same places in which the annihilation of Jews had taken place and in the midst of the same people who had been involved in it. All of these factors could spoil the integrity of the testimonies.

Furthermore, it should be admitted that there is a general problem with testimonies. That is, they reflect a witness's subjective standpoint on the traumatic events leaving their imprint on the witness, regardless of whether the witness was present at the event or heard about the occurrences second hand from eyewitnesses (which certainly diminishes the value of the evidence). This subjectivity is still present, regardless of whether the witness reported about the event during the war or dozens of years later or whether the witness was a Jewish victim, bystander, or perpetrator.

Information on the fate of the Jews in the Crimea and the North Caucasus was leaked to the press even before the Soviet authorities disclosed their declarations. The most important channel by which this information was disseminated was *Eynikayt* (Unity), the newspaper of the Jewish Anti-Fascist Committee.[48] Despite the fact that its articles reflected the Soviet doctrine of the "fraternity of nations," unlike the rest of the Soviet media (which presented the annihilation of Jews under the official Soviet stance in terms of shared suffering and "persecution of peaceful Soviet

47 Zvi Gitelman, "Internationalism, Patriotism, and Disillusion: Soviet Jewish Veterans Remember World War II and the Holocaust," in Roth and Maxwell, *Remembering for the Future* (Houndmills and New York: Palgrave, 2001), pp. 296-308. On the opposite impact of the Holocaust on Soviet Jewish identity, see Irena Cantorovich and Nati Cantorovich, "The Impact of the Holocaust and the State of Israel on Soviet Jewish Identity," in Yaacov Ro'i, ed., *The Jewish Movement in the Soviet Union* (New York: Woodrow Wilson Center Press, Johns Hopkins University Press, 2012), pp. 119-136.

48 Yosef Gorny, *Jewish Press and the Holocaust, 1939-1945: Palestine, Britain, the United States, and the Soviet Union* (New York: Cambridge University Press, 2012), pp. 185-202; Dov-Ber Kerler, "The Soviet Yiddish Press: "Eynikayt" during the War, 1942-1945," in Robert Shapiro, ed., *Why Didn't the Press Shout? American and International Journalism during the Holocaust* (Jersey City, NJ: Yeshiva University Press, 2003), pp. 221-249.

citizens"), the topic of the Jewish destruction was prominent. The articles published in *Eynikayt*, as well as certain Soviet sources such as interviews with Holocaust survivors, were reproduced in Hebrew newspapers that appeared in Mandatory Palestine and Israel. Still, it should be acknowledged that in these newspaper publications the subject of the extermination of Jews in the Crimea and the North Caucasus was never highlighted, because the regions were considered to be on the periphery of the Jewish world.

As illustrated above, every source is problematic in its own way. Therefore, I have made every effort to utilize various kinds of sources in order to present as accurate a picture as possible of the events included in this study. This was, however, not always acheivable, owing to the paucity of other sources. In such cases, I was compelled to rely on the available source and my own judgment.

A Note on Scholarly Conventions

Much of this book is based on personal testimonies or interviews of individuals housed in archives. Often these do not include first names, which is indicative of Soviet and Russian academic and naming conventions, in general. Russian publication tradition uses the standard first and sometimes patronymic initial followed by the full last name. Where there is no first name or patronymic included it should be assumed that they are unavailable. This is true for all Russian primary and secondary sources. Oftentimes, the date is unknown or estimated, in which instance I have attributed the estimated date or written 'no date' in square brackets. For testimonies of individuals, in addition to the testimonial date, I have given the individual's birth year in parentheses, if known. It has not always been practical to attribute my date assumptions throughout, but I have done so in instances where it is necessary to know precise dating.

In the German legal sources I have used, often only the first name and surname initial of an individual is available. This is not accidental, as for privacy concerns, the postwar German courts ordered the deletion of the family names of those interrogated in war- and Holocaust-related proceedings.

Both in the main text and in the footnote and bibliographic information I have maintained full spellings of the original Russian, according to the Library of Congress (ALA-LC) transliteration system, but I have not included diacritics. However, in German documents, I have maintained the German spelling of the names of localities. For the names of people and towns that are well-known in English, I use the popular spelling rather than the ALA-LC transliteration (for example, I maintain "Yalta" instead of transliterating it as "Ialta").

All secondary sources are cited in the original language according to the Chicago Manual of Style, edition 15. Yiddish and Hebrew titles are given in English followed by "Yiddish" or "Hebrew" in parentheses. All German primary documents have been rendered in German. Russian or Ukrainian primary documents with an actual title have been rendered in the original according to the ALA-LC transliteration system, with the title in quotation marks. Those that do not have official titles are given as a description of the source rendered in English. All references to Soviet *Akty* (acts, reports) are indicated as 'Akt' followed by an English description (i.e., "Akt of the Commission of Larindorfskii *raion*").

The Russian geographic and administrative indicators *krai* (territory) and *raion* (area) have been used throughout. I have retained the Russian adjectival forms for towns and cities corresponding to them. For example, instead of "Krasnodar *krai*" I retain "Krasnodarskii *krai*."

All translations throughout are my own unless otherwise indicated.

[illegible] and [illegible] the Latin names of [illegible] Hebrew [illegible] as [illegible]

[illegible] and in the footnote and bibliographic information [illegible] the original Russian [illegible] (ALA-LC) [illegible] system, but I have not included [illegible]. However, [illegible] the [illegible] spelling of the names [illegible] hundreds of [illegible] and [illegible] are well-[illegible] [illegible]

[illegible]

The Crimea and the North Caucasus: Historical Background

1. The Crimea[1]

Since its annexation by Russia in 1783 under Catherine the Great, the Crimean peninsula has become an object of intensive colonization.[2] Although the imperial government also welcomed the arrival of non-Russians, including Germans and even Jews, most of the newcomers were Russians and Ukrainians. By the end of the 19th century, Russians and Ukrainians constituted the largest national groups in the peninsula. The Russian Civil War and interwar period did not substantially change their dominance in the Crimea.

Crimean Tatars constituted another important segment of the Crimean population. Prior to the Russian conquest in 1783, they were the ruling and largest group in the peninsula.[3] After the conquest, the Russian government invested considerable efforts in diminishing the numerical prevalence of Tatars in the region.[4] This policy bore its fruits, and the proportion of Crimean

1 On the developments in the Crimea before WWII, see Alan W. Fisher, *The Russian Annexation of the Crimea* (Cambridge: Cambridge University Press, 1972); D. A. Amanzholova et al., eds., *Natsional'naia politika Rossii: Istoriia i sovremennost'* (Moscow: Informatsionno-izdatel'skoe agentstvo "Russkii mir," 1997), p. 80.

2 Kelly O'Neill, "Between Subversion and Submission: The Integration of the Crimean Khanate into the Russian Empire, 1783-1853" (PhD diss., Harvard University, 2006).

3 Brian Glyn Williams, *The Crimean Tatars: The Diaspora Experience and the Forging of a Nation* (Leiden: Brill, 2001), pp. 39-72.

4 Ibid., pp. 139-171; Justin McCarthy, *Death and Exile: The Ethnic Cleansing of Ottoman Muslims, 1821-1922* (Princeton: Darwin Press, 1995), pp. 15-18.

Tatars in the peninsula dwindled to only 34% by 1897.[5] Despite this demographic transformation, the group continued to perceive itself as an indigenous population with rights to group autonomy and independence. In 1918, the Tatars endeavored to achieve independence of, or at least autonomy in, the Crimea.[6] Their demands were at odds with the wishes of the numerically stronger Russians and Ukrainians[7] and totally rejected by the White Movement.[8] Tatar nationalists, thus, gradually gravitated toward the Bolshevik camp and by the end of the Civil War were their firm supporters.[9]

After the Soviets established power in the Crimea in 1921, the Bolsheviks took notice of widespread separatist tendencies among the Tatars and attempted to partly satisfy them by giving them a privileged position in the emerging Autonomous Republic of the Crimea.[10] This was no isolated phenomenon but part of a general policy of indigenization.[11]

5 Ibid., p. 218.

6 On the Crimean Tatars during the Civil War in Russia, see Andrei Kruchinin, *Krymsko-tatarskie formirovaniia v Dobrovol'cheskoi armii: istoriia neudachnykh popytok* (Moscow: Voenno-istoricheskaia biblioteka "Voennoi byli," 1999), pp. 5, 22; Edige Kirimal, *Der Nationale Kampf der Krimtürken: mit besonderer Berücksichtigung der Jahre 1917-1918* (Emsdetten/Wesfalen: Verlag Lechte, 1952), pp. 33-277.
On the general aspects of the situation in the Crimea in 1918-early 1919, see *Alexandr Puchenkov, Ukraina i Krym v 1918-nachale 1919 goda. Ocherki politicheskoi istorii* (St. Petersburg: Nestor-Istoriia, 2013), pp. 123-161.

7 Alexandre Bennigsen and S. Enders Wimbush, *Muslim National Communism in the Soviet Union: A Revolutionary Strategy for the Colonial World* (Chicago: University of Chicago Press, 1979), p. 25.

8 Kirimal, *Der Nationale Kampf der Krimtürken*, pp. 278-285.

9 Williams, *The Crimean Tatars*, pp. 347-348; Bennigsen and Wimbush, *Muslim National Communism in the Soviet Union*, p. 25.

10 Williams, *The Crimean Tatars*, pp. 355-365; Kirimal, *Der Nationale Kampf der Krimtürken*, pp. 287-288.
On the establishment of the Soviet regime in the Crimea in the wake of the Civil War, see Grégory Dufaud, "The Establishment of Bolshevik Power in the Crimea and the Construction of a Multinational Soviet State: Organisation, Justification, Uncertainties," *Contemporary European History* 21, no. 2 (May 2012): pp. 257-272.

11 Indigenization or nativization (*korenizatsiia*): policy conducted by the Bolshevik Party from the early 1920s aimed at upgrading the status of the local non-Russian

By 1928, the Tatar leadership of the Autonomous Republic of the Crimea fell out of favor with the central Soviet government. The reasons for why the highest-ranking Soviet officials of Tatar origin, including the influential head of the Crimean administration (*KrymTsyK*), Veli Ibraimov, were purged, i.e., deposed, arrested, and executed, are not easy to establish. Yet, it seems that the central Soviet government was not pleased with the accelerated application of the indigenization policy in the Crimea, i.e. favoring Crimean Tatars at the expense of other ethnic groups. Ibraimov's arrest was followed by large-scale arrests of those whom the Soviet central authorities and the OGPU (Joint State Political Directorate, predecessor to the NKVD) deemed as his followers.[12] On the whole, the fall of the Crimean Tatars from leadership positions in the Autonomous Republic of the Crimea in the late 1920s was likely as sharp as their ascent to power in the Republic in the early 1920s. By 1928, the central Soviet government had other plans for the Crimea. They took drastic measures to curtail Tatar involvement in active policy-making in the Crimea (*ibraimovshina*), which served as a signal of the winds of change blowing from the Kremlin at a nation-wide level. Regardless, from the early 1930s, the policies of indigenization in the Crimea were largely reversed and gradually gave way to intensive Russification.[13] By 1923, Russians and Ukrainians constituted almost half of the population, while the share of Tatars living in the peninsula constituted only 25% and continued to decrease.[14]

Ashkenazi Jewish settlements in the peninsula emerged in the first half of the 19th century, and, with certain exceptions, Jews

population. It included, among other things, an increasing use of local languages in education, culture, and bureaucracy, as well as granting employment privileges to the local non-Russian population (including local elites). Terry Martin, *The Affirmative Action Empire: Nations and Nationalism in the Soviet Union, 1923–1939* (Ithaca: Cornell University Press, 2001), pp. 31-208.

12 Vladimir Pashchenia, "Puti zavoevaniia i uderzhaniia bol'shevikami vlasti v Krymu (1905-1945 gg.)," *Kul'tura narodov Prichernomor'ia* 90 (2006): pp. 126-127.

13 Kirimal, *Der Nationale Kampf der Krimtürken*, pp. 296-299.

14 Alan W. Fisher, *The Crimean Tatars* (Stanford: Hoover Institution Press, 1978), p. 138.

were permitted to settle all over the Crimea.[15] Trade opportunities and the unique position of the peninsula as an important resort center attracted Jews from other areas of the Pale of Settlement.[16] In 1905, there were pogroms in the region.[17] By 1917, more than 68,000 Jews and Krymchaks lived in the Crimea (8.4% of the population).[18] Jewish presence in the peninsula continued uninterrupted until the outbreak of WWII, considerably reinforced by Jews whom the Soviet government wanted to transform into *kolkhozniki*. By 1939, more than 18,000 Jews (27.6% of the total Jewish population) lived in the rural areas of the peninsula.[19] This was more than twice as high as the similar figure for the entire Soviet Jewish population (13.1% by 1939), arguably making it the most distinctive feature of the Crimean Jewish community.[20] A considerable number of Crimean Jews (31.6%) dwelt in the "Jewish National Regions" (*evreiskie natsional'nye raiony)* of Fraidorf and Larindorf, two major concentrations of the Jewish population.[21]

15 With the exception of Sevastopol' (1829-1859, later the ban was partially lifted) and Yalta (since 1893).
On the general history of Jews in the Crimea, see, for example, Dan Shapira, "Some Notes on the History of Crimean Jewry from the Ancient Times until the End of the 19th Century, with Emphasis on the Qrimçaq Jews in the First Half of the 19th Century," Wolf Moskovich and Leonid Finberg, eds., *Jews and Slavs. Vol. 19: Jews, Ukrainians and Russians; Essays on Intercultural Relations* (Jerusalem: The Hebrew University of Jerusalem; Kyiv: Institute of Jewish Studies, 2008), pp. 65-92; Aleksandr Gertsen, *Evrei v Krymu: Kratkii ocherk istrorii iudeiskih obshin Kryma* (Simferopol': Tavriia-Plus, 1999).

16 Mikhail Polishchuk, *Evrei Odessy i Novorossii* (Jerusalem: Gesharim, 2002), pp. 76-77.

17 The pogroms took place in Feodosiia, Kerch, and Simferopol'. Zionist Organisation, *Die Judenpogrome in Rußland* (Köln and Leizpzig: Jüdischer Verlag, 1910), pp. 69-70, 162-8, 170-4

18 Michael Gesin, "Holocaust: The Reality of Genocide in Southern Ukraine" (PhD diss., Brandeis University, 2003), p. 153.

19 Mordechai Altshuler, *Distribution of the Jewish Population of the USSR: 1939* (Jerusalem: The Hebrew University, Center for the Research of East European Jewry, 1993), p. 63.

20 Mordechai Altshuler, *Soviet Jewry on the Eve of the Holocaust: A Social and Demographic Profile* (Jerusalem: The Hebrew University, Center for the Research of East European Jewry, Yad Vashem, 1998), p. 29.

21 "Jewish National Regions" were created in several rural areas of the Soviet Union as a part of an indigenization policy. Jews made up a considerable part,

A group of students at a Jewish school in the village of Smidovichi, "Sotsdorf" *kolkhoz*, December 30, 1937. Personal archive of M. M. Shpigel'man. Courtesy: Archive of the Russian Holocaust Center (Moscow) [RHCA]

Thus, by the time of the outbreak of Soviet-German hostilities, Jews were a highly visible minority in the otherwise ethnically heterogeneous composition of the scarcely populated peninsula. According to the 1939 population census, Jews constituted 5.8% (65,452 people) of the total population of the Crimea (approx. 1,128,500 people).[22]

The behavior of various groups during the Russian Civil War constituted a litmus test of the political orientation of the Crimean population. Although the peninsula was the last stronghold of the White Movement, this was mainly a result of the unique geographic position of the Crimea, not particularly strong local anti-Bolshevist sentiment. Significantly, no pogroms occurred in the Crimea, despite the long-term presence of White troops, and the scope of

but not necessarily the majority, of their population. See Table 3, "Rural Jewish Population in the Crimea and the North Caucasus. 1939."

22 Altshuler, *Distribution of the Jewish Population of the USSR*, pp. 9-11. See Tables 1-2.

antisemitic excesses was limited, compared to the other White-controlled areas.[23]

Insofar as the relations between the Ashkenazi Jews and the rest of the Crimean population prior to WWII were concerned, it seemed that some of the Crimean Tatars considered the Ashkenazim as a part of the Imperial and later Soviet effort to squeeze the Tatars out of their native land.[24] This tension surfaced in the late 1920s when the regional Crimean administration, led by the Tatars, endeavored to overrule the central Soviet government's decision to allocate the land to Jewish settlers.[25] It is not easy to gauge the dimensions of the discontent among the Tatars over the land distribution and redistribution during the 1930s, but some level of discontent seems to have still been present by the beginning of the war.[26]

23 Viacheslav Zarubin, "M. M. Vinaver i Krym," in Viktoriia Mochalova, et al., eds., *Materialy 11 Ezhegodnoi Mezhdistsiplinarnoi konferentsii po iudaike* (Moscow: Sefer i Institut Slavianovedeniia RAN, 2004), p. 20; Iosif Shekhtman, *Pogromy Dobrovol'cheskoi Armii na Ukraine: k istorii antisemitizma na Ukraine v 1919-1920 gg.* (Berlin: Ostjüdisches Historisches Archiv, 1932), especially p. 32.

24 Little is known about the attitudes of the Crimean Tatars towards Jews in the Tsarist Empire. Jewish sources mention that in 1905 the Tatars participated in the pogrom in Feodosiia and plundered Jewish property. Zionist Organization, *Die Judenpogrome in Rußland*, p. 171; See also Kirimal, *Der Nationale Kampf der Krimtürken*, p. 291. This book was published by a Crimean Tatar (a former high-ranking collaborator with the Nazis) and claims that the Tatars saved Jews during the pogroms, but does not go into details.

25 Jonathan Dekel-Chen, *Farming the Red Land: Jewish Agricultural Colonization and Local Soviet Power, 1924-1941* (New Haven: Yale University Press, 2005), pp. 98-100; Fisher, *The Crimean Tatars*, p. 141; Kirimal, *Der Nationale Kampf der Krimtürken*, pp. 291-2.

26 Williams, *The Crimean Tatars*, pp. 366-369.

2. The North Caucasus[27]

Russia had formally pacified the North Caucasus by 1864.[28] It was the culmination of many decades of Russian penetration into the region (since approximately 1815) that caused a bloody war between the Imperial armies and local insurgents, whose struggle against the Russians was sustained by patriotic and religious fervor. Throughout the first half of the 19th century, the Russian government encouraged colonists from elsewhere in the Empire to settle in the recently conquered areas of the North Caucasus, while others were forcefully relocated to the region. A significant number of Cossacks came to the region, as the Imperial government awarded vast land portions in the North Caucasus to thousands of them in exchange for protection from outside penetration into the Imperial hinterland.[29]

In the second part of the 19th century, newcomers (particularly Russians, Ukrainians, and, to a lesser extent, Germans) flocked to the North Caucasus.[30] Their arrival sharply transformed the ethnic

27 On the population developments in the North Caucasus prior to World War II, see Nikolai F. Bugai and Askarbi M. Gonov, *Kavkaz — narody v eshelonakh: 20-60-e gody* (Moscow: INSAN, 1998), pp. 5-117; Paul B. Henze, "Fire and Sword in the Caucasus: The 19th Century Resistance of the North Caucasian Mountaineers," *Central Asian Studies* 2, no. 1 (1983): pp. 5-44.

28 Moshe Gammer, *Muslim Resistance to the Tsar: Shamil and the Conquest of Chechnia and Daghestan* (London: Frank Cass, 1994).

29 Thomas M. Barrett, *At the Edge of the Empire: The Terek Cossacks and the North Caucasus Barrier, 1700-1860* (Boulder, CO: Westview Press, 1999).
The Cossackdom of Don was centered at Novocherkassk and numbered 1.5 million people as of 1917, possessing more than 80% of the total land assets in the area at the time. As of 1917, the Cossackdom of Kuban' numbered more than 1.3 million people and made up 45% of the province's population. Its center was in Ekaterinodar (presently Krasnodar). As of 1917, the Cossackdom of Terek numbered 278,000 and was centered in Vladikavkaz. It possessed almost 29% of land out of the total land assets in the area. Nikolai F. Bugai, ed., *Kazachestvo Rossii: ottorzhenie, priznanie, vozrozhdenie (1917-90 gody)* (Moscow: Mozhaisk-Terra, 2000), pp. 10-11.

30 Valentina Patrakova and Viktor Chernous, "Russkie na Severnom Kavkaze: Istoricheskii ekskurs" in Viktor Chernous, ed., *Russkie na Severnom Kavkaze: Vyzovy XXI veka: Sbornik nauchnykh statei*, 2nd enl. ed. (Rostov-na-Donu: Izdatel'stvo SKNTs VSh, 2002), pp. 38-40.

composition of the region. In 1897, the Orthodox Slavs made up 94% of the total population in the Stavropol' province. The figures for the Kuban' and Terek provinces were 94% and 43%, respectively.[31]

The indigenous population of the North Caucasus consisted of numerous small ethnic groups who practiced Orthodox Christianity or Islam. It is generally assumed that the Muslims constituted the backbone of the movement that opposed the Russian rule in the Caucasus, whereas smaller Christian groups were supportive of the Russian penetration. The indigenous peoples displayed increasingly conservative and traditionalist patterns of social and political behavior.

The Bolshevik Revolution and the ensuing Civil War constituted one of the most important landmarks in the history of the region.[32] Overall, the inhabitants of the North Caucasus seemed to consider Bolshevism unappealing and resisted it. The region was the cradle and the main stronghold of the White Movement. The Cossacks, whose military traditions and training made them a formidable military force, fought against the Bolsheviks with unparalleled zeal and stubbornness.[33] Significantly, the Caucasian Cossacks were actively involved in committing anti-Jewish atrocities when the White armies swept into Ukraine in 1919.[34]

Following the defeat of the White armies in the Civil War, the Cossacks were subjected to particularly cruel treatment by the victorious Bolsheviks, which decimated large numbers of the North Caucasian Cossacks.[35] During the Soviet rule, migration

31 Ibid., p. 40.

32 For some insight into this period, see Valerii Dzidzoev, *Belyi i krasnyi terror na Severnom Kavkaze v 1917-1918 gg.* (Vladikavkaz: Alaniia, 2000).

33 Bugai, *Kazachestvo Rossii*, pp. 13-31.

34 Irina Astashkevich, "The Pogroms in Ukraine in 1917-1920: An Alternate Universe," (PhD diss., Brandeis University, 2013), pp. 271-272; 284-285; 296; Peter Kenez, *Civil War in South Russia, 1919-1920: The Defeat of the Whites* (Berkeley: University of California, 1977), p. 172; Shekhtman, *Pogromy Dobrovol'cheskoi Armii na Ukraine*, pp. 31, 76.

35 Evgenii Zhuravlev, *Kollaboratsionizm na iuge Rossii v gody Velikoi Otechestvennoi voiny (1941-1945 gg.)* (Rostov-na-Donu: Izd-vo Rostovskogo universiteta, 2006), pp. 22-27, 42; Elena Khachemizova, "Obshchestvo i vlast' v 30-e-40-e gody XX veka: politika repressii (na materialakh Krasnodarskogo kraia)" (PhD diss., Adygeiskii gosudarstvennyi universitet, 2004), pp. 44-107.

to the area continued, and the composition of the local Russian population changed. The government deported a large number of Cossacks from the Caucasus (63,500 by early 1933[36]), while Russians from central and northern Russia were ordered to make their homes in the Cossack regions during collectivization.[37]

The indigenous peoples of the North Caucasus (particularly those professing Islam) did not join ranks with the Whites, who struggled under the banner of "One Russia, united and undivided." Thus, at least for a short while, many of them sympathized with the Bolsheviks, who had made successful appeals to non-Russian minorities in the region. At the same time, however, traditional and conservative ways of the mountain people prevented them from cooperating with the Reds. The result was a less institutionalized but more protracted form of guerilla warfare against the Red forces in the Caucasus. Yet, this phase of active resistance was largely over by 1932[38], as the military pressure that the Soviet regime constantly mounted against the rebels became untenable. However, manifest intensification of the Soviet anti-religious campaign from the late 1920s fueled more discontent among many indigenous peoples.[39] Thus, during the interwar period, a significant portion of the local population in the Caucasus remained or became hostile to Soviet rule.

36 Aleksandr Savochkin, "Massovye repressii 30-40kh gg XX veka na Severnom Kavkaze kak sposob utverzhdeniia i podderzhaniia iskliuchitel'noi samosotoiatel'nosti gosudarstva" (PhD diss., Vladimirskii iuridicheskii institut Federal'noi sluzhby ispolneniia nakazanii, 2008), p. 127.

37 Sergei Kisilitsyn, "Raskazachivanie — strategicheskii kurs Bolshevistskoi politicheskoi elity v 20-kh gg," in *Vozrozhdenie kazachestva: istoriia i sovremennost'* (Novocherkassk: Novocherkasskii gosudarstvennyii universitet, 2001), pp. 98-107; Natal'ia Bulgakova, "Sel'skoe naselenie Stavropol'ia vo vtoroi polovine 20-kh — nachale 30-kh godov 20 veka: Izmeneniia v demograficheskom, khoziaistvennom i kul'turnom oblike" (PhD diss., Stavropol'skii gosudarstvennyi universitet, 2003), pp. 17-18.

38 Jeronim Perović, "Highland Rebels: The North Caucasus during the Stalinist Collectivization Campaign," *Journal of Contemporary History* 0 (0), 2015: pp. 1-27.

39 Fifty-six percent of the prayer buildings were closed in Kabardino-Balkariia in 1936. State Archive of the Russian Federation (GARF), 5263/1/97, pp. 4-5, in Movsur Ibragimov, *Vlast' i obshchestvo v gody Velikoi Otechestvennoi voiny na primere natsional'nykh respublik Severnogo Kavkaza* (Moscow: Moskovskii pedagogicheskii univesitet, 1998), p. 385.

The North Caucasus was situated beyond the Pale of Settlement; therefore, apart from small privileged groups, Ashkenazi Jews were forbidden to settle in the region before 1917.[40] Those permitted to reside faced Tsarist anti-Jewish policy, conducted with particular vigor in the Cossack areas.[41] After the Bolshevik Revolution, some Jews migrated into the Caucasus, mainly into industrial[42] and resort centers.[43] As the region was primarily agricultural, it offered only modest employment opportunities for the newcomers. Yet, the mild climate, favorable food conditions in urban centers,[44] and resort capacities attracted a number of Jews, especially during the 1930s, when the overall food situation in the Soviet Union was strained.[45] By the time hostilities broke out between Nazi Germany and the Soviet Union, Ashkenazi Jews constituted a foreign and numerically negligible minority in the North Caucasus. In 1939, 4,600 Jews were recorded in Kabardino-Balkariia, 2,100 in the North Ossetiia, 7,600 in Krasnodarskii *krai*, and 7,100 in Stavropol'skii *krai*.[46]

40 Amanzholova et al., *Natsional'naia politika Rossii*, p. 151.

41 Ekaterina Norkina, "The Origins of Anti-Jewish Policy in the Cossack Regions of the Russian Empire, Late Nineteenth and Early Twentieth Century," *East European Jewish Affairs* 43, no. 1 (2013): pp. 62-76.

42 For Maikop, see *Emes*, February 20, 1925.

43 For Minvody in 1926 [1,381 Jews (2.3% of the total)], see Mordechai Altshuler, Yiztak Arad, and Shmuel Krakowski, eds., *Sovetskie evrei pishut Il'e Erenburgu, 1943-1966* (Jerusalem: Yad Vashem and Center for Research and Documentation of East European Jewry, 1993), p. 207.

44 On the situation in rural areas, see Brian J. Boeck, "Complicating the National Interpretation of the Famine: Reexamining the Case of Kuban," *Harvard Ukrainian Studies* 30, no. 1/4 (2008): pp. 31-48.

45 Robert W. Davies and Stephen Wheatcroft, *The Years of Hunger: Soviet Agriculture, 1931-1933* (New York: Palgrave Macmillan, 2009).

46 Including Mountain Jews. See Tables 1, 3 and 4.

3. The Strategic Importance of the Crimea and the Caucasus[47] for Nazi Germany

In terms of strategy, the Crimea was a valuable asset to its possessor.[48] As it juts deeply into the Black Sea, it provided the shortest route to any state in the Black Sea region and could cut off sea communications. Also, control of the Crimea stabilized the whole southern flank of any army attempting to advance into southern Ukraine. Furthermore, as long as the Soviet Union maintained possession of the peninsula, most specifically its air bases, the oil region of Ploieşti in Romania, essential for the Axis war effort, remained under threat of Soviet bombing.[49] Additionally, possession of the peninsula controlled the oil supply from the Caucasus into Romania.[50] In terms of geopolitics, the Crimea could serve as a bridgehead for a German incursion into the Caucasus and a further advance to the south or east.[51]

If the Caucasus fell into German hands, its control of the region had the potential to stabilize German relations with Turkey and Iran. Of particular significance was the role that the Caucasus played in Nazi Germany's oil calculations.[52] At that time,

47 This section deals with the entire Caucasian region, i.e., the North Caucasus and the Transcaucasus. Therefore, when reference is made to the North Caucasus, it is explicitly mentioned as such.

48 On German ideas and plans concerning the Crimea before the conquest, see Kunz, *Die Krim unter deutscher Herrschaft*, pp. 15-73.

49 On the Soviet bombardments of the Ploiesti oil centers at the first stage of the war conducted from the Crimean bases, see the diary of Pavel Mus'ianov [editor of *Krasnyii chernomorets* (Sevastopol') newspaper]. Available from: http://www.moscow-crimea.ru/history/20vek/musiakov2.html.

50 Directive of the *Reichsminister* for the Occupied Eastern Territories Rosenberg forwarded to *Reichskommissar* of Ukraine Koch on the political, ideological, and economical activities of the *Reichskommissariat*, November 18, 1941, in Orest Dziuban, Iaroslav Dashkevich, and Vasil' Kuk, eds., *Ukrain'ske derzhavotvorennia: Akt 30 chervnia 1941: zbirnyk dokumentiv i materialiv* (Lviv-Kiev: Literaturna ahentsiia "Piramida," 2001), p. 432.

51 Bentsion Vol'fson, *Krymskii poluostrov v zakhvatnicheskikh planakh nemetskogo fashizma* [before October 5, 1945], State Archive of the Autonomous Republic of the Crimea (DAARK), P-156/1/221.

52 Hilter's speech on October 2, 1942, on the strategic situation during the war and the decisive importance of the Eastern Front, particularly of the Caucasian oil

the explored oil reserves of the region were largely located in the North Caucasus and in the Caspian shelf near Baku. Additional reserves were in Iraq (near Mosul), which could be reached only by pushing through the Caucasus. Concerning population policy, the importance of the Caucasus, with its ethnically and religiously heterogeneous population, was unique. If cleverly handled, the region could become a model for German attitudes toward non-Russian nations, with further repercussions in the Muslim East.

In terms of global vision, the most fundamental aspect of Nazi Germany's perception of the Crimea and the Caucasus laid in the fact that it was part of its overall vision for the East. Concerning *Lebensraum*, the Crimea and the Caucasus belonged to a sphere of minor importance to Nazi Germany. However, this factor was partly offset by those at the helm of German military leadership, who traditionally assigned great importance to penetration into the Middle East and displayed an apparent continuity in such thinking during World War II.

Also worth consideration is the fact that during the period under review, the Crimea and the Caucasus were part of the Soviet Union. Therefore, Nazi Germany kept repercussions of activity in the region on Soviet-German relations in mind. From 1933 until the first quarter of 1939, these relations remained strained. Consequently, it enabled Germany to cultivate close relations with the groups of émigrés from the Crimea and the Caucasus.[53]

However, until 1939, Nazi Germany had reached no clear decision regarding treatment of the Crimea and the Caucasus. The rapprochement between Nazi Germany and the Soviet Union after August 1939 did not change the situation. The Germans almost completely froze the activities of the Crimean and Caucasian

fields in Joseph Goebbels, *Die Tagebücher von Joseph Goebbels*, Elke Fröhlich, ed. vol. 6 (Munich: Saur, 2004), pp. 42-53. See also Joel Hayward, "Hitler's Quest for Oil: The Impact of Economic Considerations on Military Strategy, 1941-42," *Journal of Strategic Studies* 18, no. 4 (1995): pp. 94-135.

53 Georges Mamoulia, "L'histoire du groupe Caucase (1934-1939)," *Cahiers du Monde russe* 48, no. 1 (Jan. - Mar., 2007): pp. 45-85; Patrick zur Mühlen, *Zwinschen Hakenkreuz und Sowjetstern: Der Nationalismus der sowjetischen Orientvölker im Zweiten Weltkrieg* (Düsseldorf: Droste, 1971), pp. 40, 120.

groupings under their auspices.[54] The revival of German interest in the Crimea and the Caucasus resulted from the intensification of its preparations for the attack on the Soviet Union in early 1941. However, Nazi Germany's definite notions toward the Crimea and the Caucasus came to the fore only after its invasion of the Soviet Union in June 1941.

Soon after the German attack on the Soviet Union, Hitler announced his plans for the Crimea to his inner circle of associates.[55] In accordance with these directives, the Crimea would be placed under direct German rule and renamed "*Gau Gotenland*." It would also be connected via *autobahn* to the Reich. In order to "Germanize" the Crimea, ethnic Germans from South Tyrol, Romania (including Transnistria), and Palestine would be relocated to the region.[56] The plans also included an ethnic cleansing of Russians, Ukrainians, and Tatars. In general, Hitler regarded the Crimea as "the German South," a kind of substitute for the Mediterranean coast.[57]

Considering the self-restrained German policy toward the Crimea from 1933 to 1941, Nazi Germany's expression of such profound interest in the peninsula in 1941 was an abrupt shift. A variety of reasons may account for this change in German attitude. First, it seems that Germany felt confident to lay claims to the Crimea because of its initial victories following its invasion of the Soviet Union. Second, the next drive of the Wehrmacht would be

54 Ibid., p. 19.

55 Adolf Hitler, *Monologe im Führerhauptquartier 1941-1944* in Werner Jochman, ed., *Die Aufzeichnungen Heinrich Heims* (Hamburg: A. Knaus, 1980), pp. 39, 48, 63-64, 90, 124, 128 (entries from July 5-6, July 27, August 18, September 18, November 5, 1941); Henry Picker, *Hitlers Tischgespräche im Führer-Hauptquartier, 1941-1942* (Stuttgart: Seewald Verlag, 1963), pp. 272 (entry from May 8, 1942), 290-291 (May 13, 1942); Hugh Trevor-Roper, *Hitler's Secret Conversations, 1914-1941* (New York: Farrar, Strauss and Young, 1953), pp. 16 (entry from July 27, 1941), 68, 70 (October 17, 1941).

56 Peter Witte et al., eds., *Der Dienstkalender Heinrich Himmlers 1941/42* (Hamburg: Christians, 1999), pp. 481, 566; Zur Mühlen, *Zwischen Hakenkreuz und Sowjetstern,* p. 183.

57 Hitler, *Monologe im Führerhauptquartier 1941-1944,* p. 39 (July 5-6, 1941), 91 (October 17, 1941). See also the directive of Rosenberg in Dziuban, Dashkevich, and Kuk, *Ukrain'ske derzhavotvorennia*, p. 432.

directed into the East, so the Crimea would serve as the outpost of the Reich in the south.

However, it is illuminating that even at the time of its greatest military triumphs Germany never publicly disclosed its intentions for the Crimea, let alone their implementation. As Nazi Germany began to realize that the fighting in the Eastern front would last longer than initially thought, it became willing to enlist the support of Turkey, which had traditional connections to the Crimea and the Caucasus.[58] This last factor (willingness to enlist Turkish support) should be seen in the context of Germany's decision to form military units raised from the Soviet prisoners-of-war. Non-Russian POWs from the Crimea and the Caucasus became the backbone of new troops.

Because of its complexity and rich oil reserves, the Caucasus also occupied a unique position in the German war strategy.[59] By virtue of its economic importance, the Caucasus, most specifically the oil-rich region of Baku, was included in the operational proposals for the Eastern campaign as early as July 1940.[60] The

58 A. K. Moldadossova and R. S. Zharkinbaeva, "The Problem of Turkey's Neutrality during the Second World War in the Context of International Conferences," *The Journal of Slavic Military Studies* 28, no. 2 (2015): pp. 401-413; Corry Guttstadt, *Turkey, the Jews, and the Holocaust* (Cambridge: Cambridge University Press, 2013), pp. 29-37; Kunz, *Die Krim unter deutscher Herrschaft*, pp. 19-28; Karl Heinz Roth, "Berlin-Ankara-Baghdad: Franz von Papen and German Near East Policy during the Second World War," in Wolfgang G. Schwanitz, ed., *Germany and the Middle East: 1871-1945* (Princeton, NJ: Max Wiener Publishers, 2004), pp. 199-203; Aleksei Bezugolnyi, "Ni mira, ni voiny: Polozhenie na sovetsko-turetskoi granitse i mery sovetskogo rukovodstva po predotvrashcheniiu turetskoi ugrozy v pervyi period Velikoi Otechestvennoi Voiny," *Voenno-Istoricheskii arkhiv* 5, no. 41 (2003): pp. 53-76; Yücel Güçlü, "The Uneasy Relationship: Turkey's Foreign Policy vis-à-vis the Soviet Union at the Outbreak of the Second World War," *Mediterranean Quarterly Summer* 13, no. 3 (2002): pp. 58-93.

59 Trevor-Roper, *Hitler's Secret Conversations, 1941-1944*, pp. 68 (entry from October 17, 1941), p. 593 (entry from June 26, 1942), and Picker, *Hitlers Tischgespräche im Führer-Hauptquartier, 1941-1942*, pp. 272 (entry from May 8, 1942), 274 (May 9, 1942). See also Parvin Darabadi, "Kavkaz i Kaspii v "Bol'shoi geostrategicheskoi igre" nakanune i v period Vtoroi Mirovoi voiny (geoistoricheskii ocherk)," *Kavkaz i globalizatsiia* 1 (2008): pp. 146-169.

60 Alex J. Kay, *Exploitation, Resettlement, Mass Murder: Political and Economic Planning for German Occupation Policy in the Soviet Union, 1940-1941* (New York: Berghahn, 2006), pp. 33, 57.

fate of the region was also connected with other regional players, such as Turkey and Iran.[61] In order to attract numerous small groups of Turkish origin in the Caucasus, Hitler initially planned to hand over the Caucasus to Turkey after first exploiting the region.[62] From April-June 1941, however, the Germans envisioned the Caucasus as a federal state under its protectorate. Because of the region's oil resources, its population was spared the worst effects of military hostilities.[63] Although Hitler never considered the idea of population resettlement, a Nazi politician ideologically close to Alfred Rosenberg suggested the idea of bringing German settlers (usually ethnic Germans from outside the Reich) to the region in July 1941.[64]

Finally, as already mentioned, after the successful implementation of Operation Barbarossa, Germany had planned to advance southward into the Middle East. The Caucasus would serve as a bridgehead for this drive.[65] In the special directive No. 32 "Preparations for the time after Barbarossa," signed on June 11, 1941, on the eve of the invasion of the Soviet Union, Hitler ordered the "concentric attack from Libya through Egypt, from Bulgaria through Turkey, and possibly from the Transcaucasus through Iran" and "to prepare to send a motorized expeditionary corps from the Caucasus to Iraq."[66]

61 Iran – until its occupation by the Soviet and British troops in August 1941: Aleksandr Orishev, "Politika Germanii v Irane nakanune Vtoroi mirovoi voiny," *Novaia i noveishaia istoriia* 6 (2002): pp. 25-36; Yair Hirschfeld, "Irans Bedeutung für die deutsche Kriegswirtschaft vom Beginn des Zweiten Weltkriegs bis zum anglo-russischem Besetzung Irans im August 1941," *Jahrbuch des Instituts für deutsche Geschichte* 7 (1978): pp. 421-446.

62 Kay, *Exploitation, Resettlement, Mass Murder*, pp. 71-72, Manfred Zeidler, "Das 'Kaukasische Experiment': Gab es seine Weisung Hitlers zur deutschen Besatzungspolitik im Kaukasus?" *Vierteljahre für Zeitgeschichte* 53, no. 3 (2005): pp. 477-481.

63 Kay, *Exploitation, Resettlement, Mass Murder*, p. 203.

64 Ibid., p. 102.

65 Zur Mühlen, *Zwinschen Hakenkreuz und Sowjetstern*, p. 40.

66 Walther Hubatsch, *Hitlers Weisungen für die Kriegsführung* (Frankfurt am Main: Bernard und Greaffe Verlag für Wehrwesen, 1962), pp. 129-134; Altshuler, *Jews of the Eastern Caucasus*, pp. 109-110.

fate of the region was also connected with other regional powers such as Turkey and Iran [illegible] groups of Turks [illegible] in the Caucasus. Hitler initially intended to hand over the Caucasus to Turkey after first exploiting its resources [illegible] June 1942, however, the [illegible] the Caucasus as a federal state under its protectorate [illegible] the region's [illegible] its population [illegible] of [illegible]. Although Hitler [illegible] region in July 1942 [illegible]

[illegible]

Chapter One

Jews in the Crimea from the Beginning of the German-Soviet War (June 22, 1941) to the German Occupation (November 1941)

1. Evacuation[1] into the Region

After the outbreak of the Soviet-German hostilities in June 1941, the Crimea served as an escape route for a limited number of Jewish refugees. They arrived primarily from the geographically close areas of central and southern Ukraine,[2] as well as from the republic of Moldavia.[3] The route to the Crimea was hardly a significant destination under the Soviet evacuation program,[4] if at all, as the

1 On the wartime population evacuation in the USSR, see, for example, Rebecca Manley, *To the Tashkent Station: Evacuation and Survival in the Soviet Union at War* (Ithaca: Cornell University Press, 2009), pp. 24-47; Arad, *The Holocaust in the Soviet Union*, pp. 72-87.

2 Belaia Tserkov', Dnepropetrovsk, and Izmail: Testimonies of Lea Podochiva, 1994, Yad Vashem Hall of Names (YVHN). See also the testimony of Anatolii Varshavskii, July 13, 1993, YVHN and the testimony of Sara Vainberg, April 19, 1991, YVHN.

3 Kishinev: Testimony of Kharii Daich, February 29, 1974, YVHN; Testimony of Aron Nekhama, May 31, 1994, YVHN.

4 The Soviet evacuation program was aimed first and foremost at: 1) safeguarding lives of the Party, Soviet, and security agencies functionaries of different levels; 2) moving industrial (primarily of military character) and agricultural capacities with workers employed in them; and 3) transferring whatever possible human resources out of the Germans' reach. Vadim Dubson, "On the Problem of the Evacuation of Soviet Jews in 1941 (New Archival Sources)," *Jews in Eastern Europe* 3 [40] (1999): pp. 42-43; Semeon Shveibish, "Evakuatsiia i sovetskie evrei v gody Katastrofy," *Vestnik Evreiskogo universiteta v Moskve* 2 (1995): p. 40.

authorities were aware of the vulnerability of their positions in the peninsula. Accordingly, Jews who eventually made their way to the Crimea appeared to come there on their own. By the time of the German conquest of the peninsula in November 1941, Jewish refugees were staying in the main Crimean town of Simferopol'[5] and, to a smaller extent, in other towns.[6]

There were many young[7] and middle-aged women among the newcomers,[8] while there is only a small record of the arrival of young men or elderly persons,[9] or indeed whole families.[10] The refugees coming to the Crimea had already left their native homelands and headed for a safe area, which by mid-August 1941 the Crimea could no longer be considered. After all, the Soviet-German front line was rapidly approaching its borders. Therefore, many of these Jewish refugees viewed the peninsula as a mere transition point. That is, because the Red Army seemed determined to defend the Crimea, Jewish refugees fled to the region with the assumption that it would then be possible to escape the Crimea further into the Soviet rear. Indeed, some groups were able to leave the peninsula while others remained stuck.

In the first months of 1942, the Red Army liberated part of Crimean peninsula from the Wehrmacht near the city of Kerch. This turned out to be a destination for some Jews previously evacuated from the Crimea who were eager to return to their

5 Testimony of Efim Gopshtein, August 16, 1944, Yad Vashem Archives (YVA), M.35/23, p. 58. Gopshtein's testimony is also presented in Joshua Rubenstein and Ilya Altman (Il'ia Al'tman), eds., *The Unknown Black Book: The Holocaust in the German-Occupied Soviet Territories* (Bloomington: Indiana University Press in association with the United States Holocaust Memorial Museum, 2008), pp. 338-359.

6 Kerch, Sevastopol': Testimony of Leda Kiseleva, September 28, 1992, YVHN; Testimony of Sara Vainberg, April 19, 1991, YVHN.

7 Testimony of Proszberg, October 7, 1956, YVHN; Testimony of Gila Baum, 1992, YVHN.

8 Testimony of Hania Dominitz, January 2, 1957, YVHN; Testimony of Abraham Zeifman, August 1, 1955, YVHN.

9 Testimony of Kharii Daich, February 29, 1974, YVHN.

10 Testimony of Moshe Tenebaum, October 5, 1955, YVHN; Testimony of Abraham Gis, July 1956, YVHN.

(Evacuation of) the column of the blind. Belorussia. Photo by David Abramovich Minsker. Late June-early July 1941. Courtesy: RHCA

Jewish refugees. Belorussia. Photo by David Abramovich Minsker. Late June-early July 1941. Courtesy: RHCA

native region.[11] It is not clear whether Soviet authorities supported their movement, but, at any rate, they did not oppose to it. The Jewish refugees mistakenly regarded the Soviet return to the peninsula as part of a general changing of the tide in the war. But most of the Jews apparently failed to flee the Crimea when the Red Army abandoned it in May-early July 1942 and were soon killed thereupon by the Germans.

2. Evacuation from the Region

2.1. General concerns

Jewish representation in the target groups intended for evacuation from the Crimea was of decisive importance to the possibility of the targeted groups undergoing government-sponsored evacuation. Precise data on the Jewish representation among the Soviet functionaries or the workers of armaments industries, the first two groups earmarked by the government for evacuation, remains elusive.[12] However, by and large, Soviet Jewish functionaries and their family members were likely to leave the peninsula as they were more aware of what potentially awaited them under German rule either as Jews and/or Soviet activists. One way or another, Jews/Soviet activists sensed that remaining in the peninsula might compromise their position, as was the case in an example concerning the Jewish wife of a non-Jewish Crimean Communist. She was evacuated on October 25, 1941 following her husband's warning: "You are a Jewess and will not be able to stay with me."[13] In another example, non-Jewish neighbors tried to persuade a Jewish

11 Testimony of Mikhail Hana Melinskii, January 12, 1986, December 6, 2009, available from http://www.iremember.ru/content/view/1051/75/lang.ru.

12 On the whole, the evacuation of industrial plants from the Crimea seemed relatively successful. This is acknowledged indirectly in a German report on the situation in Simferopol': "All the planes and factories were plundered (i.e. evacuated or destroyed)" OK I/853, "TB für die Zeit vom 5.-15.11.1941," Simferopol, November 14, 1941, YVA, M.29.FR/41, p. 23. For a postwar Soviet testimony on the topic, see Naum Sirota, *Tak derzhalas' Kerch* (Simferopol': Krymizdat, 1961), pp. 34-36.

13 Ivan Kozlov, *V Krymskom podpol'ie* (Moscow: Gospolitizdat, 1954), p. 19.

family to evacuate, pointing to the danger because of its affiliation with the Soviet regime by claiming: "Regardless of nationality, everyone knows that your four children are Communists."[14]

The two aforementioned groups appeared to be numerically insignificant in terms of Jewish survival, but importantly, the majority of their members were evacuated with their families. It is of note that unlike many 'ordinary' Jews, members of these groups were not given a choice whether to stay or to move but were mostly ordered to evacuate – not as Jews – but by virtue of being involved in the Soviet regime.[15] This was the case with the Secretary of the Yalta Committee of the VKP(b), who was evacuated in the obligatory manner from Kerch in early November 1941.[16] We cannot establish, however, what could have motivated Jewish members of these groups to evacuate, if given a choice, and whether or not their decisions were based on fear of being persecuted as a Jew and/or Soviet activist, if at all.

Evacuation of children constitutes another special case. The authorities were eager to evacuate minors, as was the case in Kerch. On August 5, 1941, the local administration of Kerch made the decision "to evacuate the children belonging to the following age groups: 1) day nursery 2) pre-school 3) 1-4 school grades."[17] However, it is not clear how this decision was carried out or to what extent it affected the departure of their families, if at all. Many of the institutions that enrolled Jewish children were located in the peninsula, as it was known for its favorable climatic conditions; for the most part, the children were evacuated.[18] There

14 Veniamin Dymshits, *Magnitka v soldatskoi shineli* (Moscow: Arkhitektura, 1995), p. 162.

15 Statement of Evsei Fel'dman, [no later than November 20, 1943], State Archive of the Russian Federation (GARF), 7021/9/95, p. 353.

16 Sirota, *Tak derzhalas' Kerch*, p. 45.

17 Ibid., p. 34. On the evacuation of children in the USSR, see Manley, *To the Tashkent Station: Evacuation and Survival in the Soviet Union at War*, pp. 20, 22, 31, 35-37, etc.

18 See Table 15, "Evacuation of children's homes and medical institutions from the Crimea into the North Caucasus as of 1942" and Memorandum of the Crimean District Committee of the VKP(b) "Ob evakuatsii naseleniia iz Kryma i okazanii emu pomoshi v mestakh naznacheniia", May 18, 1943, State Archive of the Autonomous Republic of the Crimea (DAARK), R-1/1/2182.

were Jews among the children placed in orphanages who either had no parents[19] or whose parents were not present in the Crimea.[20] Furthermore, the administration, staff, and students of institutes of higher education were predominantly evacuated,[21] although some students did not join this organized effort.[22]

Nevertheless, it should be emphasized that the evacuation of the target groups was far from a complete success. Authorities issued the extremely belated general evacuation decree with respect to "all communists, members of the *Komsomol*, and functionaries (*sovetskii aktiv*), except those selected to perform special tasks" on October 29, 1941, only days before German troops entered.[23] The result was that a number of lower-ranking Soviet activists, including some 3,000 Communists (15% of their total number), were unable to evacuate and remained in the Crimea.[24] Among them were also Jews, such as a Jewish *Komsomol* functionary in Simferopol' who failed to join the retreating Red Army units,[25] and a Jewish employee of the Crimean Department of Agriculture who was reportedly "forgotten by his superior in the occupied area."[26]

Most Jews who succeeded in evacuating from the Crimea fell into the third target group, loosely defined as "any possible human resources that could be transferred out of the Germans' reach." Within this group certain categories of people were denied

19 Simferopol': Testimony of Son'ia Glikman, September 12, 1985, YVA, 0.3/4325, p. 4.
20 Yalta: Testimony of Vadim Maniker, April 1975, YVA, 0.3/4108, p. 1.
21 Crimean Medical Institution in Simferopol': Beliaev and Bondar', *Kuban' v gody Velikoi Otechestvennoi voiny, 1941-1945*, pp. 181-182.
22 Testimony of Boris Brandis, April 29, 1999, YVHN; Testimony of Iakov Simin, July 10, 1998, YVHN.
23 Decree of the [Crimean] District Committee of the VKP(b) on evacuation, October 29, 1941, in Kondranov and Stepanova, *Krym v period Velikoi Otechestvennoi voiny*, p. 53.
24 Aleksei Basov, *Krym v Velikoi Otechestvennoi Voine, 1941-1945* (Moscow: Nauka, 1987), p. 21.
25 Kozlov, *V Krymskom podpol'ie*, p. 150.
26 Diary of Grigorii Ioffe, in charge of evacuation of the cattle, Head of the 1st Industrial Department of the State Commissariat for Agriculture, entry from November 9, 1941, DAARK, P-156/1/31, p. 31.

evacuation permits, mainly the seriously infirm[27] and persons with physical disabilities.[28] Overall, authorities did not clearly define who was eligible to evacuate, resulting in inconsistency in the local evacuation policy. This case in which a wife describes her Jewish husband's hindered evacuation illustrates some of this inconsistency:

> When the evacuation commenced, Isaak, my husband, who worked as a chief book-keeper of the Yalta trade syndicate (*Yalttorgsin*), was not exempt from the obligation to work. On the contrary, he received additional assignments. Trade points were not closed and he continued to work.[29]

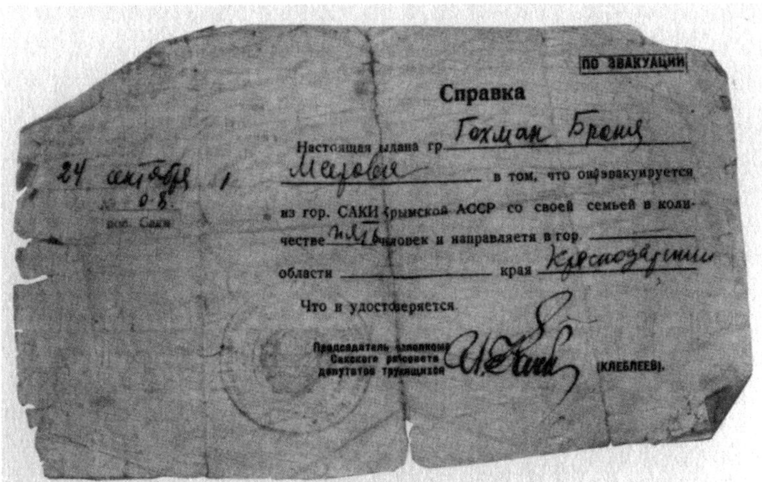

ПО ЭВАКУАЦИИ

Справка

Настоящая выдана гр. Гохман Броня Меєровна в том, что она эвакуируется из гор. САКИ Крымской АССР со своей семьей в количестве пять человек и направляется в гор. ______ области ______ края Краснодарский

Что и удостоверяется.

Председатель исполкома Сакского райсовета депутатов трудящихся (КЛЕБЛЕЕВ).

24 сентября
№ 08

Certificate of Evacuation: "Issued to the citizen Gokhman Bronia Meerovna [and confirming that] she is evacuating from the town of Saki in the Crimean ASSR [Autonomous Soviet Socialist Republic] with her family numbering five persons and is heading for Krasnodarskii *krai*. Date: September 24, 1941. Signed by the Chairman of the Saki Regional Council of the Deputies of Working People Klebleev." Courtesy: RHCA

27 Feodosiia: Interview with Savelii Al'ianaki, March 30, 2004, author's archive.

28 Simferopol': Memoirs of A. F. Peganova, November 9, 1944, DAARK, P-156/1/40, pp. 34-45.

29 Statement of Mariia Kaidanova, July 24, 1944, GARF, 7021/9/59, p. 85.

In such an atmosphere of uncertainty, personal initiative was an important factor in overcoming bureaucratic hurdles and obtaining evacuation authorization. This is indicated in a piece of postwar evidence describing the course of evacuation from the town of Evpatoriia:

> Evacuation commenced in August. There were Jews among the evacuees but not many. It was announced that everyone eager to go might do so. Yet, not everyone was given an evacuation permit. Many people remained. I don't know why, but not everyone received the permit. It was very difficult for me to get the whole of my family inscribed in the permit.[30]

As the front line drew closer to the Crimea, the circle of those eager to leave widened. At the same time, however, it was becoming more and more difficult to procure evacuation authorizations. Even once those necessary documents were in possession, actualization of evacuation had become significantly more difficult.

Members of the third group made the decision whether to evacuate or to stay on their own volition.[31] A number of factors influenced a family's or an individual's decision-making process, most specifically the degree of availability of information regarding the impending disaster. Given the relative isolation of the peninsula, it is possible that the number of people in the Crimea who did not know about the German persecution of Jews was substantial.[32] Yet, this notion is partly offset by a high share of men who were already drafted into the army, which could have enabled them to become informed of the German policies toward Jews and accordingly to alert their relatives.[33] Most importantly, the peninsula was occupied

30 Testimony of Rachel Horowitz, March 20, 1988, YVA, 0.3/4875, p. 5.

31 On the hesitations within this group, see Anna Shternshis, "Between Life and Death: Why Some Soviet Jews Decided to Leave and Others to Stay in 1941," *Kritika: Explorations in Russian and Eurasian History* 15, no. 3 (Summer 2014): pp. 477-504.

32 Testimony of Efim Gopshtein, August 16, 1944, YVA, M.35/23, p. 62; Abram Shenderovich, "Zhyzn' i sud'ba," *Paralleli* 13-14 (2015): p. 320.

33 Simferopol': Interview with Vladimir Peisakh, March 22, 2004, author's archive.

more than four months after the war began. As a result, there is no record in Crimean Jewish testimonies indicating that the German onslaught against the Jews took them by surprise.[34]

The official Soviet media was potentially an important channel through which Crimean Jews could have learned that they should evacuate, although it required an acute sense of awareness on the part of the reader. It is worth mentioning that authorities, fearful of the influence of German propaganda, ordered the local population to deliver radio sets to all Crimean citizens at the beginning of the war. In addition, because of the war chaos, it was nearly impossible to find central newspapers in the Crimea at that time.[35] The most important remaining official source was the daily newspaper *Krasnyi Krym* (Red Crimea), and its analysis predictably reveals the ambiguous message Crimean Jews who read this paper received.[36] On the one hand, quite a number of publications in *Krasnyi Krym* addressed the German maltreatment of Jews in Europe, which highlighted the especially brutal treatment of Jews compared to the rest of the population.[37] On the other hand, only one article appeared on the Nazi persecution and annihilation of Jews in the occupied Soviet territories, and it was published relatively late.[38] The gradual approach of the Wehrmacht into the Crimea was partly reflected in the newspaper, albeit delayed.[39] However, not

34 Mordechai Altshuler, "The Evacuation and Flight of Jews of Eastern Belorussia during the Holocaust: June-August 1941" (Hebrew), *Yahadut zmanenu* 3 (1986): p. 132; Rozaliia Krichevskaia, *Dvadtsat' deviat' mesiatsev iz detstva* (Beer Sheva, 1997), p. 8.

35 Testimony of Efim Gopshtein, August 16, 1944, YVA, M.35/23 p. 62.

36 Published in Simferopol' by the Crimean District Committee and Simferopol' Municipal Committee of the VKP(b) and the Supreme Council of the Crimean ASSR. I looked through all available issues from June 22 to September 18, 1941.

37 For example, I. Degtiarev, "Fashizm – zleishii vrag chelovechestva," *Krasnyi Krym*," *Krasnyi Krym*, no. 164 (6176), July 13, 1941; G. D. [full name unavailable], "Gitlerovskii 'Novyi poriadok' v Evrope," *Krasnyi Krym*, no. 167 (6179), July 17, 1941.

38 Vanda Vasil'evskaia, "Zapadnaia Ukraina istekaet krov'iu," *Krasnyi Krym*, no. 221 (6233), September 18, 1941.

39 For example, "Kiev byl i ostanetsia sovetskim," *Krasnyi Krym*, no. 207 (6219), September 2, 1941; A. Krasnov, "Na podkhodakh k Kievu," *Krasnyi Krym*, September 7, 1941; T. Zhukov, "Oborona Odessy," *Krasnyi Krym*, no. 212 (6224).

a single word was said about the evacuation from the Crimea. In fact, some articles emphasized the 'business as usual' atmosphere (e.g., school enrollments and institution openings,[40] as well as reports on the harvest collection for the fall of 1941[41]). As for the domestic military agenda, the propaganda message remained the same throughout the whole period from the outbreak of hostilities in June 1941 up to the German occupation of the Crimea in late October: "The Crimea will be defended at any cost."[42]

It should be also taken into account that possessing information of the German brutalities toward Jews did not automatically lead to evacuation. Some Jews simply discarded this news.[43] For others, the decision-making process was more nuanced: for some mixed families, such information sufficed to convince Jewish husbands to evacuate while consciously leaving their Russian wives and children behind in the due-to-be-occupied territory;[44] illness of a family member[45] or pregnancy[46] could prevent the whole family from evacuating; and memories of stability left by the German occupation during the First World War (Germany occupied the Crimea in 1918) made some elderly Jews unwilling to evacuate in 1941.[47]

40 [No title], *Krasnyi Krym*, July 19, 1941. Announcements: enrollment for 4-month long courses of foreign languages (English, French); [No title], *Krasnyi Krym*, September 10, 1941. The studies began at the Simferopol' musical school. The beginning of the school term was prolonged until October 1.

41 T. Ametshaev, "Vazhneishie zadachi sel'khozrabotnikov v Krymu," *Krasnyi Krym*, no. 218 (6230), September 14, 1941.

42 For example, "Prevratim Krym v nepristupnuiu krepost'," *Krasnyi Krym*, no. 203 (6215), August 28, 1941; Editorial "Prevratim Krym v nepristupnuiu krepost'," *Krasnyi Krym*, no. 213 (6225), September 9, 1941.

43 Kerch: "Story of Iosef Vaingarten" (Yiddish), *Eynikayt*, July 15, 1942; Lev Kvitko, "The risen from the grave recalls," (Yiddish), *Eynikayt*, October 25, 1942.

44 Simferopol'skii *raion*: Diary of Chrisanf Lashkevich, entry from August, 1942, DAARK, P-156/1/31, p. 87.

45 Simferopol' and Yalta: Memoirs of A. F. Peganova, [no date], DAARK, P-156/1/40, pp. 34-45; Statement of Khrista Zheltukhin, June 3, 1944, GARF, 7021/9/59, p. 102.

46 Simferopol': Letter of Dana Poiurovskaia, September 2, 1991, in the file of Ekaterina Kolesnikova, 1993, YVA, M.31/5541.

47 Simferopol' and Evpatoriia: Rachel Horowitz, March 20, 1988, YVA, 0.3/4875, p. 5; Interview with Vladimir Peisakh, March 22, 2004, author's archive.

The inclinations of Jews toward evacuating the Crimea and the ability to actually do so were contingent upon their location. As the Holocaust-related information was primarily disseminated by refugees in the Crimea[48] and by Red Army personnel,[49] the Jews dwelling in the capital of the peninsula, Simferopol', and the two main harbors, Sevastopol' and Kerch, had an advantage over the inhabitants of other towns and rural areas, in particular. Logistically, inhabitants of numerous harbor towns from which evacuation was conducted (e.g., Feodosiia, Kerch, Yalta, Evpatoriia) had an advantage over Jews residing inside the peninsula. Those who lived in Kerch were in a particularly advantageous position, as it was the most important evacuation harbor. No large-scale evacuation occurred in Sevastopol', another important harbor, until November 1941, which is due to the fact that prior to this point the Soviet command did not envision the possibility of the area coming under direct German attack.[50]

Concerning the spontaneous flight from the peninsula, the following consideration should be taken into account. Before the fighting began on September 24, 1941 for control of the Perekop Isthmus connecting the Crimea with southern Ukraine, Jews could move out of the Crimea by land, i.e. through this isthmus.[51] However, as the front line rapidly approached, Jews availed themselves of this possibility only in the very few cases when Soviet authorities explicitly sanctioned the evacuation by a land route.[52] In fact, the deportation of the Crimean Germans via railroad around August 18-20, 1941 is almost

48 Diary of Grigorii Ioffe, in charge of the evacuation of cattle, head of the First Industrial Department of the State Commissariat for Agriculture, entry from November 21, 1941, Commission on the History of the Great Patriotic War, DAARK, P-156/1/31, p. 67.

49 Memoirs of A. F. Peganova, [no date], DAARK, P-156/1/40, pp. 34-45.

50 This is one of very few sources of evacuation of the Jews from Sevastopol' prior to October–November 1941. Statement of Sarra Igla, August 18, 1944, GARF, 7021/9/6, p. 79.

51 Ernst Klink, "The Conduct of Operations", p. 606.

52 Evpatoriia: Testimony of Rachel Gurevich, [no date], Institute of Contemporary Jewry (ICJ), TC/2761, not transcribed.

the last account of evacuation by land route[53] – there is only one record of civilian transportation via land route from the peninsula in mid-September.[54] Of further consideration is the fact that evacuation via land was significantly hindered both by the German bombardments, which caused casualties among the evacuees,[55] and by the Soviet ban on leaving the Crimea without authorization.[56]

Thus, as a result of its unique geographic position, evacuation from the Crimea was overwhelmingly facilitated by sea routes. In order to board a ship transporting people from the peninsula, it was necessary to present an evacuation permit at the harbor.[57] Evacuation by sea was impossible without this document. It is probable that in some cases Jews were able to circumvent regulation orders by pulling strings or bribing Soviet officials. The record shows that only a very small number of Jews defied the official regulations by endeavoring to escape on their own via the sea (e.g., on private boats or rafts).[58] With the above considerations in mind, evacuation from the Crimea appears to have been predominantly officially sanctioned, with the result that those Jews unable to obtain evacuation permits were inevitably forced to stay. In rare cases, some managed to eventually evacuate, such as a witness who escaped Yalta into Kerch together with her relatives. They stayed in Kerch throughout October 1941 but could not evacuate as the area was constantly bombed. They succeeded in departing only at the end of October 1941.[59]

It must be kept in mind that possessing the necessary evacuation authorization in the Crimea did not necessarily guarantee survival during the Holocaust era. In possession of all

53 "Memories of Edgar Pape," in Vadim Garagulia, Ivan Kondranov, and Liubov' Kravtsova, eds., *Krym v Velikoi Otechestvennoi voine, 1941-1945* (Simferopol': Tavriia, 1994), p. 8. See also Manley, *To the Tashkent Station: Evacuation and Survival in the Soviet Union at War*, p. 42.

54 Shenderovich, "Zhyzn' i sud'ba," p. 322.

55 Testimony of Ekaterina Govzman, July 20, 1999, YVHN.

56 Testimony of Hana Melinskii, January 12, 1986, YVA, 0.3/4342, p. 3.

57 Ibid.

58 Testimony of Irina Chamanian, March 22, 1998, YVHN.

59 Testimony of Ol'ga Polonskaia, May 1, 1962, YVA, 0.3/2246, p. 5.

necessary papers, one Jewish man arrived at the shipment point and yet failed to evacuate because the ship was overcrowded, which sealed his fate.[60] As already mentioned, the German air force bombed several evacuation transports, killing many refugees. Evacuation from the Crimea into the North Caucasus demonstrates that Jews could escape the German occupation of the peninsula in 1941, but even so, many perished as a result of the German advance into region of their evacuation destination (North Caucasus) in 1942, as will be revealed in Chapter Four.

2.2. Prior to November 1941

Evacuation from the Crimea began at the onset of war. Given the fact that the region was not directly endangered by the German army in the first months of hostilities, in the initial phase of the warfare its dimensions were noticeable, as is exhibited by the fact that according to the data of the Council for Evacuation, some 51,000 people were evacuated from the peninsula by August 20, 1941.[61] Jews were among the evacuees,[62] and other Jews who were not included in this number still considered evacuation a possibility.[63] Although there is no appraisal of the share of the Jews among this wave of evacuees, the only available testimony, which depicts the evacuation from the Crimea by train, points out the huge Jewish dimensions of this process: "All the passengers of the train were Jews."[64]

The evacuation atmosphere fluctuated between spontaneity and calculation. The following source (from Simferopol') suggests that prior to 1941, evacuation from the Crimea was relatively

60 Yalta: Statement of Viktor Domorovskii, August 10, 1944, YVA, M.33/68, pp. 106-107.

61 Report of the Deputy People's Commissar of Transportation on the course of evacuation in accordance with the decisions of the SNK SSSR, Secret, August 22, 1941, YVA, JM/24678.

62 Feodosiia, Simferopol': Statement of Fania Shtaingard, August 22, 1944, GARF, 7021/9/6, pp. 281-282; Testimony of Liudmila Bradichevskii, May 13, 1996, ICJ, 217/183, p. 1.

63 Simferopol': Testimony of Liudmila Bradicheskii, May 13, 1996, ICJ, 217/183, p. 1.

64 Evpatoriia: Testimony of Rachel Gurevich, [no date], ICJ, TC/2761.

smooth and did not significantly affect the morale of the Jewish population:

> Grigorii Gol'dberg was willing to evacuate, but he fell short of money. He wanted to sell his house. His neighbor offered to buy his house very cheaply (for only 4,000 rubles instead of 30,000 rubles, which he had originally spent).[65]

Gol'dberg declined the proposal and consequently failed to evacuate. The fact that economic factors of this sort played a significant role for a person considering evacuation implies that during this period, at least for him, this was not a spontaneous flight at any cost but rather a well-calculated step. For such people, evacuation appeared to be seen in terms of economically-motivated migration, not as a panicked escape. Other witnesses also reasoned that economic factors played a vital role in their decision to evacuate.[66]

Significant intensification in government-sponsored evacuation may be traced to mid-August 1941, when the strategic position of the Soviet forces in southern Ukraine deteriorated considerably. Soviet authorities considered the possibility of a German thrust in the direction of the Crimea in the near future, which resulted in a growing ambiguity in Soviet plans. On the one hand, their plans involved important military preparations, such as setting up defensive positions around strategic areas[67] and organizing local armaments production.[68] On the other hand, special attention was placed on the speedy removal of

65 Testimony of D. I. Makarycheva, Commission on the History of the Great Patriotic War, DAARK, P-156/1/36, p. 59; Shenderovich, "Zhyzn' i sud'ba," p. 322.

66 Sevastopol': Testimony of Aza Tumbinskaia in Gel'man and Glubochanskii, *Kholokost*, p. 137.

67 Kerch: All works were scheduled to be over by August 26, 1941. Decree of the Bureau of the Kerch Municipal Committee of the VKP(b) on the erection of defensive objects around the town, August 11, 1941, in Kondranov, *Krym v period Velikoi Otechestvennoi voiny*, pp. 49-50.

68 Kerch: Decree of the Bureau of the Crimean District Committee of the VKP(b) on organization of armaments production in the Crimean enterprises, August 28, 1941, in ibid., pp. 54-55.

the population from the Crimea. Particularly telling of Soviet intentions concerning the Crimea was the fact that on August 13, 1941, authorities evacuated the families of NKVD employees.[69] Then, on August 14, 1941, the Supreme Command Headquarters issued the Directive to the Military Council of the 51st Army, which defended the peninsula. It stated:

> In order to defend the Crimea... everything of value but of no need for the defense is to be evacuated.[70]

This moment can be considered a turning point in the Crimean evacuation policy, as it denoted a previously unseen sort of large-scale undertaking. In fulfillment of this order, on August 19, 1941, the Council for Evacuation issued a decree providing for the evacuation of 85,000 workers and employees and their families; 35,000 people were to go by train, and the rest by sea.[71] Soviet military authorities were placed in charge of issuing evacuation permits.[72]

The evacuation efforts were accelerated in September-October. According to a high-ranking Soviet official, from the second half of October 1941 up to that point "two steamships [had] departed every day from Kerch, not to mention the small ships belonging to the Army, which also took away a considerable number of people."[73] Many Jews were able to evacuate during this period.[74] The growing scale of the evacuation from the peninsula in and of itself turned into a weighty factor for Jews still deciding whether or not to evacuate,[75] as did news of the Soviet surrender of important areas close to the Crimea.[76]

69 Diary of Chrisanf Lashkevich, entry from August 13, 1941, DAARK, P-156/1/31, p. 53.

70 Kondranov, *Krym v Velikoi Otechestvennoi voine*, p. 7.

71 Basov, *Krym v Velikoi Otechestvennoi Voine, 1941-1945*, p. 26.

72 Testimony of Hana Melinskii, January 12, 1986, YVA, 0.3/4342, p. 4.

73 Sirota, *Tak derzhalas' Kerch*, p. 35.

74 Simferopol', Yalta: Statement of Evsei Fel'dman, GARF, 7021/9/95, p. 353. Statement of Iona Achkinaz, September 18, 1944, GARF, 7021/9/95, p. 67.

75 Sirota, *Tak derzhalas' Kerch*, pp. 34-35.

76 Kherson and Nikolaev by mid-August 1941, Kiev on September 19, 1941, and

Learning by mail or other means of Jewish evacuation outside of but in close proximity to the Crimea could have also led other Jews to opt for evacuation.[77]

From the second half of October 1941, German airplanes had begun regularly bombing ships entering and exiting the Crimea, and evacuation consequently turned into a dangerous enterprise. German bombardments all but prevented daytime evacuation[78] and severely diminished its efficiency.[79] Thousands of evacuees, among them Jews, perished from the attacks on all Crimean harbors.[80] One of the most striking pieces of evidence is the sinking of the hospital ship "Armenia" on November 7, 1941, near Yalta, which had left Sevastopol' carrying some 3,000 Crimean inhabitants.[81] Among the victims were Jews, most of whom were medical personnel.[82] Other Jewish civilian evacuees and Jewish soldiers perished when their ships, departing from the Crimean harbors of Feodosiia,[83] Kerch,[84] and Yalta,[85] were blown up by underwater mines or bombed.

Not only did the German air raids in the immediate vicinity of the Crimean harbors cause a large number of casualties, but they also had particularly negative repercussions on the willingness of the potential evacuees to pursue evacuation. The following example

Odessa in mid-October 1941: Klink, "The Conduct of Operations," pp. 597, 602, 606.

77 Feodosiia: Yehezkiel Keren, *Crimean Jewry from its Inception (Beginning) to the Holocaust* (Hebrew), (Jerusalem: Reuven Mas, 1981), p. 296.

78 Kerch: Interview with Vladimir Peisakh, March 22, 2004, author's archive.

79 Ivan Oleksandrovych Herasymov, et al., eds., *Kniga skorbi Ukrainy: Avtonomnaia respublika Krym* (Simferopol': Tavrida, 2001), p. 9.

80 Ibid., p. 9. See also S. Gordon, "On the Jewish Settlements in the Crimea" (Yiddish), *Eynikayt*, August 16, 1945, p. 3.

81 Note of the Crimean District Committee of the VKP(b) on the composition and transformation of the Crimean Party organization, February 25, 1943, in Kondranov, *Krym v period Velikoi Otechestvennoi voiny*, p. 65; Il'ia Vergasov, *Krymskye tetradi* (Moscow: Sovetskii pisatel', 1971), pp. 24-25.

82 Testimony of Alexander Mikheikin, June 3, 1992, YVHN; Testimony of Viktor Frenkel, May 5, 1996, YVHN.

83 Testimony of Dainova (no first name available), n.d., YVHN. Testimony of Mikhail Girshkovich, September 22, 1992, YVHN.

84 Testimony of Mariia Paramonov, May 25, 1999, YVHN.

85 Testimony of Liza Moskovskaia, October 4, 1992, YVHN.

underscores this point. German planes bombed the "Rot Front" ship on November 4, 1941, and, as a result, "600 specialists from Voikov plant and their families" were killed.[86] The ship went down near the Kerch harbor; only around 10 people survived the attack.[87] The masses of potential evacuees waiting for their turn in Kerch quickly learned of the disaster and were reluctant to evacuate afterwards.[88] According to a statement from a high-ranking Communist Party official, in the wake of the German attack, people said "it would be better to be killed here at home while dealing with something that the army needs than somewhere at sea."[89]

The rapidly deteriorating military situation in and around the Crimea affected all aspects of evacuation. During its retreat, the Red Army requisitioned all cars and trucks,[90] while fleeing military men and civilians who possessed transport refused to pick up passengers.[91] Furthermore, the army used the same facilities (harbors and ships) meant for civilian evacuation to remove its own personnel from the embattled peninsula. As the Germans edged closer, the authorities intensified the military evacuation, which was prioritized over the removal of the civilians.[92]

2.3. November 1941-June 1942

From mid-November 1941 to early July 1942, the Red Army maintained strongholds in the Crimea. These included Sevastopol' (up to the beginning of July 1942), Kerch (January-May 1942), Feodosiia, Sudak, and Evpatoriia (from a couple of days to a couple of weeks during January 1942). The Germans had previously occupied all of these towns except Sevastopol' and conducted killing operations against the Jews, drastically decreasing their

86 Act of the Commission of the town of Kerch, August 24, 1944, YVA, M.33/61, pp. 29-30.
87 Herasymov, *Kniga skorbi Ukrainy*, p. 9.
88 Kozlov, *V Krymskom podpol'ie*, p. 51.
89 Sirota, *Tak derzhalas' Kerch*, p. 35.
90 Diary of Grigorii Ioffe, entry from October 30, 1941, DAARK, P-156/1/31, p. 29.
91 Ibid., Entry from October 31, 1941.
92 Ibid., Entry from November 2, 1941.

number.[93] Special attention should be placed on the evacuation processes from Kerch and Sevastopol', because Soviet presence remained longer in those areas than elsewhere.[94]

Despite the fact that most Soviet naval transportation capacities were used for military needs, civilians occasionally used them as well. This often occurred when the Red Army required maximum civilian abandonment of a given area, e.g., Sevastopol' (under siege). In November 1941, the Soviet command deemed the presence of numerous non-combatants in the area detrimental to the Soviet military effort:

> Sevastopol' authorities are ordered to expedite the evacuation of the population that is not employed in servicing the Army and armaments production. Heads of enterprises and institutions of the town are ordered to reduce their staff and personnel to a minimum.[95]

It is conceivable that the Soviet command was more ready to consider evacuating the civilian population in 1942 than before, but its ability to do so drastically diminished as the German air forces and Italian Navy inflicted heavy losses on the Soviet sea transports connecting Sevastopol' with the Soviet sea bases in the Black Sea. Nevertheless, evacuation from Sevastopol' continued unabated from November 1941 to July 1942.[96] Given the logistical obstacles facing Soviet authorities, the departure

93 See Chapter 3, "Destruction of the Jewish Population in the Crimea."

94 Some Jews evacuated from Feodosiia, too. "Alla-Roza Brazgol," Lev Kvitko, ed., YVA, M.35/14, p. 91. This testimony is also presented in Rubenstein and Altman, *The Unknown Black Book*, pp. 371-372. See also Moshe Gutovich, "From the conversation with Moshe Gutovich, Jewish refugee from Feodosiia" (Yiddish), *Eynikayt*, no. 1685, July 13, 1943, p. 3; Krichevskaia, *Dvadtsat' deviat' mesiatsev iz detstva*, p. 23.

95 Decree of Sevastopol' municipal committee of the VKP(b) "Ob evakuatsii naseleniia goroda", November 13, 1941, in Kondranov, *Krym v period Velikoi Otechestvennoi voiny*, p. 79.

96 Information survey of the Sevastopol' municipal committee of the VKP(b) on the situation in the city during the third onslaught by the enemy, June 19, 1942, in ibid., p. 158. Testimony of Vladimir Petrov, 2002, in Gel'man and Glubochanskii, *Kholokost*, p. 102.

of 58,000 people,[97] among them Jews,[98] was a considerable achievement.

In Kerch, the situation was different. Evacuation took place from January to mid-May 1942, but few details are known about its conditions. According to the recent testimony of a Krymchak survivor, the Soviet authorities prohibited evacuation during almost the entire period, while Soviet soldiers shot at those who attempted to escape by swimming through the Taman Straits leading to the Soviet mainland.[99] Such protocol lasted only up to about two days before the Germans seized Kerch in mid-May 1942, after which evacuation from Kerch was massive.[100] The area was close to the Soviet mainland; therefore, authorities were in the position to arrange smooth evacuation from the area. Nevertheless, evacuation from Kerch during the Soviet presence still failed, with only 12,000 people relocated during this period.[101] This was largely due to the fact that Soviet authorities were reluctant to acknowledge their vulnerability and allow evacuation until the last moment.

3.4. The evacuation of Jewish *kolkhozniki*[102]

After the beginning of the war, central Soviet authorities demanded (along the lines of the aforementioned evacuation directives) that "*kolkhozniki* remove the cattle and hand the bread over to the state bodies for safekeeping so that it can be moved to the rear areas."[103]

97 Memorandum of the Crimean District Committee of the VKP(b) "Ob evakuatsii naseleniia iz Kryma i okazanii emu pomoshi v mestakh naznacheniia", May 18, 1943, DAARK, R-1/1/2182.

98 Statements of Rozaliia Abramovich and Evgeniia Abramovich, July 17, 1944, GARF, 7021/9/101, p. 84. Statement of Naum Abramovich, Akt no. 149, August 16, 1944, GARF, 7021/9/5, p. 427.

99 Interview with Professor David Borokhov, March-April 2004, author's archive; Larisa Mangupli, *Kerosinovyi vkus detstva* (Kerch, 2003), pp. 19-21.

100 Diary of Ol'ga Mikhinina, inhabitant of Kerch, entry from May 10, 1942, DAARK, P-156/1/31; Mangupli, *Kerosinovyi vkus detstva*, pp. 19-21.

101 Memorandum of the Crimean District Committee of the VKP(b) "Ob evakuatsii naseleniia iz Kryma i okazanii emu pomoshi v mestakh naznacheniia", May 18, 1943, DAARK, R-1/1/2182.

102 For the purposes of the study, all Jewish inhabitants of Crimean rural areas are referred to in this section as 'Jewish *kolkhozniki*'.

103 Directive of the SNK SSSR and the TsK VKP(b) to the Party and the Soviet

In line with this decree, during the first half of September 1941 Crimean authorities ordered cattle flocks, grain reserves, and stations for tractors and agricultural machines (MTS) to be moved out of the peninsula.[104] Cattle were scheduled to be removed from the entire peninsula.[105] In the end, the Soviets succeeded in removing all "public" cattle (i.e., 700,000 heads of cattle) and 175,000 tons of grain from the Crimea.[106] Most of the cattle herds were led by transport through the Kerch harbor; only a small number was evacuated via land routes through southern Ukraine.

The primary problem was that the authorities were more concerned with evacuating cattle than people. This evacuation policy, according to the formula of evacuating "Jewish *kolkhozniki* with cattle or grain," may be outlined as follows: The cattle were to be accompanied by people, and as many Jewish *kolkhozy* bred cattle and grew grain, a small number of their inhabitants were assigned to accompany the transportation of flock, grain, and machinery to safety outside of the Crimea.[107] Although there is no general data shedding light on the performance of the Jewish *kolkhozy* in evacuating the cattle, a Soviet wartime report emphasizes that, despite serious logistical difficulties, many *kolkhozy* in the Fraidorfskii *raion* (i.e., predominately Jewish) excelled in fulfilling evacuation directives.[108]

organizations of the front districts, no. P509, June 29, 1941, in Vladimir Zolotarev, ed., *Velikaia Otechestvennaia voina, 1941-1945* (Moscow: Nauka, 1998), vol. 1, p. 500.

104 Sirota, *Tak derzhalas' Kerch*, p. 37.

105 Ibid., p. 37.

106 Memorandum "O rabote Krymskogo Obkoma VKP(b) po rukovodstvu partizanskim dvizheniem i podpol'noi rabotoi v Krymu," February 13, 1943, DAARK, P-1/1/2144a.

107 By 1939, Jews produced 12.5% of the Crimean grain and nearly 11% of all field crops; the colonists possessed 20% of its sheep. Jonathan Dekel-Chen, *Shopkeepers and Peddlers into Soviet Farmers: Jewish Agricultural Colonization in Crimea and Southern Ukraine, 1924-1941* (PhD diss.,. Brandeis University, 2001), p. 363. See also Keren, *Crimean Jewry from its Inception*, pp. 210-211.

108 Information resume of the Crimean District Committee of the VKP(b) on the rise of political and labor spirit in the midst of the Crimean working people as a reaction to the Hitlerite aggression, September 24, 1941, in Kondranov, *Krym v period Velikoi Otechestvennoi voiny*, p. 60.

Authorities intended to evacuate only those key workers necessary for accompanying the cattle, but the criteria for selecting these workers were not clear. According to the testimony of a contemporary high-ranking Crimean Communist official, directives were not always followed, as "the check-up revealed that in some *kolkhozy* and *sovkhozy* entirely unsuitable people – teenagers, women with small children – were assigned to this work."[109]

Jewish testimonies also suggest that lone women,[110] whole families,[111] mothers with children,[112] or elderly persons[113] were occasionally assigned to accompany the cattle. Some were evacuated, such as a Jewish woman assigned to accompany 117 cows from the Oktiabr'skii Jewish *kolkhoz* near Simferopol' towards Kerch.[114] Others were unable to leave, and stayed in the Crimea, such as the example of an elderly Jewish *kolkhoznik* who remained, despite being assigned to accompany the evacuation of the flock from the village of Friling.[115] Still others perished during the course of evacuation.[116] When the Red Army regained control over the Kerch area in January-May 1942, Soviet authorities again attempted to evacuate cattle from the area. The cattle were moved into the Soviet mainland, but the Jews who accompanied them were unable to evacuate and were murdered in the Holocaust.[117] Regardless of the result, the juxtaposition of evidence suggests that only a few Jews accompanying cattle or grain left the Crimea.

109 Sirota, *Tak derzhalas' Kerch*, p. 38.

110 Testimony of Hana Melinskii, January 12, 1986, YVA, 0.3/4342, p. 3.

111 Letter from Bluma Zlotskaia and Hannah Kaem letter to the newspaper *Shalom* (published in no. 5/34, May 1993), in Gitel Gubenko, *The Book of Sorrows* (New York: GStanislav Company, Inc., 2003), pp. 108-109. Testimony of Mikhail Shpigelman, 1999, in Elena Rivkina and Mikhail Tiaglyi, eds., *Vospominaniia zhitelei evreiskikh poselenii v Krymu* (Simferopol': BETS "Chesed Shymon," 2004), p. 14.

112 Dzhankoi: Statement of Rita Dvoretskaia, [no later than May 1945], GARF, 7021/9/193, p. 394.

113 Testimony of Il'ia Berenson, July 19, 1991, YVHN.

114 Testimony of Hana Melinskii, January 12, 1986, YVA, 0.3/4342, p. 3.

115 Pervomaisk Regional Council: Gubenko, *Kniga pechali*, p. 42.

116 From Pervoimaiskii *kolkhoz* into the Taman peninsula: Testimony of Il'ia Berenson, July 19, 1991, YVHN.

117 Zlotskaia and Kaem's letter in Gubenko, *Book of Sorrows*, pp. 108-109.

However, the impact of government policy on the evacuation of the Jewish *kolkhozniki* went beyond its narrowly defined goals. As Jewish *kolkhozy* were not on the main rescue routes by which refugees exited the Crimea, little information was available to their inhabitants on the dimensions and proximity of danger. As a result, the drastic policy of evacuating flock and grain (the *raison d'être* of the villages) in and of itself made a profound impression on the masses of Jewish *kolkhozniki* and led them to consider evacuation.[118] Evacuation from some Jewish *kolkhozy* was made easier as their administrations circumvented the complicated bureaucratic procedure and quickly issued evacuation permits for those Jews eager to leave.[119] Thus, it appears that the evacuation of masses of Jewish *kolkhozniki*, however incomplete, may be attributed largely to these 'side effects' of the Soviet evacuation policy.

Little is known about the evacuation from villages. A Soviet wartime report from September 1941 points out the enormous transportation problems that potential evacuees from the Jewish *kolkhozy* in Fraidorfskii *raion* confronted.[120] This had a detrimental effect on the evacuation of Jewish *kolkhozniki*, which was only partly offset by the allocation of some of the remaining horses for evacuees to use.[121]

The dimensions of the evacuation of Jewish *kolkhozniki* from the Crimea are difficult to determine. Appraisals made by individuals differ diametrically and range from the remark by a contemporary Jewish official in charge of evacuation of the cattle made in late October 1941:

118 Slavianskaia station, village of Zol'skoe: Diary of Grigorii Ioffe, entry from November 10, 1941, DAARK, P-156/1/31, p. 31; Akt no. 90 of the Commission of Kabardino-Balkar Republic, July 14, 1943, GARF, 7021/7/109, p. 186.

119 Village of Fraileben: Testimony of Ita Al'tman, June 28, 1999, in Rivkina and Tiaglyi, *Vospominaniia zhitelei evreiskikh poselenii v Krymu*, p. 56.

120 Information resumé in Kondranov, *Krym v period Velikoi Otechestvennoi voiny*, p. 60.

121 "Gorkii" *kolkhoz*. Letter by the *starosta* of the Gorkii farm forwarded to the *Kommandant* of the Agricultural Administration of Simferopol'skii *raion*, February 17, 1942, GARF, 7021/9/194, p. 102.

> Jewish *kolkhozy* [in Kirovskii *raion* – KF] make a sad impression since their inhabitants abandoned them.[122]

and the testimony of a Jew who encountered "the people who visited [these places] after the war":

> The larger part of Crimean Jewish population did not succeed in escaping... Many Jews, in particular the *kolkhozniki*, were forced to make their way back to their places of residence. After the occupation, the Germans began their destruction.[123]

to a Soviet cliché published in *Eynikayt* in July 1945:

> The Germans clenched their teeth on seeing the Jewish settlements in the Crimea, whose people fled in a timely fashion and took with them the cattle and harvest that they were able to collect from the fields.[124]

Numerous Jewish inhabitants of Crimean rural settlements, including Jewish *kolkhozy*, chose to stay of their own volition or were possibly ordered to do so by the Soviet authorities.[125] Other Jewish *kolkhozniki* spontaneously headed for and ended up in the central town of the peninsula, Simferopol', by the time of the German occupation.[126] This direction of migration illustrates the state of turmoil in which the Jewish villagers found themselves. Many Jewish *kolkhozniki* who succeeded in evacuating from the Crimea were murdered during the German occupation of

122 Diary of Grigorii Ioffe, entry from October 25, 1941, DAARK, P-156/1/31, p. 29.

123 Letter of Yishaiahu Shreibshtein, inhabitant of Simferopol' before the war, in Benjamin West, *In the Ropes of Destruction: Soviet Jews in the Nazi Holocaust, 1941-43* (Hebrew), (Tel Aviv: Archion Ha-avoda, 1963), p. 145.

124 *Eynikayt,* July 5, 1945, in West, *In the Ropes of Destruction*, p. 151.

125 Kolaiskii *raion* and unidentified place: Story of the chairman of "Oktiabr'" *kolkhoz* (village of Baigonchik) recorded by P. Vul, February 1945, DAARK, P-156/1/37, p. 135; Testimony of Yishaiahu Shreibshtein in West, *In the Ropes of Destruction*, p. 145.

126 Testimony of Efim Gopshtein, August 16, 1944, YVA, M.35/23, p. 58.

the Caucasus. Overall, the authorities prioritized evacuation of flock and grain over that of civilians on the *kolkhozy*. One of the consequences of this policy was the fact that important capacities allocated to evacuate cattle and grain, such as ships, were unavailable for the evacuation of people.

The only available official Soviet estimate mentions the evacuation of nearly 10,000 Jewish *kolkhozniki* (55.4% of their population as of 1939) from the Crimea.[127] This, however, was an exaggeration. Witnesses and researchers have tended to think that the Soviet authorities prioritized the evacuation of this group, yet relatively few Jewish *kolkhozniki* were assigned to accompany the removal of cattle and grain, and only part of that group actually evacuated from the peninsula.[128] Large-scale Jewish evacuation from the rural Crimean *kolkhozy* was impaired by a number of weighty factors (e.g., deficient transportation and lack of contact between the Jewish *kolkhozniki* and Jewish refugees), which arguably reduced its dimensions below the general estimate for the region to as low as 30-40%.

3. Enlistment

Following the German attack on the USSR, authorities immediately proclaimed an enlistment decree in the Crimea,[129] which called for the drafting of conscript-age men born between 1905 and 1918 into the army (those born between 1919 and 1922 had already been conscripted prior to June 22, 1941).[130] From June to November 1941,

127 Vladimir Gurkovich, "Evakuatsiia evreev i lits drugikh natsional'nostei iz Kryma v 1941 g.," *Krymskoe vremia*, December 18, 2001, in Jonathan Dekel-Chen, "Soviet-Jewish agricultural colonists, 1937-1945," *Jews in Eastern Europe* 3 [46] (2001): p. 53f.

128 Schwarz, *Evrei v Sovetskom Soiuze s nachala vtoroi mirovoi voiny (1939-1965)*, p. 58; Keren, *Crimean Jewry from its Inception*, p. 308.

129 Decree of Feodosiia's Municipal Committee of the VKP(b), June 22, 1941, in Kondranov, *Krym v period Velikoi Otechestvennoi voiny*, pp. 19-21.

130 Initially the draft applied to men born between 1905 and 1918. V. A. Vlasov, ed., *Zakonodatelnye i administrativno-pravovye akty voennogo vremeni (s 22 iunia 1941 g. po 22 marta 1942 g.)* (Moscow: Iurizdat, 1942), pp. 38-41.

the Red Army and other military institutions drafted some 93,000 people (8.25% of the prewar Crimean population).[131] Ten thousand volunteers,[132] among them Jews, were among the draftees.[133] Initially, some of the draftees were stationed far from the peninsula. However, Soviet policy changed as a result of the deterioration of the situation at the front, and after the second half of August 1941 the conscripts were mainly stationed in the Crimea.[134]

The enforcement of the enlistment order in the peninsula should be viewed with an eye to the fact that the Germans seized the Crimea over four months after the outbreak of the war. Therefore, the Soviet command had more than just a small stretch of time to make use of the Crimean human resources: In a number of cases they extended the draft to men over 40.[135] In the peninsula, the draft affected both the urban[136] and rural[137] Jewish population. Jews and non-Jews alike additionally served in the so-called *opolchenie*, another parliamentary military institution[138]

131 Novella Vavilova, *Uroki razgnevannoi Klio* (Simferopol', 1998), p. 93.

132 Ibid.

133 Memoirs of Naum Fishman, n.d., in Pavel Polian and Aron Shneer, eds., *Obrechennye pogibnut': Sud'ba sovetskikh voennoplennykh-evreev vo Vtoroi mirovoi voine: Vospominaniia i dokumenty* (Moscow: Novoe izdatel'stvo, 2006), pp. 280-281.

134 Testimony of Akhtarova, a Tatar woman married to a Jewish man, Gregorii Odesskii, who managed to escape to Istanbul at the time of the German retreat, "Tragic End of the Jewry of the Western Russia" (Hebrew), *Ha-boker* no. 2691, September 6, 1944, p. 2 from *Izvestiia*, July 2, 1944.

135 Testimony of Kucherov, [no date], YVHN; Testimony of Bella Khaimova, September 15, 1996, YVHN; Testimony of Evgeniia Dubovaia, March 14, 2000, YVHN.

136 Feodosiia, Evpatoriia. Statement of Sof'ia Gol'dshtein, July 6, 1944, GARF, 7021/9/2, p. 329; Testimony of Rachel Gurevich, [no date], ICJ, TC 2761.

137 Kolaiskii *raion*, Kurmanskii *raion*: Testimony of Nisl Leshinskii, August 26, 1992, YVHN; Testimony of Dina Arbuzova, May 9, 1991, YVHN.

138 Usually men and women exempt from the draft (e.g., children of the repressed) volunteered or were compelled to join the *opolchentsy*. These units were raised in accordance with the decisions of the Soviet government in the threatened areas. The level of compulsion increased over time as the Germans approached. It is not clear whether the *opolchentsy* knew what they were getting into when they volunteered, as they were volunteering for the sake of the war effort without necessarily knowing the specifics. After all, Soviet propaganda persisted during the German military advance. The armored Wehrmacht divisions destroyed the

established in mid-July 1941.[139] The *opolchenie* usually consisted of more elderly men than the army drafts did, including those over age 45.[140] It stands to reason that men enlisting in the *opolchenie*, particularly those serving as heads of families, had a detrimental effect on their respective families' evacuation decisions. However, it is nearly impossible to evaluate this phenomenon.

When the Germans broke through the Soviet hold in late October 1941, some of the Soviet soldiers made their way to Kerch, from where they continued on to the Caucasus.[141] A smaller group pushed its way toward the fortress of Sevastopol'. Some scattered units of the Red Army joined partisan detachments already deployed throughout the Crimea.[142] The Soviet command ordered thousands more soldiers (some of whom who had been previously serving in the Crimea itself) to the peninsula during the course of warfare around Sevastopol' and Kerch up to July 1942.[143] In the final count, no less than 20 Red Army divisions, of different combat strength, engaged in the warfare on Crimean soil.[144] A considerable number of them

masses of speedily trained and poorly equipped *opolchentsy*. On the *opolchenie* see, for example, Richard Bidlack, "The Political Mood in Leningrad during the First Year of the Soviet-German War," *Russian Review* 59, no. 1 (2000): pp. 96-113; Aleksandr Kolesnik, "V edinom boevom stroiu: Moskovskoe narodnoe opolchenie v dokumentakh arkhiva Ministerstva Oborony SSSR, 1941-1945 gody," *Sovetskie Arkhivy* [USSR], 6 (1972): pp. 27-31.

139 Kondranov, *Krym v period Velikoi Otechestvennoi voiny*, p. 43.

140 Sources include mentioning of those from both towns and villages. Sevastopol' and Simferopol': Testimony of Miriam Ashkenazi, December 11, 1995, YVHN. See also the interview with Vladimr Peisakh, March 22, 2004, author's archive, the testimony of Elena Fel'kner, July 14, 1994, YVHN. "Lunacharskii" *kolkhoz*: Testimony of Efim Lovin, [no date], YVHN.

141 Statement of Sof'ia Gol'dshtein, GARF, 7021/9/2, p. 329; Statement of Lazar' Gomel'skii, Commission of Feodosiia, [no later than 18 August 1944], GARF, 7021/9/6, p. 139. Here the "Caucasus" means the entire Caucasus, consisting of the North Caucasus and the Transcausus.

142 Testimony of Sof'ia Kantorova, February 1, 1993, YVHN; Testimony of Mark Mendeleev, September 5, 1999, YVHN.

143 Testimony of Ziskind, [no date], YVHN; Testimony of Dina Arbuzova, May 9, 1991, YVHN.

144 Klink, "The Conduct of Operations," pp. 627-631; Bernd Wegner, "The War Against the Soviet Union, 1942-1943," in Horst Boog, et al., *The Global War: Widening the Conflict into a World War and the Shift of the Initiative 1941-*

were destroyed during the Battle of the Crimea in 1941[145] and 1942,[146] while the Germans captured a smaller number. There is a record of Jewish excellence during the fighting in the Battle of the Crimea.[147]

* * *

The official Soviet estimate of the total number of evacuees from the Crimean peninsula is "more than 270,000" – i.e., 23.9% of the Crimean population as of 1939.[148] This figure is extremely high, and a clear overstatement. It does not take into account those who perished during the evacuation, but does consider the evacuation of the considerably large number of military personnel.

In dealing with the Crimea, one should consider the following factors, all of which had a detrimental effect on the dimensions of Jewish evacuation:

1) The relative isolation of the peninsula, as a result of which fewer Jewish refugees (a main source of information regarding imminent danger) passed through in the first months of the war;
2) The difficulty and (as of September 1941) actual impossibility of evacuating on one's own;
3) The absence of large concentrations of Jewish populations (with the notable exception of Jewish *kolkhozy*), which could have facilitated mass Jewish evacuation by following 'group mentality'; and

1943, vol. 6 of *Germany and the Second World War* (Oxford: Clarendon, 2001), pp. 929-941.

145 Testimony of Vera Rabinovich, January 15, 2001, YVHN; Testimony of Kucherov, [no date], YVHN.

146 Testimony of Ziskind, [no date], YVHN; Testimony of Kvashnik, [no date], YVHN.

147 Yitzhak Arad, *In the Shadow of the Red Banner: Soviet Jews in the War against Nazi Germany* (Jerusalem: Yad Vashem, The International Institute for Holocaust Research; Gefen, 2010), pp. 39-40, 50, 53.

148 Memorandum of the Crimean District Committee of the VKP(b) "Ob evakuatsii naseleniia iz Kryma i okazanii emu pomoshi v mestakh naznacheniia", May 18, 1943, DAARK, R-1/1/2182, in Kondranov, *Krym v period Velikoi Otechestvennoi voiny*, pp. 66-68.

4) The conscription of a considerable number of Jewish men in the Red Army, which detrimentally affected their families' decisions on whether or not to evacuate.

As a result, the more realistic estimate of the number of Jews evacuated from the Crimea is closer to 25,000-30,000 people (38-46% of the prewar population).[149]

149 Yitzhak Arad gives the following estimate: some 45,000 Jews remained in the Crimea, among them Karaites and Krymchaks. This figure includes 5,000 refugees who came to the peninsula from other regions. Arad, *The History of the Holocaust*, p. 374. Thus, according to this estimate, 35,702 Jews left the Crimea, among them those who were evacuated. This figure should be juxtaposed with the size of the Jewish population of 75,702 people, including Karaites and Krymchaks as of 1939 (65,452 Jews, 4,170 Karaites, and 6,080 Krymchaks).

Chapter Two

Jews in the North Caucasus from the Beginning of the German-Soviet War (June 22, 1941) to the German Occupation (August 1942)

1. Evacuation into the Region[1]

1.1. In 1941

The North Caucasus first emerged as an important evacuation destination in the summer-fall of 1941, when it was not entirely clear whether the German advance towards this region could be checked. The fact that the Soviet authorities decided to erect a defensive line and set up an extermination (*istrebitel'nyi*) battalion[2] in Stavropol'skii *krai* at the end of October 1941 proves that they had considered

1 This subject is enlarged upon in my article: Kiril Feferman, "A Soviet Humanitarian Action?: Centre, Periphery and the Evacuation of Refugees to the North Caucasus, 1941-1942," *Europe-Asia Studies* 61, no. 5 (2009): pp. 813-831.

2 Extermination (*istrebitel'nyi*) battalions were established in accordance with the decree of the Council of People's Commissars from June 24, 1941, "on the protection of enterprises and institutions and the establishment of extermination battalions in the endangered areas." Their members (both men and women) were selected based on their ideological reliability. They underwent short military training, and their service was regulated by the Military Code of the Red Army. At the same time, they maintained employment in their initial workplaces. They gathered, trained, and arm-guarded critical locations several times a week, this frequency increasing as the front line drew closer. As the Germans approached, segments of the extermination battalions participated in fighting, while the others formed the nucleus of the future partisan units.

the area in danger.[3] The Soviet policy of directing people into such a vulnerable place was attributed to their desire to relieve pressure on other rescue routes.

Tens of thousands of evacuees and refugees had made their way into the North Caucasus since the beginning of the war. From July 19-25, 1941, 37,165 evacuees arrived in Krasnodarskii *krai* alone.[4] By early September, this number had grown considerably, reaching 205,000 people by September 10, including 6,627 children from orphanages.[5] It is notable that fewer evacuees were registered in the non-Russian areas of the North Caucasus: 16,470 people by the end of 1941 in Kabardino-Balkar and 5,072 evacuated families in the North Ossetiian republics.[6]

Statistical research on the national composition of the evacuees conducted in Krasnodarskii *krai* revealed that "as of October 1, 1941, 218,000 people, 73% of them Jews, were received and accommodated in the *krai*."[7] Jewish testimonies pertaining to other areas support the claim that as of the fall of 1941, Jews constituted the majority of, or at least the considerable part of, the evacuees all over the region.[8]

3 Decree of the Bureau of the Committee of Archangel'skii *raion* of the VKP(b) on the establishment of extermination battalion, October 20, 1941, in Stepan Boiko, ed., *Stavropol'e v Velikoi Otechestvennoi voine 1941-1945 gg: Sbornik dokumentov i materialov* (Stavropol': Stavropol'skoe knizhnoe izdatel'stvo, 1962), p. 57; Decree of the Bureau of the [Stavropol'] committee of the VKP(b) on the performance of defensive works in the *krai*, October 21, 1941, in ibid., pp. 57-58. On the extermination battalions in the North Caucasus, see Elena Nikulina, "Istrebitel'nye bataliony Stavropol'ia i Kubani v gody Velikoi Otechestvennoi voiny: 1941-1945 gg," (PhD diss., Piatigorskskii gosudarstvennyi lingvisticheskii universitet, 2005).

4 Beliaev and Bondar', *Kuban' v gody Velikoi Otechestvennoi voiny, 1941-1945*, pp. 38-39.

5 Ibid., pp. 56-57. For more information, see Ilona Iurchuk, "Politika mestnykh vlastei Kubani po zashite detstva i ee prakticheskaia realizatsiia v gody Velikoi Otechestvennoi voiny (1941-1945 gg.)," (PhD diss., Armavirskii institut sotsial'nogo obrazovaniia, 2008), p. 81.

6 Balikoev, *Narody Severnogo Kavkaza v gody Velikoi Otechestvennoi voiny (1941-1945)*, p. 80.

7 Beliaev and Bondar', *Kuban' v gody Velikoi Otechestvennoi voiny, 1941-1945*, pp. 76-77

8 Uspenskaia *stanitsa* in August 1941; Krasnodar in November-December 1941; village of Slavianskaia in Krasnodarskii *krai* in November 1941: Saul

Jews came into the Caucasus from a number of places such as Moscow[9] and, significantly to the concern of this study, from the Crimea.[10] However, the biggest stream of Jewish refugees arrived from Ukraine,[11] particularly from the neighboring east, as well as from Moldavia.[12] Refugees went both via organized removal and individual initiative. The gender and age composition of the Jewish evacuees was predominately young and middle-aged women,[13] while the share of elderly persons over age 60 was significant as well.[14] There were few young and middle-aged men.[15] Family units sometimes arrived, i.e., elderly couples,[16] elderly individuals with middle-aged children,[17] or

Borovoi, *Vospominaniia: Pamiatniki evreiskoi istoricheskoi mysli* (Moscow: Evreiskii universitet v Moskve; Jerusalem: Gesharim, 1993), pp. 249-250, 252; Testimony of Rachel Gurevich (1914), the Hebrew University of Jerusalem, Intitute of Contemporary Jewry, Department of Oral History (HUJ, ICJ, DOR), TC 2761; Diary of Grigorii Ioffe, entry from November 9, 1941, State Archive of the Autonomous Republic of the Crimea (DAARK), P-156/1/31, p. 31.

9 Testimony of Dina Ostropol', April 3, 1974, YVHN; Testimony of Roza Fiks, April 20, 1994, YVHN.

10 Testimony of Liudmila Bradichevskii, May 13, 1996. ICJ, (217) 183, p. 1; Report of Moisei Evenson, Viktor Shklovskii, ed., [no date], YVA, P.21.2/1; Diary of Grigorii Ioffe, entry from November 10, 1941, DAARK, P-156/1/31, p. 31.

11 Chernovtsy: Testimony of Mina Horowitz, August 1, 1973, YVA, 0.3/3682, p. 6; Kiev, Vinnitsa: Testimony of Roza Lipkin (1904), [no date], ICJ, TC 2860, not transcribed; Testimony of Sarra Labinov, [no date], ICJ, TC 2773, side A, not transcribed; Odessa: Borovoi, *Vospominaniia*, p. 249; Testimony of Semeon Rechister, December 20, 1991, YVHN.

12 Khar'kov and Krivoi Rog: Testimony of Mordukhai Cherkasskii, January 25, 1991, YVHN; For more information, see testimony of Anfisa Kalnitskaia, 1926 [no date], ICJ, TC 2759, not transcribed; Moldavia, Kishinev and other areas: Testimony of Sarra Gisa, May 15, 1955, YVHN; Testimony of Boris Levit, May 16, 1999, YVHN.

13 Testimony of Leonid Luda, April 29, 2000, YVHN; Testimony of Stepanskaia, [no date], YVHN; Testimony of Semeon Rechister, December 20, 1991, YVHN.

14 Kishinev and other areas: Testimony of Sarra Gisa, May 15, 1955, YVHN; Testimony of Bella Gol'dshtein, October 6, 1992. YVHN.

15 Testimony of Geniia Shaulov, November 1, 1956, YVHN; Testimony of Mikhail Skladman, October 22, 1979, YVHN.

16 Testimony of Fedor (Froim) Berezovskii, September 5, 2000, YVHN.

17 Testimony of Mordukhai Cherkasskii, January 25, 1991, YVHN; Testimony of Josef Kodner, March 18, 1975, YVHN.

mothers with small children.[18] For lack of available data, it was impossible to draw precise conclusions about the social composition of the newcomers. Yet, the sizable presence of housewives stands out.[19]

Of particular note is the very high number of children among the evacuees in the North Caucasus. Many of them were brought as a part of the organized evacuation of 24 children's homes.[20] Their share was high from the beginning of evacuation into the region but particularly increased by January 1942 (at which point they constituted almost half out of 51,353 refugees who remained in Krasnodarskii *krai*).[21] The reason for this growth has to do with the fact that many adults abandoned the Caucasus individually. Unlike them, children placed in special state institutions could not evacuate on their own, and there was no order from the Soviet authorities for their organized evacuation.

The authorities attempted to organize the incoming evacuation of both refugees as well as those who were systematically brought into the region. The newcomers were both registered[22] and non-registered,[23] and apparently the great majority were supplied with food. The refugees were accommodated free of charge in private homes or state-owned buildings, yet the conditions in which they had to

18 Testimony of Inda Bergman, 1993, YVHN; Testimony of Anna Kliatskina, May 26, 1974, YVHN; Testimony of Semeon Rechister, December 20, 1991, YVHN; Testimony of Sima Cherchikova, October 18, 1999, YVHN.

19 Testimony of Mordukhai Cherkasskii, January 25, 1991, YVHN; Testimony of Leonid Luda, April 29, 2000, YVHN.

20 See Table 15, "Evacuation of children's homes and medical institutions from the Crimea into the North Caucasus as of 1942" and "From Odessa and Yalta," Akt of the Commission on the Odessa orphanage No 6 evacuated into the Caucasus, [no date], Yad Vashem Archives (YVA), M.33/286, pp. 5-8; Testimony of Vadim Maniker, April 1975, YVA, 0.3/4108, p. 2.

21 Testimony of Vadim Maniker, April 1975, YVA, 0.3/4108, p. 2.

22 Krasnodar and elsewhere in the region: Diary of Grigorii Ioffe, entry from November 12, 1941, DAARK, P-156/1/31, p. 31; Memorandum of the Crimean District Committee of the VKP(b) "Ob evakuatsii naseleniia iz Kryma i okazanii emu pomoshi v mestakh naznacheniia", May 18, 1943, DAARK, R-1/1/2182.

23 Village of Slavianskaia: Diary of Ioffe, entry from November 9, 1941, DAARK, P-156/1/31, p. 31.

live were sometimes difficult.[24] An excerpt from a wartime letter pertaining to the situation in the town of Budennovsk (Stavropol'skii *krai*) in October 1941 is illuminating:

> Upon our arrival it was proposed to relocate to *kolkhozy* situated some 50-70-100 km from Budennovsk, but we decided to stay in the town. We live with two wives of the military men in the room allocated by the Military Commissariat (*voenkomat*)... It was proposed [for one of the female respondents – KF] to work as a book-keeper in a kindergarten. We decided not to move anywhere. We were provided with a room and firewood... People experience enormous difficulties with fuel; coal cannot be procured at any price... As compared to other people we fare really well; many are envious of us.[25]

As suggested in the previous testimony, there was a connection between accommodation and employment of the newcomers. The evacuees willing to stay in the region desired work, as it served as an additional source of food and material provision. However, the local employment policy was inconsistent throughout the period under review. In the early stages of the war, the refugees were provided with work in towns[26] and rural areas,[27] which may be indicative of long-term Soviet plans to accommodate the refugees in the region. But in retrospect, employment turned out to be a trap for the evacuees, as the employed were less inclined to move

24 Budennovsk and village of Slavianskaia: Letters received by Efim Ginzburg, November 18, 1941, YVA, 0.75/324, p. 74; Diary of Grigorii Ioffe, entry from November 9, 1941, DAARK, P-156/1/31, p. 31.

25 Diary of Grigorii Ioffe, entry from November 9, 1941, DAARK, P-156/1/31, pp. 74-76.

26 Krasnodar, Mikoianshakhar, Piatigorsk: Borovoi, *Vospominaniia*, p. 251; File of Shamail, Ferdaus, Sultan, and Muchtar Khalamliev, 1994, YVA, M.31/6228; Testimony of Khania Knor (1918), [no date], ICJ, TC 2772, not transcribed.

27 Labinskaia *stanitsa*, Stavropol'skii *krai*: File of Klavdiia Siosoeva, Agripina Dedova, and others, [no date], YVA, M.31/8884; Testimony of Ida Mandel'blat, May 25, 1998, YVA, VT/1911, not transcribed.

on.[28] As the influx of refugees continued to grow throughout the summer-fall of 1941, the government program became increasingly strained. Consequently, those who came in the fall were not always guaranteed employment or food,[29] as illustrated by the fact that by the late November 1941, only up to 20% of able-bodied evacuees were employed in North Ossetiia.[30]

Many newcomers were reluctant to follow the evacuation regulations, and settled down where they thought fit and not where the authorities wanted. A document of the local Krasnodar agency in charge of the "resettlement" policy dated September 1941 is instructive:

> The evacuees are constantly leaving the areas assigned them and bombarding the Resettlement Department with persistent requests to send them to other areas and territories.[31]

The Soviet military meticulously checked evacuees, including body searches at transfer points.[32] Nevertheless, the authorities were alarmed by the "penetration of the enemy agents" under the guise of refugees as the "Directive letter of the Committee of the VKP(b) of Krasnodarskii *krai* on the work with the evacuees" from September 1941 demonstrates:

> Fascists dispatch inhabitants of the occupied areas... to the Red Army's rear with the task of conducting diversions,

28 Budennovsk: Letters received by Efim Ginzburg, November 18, 1941, YVA, 0.75/324, p. 75.

29 Village of Ivanovka, Krasnodar: Testimony of Rachel Gurevich, ICJ, TC 2761; Diary of Grigorii Ioffe, entry from November 19, 1941, DAARK, P-156/1/31, p. 33.

30 Alexander Israpov, "Gosudarstvennye organy upravleniia i narod v 1941-1945 gg.: Aspekty politicheskogo, ekonomicheskogo i organizatsionno-pravovogo vzaimodeistviia na materialalkh avtonomnykh respublik Severnogo Kavkaza," (PhD diss., Dagestanskii nauchnyi tsentr Rossiiskoi Akademii nauk, 2004), p. 165.

31 Note of the Resettlement Department of the Executive Committee of Krasnodarskii *krai,* in Beliaev and Bondar', *Kuban' v gody Velikoi Otechestvennoi voiny, 1941-1945*, pp. 56-57.

32 Peresyp ferry: Diary of Grigorii Ioffe, entry from November 6, 1941, DAARK, P-156/1/31, p. 31.

> reconnoitering the location of Soviet troops undermining Soviet defense, signaling with rockets to show German planes the location of military units, and circulating panic rumors on the might of the German army and on [its] allegedly good attitudes towards the POWs and local population. It is necessary to check all the suspects thoroughly.[33]

Finally, on October 6, 1941, the NKVD Administration for Krasnodarskii *krai* ordered a security check of all the newcomers.[34]

As a result of security and logistical problems, the Soviet authorities became increasingly concerned with the incessant influx of evacuees. They attempted to solve the problem by limiting incoming evacuation. From September 30, 1941, they banned the registration of new arrivals and empowered local authorities to dispatch unemployed people within two days of their arrival to work in key industrial and military centers.[35] Local authorities evidently took an even more restrictive step by seeking to limit the number of incoming evacuees by deciding "to entrust the issuance of resettlement permits to the military authorities."[36] However, the problem was solved only several months later, when the larger part of the newcomers left the North Caucasus for the deep Soviet rear. According to the Soviet report, "as of January 1942, 51,353 people remained in Krasnodarskii *krai* out of 226,000 who had been evacuated there. The rest departed to the far rear areas."[37]

Jewish evacuees were dispatched all over the North Caucasus from towns[38] to numerous Russian villages,[39] including Cossack

33 Beliaev and Bondar', *Kuban' v gody Velikoi Otechestvennoi voiny, 1941-1945*, pp. 56-57.

34 Ibid., pp. 76-77.

35 Krasnodar, Maikop, Novorossiisk, Tuapse: Ibid.

36 Ibid., pp. 56-57.

37 Ibid., pp. 181-182.

38 Elista and Nal'chik: Testimony of Liudmila Bradichevskii, ICJ, (217) 183, p. 1; Testimony of Iurii Piler, July 16, 1990, YVHN.

39 Villages of Naturbovo and Levokumskoe: Interrogation of Klavdiia Parshikova, August 12, 1942, YVA, M.33/291, p. 98; Memoirs of Peotr Belokurov, November 13, 2002, YVA, 0.33/6783, pp. 1-2.

settlements – *stanitsy*.[40] According to a Soviet wartime report, 39,100 out of 51,353 evacuees in Krasnodarskii *krai* were sent to villages as of January 1942.[41] No record exists of Jewish refugees ever having been sent to Muslim villages, which is perhaps indicative of the reluctance of the Jews themselves to stay in an entirely unfamiliar setting. Alternatively, it may indicate that Soviet authorities had a certain lack of confidence in the Muslim villagers because of the prewar record of armed resistance to the Soviet rule in many Muslim-dominated areas in the Caucasus. Overall, the rationale behind the Soviet policy was to lessen the friction between the newcomers and native population, as well as to distribute fairly the burden of accommodation among many localities.

1.2. In 1942

As the situation in the southern flank of the Soviet-German front stabilized in the winter of 1941-1942, the Soviet authorities began to view the North Caucasus as a relatively safe shelter for refugees from other regions. It is against this backdrop that the Soviets made the decision to direct a large number of people from besieged Leningrad into the North Caucasus, primarily into the territories of Krasnodar and Stavropol'.[42] The decision was carried out in the winter of 1941-1942, when the evacuation from Leningrad was made possible through the frozen lake of Ladoga.[43] 36,000 evacuees from Leningrad were accommodated in Krasnodarskii *krai* alone in April 1942.[44] In addition, in the course of the first half of 1942, Jews and non-Jews from other endangered areas (the Crimea and

40 Labinskaia and Tbilisskaia *stanitsy*: Questioning of Leonid Borukhovich, September 6, 1943, YVA, M.33/292, p. 18; Questioning of Anna Suzdalenko, May 10, 1944, YVA, M.33/308, p. 29.

41 Beliaev and Bondar', *Kuban' v gody Velikoi Otechestvennoi voiny, 1941-1945*, pp. 181-182.

42 Decree of the Bureau of the Committee of the VKP(b) of [Stavropol'skii] *krai* and the Executive Council of *krai*, "O razmeshenii naseleniia, evakuirovannogo iz Leningrada," February 10, 1942, in Boiko, *Stavropol'e v Velikoi Otechestvennoi voine 1941-1945 gg.*, p. 75.

43 Testimony of Tsilia Gadleva, October 25, 1990, YVA, 0.3/4391, p. 8.

44 Beliaev and Bondar', *Kuban' v gody Velikoi Otechestvennoi voiny, 1941-1945*, p. 249.

Rostov) were also evacuated into the Caucasus.[45] At the same time, it should be emphasized that in the first half of 1942 there were no new German conquests of territories with considerable Jewish populations, and, as a result, there was no visible influx of non-organized Jewish refugees into the North Caucasus.

Incoming Jews were dispatched all over the North Caucasus, especially into the resort towns of Stavropol'skii *krai*.[46] They were also brought on a smaller scale into Russian villages,[47] including Cossack settlements.[48] As in 1941, there is no record of Jewish refugees having been sent to Muslim villages in 1942 – nor is there evidence that they were provided with employment. This may be the result of the Soviets' logistical inability to provide masses of newcomers, including many white-collar workers, with suitable employment in the region. Alternatively, it cannot be ruled out that the authorities may not have considered the presence of these evacuees in the Caucasus a long-term project.

The staff, and in particular, young students of Leningrad's institutions of higher education were also among the evacuees into the region in 1942.[49] Elderly family members were sometimes able to accompany the students, while at other times the students arrived alone.[50] There were many children among the evacuees: of the

45 Memorandum of the Committee of the VKP(b) of the Karachaevo Autonomous *raion*, [no later than June 24, 1943], GARF, 7021/17/8, pp. 2-3; Testimony of Vladimir Shpits, June 7, 1992, YVHN.

46 Essentuki, Piatigorsk: Testimony of Debora Shklovskaia, March 5, 1991, YVHN; Testimony of Sima Roiak, September 24, 1994, YVHN.

47 Village of Novozavedennoe: Statement of Anna Shlaen, 1943, GARF, 7021/17/11, p. 114.

48 Kotliarevskaia and Aleksandriiskaia *stanitsy*: Akt no. 75 of the Commission of the Kabardino-Balkarsk Republic, June 24, 1943, GARF, 7021/7/109, p. 171; Akt of the Commission of the village of Aleksandriiskaia, January 25, 1943, GARF, 7021/17/9, p. 12.

49 Kislovodsk and Piatigorsk: Testimony of Tsilia Gadleva, October 25, 1990, YVA, 0.3/4391, p. 9; Dobruskin, Leningrad Polytechnical Institute, *Nash Politekh*, "V blokade i evakuatsii," February 22, 2005, available from http://nashpolytech.ru/index.php?id=59; Testimony of Evgeniia Tukhshnaid, [no date], YVHN; Testimony of Khasia Epshtein, November 8, 1992. YVHN; Testimony of Sima Roiak, September 24, 1994, YVHN.

50 Essentuki and Kislovodsk: Testimony of Mira Idina, April 1, 1991. YVHN; Testimony of Tukhshnaid, YVHN. Testimony of Debora Shklovskaia, March 5,

36,000 evacuees from Leningrad accommodated in Krasnodarskii *krai* in April 1942, there were more than 10,000 children, i.e., almost 28% of the group.[51] As a result, by the time of the German occupation in August 1942, Jewish evacuees overshadowed the small native Jewish population of the region.

It is difficult to ascertain how many Jews stayed in the North Caucasus before the German takeover. According to the data of the Soviet Council for Resettlement, as of July 7, 1942, 60,397 people were registered in Krasnodarskii *krai*, while 53,000 were registered in Stavropol'skii *krai*.[52] The share of Jews among them is unknown, and there is no data on the number of evacuees in other areas of the North Caucasus. These appraisals are somewhat higher than the ones used in this study. In any case, it seems safe to estimate the number of the evacuated Jews in the entire region as of July-August 1942 at about 50,000.

2. Evacuation from the Region

2.1. General concerns

Jewish representation in the target groups that the government designated for evacuation, which was elsewhere a crucial factor in the dimensions of the number of Jews evacuated, took on a specific form in the North Caucasus. As the majority of Jews were newcomers to the region, they were not included in the circle of local high- or low-ranking officials, whose departures the authorities prioritized. Nor did they belong to the workers in key industries also earmarked for priority evacuation. At the same time, certain Jewish evacuees the government had placed in villages might have been included in the evacuation of what one Soviet directive referred to as "agricultural capacities

1991, YVHN.

51 Beliaev and Bondar', *Kuban' v gody Velikoi Otechestvennoi voiny, 1941-1945*, p. 249; File of Vera Buriachok, 1996, YVA, M.31/7789; File of Natal'ia Dudnik, 1997, YVA, M.31/7704.

52 Details on the number of accommodated evacuated people, YVA, JM/24745, originally from GARF, A-327/2/67.

with workers employed in them." More Jews belonged in a third (albeit lower prioritized) category of "whatever possible human resources." This mainly included students and teaching staff of institutes of higher education and children of state-run institutions, in particular. Thus, on the face of it, many Jewish refugees in the Caucasus could have potentially benefited from the state-sponsored evacuation program.

In the North Caucasus, Jews based their evacuation decisions on their knowledge of the proximity of the Germans. In this respect, the local press, such as the main newspapers of Stavropol'skii and Krasnodarskii *kraia* [*Ordzhonikidzevskaia Pravda* (Ordzhonikidze's Truth) and *Bol'shevik*] could serve as an important source of information.[53] However, on the whole, there was not a single word about evacuation from the North Caucasus. Soviet propaganda in the North Caucasus, as seen from the newspapers, persisted in "business as usual" up to the point when the Germans reached critical proximity to the region.[54] References to the Germans' particular maltreatment of Jews were extremely rare.[55] Furthermore, information on the advance of the German armies towards the Caucasus was infrequent and clearly outdated.[56] Despite the relative length of the period under review (the summer of 1941 to the summer of 1942), there was less potential evacuation-inducing information published in

53 *Ordzhonikidzevskaia Pravda* was published daily by the Ordzhonikidze District (*krai*) Committee of the VKP(b), the District Council of the Deputies of Workers, and the Voroshilovsk [Stavropol' – KF] Municipal Committee of the VKP(b). *Bol'shevik* was published daily by the Krasnodar District (*krai*) and the Municipal Committee of the VKP(b) and the District Council of the Deputies of Working People. I looked through all the issues of these two newspapers from June 22, 1941 to late July 1942, when their publication ceased.

54 Editorial "O khode sbora urozhaia," Decree of the Bureau of the Ordzhonikidze District Committee of the VKP(b) from July 9, 1942, *Ordzhonikidzevskaia Pravda*, no. 159, July 10, 1942, p. 1. Editorial "Rabotat', ne shadia sil dlia fronta," *Bol'shevik*, no. 176, July 26, 1942, p. 1.

55 A. Faigelman, "V lapakh gitlerovskikh banditov," *Ordzhonikidzevskaia Pravda*, no. 154 (2218), July 2, 1941.

56 Editorial "Otbit' napadenie vraga!" *Ordzhonikidzevskaia Pravda*, no. 175 (2550), July 29, 1942, p. 1. Editorial "Rabotat', ne shadia sil dlia fronta," *Bol'shevik*, no. 176, July 26, 1942, p. 1.

Caucasian newspapers for Jews to discern than in four months (June 22 to mid-September 1941) in the Crimea.[57]

Thus, rumors served as a source of this information, as indicated by a postwar Jewish testimony pertaining to Krasnodarskii *krai*:

> My family, which consisted of five persons, stayed in the village of Ivanovka for one to one-and-a-half months. In approximately November-December 1941, it was rumored that Jews were gradually abandoning the village. So, my family made up its mind to move to Krasnodar.[58]

This wartime letter, which arrived from Budennovsk in October 1941, is also indicative of the influence of rumor:

> Minvody was bombed. Many of the evacuees have begun to move away from here to Makhachkala. Rumors were circulating that it was impossible to reach Makhachkala, that on the way people were taken off [the trains] and dispatched to *kolkhozy*, and that an epidemic of typhus broke out in Makhachkala.[59]

The latter testimony suggests that information about the various effects of the Soviet evacuation program played a certain role in the behavior of Jews. However, according to another source, when Jews grasped the devastating nature of the situation, their knowledge of the negative effects of the Soviet evacuation procedure had a negligible impact on their decisions.[60]

Of note is the fact that there was almost no German presence in the Caucasus during the First World War. As a result, whereas some elderly Jews in the Crimea may have had memories of a

57 I analyzed the following newspapers: 1) *Ordzhonikidzevskaia Pravda*, 2) *Bol'shevik*, and 3) *Krasnyi Krym*.

58 Testimony of Rachel Gurevich, ICJ, TC 2761.

59 Letters received by Efim Ginzburg, November 18, 1941, YVA, 0.75/324, p. 75.

60 Stavropol' in the fall of 1941, Georgievsk in the spring of 1942: Testimony of Ida Mandel'blat, May 25, 1998, YVA, VT/1911; Testimony of Anfisa Kalnitskaia, [no date], ICJ, TC 2759.

certain stability left by the German occupation of the Crimea, such memories of stability associated with the First World War did not influence the decisions of native Caucasian Jews on whether to stay or to escape. The available testimonies indicate that by mid-1942, the number of Ashkenazi Jews residing in the Caucasus who did not know of the German discrimination against Jews was low. However, some Jewish intellectuals disregarded the revelations, such as one professor who claimed, "I do not believe that the civilized nation of Göthe and Schiller can behave like barbarians."[61] The role of Holocaust survivors from the neighboring city of Rostov-na-Donu in facilitating information transfer should also be emphasized. The temporary German occupation of the city from November 20-28, 1941 and the intensive mistreatment of Jews caused local Jews to escape the area expediently.[62] Although many of these refugees were eventually unable to leave the North Caucasus, as they were swept up by the new German offensive in the summer of 1942,[63] some of them were able to share with other Jews their first-hand experience of living under German rule.[64]

It should be borne in mind that Jews were often puzzled over the military developments in the southern part of the Soviet-German war in 1941-42, while analyzing them for an indication of whether or not to flee. On the one hand, Red Army victories during the winter campaign of 1941-1942 partly assuaged Jewish fears.[65] On the other, the fiasco of Soviet forces near Khar'kov in

61 Dobruskin, "V blokade i evakuatsii," February 22, 2005, available from http://nashpolytech.ru/index.php?id=59. For Mikoianshakhar, see Nicholas Poppe, *Reminiscences* (Bellingham: Western Washington University Press, 1983), p. 161.

62 Ernst Klink, "The Conduct of Operations," p. 619; On the Battle of the Caucasus in 1941, see Chapter 4, "Destruction of the Jewish Population in the North Caucasus," in this book.

63 Schwarz, *Evrei v Sovetskom Soiuze s nachala vtoroi mirovoi voiny (1939-1965)*, p. 58; Report of Moisei Evenson, Viktor Shklovskii, ed., [no date], YVA, P.21.2/1.

64 Testimony of Anfisa Kalnitskaia, [no date], ICJ, TC 2759; Testimony of Ida Mandel'blat, YVA, May 25, 1998, VT/1911.

65 B. I. Nevzorov, "Sokrushenie Blitskriega," in *Velikaia Otechestvennaia voina: 1941-1945*, vol. 1, Zolotarev, *Velikaia Otechestvennaia voina, 1941-1945*, pp. 248-284; Idem., "Zimnee nastuplenie Krasnoi Armii," ibid., pp. 285-318.

mid-May, the fall of Sevastopol' on July 2, and, particularly, the abandonment of Rostov on July 23, 1942, caused Jews to consider evacuating the Caucasus.[66]

Increasing outbursts of antisemitism from the local Russian population might potentially cause Jews to conclude that they were vulnerable in the region.[67] Antisemitism was clearly evident in a number of Russian — and to a lesser extent non-Russian — areas from the beginning of the war.[68] According to the postwar memories of a Jewish escapee, in Krasnodar in the fall of 1941 local people let one another pass in lines at the expense of Jews and made derogatory antisemitic remarks.[69] Importantly, the same author noticed that as the Germans approached in the fall of 1941, the enmity towards Jews increased.[70] In January 1942, the Party authorities in Stavropol'skii *krai* recorded that in one of its regions "draftees were saying 'Beat *Zhidy* and Communists!'"[71]

Anti-Jewish attitudes were sometimes more extreme. For example, a sixth-grade Jewish schoolboy was repeatedly beaten because he was a Jew.[72] Another Jewish refugee mentions in her

66 O. N. Kudriashov and P. P. Chevela, "Oborona Stalingrada i Severnogo Kavkaza," in *Velikaia Otechestvennaia voina*, Zolotarev, *Velikaia Otechestvennaia voina, 1941-1945*, p. 369. For more testimonies regarding Jewish decisions to flee the Caucasus, see Testimony of Iakov Vinokurov, October 19, 1999, YVA, VT/2489, not transcribed; Testimony of Barukh Iafit, September 4, 1999, YVHN.

67 Uspenskaia *stanitsa* and Krasnodar in the fall of 1941: Borovoi, *Vospominaniia*, pp. 250, 252.

68 Testimony of Anfisa Kalnitskaia, [no date], ICJ, TC 2759; Testimony of Liudmila Bradichevskii, ICJ, (217) 183, p. 3; See the report of Stavropol'skii *krai* Committee of the VKP(b) in September 1941 in Maksim Andrienko, "Naselenie Stavropol'skogo kraia v gody Velikoi Otechestvennoi voiny: otsenka povedencheskikh motivov," (PhD diss., Piatigorskii gosu-darstvennyi lingvisticheskii universitet, 2005), p. 57.

69 Borovoi, *Vospominaniia*, p. 252.

70 Ibid., p. 254.

71 Andrienko, "Naselenie Stavropol'skogo kraia v gody Velikoi Otechestvennoi voiny," p. 57.

72 Vyselkovskaia *stanitsa* in Krasnodarskii *krai*; Document from the Russian State Archive of Social and Political History (RGASPI), 17/88/131, pp. 75-76 in Iurchuk, "Politika mestnykh vlastei Kubani po zashite detstva i ee prakticheskaia realizatsiia v gody Velikoi Otechestvennoi voiny (1941-1945 gg.)," 2008, p. 82.

postwar interview that from early August to mid-November 1941, dreadful antisemitism prevailed in Vyselkskaia *stanitsa*[73] (Krasnodarskii *krai*) where she settled:

> Neither I nor my brother could actually learn in school: Children offended us by crying "*Zhid*!" In the school, teachers used to say to the children: "Why do you bother them? It is not their fault that they are *Zhidy*."

When the Germans captured Rostov-na-Donu for the first time (mid-November 1941), her family moved away towards the Transcaucasus. She says that when "we entered local villages to procure food, the population was ill-disposed towards us and even behaved in a belligerent fashion. We were never invited to enter houses in order to clean up. It was even a feeling of terror."[74] Yet, in many cases it cannot be established whether this hostile attitude was due to the fact that the witness was Jewish or a refugee. In a limited number of sources, the Russian population displayed neutral or even positive attitudes towards Jewish refugees.[75] Yet, such examples stand out as an exception to the trend, which, with some deviations, was indicative of the increase in antisemitism among the local Slavic people on the eve of the German occupation of the North Caucasus.

By mid-1942, they could hardly attain Holocaust-related information by radio.[76] It is worth mentioning the Note of the Soviet Commissar for Foreign Affairs, Viacheslav Molotov,

73 Cossack village. Before the Bolshevik Revolution this was indeed the village whose inhabitants were exclusively or overwhelmingly Cossacks. However, due to the Soviet population policies in the 1920-30s, in some cases ethnic Russians or Ukrainians were settled in *stanitsy* whose Cossack inhabitants had been previously deported by the Soviets. These *stanitsy* continued to be referred to as *stanitsy* even after the population "exchange."

74 Testimony of Anfisa Kalnitskaia, [no date], ICJ, TC 2759.

75 Testimony of Sarra Labinov, [no date], ICJ, TC 2773, side A, not transcribed; Testimony of Ida Mandel'blat, May 25, 1998, YVA, VT/1911.

76 Inna Somova, "Kul'turnye i religioznye uchrezhdeniia Stavropol'skogo kraia v period Velikoi Otechestvennoi voiny," (PhD diss., Piatigorskii gosudarstvennyii lingivisticheskii universitet, 2004), pp. 47-48.

published by the central and regional Soviet media on January 6, 1942, which invoked the special maltreatment the Germans inflicted upon Jews in Lvov and Kiev:

> Horrible slaughter and pogroms were committed by the German invaders in the Ukrainian capital, Kiev. In only a few days, the German bandits killed and tortured 52,000 men, women, old men, and children, mercilessly dealing with all Ukrainians, Russians, and Jews who in any manner displayed their loyalty to the Soviet Government. Soviet citizens who have escaped from Kiev described the astounding picture of these mass executions. A large number of Jews, including women and children, were assembled together in the Jewish cemetery. Before shooting, all of them were stripped naked and beaten up... and were shot with automatic rifles.[77]

However, the importance of this information was partly offset by the skepticism that average Soviet people felt toward the official propaganda. Therefore, it seems that the main source of the Holocaust-related information were the evacuees escaping from areas such as Ukraine, as well as the Red Army personnel (especially, if there were Jews among them).[78] A piece of postwar evidence of a Jewish survivor underscores this point:

> Apparently in the winter months of 1941-1942, my infant, sister-in-law with her child, and I found ourselves in the village of Dzhiginka. Near the village there was an air base. One of the pilots learned that we were Jews and told us to escape as the Germans were approaching and that they

77 Note, "O povsemestnykh grabezhakh, razorenii naseleniia i chudovishnikh zversvakh germanskikh vlastei na zakhvachennykh imi sovetskikh territoriiakh," *Pravda*, January 6, 1942. Translation is in Viacheslav Molotov, *Soviet Government Statements on Nazi Atrocities* (London: Hutchinson, 1946), p. 22.

78 Testimony of Aleksandr Simakhov, January 8, 1998, in Svetlana Danilova, ed., *Iskhod gorskikh evreev: razrushenie garmonii mirov* (Nal'chik: Poligrafservis IT, 2000), p. 171; Testimony of Anfisa Kalnitskaia, [no date], ICJ, TC 2759.

> would kill us. He advised us to talk to the Major who was a Jew and to speak Yiddish to him. The Major issued us certificates that we belonged to the military personnel and gave us a car.[79]

This evidence also depicts one of the few manifestations of Jewish solidarity in the course of evacuation. Also evident is the extremely important role the army played during the evacuation of civilians: Military men issued the evacuation permits (and also verified/ annulled them),[80] accommodated,[81] or provided transportation for those "related" to the army. Another postwar Jewish testimony pertaining to an evacuation from Piatigorsk in August 1942 is instructive in this respect:

> There was no transportation. So my family put its possessions in the cart and left in the direction of Nal'chik. It took five days to get from Piatigorsk to Nal'chik. Among the refugees were also the wives of Red Army officers. On the way, they were greatly assisted by the military men with food and water.[82]

Jews in the North Caucasus were motivated by personal circumstances in considering the possibility of evacuation. These included illnesses and physical disabilities, as well as personal reluctance. One disabled Jew considered under official Soviet classification as "of the 2nd category" (which implied that he was a person of "serious disabilities") did not succeed in evacuating from Essentuki due to his disabilities;[83] in Krasnodar another Jew's wife was ill, and because "it was difficult for her to leave with her children"[84], she opted to stay. Illness and physical disabilities

79 Testimony of Hana Melinskii, January 12, 1986, YVA, 0.3/4342, p. 4.

80 Krasnodar: Ibid.

81 Budennovsk: Letters received by Efim Ginzburg, November 18, 1941, YVA, 0.75/324, p. 74.

82 Testimony of Khania Knor, [no date], ICJ, TC 2772, not transcribed.

83 Testimony of Samuil Belenkov, August 10, 1943, GARF, 7021/17/4, p. 24.

84 Testimony of Mikhail Shapiro, February 16, 1974. YVA, 0.3/6019, p. 5.

became a prominent factor in the region due to a high proportion of mothers with children, as well as lone children and elderly persons, among the Caucasian evacuees. Reluctance to leave one's native area was also a significant consideration. For example, the father of the above-mentioned witness in Nal'chik suggested evacuation, but her mother refused on the following grounds: "Why should I abandon my house and go?"[85]

Several general factors also influenced Jews considering evacuation, including the unavailability of transport necessary for the evacuation from the Caucasus.[86] This unavailability became particularly acute after the beginning of the German drive into the region, and units of the retreating Red Army began to requisition all transport capacities.[87] Economic hardships involved in the evacuation were also at play.[88] It should be taken into account that to evacuate, particularly on one's own, was a costly enterprise. To quote a wartime testimony — "one should have paid for everything."[89] An additional factor was the malfunctioning of the Soviet bureaucracy. In Krasnodar, a Jewish woman received evacuation authorization but was not allowed to leave until her storage was emptied of goods.[90]

The impact of the food conditions in the region also influenced the behavior of Jewish refugees. In contrast to many other Soviet rear areas, in the North Caucasus the food situation was relatively satisfactory. This was a particular consideration for Jewish refugees from Leningrad, who had already experienced severe starvation during the siege of the city since September 1941.[91] Evacuation elsewhere from such a "blessed" region as the

85 Testimony of Elizaveta Nazarova, January 6, 1998, in Danilova, *Iskhod gorskikh evreev*, p. 131.

86 Kislovodsk: Testimony of Tsilia Gadleva, October 25, 1990, YVA, 0.3/4391, p. 9.

87 Nal'chik: Testimony of Noshum Shamilov, October 11, 1988, YVA, 0.3/5157, p. 12.

88 Nal'chik: Testimony of Liviia Digilova, August 19, 1999, in Danilova, *Iskhod gorskikh evreev*, p. 45; Testimony of Noshum Shamilov, October 11, 1998, YVA, 0.3/5157, p. 12.

89 Testimony of Ida Mandel'blat, May 25, 1998, YVA, VT/1911.

90 Testimony of Natal'ia Krechetovich, August 29, 1999, YVA, 0.33.C/5961.

91 E.g., Nadezhda Cherepenina, "Assessing the Scale of Famine and Death in the

North Caucasus was fraught with uncertainty and frowned upon by the potential refugees.[92]

Like everywhere, the intention and ability of Jews who found themselves in the Caucasus to escape the approaching German forces were contingent upon their location. It seems that, all other conditions being equal in 1941, the best sources of Holocaust-related information were in the towns, which served as transportation centers through which Jewish refugees tried to make their way eastwards. However, this information was more difficult to come by in some towns, more so than others. Villages were particularly problematic, as long distances became an effective barrier preventing Jews from learning about the proximity of danger.[93] Jews staying in large transportation centers found it easier to evacuate.

In the summer of 1942, the situation changed. Despite the fact that "urban" Jews seemed better informed of the proximity of the Germans, their ability to evacuate decreased considerably due to the enormous transportation problems. Conversely, those Jews who resided in rural areas had chances to escape on their own, provided their location was far enough from the advancing German troops. Regardless, it should be remembered that evacuation via such a vast area as the North Caucasus was a multi-stage process: One could escape the first wave of the German attack in the region only to find oneself swept up by the second.[94]

Besieged City," in John Barber and Andrei Dzeniskevich, eds., *Life and Death in Besieged Leningrad, 1941-44* (Basingstoke: Palgrave Macmillan, 2005), pp. 28-70.

92 See section 4A, "Food conditions."

93 Villages of Dzhiginka in the winter of 1941-1942 and Ivanovka in November-December 1941: Testimony of Hana Melinskii, January 12, 1986, YVA, 0.3/4342, p. 4; Testimony of Rachel Gurevich, ICJ, TC 2761.

94 From Krasnodar into Nal'chik: Testimony of Aron Gurevich, [no date], GARF, 7021/17/206, p. 329; Testimony of Lidiia Amchislavskaia, May 17, 1989, YVHN; Testimony of Izrail' Tomachevskii, October 3, 1999, YVHN.

2.2. In 1941 and 1942[95]

Movement of refugees from the North Caucasus eastwards had been noticeable from the summer of 1941, when the possibility of the German offensive towards the region was far from a reality. Testimonies, mainly from Jewish survivors, paint a controversial picture. Many of the Jews who had been relocated in the summer-fall of 1941 passed through the region but, as previously stated, did not settle there – regardless of whether they fled on their own initiative, or were systematically evacuated by authorities.[96] For them, the North Caucasus served as a transition point on their way to the Soviet deep rear. Others, however, were advised or forced to settle in the Caucasus, and were often dispatched to remote Caucasian areas.[97] A sort of second "intermediary" evacuation occurred when the authorities sent refugees further east into the vast North Caucasian lands as the situation on the fronts deteriorated – a phenomenon noticeable in 1941.[98] Although there is no clear-cut explanation for these ostensibly contradictory policies, it seems that they were a result of the general disorder, personal deviations by the evacuees from the original state-issued evacuation plans, and the personal initiative they displayed vis-à-vis the authorities.

In the fall of 1941, Jews were able to utilize an already malfunctioning but still active transportation system.[99] However, serious troubles were already manifest – i.e., it was extremely difficult to obtain tickets, which were often not honored; there were many more potential escapees than the actual number of

95 Linets, *Severnyi Kavkaz nakanune i v period nemetsko-fashistskoi okkupatsii*, pp. 51-80.

96 Elista and Starominskaia *stanitsa*: Testimony of Liudmila Bradichevskii, ICJ, (217) 183, p. 1; Borovoi, *Vospominaniia*, p. 256.

97 Labinskaia *stanitsa*, villages of Slavianskaia and Vyselki: Questioning of Raisa Niminskaia, August 24, 1943, YVA, M.33/292, p. 105. Diary of Giorgii Ioffe, entry from November 10, 1941, DAARK, R-156/1/31, p. 31; Testimony of Anfisa Kalnitskaia, [no date], ICJ, TC 2759.

98 Statement of Sarra Igla, August 18, 1944, GARF, 7021/9/6, p. 79; Testimony of Anfisa Kalnitskaia, [no date], ICJ, TC 2759.

99 Diary of Grigorii Ioffe, entry from November 9, 1941, DAARK, P-156/1/31, p. 31; Letters received by Ginzburg, November 18, 1941, YVA, 0.75/324, p. 74.

seats and trains;[100] it was difficult to evacuate from remote localities because of the unavailability of transport;[101] and sporadic German bombardments of railways and railway stations caused casualties among the Jewish refugees, and resulted in delays in the railway traffic.[102]

In almost all the documented cases, it is unobservable whether local authorities encouraged or discouraged Jewish refugees from moving eastwards. Those earmarked for evacuation were systematically evacuated in accordance with the authorities' orders, as exemplified by the orphanage evacuated from the village of Starominskaia in late October 1941.[103] Acting on their own initiative, local officials sometimes aided Jews in getting onto trains.[104] However, after the situation in the Soviet southern flank improved, from December 1941 the authorities imposed a complete ban or severe limitations on leaving the area.[105]

Evacuation from the North Caucasus took place prior to the German offensive into the region in the summer of 1942, and may be seen as a continuation, albeit on a smaller scale, of what had begun during the last months of 1941. Though numerically insignificant, it again revealed severe transportation problems, which had considerably worsened in July-August 1942, as demonstrated in this postwar Jewish testimony:

> By May 1942, we asked to be evacuated to the Urals. It was a complicated process that was expected to be quite long. It took the train 40 days to get from Minvody to Makhachkala. There were numerous stops.[106]

100 Diary of Grigorii Ioffe, entries from November 28 and 29, 1941, DAARK, P-156/1/31, p. 34.

101 Testimony of Ida Mandel'blat, May 25, 1998, YVA, VT/1911.

102 Testimony of Lidiia Iundina, October 4, 1988, YVHN; Letters received by Efim Ginzburg, November 18, 1941, YVA, 0.75/324, p. 75.

103 Testimony of Son'ia Glikman, September 12, 1985, YVA, 0.3/4325, p. 5.

104 Krasnodar: Testimony of Rachel Gurevich, ICJ, TC 2761.

105 Complete ban in Budennovsk: Letters received by Efim Ginzburg, entry from December 13, 1941, YVA 0.75/324, p. 76; Severe limitations in Krasnodar: Testimony of Hana Melinskii, January 12, 1986, YVA, 0.3/4342, p. 4.

106 Testimony of Anfisa Kalnitskaia, [no date], ICJ, TC 2759.

Evacuation became increasingly difficult as the Red Army rapidly retreated from the North Caucasus in the summer of 1942.[107] The authorities still sought to continue systematic evacuation and maintain a delicate balance between the necessity to begin evacuation when the Germans were critically close and the unwillingness to initiate it when the military situation was, arguably, still bearable. The directives received by the authorities of Kalmykiia from the center are instructive in this respect:

> Kamykiian authorities worked on the assumption that the population should be evacuated if the front line was 30 km off. Such were the responses given to the Kamykiian committee of the VKP(b) by the member of the Council for Evacuation Mikoian and the member of the Military Council of the Stalingrad Front, Khrushev.[108]

On July 24, the Stavropol' District Committee of the VKP(b) under Mikhail Suslov conducted a conference to study the evacuation of civilians. However, it could not reach any decision because it did not possess any real-time information on what had transpired on the southern front.[109] The Military Council of the North Caucasian Front sanctioned evacuation from the region on July 28, 1942.[110] In Stavropol', the order to evacuate the

107 Kudriashov and Chevela, "Oborona Stalingrada i Severnogo Kavkaza," in *Velikaia Otechestvennaia voina*, pp. 369-376.

108 S. A. Gladkova, "Organizatsiia evakuatsii liudskikh i materialnykh resursov," in Kalmytskii institut gumanitarnykh issledovanii Rossiiskoi akademii nauk, et al., p. 73.

109 Tat'iana Petrenko, "Evakuatsionnyi protsess na Stavropol'e letom 1942 goda: uspekhi i trudnosti," (PhD diss., Piatigorskii gosudarstvennyi tekhnologicheskii universitet, 2004), p. 39.

110 Decree of the Military Council of the North Caucasian Front, "O podgotovke unichtozheniia zapasov khleba, topliva, skota i prochego tsennogo imushestva, esli ikh vyvoz stanet nevozmozhnym," July 28, 1942, in Beliaev and Bondar', *Kuban' v gody Velikoi Otechestvennoi voiny, 1941-1945*, pp. 315-316.
The evacuation from Nal'chik, occupied on October 29, 1942, was also authorized only two days before the Germans' entry: Raisa Ashkhotova, ed., *Liki voiny: Sbornik dokumentov po istorii Kabardino-Balkarii v gody Velikoi Otechestvennoi voiny (1941-1945 gg.)* (Nal'chik: El'brus, 1996), pp. 144-145.

population was issued only on August 1, 1942, that is, two days before the town was occupied by the Germans;[111] yet, it was not announced to the population.[112] Evacuation commenced in Kislovodsk on August 5 as the advancing German troops stood at the gate of the neighboring town of Minvody.[113] In Krasnodar, the population had been scheduled to be evacuated from August 4,[114] but Soviet functionaries fled as chaos ensued.[115] The evidence pertaining to Beloglinskii *raion* (Krasnodarskii *krai*) contains no specific reference to the evacuation of Jews, but is indicative of the belatedness of Soviet measures:

> On July 29, 1942, a representative of the District Committee of the VKP(b), Comrade Stepanov, arrived and proposed to proceed with the bread harvesting. Battles on the area's territories commenced after dinner on July 30. Only thereupon, without receiving any directions whatsoever, the evacuation of people and machinery began... All draught animals were distributed on July 30, 1942 to the evacuating institutions of the raion, as well as to the families of Red Army commanders and political workers [*kompolitsostav*]. But it was impossible to provide everyone with draught animals. Therefore, part of the families of the military men and communists remained in the raion.[116]

It appears that the authorities attempted to carry out evacuation according to the well-established order of priorities until the very end. But even when the evacuation of the "target groups"

111 Boiko, *Stavropol'e v Velikoi Otechestvennoi voine 1941-1945 gg.*, p. 106.

112 Petrenko, "Evakuatsionnyi protsess na Stavropol'e letom 1942 goda," pp. 40-41.

113 Report of Moisei Evenson, Viktor Shklovskii, ed., [no date], YVA, P.21.2/1, P.21.2/1.

114 Beliaev and Bondar', *Kuban' v gody Velikoi Otechestvennoi voiny, 1941-1945*, pp. 341-342.

115 Kislovodsk, Nal'chik: Testimony of Fania Skliar, September 1975, YVA, 0.3/3934, p. 3; Testimony of Sarra Golan, July-August 1974, YVA, 0.3/6039, p. 2.

116 A. A. Griniuk, explanatory note of the second Secretary of the Committee of the VKP(b) of [Krasnodarskii] *krai*, August 1942, in Beliaev and Bondar', *Kuban' v gody Velikoi Otechestvennoi voiny, 1941-1945*, pp. 334-335.

was successfully implemented, it could later fail as the general situation grew out of the Soviet authorities' control:

> On August 8, the order came for the entire population to evacuate from Mikoianshakhar and to go by foot about 300 km to Kizliar near the Caspian Sea. Nothing came of the order as the only people who actually left were civilian and Party officials, as well as party members... The local mountaineers ambushed the commandant and his entire convoy. Everybody was killed.[117]

Other sources also indicate that in a number of important centers in the North Caucasus, the non-Russian population deposed the Soviet administration some time prior to the arrival of the German troops. These anti-Soviet forces came effectively to control the roads and prevented the evacuation and flight of civilians, as well as that of retreating Red Army troops.[118]

It is evident that under such circumstances, it was also difficult for the Jews who belonged to the "target" groups to be evacuated from the North Caucasus at this time. In Stavropol', a Jewish militia captain was able to evacuate himself, but was powerless to take anyone from his family with him.[119] In the same city, a Jewish book-keeper was evacuated with some of his institution staff. Yet, "all members of his family numbering 14 persons were unable to be evacuated owing to bad transport conditions."[120] Twenty-eight percent of all pupils in the state-run orphanages (which hosted a considerable number of Jewish pupils)[121] failed to evacuate from Stavropol'skii *krai*,[122] and more than 60% from Krasnodarskii *krai*

117 Poppe, *Reminiscences*, p. 160.

118 See, for example, Iurii Klychnikov and Sergei Linets, *Severokavkazskii uzel: osobennosti konfliktnogo potentsiala (istoricheskie ocherki)* (Piatigorsk: Reklamno-informatsionnoe agenstvo na KMV, 2006), p. 145.

119 Statement of Efrem Peikhvasser, July 2, 1943, GARF, 7021/17/1, p. 26.

120 Statement of Abram Nankin, 1943 (author's suggestion), GARF, 7021/17/1, p. 24.

121 Petrenko, "Evakuatsionnyi protsess na Stavropol'e letom 1942 goda," p. 54.

122 Armavir and Teberda: Questioning of Vera Olshevskaia (1906), August 13, 1943. YVA, M.33/286, pp. 7-9. For more information, see Testimony of Vadim

failed (in the latter case, 9,750 pupils out of 15,730 stayed in the occupied territory).[123]

Despite unfavorable conditions, the authorities did their best to remove cattle from the Germans' reach. In almost all the cases, those who accompanied the cattle were Jews. It seems that the Jews volunteered to do it, and in this case their desire to leave the region coincided with the interests of authorities. The Soviets claimed that they succeeded in removing a lot of cattle from the region, and some Jews probably saved themselves in this way.[124] On the other hand, many wartime sources indicate that these attempts were often a complete failure as the Jewish cattle-drivers were forestalled by the advancing German troops.[125] According to a wartime Soviet report, "The enemy advanced quickly with regard to the pace of the evacuation of cattle, and a considerable part of cattle was cut off by the enemy."[126]

Evacuation or, to be more precise, the flight of masses of Jews from the North Caucasus in late July to early August 1942 spontaneously commenced before the authorities had made any official announcement. To quote a Russian witness of the events that took place in Stavropol', "Those who attempted to escape through the railway were doomed: There were not enough trains. Besides, the Germans would have soon cut off the railroad."[127]

Jewish testimonies and official Soviet reports depict the same picture – the transportation system collapsed entirely at that time.[128] A postwar Jewish testimony is instructive in this respect:

Maniker, April 1975, YVA, 0.3/4108, p. 2.

123 Iurchuk, "Politika mestnykh vlastei Kubani po zaschite detstva i ee prakticheskaia realizatsiia v gody Velikoi Otechestvennoi voiny (1941-1945 gg.)," p. 96.

124 See section 4A, "Food conditions."

125 Akt of the Commission of Dovsun Country Council, July 18, 1943, GARF, 7021/17/10, p. 15. See also the Akt of the Commission of Sovetskaia *stanitsa*, 1943, YVA, M.33/301, pp. 95-96.

126 Telegram of the [Stavropol'] Committee of the VKP(b), in Boiko, *Stavropol'e v Velikoi Otechestvennoi voine 1941-1945 gg.*, pp. 109-110.

127 Belikov, *Okkupatsiia*, pp. 21-25.

128 Village of Izobil'noe, Krasnodar: Akt of the Commission of Izobil'nenskii *raion*, June 29, 1943, GARF, 7021/17/10, p. 121; Testimony of Tsilia Gadleva, October 25, 1990, YVA, 0.3/4391, p. 9.

> There were many hundreds of evacuees, including many college teachers... one of my relatives intended to evacuate, and waited for the train for some days, but it did not arrive. The Germans came.[129]

The efficient German bombardments of railway centers resulted in bringing the still-functioning transportation capacities to a halt.[130]

Unable to evacuate by train, masses of Jews endeavored to escape on their own by whatever means of transportation was available, which meant carts, horses, and feet.[131] Most of the Jewish refugees were forestalled by the advancing Wehrmacht troops and Soviet insurgents.[132] Nevertheless, a small record of Jews who were able to make their way outside of the German occupation area, even in such unfavorable conditions, exists.[133]

3. Enlistment

In accordance with the directives of the Soviet government, from the beginning of the German invasion of the USSR the conscript-age men were enlisted in the Red Army, at least in a number of the North Caucasian areas.[134] The enlistment was initially

129 Testimony of Tsilia Gadleva, YVA, 0.3/4391, p. 9.

130 Testimony of Lidiia Iundina, October 4, 1988, YVHN; Testimony of Vladimir Shpits, June 7, 1992, YVHN. For more information, see the testimony of Mikhail Skladman, October 22, 1979, YVHN and the testimony of Sima Cherchikova, October 18, 1999, YVHN.

131 From Essentuki towards Elista and Budennovsk: Testimony of Abraham Wein, August 3, 1988, YVA, 0.3/4822, p. 15.

132 Testimony of Fania Skliar, [no date], YVA, 0.3/3934, p. 3; Poppe, *Reminiscences*, p. 160.

133 Testimony of Khania Knor, [no date], ICJ, TC 2772: Testimony of Mikhail Mil'grom [no date], GARF, 7021/17/206, p. 43.

134 Krasnodar and Stavropol': Beliaev and Bondar', *Kuban' v gody Velikoi Otechestvennoi voiny, 1941-1945*, pp. 25-26. Decree of the Presidium of the Supreme Council of the USSR on the enlistment of conscript-age persons from a number of areas, June 22, 1941, in Boiko, *Stavropol'e v Velikoi Otechestvennoi voine 1941-1945 gg.*, p. 27.

introduced for the draftees born between 1905 and 1918,[135] and the enlistment quotas for the region were filled.[136] Despite the actual lack of relevant evidence, it stands to reason that Jewish residents of the region were affected by the draft similarly to the rest of the population. As a result of new waves of enrollment, in 1941 (June 22-December 31) every eighth inhabitant (sic) of Krasnodarskii *krai* was conscripted,[137] and by the spring of 1942, the great majority (98.2%) of draftable men up to age 46 in the North Caucasian Military District were drafted.[138]

However, it seems that the refugees evacuated into the North Caucasus were affected by the enlistment to a lesser extent. This was the case in the first months of the evacuation, when many conscript-age Jewish men were visible in the midst of the North Caucasian population already depleted by Red Army drafts.[139] The ensuing growth of anti-Jewish feelings was duly recorded in a Soviet report.[140] Although some refugees who settled down in the Caucasus were conscripted into the Red Army, new drafts obviously did not cover all conscript-age Jewish men, as may be inferred from the study of a sizable number of Jewish conscript-age men and women recorded in the lists of evacuees and victims of the German occupation.[141] It is probable that their inadequate

135 Ibid.

136 Note submitted by the information sector of the Committee of the VKP(b) on the pace of enlistment in the Red Army and the work of enterprises, *kolkhozy*, *sovkhozy*, MTS in the conditions of the Patriotic War, August 1, 1941, in ibid., pp. 38-39.

137 Khachemizova, "Obshestvo i vlast'", p. 130.

138 Alexei Bezugol'nyi, "Narody Kavkaza v Vooruzhennykh silakh SSSR v gody Velikoi Otechestvennoi Voiny 1941-1945 gg," (PhD diss., Stavropol'skii gosudarstvennyi universitet, 2004), p. 38.

139 Information provided by the Head of Military Department of Soldatsko-Akeksandrovsk area committee of the VKP(b) B. Fadeev, top secret, August 30, 1941, in V. Belokon', T. Kolpikova, Ia. Kol'tsova, and V. Maznitsa, eds., *Stavropol'e: Pravda voennykh let: Velikaia Otechestvenaia v dokumentakh i issledovaniiakh* (Stavropol': Stavropol'skii gosudarstvennyi universitet, 2005), p. 35.

140 Andrienko, "Naselenie Stavropol'skogo kraia v gody Velikoi Otechestvennoi voiny," p. 57.

141 This suggestion is based on the analysis of many testimonies available in the Hall of Names in Yad Vashem.

army enlistment in the Caucasus had to do with a number of factors: the unclear status of the newcomers with respect to the possibility of their further evacuation from the region, the logistic problems resulting from the inadequate coordination between civil bureaucracy in charge of evacuation and military authorities in charge of conscription, and the lack of confidence towards those Jews who had been evacuated from the territories recently annexed by the Soviet Union. Likewise, Jewish participation was hardly visible in the ranks of the local *opolchenie* and "extermination battalions" because they were apparently comprised solely of the native inhabitants of the North Caucasus.[142]

* * *

The evaluation of the dimensions of the Jewish survival due to evacuation from the North Caucasus constitutes a problem for a number of reasons. The region incorporated heterogeneous territories, which diverged in relation to the density and quantity of the Jewish population, its closeness to the front line, and the timing of the German occupation. In this respect, information on the prewar Jewish population of the region is only of secondary importance, as considerable displacement of the Jewish population in the Caucasus occurred by the time of the German occupation.

Nonetheless, if the region is regarded as a single unit, regarding evacuation it should be borne in mind that the greater part of the region was seized by the Germans as a result of the thrust that was all too reminiscent of the first months of the Blitzkrieg in the Soviet-German warfare. In the Caucasus, the Soviets again failed to implement their large-scale evacuation plans. The fact that the Soviet authorities evacuated masses of people from other endangered areas to the region demonstrates that they did not envision any German drive into the Caucasus. Therefore, in terms of "evacuation resulting in survival," the North Caucasus was on

142 Testimony of Liudmila Freidlin, November 20, 1999, YVHN; the testimony of Mikhail Koltun in *Stavropol'skaia Pravda*, August 9, 2005, available at http://vechorka.ru/index.php?c=prin&st=1694&arh=1.

par with those territories occupied by the Germans by the end of July 1941. In these regions, the percentage of evacuees/refugees able to flee from the advancing German armies fluctuated around 35-45%.[143]

However, the impact of the full year of the Soviet-German war on the dimensions of evacuation/flight from the North Caucasus must also be assessed. It goes without saying that the danger Jews perceived as a result of the German occupation was by far more evident for them in 1942 than in 1941. Also, most of the Jews residing in the North Caucasus by the summer of 1942 were non-organized refugees who were psychologically prepared to continue their flight eastwards, even in the absence of directives and aid from the authorities. As a result, despite the government policy, some Jews were still able to flee the North Caucasus, mostly on their own, and a certain upward correction in the evacuation assessment from the region is in order. On the whole, I estimate that about 40-50% of the Jews were able to evacuate from the North Caucasus by the time of the German occupation in the summer of 1942.

143 Schwarz, *Evrei v Sovetskom Soiuze s nachala vtoroi mirovoi voiny (1939-1965)*, pp. 47-51. See also Altshuler, Arad, and Krakowski, *Sovetskie evrei pishut Ilie Erenburgu*, p. 97.

Chapter Three

Destruction of the Jewish Population in the Crimea

1. German Institutions Involved in the Holocaust in the Crimea

1.1. The 11th Army[1]

The German Army exerted executive authority as an institution in the occupied Crimea from the moment it entered the peninsula in the fall of 1941 and throughout the period of the mass destruction of the Jewish population of the Crimea.[2] The Commander of the 553rd Rear Army,[3] subordinate to the Commander of the

1 On the 11th Army in the Crimea, see Pohl, *Die Herrschaft der Wehrmacht*, pp. 262-268; Marcel Stein, ed., *Die 11. Armee und die "Endlösung" 1941/42: eine Dokumentensammlung mit Kommentaren* (Bissendorf: Biblio Verlag, 2006); Oldenburg, *Ideologie und militärisches Kalkül*, pp. 259-306.

2 For the German view of the warfare in the Crimea in 1941, see Klink, "The Conduct of Operations," pp. 627-631. For the German view of the warfare in the Crimea in 1942, see Wegner, "The War Against the Soviet Union, 1942-1943," pp. 929-941; Joel Hayward, "A Case Study in Early Joint Warfare: An Analysis of the Wehrmacht's Crimean Campaign of 1942," *Journal of Strategic Studies* 22, no. 4 (1999): pp. 103-130.
For the Soviet insight into the warfare in the peninsula in 1941 and 1942, see Aleksei Basov, *Krym v Velikoi Otechestvennoi Voine, 1941-1945* (Moscow: Nauka, 1987), pp. 46-81; 84-191.

3 553rd Rear Army, in German "*Kommandant des rückwärtigen Armeesgebietes* 553", or *Korück* 553 – Commander of the Rear Army Group 553. The term refers to both the unit and its commanding office.

11th Army,[4] was responsible for the rear of the 11th Army. After the seizure of Sevastopol', followed by the removal of the bulk of the 11th Army from the Crimea, the Commander of the German troops in the peninsula (*Befehlshaber Krim*) attained ultimate control.[5] In September 1942, the supreme authority in the Crimea was transferred to the German civil administration under Alfred Frauenfeld as *Generalkommissar für Taurien* (part of the *Reichskommissariat Ukraine)*, although the Wehrmacht remained an important factor because of its role in combatting Soviet partisans.

Of note is AOK 11 commander General Erich von Manstein's[6] position regarding army involvement in anti-Jewish actions during the Battle of the Crimea. Some days after he took over the command of the Army in September-October 1941, Manstein announced that

> it was unworthy of an officer to participate in the execution of Jews… What the SS are doing is dirty work, but we know that is must be done. We'll not stop it and generally support

4 In German — AOK 11, or "*Armeeoberkommando* 11" — the Army High Command 11. The term refers to both the unit and its commanding office.

5 Under this name, the XXXXII Corps HQ took over command in the Crimea from the 11th Army HQ on August 24, 1942. Wegner, "The War Against the Soviet Union, 1942-1943," p. 1032.

6 Erich von Manstein (1887-1973): son of an artillery general; German military commander; author of the plan to invade France by a concentrated armored thrust through the Ardennes Forest; became commander of the 11th Army on September 12, 1941; promoted to *Generalfeldmarschall* for the successful termination of the Battle of the Crimea in July 1942; on November 21, 1942, became commander of the Army Group (*Heeresgruppe*) Don that attempted to break through the Soviet siege of the German 6th Army at Stalingrad; removed from the army over strategic disagreement with Hitler in March 1944; found guilty by the British court for "violation of laws of war" and sentenced to 18 years in prison in 1949; granted an early release due to poor health in 1952; later served as counselor to Adenauer and the *Bundeswehr*. On Erich von Manstein, see Lemay Benoít, "Le feld-maréchal Erich von Manstein: un instrument docile dans une entreprise criminelle," *Revue d'Histoire de la Shoah* 187 (2007): pp. 177-192; Oliver von Wrochem, *Erich von Manstein: Vernichtungskrieg und Geschichtspolitik* (Paderborn: Ferdinand Schöningh Verlag, 2006); Marcel Stein, *Der Januskopf: Feldmarschall von Manstein; eine Neubewertung* (Bissendorf: Biblio Verlag, 2004).

> it; our people must, however, be prevented from observing the executions.[7]

That Manstein embraced Nazi anti-Jewish genocidal policies is further reflected in his order from November 20, 1941, when his Army was already stationed in the Crimea:

> This struggle is not being carried against the Soviet Armed Forces alone in the established form laid down by European rules of warfare. Behind the front, too, the fighting continues.

Manstein depicted Jewry as an "intermediary" between the two:

> Jewry is the middleman between the enemy in the rear and what remains of the Red Army and the Red leadership still fighting. More strongly than in Europe, they hold all key positions of political leadership, administration, trade, and crafts, and constitute a cell for all unrest and possible uprisings.

He described the aim of the war:

> The Jewish Bolshevik system must be wiped out once and for all, and should never again be allowed to invade our European living-space.[8]

Yet, until July 1942, when the 11th Army captured the last Soviet stronghold in the Crimea (Sevastopol'), its regular units engaged in intensive warfare throughout the Crimean peninsula. As Manstein put it:

7 Statement of the AOK Chief of HQ (Stabschef) Wöhler, in "Die Anklage gegen Manstein," *Neue Zürerei Zeitung*, December 1, 1949, p. 2, Yad Vashem Archives (YVA), P.13/32.

8 Secret circular by the Commander of the 11th Army N 2379/41, November 20, 1941, translated into Russian, State Archive of the Autonomous Republic of the Crimea (DAARK), P-156/1/24, p. 1. See also Armeebefehl Mansteins, AOK 11/1c/AO, Nr. 2379/41 geh., November 20, 1941, in Ueberschär and Wetter, *Der deutsche Überfall auf der Sowjetunion*, p. 343f.

> Our troops, almost down to the last man, in the Crimea particularly, were being used in the battle at the front, and even our clerks sometimes had to be sent into battle. The entire rear area was more or less devoid of troops and only the most important supply points were manned.[9]

As a result, fewer Wehrmacht personnel were available for various security operations. Consequently, despite the fact that securing its living space was critical to considerations, the AOK 11 often did not possess sufficient forces to support the *Einsatzgruppe* in its security missions, such as the mopping-up of towns, anti-partisan fighting, and "clearing" the area of Jews.[10]

However, whenever this goal was considered most urgent and it was compatible with its resources, the Army did help. The fulfillment of the task was the primary responsibility of the military agencies permanently stationed in strategic places all over the peninsula — 11 Local HQs (*Ortskommandaturen*, or OK) and three Local Field HQs (*Feldkommandaturen*, or FK) subordinated to Commandant of the Rear Area (*Korück*) 553,[11] himself under Erich Manstein's authority.[12] OK/FK were occasionally strengthened by mobile *Feldgendarmerie* units,[13] Romanian troops,[14] and local militias.[15]

9 Testimony of Erick von Manstein, August 12, 1946, *The Trial of German Major War Criminals: Proceedings of the International Military Tribunal Sitting at Nuremberg, Germany* (PNWCT) (London: International Military Tribunal, 1946-51), vol. 20, p. 618.

10 Arnold, *Die Wehrmacht und die Besatzungspolitik*, pp. 203-209.

11 On the involvement of OK/FK in the extermination of the Jews in the occupied Soviet territories, see Matthäus Jürgen, "Beteiligung der Ordnungspolizei am Holocaust" in Kaiser, *Täter im Vernichtungskrieg*, pp. 166-185. On the OK/FK murderous activities in the Crimea in 1941-1942, see Kunz, "Die Feld- und Ortskommandaturen, pp. 54-70. The number of FK/OK is given as of the summer of 1941 in ibid, p. 57.

12 "Strafsache gegen Walter Bierkamp," Der Untersuchungsrichter I bei dem Landgericht Düsseldorf, Stuttgart, Wilhelm F. Friedrich, April 30, 1963, YVA, TR.10/1147, p. 358.

13 "Strafsache gegen Walter Bierkamp," Der leitende Oberstaatsanwalt bei dem Landesgericht Hamburg, Z. Zt. Munich, Vernehmungsniederschrift, Horst E., August 13, 1964, YVA, TR.10/1147, p. 479.

14 Ibid.

15 OK I/742, FG, "TB für April 1942," Fraidorf, April 26, 1942, YVA, 0.51/185 II, p. 3.

Often, the *Kommandaturen* emerged in the Crimean countryside before the *Einsatzgruppe* D (EG D), and were the first German agency to deal with Jews. Especially in the first months of the occupation, scattered OK/FK served as an instrument to enforce movement and residential restrictions as well as the Jewish policy all over the peninsula. The patterns of OK/FK behavior with respect to Jews were different. Even prior to the large-scale killing operations conducted in late November-December 1941, they reported Jewish presence to the *Einsatzgruppe*.[16] An excerpt from the military report related to Simferopol' is typical in this respect. On November 22, 1941, the local OK II/915 reported that in its field of activity "Mark Kamzahn, Jew, was arrested and handled to SK 10b for his appeal to resist the German army."[17] After the actions, the *Kommandaturen* continued to reveal Jews and to report these cases to the *Einsatzgruppe*.[18]

In certain cases, the OK/FK transferred the arrested Jews to the Secret Field Police,[19] which was in charge of internal military security.[20] The Secret Field Police enjoyed a considerable measure of independence but, unfortunately, there are few accounts of its onduct against the Jews in the Crimea. In the first months of the occupation, GFP units participated in large-scale anti-Jewish

16 Simferopol, OK II/915, FG, "TB für die Zeit vom 21.-29.11.1941," O.U., November 29, 1941, YVA, M.29.FR/41, p. 34; 1./Feldgend, Abt., Mot., 683, "TB für die Zeit vom 28.-30.11.1941," O.U., December 1, 1941, YVA, M.29.FR/41, p. 36.

17 OK II/915, FG, "TB für die Zeit vom 21.-29.11.1941," O.U., November 29, 1941, YVA, M.29.FR/41, p. 33.

18 Sargil, village of Kolai, Stabsoffz. d. Feldgend, "TB als Beilage zum KTB für die Zeit vom 1.-31.3.1942," April 2, 1942, YVA, M.29.FR/118, p. 24; FK 608, "TB für die Zeit vom 13.-27.4.1942," April 28, 1942, YVA, M.29.FR/37, p. 20; Oldenburg, *Ideologie und militärisches Kalkül*, p. 164.

19 The Secret Field Police (*Geheime Feldpolizei*, or GFP) belonged to the order troops of the Wehrmacht. Their 50 man-strong mobile units were staffed by the Security Police, Gestapo, and Criminal Police. Arnold, *Die Wehrmacht und die Besatzungspolitik in den besetzten Gebieten der Sowjetunion*, pp. 468-474; Paul B. Brown, "The Senior Leadership of the Geheime Feldpolizei," *Holocaust and Genocide Studies* 17, no. 2 (2003): pp. 278-304.

20 Unidentified locality, Staboffz, der FG, "TB als Anlage zum KTB für die Zeit vom 1.-30.11.1941," December 2, 1941, YVA, M.29.FR/118, p. 6.

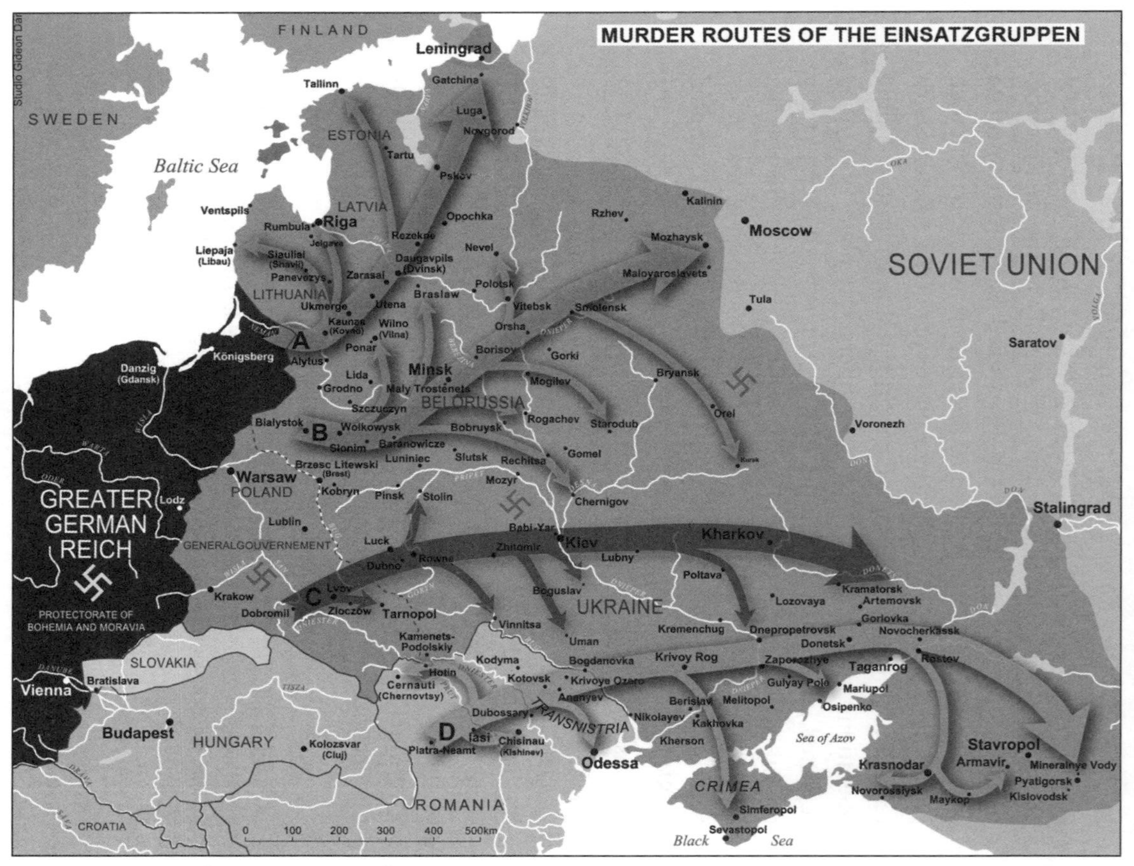

Courtesy: U.S. Holocaust Memorial Museum

actions, presided over by the EG D.[21] The Secret Field Police occasionally served as the final authority on where the arrested Jews were sent. This sometimes meant that they verified Jewish identities and killed them summarily without transferring them to the EG D. The following report of the GFP from November 11, 1941 illustrates this notion:

> A Jew was arrested. He turned out to be an NKVD agent and plunderer. He was shot. The report was made to the SD.[22]

The Secret Field Police, in contrast to the EG D, did not initiate anti-Jewish actions.

When the *Kommandaturen* discovered Jews, the common response was first to arrest and then shoot them. In April 1942, the *Ortskommandatur* I(V)/287, in charge of Feodosiia, exterminated 23 Jews.[23] In the first half of May, it shot 34 more Jews.[24] The German military reports justified these killings by referring to "an alien behavior towards Germany"[25] or to suspicions that the arrested Jew was a spy.[26] The words "execution" or "shooting" were often avoided and substituted with "treated appropriately"[27] or,

21 Sevastopol', areas Sarabus and Spath, "Verdict against Ernst Schrewe," November 12-23, 1947, United States Holocaust Memorial Museum Archives (USHMMA), RG-31.018M, reel 7; Staboffz, der FG, "TB als Anlage zum KTB für die Zeit vom 1.-31.1.1942," February 2, 1942, YVA, M.29.FR/60, p. 9. See also Oldenburg, *Ideologie und militärisches Kalkül*, pp. 207-208.

22 Wehrmachtsdienststelle, GFP 647, *Kommando* Simferopol, "TB für die Zeit vom 2.-11.11.1941," November 11, 1941, YVA, M.29.FR/120, p. 4; GFP 647, "TB für den Monat Juni 1942," O.U., June 26, 1942, YVA, M.29.FR/59, p. 30.

23 OK I (V)/287, "TB für die Zeit vom 16.-30.4.1942," Feodosia, May 1, 1942, YVA, M.29.FR/37, p. 23.

24 OK I (V)/287, "TB für die Zeit vom 1.-13.5.1942," Feodosia, May 13, 1942, YVA, M.29.FR/37, p. 36.

25 Evpatoriiskii *raion*, FK 810, FG, "TB über die im Gebiete der FK 810 durchgeführten Streifen," O.U., February 15, 1942, YVA, M.29.FR/40, p. 8.

26 Fraidorfskii *raion*, 3./Feldgend, Abt., (mot) 683, "TB des im Freidorfer Gebiet eingesetzten Zuges," O.U. February 11, 1942, YVA, M.29.FR/40, p. 5.

27 Evpatoriiskii *raion*, FK 810, FG, "TB über die im Gebiete der FK 810 durchgeführten Streifen," O.U., February 15, 1942, YVA, M.29.FR/40, p. 8; FK 810, "TB für die Zeit vom 27.2-13.3.1942," March 13, 1942, ibid., p. 28.

more revealingly, "shot in attempted escape",[28] "shot because of revolt and jeopardizing the civilian population,"[29] or "resettled."[30] The following *Feldgendarmerie* report from February 11, 1942, is illuminating:

> The Militia had finally discovered 5 Jews (3 men, 2 women) outside of the locality in the steppe and delivered them to the [*Feldgendarmerie*] section; the latter executed them because they were suspected of spying. They had long stayed in the given area without permanent residence.[31]

Aside from the German occupation forces, there was also some Romanian involvement in the Crimea, for which general observations are in order. From October 1941 to July 1942, considerable Romanian forces, subordinated to the Wehrmacht command on an operational level and sometimes placed under direct German command, also occupied and "pacified" the Crimea, as well as engaged in actual fighting.[32] The Germans preferred to use the Romanian units in operations against non-regular forces, such as in anti-partisan warfare, combings, and round-ups, due to their perception of them as having relatively low combat strength.[33]

28 Evpatoriiskii *raion*, FK 810, "TB für die Zeit vom 27.4-10.5.1942," May 12, 1942, YVA, M.29.FR/37, p. 32.

29 Dzhankoi, OK II/939, "TB für die Zeit vom 1.-10.12.1941," Dzhankoi, December 10, 1941, YVA, M.29.FR/41, p. 46.

30 Area of Pervomaisk and Kangil, Staboffz, der FG, "TB als Anlage zum KTB für die Zeit vom 1.-31.1.1942," February 2, 1942, YVA, M.29.FR/60, p. 8.

31 3./Feldgend., Abt., (mot) 683, "TB des im Freidorfer Gebiet eingesetzten Zuges," O.U., February 11, 1942, YVA, M.29.FR/40, p. 5.

32 On the military aspect of the Romanian involvment in the warfare in the Crimea and the Caucasus, see Jipa Rotaru, Oroian Teofil, Zodian Vladimir, and Leonida Moise, *Hitler, Antonescu, Caucazul si Crimea: Sange romanesc si German pe frontul de Est* (Bucharest: Paideia, 1999). See also Grant T. Harward, "First among Un-Equals: Challenging German Stereotypes of the Romanian Army during the Second World War," *The Journal of Slavic Military Studies* 24, no. 3 (2011): pp. 461-462, 467; Adrian Pandea and Eftimie Ardeleanu, *Românii în Crimeea, 1941-1944* (Bucharest: Editura Militară, 1995).

33 Gottlob Herbert Bidermann, *In Deadly Combat: A German Soldier's Memoir of the Eastern Front* (Lawrence, Kansas: University Press of Kansas, 2000), pp. 121-122.

The Romanian units were also involved in implementing the "Final Solution" in the Crimea.[34] The Romanians became instrumental in their own right in a number of locations lacking sufficient German troops. Overall, Romanian soldiers were less strict toward Jews, in that they were more content with superficial check-ups and were apparently more inclined to bribery.[35] On the other hand, the Romanian soldiers often physically maltreated the local people and plundered their property, targeting Jews in particular.[36] By and large, the Romanian troops stationed in the Crimea from October 1941 to July 1942 did not substantially change their conduct toward Jews. This was a reflection of, with some reservations, the ambiguity of the Romanian stance toward the Jews in Transnistria during this period.[37] Although the Romanian military in the Crimea occasionally killed Jews, the Romanians frequently accepted bribes and let Jews survive, especially when there were no Germans in the vicinity. A last note regarding Italian presence in the Crimea – judging by the small available evidence, personnel of the Italian navy, which had been active in the Crimea since late May 1942, was not involved in the persecution of Jews in the region.[38]

34 Dzhankoi, village of Topalovka, "Interrogation of Il'ia Sirota," June 16, 1944, State Archive of the Russian Federation (GARF), 7021/9/194, pp. 155-157 and in DAARK, P-156/1/34, p. 19. "Story of Iakov Granovskii," account of D. I. Makarycheva, DAARK, P-156/1/36, p. 92.

35 Sargil, Simferopol': Staboffz, der FG, "TB als Anlage zum KTB für die Zeit vom 1.-31.3.1942," April 2, 1942, YVA, M.29.FR/118, p. 24; Letter of Dana Poiurovskaia, file of Ekaterina Kolesnikova, YVA, M.31/5541.

36 Yalta, Fraidorfskii *raion*: Diary of O. I. Shargorodskaia, entries from November 21 (28), December 4, 1941, DAARK, P-156/1/31, pp. 154, 156-157; 3./ Feldgend., Abt., (mot) 683, "TB des im Freidorfer Gebiet eingesetzten Zuges," O.U., February 11, 1942, YVA, M.29.FR/40, p. 5.

37 Dennis Deletant, "Transnistria and the Romanian Solution to the 'Jewish Problem,' in Ray Brandon and Wendy Lower, eds., *The Shoah in Ukraine; History, Testimony, Memorialization* (Bloomington: Indiana University Press in association with the United States Holocaust Memorial Museum, 2010), pp. 156-189.

38 Valerio Borgese, "10th Navy group in the Black Sea: Participation in the Siege of the Black Sea," in Garagulia, Kondranov, and Kravtsova, *Krym v Velikoi Otechestvennoi voine,* pp. 28-34.

1.2. *Einsatzgruppe* D[39]

The *Einsatzgruppe* D (EG D) numbered approximately 500 to 600 members enlisted from the Security Police, the SD, the SS, and the Order Police.[40] When Romania decided to join Nazi Germany's attack on the Soviet Union in May-June 1941, the Reich Chief Security Administration (RSHA)[41] responded by creating this special *Einsatzgruppe*, in order to act in the areas in which Romania would later be fighting. SS-*Standartenführer* Otto Ohlendorf[42] was appointed to the position of the *Einsatzgruppe* leader, retaining it until July 1942.

In terms of internal structure and organization, the EG D was made up of *Sonderkommando* (Sk) 10a, 10b, and *Einsatzkommando* (Ek) 11a, 11b, 12. After the outbreak of the war, the EG D was attached to the Army Group South[43] and, in addition to its own

39 For an overview of the activity of the *Einsatzgruppe* D in the Crimea, see Angrick, *Besatzungspolitik und Massenmord*, pp. 323-361.

40 "Affidavit of Heinz Hermann Schubert," December 7, 1945, Prosecution Exhibit 193, doc. NO 5111 (M895, roll 12 RG 238), page 1 of original in *PNWCT.*

41 The Reich Chief Security Administration (*Reichssicherheitshauptamt*, or RSHA) was created by Himmler on September 27, 1939. It incorporated the Security Police (*Sicherheitspolizei*, or *Sipo*) and Security Service (*Sicherheitsdienst*, or SD). It was headed by Heydrich until his assassination on June 4, 1942; Himmler superseded him until he appointed Ernst Kalntebruner as the new RSHA Chief on January 30, 1943. On RSHA, see Michael Wildt, *Generation des Unbedingten: Das Führungskorps des Reichssicherheitshauptamtes* (Hamburg: Hamburger Edition, 2002).

42 Otto Ohlendorf (1907-1951): 1925 — member of the NSDAP; 1927 — member of the SS; 1933-34 — lecturer at the Kiel Institute of World Economy; 1936 — economic referent of the SD; 1939-1945 — chief of Department III, German living area (*Deutsche Lebensgebiete — SD Inland*) of the RSHA; May 1941-June 1942 — commander of the *Einsatzgruppe* D; November 1942 — head of a department in the Ministry of Economics; approx. 1942 — awarded *Freundeskreuz* of the *Reichsführer*-SS; 1944 — SS *Gruppenführer*; 1948 — chief defendant in the *Einsatzgruppen* trial, condemned to death; 1951– hanged. On Ohlendorf, see Jörg Pache and Friederike Scharlau, "Akteure der Vernichtung: Deutsche und sowjetische Täter - ein Vergleich," *Zeitschrift für Geschichtswissenschaft* 57, no. 12 (2009): pp. 973-985.

43 Army Group South (*Heeresgruppe Süd*): In 1941 it consisted of the Tank Group (*Panzergruppe*) 1, Armies 6, 11, and 17, as well as two Romanian armies (3 and 4). *Generalfeldmarschall* Gerd von Rundstedt was its first commander (until December 3, 1941); he was followed by *Generalfeldmarschall* Walter von Reichenau (until January 12, 1942) and *Generalfeldmarschall* Fedor von Bock (till February 12, 1943).

assignment, acted in the field of the Rear Army Group. From November 1941 until the summer of 1942, most units of the EG D, with the exception of Sk 10a and part of Ek 12, were stationed in the Crimea and operated in the field of activity of the 11th Army.[44] Until May 1942, the EG D was the sole SS agency in the Crimea. After the end of May, the SS and Police Leader for Tauria, Ludolf von Alvensleben,[45] was installed in Simferopol'. In July-August 1942, the EG D was withdrawn from the peninsula; Sk 11b was transformed into *Dienststelle des KdS Simferopol*[46] and subordinated to the head of the SS and police in the *Reichskommissariat Ukraine*.[47]

Apart from its own forces, the *Einsatzgruppe* also operated some local police forces. They were raised in the first half of 1942 among the Soviet POWs who were primarily of Crimean Tatar[48] (but also of Caucasian and, to a lesser extent, Russian) descent. The prisoners, who were detained mostly in the Crimea but also

44 Coordination between the EG D and AOK 11 was achieved by means of a liaison officer in the person of the SS-*Hauptführer* S. delegated to the Army: "Strafsache gegen Walter Bierkamp," Staatsanwaltschaft bei dem Landgericht München I, Versuchungsniederschrift, Heinz S. Hermann, July 16, 1959, YVA, TR.10/1147, p. 4.

45 Ludolf von Alvensleben (1901-1970): son of a Mayor-General; 1920 – service in Freikorps; 1929 – member of the NSDAP and the SA; NSDAP leader (*Kreisleiter*) in Mansfeld; 1934 – member of the SS; 1938 – Himmler's Chief aide-de-camps; October 1939 to July 1940 – *Selbstschutz-Führer* in Danzig and West Prussia; May 1942 – SS and Police Leader in Tauria; 1943 – SS *Oberführer*; October 1943 – High SS and Police Leader in southern Russia in the area of the Army Group A; 1946 – escape from the internment camp Neuengamme to Argentina.

46 Andrej Angrick, "Die Einsatzgruppe D," p. 102.

47 The *Reichskommissariat Ukraine*, with its capital in Rovno, took over the territories seized by the Wehrmacht on September 1, 1941. It was part of the civil administration subordinated to the Reich Ministry of the Occupied Eastern Territories under Alfred Rosenberg. Erich Koch, the Nazi leader from East Prussia, served as the Reichskommissar. On the Holocaust in the *Reichskommissariat Ukraine*, see Dieter Pohl, "The Murder of Ukraine's Jews under German Military Administration and in the *Reichskommissariat* Ukraine," in Brandon and Lower, *The Shoah in Ukraine*, pp. 23-76.

48 "Interrogation of Edem Khalilev," May 27, 1944, GARF, 7021/9/194, p. 240; OSR USSR, no. 157, CSPSS, Berlin, January 19, 1942, in Yitzhak Arad, Shmuel Krakowski, and Shmuel Spektor, eds., *The Einsatzgruppen Reports: Selection from the Dispatches of the Nazis' Death Squads Campaign against the Jews (July 1941-January 1943)* (New York: Holocaust Library, 1989), pp. 284-286.

elsewhere in the occupied territories, were brought to the Crimea and selected for service in the local police units and released in the Crimea.[49] They eventually formed a single 100-120- (although, according to another source, only 50-) man-strong "Caucasian" or "Tatar" unit, which was headed by the SS-*Oberscharführer* Walter Kehrer and subordinated directly to the *Einsatzgruppe* HQ.[50]

Unlike other areas treated by the EG D, prior to its arrival in the Crimea the extermination of Jews occurred at a relatively slower pace in the peninsula. Several factors contributed to this, including the fact that some of the *Einsatzgruppe* forces were engaged in various security operations in the Crimea conducted jointly with the army.[51] Other EG D troops participated in the extermination of Jews in the territories previously captured by the German and Romanian armies in the southern part of the Soviet Union.[52] By October-November 1941, part of the EG D forces were attached to the Wehrmacht troops advancing towards the Caucasus.[53] Nevertheless, although the EG D operations from November 1941-June 1942[54] had an incredible geographic expanse, during this period the bulk of its forces were deployed in the Crimea.

The work of the EG D in the peninsula turned out to be efficient. In a series of killing operations conducted in towns and

49 Simferopol: "Landgericht München, Nachtragsanklageschrift in der Strafsache gegen Walter Kehrer und Max Drexler," October 28, 1970, YVA, TR.10/802, p. 10.

50 Martin C. Dean, "Gutachten in dem Verfahren gegen Alfons Götzfried beim Landsgericht Stuttgart Az. August 25, 1998," p. 15. I am grateful to Dr. Martin Dean from the United States Holocaust Memorial Museum for sharing this document with me. See also "Urteil in der Strafsache gegen Walter Kehrer und Max Drexler," September 17, 1975, YVA, TR.10/865, p. 33. On this unit, see Pieper Henning, "*SS-Oberscharführer* Walter Kehrer und die 'Kaukasier-Kompanie': Eine Sondereinheit und ihre Rolle im Zweiten Weltkrieg 1942-1944," *Zeitschrift für Geschichtswissenschaft* 56, no. 3 (2008): pp. 197-221.

51 See further on in the chapter.

52 OSR USSR, no. 134, November 17, 1941, YVA, 0.51/165 I. See also OSR USSR, no. 141, December 3, 1941, YVA, 0.51/165 II.

53 Angrick, *Besatzungspolitik und Massenmord*, p. 244.

54 At this time, the *Einsatzgruppe* D "zone [of operations] reached Cernauti, that is, Carpathians, to Rostov; that is, approximately 1,200 kilometers long and probably from 300 to 400 km broad. In this huge zone not only the 11th Army but also the First Armored Army, and the 3rd and 4th Romanian armies." Testimony of Erick von Manstein, August 12, 1946, *PNWCT*, vol. 20, pp. 617-618.

villages from mid-November 1941 to mid-January 1942, its small but mobile forces liquidated the great majority of Crimean Jewry. Afterwards, the EG D began pursuing Jews who had gone into hiding. At the same time, the *Einsatzgruppe* teams established local police infrastructures and began actively to incorporate them, as well as local informers, in its pursuit of Jews. Large groups of Jews managed to survive until 1942, either because the EG D had exempted them from extermination in 1941 (Jews in mixed marriages, their children, and converts)[55] or because the area in which they resided had not been under effective German control in 1941. In the Crimea, most of the EG D's Jewish victims were killed by automatic fire by the relatively small (20-men-strong or so) execution squads (*Erschiessungskommandos*).[56] After 1942, murders were increasingly carried out by means of gas vans.[57] There exists almost no record of non-compliance with execution orders in the Crimea on the part of the EG D men.[58]

Some of the EG D forces in the Crimea hunted down partisans, Soviet soldiers, or other "suspects," and participated in the warfare against the partisans in November 1941,[59] January 1942[60] and later on. The EG D's focus on the "Solution of the Jewish Problem" in the Crimea was deterred by its involvement in fighting and, thus, resulted in a temporary delay in the German

55 Memoirs of A. M. Berliand, November 1944, DAARK, P-156/1/37, pp. 27-33.

56 *PNWCT*, Band IV (Einsatzgruppen-Prozeß), Bl. 37, p. 326. See also "Strafsache gegen Bierkamp," "Bayerisches Landeskriminalamt," Versuchungsniederschrift, Hans G., (Exekutionskommando und Gruppenstab der EG D), June 26, 1962, YVA, TR.10/1147, p. 272.

57 Simferopol and Simferopol'skii *raion*: "Strafsache gegen Bierkamp," Staatsanwaltschaft Munich I, z. Zt. Berlin, Versuchungsniederschrift, Alfred M., December 10, 1963, YVA, TR.10/1147, p. 398. Akt of Pervomaiskii rural council, June 10-15, 1944, DAARK, R-1289/1/1, p. 90.

58 There were probably a very few exceptions to this rule, as indicated in a testimony, related to the EG driver in the Crimea. "Strafsache gegen Walter Bierkamp," Bayerisches Landeskriminalamt, Vernehmungsunterschrift, Alex H. Richard, March 22, 1972, YVA, TR.10/1147, p. 635.

59 OSR USSR, no. 139, CSPSS, Berlin, November 28, 1941, YVA, 0.51/165 I.

60 "Strafsache gegen Walter Bierkamp," Bayerisches Landeskriminalamt, Z. Zt. Nördlingen, September 8, 1965, Versuchungsniederschrift, Theodor B., 1 Generalstaboffizier des AOK 11 until November 1942, YVA, TR.10/1147, p. 499; Testimony of Erick von Manstein, August 9, 1946, *PNWCT*, vol. 20, p. 619.

onslaught on the local Jews. However, it should be mentioned that the line between solving the "Jewish Problem" and strictly military tasks was sometimes blurred. Taking hostages from the Jewish population and shooting them as "retaliation" for casualties inflicted by a partisan assault clearly underscores this point.[61]

2. The "Final Solution" in the Crimea[62]

2.1. General concerns

The unfolding of the Holocaust in the Crimea should be analyzed with an eye to the peculiarity of warfare in the peninsula from 1941-1942. It was not until July 1942 that the Wehrmacht entirely crushed the resistance of regular Soviet troops by seizing the fortress of Sevastopol'. Prior to this point, at various times the Red Army and Soviet partisans had controlled some urban centers with small adjacent rural areas. Many soldiers from the defeated Soviet units had wandered around the peninsula, some of them having gradually made their way to the partisans. The latter could be found in inaccessible hiding places, most specifically in the Crimean mountains. These forces had attacked and inflicted losses on the Wehrmacht since November 1941.[63]

For its part, the German command was willing to capitalize on the feeling of panic and disorder among the disintegrating Soviet regular and partisan units. It also desired to maximize the use of the troops at its disposal because it had been scheduled that the bulk of these forces would be transferred to other areas of the Eastern front after the rapid end of the Battle of the Crimea. As a result, after November 1941 the German command sanctioned

61 Area of Bium-Lambat and Alushta, Feodosiia (?) [not clear from the report itself]: OSR USSR, no. 156. CSPSS, Berlin, January 16, 1942, YVA, 0.51/165 III. See also Angrick, *Besatzungspolitik und Massenmord*, pp. 333-334.

62 Norbert Kunz, *Die Krim unter deutscher Herrschaft*, pp. 179-187; Arad, *The History of the Holocaust*, pp. 373-389; Al'tman, *Zhertvy nenavisti*, pp. 287-289; Gubenko, *Kniga pechali*.

63 OSR USSR no. 156, CSPSS, Berlin, January 16, 1942, YVA, 0.51/165 III. See also Arad, Krakowski, and Spektor, *The Einsatzgruppen Reports*, p. 283.

large-scale combing operations throughout the peninsula.[64] Rural areas beyond direct German control were constantly searched or, at least, regularly supervised. The situation in the towns was likely even graver, as the Germans usually maintained the necessary manpower in them to manage the local population and did not hesitate to use it. Round-ups in the towns, primarily in Simferopol', were persistently carried out for the same purpose.[65] By means of its security branches (*Feldgendarmerie* and *Geheime Feldpolizei*), the army was deeply engaged in these procedures. This supervision policy was especially pronounced during the first months of the occupation, when comprehensive killing operations against Jews were conducted.[66] This made the pursued Jews' survival in the peninsula far more difficult.

As elsewhere in the occupied Soviet territories, the German army imposed severe restrictions on population movement. In the Crimea, this policy had an added dimension. Owing to the unique geographic position of the peninsula, it was easily isolated from the rest of the occupied territories. The respective order of the Commander of the 11th Army, General von Manstein, was issued on December 20, 1941,[67] and remained in effect for a long period of time.[68] In order to prevent the free movement of the population into and out of the Crimea (on the grounds of impeding communication and supply of Crimean partisans), the army installed cordons on the few roads connecting the peninsula with the rest of the occupied territory.[69] In line with this policy,

64 Wehrmachtsdienststelle, GFP 647, *Kommando* Simferopol', "TB für die Zeit vom 2.-11.11.1941," November 11, 1941, YVA, M.29.FR/120, pp. 3-4.

65 Staboffz. der FG, "TB als Anlage zum KTB für die Zeit vom 1.-30.11.1941," December 2, 1941, YVA, M.29.FR/118, p. 6; Testimony of Efim Gopshtein, August 17, 1944, YVA, M.35/21, p. 162.

66 Staboffz, der FG, "TB als Anlage zum KTB für die Zeit vom 1.-31.12.1941," January 2, 1942, YVA, M.29.FR/118, p. 8; Staboffz, der FG, "TB als Anlage zum KTB für die Zeit vom 1.-30.12.1941," December 2, 1941, YVA, M.29.FR/118, p. 6.

67 Staboffz, der FG, "TB als Anlage zum KTB für die Zeit vom 1.-31.12.1941," January 2, 1942, YVA, M.29.FR/118, p. 9.

68 FK 608, "TB für die Zeit vom 28.4-12.5.1942," May 13, 1942, YVA, M.29.FR/37, p. 29.

69 EM UdSSR no. 190, April 8, 1942, Russian State Military Archive (RGVA),

severely strict residence regulations were also imposed. In towns, the passports of all legal residents were stamped; often the authorities changed the requirements for what constituted a valid passport in order to fight fraud, and therefore the types of stamps changed depending on the period in which it was issued. People caught without valid IDs were doomed. In the villages, whole populations were registered, and any newcomers were also obliged to register.[70] Movement between the villages was forbidden; those able to secure leave from the villages were given only limited permits.[71] Highlighting this notion is an order of German police in Kerch, dated December 19, 1941:

1. It is forbidden to abandon apartments and to stay outside and in public places after dark. Whoever is found after dark without a written permit from the German command will be shot.
2. In daytime, it is forbidden to move along highways and country roads or outside of the roads (in fields) without a written permit from the German command. Trespassers will be shot.
3. Movement from the town into villages and settlements of the area, as well as from the countryside into the town, in daytime is permitted only with a written permit from the German command.[72]

The residence and movement restrictions in the Crimea would soon have a devastating effect on the Jews' prospects for survival.

After the conquest of the Crimea was completed in the summer of 1942, the bulk of the Wehrmacht troops and EG D

500/1/773, p. 241; Testimony of Zalman Uzikov, December 14, 1987, YVA, 0.3/4939, p. 20.

70 Supreme Commander of the German Forces in the Crimea, directive to the heads of localities in the Crimea, DAARK, P-156/1/24, p. 37.

71 Report of the Commander of the North Caucasian Front Semeon Budennyi, July 1942, Russian State Archive of Social and Political History (RGASPI), 69/1/622, p. 9.

72 Announcement of the German Police, Kerch, December 19, 1941, USHMMA, RG-31.030M, reel 1.

withdrew from the peninsula, while relatively small German military and security forces, reinforced by local auxiliary troops, managed security. Following this, the active phase of the Jew-hunt in the Crimea by numerous German and Romanian forces available in the peninsula was over. From then on, the onslaught against Jews centered on their having been revealed from hiding by a ramified network of local collaborationists.[73]

2.2. Simferopol'[74]

The 11th German Army seized Simferopol', the capital town of the Crimea, in early November 1941 without engaging in heavy fighting, and retained it until the general German withdrawal from the peninsula in the spring of 1944. The town hosted the largest Ashkenazi Jewish and Krymchak communities in the Crimea. A considerable number of Jews in the peninsula had also found themselves there by the time of the German occupation. Other than those who had resided in Simferopol' prior to the war and who did not evacuate, additional Jews arrived there from some Ukrainian towns as well as from the Crimean Jewish agricultural colonies of Fraidorf and Larindorf.[75] The Soviet failure to check the rapid German advance into the peninsula took everyone by surprise. Unable to leave the Crimea, many Jews clustered together in what was the biggest Jewish center in the peninsula.

There are different estimates of the number of Jews in Simferopol' in November 1941. The German military provided a highly exaggerated figure of about 20,000.[76] Some 14,000 Jews, including 1,500 Krymchak Jews, had complied with the registration order in Simferopol'.[77] Considering that the number

73 OSR USSR, no. 157, CSPSS, Berlin, January 19, 1942, in Arad, Krakowski, and Spektor, *The Einsatzgruppen Reports*, pp. 284-286.

74 On the Holocaust in Simferopol', see for example, D. Stanov, "There are no Jews among us" (Yiddish), *Eynikayt*, September 21, 1944, p. 3; "From Day to Day: The Destruction of the Crimea" (Yiddish), *Eynikayt*, March 17, 1945, p. 2; D. Braginski, "Raised as a Patriot" (Yiddish), *Eynikayt*, October 2, 1945, p. 3.

75 Testimony of Efim Gopshtein, August 16, 1944, YVA, M.35/23, p. 58.

76 OK I/85, "TB für die Zeit vom 5.-15.11.1941," Simferopol', November 14, 1941, YVA, M.29.FR/41, p. 23.

77 Testimony of Efim Gopshtein, August 16, 1944, YVA, M.35/23, p. 58. See also

of Jews, presumably with the Krymchaks, registered in the 1939 Soviet population census was 22,791 (out of the total population of 142,500 people), an evaluation of 14,000 Jews seems well-grounded.[78] On the whole, some 50% of all Crimean Jews ended up in Simferopol' by the time of the German occupation.

The German military administration established in Simferopol' (OK I/853) was either unable or reluctant to enforce order. Against the general background of summary executions of civilians,[79] curfew (17:00-5:00),[80] and isolation due to the town being cordoned off from the rest of the country, the Jews of Simferopol' endured particularly intensive maltreatment and depredations. This included searches of Jewish houses for weapons (in vain),[81] outdoor beatings,[82] rapes,[83] plunder,[84] and executions of Jews accused as Soviet agents and plunderers.[85] Then there were executions without any pretext whatsoever:

> In the first days after the occupation of the town, two Germans entered one of the houses on Tolstoy Street at the bookkeeper Peckerman's residence. When one of them saw an infant in its mother's arms, he took it and put it in an oven. The mother attacked him but the second German shot her. The father

Gilbod, *Jewish Account* (Yiddish) (St. Louis, Missouri), June 16, 1944, p. 5.

78 Altshuler, *Distribution of the Jewish Population of the USSR* , pp. 30-31.

79 As a reprisal for the murder of Germans: Interrogation of Mikhail Petukhov, April 10, 1943, GARF, 7021/148/46, p. 587; Akt of the Commission of the town of Simferopol', November 1, 1944, DAARK, R-1289/1/1, pp. 23-24.

80 Staboffz. der FG, "TB als Anlage zum KTB für die Zeit vom 1.-30.11.1941," December 2, 1941, YVA, M.29.FR/118, p. 6.

81 OK II/915, FG, "TB für die Zeit vom 21.-29.11.1941," November 29, 1941, YVA, M.29.FR/41, p. 33.

82 Diary of Chrisanf Lashkevich, entry from November 9 and 22, 1941, DAARK, P-156/1/31, pp. 66, 69.

83 Memoirs of A. F. Peganova, "Chetyre kamery smerti," DAARK, P-156/1/40, p. 44.

84 Testimony of Musia Leikin (Iofin), December 27, 2000, YVA, 0.33.C/6428 (not transcribed); Diary of Chrisanf Lashkevich, entry from November 9, 1941, DAARK, P-156/1/31, p. 66.

85 Wehrmachtsdienststelle GFP 647, *Kommando* Simferopol', "TB für die Zeit vom 2.-11.11.1941," November 11, 1941, YVA, M.29.FR/120, p. 4.

> attacked them, too, but they prevailed upon him, broke his legs, and dragged him out.[86]

On November 18, 1941, the Jewish Council (*Judenrat*) arranged for the registration of the entire Jewish population.[87] The German military rigidly enforced the orders for Jewish registration and begun the policy of requiring Jews to bear six-pointed stars on their clothing. The "transgressors" were detected and executed, sometimes publicly.[88] After the establishment of the *Judenrat*, the Germans plundered the Jews in the "organized" way, by demanding a wide range of property and valuables.[89] Jews were obliged to present themselves at the Jewish Council on a daily basis,[90] from where they were sent to labor at various tasks.[91]

On December 9 or 10, 1941, the Jewish Council ordered the Ashkenazi Jews of Simferopol' to assemble in the building of the former Regional Committee of the Communist Party on December

86 Testimony of Max Solomin from Simferopol', recorded by Lev Kvitko, 1944, YVA, M.35/14, p. 86. Solomin's testimony is also presented in Rubenstein and Altman, *The Unknown Black Book*, pp. 363-365.

87 Testimony of Efim Gopshtein, August 16, 1944, YVA, M.35/23, p. 55.

88 1./FG Abt. Mot. 683, "TB für die Zeit vom 28.-30.11.1941," O.U., December 1, 1941, YVA, M.29.FR/41, p. 36. Ivan Genov, *Dnevnik partizana* (Simferopol': Krymizdat, 1963), p. 87 (entry from December 27, 1941).

89 Diary of Chrisanf Lashkevich, entry from November 22, 1941, DAARK, P-156/1/31, p. 70. Testimony of Efim Gopshtein, August 16, 1944, YVA, M.35/23, pp. 51-52.
The plunderings were carried out "by order of the Command" – hence, the use of the phrase "organized way" – in contrast to non-organized plunder conducted on the soldiers' own initiative. In principle, the property requisitioned from the Jews in the first case had to be delivered to the German authorities, who then further channeled it to the Reich or allocated it for domestic needs (for example, rewarding the collaborators). Yet, the border between these two types of the plunder was often blurred. It seems plausible that part of the "orderly" confiscated Jewish property passed through the hands of the individual German involved. This was also the case with the "unorganized" plunder. Sometimes German military and security personnel stole Jewish possessions confiscated in organized plunder, while other times part of what the Germans plundered in a non-organized manner was delivered to the German authorities.

90 Testimony of Efim Gopshtein, August 16, 1944, pp. 51-53.

91 Ibid, pp. 51-52.

10 and 11.[92] They were allowed to bring with them up to 25 kg of personal possessions.[93] The pretext for the assembly was their alleged evacuation to Ukraine.[94] Non-compliance was met with capital punishment, and corpses of those who failed to comply with the order were hung around the town.[95] In some neighborhoods, Russian policemen went from house to house and took Jews away.[96] SS-men cordoned streets leading to the assembly point, and conducted thorough searches in several neighborhoods.[97] At the same time, a Jewish witness mentions that the Germans were polite and refrained from beating Jews outdoors.[98] Apparently, in doing so, the Germans succeeded in misleading some of their victims about their real intentions.

Once the Jews entered the building, they were stripped of their possessions.[99] From this point on, they were handled by the *Einsatzgruppe* men,[100] who did not even supply the assembled Jews with water.[101] Any pretense of politeness ended, and the Germans no longer concealed their true intentions regarding the Jews: [In the building] the German night guards said: "It is all over with the *Zhidy*."[102] More than 10,000 Jews were killed by automatic fire in anti-tank trenches near Simferopol' from December 11-13,

92 Memoirs of Il'ia Sirota, February 16, 1945, DAARK, P-156/1/40, p. 114.

93 "Strafsache gegen Bierkamp," Bayerisches Landeskriminalamt, Vernehmungsniederschrift, Georg. Einsatzkommando 12, March 7, 1962, YVA, TR.10/1147, p. 233.

94 Ibid., pp. 353-354; Testimony of Lev Iurovskii, recorded by Lev Kvitko 1944, YVA, M.35/14, p. 81. Iurovskii's testimony is also presented in Rubinstein and Altman, *The Unknown Black Book*, pp. 359-363.

95 Ibid., p. 368; Testimony of Zalman Uzikov, December 14, 1987, YVA, 0.3/4939, p. 15.

96 Testimony of Efim Gopshtein, August 16, 1944, YVA, M.35/23, p. 64.

97 Testimony of V. Davydov in Vasilii Grossman and Il'ia Erenburg, *Chernaia kniga*, vol. 2 (St. Petersburg: Interbook, 1991), p. 63. Also in Gubenko, *Kniga pechali*, pp. 51-52.

98 Testimony of Max Solomin, recorded by Lev Kvitko, 1944, YVA, M.35/14, p. 87.

99 Memoirs of Il'ia Sirota, February 16, 1945, DAARK, P-156/1/40, p. 114.

100 "Strafsache gegen Bierkamp," Bayerisches Landeskriminalamt, Vernehmungsniederschrift, Georg. Einsatzkommando 12, March 7, 1962, YVA, TR.10/1147, p. 234.

101 Memoirs of Il'ia Sirota, February 16, 1945, DAARK, P-156/1/40, p. 114.

102 Ibid., p. 114.

1941.[103] According to one seemingly reliable eyewitness testimony, the *Einsatzgruppe* allowed the young German members of the RAD[104] to attend and participate in the Jewish extermination at Simferopol'.[105] The execution site was heavily guarded; it was impossible for Jews to escape.[106]

Although the permanent German security presence in Simferopol' was limited in scope, its annihilation of the largest concentration of Jews in the Crimea happened rather smoothly.[107] The gradual annihilation of Simferopol''s Jews until the Great *Aktion* that murdered 10,000 Jews lasted almost six weeks. In the meantime, it had become increasingly difficult to flee the

103 The final data for the number of *Soviet people* that the Germans victimized in Simferopol' range from 16,912 (ESC unpublished report on the Crimea, GARF, 7021/116/154, p. 68) to 18,912 (ESC unpublished report on the Crimea, GARF, 7021/116/154, p. 73). This figure can be juxtaposed with the most relevant German assessment of the number of *Jews* killed from November 16 to December 15, 1941 — 17,645. However, this figure refers to the Jewish victims killed not only at Simferopol' but also at Evpatoriia, Alushta, Karasubazar, Kerch, and Feodosiia: OSR USSR, no. 150, CSPSS, Berlin, January 2, 1942, YVA, 0.51/165 II. See also Arad, Krakowski and Spektor, *The Einsatzgruppen Reports,* pp. 266-267. The number of the Holocaust victims in Simferopol' referred to in the Jewish press is 14,000 people: Gilbod, *Jewish Account*, p. 5.

104 RAD: In 1931, it was founded as *Freiwilliger Arbeitsdienst* (Voluntary Labor Service), and participation was optional. Upon the Nazi rise to power, the name was changed to *Nationalsozialistischer Arbeitsdienst* (National Socialist Labor Service), and in 1934 it was changed for the final time to RAD *Reichsarbeitdienst* (Reich Labor Service). At this time, participation was mandatory for certain age groups, who served for set terms. On RAD, see e.g., Kiran Klaus Patel, *Soldiers of Labor. Labor Service in Nazi Germany and New Deal America, 1933–1945* (New York: Cambridge University Press, 2005), pp. 64-395.

105 "Strafsache gegen Bierkamp," Abschrift, Dr. A. FK 810, April 13, 1967, YVA, TR.10/1147, pp. 596-597, 599.

106 "Strafsache gegen Walter Bierkamp," Staatsanwaltschaft, Munich, Berlin, Herr Fritz U., Versuchungsniederschrift, December 6, 1962, YVA, TR.10/1147, p. 387.

107 Apart from *Einsatzkommando* 11b, Headquarters of the EG D, OK I/853, the Headquarter of Army Rear Group (*Korück*) 553 were also stationed permanently in Simferopol' during the period under review. Landgericht Düsseldorf, "Urteil gegen Karl R. Pallmann, Paul H. Lorenz, Hans H. Jakob, Erich Buballa, Otto Dolezych, Josef Kappl, Carl Friedrich M. Berherns wegen Mordes," July 22, 1971, YVA, TR.10/724, p. 58.

town because of various German measures directed against the population in general, not only against the Jews. The influx of numerous Jews who were not previously inhabitants of Simferopol' made it much more complicated for the newly arriving Jews to find shelter anywhere in the town. Organized depredations were accompanied by a previously unseen (by Crimean standards) plundering of Jewish property and the physical maltreatment of the Jews.

The *Einsatsgruppe* had destroyed almost all of Simferopol''s Jews by the end of December 1941. However, despite constant searching and combing for Jews, there was still some possibility for rescue by the virtue of its position as the peninsula's largest town. The Germans were fully aware of such possibilities, and therefore repeatedly conducted mop-ups and searches in Simferopol'. These measures were most intensive in December 1941,[108] but were on the ebb towards the second quarter of 1942.[109]

As mentioned, the first mass killing in Simferopol' was the automatic shooting of 10,000 Jews in December 1941. However, in 1942, a gas van was brought to Simferopol'. From then on, the murder of Simferopol''s Jews was carried out largely by rounding up Jews and killing them in the gas van.[110] Although the Germans never completely ceased combing operations (and applied them with various degree of comprehensiveness throughout the entire occupation period),[111] from the start of the occupation to its end many, if not most, of Simferopol''s hidden Jews were found by German police agents and denouncers.

108 Interrogation of Ekaterina Sirota, GARF, 7021/9/194, p. 162; OK II/939, "TB für die Zeit vom 21.-31.12.1941," Dzhankoi, January 1, 1942, YVA, M.29. FR/40, p. 1.

109 Testimony of Efim Gopshtein, YVA, M.35/21, p. 162; Staboffz. der FG, "TB als Anlage zum KTB für die Zeit vom 1.-31.1.1942," February 2, 1942, YVA, M.29. FR/118, p. 17.

110 "Strafsache gegen Walter Bierkamp," Staatsanwaltschaft Munich, I. z. Zt., Berlin, Vernehmungsniederschrift, Alfred M., December 10, 1963, YVA, TR.10/1147, p. 398. Nachtragsanklageschrift in der Strafsache gegen Kehrer, YVA, TR.10/802, pp. 3-4.

111 Testimony of Efim Gopshtein, August 16, 1944, YVA, M.35/21, p. 162.

2.3. Cooperation between the AOK 11 and EG D in Implementing the "Final Solution" in Simferopol'

The cooperation between the AOK 11 and EG D in "solving the Jewish Question" in the Crimea took on different forms.[112] Echoing the agreement between the RSHA and the Army[113] (and similar to the patterns of cooperation between these two agencies in neighboring Ukraine),[114] the process varied from joint patrolling and combing operations[115] to reporting cases of Jews discovered in hiding and their extradition by the Army over to the *Einsatzgruppe*. The 1c (intelligence) section of the Army coordinated these joint activities.[116] The following section examines the cooperation between the two bodies in question in the destruction of the largest Jewish community in the Crimea – Simferopol'.

According to various sources, the Germans killed between 11,000 and 17,000 Jews and Krymchaks from December 9-13, 1941, in Simferopol' – the majority of the town's Jews.[117] Afterwards, the strictest police regime was established, which involved, among other actions, frequent combings of the entire town and its separate neighborhoods for Jews.[118] The remaining Jews were either arrested

112 Oldenburg, *Ideologie und militärisches Kalkül*, pp. 163-224; Roni Shtauber, "Cooperation between the Wehrmacht and the Einsatzgruppe D in the extermination of the Crimean Jews" (Hebrew), *Massuah* 15 (1987): pp. 212-221.

113 See Introduction.

114 Wendy Lower, "The 'reibungslose' Holocaust? The German Military and Civilian Implementation of the 'Final Solution' in Ukraine, 1941-1944," in Gerald D. Feldman and Wolfgang Seibel, eds., *Networks of Nazi Persecution: Bureaucracy, Business and the Organization of the Holocaust* (New York: Berghahn, 2005), pp. 236-256.

115 Dzhankoi, Kerch: 1c/AOK 11, "Bericht für die Zeit vom 16.-31.12.1941," January 1, 1942, NOKW-1866, National Archives and Records Administration (NARA), T-501, roll 59, frame 291; Staboffz. der FG, "TB als Anlage zum KTB für die Zeit vom 1.-31.1.1942," February 2, 1942, YVA, M.29.FR/60, p. 9.

116 "Urteil gegen Pallmann," July 22, 1971, YVA, TR.10/724, p. 60.

117 Bentsion Vol'fson, *Krovavye zlodeianiia nemtsev v Krymu*, DAARK, P-156/1/34; OSR USSR, no. 157, CSPSS, Berlin, January 19, 1942, in Arad, Krakowski, and Spektor, *The Einsatzgruppen Reports*, pp. 284-286.

118 OK II/939, "TB für die Zeit vom 21.-31.12.1941," January 1, 1942, YVA, M.29. FR/40, p. 1; Interrogation of Ekaterina Sirota, GARF, 7021/9/194, p. 162.

and almost immediately executed[119] or forced to escape the town clandestinely.[120] Therefore, the German claim in later reporting that no more Jews remained in Simferopol' was well-founded.[121]

In order to ensure the murder of Simferopol''s Jews, the Germans needed to balance their modest resources, that is, their relatively low manpower in the region. The overall process for doing so developed along the following lines: By late November 1941, the Germans, namely the Wehrmacht and local auxiliary police forces, had finished preparations for the final annihilation of Jewry in Simferopol'.[122] On the eve of the *Aktion*, the EG D had at its disposal the incomplete Ek 11b, numbering some 100 people,[123] and Ohlendorf's headquarters (guarded by some 20 men).[124] It is probable that some additional EG D forces were brought from elsewhere in the Crimea.[125] Therefore, one could cautiously suggest that the extermination of the Jewish community in Simferopol' was supposed to take place at a later stage. It could have been carried out after the Ek 11b had the chance to regain some of its forces employed outside of Simferopol', and additional EG D units would have provided more forces for a smooth implementation of the action. This could have likely taken place by late December 1941.[126]

119 "Nachtragsanklageschrift in der Strafsache gegen Kehrer," October 28, 1970, YVA, TR.10/802, pp. 3-4.

120 See Chapter 6, "Jewish Responses to the Holocaust in the Crimea."

121 OSR USSR, no. 150, CSPSS, Berlin, January 2, 1942, YVA, 0.51/165 II; Arad, Krakowski, and Spektor, *The Einsatzgruppen Reports*, pp. 266-267.

122 OSR USSR, no. 142, CSPSS, Berlin, December 5, 1941, in Arad, Krakowski and Spektor, *The Einsatzgruppen Reports*, p. 250.

123 Some of the Ek 11b detachments were deployed outside of the town. OSR No. 141, December 3, 1941 YVA, 0.51/165 II; OSR No. 144, December 10, 1941, ibid.; and OSR No. 146, December 15, 1941, ibid.

124 "Strafsache gegen Walter Bierkamp," Staatsanwaltschaft bei dem Landgericht Munich I. Versuchungsniederschrift, Heinz S. Hermann, July 16, 1959, YVA, TR.10/1147, p. 4.

125 *PNWCT*, Band IV (Einsatzgruppen-Prozeß), vol. 37, p. 323.

126 The estimate that the *Einsatzgruppe* D initially intended to kill all of Simferopol''s Jews only in March 1942 (Oldenburg, *Ideologie und militärisches Kalkül*, p. 167), based on Friedrich Jörg, *Das Gesetz des Krieges. Das deutsche Heer in Russland, 1941 bis 1945: Der Prozess gegen das Oberkommando der Wehrmacht* (Munich: Piper, 1993), p. 661 seems to be groundless, given the actual pace of extermination of Jews in the Crimea.

Thus, given the serious lack of EG D manpower in Simferopol', the relatively early implementation of such major action gives rise to several questions, the most important of which is – how could the EG D have carried out this central killing operation on the Crimean peninsula with such relatively small resources?

The answer to this question was given only after the war. During the postwar criminal proceedings against former members of the EG D, those charged repeatedly claimed that it was the AOK 11 that ordered the action in Simferopol'.[127] The AOK 11 was willing to get rid of the Simferopol' Jews in light of "the gravity of the food situation" in the peninsula. In other words, it was reluctant to provide food for the town's more than 10,000 Jews (with possible ramifications on the rest of the Crimean Jewry[128]). Another motive included the Army command's "desire to avoid alienation of the local population and ensuing disorder."[129] The Quartermaster of the 11th Army stated to this regard in the postwar criminal proceedings that

> The SD would have conducted the extermination *Aktion* in any case. It was entirely impossible to do anything against it, since Hitler and Himmler were behind this killing operation... I was guided solely by military standpoint, namely, to safeguard the Army from what I regarded as certain consequences of the SD-launched *Aktion* if it were drawn out for a longer time.[130]

According to the testimonies of the EG D men, the Army went to great lengths to make it possible for the *Einsatzgruppe* to kill the Simferopol' Jews as soon as possible (preferably before Christmas 1941[131]). To this end, the Wehrmacht provided the EG D with

127 Testimony of Otto Ohlendorf, January 3, 1946, *PNWCT,* vol. 4, p. 318.

128 OK I (V)/287, "TB für die Zeit vom 23.-27.11.1941," Kerch, November 27, 1941, YVA, M.29.FR/41, p. 30.

129 "Strafsache gegen Bierkamp," Bayerisches Landeskriminalamt, IIIa/SK, Munich, Karl R. Werner, Major i. Generalstab., October 31, 1965, YVA, TR.10/1147, p. 549.

130 Ibid., p. 550.

131 Testimony of Werner Braune, November 25, 26 and December 1, 2, 1947, *PNWCT, Green Series,* pp. 323-324.

soldiers and logistical assistance, such as trucks, gasoline, and drivers to transport the detained Jews.[132] It is noteworthy that such presentation of the developments is only partly corroborated by German wartime documents, namely only with respect to the assignment of a small number of *Feldgendarmen*.[133] As for the rest of the statements, they are not supported by contemporary evidence. Furthermore, they are partly[134] or entirely[135] refuted in the postwar testimonies offered by former AOK 11 men.

In discussing the cooperation between the EG D and the AOK 11 in the elimination of Simferopol"s Jews, the following considerations should be taken into account. Under the legal proceedings, the EG D men blamed the Army not only for logistical help but also for issuing the very order to execute the Jews in the town. Conversely, the AOK 11 officers and soldiers eagerly downplayed the scope of the Army's involvement in the massacre of Jews.[136] Nevertheless, the statement that the Army issued the order to execute Simferopol"s Jews seems problematic. Legally, the Army command was in no position to issue such an order, as the EG D was not subordinated to it. Yet, the Army could certainly *request* that the EG D precipitate the *Aktion*, in accordance with military needs as the Army command saw them, and could offer logistical assistance for this purpose.

In order to resolve the quandary of who was ultimately responsible, it is essential to determine the character of the relations between the command of the AOK 11 and the EG D. The following episode mentioned in a diary of a Jewish survivor

132 "Strafsache gegen Walter Bierkamp," Munich, July 16, 1959, YVA, TR.10/1147, p. 19; "Strafsache gegen Nosske," Staatsanwahltschaft bei dem Landesgericht München, I, Vernehmungsniederschrift, Heinz S. Hermann, July 16, 1959, YVA, TR.10/1156, p. 92.

133 Staboffz. der FG, "TB als Anlage zum KTB für die Zeit vom 1.-31.12.1941," January 2, 1942, YVA, M.29.FR/118, p. 8.

134 "Strafsache gegen Walter Bierkamp," Der leitende Oberstaatsanwalt bei dem Landesgericht Hamburg, Z. Zt. München, Vernehmungsniederschrift, E. Horst, August 13, 1964, YVA, TR.10/1147, p. 483.

135 "Strafsache gegen Walter Bierkamp," Versuchungsniederschrift, S. Oberst, i.G. Oberquartiermeister der 11 Armee, December 18, 1961, YVA, TR.10/1147, pp. 187-188.

136 Testimony of Erich von Manstein, August 12, 1946, *PNWCT*, vol. 21.

may shed light on these relations.[137] Apparently, in the first part of November 1941, the Commander of the 11th Army General von Manstein arranged a banquet for senior officers to celebrate the conquest of the Crimea. In order to hold the banquet, the Germans needed 40 tablecloth sets. Those in the Army in charge of the banquet (the department of the Quartermaster) made a request to this effect to the EG D. It is not clear whether the Army knew from what source the sets would be received. But certainly they realized that the *Einsatzgruppe* would not order the sets from Berlin. Nor did it carry them in its trucks. It could requisition everything it wished from the local population, of which the Jews were the most vulnerable part and whose lives and property belonged entirely to the Reich. Certainly the Germans could also "ask" the Jews to provide the sets free of charge, a "request" the Jews were in no position to deny. Indeed, the EG D ordered the Jewish Committee of Simferopol' to provide the lacking sets. The order was fulfilled.

This background illustrates early EGD and AOK11 cooperation, based on total disregard for Jewish property. Both institutions collaborated closely in the implementation of the "Final Solution" even before the Battle of the Crimea, and therefore we can understand why the road between the episode with the tablecloth sets and that of killing Jews was so short and smooth as suggested by the efficient results of the killings carried out near Simferopol' on December 9-13, 1941. It is evident that the Army provided the logistical support and placed some of its special units at the disposal of the EG D. It is rather doubtful that the Army issued the order to conduct the killing operation in Simferopol', but it welcomed the outcome. On the other hand, it should be stressed that, overall, the *Einsatzgruppe* initiated, prepared, and conducted the killing action. While the Army was certainly of help, it was an auxiliary factor in carrying it out. At the same time, there exists contradictory evidence regarding the involvement of regular units of the AOK 11 in the extermination

137 Testimony of Efim Gopshtein, August 16, 1944, YVA, M.35/23, p. 52.

of the Jews in the Crimea.[138] Even though wartime and postwar German sources maintain that the AOK regular forces were explicitly banned from getting involved in the *Einsatzgruppe* activity in the region, this evidence should be read in the context of the Wehrmacht trying to put all the blame for the murder of Jews in the Crimea on the SS.[139] Overall, it is plausible that AOK 11 regular units participated in the genocide of the Jews on Crimean soil to some extent.

A memorial plaque on the building that served as the gathering point for Jews in Simferopol', December 2009. Courtesy: RHCA

138 Sönke Neitzel, ed., *Tapping Hitler's Generals: Transcripts of Secret Conversations, 1942-1945* (St. Paul: Frontline Books and MBI Publishing, 2007), pp. 192, 195, 219.

139 "Strafsache gegen Walter Bierkamp," Bayerisches Landeskriminalamt, IIIa/SK, Munich, Friedrich H. Wilhelm (Major i. Generalstab), October 31, 1965, YVA, TR.10/1147, p. 552.

What happened in Simferopol' in December 1941 was no exception to the rule. The 11th Army and the EG D also cooperated closely elsewhere in the Crimea, complementing each other in accomplishing security tasks. Although the Wehrmacht conducted combing operations in Crimean towns, it was the EG D men who guided them.[140] Conversely, when short of manpower, the EG D explicitly requested that the Army handle the matters [within the *Einsatzgruppe* competence] by itself.[141] As the *Einsatzgruppe* later experienced difficulties in manning its execution squad, the Army secured assistance by placing its *Feldgendarmen* at the EG D's disposal.[142] Also significant is the fact that General von Manstein awarded iron crosses and Army merit crosses to the *Einsatzgruppe* men.[143] The Army requested that all wristwatches belonging to Jews killed by the EG D be turned in to the Army.[144] Such developments reflected close mutual confidence and cooperation between the AOK 11 and the EG D in the Crimea.

2.4. Other Crimean towns[145]

Concerning the mass murder of Jews in the Crimean towns, a distinction must first be made between those captured in 1941 and those in 1942. Sevastopol' was the only town never to have been under German control until July 1942. Other towns, namely Kerch and to a much lesser degree, Feodosiia, Sudak, and Evpatoriia, were temporarily recaptured from German control and held by the Red Army in the first half of 1942. The Soviet Army controlled Kerch from late December 1941 (there is some controversy concerning dates) to between May 15-21, 1942; Feodosiia from late December

140 Simferopol, Staboffz. der FG, "TB als Anlage zum KTB für die Zeit vom 1.-31.1.1942," February 2, 1942, YVA, M.29.FR/60, p. 9.

141 Simferopol': Wehrmachtsdienststelle, GFP 647, *Kommando* Simferopol', "TB für die Zeit vom 2.-11.11.1941," November 11, 1941, YVA, M.29.FR/120, p. 3.

142 Feodosiia: "Urteil gegen Pallmann," YVA, TR.10/724, p. 82.

143 Valerie Hebert, *Hitler's Generals on Trial: The Last War Crimes Tribunal at Nuremberg* (Lawrence, KS: University of Kansas Press, 2010), p. 119.

144 Ibid., p. 265.

145 For the general presentation of the course of the Holocaust in some Crimean towns, see Table 5, "Course of the Holocaust in Crimean towns." See also Oldenburg, *Ideologie und militärisches Kalkül*, pp. 182-209.

1941 to January 15, 1942; Sudak from January 6-25, 1942; and Evpatoriia from January 5-7, 1942.[146] For these towns captured in 1942, there had existed a possibility that the advancing Soviet troops would liberate the remaining Jews and then evacuate them as the Red Army retreated. However, it should be remembered that the towns pertaining to the latter group (i.e., all the towns except Sevastopol') had already been occupied by the Germans since November 1941. To put it otherwise, large-scale extermination had already been carried out there, and the Germans had already killed all registered and detected Jews in these towns.[147]

By the time of the German conquest, the Jewish population of Crimean towns was made up largely of those who had lived there before the occupation. In addition to those in Simferopol', more than 22,000 Jews had lived in the Crimean towns[148] as of 1939.[149] Prior to the German occupation, the native Jewish population in the Crimea had decreased considerably, owing to evacuation and enlistment in the Red Army. This process was only partly offset by the arrival of Jewish refugees from outside of the peninsula.[150] The only important exception to this trend was the harbor town of Kerch, where thousands of Jews who had endeavored to evacuate by sea were caught unawares by the rapid retreat of the Soviet troops, who had defended the town. Kerch turned out to be the only Crimean town whose Jewish population had increased by the time of the German occupation in comparison with the prewar period.[151] For them,

146 Basov, *Krym v Velikoi Otechestvennoi voine*, p. 6.

147 See Table 5, "Course of the Holocaust in Crimean towns."

148 Only cities whose population exceeded 1,000 Jews are included in this calculation.

149 Altshuler, *Distribution of the Jewish Population of the USSR* , pp. 30-31.

150 Izmail, Zaporozh'e: Testimony of Leda Kiseleva, September 28, 1992, YVHN; Testimony of Sara Vainberg, April 19, 1991, YVHN.

151 As of 1939, 5,573 Jews lived in Kerch. Altshuler, *Distribution of the Jewish Population of the USSR*, pp. 30-31. The assessment of the number of Jewish victims fluctuates between more than 7,000 (Akt of the Commission of the town of Kerch, August 2, 1944, DAARK, R-1289/1/2, p. 35) to more than 11,600 (the latter figure refers not solely to the Jews but to all Soviet people qualified in the report as "women, children and old men" – ESC unpublished report on the Crimea, GARF, 7021/116/154, p. 67).

Kerch became a death trap with no way out.[152] Furthermore, the singularity of the case of Kerch is expressed in the fact that when the German army seized the town for the second time in May 1942, a considerable number of Jews[153] were again caught and killed there.[154]

The available sources allow for the reconstruction of only some of the developments that preceded Jewish extermination in the Crimean towns. Some common traits are discernible in most of the localities. These include the obligations to register,[155] to bear six-pointed stars for Jews over age 16,[156] to pay high monetary contributions (in Yalta – equivalent of 1 million golden rubles[157]), and for Jews ages 16-70 to perform forced labor (cleaning lavatories, dragging stones, digging ditches, etc.).[158] The following first order of the *Kommandant* of Feodosiia concerning the town's Jews underscores this point, and particular attention should be drawn to the promptness and comprehensiveness of German measures:

> All *Zhidy* of both sexes are obliged to bear a white band with a six-pointed star on both arms. All *Zhidy* of both sexes

152 Akt of the Commission of the town of Kerch, August 2, 1944, DAARK, R-1289/1/2, p. 35; "Strafsache gegen Alois Persterer," Bayer, Landeskriminalamt, IIIa/SK, Berlin, Vernehmung - Helmut, September 12, 1961, YVA, TR.10/1158, pp. 24-28; Bentsion Vol'fson, "Krovavye prestupleniia nemtsev v Kerchi," *Istoricheskii zhurnal* 8 (1942): pp. 33-36.

153 Remaining residents of the area and those who flocked to Kerch from all over the peninsula. Story of Solomon Belkin, former chairman of one of *kolkhozy* in Larindorfskii *raion*, in Il'ia Vergasov, *Krymskie tetradi* (Moscow: Sovetskii pisatel', 1971), p. 100 in YVA, 0.32/62, pp. 16-17.

154 OK I(V)/287 und 46 Infanteriedivision, "TB für die Zeit vom 15.-30.6.1942," Kerch, June 30, 1942, YVA, 0.51/185 II, p. 8.

155 Feodosiia, Yalta: Order of the German *Kommandatur* to the Municipal Authority of Feodosiia, [no date], DAARK, R-1458/1/2, p. 5; Report of Margarita Frolova-Meltsyna, [no date], YVA, 0.33/626, p. 1.

156 Sevastopol', Yalta: "Tragic End of the Jewry in Western Russia" (Hebrew), *Ha-boker* no. 2691, September 6, 1944, p. 2 from *Izvestiia*, July 2, 1944; Akt no. 64 of the Commission of the town of Yalta, July 17, 1944, DAARK, R-1289/1/4, p. 96; Diary of O. I. Shargorodskaia, entry from November 21 (28), 1941, DAARK, P-156/1/31, p. 154; Akt of the Commission of the town of Evpatoriia, July 5, 1944, GARF, 7021/9/57, p. 19.

157 Vergasov, *Krymskie tetradi*, p. 32, in YVA, 0.51/185 II.

158 Sevastopol', Yalta: Statement of Devlikanova, June 23, 1944, GARF, 7021/9/46, p. 84; Report of Margarita Frolova-Meltsyna, [no date], YVA, 0.33/626, p. 1.

> are subject to immediate registration. All *Zhidy* are strictly forbidden to move freely from one place to another. Failure to do so will lead to the strictest punishment. All *Zhidy* of both sexes between ages 16-50 are placed at the disposal of a headman (*starshyna*) of the community who assigns them to work.[159]

The Germans rigidly enforced the anti-Jewish orders. Failure to bear identifying stars led to execution on the spot.[160] They also occasionally imposed curfews[161] and conducted large-scale arrests of Jews even before a mass assembly.[162] German measures were accompanied by the physical maltreatment of Jews[163] to the point of murder.[164] The dispossession of Jews was especially severe in Yalta, where the Germans demanded that the Jews deliver all money and gold to the Jewish Committee,[165] as well as in Evpatoriia[166] where, in addition to monetary contributions, the Germans plundered Jewish property on numerous occasions.[167]

In order to ensure that Jews arrived at the assembly points, the Germans often dissimulated their true intent. The grave food situation in many towns provided the Germans

159 Order of the German *Kommandatur* to the municipal authority of Feodosiia, [no date], DAARK, R-1458/1/2, p. 5.

160 Kerch, Sevastopol': OK I(V)/287, "TB für die Zeit vom 16.-30.4.1942," Kerch, May 25, 1942, YVA, M.29.FR/37, p. 41; Sevastopol' trial, Statement of V. N. Romanova-Petrova, 1947, USHMMA, RG-06.02505.

161 Kerch, Yalta: OK I(V)/287, "TB für die Zeit vom 16.-30.4.1942," Kerch, May 25, 1942, YVA, M.29.FR/37, p. 41; Interrogation of Neish Kemilev, June 8, 1944, GARF, 7021/9/194, p. 200.

162 Kerch: "Story of Iosef Vaingarten" (Yiddish), *Eynikayt*, July 15, 1942.

163 Karasubazar, Yalta: Landgericht München, "Anklageschrift in der Strafsache gegen Johannes Schlupper, Heinrich Winterstein, Rudolf Eschenbacher," July 27, 1973, YVA, TR.10/775, p. 6; Diary of O. I. Shargorodskaia, entry from November 21 (28), 1941, DAARK, P-156/1/31, p. 154.

164 Yalta: Report of Margarita Frolova-Meltsyna, [no date], YVA, 0.33/626, p. 1.

165 Akt of the Commission of the town of Yalta, July 17, 1944, GARF, 7021/9/59, p. 24 and DAARK, R-1289/1/4, p. 96.

166 Akt of the Commission of the town of Evpatoriia, 1944, YVA, M.33/57, pp. 50-51.

167 Report of the Crimean Commission on the conclusion of the investigation of the outcome of the German occupation of the Crimea, December 16, 1941, DAARK, P-156/1/32, p. 15.

with the convenient pretext of "sending of Jews to work in the countryside."[168] Sometimes the Germans employed more sophisticated methods. In Feodosiia, the assembled Jews were released from the prison on December 1, 1941, in order "to be able to retrieve all valuables, as a long way awaited them."[169] According to the testimony of a Russian witness, this camouflage policy was also applied in Sevastopol':

> After the Jews were assembled at the stadium, the Germans let them go home. At this time, the Germans behaved so well towards the Jews that my Jewish neighbor told me, with joy, that she had been deceived by the talk that the Germans were beasts. After the Jews spent a night at home, they were again assembled at the stadium.[170]

The outcome of the "Final Solution" in the Crimean towns regarding the chances of Jewish survival was also related to the fact that German security, enforcement, and retaliation measures were harsher in some places than in others. Although these steps were directed against the whole population, they had severely negative effects on the chances for Jewish survival. In early January 1942, after the Germans recaptured Evpatoriia, they shot some 3,000 men suspected of taking sides with the Soviets.[171] In fear of another Soviet landing attempt, the Germans dispatched some 1,500 members of the general male population of Yalta to the recently established labor camp at Simferopol', where one-third of them

168 Feodosiia, Sevastopol': Akt of the Commission of the town of Feodosiia, 1944 (?) [not clear in the report itself], GARF, 7021/9/57, p. 1; Statement of V. N. Romanova-Petrova, 1947, USHMMA, RG-06.02505.

169 Questioning of Ol'ga Korchagina, May 10, 1944, GARF, 7021/9/58, p. 103.

170 Interrogation of Ivan Volkov, June 21, 1944, GARF, 7021/9/194, pp. 234-235.

171 "Strafsache gegen Walter Bierkamp," Bayerisches Landeskriminalamt, IIIa/SK, Munich, Karl R. Werner, Major i. Generalstab., October 31, 1965, YVA, TR.10/1147, p. 515. See also, Akt of the Commission of the town of Evpatoriia, July 5, 1944, GARF, 7021/9/57, p. 19.

perished.[172] Because of "the special situation" (i.e., the fear of Soviet landing and infiltration into the town), the Germans searched Feodosiia three times for any remaining Soviet soldiers, as well as those civilians who had allegedly helped them.[173] Immediately after the capture of Sevastopol' in July 1942, the Germans brought a great number of the surviving civilians to the camps for security screening.[174] Consequently, the chances for Jews to survive in such places diminished considerably.

Holocaust memorial in Sevastopol', October 2008. Courtesy: RHCA

As a rule, small *Teilkommandos* of the EG D were responsible for the whole process of the "treatment" of the Jews in the Crimean

172 Akt of the Commission of the town of Yalta, August 19, 1944, GARF, 7021/9/59, p. 183; Akt no. 64 of the Commission of the town of Yalta, July 22, 1944, YVA, M.33/368, p. 29.

173 OSR USSR, no. 184, CSPSS, Berlin, March 23, 1942, in Arad, Krakowski, and Spektor, *The Einsatzgruppen Reports*, pp. 317-318.

174 OK II/576 (V), "TB für die Zeit vom 1.-15.7.1942," Bakhchisarai, July 16, 1942, YVA, 0.51/185 II, p. 6.

towns, including their extermination.[175] However, they were often badly under-manned to cope with this task, and therefore worked in close cooperation with local HQs established by the 11th Army. In Feodosiia, the *Ortskommandatur* I/287 had conducted a census of the population and required that the Jewish population register with officials; therefore, the EG D unit that arrived afterwards only dealt with the Jews who were already registered.[176] Local police, especially in the Tatar-dominated towns,[177] and, to a lesser extent, in Russian localities,[178] assisted the Germans in the logistical organization of the actions. The number of survivors of the extermination procedures was low,[179] and those who did manage to survive were sometimes finished off.[180] In the Crimea, the Germans carried out most Jewish exterminations in one all-encompassing action, in that they assembled all Jews at a specific pre-planned point and time and killed them all swiftly and collectively, regardless of gender, ability, health, etc. However, there were some instances that deviated from the general protocol, such as in Yalta, where initially healthy Jewish males were killed, followed by the

175 Bakhchisarai, Kerch: OK Bachtschisaray, TB, December 14, 1941, YVA, M.29.FR/41, p. 49; See also "Strafsache gegen Alois Persterer," Bayer, Landeskriminalamt, IIIa/SK, Berlin,Vernehmung – Helmut, September 12, 1961, YVA, TR.10/1158, pp. 24-28.
The only exception was likely Feodosiia, where the *Feldgendarmen* were also involved: "Urteil gegen Pallmann," YVA, TR.10/724, p. 82.

176 OK I/287, "TB für die Zeit vom 13.-16.11.1941," November 16, 1941, YVA, M.29.FR/41, p. 25; Order of the German *Kommandatur* to the municipal authority of Feodosiia, [no date], DAARK, R-1458/1/2, p. 5. See also Oldenburg, *Ideologie und militärisches Kalkül*, pp. 186-187.

177 Bakhchisarai, Dzhankoi: "Strafsache gegen Bierkamp," Staatsanwaltschaft, München, Berlin, Vernehmungsniederschrift, Herr U. Fritz, December 6, 1962, YVA, TR.10/1147, p. 377; OK II/939, "TB für die Zeit vom 11.-20.12.1941, Dzhankoi, December 20, 1941, YVA, M.29.FR/41, p. 50.

178 Evpatoriia: Interrogation of Ul'ian Kravchik, June 30, 1944, YVA, M.33/57, p. 48.

179 Dzhankoi, Kerch: Interrogation of Il'ia Sirota, GARF, 7021/9/194, pp. 155-157; Report of the Metropolitan Nikolai (member of the ESC), "From Day to Day," (Yiddish), *Eynikeyt*, March 17, 1945, p. 2.

180 Karasubazar: Commission on the History of the Great Patriotic War, DAARK, P-156/1/34, p. 19.

rest of the Jews on the next day.[181] It is probable that the fact that Yalta's Jews were confined to a ghetto (and, thus, had fewer chances to escape) accounted for the Germans' "tardiness" in this case.

Killing operations against the Ashkenazi and Krymchak Jewish populations in most of the Crimean towns were conducted within the relatively short period of time from November 23 to December 18, 1941: Evpatoriia (November 23),[182] Kerch (December 1),[183] Feodosiia (December 3),[184] Bakhchisarai (December 13),[185] Simferopol' (December 11-13),[186] and Yalta (December 18).[187] This was followed by the second wave of the executions directed against the Krymchak population, whom the Germans eventually recognized as Jewish:[188] Karasubazar (mid-January 1942),[189] and Dzhankoi (January or February 1942).[190] Finally, the Germans annihilated Jews and Krymchaks in the two Soviet enclaves seized during the course of the May-June 1942 offensive: Kerch (mid-May)[191] and Sevastopol' (first ten days of July).[192] It is significant that the actions were not carried out simultaneously. The Germans relied on the ramified

181 Il'ia Erenburg, ed., *Murder of a People* (Yiddish), 2nd ed., (Moscow: Der Emes, 1945), pp. 63-65; West, *In the Ropes of Destruction*, p. 141; Vol'fson, "Krovavye prestupleniia nemtsev v Kerchi," pp. 33-36.

182 Akt of the Commission of the town of Evpatoriia, May 9, 1944, GARF, 7021/9/57, p. 30.

183 "Story of Iosef Vaingarten," (Yiddish), *Eynikayt*, July 15, 1942.

184 Questioning of Ol'ga Korchagina, May 10, 1944, GARF, 7021/9/58, p. 103.

185 OK Bachschisarai, TB, December 14, 1941, YVA, M.29.FR/41, p. 49.

186 Memoirs of Il'ia Sirota, February 16, 1945, DAARK, P-156/1/40, p. 114.

187 Akt no. 64 of the Commission of the town of Yalta, July 17, 1944, DAARK, R-1289/1/4, pp. 98-103.

188 See Chapter 5, "The Fate of Karaites and Krymchaks in the Crimea and Mountain Jews in the North Caucasus during the Holocaust."

189 Commission on the History of the Great Patriotic War, DAARK, P-156/1/34, p. 19; Akt of the Commission of the town of Yalta, May 13, 1944, DAARK, R-1289/1/11, pp. 6-7.

190 Interrogation of Dmitrii Pankeev, July 14, 1944, DAARK, R-1289/1/16, p. 24; Interrogation of Aleksandra Podgornaia, June 28, 1944, GARF, 7021/9/193, p. 19.

191 OK I(V)/287 and 46th Infanteriedivision, "TB für die Zeit vom 15.-30.6.1942," Kerch, June 30, 1942, YVA, 0.51/185 II, p. 8.

192 "Tragic End of the Jewry in the Western Russia."

system of movement restrictions designed *inter alia* to prevent Jews and non-Jews from spreading the information concerning extermination and persecution of Jews in the Crimea.

Concerning the possibilities for Jewish survival in the Crimean urban setting, it should be emphasized that military *Ortskommandaturen* were established in every Crimean town. Although they had to cope with many tasks, the "Jewish Problem" was among them, and it is critical to consider that the sole (or at least a main) function of the EG D troops was to kill the Jews. As of November 12, 1941, the EG D units were present exclusively in Alushta, Bakhchisarai, Feodosiia, Sudak, and Yalta,[193] – and at that time, the Jews were still alive in these towns. As of December 15, 1941, the *Einsatzgruppe* troops were present in Alupka, Alushta, Bakhchisarai, Evpatoriia, Feodosiia, Karasubazar, Kerch, Sudak, and Yalta.[194] By that time, extermination actions had already been conducted in all of these towns except Yalta.[195] As of January 26, 1942, they were stationed in Alushta, Bakhchisarai, Dzhankoi, Evpatoriia, Feodosiia, Karasubazar, Staryi Krym, and Yalta.[196] By that time, all registered Jews in these towns had already been killed. As of March 27, 1942, the *Einsatzgruppe* troops were still deployed in Alushta, Dzhankoi, Evpatoriia, Feodosiia, Karasubazar, and Sudak.[197] By this point, there was no recorded Jewish presence in these towns.

As depicted, the *Einsatzgruppe* forces remained in some of the locations long after the killing operations against the Jews, while they abandoned others for reasons of their own. It appears that in cases where their presence was permanent, the chances for hidden Jews to survive were sharply diminished. EG D troops, supported by the German Army and local police (and also aided by a ramified network of informers[198]), carried out "post-

193 OSR USSR, no. 132, November 12, 1941, YVA, 0.51/165 I.

194 OSR USSR, no. 146, December 15, 1941, YVA, 0.51/165 II.

195 See Table 5, "Course of the Holocaust in Crimean towns."

196 OSR USSR, no. 160, January 26, 1942, YVA, 0.51/165 III.

197 EM UdSSR, No. 186, March 27, 1942, RGVA, 500/1/773, p. 127.

198 Karasubazar, Sevastopol': Interrogation of Neish Kemilev, June 8, 1944, GARF, 7021/9/194, p. 200; Statement of V. N. Romanova-Petrova, [no later than July 1944], GARF, 7021/9/46, pp. 71-72.

extermination" searches for hidden Jews in the Crimean towns – and discovered many of them.[199]

2.5. Rural areas[200]

Thousands of Jews had lived in the rural areas of the Crimea by the time of the German occupation (as of 1939, some 18,000[201]). A considerable number of them were concentrated in the two "Jewish National Regions" of Fraidorf and Larindorf, while the others were scattered in many villages throughout the peninsula. The German military and security forces were not permanently stationed in the rural areas[202] because the German command did not have enough troops in the Crimea to deploy them there.[203] This was of little significance, though, as the Jewish rural population was often quickly exterminated upon the Germans' first appearance in their area.[204]

In other cases, 'rural' Jews were exterminated during the second arrival of the Germans, as during this interim period they were mainly at the mercy of collaborators in the recently established local administrations.[205] In the meantime, they

199 Feodosiia, Sevastopol': OK I(V)/287, "TB für die Zeit vom 16.-30.4.1942," Feodosiia, May 1, 1942, YVA, M.29.FR/37, p. 23; Rozaliia Krichevskaia, *Dvadtsat' deviat' mesiatsev iz detstva* (Beer Sheva, 1997), pp. 27-28; Interrogation of Nikolai Madatov, March 11, 1947, USHMMA, RG-31.018M, reel 7.

200 See Table 6, "Course of the Holocaust in a Crimean countryside, by *raiony* and villages"; Rubinstein and Altman, *The Unknown Black Book*, pp. 372-376 and Oldenburg, *Ideologie und militärisches Kalkül*, pp. 176-182.

201 Altshuler, *Distribution of the Jewish Population of the USSR*, p. 63.

202 Except for the village of Bakhcheli: Story of Fania Margolina in Gubenko, *The Book of Sorrows*, p. 56.

203 "Urteil gegen Pallmann," YVA, TR.10/724, p. 54; OSR USSR, no. 170, CSPSS, Berlin, February 18, 1942, in Arad, Krakowski, and Spektor, *The Einsatzgruppen Reports*, p. 296; EM UdSSR, No. 178, CSPSS, Berlin, March 9, 1942, RGVA, 500/1/773, pp. 42, 45.

204 Villages of Peretsfeld (November 15, 1941) and Sverdlovka (December 7, 1941): Akt of the Commission of Fraidorfskii *raion*, October 15, 1944, DAARK, R-1289/1/12, p. 14; Questioning of Savelii Kulikov, July 24, 1944, YVA, M.33/63, p. 25.

205 Akt of the Commission of Larindorfskii *raion*, October 16, 1944, DAARK, R-1289/1/13, pp. 8-9.

experienced the same stages characteristic for the Holocaust in the Crimean towns, i.e., registration,[206] bearing six-pointed stars,[207] forced labor,[208] physical maltreatment,[209] rape,[210] organized and sporadic plunder of Jewish property,[211] movement restrictions,[212] and segregation[213] to the point of ghettoization.[214]

In the exceptional cases when German troops were deployed to Jewish rural settlements, it was the inherent nature of their presence that determined the conditions of Jews in the interim period. In the case of the village of Pervomaiskoe, an unidentified German unit was stationed there, and its permanent presence fostered such conditions so that rigid adherence toward many components of the anti-Jewish policy was implemented:

> Jewish houses were marked. Six-pointed stars were put on their clothes. For fear of execution, Russians were forbidden

206 "Gorkii" *kolkhoz* and "Frunze" village: Interrogation of Galina Nazarenko, April 27, 1944, GARF, 7021/9/194, p. 83; Story of Mariia Rashkovskaia in Gubenko, *The Book of Sorrows*, p. 98.

207 Villages of Sverdlovka and Pervomaiskoe: Questioning of Savelii Kulikov, July 24, 1944, YVA, M.33/63, p. 25; Interrogation of Stepan Beznos, May 27, 1944, GARF, 7021/9/194, p. 89.

208 Villages of Kalinskoe and Pervomaiskoe: Interrogation of Konstantin Zhukovskii, May 27, 1944, GARF, 7021/9/194, p. 87; Interrogation of Stepan Beznos, May 27, 1944, GARF, 7021/9/194, p. 89.

209 "Frunze" village and "Gorkii" *kolkhoz*: Questioning of Mariia Rozhkovskaia, July 22, 1944, YVA, M.33/63, p. 28; Interrogation of Galina Nazarenko, April 27, 1944, GARF, 7021/9/194, p. 83.

210 Village of Lekkert: Questioning of Evgeniia Padaia, July 23, 1944, YVA, M.33/63, p. 35.

211 Kolaiskii *raion*, "Gorkii", Kalinskoe: Akt of the Commission of Kolaiskii *raion*, November 29, 1944, GARF, 7021/9/61, p. 20; Interrogation of Nadezhda Bykova, May 27, 1944, GARF, 7021/9/194, p. 84; Interrogation of Konstantin Zhukovskii, May 27, 1944, GARF, 7021/9/194, p. 87.

212 Kalininskoe, Pervomaiskoe, "Gorkii": Conclusion of the Deputy Military Prosecutor of the military unit 34500 Mayor Rasponomarev, June 18, 1944, GARF, 7021/9/194, p. 112.

213 Villages of Lekkert and Pervomaiskoe: Questioning of Evgeniia Padaia, July 23, 1944, YVA, M.33/63, p. 35; Interrogation of Stepan Beznos, May 27, 1944, GARF, 7021/9/194, p. 89.

214 Village of Voikovstat: Zlotskaia and Kaem's letter, in Gubenko, *The Book of Sorrows*, pp. 108-109.

> from visiting Jews or giving them anything. A *starosta* [headman] was ordered to take foodstuffs away from the Jews. The Jews were sent to carry out hard labor. They were murdered on January 21, 1942, in a gas van.[215]

Another case, which can only be corroborated by a single piece of postwar Soviet evidence, demonstrates that on rare occasions the German military presence temporarily alleviated the Jews' suffering. In line with this evidence, a unit of older-aged German soldiers was stationed on an unknown Jewish *kolkhoz* in Larindorfskii *raion*. According to this testimony, not only did those soldiers "[do] no harm to the Jews, but they also brought water from a clean fountain situated 3-4 km off, sawed wood, and gave bread and sugar to children... Generally speaking, they behaved in a human way."[216] However, on the whole, such occurrences seem to be almost non-existent and are an extreme exception to the rule.

At the final stage, the Germans usually herded the Jews into one building, then marched them outside and shot them before typically throwing their corpses into wells.[217] The majority of the inhabitants of "Jewish National Regions" were killed in November-December 1941.[218] Jews scattered in smaller villages were murdered as a result of thorough combing operations conducted by the forces of the EG D[219] or OK/FK.[220] Local collaborators were actively involved in the Holocaust in the

215 Interrogation of Stepan Beznos, May 27, 1944, GARF, 7021/9/194, p. 89.

216 Story of Belkin in Bergasov, *Krymskie tetrad*, YVA, 0.32/62, pp. 16-17.

217 Villages of Peretsfeld, Vuzul-Montanai, and Ikor: Akt of the Commission of Fraidorfskii *raion*, October 15, 1944, DAARK, R-1289/1/12, p. 14; Idem., DAARK, R-1289/1/12, p. 15; S. Gordon, "On the Jewish settlements in the Crimea" (Yiddish), *Eynikayt*, August 16, 1945, p. 3.

218 See Table 6, "Course of the Holocaust in a Crimean countryside, by *raiony* and villages."

219 Northern Crimea: OSR USSR, no. 170, CSPSS, Berlin, February 18, 1942, in Krakowski and Spektor, *The Einsatzgruppen Reports,* p. 296.

220 Villages of Fraidorf, Voinka and elsewhere: 3./ Feldgend. Abt. (mot) 683, "TB des im Freidorfer Gebiet eingesetzten Zuges," O.U., February 11, 1942, YVA, M.29.FR/40, p. 5; Staboffz. der FG, "TB als Anlage zum KTB vom 1.3-31.3.1942," April 2, 1942, YVA, M.29.FR/118, p. 24.

Holocaust memorial in Ikor-Romashkino, Crimea. December 2014. Courtesy: RHCA

Crimean rural areas before and after the killing operations. From February 1942, a gas van was brought to Fraidorfskii *raion* because there were apparently still enough Jews to "justify" its use.[221] Murders of Jews in rural areas were recorded throughout the first half of 1942 until the summer; the fact that increasingly fewer Jews remained alive accounts for the decreases in the numbers of recorded Jewish victims.[222] Only a small number of Crimean Jewish villagers survived the Holocaust, mainly by joining the partisans.

221 3./ FG Abt. (mot) 683, "TB des im Freidorfer Gebiet eingesetzten Zuges," O.U., February 11, 1942, YVA, M.29.FR/40, p. 5.

222 See Table 6, "Course of the Holocaust in a Crimean countryside, by *raiony* and villages."

3. Internal Organization of Jewish Life

3.1. Jewish Councils

In the Crimea there were four Jewish Councils (also known as Jewish committees or *Judenräte*): Evpatoriia,[223] Simferopol',[224] Sevastopol',[225] and Yalta.[226] Additionally, the Germans appointed a *starosta* of the Jewish community in Feodosiia and Karasubazar.[227] Thus, it turns out that in the peninsula, the Jewish Councils were established only in a minority of the localities. In order for its own Jewish Council to be established, the Jewish community had to be large enough (more than 500 people) and to reside in a town. There is no record of any Jewish Councils in the Crimean countryside. The Councils were usually appointed within the first two weeks of occupation, and existed throughout the whole period of the Jewish "legal" existence, i.e., up until the Germans began exterminating Jews.

Members of the Jewish Councils were selected on account of their accidental contacts with the German authorities. Such, for example, was the case in Evpatoriia, when on November 5, 1941, ten Jews were randomly detained outdoors and appointed to serve on the Jewish Council.[228] This pattern stemmed not only from the arbitrary decisions of German officers, but also from the absence of identifiable leaders in the Jewish public. The Jewish Councils consisted of several (up to six) persons, and in two cases there were *Obmann* (headmen, also referred to as *starosta*, in the

223 Testimony of the inhabitant of Evpatoriia Mina Fishgoit, [no date], YVA, P.21.2/9; OSR USSR, no. 149, CSPSS, Berlin, December 22,1941, in Arad, Krakowski, and Spektor, *The Einsatzgruppen Reports,* p. 265.

224 Testimony of Efim Gopshtein, August 16, 1944, YVA, M.35/23, p. 50.

225 Excerpts from the diary of Boris Pekarchuk, [no date], GARF, 7021/9/46, pp. 56-57.

226 Akt of the Commission of the town of Yalta, July 17, 1944, GARF, 7021/9/59, p. 24; Report of Margarita Frolova-Meltsyna, [no date], YVA, 0.33/626, p. 1.

227 Order of the German *Kommandatur* to the municipal authority of Feodosiia, [no date], DAARK, R-1458/1/2, p. 5; Akt of the Commission of the town of Karasubazar, May 13, 1944, DAARK, R-1289/1/11, pp. 6-7.

228 Testimony of the inhabitant of Evpatoriia Mina Fishgoit, [no date], YVA, P.21.2/9.

German documentation). There is no evidence that in the Crimea members of the Jewish Councils advocated any other policy except complete compliance with German orders. The Council members did not enjoy privileges. On the contrary, they were sometimes beaten and threatened with execution if the Germans' demands were not met.[229]

The EG D was the German body responsible for the establishment of the Jewish Councils in the peninsula.[230] The Germans applied arbitrarily unrestrained rules towards the Council members.[231] The Jewish Council had the unfortunate responsibility of relaying most of the Germans' orders regarding Jews to their community.[232] The Councils also served the Germans as a convenient tool for confiscating property and valuables from the Jews.[233] By means of the Jewish Councils, the Germans exploited Jewish manpower by placing orders on the Jews to perform various kinds of forced labor.[234] The Jewish Council[235] (or sometimes the *starosta*[236]) was also responsible for conveying the "resettlement" order. The Jewish Committee was ultimately in charge of confirming the list of the Jews designated for the "resettlement."[237]

Ultimately, the Jewish Councils in the Crimea were short-lived institutions that did not have enough time to develop enough

229 Simferopol', Yalta: Memoirs of A. F. Peganova, "Chetyre kamery smerti," DAARK, P-156/1/40; Statement of Aleksandr Ponomarev, June 30, 1944, GARF, 7021/9/59, p. 84 (?) [page illegible in the report itself].

230 Yalta: Memoirs of A. F. Peganova, "Chetyre kamery smerti," DAARK, P-156/1/40.

231 Simferopol': Ibid.

232 Simferopol': "Strafsache gegen Alois Persterer," Bayer, Landeskriminalamt, IIIa/SK, Berlin, Vernehmung – Losansky, September 15, 1961, YVA, TR.10/1158, p. 68; Testimony of Efim Gopshtein, August 16, 1944,YVA, M.35/23, p. 50.

233 Simferopol': Testimony of Lev Iurovskii, recorded by Lev Kvitko, 1944, YVA, M.35/14, p. 80.

234 Simferopol': Testimony of Efim Gopshtein, August 16, 1944, YVA, M.35/23, pp. 50-51.

235 Simferopol': Ibid., p. 60.

236 Karasubazar: Akt of the Commission of Karasubazarskii *raion*, May-October 1944, YVA, M.33/82, p. 4.

237 Yalta: Report of Margarita Frolova-Meltsyna, [no date], YVA, 0.33/626, p. 6.

of a full structure significantly to influence Jewish life. The fields of activity characteristic of Jewish Councils in Eastern Europe, such as welfare and law enforcement (Jewish police), etc., did not develop (to be more precise, the Germans did not *allow* them to develop) apart from certain exceptions. Also, the short existence of the Jewish Councils in the peninsula excluded any possibility of laying the groundwork for waging resistance in the region. The structure of the Jewish Councils was simpler, and designed solely in order to fulfill the concrete tasks set by the Germans. This had to do with the fact that the Germans had set up Jewish Councils in the Crimea without intending later to relocate the Jews to ghettos, i.e., without envisaging a more protracted Jewish existence in the peninsula. The absence of ghettos in most of the Crimean towns diminished the authority of the Jewish Councils. Without being confined to a space in which they were easily identified as Jews, some were able to evade Jewish Council orders by virtue of their non-Jewish appearance, possession of "Aryan" documents,[238] and other reasons.

3.2. Ghettos[239] and the Camp[240]

The Germans established ghettos in Yalta and in the village of

238 An "Aryan" document was most often a Soviet passport wherein the nationality of the passport owner was inscribed in the fifth paragraph. Nationality was also recorded in some other Soviet documents, such as birth certificates. In this section and elsewhere in the study, "Aryan" document or ID means Soviet passport, unless stated otherwise.

239 On ghettos in the occupied Soviet territories, see Petra Rentrop, "Weißrussland," in Wolfgang Benz and Barbara Distel, eds., *Der Ort des Terrors: Geschichte der nationalsozialistischen Konzentrationslager*, vol. 9 (Munich: C. H. Beck, 2009), pp. 378-381; Martin Dean, "Lebensbedingungen, Zwangsarbeit und Überlebenskampf in den kleinen Ghettos: Fallstudien aus den Generalkommissariaten Weissruthenien und Wolhynien-Podolien," in Christoph Dieckmann und Babette Quinkert, eds., *Im Ghetto 1939-1945; neue Forschungen zu Alltag und Umfeld* (Göttingen: Wallstein Verlag, 2009), pp. 54-73; Wendy Lower, "Facilitating Genocide: Nazi Ghettoization Practices in Occupied Ukraine, 1941-1944," in Eric J. Sterling, ed., *Life in the Ghettos During the Holocaust* (Syracuse, NY: Syracuse University Press, 2005), pp. 120-144.

240 On the camps in the occupied Soviet territories, see Mario Wenzel, "Zwangasarbeiterslager für Juden in den besetzten polnischen und sowjetischen Gebieten," in Benz and Distel, *Der Ort des Terrors*, pp. 139-153.

Voikovstat,[241] as well as a camp for Jews in Dzhankoi.[242] For the purposes of study, all of them are referred to as ghettos, unless otherwise stated. The only full-fledged ghetto in the Crimea was in Yalta. It is not clear why the Germans decided to establish a ghetto there. In early December 1941, the Sk 11a issued the order for Jews to settle within three days (by December 5) in the building of the former Massanrovskie barracks situated on a mountain 2-3 km from the town.[243] Apparently, the order was applied solely to Jews from Yalta, and not to those from the surrounding areas. It was announced that failure to comply with the three-day term would lead to execution.[244] Prior to the resettlement, the German *Kommandant* von de Reck had announced to the Jewish Council that the Jews were to be kept in the ghetto for three to four months until March, and then would be sent outside of Simferopol', where "everyone would live as he can, that is outside of other peoples."[245]

Up to 1,500 Jews were crammed into the building; in every room there were ten or more families. They were subject to ceaseless depredations. *Kommandant* von de Reck was reported as at times driving the Jews around the house for 1.5-2 hours by shouting and

241 Untitled document, DAARK, R-137/9(d)/7, p. 32; Diary of O. I. Shargorodskaia, entry from November 21 (28), 1941, DAARK, P-156/1/31, p. 154. Although Germans explicitly referred to confinement in Evpatoriia as a ghetto, it was too short-lived, even by the Crimean standards (two days), and therefore is not examined in the study. OSR USSR, no. 149, CSPSS, Berlin, December 22, 1941, in Arad Krakowski and Spektor, *The Einsatzgruppen Reports*, p. 265; Akt of the Commission of the town of Evpatoriia, July 5, 1944, GARF, 7021/9/57, p. 19.

242 OK II/939, "TB für die Zeit vom 11.-20.12.1941," Dzhankoi, December 20, 1941, YVA, M.29.FR/41, p. 50; See also sections from Lev Kvitko in Vasilii Grossman and Il'ia Erenburg, eds., *Chernaia kniga o zlodeiskom povsemestnom ubiistve evreev nemetsko-fashystskimi zakhvatchikami vo vremenno-okkupirovannykh raionakh Sovetskogo Soiuza i v lageriakh unichtozheniia Pol'shi vo vremia voiny 1941-1945 gg.* (Jerusalem: Tarbut, 1980), pp. 291-294.

243 Report of Margarita Frolova-Meltsyna, [no date], YVA, 0.33/626, pp. 2-7; Akt of the Commission of the town of Yalta, July 17, 1944, GARF, 7021/9/59, p. 24. According to another source, the ghetto was established in the buildings of a former Workers' Faculty (*rabfak*) of the Agricultural Institute: Letter of P. Nesterenko, July 5, 1944, YVA, P.21.2/8.

244 Report of Margarita Frolova-Meltsyna, [no date], YVA, 0.33/626, p. 1.

245 Ibid., p. 2.

beating them with a stick; in this way he killed two people.[246] The inmates of the ghetto suffered from malnourishment[247] and two Jews died from starvation.[248] Some Jewish women were raped.[249] According to the German order, the Jewish Council instructed Jewish men and women to greet the German officers by taking off their hats in front of them and bowing from the waist.[250]

Jews worked from morning to evening.[251] A garment workshop was opened in the ghetto to service the Germans.[252] The Jews were constantly demanded to provide the Germans with all kinds of goods: blankets, linen, covers, women's dresses, men's suits, etc. It was announced that failure to comply with the order by a certain deadline would lead to the "arrest of the Board [of the Jewish Committee] and then, to their execution."[253]

In order to deprive the Jews of their last means, two days prior to the liquidation of the ghetto the Germans demanded that the Jews establish a bank and a cooperative society and deposit all valuables and money in them, retaining for themselves no more than 50 rubles.[254]

Yalta's ghetto was the only urban place in the Crimea where the Germans segregated Jews from non-Jews. Jews were not allowed to go out in the streets after 2 p.m.[255] The ghetto was surrounded by a barbed-wire fence[256] and guarded by Russian or, according to

246 Report of Margarita Frolova-Meltsyna, [no date], YVA, 0.33/626, p. 2; Statement of Mariia Rokhman, August 2, 1944, GARF, 7021/9/59, p. 112; Erenburg, *Murder of a People* (Yiddish), pp. 63-65.

247 Erenburg, *Murder of a People* (Yiddish), pp. 63-65; West, *In the Ropes of Destruction*, p. 141.

248 Report of Margarita Frolova-Meltsyna [no date], YVA, 0.33/626, p. 4.

249 Letter of P. Nesterenko, July 5, 1944, YVA, P.21.2/8.

250 Ibid., pp. 2-3.

251 Statement of Mariia Rokhman, August 2, 1944, GARF, 7021/9/59, p. 112.

252 Ibid., p. 2.

253 Report of Margarita Frolova-Meltsyna, [no date], YVA, 0.33/626, p. 3.

254 Ibid., p. 5.

255 Akt of the Commission of the town of Yalta, July 17, 1944, GARF, 7021/9/59, p. 24.

256 Erenburg, *Murder of a People* (Yiddish), pp. 63-65; West, *In the Ropes of Destruction*, p. 141.

another source, Jewish policemen.[257] Non-Jews who dared come to the ghetto were punished: a friend of the Jewish Council Chairman who came to see him was arrested for "illegal presence and a visit to the ghetto."[258]

The ghettoized Jews were also denied the medical services available in the town of Yalta:

> The Chairman of the Jewish Committee doctor… Kazirinskii… fell ill and needed to be treated by a surgeon. He asked the *Kommandant* for the permission to be operated on in the appropriate medical institution in the town. The *Kommandant* shouted at him: "The ghetto is supposed to meet all your needs – open hospitals, treat yourselves, and operate on yourselves!"[259]

At the same time, the segregation was inconsistent. Everyday contact between Jewish inmates of the ghetto and their non-Jewish spouses residing outside of the ghetto was tolerated.[260] During the first four days of the ghetto's establishment, Jews were permitted to leave the town but had to return by a certain hour.[261] It seems that the German segregation policy in Yalta was only partly successful, mainly because they were short of manpower.

Fewer details are known about the ghetto in the village of Voikovstat (Kerchenskii *raion*), the only one established in a Crimean rural area. Here, Jewish segregation was rigidly enforced. More than 100 Jews registered in the village were ordered to bear six-pointed stars and forced to march out to the edge of the village, where they were placed in houses encased in barbed wire.[262] All of their livestock was taken. A roll-call was conducted every evening.

257 Report of Margarita Frolova-Meltsyna, [no date], YVA, 0.33/626, p. 2; Letter of P. Nesterenko, July 5, 1944, YVA, P.21.2/8.

258 Report of Margarita Frolova-Meltsyna, [no date], YVA, 0.33/626, p. 4.

259 Ibid.

260 Statement of Aleksandr Ponomarev, August 30, 1944, GARF, 7021/9/59, p. 84 (?) [page illegible].

261 Report of Margarita Frolova-Meltsyna, [no date], YVA, 0.33/626, p. 2.

262 Untitled document, DAARK, R-137/ 9 (d)/7, p. 32, courtesy of Dr. Martin Dean.

Romanian soldiers guarded the ghetto.[263] Yet, it seems that the Jews were not sent to perform forced labor.[264] The existence of the ghetto in Voikovstat, relatively lenient conditions for the Jewish inmates, and their survival as of late 1941 can be probably explained by the fact that Romanians and not Germans were in charge of the ghetto. The ghetto's survival indicates that the beginning of the Romanian army's de-escalation in its murder of Jews was also noticeable in the Crimean peninsula. The ghetto was liberated by Soviet troops that landed in the area in the late December 1941.[265] Most of its inmates escaped to the Soviet mainland during the period of Soviet control of the area until May 1942, but some 20 Jews were murdered during the second German occupation of the region.[266]

More than 700 Jews from the town of Dzhankoi, its surrounding area,[267] and elsewhere in the Crimea[268] were brought to the camp erected by the Germans in Dzhankoi in mid-December 1941. It is not clear what considerations the Germans had in sending Jews there, but they likely envisaged establishing one large Jewish camp for the whole peninsula. It is also probable that the local mayor set up the ghetto without informing the Germans.[269] Prior to the ghetto's establishment, 15 Jewish men had been killed in an *Aktion*.[270] This minor killing operation preceding the mass extermination was a unique development in the Crimea, and may be seen within the context of German attempts to enforce the order to resettle the Jews in the camp.

263 Mark Goldenberg, "Kerchensko-Feodosiiskaia desantnaia operatsiia v sud'be evreev i krymchakov Vostochnogo Kryma," *Tkuma, Vestnik nauchno-prosvetitel'skogo tsentra "Tkuma" (Dnepropetrovsk, Ukraine)*, 47-48, no 4-5 (2004): p. 2.

264 Testimony of Roman Kapelevich, December 12, 2008, available from http://www.iremember.ru/content/view/736/75/lang.ru.

265 Zlotskaia and Kaem's letter in Gubenko, *The Book of Sorrows*, pp. 108-109.

266 Ibid., pp. 108-109.

267 OK II/939, "TB für die Zeit vom 11.-20.12.1941," Dzhankoi, December 20, 1941, YVA, M.29.FR/41, p. 50.

268 Testimony of Mark Al'ianaki, [no later than July 4, 1944], GARF, 7021/9/5, p. 76.

269 1c/AOK 11, "Bericht für die Zeit vom 16.-31.12.1941," January 1, 1942, NOKW-1866, NARA, T-501, roll 59, frame 291.

270 OK II/939, "TB für die Zeit vom 1.-10.12.1941," Dzhankoi, December 10, 1941, YVA, M.29.FR/41, p. 46.

In the camp itself, according to a German report, "Jews were used for all available labor in the town."[271] Only able-bodied Jews had a chance to survive, as those incapable of working were shot on the spot.[272] The ghettoized Jews were severely undernourished[273] and sanitary conditions were appalling.[274] The camp in Dzhankoi also held non-Jewish inmates; the Germans sent Soviet peasants accused of rendering aid to Jews to Dzhankoi.[275] In addition, the place served as a POW camp.[276] It was guarded by German and Russian policemen,[277] who frequently maltreated and even killed Jews.[278] On December 30, 1941, the SD detachment in charge of guarding the EG D headquarters in Simferopol' was sent to Dzhankoi, killing 443 Jews in a hilly area near the road to Simferopol'.[279]

There is no evidence that the Germans ever exploited the ghetto inmates in the Crimea in industrial or military production. Such a step would have implied the Germans' tacit consent to a more protracted Jewish existence in the peninsula, which was not compatible with German policies. Jews were mostly used in hard physical labor of no industrial significance, such as stone hewing.[280] As Jewish Councils in the Crimea were weak

271 OK II/939, "TB für die Zeit vom 11.-20.12.1941," Dzhankoi, December 20, 1941, YVA, M.29.FR/41, p. 50.

272 Sections from Lev Kvitko in Grossman and Erenburg, *Chernaia kniga*, pp. 291-294.

273 Testimony of Zalman Uzikov, December 14, 1987, YVA, 0.3/4939, p. 22.

274 1c/AOK 11, "Bericht für die Zeit vom 16.-31.12.1941," January 1, 1942, NOKW-1866, NARA, T-501, roll 59, frame 291.

275 Sections from Lev Kvitko in Grossman and Erenburg, *Chernaia kniga*, pp. 291-294.

276 Testimony of Zalman Uzikov, December 20, 1941, YVA, 0.3/4939, p. 22.

277 OK II/939, "TB für die Zeit vom 11.-20.12.1941," Dzhankoi, December 20, 1941, YVA, M.29.FR/41, p. 50.

278 Sections from Lev Kvitko in Grossman and Erenburg, *Chernaia kniga*, pp. 291-294; Testimony of Zalman Uzikov, YVA, 0.3/4939, p. 22.

279 Untitled document, NOKW-2231, OK II/939, January 1, 1942, NARA, T-501, roll 57, frame 218; Statements of Oskar Rimmele, Staatsanwaltschaft Munich I, 22 Js 203/61, Bd. 6, USHMMA, pp. 1347R-1349 & Bd. 11, courtesy of Dr. Martin Dean.

280 Dzhankoi: Sections from Lev Kvitko in Grossman and Erenburg, *Chernaia kniga*, pp. 291-294.

institutions, German control and intervention in Jewish life was more visible and comprehensive. Illegal activity characteristic for East European ghettos, such as smuggling food or weapons, youth movements, and cultural and religious events – and certainly Jewish resistance[281] – was not recorded in the Crimea.

It is noteworthy that Jewish inmates of the Crimean ghettos were exterminated later than the majority of Jews in other Crimean towns. The ghetto in Yalta existed until December 18, 1941,[282] and the ghetto in the village of Voikovstat was not liquidated at all before the Soviet seizure of the area in late December 1941. The killing operation in Dzhankoi took place in early January 1942 or perhaps even later.[283] It may be suggested that the Germans felt confident enough of the possibility to kill the Jews interned in ghettos at any propitious moment.

In comparison, the ghettos in the Crimea were not in operation long enough to render such a devastating effect on Jewish life as did the ghettos in Eastern Europe. As the ghettos in the peninsula were not designated to provide for Jewish existence for a continuous stretch of time, segregation components were less comprehensive: it is not known that gates and guards were put around the entirety of the ghettos. It should be remembered that the Germans generally regarded the establishment of ghettos as a provisional measure to control and segregate Jews. In the Crimea, the ghettos also served as a provisional measure that facilitated German exploitation of Jews and their further extermination.

281 Dan Michman, *The Emergence of Jewish Ghettos during the Holocaust*, translated by Lenn. J. Schramm (New York: Cambridge University Press, 2011), pp. 122-144.

282 Akt of the Commission of the town of Yalta, July 17, 1944, GARF, 7021/9/59, p. 24.

283 Interrogation of Aleksandra Podgornaia, June 28, 1944, GARF, 7021/9/193, p. 19; Interrogation of Dmitrii Pankeev, July 14, 1944, DAARK, R-1289/1/16, p. 24.

4. Special Cases

4.1. The medical domain[284]

This small section explores two cases: German policies regarding the Jewish patients of Crimean hospitals, and those towards Jewish medical workers (doctors, nurses, etc.). Like many other occupied Soviet territories,[285] in the Crimea the Germans annihilated all the patients of the psycho-neurological hospitals, with Jews among them.[286] Furthermore, in a number of Crimean hospitals, specifically Jewish patients were shot while the rest of the patients were not touched.[287]

There exists more ambiguity concerning the German attitudes towards the Jewish medical workers in the Crimea. Despite the fact that Soviet authorities prioritized the evacuation of medical workers, a certain number of Jews among them remained in the peninsula. The Soviet list of the victims in Feodosiia reveals this, although the precise figures for the rest of the Crimea cannot be extrapolated. According to this list, out of 711 Jews, nine Jewish doctors and 13 nurses stayed in Feodosiia.[288] Furthermore, in all probability, there was no evacuation of medical personnel from places where warfare was underway. As

284 Al'tman, *Kholokost na territorii SSSR*, pp. 575-578.

285 Alexander Kruglov, "German Sources on the Holocaust in the Territory of the Former USSR," in Il'ia Altman, ed., *The Holocaust and the Case of the Jewish Anti-Fascist Committee: Proceedings of the Fourth International Conference "Lessons of the Holocaust in Contemporary Russia" held in Moscow on 1-2 October, 2002*, (Moscow: Fond "Kholokost," 2002), p. 83.

286 Locality of Aleksandrovka near Karasubazar: AOK 11, IV Wi., "Bericht für die Zeit vom 1.-31.3.1942," March 31, 1942, in *Der Dienstkalender Heinrich Himmlers 1941/42*, Auszug III, p. 19; Zheleznodorozhnyi neighborhood of Simferopol': Akt of the Commission of Simferopol', [no date], GARF, 7021/9/49, pp. 1-2.

287 Feodosiia, Sevastopol': Questioning of Elizabeta Samborskaia, June 21, 1944, GARF, 7021/9/58, p. 43; Statement of Aleksandra Radziuk, June 22, 1944, GARF, 7021/9/46, p. 92.

288 The list covers only 711 out 7,993 victims, i.e., 8.9% of those who perished during the time of the German occupation: the rest were not identified. List of civilians executed by the Germans since November 3, 1941, until April 13, 1944, YVA, M.33/76, pp. 3-22.

a result, numerous Jewish doctors and nurses fell under German captivity.[289]

Although the general German policy in the Crimea was to annihilate the Jews as soon as possible, their desire to preserve the sanitary conditions in Crimean towns accounted for a periodic shift in their policy towards Jewish medical workers. This policy was not applied solely to the Crimea, but also to all occupied Soviet territories.[290] To counter sanitary problems, the Germans needed doctors, nurses, and pharmaceutical workers. It happened that a number of such workers were Jewish. Incidentally, a small fraction of those Jewish medical workers were Ashkenazi Jews – they turned out to be the only Ashkenazi Jews who managed "legally" to survive the Holocaust in the Crimea, at least its initial phase.[291]

Not only were Jewish medical personnel registered in a special category by the Germans and the Jewish Councils, but the medical institutions in which they had been previously employed also had special registration categories for them.[292] The latter registration provided the Germans with information of how sizable the share of Jewish medical workers was, and to what extent it would be possible to maintain the sanitary conditions if the Jewish medical personnel were to be eliminated. Then, the local German administration decided whether these conditions were grave enough to allow a certain number of Jewish medical workers to be exempt (at least, temporarily) from extermination. In some towns, the sanitary problems were acute, particularly if fierce fighting had occurred there prior to the German occupation. This was the case in Kerch (mid-November 1941) and Sevastopol' (July 1942). It is

289 Sevastopol': Gel'man and Glubochanskii, *Kholokost*, pp. 69-71.

290 Reinhard Heydrich's "Einweisung," July 2, 1941, in *Die Einsatzgruppen in der besetzten Sowjetunion 1941/42*, pp. 326, 357.

291 Another very small group of Ashkenazi Jews who were also granted exemption from extermination included a small number of craftsmen. Some Jewish craftsmen were actually enslaved and forced to work for the EG D. They were taken further into the Caucasus when the EG D moved there. "Strafsache gegen Bierkamp," Staatsanwaltschaft Munich I. Versuchungsniederschrift, Alfred M., December 10, 1963, YVA, TR.10/1147, p. 396.

292 Feodosiia: Municipal Department of Medicine and Sanitation, December 2, 1941, DAARK, R-1458/2/1, p. 41.

primarily in these towns that Jewish medical workers were exempt from annihilation. In Kerch, nine Jewish doctors were exempted,[293] while in Sevastopol' exemption was granted to one male civil doctor (who refused it)[294] and several female military nurses in POW camps (who managed to survive the Holocaust).[295] Three Jewish doctors in Simferopol' survived the actions in December 1941, only to be killed three months later.[296]

Most Jewish medical personnel were killed following a general stabilization of the sanitary situation[297] or at a time when the German hold on the peninsula appeared to be especially weak.[298] Moreover, it must be emphasized that the policy of granting exemptions to Jewish medical workers was not always applied, even in war-stricken places where sanitary conditions were dire. According to testimonies of Russian survivors, in Sevastopol' the Germans murdered the Jewish doctors in POW camps immediately after they occupied the area, even as the sanitary conditions in the area were deplorable.[299] Finally, the Germans did not spare Jewish medical personnel from executions in the Crimean areas in which they regarded the sanitary conditions as satisfactory.[300]

4.2. Mixed couples[301]

Nazi policies towards mixed marriages (i.e., when a Jewish man was married to a non-Jewish woman or a non-Jewish man

293 OK I (V), "TB für die Zeit vom 28.11-7.12.1941," December 7, 1941, in Angrick, *Besatzungspolitik und Massenmord*, p. 359; Gubenko, *Kniga pechali*, 1991, p. 25.

294 Excerpts from the diary of Boris Pekarchuk, [no date], GARF, 7021/9/46, p. 56 and YVA, M.33/65, p. 12.

295 Statement of M. T. Kazarnovskaia, June 24, 1944, GARF, 7021/9/46, p. 87 and YVA, M.33/66, p. 17.

296 Gilbod, *Jewish Account*, p. 5; Akt of the Commission of Simferopol', October 4, 1944, YVA, M.33/70, pp. 6-7.

297 Sevastopol': N. F. Kharlamova, "Tri goda v fashystskom plenu," manuscript, 1960, in Gel'man and Glubochanskii, *Kholokost*, pp. 106-107.

298 Simferopol': Ibid., p. 5.

299 Ibid., pp. 70-71.

300 Yalta: Untitled document, [no date], YVA, P. 21.2/5.

301 Arad, *The Holocaust in the Soviet Union*, pp. 359-376; Hadas Shtoer, "Neither Here, Nor There: *Mischlinge* under the Nazi Regime: Comparative Aspects" (Hebrew) (MA Thesis: The Hebrew University of Jerusalem, 1999).

was married to a Jewish woman) and their common children were not uniform. As is generally known, Nazi attitudes in this respect were more stringent in the occupied Soviet territories than inside Nazi Germany.[302] The phenomenon of mixed couples was hardly a marginal phenomenon in the Crimea. It is suggested that about 30-35% of the Jews living in the peninsula intermarried, in line with the trend in geographically close Soviet Ukraine (26.53% as of 1936) but much lower than in the RSFSR (55.98% as of 1936), of which the Crimean Autonomous Republic was formally a part.[303]

Either the Jewish parents in mixed families or the whole family itself were required to register on a special list during the course of the general registration of the Jewish population.[304] However, in Yalta the registration of Jews initially covered some non-Jewish members of the mixed families.[305] At the next stage, Jewish spouses in mixed families became subject to most of the calamities that befell the rest of the Jewish population, such as forced labor or confinement in a ghetto.[306] Sometimes this was also the fate of the registered children from the mixed marriage.[307] In some places, the Jewish members of mixed families were granted an exemption from the obligation to bear identifying stars.[308]

302 Yitzhak Arad, "White Stains in the Historiography of the Holocaust in Nazi-Occupied Territories of the Soviet Union," in Altman, *The Holocaust and the Case of the Jewish Anti-Fascist Committee*, p. 76; Mordechai Altshuler, "The Unique Features of the Holocaust in the Soviet Union," in Yaakov Ro'i, ed., *Jews and Jewish Life in Russia and the Soviet Union* (Ilford, Essex: F. Cass, 1995), pp. 180-181.

303 Altshuler, *Soviet Jewry on the Eve of the Holocaust*, p. 270; ibid., "Intermarriage among Soviet Jews between the World Wars" (Hebrew), *Shvut* 13 (1988): p. 38.

304 Simferopol', Yalta: Conversation with the doctor Mariia Borodina, 1945 (?), DAARK, P-156/1/37; File of Mariia Frolova, Porfirii Kulik, and Anton and Elena Artemis, 2003, YVA, M.31/9983.

305 Report of Margarita Frolova-Meltsyna, [no date], YVA, 0.33/626, p. 1.

306 Yalta: Statement of Mariia Rokhman, August 2, 1944, GARF, 7021/9/59, p. 112; Statement of Aleksandr Ponomarev, August 30, 1944, GARF, 7021/9/59, p. 84(?).

307 Feodosiia: Testimony of Mark Al'ianaki, [no later than July 4, 1944], GARF, 7021/9/5, p. 76.

308 Yalta: Diary of O. I. Shargorodskaia, entry from November 29, 1941, DAARK, P-156/1/31, p. 160; Eduard Levin, *Sorok dnei do rasstrela* (Moscow: GPNTB Rossii, 2001), p. 67.

However, Jewish members of mixed couples were usually at first exempted from the assembly for execution that was obligatory for the rest of the Jews.[309] This ostensibly had to do with the lack of clarity regarding the fate of these people. However, this initial procedure was in no way automatic: sometimes such Jews were ordered to assemble,[310] whereas others were exempted at the very last minute.[311] Occasionally, an inscription was made in German in the passports of Jewish spouses who did present themselves at the assembly points – "*wird nicht umgebracht*" – which apparently meant that they were not subjected to annihilation at that time.[312] Furthermore, sometimes Jewish spouses were initially exempted but arrested after the *Aktion* was under way and murdered.[313] The variety of these patterns indicates that the Germans were inconsistent in their initial treatment of Jews of mixed couples at the beginning of the occupation.

Nevertheless, the annihilation of Jewish spouses and their children in the mixed families usually happened after the extermination of the bulk of Jews in a given locality. As stated above, most of these people were already registered. This fact facilitated their arrest and extermination, which was typically initiated by summoning Jewish spouses and their children to the local or German police station. There exists no record of the original intentions regarding the *Aktion* plans specifically against this group. Nor was there any public announcement posted to the effect that these people were to present themselves, as they were either individually summoned or retrieved by the

309 Feodosiia, Simferopol': Interrogation of Ekaterina Sirota, June 22, 1944. GARF, 7021/9/194, p. 162; Diary of Chrisanf Lashkevich, entry from July 30, 1942, DAARK, P-156/1/31, p. 101.

310 Sevastopol': File of Boris Korchminov (Nekrasov) and Valentina Gornostai (Nekrasova), interrogation of Anna Sechnaia, December 12, 1950, USHMMA, RG-31.018M, reel 7.

311 Simferopol': Story of Minkova, Memoirs of A. F. Peganova, "Chetyre kamery smerti," DAARK, P-156/1/40, pp. 34-45.

312 Simferopol': Testimony of Efim Gopshtein, August 16, 1944, YVA, M.35/21, pp. 60-61.

313 Simferopol': Statement of Viktor Domorovskii, August 10, 1944, YVA, M.33/68, pp. 106-107; Statement of Vera Sigalenko, August 3, 1944, YVA, M.33/68, p. 163.

police. In the Crimean towns, killings of the Jews pertaining to this group (which occurred after the original executions of full-fledged Jews) happened along the same paradigm as the general Jewish extermination. That is, they commenced in late December 1941,[314] continued throughout 1942,[315] and did not cease until the liberation of the Crimea in April 1944.[316] In most cases, they were killed in gas vans.[317] The crucial difference is that non-Jews of mixed couples were sometimes given a choice to follow their Jewish spouses and joint children (which meant certain death) or not (which meant life but without their beloved ones).

Still, in several cases in the Crimea the Germans placed the non-Jewish spouses of mixed couples on the same footing as the Jews and killed them, too.[318] Apparently, in such instances, the non-Jewish spouse was legally regarded as a full-fledged accomplice to the "crime of sheltering the Jew." The following statement of a Russian man whose brother was married to a Jewish woman in Simferopol' is typical in this respect:

314 Simferopol', Yalta. Memoirs of A. F. Peganova, "Chetyre kamery smerti," DAARK, P-156/1/40, p. 45; Statement of Khrista Zheltukhin, June 3, 1944, GARF, 7021/9/59, p. 102; File of Mariia Frolova, Porfirii Kulik, and Anton and Elena Artemis, 2003, YVA, M.31/9983.

315 Simferopol': Diary of Chrisanf Lashkevich, entry from July 30, 1942, DAARK, P-156/1/31, p. 101; Statement of Elena Grammatik, June 9, 1944, GARF, 7021/9/95, p. 130.

316 Feodosiia: Questioning of Evgeniia Shvarts, June (July?) 20, 1944, GARF, 7021/9/58, p. 16; Krichevskaia, *Dvadtsat' deviat' mesiatsev iz detstva*, pp. 52-53; Letter of Grigorii Zhoga, April 17, 1944 in Il'ia Altman and Leonid Terushkin, eds., *Sokhrani moi pis'ma. Sbornik pisem i dnevnikov evreev perioda Velikoi Otechestvennoi voiny* (Moscow: Tsentr i Fond "Kholokost", izdatel'stvo "MIK", 2007), pp. 255-256.

317 Simferopol': "Strafsache gegen Walter Bierkamp," Bayerisches Landes-kriminalamt, Vernehmungniederschrift, W. Max Wilhelm, May 22, 1964, YVA, TR.10/1147, pp. 426-427.

318 Simferopol': Statement of Elena Grammatik, June 9, 1944, GARF, 7021/9/95, p. 130; Memoirs of A.F. Peganova, "Chetyre kamery smerti," DAARK, P-156/1/40, p. 45; Diary of Chrisanf Lashkevich, entry from January 1942, DAARK, P-156/1/31, p. 87; GFP 647, "TB für den Monat Juli 1942," O.U., July 26, 1942, YVA, M.29.FR/59, p. 3.

The family that consisted of Vasilii Podymov (1891, Russian), Raisa Podymova (1889, Jewish), and their daughter Lidia Podymova (1923) was shot as a Jewish family. When the Fascists began to arrest mixed families in January 1942, the Podymov family moved away to his brother's family in Simferopol'. On May 1, 1942 the Gestapo arrested the wife, on May 6 – the husband and the daughter. They were not seen any longer. On May 10, their possessions were taken away."[319]

4.3. Jewish prisoners-of-war[320]

The imperatives of the war of annihilation generally predetermined the treatment that Soviet soldiers faced in German captivity in the Crimea. In this, the Germans killed tens of thousands of captured Soviet soldiers by starvation.[321] In addition, the fact that the Commander of the 11th Army General von Manstein had stringent views toward Soviet prisoners-of-war (POWs) influenced the conditions those captured in the Crimea faced.[322] This was significant, as it was the Army that was in charge of Soviet POWS once they surrendered and were transferred to and detained in POW camps.

Once placed in POW camps, Soviet prisoners' chances to survive were not high, especially in the first months of the German occupation, which occurred during the hard winter of 1941-42. The captives had to endure the terrible treatment the Germans meted out to all Soviet POWs.[323] In the Crimea, the mortality

319 Statement of Arsenii Podymov, before November 1944, YVA, M.33/70, p. 106.

320 Arad, *The Holocaust in the Soviet Union*, pp. 376-387; Altman and Rubinstein, *The Unknown Black Book*, pp. 364-368; Polian and Shneer, *Obrechennye pogibnut'*; Pavel Polian, "First Victims of the Holocaust: Soviet-Jewish Prisoners of War in German Captivity," *Kritika: Explorations in Russian and Eurasian History* 6, no. 4 (2005): pp. 763-787.

321 Pohl, *Die Herrschaft der Wehrmacht*, pp. 201-238; Karel C. Berkhoff, "The 'Russian' Prisoners of War in Nazi-Ruled Ukraine as Victims of Genocidal Massacre," *Holocaust and Genocide Studies* 15, no. 1 (2001): pp. 1-32; Christian Streit, *Keine Kameraden: die Wehrmacht und die sowjetischen Kriegsgefangenen 1941-1945* (Stuttgart: Deutsche Verlags-Anstalt, 1978).

322 Förster, "Hitler's Decision," pp. 1213-1214.

323 Testimony of Zalman Uzikov, December 14, 1987, YVA, 0.3/4939, p. 22.

Красноармейцы!

Вам известна судьба красной армии на всем протяжении от Ледовитаго - Океана до Днепра: разбита, уничтожена, в отступлении и в разложении!

Оборона Крыма — безнадежное дело.

Вам остается лишь выбор между полным уничтожением или погибелью в волнах Черного моря, если вы попытаетесь бежать на пароходах.

Всякая связь в северном направлении прервана.

Сдавайтесь! Ваше сопротивление бессмысленно.

Спасайте вашу жизнь!

Переходите к нам! Всем пленным живется хорошо. Мы пленных ни расстреливаем.

Десятки тысячь ваших товарищей украинцев перешли к нам, все они уже отпущены по домам и работают на своих собственных полях, но без жидов и комиссаров!

ГЛАВНОКОМАНДУЮЩИЙ ГЕРМАНСКИМИ ВОЙСКАМИ

Судьба Крыма решена! Сохраните его в целости для народа!

Nazi propaganda leaflet directed to the Red Army soldiers defending the Crimea. It mentions "dozens of thousands of your Ukrainian comrades who defected to us. All of them were allowed to go home, they work their own fields, but without *Zhidy* and Commissars!" Apparently the fall of 1942. Courtesy: RHCA

rate among the Soviet POWs was somewhat lower in comparison to the rest of the occupied territories, owing to milder weather conditions. In this respect, one has to emphasize that those Soviet soldiers captured in the Crimea throughout 1942 were treated better by the Germans overall, owing to a general moderation of the German policies towards the Soviet POWs, and had therefore higher chances to survive.[324]

Some testimonies imply that the Soviet soldiers captured during a smooth German takeover were usually better treated (this would have constituted most of the warfare in the initial phase of the Battle of the Crimea).[325] Unlike such soldiers, those who were captured during the course of fierce fighting (i.e., the Battles of Feodosiia, Kerch, and Sevastopol') faced especially severe maltreatment.[326]

Apart from the above-mentioned general observations, which applied to all Soviet POWs captured in the Crimea, regardless of their origin, there was no deviation from the established pattern of the German policy towards Jewish soldiers either in 1941 or 1942, or later: once revealed, they were killed. The mechanics of destruction involved the constant screening of the captives for Jews, including denunciations and interrogations. A number of Jewish soldiers were discovered and killed on the

324 Peter Black, "Foot Soldiers of the Final Solution: The Trawniki Training Camp and Operation Reinhard," *Holocaust and Genocide Studies* 25, no. 1 (2011): pp. 6, 8-9. Although in general it is true that captured Soviet soldiers in the Crimea had greater chances of survival, there were, nevertheless, some exceptions to the rule. Such was the case, for example, with the Battle of Evpatoriia. According to German claims, Soviet soldiers captured by the Germans after the recapture of Evpatoriia by the Wehrmacht were usually killed on the spot as retaliation for the Red Army having maltreated hundreds of injured German soldiers placed in the military hospital in Evpatoriia by mutilating and brutally killing them. "Strafsache gegen Walter Bierkamp," Bayerisches Landeskriminalamt IIIa/SK, Munich, Karl R. Werner, Major i. Generalstab, October 31, 1965, YVA, TR.10/1147, p. 515.

325 Testimony of Zalman Uzikov, YVA, December 14, 1987, YVA, 0.3/4939, pp. 11-15.

326 "Tragic End of the Jewry in the Western Russia"; See also Gel'man and Glubochanskii, *Kholokost*, pp. 69-71, 76, 106.

spot,[327] while others were killed through terrible and prolonged physical maltreatment.[328]

POW camps proved to be one of few places in the Crimea where Jews were publicly maltreated.[329] At such times, it was the result of collaborators who instigated the rest of the POWs to beat Jews – such as this instance from the camp "Kulikovo Pole" near Sevastopol':

> On July 5-7, [1942] people, mainly Tatars with stripes on the sleeves indicating their affiliation with the police, came to the camps where the Germans had driven the male population [of Sevastopol'] and POWs. They provoked beatings of the imprisoned Jews, explaining to the people that they [Jews] were the reason for the people's sufferings. On July 4, the beating of 12 Jews imprisoned in the camp at the Kulikovo field was arranged. Twelve male Jews were driven out of the crowd and dragged to the edge of the crater. After a short appeal to "Beat the *Zhidy!*" the pogromists began to strike the victims.[330]

* * *

As shown, the destruction of the Ashkenazi Jewish population in the Crimean peninsula by the Germans, aided by their allies and local collaborators, was all-encompassing. To assess it numerically, various German and Soviet sources should be compared, as each of them, individually, cannot be considered entirely reliable for various reasons. The initial figure of the number of Jews who resided in the Crimea prior to the war is 65,000 (as of 1939).[331]

327 POW camp near Sevastopol', camp Tole: Statement of Giul'nara Khalilova (Seidova), April 7, 1947, USHMMA, RG-31.018M, reel 7, OK II/576 (V); "TB für die Zeit vom 1.-15.7.1942," Bakhchisarai, July 16, 1942, YVA, 0.51/185 II, p. 6.

328 Near Bakhchisarai: *Krasnyi Krym*, March 22, 1944, in Kondranov and Stepanova, *Krym v period Velikoi Otechestvennoi voiny*, p. 188.

329 Sevastopol'skii *raion*: Gel'man and Glubochanskii, *Kholokost*, pp. 69-71.

330 Statement of V.N. Romanova-Petrova, [no later than July 1944], GARF, 7021/9/46, pp. 71-72.

331 Altshuler, *Distribution of the Jewish Population of the USSR*, pp. 9-11.

The evacuation of more than 50% of the native Crimean Jewish population from the peninsula before the German occupation was partly offset by the influx of Jews from elsewhere.[332] Their survival in the German-occupied peninsula depended on a number of factors, most specifically the relative isolation of the Crimea, grave weather and food conditions, collaboration by some segments of the local population (especially the Tatars), intensive anti-partisan warfare, and the permanent presence of most units of the EG D in the small territory of the peninsula for more than eight months (November 1941-June 1942). Bearing all this in mind, it may be cautiously claimed that by the time of the German occupation, from the 30,000 to 35,000 Ashkenazi Jews who were present in the peninsula, almost all were annihilated.[333]

332 See Chapter 1, "Jews in the Crimea from the Beginning of the German-Soviet War (June 22, 1941) to the German Occupation (November 1941)."

333 Other authors present estimates lower or higher than in this study: 1) 25,000-27,000 Jews and Krymchaks: Alexandr Kruglov, *Unichtozhenie evreiskogo naseleniia Ukrainy v 1941-1944 gg.: khronika sobytii* (Mogilev-Podolskyi: Kruglov A. I., 1997), p. 96; 2) 25,000-27,000 Jews and Krymchaks: Mark Goldenberg, "K voprosu o chisle zhertv sredi mirnogo naseleniia Kryma v period natsystskoi okkupatsii (1941-1944 gg.)," *Buleten: 'Golokost i suchasnist'* 3, no. 4, (9, 10), (2003) 3) 40,000 Jews: Gubenko, *Kniga pechali*, p. 49; A Soviet source based on the ESC findings mentions "35,000 Jews and Krymchaks" killed by the Germans in the Crimea: Vol'fson, *Krovavye zlodeianiia nemtsev v Krymu*, DAARK, P-156/1/34.

Chapter Four

Destruction of the Jewish Population in the North Caucasus

1. German Institutions Involved in the Holocaust in the North Caucasus

1.1. Army Group A

The German conquest of the North Caucasus with its vast oil fields was regarded as one of two main goals of the 1942 summer offensive.[1] In the area of the North Caucasus, the operations were conducted by the forces of the Army Group (*Heeresgruppe*) A under the command of Wilhelm List[2] from July 7 to September 10. Then Hitler himself

1 Alongside the thrust northeastward against Stalingrad. For the German view of the warfare in the Caucasus in 1941, see Klink, "The Conduct of Operations," pp. 613-627. For an analysis of military aspects of the Battle of the Caucasus in 1942-1943, see Wegner, "The War Against the Soviet Union, 1942-1943," pp. 1022-1048, 1173-1177; David M. Glantz, "The Struggle for the Caucasus," *The Journal of Slavic Military Studies* 22, no. 4 (2009): pp. 588-711; Joachim Hoffmann, *Kaukasien, 1942-1943: Das deutsche Heer und die Orientvölken der Sowjetunion* (Freiburg: Rombach Verlag, 1991), pp. 63-66, 80-81; V. V. Gurkin and A. I. Kruglov, "Oborona Kavkaza: 1942 god," *Voenno-Istoricheskii Zhurnal* 10 (1992): pp. 11-18; Andrei Grechko, *Bitva za Kavkaz* (Moscow: Ministerstvo Oborony SSSR, 1971), pp. 17-27; Joel Hayward, "Too Little, Too Late: An Analysis of Hitler's Failure in August 1942 to Damage Soviet Oil," *The Journal of Military History* 64, no. 3 (July 2000): pp. 769-794.

2 Siegmund Wilhelm Walther List (1880-1971): German military commander; became *General-feldmarschall* on July 19, 1940; served as supreme Wehrmacht

took over the command. On November 22, 1942, he passed the authority over to *Generaloberst* Ewald von Kleist.[3]

The Command of the Army group comprised some 15 German (among them, one Waffen-SS "Wiking" division), six Romanian, and one Slovak division at its disposal. The Germans abandoned most of the North Caucasian region in January 1943,[4] but retained some areas, most specifically Novorossiisk, until September 1943.[5] Regarding the Holocaust, the importance

commander in the South-East from the end of the Balkan wars to October 1941; served as commander of the Army Group A from July 7-September 10, 1942; sentenced to life imprisonment in 1948 for his participation in the Yugoslavian and Greek campaigns; released in 1952 on grounds of ill health.

3 Paul Ludwig Ewald von Kleist (1881-1954): German military commander; recalled to service in 1939, although retired, upon the beginning of WWII; served as commander of the Tank Army (*Panzergruppe*) A in 1941; participated in the encirclement of the Soviet armies at Kiev; became commander of the Army Group A on November 22, 1942; promoted to *Generalfeldmarschall* for having organized the successful pullout of the Wehrmacht from the North Caucasus on February 1, 1943; relieved of his duties in 1944 over disagreements with Hitler on the conduct of war; sentenced to 15 years' imprisonment in 1946 by a Yugoslavian court for the crimes committed in the Yugoslavian campaign; extradited to the Soviet Union in 1948; sentenced to 10 years' imprisonment by the Special Conference (OSO) of the Ministry of State Security in 1952; died in 1954 in a Soviet prison, making him the highest-ranking German general to die in Soviet captivity.
The protocols of von Kleist's interrogation by the Soviet authorities from April 1949 to November 1951 are available in Vladimir Makarov and Vasilii Khristoforov, eds., *Generaly i ofitsery Vermakhta rasskazyvaiut: Dokumenty iz sledstvennykh del nemetskikh voennoplennykh 1944-1951* (Moskva: MFD, 2009), pp. 46-83. Unfortunately, these documents indicate that Soviet interrogators never inquired in a pointed manner about German treatment of the local population, most specifically of the Jews in the German-occupied North Caucasus. When a Soviet interrogator just once posed this question, Ewald von Kleist confined himself to remark only that what occurred with the North Caucasian population during the German occupation was within the competence of the *Einsatzgruppe* and had nothing to do with the activities of the Wehrmacht.

4 The withdrawal order was announced on December 28, 1942, while the actual retreat of the German troops began on December 31: "Der Bevollmächtigte beim Ob.Kdo. der Heereesgruppe A. an den Oberbefehlshaber der Heeresgruppe A," Woroschilowsk, Geheime Reichssache, December 31, 1942, Yad Vashem Archives (YVA), JM/5640.

5 E.g., David R. Galbraith, "The Defence and Evacuation of the Kuban Bridgehead, January – October 1943," (MA Thesis, National University of Ireland, Maynooth, 2014).

of what occurred in the German-controlled parts of the North Caucasus in 1943 will receive less attention in this chapter, as the absolute majority of the Jews in these places had already been destroyed in 1942.

The German advance into the North Caucasus in the summer of 1942, reminiscent in many aspects of their 1941 Blitzkrieg-style victories, disorganized the Soviet war machine.[6] Masses of Soviet soldiers retreated in disorder. Yet, unlike the campaigns of 1941, there was no large-scale encirclement of the Soviet troops in the Caucasus. Consequently, the number of Soviet soldiers, including Jews, who fell under German captivity in the region, was small. As a result, the Wehrmacht refrained from conducting combing operations in the region, which usually led to heavy limitations on the civilians' freedom of movement.

The Wehrmacht oversaw the developments in the North Caucasus, including the supervision of the local population, primarily by means of a ramified network of *Orts-* and *Feldkommandaturen*.[7] The heads of local collaboration administrations underwent close security and ideological scrutiny. One of the Germans involved in this process in the region was Theodor Oberländer.[8]

6 The Soviet troops that fought against the Wehrmacht in the North Caucasus throughout the period under review involved the following forces: Caucasian, Transcaucasian, South-Eastern, Southern, and Stalingrad fronts, as well as the Black Sea Group [of troops] and the North Group. It should be noted that the composition of the Soviet fronts was frequently changed and reshaped. Therefore, it was common during 1942-1943 for the same troops to belong to permanently changing fronts and groups.

7 "Strafsache gegen Theodor Oberländer," Vernehmungsprotokoll des Zeugen Kerrar Gaidar-Ogly Aliskerov, Berlin, April 18, 1960, YVA, TR.10/2147, p. 580.

8 Theodor Oberländer (1905-1998): Took part in Hitler's Beer Putsch in 1923; became a member of the NSDAP in 1933; served as Director of the Institute for East European Economics at the University of Königsberg in 1934; became Professor at the University of Königsberg in 1937; served as one of the regional leaders of the NSDAP in East Prussia in 1937; served as an expert on Eastern Europe at Abwehr in 1939; served as Professor of Political Science at the German Karl University at Prague in 1940; served as organizer and commander of the "Nachtigall" (raised from Ukrainians) and "Bergmann" (raised from Caucasian POWs) diversion battalions from 1940-1942; served as Federal Minister for Displaced Persons, Refugees, and Victims of War in Adenauer's government from 1953-1960; served as a member of the Christian Democratic Union from 1953-1960; was sentenced

The army was the first, and often the only, German agency to operate in Caucasian towns and villages.[9] However, the military did not maintain enough strength to make its presence felt uniformly throughout the vast newly conquered territories; at times, there was no permanent German presence in some villages[10] or even in whole regions.[11]

Scholars of the subject have long accepted Alexander Dallin's authoritative view expressed in the 1950s that North Caucasus was placed under special military administration not subordinated, even on paper, to the Ministry for the Occupied Eastern Territories, and that the Führer himself granted the region its special status.[12] Yet, Hitler's original directive has never been found, and the evidence adduced from other sources contradicts this standpoint.[13] At any rate, it was the Military Commander-in-Chief of the Army Group A (*Oberbefehlshaber der Heeresgruppe* A) who exercised the supreme authority throughout the whole North Caucasus. As a result, there was a change in the balance of forces between the Wehrmacht and the SS agencies in the region in favor of the military.[14]

Concerning the relationship between the *Heeresgruppe* A and the SS, there are contradictory testimonies. A German military source claimed at the Nuremberg Trial that:

in absentia by the East German court to a life sentence in 1960.

9 *Stanitsy* - Gul'kevichi and Tbiliiskaia: Interrogation of Irina Saksina, 1943, YVA, M.33/303, p. 85; Questioning of Anna Suzdalenko, May 10, 1944, GARF, 7021/16/464, p. 231.

10 Otradnenskaia *stanitsa*: Testimony of Roza Lipkin (1904), [no date], (Institute of Contemporary Jewry) ICJ, TC 2860.

11 Adygeiskaia Autonomous *oblast'*: Intelligence survey of the Southern Headquarters of the Partisan Movement, November 1942 (?), in Beliaev and Bondar', *Kuban' v gody Velikoi Otechestvennoi voiny, 1941-1945*, pp. 606-607.

12 Alexander Dallin, *Deutsche Herrschaft in Rußland 1941-1945: Eine Studie über Besatzungspolitik* (Düsseldorf: Droste, 1958), p. 252.

13 Manfred Zeidler, "Der Minsker Kriegsverbrechenerprozeß vom Januar 1946: Kritische Anmerkungen zu einem Sowjetischem Schauprozeß gegen Deutsche Kriegsgefangenen," *Vierteljahrshefte für Zeitgeschichte* 52, no. 2 (2004): pp. 487-500.

14 *Kommandant des rückwärtigen Armeesgebietes* (*Korück*), p. 531, October 1, 1942, Bundesarchiv-Militärarchiv (BA-MA), RH 23/16, in Hoffmann, *Kaukasien, 1942-1943*, p. 439.

> Field Marshal von Kleist, as commander of an Army Group, on a mere rumor that Jews were being murdered, immediately intervened, summoned the Higher SS and Police Leader, and told him that he would not permit excesses against the Jews. This SS-*Führer* assured him that no excesses against the Jews took place, and that he had no orders to that effect.[15]

This evidence appears to be dubious in several aspects. First, when von Kleist held the position of the Army Group commander (from November 22, 1942, until the retreat of the Wehrmacht from the region in January 1943), the murder of the Ashkenazi Jews was indeed on the ebb in numerical terms. Second, it is within this period that the saga of Mountain Jews, when most of them managed to survive, evolved.[16] At the same time, the small number of the Jews killed at that time in the Caucasus has to do with the fact that the most of them had already been annihilated. It seems hardly possible that von Kleist, who, prior to November 22, 1942, had held an important position in the Wehrmacht hierarchy in the region (i.e., Commander of the 1st Tank Army), was entirely ignorant of these murders. Still, if we note the remarkably low level of involvement of the 1st Tank Army under Kleist in the persecution of Jews in 1941,[17] it seems plausible that von Kleist's stance towards the extermination of Jews was generally restrained, and that it had a certain degree of moderating the Wehrmacht involvement in the murder of Jews in the North Caucasus in 1942.

There are numerous sources demonstrating that the Wehrmacht was involved in carrying out some phases of the Holocaust in the North Caucasus, in particular those preceding the physical onslaught against the Jews. The army, most specifically branches at the Local and Field Headquarters established in the

15 Testimony of Dr. Laternser, August 21, 1946, Affidavit 706, *The Trial of German Major War Criminals*, p. 395.

16 See Chapter 5, "The Fate of Karaites and Krymchaks in the Crimea and Mountain Jews in the North Caucasus during the Holocaust."

17 Johannes Hürter, *Hitlers Heerführer: Die deutschen Oberbefehlshaber im Krieg gegen die Sowjetunion 1941/42*, 2nd ed. (Munich: R. Oldenbourg Verlag, 2007), pp. 587-588.

main urban centers where the Jewish population was registered,[18] established *Judenräte* and put them in operation[19] and then proclaimed assembly orders for the Jews.[20] The army was sometimes also involved in carrying out the execution of Jews.[21] Of note is also the fact that even in mid-December 1942, when the bulk of the region's Jews had long since been killed, the Army Group A continued to consider Jews as belonging to the hostile segment of the Caucasian population, against which unrestrained harshness should be applied.[22] At the same time, judging by indirect evidence, such as the restrictive orders issued to the army regarding its behavior in the Caucasian space, it may be cautiously suggested that the Wehrmacht commanders were loath to see their soldiers participating in anti-Jewish actions in the region.[23]

Of note is the fact that Quartermaster-General *Generalleutenant* Eduard Wagner, belonging to the supreme leadership of the German Army, regarded the attitudes towards Jews of the peoples in the North Caucasus as a sensitive problem. Wagner's report from September 1942 did not make it clear whether he meant all Jews or only Mountain Jews. Still, his recommendation is telling: At a time when the "Final Solution" was long since a *fait accompli* in almost all occupied Soviet territories, he advised putting the extermination of Jews in the North Caucasus on

18 Elista, Kislovodsk: Report of the ESC, State Archive of the Russian Federation (GARF), 7021/8/26, pp. 10-11; Akt, July 5, 1943, GARF, 7021/17/5, pp. 35-36.

19 Essentuki, Kislovodsk: Testimony of Samuil Belenkov, (1894), August 10, 1943, GARF, 7021/17/4, p. 22; Interrogation of Mikhail Fingerut, (1880), June 25, 1943, GARF, 7021/17/5, p. 30.

20 Cherkessk, Elista: Akt of the Commission of Cherkessk, July 13, 1943, GARF, 702/17/12, pp. 68-69; "And This is the First News… What the Nazis are Doing with the Jewish Population before their Retreat in Russia" (Hebrew), *Davar*, no. 5366, February 24, 1943, p. 1 (source: Moscow, special telegram to *Davar* dated February 22, 1943).

21 Armavir, Dzhinskaia *stanitsa*: "Strafsache gegen Walter Bierkamp," Staatsanwaltschaft. Munich, Berlin, Vernehmungsniederschrift, Herr Fritz U., December 6, 1962, YVA, TR.10/1147, p. 377; Akt of the Commission of Suvorovskii *raion*, July 26, 1943, GARF, 7021/17/12, pp. 1-3.

22 Oberkommando der Heeresgruppe A 1a Nr. 4498/42 geh. An Befh.H.Geb.A, Abt. Ia, betr: Bandenbekämpfung, December 16, 1942, BA-MA, RH 22/221b, in Oldenburg, *Ideologie und militärisches Kalkül*, p. 299.

23 Ibid, p. 306.

hold until the completion of the conquest of the Caucasus. If Wagner was referring to all Jews, the report indicates that he was aware of the actual pace of the Holocaust in the region. By the time he signed his report in early September 1942, the absolute majority of Jews residing in the North Caucasus had already been killed by the SS. If he meant only Mountain Jews, then Wagner's remarks were indicative of a future change in the Nazi attitudes towards this group. However, these views became the *de facto* German policy only towards the end of 1942; in the meantime, hundreds of Mountain Jews were killed. One way or another, Wagner's report did signal some recognition of the special conditions in the North Caucasus in contrast to other German-occupied Soviet areas; the army's concerns about winning the cooperation of the local population caused it partially to take these conditions into account, even with respect to the "Jewish Question."[24]

Alongside the army, Alfred Rosenberg's Ministry for the Occupied Eastern Territories was influential in outlining German population policies in the region. This was achieved due to a number of Sovietologists and Turkologists in its service (most prominent among them, Professor Gerhard von Mende) and through the specially created position of the Ministry's envoy at the Headquarters of the Army Group A (*Bevollmächtgier des Reichsministerium für den besetzten Ostgebieten beim Oberkommando der Heeresgruppe A*), occupied by a former German General Consul at Batumi, Dr. Otto von Bräutigam.[25] Yet, it appears that the Ministry did not voice any reservation towards the established genocidal pattern of German policy in considering the "Final Solution of the Jewish Question" in the North Caucasus. Its stance (or that of Otto von Bräutigam)

24 "Notizen für Führer-Vortrag," Eduard Wagner, September 1942, in Zeidler, "Das 'Kaukasische Experiment': Gab es seine Weisung Hitlers zur deutschen Besatzungspolitik im Kaukasus?" pp. 490-491, 497-498.

25 Heinz Schneppen, "Generalkonsul a. D. Dr. Otto Bräutigam: Widerstand und Verstrickung: Eine quellenkritische Untersuchung," *Zeitschrift fur Geschichtswissenschaft* 60, 4 (2012): pp. 301-330.

towards Mountain Jews constitutes a special case, and will be dealt with in Chapter Five.

Romanian troops were also involved in carrying out the anti-Jewish policy in the Caucasus. However, the few available sources are contradictory: there is an extremely limited record of one extermination action in the Caucasus conducted solely by a Romanian unit[26] and their participation alongside other forces in killing the Jews.[27] However, when the Romanians were in control of some Caucasian towns, there is proof of "only" sporadic killings of the Jews, if any at all.[28] There is more evidence suggesting that the Romanian soldiers behaved more loosely towards the Jews, including rapes and, in particular, plunder of property.[29]

1.2. *Einsatzgruppe* D[30]

The penetration of the Wehrmacht into the North Caucasus was followed by the entry and fast deployment of almost all units of the *Einsatzgruppe* D (EG D). Prior to the Battle of the Caucasus, the leadership and composition of the EG D had undergone a transformation. In June 1942, SS-*Oberführer* Walter Bierkamp[31]

26 Ibid., p. 175.

27 Village of Apsheronskaia: Report by the Intelligence Department of the Southern Headquarter of the Partisan Movement "O massovykh ubiistvakh, nasilii i izdevatel'stvakh nemetskikh fashystov v okkupiorvannykh raionakh," December 4, 1942, Russian State Archive of Social and Political History (RGASPI), 69/1/1048, p. 8.

28 Anapa, Teberda: Akt of the Commission of the town of Anapa, February 27, 1944, GARF, 7021/16/460, pp. 1-2; Testimony of Vadim Maniker, April 1975, YVA, 0.3/4108, p. 2.

29 *Stanitsa* of Dzhiginka, village of Krasnyi: Interrogation of Alexander Chebanenko, January 25, 1944, GARF, 7021/16/461, p. 94; Report by the Intelligence Department of the Southern Headquarters of the Partisan Movement "O politicheskikh nastroeniiakh naseleniia na vremenno okkupirovannykh fashistami territoriiakh Kryma i Kavkaza," December 23, 1942, RGASPI, 69/1/1048, p. 8.

30 For a general overview of the activity of the *Einsatzgruppe* D in the Caucasus, see Angrick, *Besatzungspolitik und Massenmord*, pp. 545-669.

31 Walter Bierkamp (1901-1945): Received his law degree in 1928; became a member of the NSDAP in 1932; became Chief of the Criminal Police in Hamburg in 1937; served as inspector of the Security Police and the SD in Düsseldorf from February 1941-June 1942; served as commander of the *Einsatzgruppe* D in

superseded Otto Ohlendorf as the EG D leader,[32] and the *Sonderkommando* 11b was left in the Crimea to take care of police and security tasks in the peninsula.[33] In the North Caucasus, the EG D operated a "Caucasian" unit, raised from Soviet prisoners-of-war of Caucasian and Crimean Tatar descent.[34]

Given the enormous size of the Caucasian territory, which fell under the German control, special attention should be given to the extremely fast pace of deployment of the *Einsatzgruppe* forces. Within one-two weeks, they had firmly established themselves in the main Caucasian centers. With the EG D headquarters stationed in Stavropol', its smaller units began relentlessly to comb the territory of the region in pursuit and execution of Jews. Its analytical work in the Jewish domain, as reflected in the "Reports from the Occupied Eastern Territories" (*Meldungen aus den besetzten Ostgebieten* (MbOg)) series, was limited, and was for the most part conducted subsequent to the extermination of the Jews. The annihilation of Jews in the vast territories of the North Caucasus conducted predominantly by the EG D was so comprehensive that a German military observer had good reasons to claim that as of October 1942 no more Jews remained in the region.[35]

Apparently because of the manpower shortage and the ensuing logistical shortcomings, the *Einsatzgruppe* involvement in the establishment and functioning of *Judenräte* in the Caucasus was rather insignificant. There exists a record of such activity only in two Caucasian towns: Kislovodsk and Piatigorsk.[36] When

June 1942-May 1943; became SS-*Brigadeführer* in 1944; served as commander of the Security Police and the SD in the Generalgouvernement from June 1943-February 1945; committed suicide on May 15, 1945.

32 Berlin: "Himmlers Brief an Walter Bierkamp in Düsseldorf," June 24, 1942, Russian State Military Archive (RGVA), 1323/1/51, p. 147.

33 Andrej Angrick, "Die Einsatzgruppe D," p. 102.

34 On the activities of this unit in the Crimea, see also chapter 8, "The Local Population and the Holocaust in the Crimea".
For the North Caucasus, see Chapter 9, "The Local Population and the Holocaust in the North Caucasus."

35 "Bericht über Das 'Versuchsgebiet' im Kuban-Kosaken-Raum zur Klärung des gesamten Kosakenproblems," Kdt. zum Befehlsh. H. Geb. A. O.U., Geheim Kommandosache, Sonderführer K., [no name], January 10, 1943, YVA, JM/5716.

36 Akt of July 5, 1943, GARF, 7021/17/5, pp. 35-36; Testimony of the Ek 12 man

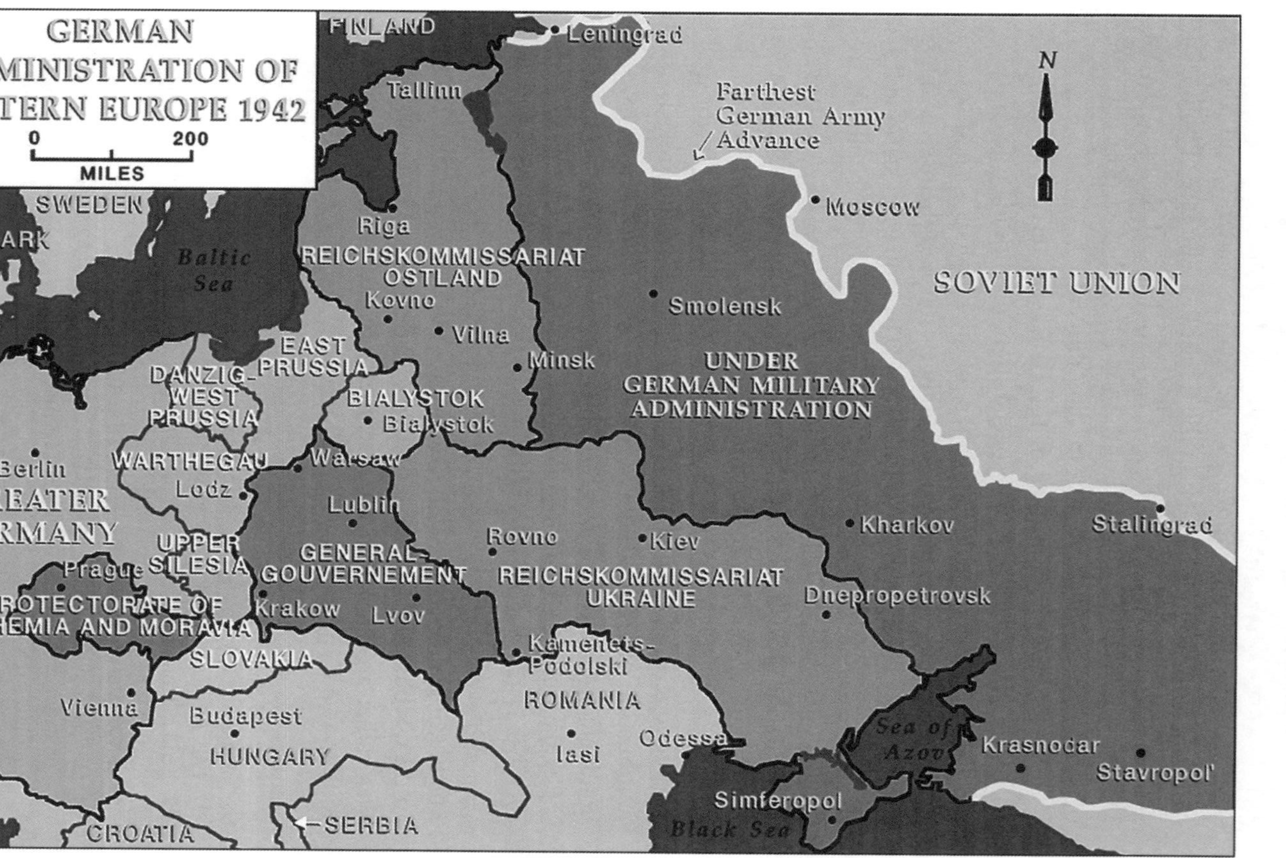

Courtesy: U.S. Holocaust Memorial Museum

it came to issuing and enforcing the assembly order, the EG D involvement increased slightly[37] growing considerably only during the extermination *Aktionen*. By virtue of being the most important and often the sole executioner, the EG D was in the position to set the time of the killing operations. Indeed, there are several records of the *Einsatzgruppe* conducting the *Aktion* and "post-action" killing of the Jews in North Caucasian towns and villages.[38] The EG D also handled special cases, such as the murder of Jewish children in Caucasian orphanages.[39]

Almost simultaneously with the appearance of the EG D in the region (August 6, 1942) another SS agency – the permanent institution of High SS and Police Leader of the Caucasus (*Höhere SS- und Polizeiführer Kaukasien*; in short, *HSSPF Kaukasien*) headed by SS-*Gruppenführer* Gerret Korsemann[40] – was established in the occupied North Caucasus.[41] The HSSPF

Pffeifer during the trial in Piatigorsk, 1968, in Yitzhak Arad, ed., *Unichtozhenie evreev SSSR v gody okkupatsii (1941-1944): Sbornik dokumentov i materialov* (Jerusalem: Yad Vashem, 1991), p. 242.

37 Kislovodsk and Stavropol': Akt, July 5, 1943, GARF, 7021/17/5, pp. 35-36; "Nachtragsanklageschrift in der Strafsache gegen Kehrer," October 28, 1970, YVA, TR.10/802, p. 15.

38 Elista and Krasnodar: Report of the ESC, GARF, 7021/8/26, pp. 10-11; "Anklageschrift in der Strafsache gegen Christmann," September 29, 1971, YVA, TR.10/822, pp. 1179, 1185.

39 Akt of the Commission of Besskorbnaia *stanitsa*, December 12, 1943, YVA, M.33/301, pp. 93-94.

40 Gerret Korsemann (1895-1958): Became a member of Freikorps Grodno in 1918; became a member of the NSDAP and the SA in 1926; became a member of the SS in 1939; became commander of the Order Police in Lublin in 1940; became SS-*Gruppenführer* in 1942; became High SS and Police Leader in the Caucasus in August 1942; reduced to service in Waffen-SS "for cowardly conduct" in 1943; imprisoned in Poland from 1945-1949.

41 "Beurteilung (Gerret) Korsemanns durch Prützmann," September 17, 1943, BDC, SSO, Akte Gerret Korsemann, in Witte, *Der Dienstkalender Heinrich Himmlers*, p. 510. It should be mentioned that the overoptimistic Germans had already assigned Korsemann to this position as early as in the first phase of the war. The location of his office was constantly recorded in the operational reports of the *Einsatzgruppe*: Standorte, HSSPF z.b.V. (Korsemann) – Rowno, EM no. 179, March 11, 1942, RGVA, 500/1/773, p. 49 and Standorte, HSSPF z.b.V. (Korsemann) – Rowno, EM no. 186, March 27, 1942, RGVA, 500/1/773, p. 126.

could make use of police and Waffen-SS units available in the region. The sole Waffen-SS division, "Wiking," was dispatched to the front-line in Chechnya immediately upon its arrival in the region,[42] but some police forces subordinated to the *HSSPF Kaukasien* maltreated and killed Jews. The following excerpt from the war diary of a police unit dated August 22, 1942, operating in Brod-Grushevskii area underscores the point:

> Jews and Russian soldiers detained in the streets were eliminated as they were sent to mark mine fields. In the course of this work, two Jews attempted to escape and were shot… In particular, the unit (*Kommando*) in the area of Bolshekpinskaia can report a successful activity… The head of this unit, Lieutenant Hoffmann, has promptly forced the inhabitants of the area to collaborate. Jews, bandits, and escaping Russian POWs were also arrested, and after a short interrogation transferred to the GFP or the SD.[43]

German wartime correspondence mentioned rivalry between two overlapping SS authorities in the region (EG D and *HSSSP Kaukasien*).[44] Yet, there is no indication that it affected the murder of the Jews.

42 Town of Malgobek: Khadzhi Ibragimbejli, "Krakh gitlerovskogo okkupatsionnogo rezhima na Kavkaze," in Basov and Kumanev, *Narodnyi podvig v bitve za Kavkaztei*, p. 275.

43 "Anlage zu II./Pol.Rgt. Einsatz- und TB des Batallions für die Zeit vom 1.–31.8.1942," (Auszug aus dem KTB), September 12, 1942, RGVA, 1358/1/9, pp. 106-107.

44 *HSSPF Kaukasien*, translation from German into Russian, September 24, 1942, RGVA, 1323/2/263, pp. 156-157.

2. The "Final Solution" in the North Caucasus[45]

2.1. Towns[46]

2.1.1. General concerns

The Germans' initial methods for dealing with the Jewish population differed from place to place. At times, the Germans personally approached the Jewish public or individual Jews in order to assuage their fears resulting from the fact that the Jews were singled out in German orders.[47] The Germans also promised that absolute compliance with their orders would safeguard the Jews' future.[48] It is noteworthy that the Germans occasionally addressed the rumors that they killed Jews, claiming that they were false.[49] The explanation provided by a German representative to Professor Naum Vilik, appointed as a *starosta* of the Jewish community in Krasnodar, is illuminating. According to a Soviet report:

> N. Vilik told the officer that rumors circulated saying that the Germans exterminated Jews. The German said: "Do you still believe in this Bolshevik lie? No one executes them. Look! In Taganrog they were allocated a separate

45 For general literature on the Holocaust in the Caucasus, see Arad, *The History of the Holocaust*, pp. 525-530; Al'tman, *Zhertvy nenavisti*, pp. 272-286.

46 See Table 8, "Course of the Holocaust in North Caucasian towns."

47 Krasnodar and Novorossiisk: In Krasnodar, the registration of the whole population took place in September 1942, i.e., more than two weeks after the registration and murder of the Jews. Intelligence survey No. 6, in Beliaev and Bondar', *Kuban' v gody Velikoi Otechestvennoi voiny, 1941-1945*, pp. 460-461. In Novorossiisk, the registration of all the inhabitants not engaged in the German-initiated works was conducted only from May 28, 1943: Akt of the Commission of Novorossiisk, October 18, 1943, GARF, 7021/16/11, p. 14.

48 Cherkessk and Stavropol': "Urteil gegen Johannes Schlupper, Heinrich Winterstein, Rudi Eschenbach," Landesgericht Munich I, July 24, 1974, YVA, TR.10/956, pp. 34-35; Document of the Stavropol' Medical Institute, July 2, 1943, GARF, 7021/17/294, p. 7.

49 Essentuki, Novorossiisk: Testimony of Samuil Belenkov, August 10, 1943, GARF, 7021/17/4, p. 24; Questioning of Zoia Chernova, October 14, 1943, GARF, 7021/16/11, p. 118.

> neighborhood and they live there in complete safety and pursue their business. That's what will happen in Krasnodar."[50]

Taganrog's Jews had been all killed by the Germans in the late October 1941, i.e., some nine months before this conversation. Afterwards, this murder was reported in the Soviet media, although in a veiled manner, without emphasizing the fact that the victims of this killing operation were exclusively Jews.[51] But beyond this, the Soviets were in no position to corroborate their claims, as long as the Germans were in control of Taganrog and adjacent areas. It is unknown how Professor Vilik received the news that the fate of Krasnodar's Jews would be similar to that of those in Taganrog, but it is likely the assurances of the Nazi officer made an impression on him — and on the local Jews — via this encounter.

In Kislovodsk, where the Germans faced a large-scale Jewish escape from the town, their tactics were different. The Germans made serious efforts to persuade the Jews that they had nothing to fear under German rule:

> Almost every day, the German occupation authorities pasted announcements warning Jewish inhabitants not to believe "false rumors" that the Nazis intended to annihilate the Jewish people. Their only intention was to separate them from the "Aryan" population by means of marking clothes, but they were ready to guarantee their existence "in respect and quiet."[52]

In the war-stricken harbor town of Novorossiisk, the Wehrmacht controlled only half of the town. Here, the Germans had to reckon with the theoretical possibility of a mass movement of Jews into the Soviet-dominated part of the town. Therefore, in appealing to the Jewish population, the Germans took into account the peculiar

50 Akt of the Commission of Krasnodar, March 25, 1943, YVA, M.33/293, pp. 5-6.

51 See, for example, "Pod gitlerovskoi piatoi," *Molot* (Rostov-na-Donu), December 21, 1941, no. 302, (6180), p. 2; "Uzhasnye zlodeianiia nemtsev v Taganroge," March 20, 1942, *Molot*, no. 67 (6258), p. 1.

52 West, *In the Ropes of Destruction*, pp. 108-109.

situation in Novorossiisk, addressing the rumors related to their persecution and killing of Jews: "The rumors that the Germans killed Jews were false. The German command is willing to grant shelter for the Jews, as the town is temporarily bombarded."[53]

In many places, the Germans assured the Jews that the aim of "resettlement" was simply to send them elsewhere.[54] This policy should be regarded as part of their camouflage tactics. Concomitantly, from time to time the Germans' policy also involved threats against entire communities or individual Jews, such as *Judenräte* members. In such instances, the Germans warned the Jews that non-compliance with their order would lead to heavy retribution, including capital punishment.[55] It must be emphasized that in all of the aforementioned cases, the Germans were determined to prevent Jews from escaping the occupied areas. In terms of the Germans' genocide policy, unlike an ordinary Soviet citizen, whose presence or absence usually mattered little to the Germans, a Jew was to be caught and murdered everywhere.

2.1.2. From Registration to Killing Operations

The German pre-destruction phase in its onslaught against the Jews in the North Caucasus involved several steps. First, the Germans forced the entire Jewish population to register immediately upon occupation. In most Caucasian towns[56] Jews were initially only required to register, as the assembly for forced labor, maltreatment, and eventually the exterminations, did not happen right away. The notable exception was Stavropol', where the Jews were almost

53 Questioning of Zoia Chernova, October 14, 1943, GARF, 7021/16/11, p. 118.

54 Essentuki, Minvody: "Massacre of the Caucasus Jews" (Hebrew), [Jewish Anti-Fascist Committee, source: letters from the local inhabitants], *Ha-tsofe* (Tel Aviv), no. 1702, August 4, 1943, p. 3; Statement of Matvei Makogonenko, August 13, 1943, GARF, 7021/17/2, pp. 14-15.

55 Cherkessk, Stavropol': Akt of the Commission of Cherkessk, July 13, 1943, GARF, 702/17/12, pp. 68-69; Akt of the Commission of Stavropol', July 11, 1943, GARF, 7021/17/1, pp. 95-96.

56 Elista, Krasnodar: Report of the ESC on the atrocities of the German Fascist occupiers in the occupied *ulusy* and the town of Elista, no later than September 10, 1943, GARF, 7021/8/26, pp. 10-11; Akt of the Commission of Krasnodar, June 30, 1943, GARF, 7021/16/5, p. 12.

immediately called to assemble.[57] Special registration directives were issued for mixed couples.[58] In the unique case of Nal'chik, all Ashkenazi Jews were arrested during registration.[59] Usually it was the Jewish Council that carried out the registration, but sometimes the Germans did it alone.[60] The local police only rarely participated in enforcing the registration order.[61]

After registration, the next stage involved forcing adult Jews, including children over 12, to wear six-pointed stars as identification badges.[62] The Germans applied this policy in most Caucasian towns.[63] In most cases, Jews were ordered to wear the stars immediately upon registration.[64] However, sometimes there was a small interval between the two procedures, as the Germans faced problems in applying the identification order.[65] This was due to poorly synchronized anti-Jewish measures in some Caucasian towns close to each other. As a result, the Military *Kommandant* of Essentuki von Beck even went so far as

57 Akt of the Commission of Stavropol', July 11, 1943, GARF, 7021/17/1, pp. 95-96; "And This is the First News" (Hebrew), *Davar*, no. 5366, February 24, 1943, p. 1.

58 See the section on mixed couples further on in the chapter.

59 Akt no. 98, GARF, 7021/7/109, p. 202.

60 Kislovodsk, Minvody: Testimony of Fania Skliar, September 1975, YVA, 0.3/3934, p. 6; "How the Jews were murdered" (Hebrew), *Ha-tsofe*, April 8, 1943, p. 1.

61 Testimony of Ia. Talianskii, [no date], GARF, 7021/17/4, p. 31.

62 Kislovodsk: Testimony of Fania Skliar, September 1975, YVA, 0.3/3934, p. 6.

63 Armavir, Zheleznovodsk: Akt of the Commission of Armavir, January 28, 1943, Central Archive of the Ministry of Defense of the Russian Federation (TsAMO RF), 51/958/52, pp. 91-92, courtesy of the United States Holocaust Memorial Musuem (USHMM); Akt of the Commission of Zheleznovodsk, July 12, 1943, GARF, 7021/17/6, p. 1. The order to wear the stars was issued and enforced by the Germans – with the exception of Tikhoretsk and probably Kislovodsk where the orders were given by the German-installed Russian heads of the towns. Beliaev and Bondar', *Kuban' v gody Velikoi Otechestvennoi voiny, 1941-1945*, pp. 464-465; Report of Moisei Evenson, Viktor Shklovskii, ed., [no date], YVA, P.21.2/1.

64 Kislovodsk, Minvody: Testimony of Fania Skliar, September 1975, YVA, 0.3/3934, p. 6; Statement of Andrei Pavlov, June 26, 1943, GARF, 7021/17/2, p. 13.

65 Essentuki and Krasnodar (?): Testimony of Samuil Belenkov, August 10, 1943, GARF, 7021/17/4, p. 24; Testimony of Nataliia Krechetovich, (1931), August 29, 1999, YVA, 0.33.C/5961.

to promise to the Jews that the order to wear stars would not be adhered to in "his" town. This was done after it became known in Essentuki that in neighboring Piatigorsk it was obligatory to bear the stars. But two days later, the order was extended to Essentuki's Jews, too.[66]

In the initial phases, Caucasian Jews were occasionally physically maltreated by their German oppressors.[67] This included German guards beating Jews and raping Jewish women in places where the non-Jewish population could not witness maltreatment, such as the apartments of Jews and detention centers.[68] But sometimes Jews were beaten in public or while performing forced labor.[69] In Nal'chik, an elderly Jew was executed while attempting to bury the corpse of his son who had been publicly shot (apparently as a POW).[70] The acts of violence were primarily committed by the Germans. When the mass murder of Jews in Caucasian towns was not immediate, the Germans required them to perform forced labor.[71] The forced labor order applied to almost the whole Jewish population, including children over 10, pregnant women and those with small children, and old

66 Testimony of Samuil Belenkov, August 10, 1943, GARF, 7021/17/4, p. 24

67 Cherkessk and Mikoianshakhar: Akt on the atrocities and maltreatment committed by the German Fascist occupiers towards the peaceful population of Pregranenskii *raion*, June 28, 1943, in Boiko, *Stavropol'e v Velikoi Otechestvennoi voine 1941-1945 gg.*, p. 135; Testimony of Ida Nikeeva, July 29, 1943, GARF, 7021/17/10, p. 204.

68 For apartments, see Essentuki: Testimony of Faina Gulianskaia, July 2, 1943, GARF, 7021/17/4, p. 17. For detention centers, see Akt of the Commission of Cherkessk, July 13, 1943, GARF, 702/17/12, pp. 68-69; Akt of the Commission of the resort of Teberda, July 5, 1943, GARF, 7021/17/7, pp. 4-5.

69 For public, see Mikoianshakhar: Testimony of Ida Nikeeva, July 29, 1943, GARF, 7021/17/10, p. 204. For forced labor, see Essentuki: Testimony of Samuil Belenkov, August 10, 1943, GARF, 7021/17/4, p. 23; Akt of the Commission of Essentuki, July 10, 1943, GARF, 7021/17/4, p. 1.

70 "Nazis' Atrocities" (Hebrew), *Ha-tsofe*, no. 1717, August 19, 1943.

71 Essentuki, Kislovodsk, and Zheleznovodsk: Letter by the painter L. N. Tarabukin and his wife D. R. Gol'dshtein to the writer Iu. Kalugin, [1943], YVA, M.35/25, p. 86 (also available in Rubinstein and Altman, *The Unknown Black Book*, pp. 384-385). Testimony of Fania Skliar, September 1975, YVA, 0.3/3934, p. 7; Statement of the doctor T. Z. Kairov, 1943 (?), GARF, 7021/17/6, p. 4.

persons up to 90 years of age.[72] It was impossible to evade labor on medical grounds.[73]

The Jews were only occasionally exploited for work having to do with maintaining satisfactory sanitary conditions in the occupied towns, such as cleaning and sweeping the streets[74] or burying the corpses of dead people and animals.[75] Jewish labor was also sometimes used for construction projects of military significance.[76] For the most part, however, the Jewish population was exploited for the most difficult and most humiliating works: cleaning lavatories and carrying stones.[77] Unlike in some other places in the occupied Soviet territories, the Germans never paid the Jewish forced laborers in Caucasian towns.[78] Jews were exploited over the course of a lengthy working day often without intervals[79] and with no food supplied.[80] They fared better if the order was enforced by Jewish councils or heads of Jewish

72 Akt of the Commission of Essentuki, July 10, 1943, GARF, 7021/17/4, p. 1; Nal'chik: Testimony of Avgosh Shamilova, January 8, 1998, in Danilova, *Iskhod gorskikh evreev*, p. 26; Nal'chik: "Nazis' Atrocities."

73 Essentuki and Zheleznovodsk: Testimony of Samuil Belenkov, August 10, 1943, GARF, 7021/17/4, p. 23; Statement of the doctor K. T. Gavrilova, 1943, GARF, 7021/17/6, p. 25.

74 Essentuki and Kislovodsk: Akt of the Commission of Essentuki, July 10, 1943, GARF, 7021/17/4, p. 1; Report of Moisei Evenson, Viktor Shklovskii, ed., [no date], YVA, P.21.2/1; Testimony of Fania Skliar, September 1975, YVA, 0.3/3934, p. 6.

75 Zheleznovodsk: Statement of T. Z. Kairov, approximately 1943, GARF, 7021/17/6, p. 4.

76 Elista, Kislovodsk, and Nal'chik: Report of ESC, GARF, 7021/8/26, pp. 10-11; Akt of the Commission of Kislovodsk, July 5, 1943, GARF, 7021/17/5, pp. 35-36; *Dokumenty obviniaiut, Sbornik materialov o chudovishnykh zverstvakh Germanskich vlastei na vremenno okkupirovannykh Sovetskikh territoriiakh*, 2nd ed., (Moscow: Gospolitizdat, 1945), pp. 140-142; Testimony of Avgosh Shamilova, January 8, 1998, in Danilova, *Iskhod gorskikh evreev*, p. 26.

77 Armavir and Essentuki: Akt of the Commission of Armavir, January 28, 1943, TsAMO RF, 51/958/52, pp. 91-92, courtesy of the USHMM; Akt of the Commission of Essentuki, July 10, 1943, GARF, 7021/17/4, p. 1.

78 Kislovodsk and Piatigorsk: Akt, July 5, 1943, GARF, 7021/17/5, pp. 35-36; Akt of the Commission of Piatigorsk, April-March 1943, GARF, 7021/17/3, p. 8.

79 Akt of the Commission of Essentuki, July 10, 1943, GARF, 7021/17/4, p. 1.

80 Essentuki and Nal'chik: Akt of the Commission of Essentuki, July 10, 1943, GARF, 7021/17/4, p. 1; Testimony of Avgosh Shamilova, January 8, 1998, in Danilova, *Iskhod gorskikh evreev*, p. 26.

communities.[81] They fared worse when either local collaborators or the Germans were involved in enforcing it.[82] Jews placed in small ghettos underwent the harshest treatment during forced labor, as their entire lives (before, during, and after the day's labor) were regulated by a vicious German administration.[83]

In the North Caucasus, the Germans widely resorted to exerting economic pressure on the Jews. Imposition of monetary indemnity (*kontributsiia*) on the Jewish communities was one such measure.[84] The price of indemnity was high (in Kislovodsk – 100,000 rubles, Cherkessk – 135,000 rubles, Mikoianshakhar – 500,000 rubles[85]). The required sum had nothing to do with the actual number of Jewish inhabitants of the town in question: In Kislovodsk, 2,000 Jews were registered, while there were 820 in Cherkessk and 129 in Mikoianshakhar. The enormous size of the indemnity can be explained by the German assumption that the Jewish population, which consisted mainly of the evacuees from big Soviet cities, was well-off.

The indemnity order was interwoven with other German steps aimed at dispossessing the Jews. The example of Kislovodsk underscores the point. Alongside the indemnity worth "100,000 rubles in cash," the German authorities demanded the Jewish committee to deliver "530 articles made of gold or silver, rings, watches, cigarette cases, 105 dozen silver spoons, 230 pairs of shoes, men's suits, coats, and carpets."[86] Usually "organized" plunder

81 Akt of the Commission of Piatigorsk, April-March 1943, GARF, 7021/17/3, p. 8; Akt of the Commission of Cherkessk, July 13, 1943, GARF, 702/17/12, pp. 68-69.

82 Nal'chik, Tikhoretsk: Testimony of Avgosh Shamilova, January 8, 1998, in Danilova, *Iskhod gorskikh evreev*, p. 26; Beliaev and Bondar', *Kuban' v gody Velikoi Otechestvennoi voiny, 1941-1945*, pp. 464-465.

83 Elista, Mikoianshakhar and Zheleznovodsk: Report of the ESC, GARF, 7021/8/26, pp. 10-11; Akt of the Commission of Mikoianshakhar, June 20, 1943, GARF, 7021/17/10, p. 195; Statement of T. Z. Kairov, approximately 1943, GARF, 7021/17/6, p. 4.

84 Cherkessk (?), Essentuki: "Urteil gegen Schlupper," Landesgericht Munich, I., YVA, TR.10/956, p. 63; Akt of the Commission of Essentuki, July 10, 1943, GARF, 7021/17/4, p. 1.

85 Commission of Kislovodsk, June 21, 1943, GARF, 7021/17/5, p. 39; Testimony of Ida Nikeeva, July 29, 1943, GARF, 7021/17/10, p. 204.

86 Akt, July 5, 1943, GARF, 7021/17/5, pp. 35-36.

took on the form of orderly arranged "requisitions" effected largely by means of the *Judenräte*[87] or under the pretext of legal searches of Jewish apartments for weapons or unregistered Jews.[88] It is noteworthy that there exists no record of "non-organized" plunder of Jewish property in the Caucasus. This is explained by a more stringent German policy of enforcing discipline in the Wehrmacht vis-à-vis the local population in Caucasian towns. In many localities, the Germans took away all Jewish property.[89] In other places, less valuable articles were allotted for the local policemen[90] and then sometimes distributed, sold, or left to the local population.[91]

In a few Caucasian towns, regardless of the size of the Jewish population, Jews were subjected to various forms of economic or political boycott. This was most comprehensive in Essentuki, where inscriptions were placed on the stores, saying: "No sale for Jews," or on commission shops and buyer-up (*skupochnyi*) shops,[92] saying: "We do not accept [goods] from Jews."[93] In Essentuki and Krasnodar, the Germans imposed a complete ban on the employment of Jews.[94] In contrast, in Piatigorsk the occupational boycott was only partial and more ideologically refined, i.e., "Jews were forbidden to carry out any paid work in organizations

87 Essentuki and Kislovodsk: Statement of Professor Vladimir Dik, June 27, 1943, GARF, 7021/17/4, p. 9; Report of Moisei Evenson, Viktor Shklovskii, ed., [no date], YVA, P.21.2/1.

88 Essentuki and Nal'chik: Testimony of Samuil Belenkov, August 10, 1943, GARF, 7021/17/4, p. 24; "Nazis' Atrocities."

89 Cherkessk and Mikoianshakhar: Akt of the Commission of Pregranenskii *raion*, June 28, 1943, in Boiko, *Stavropol'e v Velikoi Otechestvennoi voine 1941-1945 gg.*, p. 135; Testimony of Ida Nikeeva, July 29, 1943, GARF, 7021/17/10, p. 204.

90 Piatigorsk, Stavropol': Akt of the Commission of Piatigorsk, GARF, 7021/17/3, p. 8. Report of Abram Nankin in Grossman and Erenburg, *Chernaia kniga*, pp. 272-273

91 Elista and Essentuki: Statement of D. Babkina, July 20, 1943, GARF, 7021/8/27, p. 91; Testimony of Samuil Belenkov, August 10, 1943, GARF, 7021/17/4, p. 26.

92 These shops were created under Soviet rule in order to buy luxury goods from the local populations.

93 Akt of the Commission of Essentuki, July 10, 1943, GARF, 7021/17/4, p. 1.

94 Statement of the doctor Sokol'skii, June 30, 1943, June 30, 1943, GARF, 7021/17/4, p. 57(?); Krasnodarskii *krai*: Krinko, *Zhizn' za liniei fronta*, p. 104.

related to crafts and trade."[95] Occasionally the Jews were subjected to political boycott. When the mayor (*burgormistr*) of Krasnodar was "elected," the Germans inserted the provision that a candidate for the position should "be no younger than 25 years old, neither Communist nor Jewish."[96] There is also evidence that the Germans imposed a ban on Jews visiting public places in Kislovodsk.[97] In an even more localized initiative, there was a prohibition on the Jews entering the dancing club in Krasnodar.[98] Yet, on the whole, it should be emphasized that the boycott was far from a comprehensive and consistent policy in Caucasian towns. Rather, it seems that given the brevity of the pre-destruction period in the North Caucasus, the majority of Jewish population did not feel the boycott. However, it could still have influenced the public opinion towards the Jewish population.

The Germans sometimes employed segregation, another component of their restrictive policy towards the Jews in the Caucasus, amidst the background of general residence and movement restrictions. The German restriction policies were relatively lenient in the region, but there were several deviations from this pattern. In Essentuki, Jews were prohibited from changing apartments.[99] In Novorossiisk, Jewish houses and apartments were earmarked.[100] According to a Soviet report, in Essentuki the Jews were also banned from moving around the town.[101] It was only in Essentuki that the Jews were prohibited from moving away to other towns.[102] The Germans also introduced a curfew, which applied to everyone except for German-authorized personnel and

95 Akt of the Commission of Piatigorsk, March-April 1943, GARF, 7021/17/3, p. 8.

96 Beliaev and Bondar', *Kuban' v gody Velikoi Otechestvennoi voiny, 1941-1945*, p. 459.

97 Alexei Tolstoi, "Korichnevyi durman," *Pravda*, August 5, 1943.

98 Intelligence survey no. 6 of the NKVD Administration, September 12, 1942, in Beliaev and Bondar' eds., *Kuban' v gody Velikoi Otechestvennoi voiny, 1941-1945*, pp. 460-461.

99 Akt of the Commission of Essentuki, July 10, 1943, GARF, 7021/17/4, p. 1.

100 Questioning of Anna Alekseeva (1905), October 14, 1943, GARF, 7021/16/11, p. 77.

101 Alexei Tolstoi, "Korichnevyi durman," *Pravda*, August 5, 1943.

102 Akt of the Commission of Essentuki, July 10, 1943, GARF, 7021/17/4, p. 1.

Iona L'vovich Baumgolts (b. 1871) (right), a prominent doctor and author of a work on the impact of magnetic fields on human beings (1936), worked in St. Petersburg before the Bolshevik Revolution. During the Soviet period, he resided in Kislovodsk. He was shot alongside his sister, Avgustina Ionshtein (left), and other local Jews in September 1942. Courtesy: RHCA

was a part of the German population policy almost everywhere in the occupied territories. However, in this case, it is not clear whether the "general" curfew was meant to apply to everyone, or if this provision was applied specifically to the Jews.

2.1.3. Extermination and the aftermath

Jewish inhabitants of North Caucasian towns were ordered to assemble after a period ranging from one-two weeks and up to four months.[103] They were often threatened with severe

103 Krasnodar, Stavropol': Intelligence survey no. 21 of the NKVD Administration, October 6, 1942, in Beliaev and Bondar', *Kuban' v gody Velikoi Otechestvennoi voiny, 1941-1945,* p. 461; Report of Abram Nankin in Grossman and Erenburg, *Chernaia kniga*, pp. 272-273; Essentuki, Kislovodsk: Akt of the Commission of Essentuki, July 10, 1943, GARF, 7021/17/4, p. 1, in *Dokumenty obviniaiut,* pp. 140-142; Akt of the Commission of Cherkessk, July 13, 1943, GARF,

punishment for failure to comply with the order.[104] The Germans eagerly provided the pretext behind the assembly order in only one case: In Stavropol' it was announced that the assembly was due to "the necessity to resettle the Jews into the areas free of population owing to military operations."[105] Jews were required to leave their apartments intact and were permitted to take with them certain amounts of money, valuables, and personal possessions.[106] After the Germans ordered the Jews in Stavropol' to assemble with their permitted possessions, they were forbidden to leave the town on their own and were allowed to proceed only to the assembly point. This ban was to combat the possibility of Jews escaping the town, as the assembly order was issued one to two days in advance, allowing Jews potentially to have time to flee.[107]

The German administration normally proclaimed the order to assemble, although at rare times the local authorities or the Jewish Council issued it.[108] For the most part, the Germans intervened overtly only at the gathering points, which they did by placing armed guards to prevent Jews from leaving these locations.[109] The Germans enforced the assembly immediately and vigorously

702/17/12, pp. 68-69; Akt of the Commission of the resort of Teberda, July 5, 1943, GARF, 7021/17/7, pp. 4-5.

104 Essentuki, Stavropol'. Akt of the Commission of Essentuki. July 10, 1943, GARF, 7021/17/4, p. 1; Akt of the Commission of Stavropol', July 11, 1943, GARF, 7021/17/1, pp. 95-96.

105 Akt of the Commission of Stavropol', July 11, 1943, GARF, 7021/17/1, pp. 95-96.

106 Kislovodsk, Piatigorsk, Teberda: Testimony of Fania Skliar, September 1975, YVA, 0.3/3934, p. 7; Akt of the Commission of Piatigorsk, April-March 1943, GARF, 7021/17/3, p. 8; Akt of the Commission of Teberda, July 5, 1943, GARF, 7021/17/7, pp. 4-5.

107 Akt of the Commission of Stavropol', July 11, 1943, GARF, 7021/17/1, pp. 95-96.

108 Akt of the Commission of Essentuki, July 10, 1943, GARF, 7021/17/4, p. 1; Akt of the Commission of Piatigorsk, April-March 1943, GARF, 7021/17/3, p. 8; Cherkessk: "Strafsache gegen Schlupper," Der Untersuchungsrichter 115 Ks 6a-c/71, Vernehmungsniderschrift, Schlupper, December 14, 1971, YVA, TR.10/1081, p. 56; Krasnodar: Intelligence survey no. 21 in Beliaev and Bondar', *Kuban' v gody Velikoi Otechestvennoi voiny, 1941-1945*, p. 461.

109 Cherkessk, Novorossiisk: Akt of the Commission of Cherkessk, July 13, 1943, GARF, 702/17/12, pp. 68-69; Questioning of Anna Silina (1910), October 16, 1943, GARF, 7021/16/11, p. 28.

only in Teberda.[110] In larger towns, the Germans assembled the Jews at squares and then immediately marched them out towards execution sites.[111] In smaller towns, they herded Jews into one location and kept them there up to two days, usually without food or water, before driving them to extermination sites or placing them in gas vans.[112]

The Germans conducted killing operations in Caucasian towns throughout almost the whole occupation period. Annihilation of the Jewish population was constrained largely by the logistics necessary for the Germans to prepare the ground for the actions to be smoothly carried out (most specifically, by the redeployment of the *Einsatzgruppe* forces).[113] In August, killing operations began against the Jews residing in Stavropol' and Krasnodar, the most populous and presumably most important regional centers of the German-controlled Caucasus. On August 12 and 15, 1942, the Germans destroyed the biggest Jewish communities of Stavropol' (4,000 people altogether).[114] On August 21, they killed between 1,800 to more than 3,000 Jews in Krasnodar.[115] Hundreds of Jews

110 Akt of the Commission of Teberda, July 5, 1943, GARF, 7021/17/7, pp. 4-5.

111 Stavropol': Akt, July 14, 1943, GARF, 7021/17/1, pp. 3, 5.

112 Cherkessk, Essentuki: Akt of the Commission of Cherkessk, July 13, 1943, GARF, 702/17/12, pp. 68-69; Testimony of Samuil Belenkov, August 10, 1943, GARF, 7021/17/4, pp. 25-26.

113 The exceptional case of Teberda, where numerous Jewish doctors and medical workers were kept alive until December 1942, is dealt with in the section of the current chapter dealing with this professional group. The small community of Mikoianshakhar, numbering a few dozen Jews, which was also destroyed in December 1942, is too small to be regarded as a deviation from the German policy. Rather, because of the small number of the Jews in the town, it may be compared with the similar sized Jewish rural communities in the North Caucasus, some of which were annihilated in December 1942.

114 Untitled document, GARF, 7021/116/11a, p. 24.

115 Intelligence survey no. 21 of the NKVD Administration, October 6, 1942, in Beliaev and Bondar', *Kuban' v gody Velikoi Otechestvennoi voiny, 1941-1945*, p. 461; Akt of the Commission of Krasnodar, June 30, 1943, GARF, 7021/16/5, pp. 11-12, 14; Krasnodar trial, Military court of the North Caucasian Front, July 14-17, 1943, in *Dokumenty obviniaiut*, p. 104.

Dr. Yitzhak Arad gives credit to an estimate of 13,000 victims in Krasnodar, "of whom probably all were Jews." Arad, *The History of the Holocaust*, p. 535. This assessment seems to be an exaggeration; I am inclined to an estimate of more than 3,000 Jewish victims given by a local Russian researcher (albeit

residing in the smaller towns of Stavropol'skii *krai* were also exterminated in August 1942.[116]

In September 1942, the Germans wiped out the bulk of Caucasian Jewry. The destruction was primarily concentrated in four neighboring resort towns of Stavropol'skii *krai*: Essentuki, Kislovodsk, Minvody, and Piatigorsk. The Jews were all murdered at the same site near the Glass Workshop near Minvody. The total number of the victims approached 10,000 people.[117] On September 6, 2,800 Jews of Piatigorsk were murdered;[118] three days later, up to 2,000 Jews of Essentuki, 2,000 Jews of Kislovodsk, and 1,800 Jews of Minvody were killed.[119] On the same day, more than 300 Jews were annihilated in Elista, another part of the occupied Caucasus.[120] At the end of the month, over 800 Jews were exterminated in the town of Cherkessk.[121]

Thereupon, the pace of the annihilation of Jewry in Caucasian towns was constantly on the ebb. In October 1942, more than 1,000 Jews were murdered in the partly occupied harbor town

without any source): Elena Voitenko, "Kholokost na iuge Rossii v period Velikoi Otechestvennoi voiny (1941-1943 gg.)," (PhD diss., Stavropol'skii gosudarstvennyi universitet, 2005), p. 139.

116 Georgievsk, Nevinnomyssk: Akt of the Commission of Georgievsk, July 28, 1943, GARF, 7021/17/10, p. 65; Akt of the Commission of Nevinnomyssk, July 20, 1943, GARF, 7021/17/11, p. 17.

117 Akt of the local Commission on the investigation of the Nazi German atrocities, January 21, 1943, TsAMO RF, 51/958/52, p. 85, courtesy of the USHMM.

118 Akt of the Commission of Piatigorsk, GARF, 7021/17/3, p. 8; David Bergelson, "Who Will Pay for the Suffering of Israel? [News on the Destruction of Jews in the Territories of the Soviet Union that were Occupied by the Nazis]" (Hebrew), *Davar*, no. 5349, February 4, 1943, p. 1 [Source: Kuibishev, special telegram to *Davar*].

119 Akt of the Commission of Essentuki, July 10, 1943, GARF, 7021/17/4, p. 1; Kislovodsk: Akt of the Commission of the North Caucasian Front, January 13, 1943, TsAMO RF, 51/958/52, pp. 67-68, courtesy of the USHMM; Statement of Aleksei Sapunov, June 26, 1943, GARF, 7021/17/2, p. 11.

120 ESC unpublished report on Kalmykiia, [no date], GARF, 7021/116/149, p. 11; "And This is the First News" (Hebrew), *Davar*, no. 5366, February 24, 1943, p. 1.

121 Akt of the Commission of Cherkessk, July 13, 1943, GARF, 702/17/12, pp. 68-69; Igor' Mikhailov, *Okkupatsiia ili 160 dnei po germanskomu vremeni* (Stavropol': Servisshkola, 2007), pp. 48-50.

of Novorossiisk,[122] captured in early September, as well as more than 600 Jews in Kislovodsk and Essentuki (who were most likely brought there from other urban or rural places).[123] Some 600 Ashkenazi Jews were killed in November in the town of Nal'chik, seized in late October 1942.[124] Finally, the last large-scale wave of the actions swept the towns in the form of "mopping-up" operations in light of a possible German withdrawal from the North Caucasus. In December 1942, the last remaining Jewish communities of Mikoianshakhar and Teberda, numbering up to 350 people altogether,[125] were destroyed, as well a large number of Jewish women and girls in Minvody.[126]

Most of the Jews were killed by fire from automatic guns.[127] According to Soviet sources, the children were occasionally poisoned, a method of murder sometimes also applied elsewhere in the occupied Soviet areas.[128] In Nevinnomyssk and Cherkessk, Jews were killed by gas.[129] The sites of *Aktionen* varied from anti-tank trenches situated just outside the towns[130] to abandoned

122 Akt of the Commission of Novorossiisk, October 18, 1943, GARF, 7021/16/11, p. 1, YVA, M.33/306, pp. 56-57.

123 Letter by the painter L. N. Tarabukin and his wife D. R. Gol'dshtein to the writer Iu. Kalugin, 1943, YVA, M.35/25, p. 86.

124 Akt no. 98, GARF, 7021/7/109, p. 202; "Nazis' Atrocities"; "And This is the First News" (Hebrew), *Davar*, no. 5366, February 24, 1943, p. 1.

125 Akt of the Commission of Mikoianshakhar, June 20, 1943, GARF, 7021/17/10, p. 195; Akt of the Commission of Teberda, July 5, 1943, GARF, 7021/17/7, pp. 4-5; *Dokumenty obviniaiut*, pp. 163-164.

126 "And This is the First News" (Hebrew), *Davar*, no. 5366, February 24, 1943, p. 1.

127 Kislovodsk: Akt, July 5, 1943, GARF, 7021/17/5, pp. 35-36; See also, *Dokumenty obviniaiut*, pp. 140-142.

128 Elista and Kislovodsk: ESC unpublished report on Kalmykiia, [no date], GARF, 7021/116/149, p. 11; Akt no. 5, January 1943, "Iz billiutenia Nomer 2 o faktakh zlodeianii nemetsko-fashistskikh prestupnikov v techenie perioda okkupatsii Kalmykskoi ASSR," Political Department of the 28th Army, YVA, M.40. MAP/108, p. 1.

129 "Strafsache gegen Schlupper," Der Untersuchungsrichter 115 Ks 6a-c/71, Vernehmung des Angeschuldigten Rudolf Eschenbacher, December 21, 1971, YVA, TR.10/1081, p. 95; Akt of the Commission of Nevinnomyssk, July 20, 1943, GARF, 7021/17/11, p. 17.

130 Essentuki, Kislovodsk, and Nal'chik: Alexei Tolstoi, "Korichnevyi durman," *Pravda*, August 5, 1943; Akt no. 98, GARF, 7021/7/109, p. 202.

industrial or military facilities.[131] Usually they were heavily guarded, and most of the last-minute escape attempts were prevented.[132] Yet, some Jews managed to survive the actions.[133] The Germans conducted the majority of the killing operations, with "native" formations only rarely involved.[134] After the killing operations of August-September 1942, the Germans frequently used gas vans to murder smaller groups of Jews in the Caucasian towns.[135] Gas vans were also used to "cleanse" prisons[136] and to murder Jewish orphans selected from orphanages.[137]

After the actions in Caucasian towns, the Germans found Jews who were still hiding following all-encompassing security steps directed against the general population. However, due to the milder character of the occupation of the Caucasus, the Germans rarely adhered to this policy. Round-ups in Caucasian towns,[138] in which whole areas were cordoned off for house-to-house searches for Jews or other suspects, in the wake of the extermination action[139] were rare. Most of the hiding Jews

131 Elista and Minvody: Akt of the Commission of Minvody, July 15, 1943, GARF, 7021/17/2, p. 3; ESC unpublished report on Kalmykiia, [no date], GARF, 7021/116/149, p. 11.

132 Kislovodsk and Minvody: Akt, July 5, 1943, GARF, 7021/17/5, pp. 35-36; Statement of Nikolai Mikheev, July 8, 1943, GARF, 7021/17/2, p. 16.

133 Essentuki and Kislovodsk: Letter of L.N. Rubanenko to Il'ia Erenburg, October 6, 1944, YVA, P.21.3/41; Testimony of Fania Skliar, September 1975, YVA, 0.3/3934, p. 11.

134 Kislovodsk: Interrogation of Mikhail Fingerut, June 25, 1943, GARF, 7021/17/5, p. 31; See also Chapter 9, "The Local Population and the Holocaust in the North Caucasus."

135 Cherkessk and Teberda: Akt of the Commission of Cherkessk, July 13, 1943, GARF, 702/17/12, pp. 68-69; Testimony of Oleg Kurikhin in N.M. Frolov, *Znak sud'by: Vospominaniia i tvorchestvo zhertv natsyzma* (Moscow: Mysl', 2001), pp. 140-141.

136 Krasnodar and Stavropol': "Das Schwurgericht des Landesgerichts München I. Anklageschrift gegen Dr. Kurt Christmann, [no date], YVA, TR.10/890, p. 2; Akt of the Commission of Stavropol', July 3, 1943, GARF, 7021/17/1, p. 74.

137 Akt of the Commission of Teberda, July 5, 1943, GARF, 7021/17/7, p. 3.

138 Stavropol': "Strafsache gegen Walter Bierkamp," Auswertung der Vernehmungsprotokolle russischer Zeugen von Bl. 1/92-65/40 d. Akte. B. 7-8, Iwan D. ab Okt. 41 bei der Tataren-Komp, Woroschilowsk – K, YVA, TR.10/1147, p. 576.

139 Stavropol': "And This is the First News" (Hebrew), *Davar*, no. 5366, February 24, 1943, p. 1.

Holocaust memorial near Kislovodsk, 2010. Courtesy: RHCA

were detected as a result of denunciations.[140] On the whole, the nature of the German occupational regime in the Caucasus in comparison to that in other areas and its brevity in Caucasian towns presented some opportunities for persecuted Jews to

140 Kislovodsk, Krasnodar: Testimony of Faina Leina, [no date], GARF, 7021/17/206, p. 85; Krasnodar trial, Interrogation of Ivan Paramonov, June 26, 1943, Archive of the Federal Security Service of the Russian Federation (AFSB RF), H-16708, p. 657, courtesy of the USHMM.

Holocaust memorial plaque in Stavropol', 2009. Courtesy: RHCA

survive. The prompt withdrawal of the German forces from the region in late 1942 contributed to the rescue of a certain number of already detained people; in all probability, there were also Jews among them.[141]

141 Mozdok: Testimony of Alexander Guseev, After 1976, YVA, 0.3/6970, pp. 4-5.

2.2. Rural areas[142]

2.2.1. General concerns

On the whole, German attitudes towards the Jewish rural population ranged from the "carrot to the stick" approach, regardless of whether they were pursued by individual soldiers of Axis powers or representatives of the German administration. In the village of Naturbovo, superficial promises for security were given to Jews on an individual basis, as opposed to general declarations to the Jewish community as a whole. According to the wartime testimony of a Russian witness:

> My acquaintance, the tailor Khaim Mapilis, recalled to me that a Czech [apparently, Slovak – KF] from the German Army calmed him down. He said that the Germans killed solely profiteers, dealers (*gesheftmakhery*), and exploiters, whereas honest Jewish workers were not touched.[143]

In the village of Dzhiginka, the authorities made explicit pronouncements to the groups of hiding Jews, as illustrated by this citizen's claim that:

> Initially Jewish families went into hiding. Then it was announced that they would not be done any harm.[144]

In another village, polite German guards led the arrested Jews to believe up until the last moment that only resettlement was involved:

> [The guards] behaved in a very polite and attentive fashion. This calmed down the depressed and doomed people. It was said that the Germans had politely allowed the Jews to pack their possessions. Those who did not have enough bread

142 See Tables 9-13.

143 Interrogation of Klavdiia Parshikova, August 12, 1942, YVA, M.33/291, pp. 98-99.

144 Dzhiginka: Interrogation of Aleksandr Chebanenko, January 25, 1944, GARF, 7021/16/461, p. 94.

> [for a long way] were proposed to buy half a loaf of bread. Russian and German guards collected 2.50 rubles from those willing to do it and indeed brought and distributed bread. People were allowed to make breakfast and give food to the children.[145]

It is noteworthy that sometimes the German authorities sought to provide "convincing" reasons in order to account for the specifically Jewish orders – e.g., "these people are proficient in the German language and, therefore, have to be employed by the Germans."[146] Yet, in other places, the Germans did not hesitate to issue open threats. In the Aleksandriiskaia *stanitsa*, the Shekhet family, which was Jewish, was intimidated by frequenting German soldiers:

> During the night, the Germans entered their apartment, claiming that the Shekhets' days were numbered [*zhyt' vam ostalos' nedolgo*].[147]

In the *stanitsa* of Novo-Aleksandrovskaia, the Germans issued orders stipulating that non-compliance with registration would be severely punished. The order declared that "those evading the registration of the Jewish population would be punished severely. People who give shelter to the Jews will also be rendered accountable according to laws of the war period."[148] On the whole, the Germans were overconfident of the prospects for killing Jews in rural areas at any moment without being seriously hindered and, therefore, only rarely employed strict enforcement measures. On the other side of the coin, the destruction of Jewish life in rural areas was more overt and frequently involved physical maltreatment of Jews and "non-organized" plunder of their property.

145 "Molotov" *kolkhoz*: Statement of Suzanna Busilovskaia, August 2, 1943, GARF, 7021/17/11, p. 109.

146 Novozavedennoe: Statement of Anna Shlaen, 1943, GARF, 7021/17/11, p. 114.

147 Akt of the Commission of Aleksandriiskaia *stanitsa*, January 25, 1943, GARF, 7021/17/9, p. 12.

148 Akt of the Commission of Novo-Aleksandrovskaia *stanitsa*, June 24, 1943, GARF, 7021/17/11, p. 28.

When analyzing the Germans' tactics in "solving the Jewish Question" in the Caucasian rural areas, one basic fact should be borne in mind: The scarce German security and military presence in the vast Caucasian countryside was connected with a higher measure of reliance on collaborators. As a result, local headmen and policemen were actively involved in the killing of Jews. Nevertheless, when there were sufficient German troops they also took necessary precautions, such as cordoning off the assembly sites or transporting Jews in hermetically closed vehicles.[149]

2.2.2. From registration to killing operations

In the Caucasian rural areas, Jews were required to register in a few places. At times, German orders included explicit threats directed not only against the Jews who failed to register, but also against the local people who gave shelter to the Jews.[150] The registration of Jews was ordered primarily by the military administration.[151] Occasionally, after a relatively lengthy period of quiet had passed in some places, a second registration preceding the annihilation would be conducted.[152] In other places, only one order was issued, which provided for both the registration and the immediate assembly of the Jewish population.[153] Sometimes it was demanded that Jews wear identifying stars immediately upon having being registered.[154]

149 Petrovskii *raion* in Stavropol'skii *krai,* village of Rozhdenstvennskoe: Akt of the Commission of Petrovskii *raion*, July 10, 1943, GARF, 7021/17/1, p. 106; Statement of Evgeniia Penner, June 25, 1943, GARF, 7021/17/10, pp. 174-175.

150 Akt of the Commission of Novo-Aleksandrovskaia *stanitsa*, June 24, 1943, GARF, 7021/17/11, p. 28.

151 Akt of the Commission of Staro-Sherbinskaia *stanitsa*, September 1943, GARF, 7021/16/12, p. 195.

152 November 1942, village of Blagodatnoe: Akt of the Commission of Shpakovskii *raion*, July 30, 1943, GARF, 7021/17/12, p. 55.

153 Staro-Sherbinovskaia *stanitsa*; Korenovskaia *stanitsa*: Akt of the Commission of Korenovskaia *stanitsa*, April 15, 1943, GARF, 7021/16/461, p. 105.

154 Villages of Blagodatnoe and Zol'skoe: Akt of the Commission of Shpakovskii *raion*, July 30, 1943, GARF, 7021/17/12, p. 55; Akt no. 90 of the Republican Commission of the Kabardino-Balkar Republic, July 14, 1943, GARF, 7021/7/109, p. 186.

Other times, Jews were not required to register at all but only to wear identifying bands.[155]

The Germans widely employed forced labor of Jews in rural areas, primarily in collecting the harvest[156] and, to a much lesser extent, in military construction works[157] or humiliating cleaning jobs.[158] Their conditions during the forced labor depended on the extent of the German presence. When the Germans supervised Jewish labor, Jewish existence was made unbearable and involved physical maltreatment, the most difficult assignments, and critically unsanitary conditions, which resulted in a high mortality rate.[159] Jews faced very long working days and unrealizable production norms.[160] It was forbidden for the local population to give them food, and the Jews themselves were not supplied with any.[161] Conversely, Jews were better off when the local collaborators supervised their labor.[162]

The Germans and their local collaborators widely practiced the unrestrained plunder of Jewish property, in addition to orderly arranged "requisitions."[163] Judging by Soviet reports, the German

155 Labinskaia and Gul'kevichi *stanitsy*: Conversation with Mariia Doragan, June 4, 1943, YVA, M.33/298, p. 17; Interrogation of Anastasiia Gur (Kondrat'ev), May 15, 1944, GARF, 7021/16/435, p. 130.

156 Bekeshevskaia and Sovetskaia *stanitsy*: Akt of the Commission of Suvorovskii *raion*, July 26, 1943, GARF, 7021/17/12, p. 3; Akt of the Commission of Sovetskaia *stanitsa*, August 15, 1943, GARF, 7021/16/435, p. 184.

157 Akt of the Commission of Novo-Aleksandrovskaia *stanitsa*, June 24, 1943, GARF, 7021/17/11, p. 28.

158 Village of Vorontsovo-Aleksandrovskoe: Statement of Lidiia Brailovskaia, 1943, GARF, 7021/17/10, p. 33.

159 Akt of the Commission of Novo-Aleksandrovskaia *stanitsa*, June 24, 1943, GARF, 7021/17/11, p. 28; Akt of the Commission of the village of Menzhynskoe, June 27, 1943, GARF, 7021/17/10, pp. 155-156.

160 Village Menzhynskoe, Bekeshevskaia *stanitsa*: Akt of the Commission of the village of Menzhynskoe, June 27, 1943, GARF, 7021/17/10, pp. 155-156; Akt of the Commission of Suvorovskii *raion*, July 26, 1943, GARF, 7021/17/12, p. 3.

161 Bekeshevskaia *stanitsa*: Akt of the Commission of Suvorovskii *raion*, July 26, 1943, GARF, 7021/17/12, p. 3.

162 Sovetskaia *stanitsa*, and village of Troitskoe: Akt of the Commission of Sovetskaia *stanitsa*, August 15, 1943, GARF, 7021/16/435, p. 184; Testimony of German, GARF, 7021/8/27, p. 55.

163 Villages of Ol'giniskoe and Stepnoe: Statement of A. Kureshov, June 25, 1943,

military and security command tacitly approved a free-hand policy. This regarded not only those whose direct responsibility it was to "handle the Jewish Question" (i.e., the officers and soldiers of the *Einsatzgruppe* and *Kommandaturen*[164]), but also other sectors of the army, which had only casual contact with the Jewish population,[165] as well as local collaborators.[166] The German commanders were less concerned with local public opinion in the countryside. Thus, they turned a blind eye to the loose behavior of the Wehrmacht personnel assisted by the local collaborators who plundered the Jews' property. Besides, the German authorities also hoped to gain the sympathies of the local inhabitants by distributing the plundered Jewish property to those discriminated against under the Soviet regime.[167] Furthermore, in many cases the local population in the Caucasian rural areas was more ill-disposed towards Soviet power (and everything associated with it, including Jews) and was, therefore, more inclined to adopt a favorable stance towards the German onslaught against the Jews.[168]

Jews residing in North Caucasian villages were frequently

GARF, 7021/17/10, p. 162; Akt of the Commission of the village of Stepnoe, July 22, 1943, GARF, 7021/17/11, p. 147.

164 Aleksandriiskaia *stanitsa*, village of Sukhoe: Akt of the Commission of Aleksandriiskaia *stanitsa*, January 25, 1943, GARF, 7021/17/9, p. 12; Statements of the inhabitants of the village of Sukhoe, N. Zhdanova, A. Parashuk, O. Sankova, 1943, GARF, 7021/17/10, p. 137.

165 Izobil'nenskii *raion*, Stavropol'skii *krai*: Akt of the Commission of Izobil'nenskii *raion*, June 29, 1943, GARF, 7021/17/10, pp. 121-122.

166 Villages of Beluevskii (in Libkhnetskii *raion*) and Blagodatnoe: Statement of Nina Zaitseva, 1943, GARF, 7021/17/10, p. 166; Akt of the Commission of Shpakovskii *raion*, July 30, 1943, GARF, 7021/17/12, p. 55.

167 Clarification of the *Oberburgomistr* of Stavropol', Krivokhatskii, sent to the *starosta* of the village of Spitsevka about the property of the destroyed citizens, October 1942, in Valeriia Vodolazhskaia, Mariia Krivneva, and Nelli Mel'nik, eds., *Stavropol'e v period nemetsko-fashistskoi okkupatsyi (avgust 1942-ianvar' 1943): Dokumenty i materialy Komiteta po delam arkhivov Stavropol'skogo kraia, Gosudarstvennogo arkhiva Stavropol'skogo kraia, Tsentra dokumentatsii noveishei istorii Stavropol'skogo kraia* (Stavropol': Knizhnoe izdatel'stvo, 2000), p. 48.

168 Anlage zu II./Pol.Rgt. Einsatz- und Tätigkeitsbericht des Batallions für die Zeit vom 1.-31.8.1942. (Auszug aus dem KTB), September 12, 1942, RGVA: 1358/1/9, p. 106. See also, "Merkblatt für das Verhalten gegenüber kaukasischen Völkern," [no date], RGVA, 1323/2/263, p. 219.

subjected to physical maltreatment. Sometimes the local police used force in order to make the Jews deliver their property.[169] Occasionally, the only aim was to demean and to humiliate Jews.[170] The Jews who had been segregated from the rest of the population suffered especially systematic and brutal physical abuse, as opposed to those who were not.[171] The Wehrmacht soldiers,[172] special forces assigned to deal with the Jews,[173] and Romanian soldiers[174] raped Jewish women. Maltreatment, in general, was widely practiced during the actions.[175]

Occasionally, Jews residing in the Caucasian rural areas were subjected to movement and residence restrictions. Bans on Jewish employment[176] and their disfranchisement in many villages[177] were a symbolic encroachment on Jews' rights. In the village of

169 Village of Dubovo-Balkavskoe in Kursavskii *raion*, Stavropol'skii *krai*: Akt of the Commission of Dubovo-Balkavskoe, July 10, 1943, GARF, 7021/17/10, p. 149.

170 Aleksandriiskaia *stanitsa*, village of Novo-Alekseevskoe in Belorecheskii *raion*, Krasnodarskii *krai*: Akt of the Commission of Aleksandriiskaia, January 25, 1943, 7021/17/9, p. 12; Interrogation of Stepan Bogoslavskii, August 28, 1943, GARF, 7021/16/12, p. 141.

171 Akt of the Commission of Novo-Aleksandrovskaia *stanitsa*, GARF, 7021/17/11, p. 28; Akt of the Commission of Menzhynskoe, June 27, 1943, GARF, 7021/17/10, pp. 155-156.

172 Statements of inhabitants of the village of Izobil'noe, Isaak Umanskii, Raisa Sergo, Valentina Bystrova, Nataliia Rudenko, Evgeniia Maizetbert, Anna Zhernova, July 19, 1943, GARF, 7021/17/10, pp. 131-132.

173 Akt of the Commission of Suvorovskii *raion*, July 26, 1943, GARF, 7021/17/12, p. 2.

174 Krasnyi farm, unknown region: Report by the Intelligence Department of the Southern Headquarters of the Partisan Movement, "On Political Attitudes of the Population in the Temporarily Occupied by the Fascists Territories of the Crimea and the Caucasus," December 23, 1942, RGASPI, 69/1/1048, p. 8.

175 Villages of Novo-Alekseevskoe and Dzhiginka: Interrogation of Stepan Bogoslavskii (1903), August 28, 1943, GARF, 7021/16/12, p. 141; Testimony of Ol'ga Polonskaia (1903), May 1, 1962, YVA, 0.3/2246, p. 6.

176 Village of Blagodatnoe: Akt of the Commission of Shpakovskii *raion*, GARF, 7021/17/12, p. 55.

177 Village of Blagodatnoe: Akt of the Commission of Shpakovskii *raion*, July 30, 1943, GARF, 7021/17/12, p. 55; Krasnodarskii *krai*, villages of Bagovskaia, Gubskaia, Barakaevskaia, Novoslobodnaia, and Kastromskaia: Holdings of the Southern Headquarters of the Partisan Movement in Beliaev and Bondar', *Kuban' v gody Velikoi Otechestvennoi voiny, 1941-1945*, p. 469.

Bogdanovka, Jews were even banned from meeting and talking to their neighbors and from appearing in the streets after 6 p.m.[178] However, ghettoization was the most severe restriction on the Jews' freedom of movement.[179]

The Germans sought to register the entire rural population in the Caucasus in order to prevent the infiltration of Soviet agents.[180] German regulations contained a special emphasis on the necessity of pinpointing those who had arrived in the given locality after the outbreak of the war, i.e., evacuees or refugees:

> Heads of municipalities have to draw up... The second list encompasses strangers for a given locality who settled there after June 23, 1941. Jews and foreigners have to be specially marked.[181]

Local authorities in the villages were also required to state the nationality of the newcomers, with a particular emphasis on Jews.[182] This was followed by the annihilation of the registered Jews.[183]

As the Wehrmacht's control in the region deteriorated, more

178 Akt of the Commission of Bogdanovka, June 29, 1943, GARF, 7021/17/10, p. 158.

179 Village of Ol'giniskoe and Novo-Aleksandrovskaia *stanitsa* in Stavropol'skii *krai*: Akt of the Commission of Ol'giniskoe, June 26, 1943, GARF, 7021/17/10, p. 190; Akt of the Commission of Novo-Aleksandrovskaia *stanitsa*, June 24, 1943, GARF, 7021/17/11, p. 28.

180 Service instruction of the councilor of the military administration Dr. Mantel directed to heads of areas and towns on the establishment of the new order, Article 4, September 19, 1942, in Vodolazhskaia, Krivneva, and Mel'nik, *Stavropol'e v period nemetsko-fashistskoi okkupatsii (avgust 1942-ianvar' 1943)*, pp. 44-46. See also, letter-instruction of the *starosta* of the Aragir regional administration [*raiuprava*] sent to the *starosta* of the village of Mussa-Ardzhin, Stavropol'skii *krai*, October 27, 1942, GARF, 7021/17/14, p. 34.

181 Service instruction of the Councilor of the military administration Dr. Mantel directed to heads of areas and towns on the establishment of the new order, Article 4, September 19, 1942, in Vodolazhskaia, Krivneva, and Mel'nik, *Stavropol'e v period nemetsko-fashistskoi okkupatsii (avgust 1942-ianvar' 1943)*, pp. 44-46.

182 Ibid. See also, Akt of the Commission of Troitskoe, July 16, 1943, GARF, 7021/8/27, p. 54.

183 Villages of Troitskoe and Levokumskoe: Akt of the Commission of Troitskoe, July 16, 1943, GARF, 7021/8/27, p. 54; Memoirs of Peotr Belokurov, November 13, 2002, YVA, 0.33/6783, pp. 3-5.

stress was placed on their overstretched security and military personnel. As a result, the Germans began to demand that the rural authorities adhere to their requirements and that the local collaborationist administration strictly enforce the residence restrictions in Caucasian villages.[184] It is difficult to establish to what extent the German restrictive policy had a desirable effect (from the German point of view). Overall, this policy was applied at the advanced stage (2.5-3 months at the earliest) of the occupation. In many Caucasian villages there was no German presence, and handling the Jews was the responsibility of the local collaborators' administration. By November-December 1942, the collaborators became more susceptible to Soviet appeals to help fellow patriots and threats against anyone rendering aid to Germans. Therefore, it may be cautiously suggested that after this shift in local attitudes in the late fall of 1942, the Jews had some chances for finding shelter in the Caucasian countryside, or at least of not being denounced or killed (that is, if they had succeeded in surviving up to that point).

2.2.3. Extermination and the Aftermath

Authorities ordered Jews in Caucasian villages to present themselves at the assembly points, which were mainly in public buildings, such as schools[185] or posts of the *Kommandaturen*.[186] The assembly order was occasionally announced personally to Jews

184 Letter-instruction of the *starosta* of the Aragir regional administration [*raiuprava*] sent to the *starosta* of the village of Mussa-Ardzhin, Stavropol'skii *krai*, October 27, 1942, GARF, 7021/17/14, p. 34; Directive of the *starosta* of the village of Medvezh'e to the chairman of "*Vtoraia piatiletka*" *kolkhoz* on the registration of the arriving population, December 2, 1942, in Vodolazhskaia, Krivneva, and Mel'nik, *Stavropol'e v period nemetsko-fashistskoi okkupatsii (avgust 1942-ianvar' 1943)*, p. 56.

185 Villages of Menzhynskoe and Bogdanovka: Minutes of the Plenary meeting of the Ordzhonikidzevskii District Committee of the VKP(b) on the terror of the occupiers in the occupied territory and their plans to use lands of *kolkhozy* and *sovkhozy*, March 9, 1943, in Vodolazhskaia, Krivneva, and Mel'nik, *Stavropol'e v period nemetsko-fashistskoi okkupatsii (avgust 1942-ianvar' 1943)*, p. 81.

186 Villages of Stepnoe and Starominskaia: Akt of the Commission of Stepnoe, July 22, 1943, GARF, 7021/17/11, p. 147; Akt of the Commission of Starominskii *raion*, December 12, 1943, YVA, M.33/302, p. 32.

after they were summoned to a *Kommandatur*,[187] but was more often proclaimed as a community-wide order.[188] Sometimes the orders contained stipulations, such as the requirement to "perform permanent work,"[189] "resettlement,"[190] or "evacuation into the deep rear."[191] Occasionally the German forces skipped most of the stages preceding assembly, and ordered the Jews to assemble almost immediately upon their arrival in the area.[192]

The *Kommandaturen* usually proclaimed the assembly order.[193] The Germans rarely used enforcement measures to ensure that Jews complied with the order, particularly to ensure that they did so willingly.[194] After the assembly, the Jews were isolated for some time and then marched out to be killed – usually in the immediate vicinity of the village.[195] Jewish women were occasionally raped during the killing operations.[196] On the whole, during the Holocaust in the Caucasian rural areas, the small German forces carried out this final stage in their

187 Akt of the Commission of Aleksandriiskaia *stanitsa*, January 25, 1943, GARF, 7021/17/9, p. 12.

188 Borguevskii rural council: Akt of the Commission of Suvorovskii *raion*, July 26, 1943, GARF, 7021/17/12, p. 2.

189 Village of Soldatsko-Aleksandrovskoe: Akt of the Commission of Soldatsko-Aleksandrovskii *raion*, July 17, 1943, GARF, 7021/17/11, p. 112. Since this was a part of the German camouflage, it had to be regarded as a promise of a permanent source of wages and, most importantly, food provision awarded for permanent work.

190 Otradnenskaia *stanitsa*, Stepnoe: Akt of the Commission of Otradnenskii *raion*, Krasnodarskii *krai*, July 6, 1944, GARF, 7021/16/464, p. 19; Akt of the Commission of Stepnoe, July 22, 1943, GARF, 7021/17/11, p. 147.

191 Starominskaia *stanitsa*: Akt of the Commission of Starominskii *raion*, December 12, 1943, YVA, M.33/302, p. 32.

192 Labinskaia *stanitsa*: Conversation with Mariia Doragan, June 4, 1943, YVA, M.33/298, p. 17.

193 Villages of Bogdanovka and Stepnoe: Akt of the Commission of Bogdanovka, June 29, 1943, GARF, 7021/17/10, p. 158; Akt of the Commission of Stepnoe, July 22, 1943, GARF, 7021/17/11, p. 147.

194 Akt of the Commission of Bogdanovka, June 29, 1943, GARF, 7021/17/10, p. 158.

195 Borguevskii rural council: Akt of the Commission of Suvorovskii *raion*, July 26, 1943, GARF, 7021/17/12, p. 2.

196 Ladozhskii *raion*: Akt of the Commission of Ladozhskaia *stanitsa*, February 1, 1943, YVA, M.33/292, p. 30.

annihilation of the Jews rather smoothly, as compared to the previous stages.

Jews were exterminated in Caucasian villages throughout the entire period of the German occupation of the region.[197] In the initial phase of the occupation, smaller groups of Jews, in particular, were targeted.[198] However, sizeable groups were affected, as well.[199] The initial destruction affected all areas but only some villages. In these cases, the extermination of the Jews was usually all-encompassing. However, Jews living in other, sometimes even neighboring, localities were spared, or only partly affected by the German murderous policy.[200] A certain number of Jews found themselves captured in the war-stricken zone of the Stalingrad region to the north of the North Caucasus; they were brought to the Caucasus (apparently because no SS troops operated in the Stalingrad region) and executed there.[201]

The mass murder was intensive in the first weeks following the German occupation (August 1942).[202] Sometimes the Germans would occupy a locality for some period, leave, and then return later. In many cases, the German forces destroyed the Jewish population upon their first arrival in the village. The

197 See Tables 9-13.

198 Stavropol'skii *krai*, village of Alekseevka — 26 Jews; Burlazkii *raion* — 29 Jews; village of Don-Balka — 17 Jews: Akt of the Commission of Alekseevka, June 25, 1943, GARF, 7021/17/10, p. 9; Akt of the Commission of Dovsunii country council, July 18, 1943, GARF, 7021/17/10, p. 15; Akt of the Commission of Don-Balka, July 30, 1943, GARF, 7021/17/10, p. 80.

199 Village of Donskoe — 112 Jews: Akt of the Commission of Trunovskii *raion*, July 30, 1943, GARF, 7021/17/12, p. 39.

200 Krasnodarskii *krai*, village of Uspenskoe; Labinskaia *stanitsa*: Akt of the Commission of Uspenskoe, May 11, 1944, GARF, 7021/16/465, p. 259; Conversation with Mariia Doragan, June 4, 1943, YVA, M.33/298, p. 17.

201 Akt of the Commission of village of Plodovitoe, Maloderbetovskii *ulus*, Kalmytskaia ASSR, September 21, 1943, in Shaldanova, "Kholokost na territorii Kalmykii," p. 175. See also, Gert C. Lübbers, "Die 6. Armee und die Zivilbevölkerung von Stalingrad," *Vierteljahrshefte für Zeitgeschichte* 54, no. 1 (2006): pp. 110-111.

202 Villages of Alekseevka and Uspenskoe: Akt of the Commission of Alekseevka, GARF, 7021/17/10, p. 9; Akt of the Commission of Uspenskoe, GARF, 7021/16/465, p. 259.

extermination of the Jews was usually immediate.[203] It was rarely delayed, but when it was, it was for only some days – during which time the Jews were usually imprisoned.[204] During these first few occupational weeks, almost all of the "formal" stages preceding the physical annihilation (i.e., registration, forced labor, etc.) were skipped. It was during this period that masses of Jews who attempted to escape but were caught by the advancing German troops were killed. German execution squads usually carried out the exterminations.[205]

In September-October 1942, hundreds of Jews were murdered, destroying the bulk of the rural Jewish rural population.[206] The pace of the destruction decreased in November, but in December 1942 the North Caucasian villages were swept up in a new wave of mass murders. Like in the towns, it consisted of the last-minute mopping-up of the whole region (on the eve of the possible German withdrawal from the Caucasus) and the cleansing of all undesirable elements, including Jews. Remnants of the legally registered Jewry, such as inmates of camps[207] and those detected as a result of intensified searches, were killed during the German retreat from the region in January 1943.[208]

In most cases, the Germans only involved their own forces. They destroyed the Jews by shooting them,[209] while children were sometimes given poison.[210] The use of gas vans was extensive throughout the whole occupation period and

203 Villages of Dovsun and Don-Balka: Akt of the Commission of the Dovsun country council, GARF, 7021/17/10, p. 15; Akt of the Commission of Don-Balka, July 30, 1943, GARF, 7021/17/10, p. 80.

204 Akt of the Commission of Uspenskoe, May 11, 1944, GARF, 7021/16/465, p. 259.

205 Village of Uspenskoe: Ibid.

206 See Tables 9-13.

207 Goriachevskaia *stanitsa*: Interrogation of Vasilii Miroshnichenko (1877), June 24, 1943, GARF, 7021/17/10, p. 74.

208 "Kirov" *kolkhoz*: Akt of the Commission of "Kirov" *kolkhoz*, January 15, 1943, GARF, 7021/17/11, p. 151.

209 Akt of the Commission of Arzyrskii *raion*, June 28, 1943, GARF, 7021/17/9, p. 49; Akt of the Commission of Arkhangel'skii *raion*, July 20, 1943, GARF, 7021/17/9, p. 50.

210 Udobnenskaia *stanitsa*, memoirs of Mikhail Bugakov, 2005, YVA, 0.33/7074.

thousands of Jews were killed in this way in August,[211] September,[212] November,[213] and December 1942.[214] The Germans rarely used local collaborators in the extermination actions,[215] but they proved indispensable during the "post-action" phase when they revealed hiding Jews.[216]

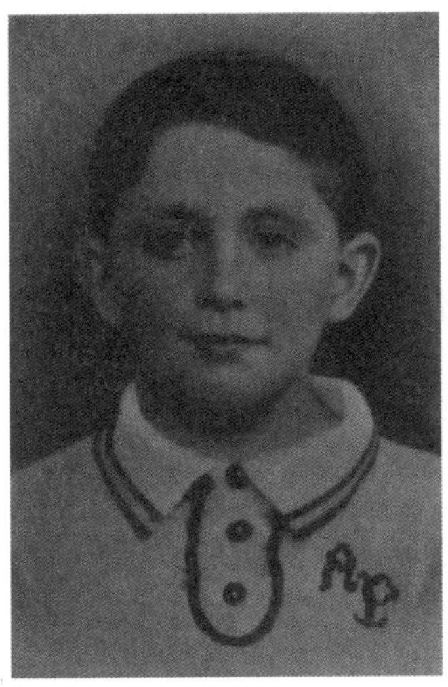

Musia (Abram) Pinkenzon was born in 1930 in Balti, Romania; the USSR annexed the area in 1940. After the German invasion, Abram's family fled to Ust'-Labinskaia *stanitsa* in Krasnodarskii *krai.* Abram was a talented violinist. He was also a member of the Communist organization for children (*pionery*). On December 15, 1942, when 387 Jews from Ust'-Labinskaia *stanitsa* were brought to execution he began to play "The International" (Bolshevik anthem) on the violin and was immediately shot. In the Soviet Union, Musia (Abram) Pinkenzon became a symbol of the Soviet resistance. An impressive monument dedicated to him was erected on the site of his murder during the Soviet era. Courtesy: RHCA

211 Akt of the Commission of Trunovskii *raion*, July 30, 1943, GARF, 7021/17/12, p. 39.

212 Akt of the Commission of Petrovskii *raion*, July 10, 1943, GARF, 7021/17/1, p. 106; Akt of the Commission of Staro-Mar'evskii *raion*, July 23, 1943, GARF, 7021/17/11, p. 125.

213 Akt of the Commission of Trunovskii *raion*, July 30, 1943, GARF, 7021/17/12, p. 39; Akt of the Commission of Shpakovskii *raion*, July 30, 1943, GARF, 7021/17/12, p. 55.

214 Akt of the Commission of Spitsevskii *raion*, June 28, 1943, GARF, 7021/17/11, p. 119; Akt signed by the inhabitants of the village of Spitsevka, January 20, 1943, TsAMO RF, 51/958/52, p. 80, courtesy of the USHMM.

215 Report on the partisan activity by the Secretary of District Committee of the VKP(b) Mikhail Suslov, Top Secret, October 25, 1942, RGASPI, 69/1/619, page illegible; Akt of the Commission of Dubovo-Balkavskoe, July 10, 1943, GARF, 7021/17/10, p. 149.

216 Statement of Evdokiia Bakaushina, 1943, GARF, 7021/17/11, p. 90. See also, Akt of the Commission of Neftegorskii *raion*, November 30, 1943, YVA, M.33/302, p. 6.

In summation, it may be said the Germans' permanent presence in the Caucasian rural localities (especially in the smaller ones) presented some chances for the persecuted Jews to survive, due to the irregular and chaotic nature of that presence. However, in order to obtain a clear picture, the discussion on the subject must also consider attitudes of the local people to the Jewish plight, as it was the local population that administered most of the Jews' affairs in the North Caucasian villages[217] (see Chapter 9, "The Local Population and the Holocaust in the North Caucasus").

3. Jewish Councils, Ghettos, and Camps

In the North Caucasus, Jewish Councils were set up in the towns with the largest Jewish communities: Essentuki, Kislovodsk, Krasnodar, and Stavropol'.[218] In Cherkessk and Novorossiisk, their functions were assigned to a single person, the *starosta*.[219] *Judenräte* were set up soon after the beginning of the occupation.[220] Occasionally, the Germans explained this by citing the need "to protect the interests of the Jewish population" (Stavropol'[221]), "to ensure the proper

217 See Chapter 9, "The Local Population and the Holocaust in the North Caucasus."

218 Essentuki, Kislovodsk, Krasnodar: Akt of the Commission of Essentuki, July 10, 1943, GARF, 7021/17/4, p. 1; V. Karl, "Destruction of the Caucasian Jewry" (Hebrew), (Descriptions of the Soviet writer Alexei Tolstoi on the basis of the eyewitnesses of the anti-Jewish atrocities), *Ha-tsofe*, no. 1842, January 26, 1944, p. 3; Interrogation of Nikolai Poznanskii, January 10, 1944, GARF, 7021/16/462, p. 205.

219 Akt of the Commission of Cherkessk, July 13, 1943, GARF, 702/17/12, pp. 68-69; Memorandum of the command of the Krasnodar group [*kust*] of partisan detachments, October 1942 (?), Center of Documentation of the Contemporary History of Krasnodarskii *krai* (TsDNIKK), 4373/1/35, pp. 62-66, in Beliaev and Bondar', *Kuban' v gody Velikoi Otechestvennoi voiny, 1941-1945*, p. 557.

220 With the exception in Novorossiisk, where the establishment of the *Judenrat* was announced more than one month later after the Germans' entry. This development can likely be explained by the fact that the town was only partly seized by the Wehrmacht, and the protracted warfare inside of it never ceased. Akt of the Commission of Novorossiisk, October 18, 1943, GARF, 7021/16/11, p. 1, YVA, M.33/306, pp. 56-57.

221 Report of Abram Nankin in Grossman and Erenburg, *Chernaia kniga*, pp. 272-273.

arrangement of the Jewish community" (Krasnodar[222]), or even "to improve the life [*byt*] of the Jews and to enable them to trade" (Novorossiisk[223]). *Judenräte* in Caucasian towns were a convenient instrument in German hands for a smooth conduction of the whole complex of anti-Jewish measures, from registration of the Jewish population[224] to assigning forced labor.[225] Finally, it is via Jewish Councils that Jews were squeezed of their property[226] and forced to assemble.[227]

The *Judenräte* members were appointed in accordance with the explicit directives of the German command.[228] The profile of an average member of a Jewish Council in the Caucasus was as follows: He was middle-aged male Caucasian Jew (not evacuee) and was a doctor or lawyer by profession.[229] In most cases, he was rather popular in his community.[230] The Germans did not single out the *Judenräte* members for special treatment. The only relevant evidence for Essentuki concerns one member of the *Judenrat* and indicates that he performed forced labor like ordinary Jews, was severely punished for non-compliance with the German order,[231]

222 Interrogation of Nikolai Poznanskii, January 10, 1944, GARF, 7021/16/462, p. 205.

223 Akt of the Commission of Novorossiisk, October 18, 1943, GARF, 7021/16/11, p. 1.

224 Essentuki, Krasnodar: Akt of the Commission of Essentuki, July 10, 1943, GARF, 7021/17/4, p. 1; Statement of Anna Sokolitskaia-Vasser, January 11, 1944, GARF, 7021/16/462, p. 204.

225 Akt of the Commission of Cherkessk, July 13, 1943, GARF, 702/17/12, pp. 68-69; Akt of the Commission of Piatigorsk, GARF, 7021/17/3, p. 8.

226 Kislovodsk and Piatigorsk: Akt of the Commission of Kislovodsk, June 21, 1943, GARF, 7021/17/5, p. 39; Akt of the Commission of Piatigorsk, GARF, 7021/17/3, p. 8.

227 Krasnodar: Intelligence survey no. 21 of the NKVD Administration, October 6, 1942, in Beliaev and Bondar', *Kuban' v gody Velikoi Otechestvennoi voiny, 1941-1945*, p. 461.

228 Essentuki and Krasnodar: Akt of the Commission of Essentuki, July 10, 1943, GARF, 7021/17/4, p. 1; Interrogation of Nikolai Poznanskii, January 10, 1944, GARF, 7021/16/462, p. 205.

229 Kislovodsk and Novorossiisk: *Dokumenty obviniaiut*, pp. 140-142; Akt of the Commission of Novorossiisk, October 18, 1943, GARF, 7021/16/11, p. 1.

230 Essentuki, Kislovodsk: Testimony of Raisa Kogan, June 29, 1943, GARF, 7021/17/4, p. 12; Report of Moisei Evenson, Viktor Shklovskii, ed., [no date], YVA, P.21.2/1.

231 Testimony of Samuil Belenkov, August 10, 1943, GARF, 7021/17/4, p. 23.

and was threatened with execution provided further German demands were not met.[232] The only evidence for privileged treatment of the *Judenräte* members is the allocation of a special coach for them during the deportation from the Kislovodsk railway station.[233] This clearly stands out, but cannot be corroborated by other sources.

In the unique case of Essentuki, the Germans allowed the *Judenrat* to pursue activities in the medical and social fields, albeit only for several days.[234] A medical commission was established under the auspices of the *Judenrat*, which examined the patients and, if need be, directed them to a Jewish hospital.[235] Only in Essentuki was the Jewish Council permitted to establish a hostel for sick and homeless Jews.[236] A commission for social affairs handled the requests of Jewish refugees who flocked to the town from the neighboring villages.[237] Lastly, the *Judenrat* in Essentuki rationed out bread to the Jews who performed forced labor.[238]

In the North Caucasus, the policy of confining Jews to ghettos was applied only to a few of the towns containing medium- (several hundreds) and small-sized (up to one hundred people) Jewish populations.[239] In the ghettos, the Jews were placed in separate locations hardly fit for human beings, and were forbidden to go outside without the authorization of the Germans or local administration unless they were sent to perform forced labor.[240] Jewish Councils were not involved in running the ghettos: They simply did not exist in these towns. The life of the ghettoized Jews was regulated solely by the Germans. The ghetto inmates did not

232 Ibid.

233 Alexei Tolstoi, "Korichnevyi durman," *Pravda*, August 5, 1943, in Al'tman, *Zhertvy nenavisti*, p. 278.

234 Testimony of Samuil Belenkov, August 10, 1943, GARF, 7021/17/4, p. 24.

235 Statement of Aleksandr Gontov, June 30 1943, GARF, 7021/17/4, p. 61.

236 Testimony of Samuil Belenkov, August 10, 1943, GARF, 7021/17/4, p. 24.

237 All the testimonies likely refer to the same commission. Statement of Aleksandr Gontov, June 30 1943, GARF, 7021/17/4, p. 61.

238 Testimony of Samuil Belenkov, August 10, 1943, GARF, 7021/17/4, p. 24.

239 Elista and Zheleznovodsk: Report of the ESC, GARF, 7021/8/26, pp. 10-11; Akt of the Commission of Zheleznovodsk, July 12, 1943, GARF, 7021/17/6, p. 1.

240 Cherkessk and Elista: Akt of the Commission of Cherkessk, July 13, 1943, GARF, 702/17/12, pp. 68-69; Report of the ESC, GARF, 7021/8/26, pp. 10-11.

work in industrial production but only in humiliating jobs, such as cleaning lavatories and sweeping streets.[241] There were no provisions in return for their labor. In order to survive, the Jews had to sell their possessions and rely on handouts from the local people when they went out to perform forced labor. As a result, the Jews suffered from terrible undernourishment.[242] In almost all the ghettos in the North Caucasus, Jews were subjected to physical maltreatment and continual plunder of their property.[243] Almost all the ghettos were liquidated during the great wave of extermination in August-September 1942.[244]

4. Special Cases

4.1. The medical domain

This section examines two cases: German policies towards the Jewish patients of hospitals and towards medical workers (doctors, nurses, etc.) of Jewish nationality in the Caucasus. The Soviet evacuation policy benefited these groups, and, as a result, many Jews belonging to them found themselves in the North Caucasus.

241 Mikoianshakhar – 1st ghetto, Zheleznovodsk: Akt of the Commission of Mikoianshakhar, June 20, 1943, GARF, 7021/17/10, p. 195; Statement of T. Z. Kairov, approximately 1943, GARF, 7021/17/6, p. 4.

242 Akt of the Commission of Mikoianshakhar, June 20, 1943, GARF, 7021/17/10, p. 195.

243 Elista, Mikoianshakhar, Zheleznovodsk: Report of the ESC, GARF, 7021/8/26, pp. 10-11; Akt of the Commission of Mikoianshakhar, June 20, 1943, GARF, 7021/17/10, pp. 195-196; Akt of the Commission of Zheleznovodsk, July 12, 1943, GARF, 7021/17/6, pp. 1-2.

244 Akt of the Commission of Cherkessk, July 13, 1943, GARF, 702/17/12, pp. 68-69; Report of the ESC, no later than September 10, 1943, GARF, 7021/8/26, pp. 10-11; Akt of the Commission of Mikoianshakhar, June 20, 1943, GARF, 7021/17/10, p. 196; Statement of T. Z. Kairov, 1943 (?), GARF, 7021/17/6, p. 4. It should be mentioned that Dr. Il'ia Al'tman claims that there was also a ghetto in Essentuki, which initially contained 2,000 Jews and by the end of its existence in October 1942 some 500 people. However, he does not quote the source on which he based this statement. (Al'tman, *Zhertvy nenavisti*, p. 97). For my part, I was unable to reveal any information concerning the ghetto in Essentuki. In Mikoianshakhar, one of two ghettos existed until December 1942. Akt of the Commission of Mikoianshakhar, June 20, 1943, GARF, 7021/17/10, p. 195.

The Soviets generally placed Jewish and non-Jewish patients, as well as Jewish medical personnel, from the evacuated hospitals in the large towns of Stavropol' and Krasnodar or in the resort center of Teberda, apparently on medical grounds (e.g., more developed infrastructure, etc.).[245] Many of these institutions, as well as the Caucasian hospitals (e.g., in Novo-Aleksandrovskaia *stanitsa*), failed to evacuate in July-August 1942.

The Germans did not spare the Jewish patients of the hospitals in the Caucasus. A special procedure usually took place, which included the selection and killing of specifically Jewish patients. Once German representatives arrived at a hospital, they demanded the administration of the hospitals to produce the list of patients, claiming the need to dispatch the Jews to a specially designated hospital.[246] In the late period of the occupation, the Germans no longer concealed their intentions for the Jewish patients. One Jewish patient was killed on the spot by a German guard as he tried to escape from the mental hospital in Krasnodar during an arrest conducted on December 18, 1942.[247] During the late occupational period, arrested Jewish patients were harshly treated in front of the hospital personnel.[248] After consulting the administration's list, the Germans selected the Jews and took them away.[249] The Jewish patients of hospitals were often killed by means of gassing.[250]

245 See Table 15, "Evacuation of children's homes and medical institutions from the Crimea into the North Caucasus as of 1942."

246 Statement of the workers of the Stavropol' Medical Institute, July 12, 1943, GARF, 7021/17/1, p. 79.

247 Akt of the Commission of Krasnodar, January 21, 1944, GARF, 7021/16/462, p. 88.

248 Akt of the Commission of Teberda, July 5, 1943, GARF, 7021/17/7, p. 3.

249 Stavropol', Novo-Aleksandrovskaia *stanitsa*: Statement of the workers of the Stavropol' Medical Institute, July 12, 1943, GARF, 7021/17/1, p. 79; Akt of the Commission of Novo-Aleksandrovskaia *stanitsa*, June 24, 1943, GARF, 7021/17/11, p. 28.

250 Teberda, Novo-Aleksandrovskaia *stanitsa*: Akt of the Commission of Teberda, July 5, 1943, GARF, 7021/17/7, p. 3; Akt of the Commission of Novo-Aleksandrovskaia *stanitsa*, June 24, 1943, GARF, 7021/17/11, p. 28.

Such actions were conducted either simultaneously with[251] or several days after the destruction of the bulk of the Jewish community in the respective localities.[252] If not then, it happened at the very end of the occupation period.[253] The German actions covered all medical institutions in the region and included general,[254] children's,[255] and mental hospitals.[256] In mental hospitals, all of the patients—not only Jews—were killed.[257]

In the occupied Soviet territories, the Germans occasionally exempted Jewish medical personnel from destruction due to the need to maintain satisfactory medical conditions. Yet, the fact that Caucasian towns were mainly spared from heavy fighting and resulting devastation,[258] possibly due to the timing of the German conquest (summer) and generally mild climate, usually led the Germans to conclude that the sanitary conditions in the region were satisfactory and did not necessitate the use of Jewish medical workers. Therefore, the German policy towards the Jewish

251 Krasnodar—1st case, August 22; Stavropol'—August 14: Akt of the Commission of Krasnodar, February 22, 1943, GARF, 7021/16/5, p. 5; Testimony of Abram Konevskii, July 3, 1943, GARF, 7021/17/1, p. 67.

252 Novo-Aleksandrovskaia *stanitsa* – late September: Akt of the Commission of Novo-Aleksandrovskaia *stanitsa*, June 24, 1943, GARF, 7021/17/11, p. 28.

253 Krasnodar, 2nd case – December 18; Teberda – December 22: Akt of the Commission of Krasnodar, January 21, 1944, GARF, 7021/16/462, p. 88; Akt of the Commission of Teberda, July 5, 1943, GARF, 7021/17/7, p. 3.

254 Stavropol'—unknown number; Novo-Aleksandrovskaia *stanitsa*—541 people, mostly Jews: Testimony of Abram Konevskii, July 3, 1943, GARF, 7021/17/1, p. 67; Statement of the workers of the Stavropol' Medical Institute, July 12, 1943, GARF, 7021/17/1, p. 79; Akt of the Commission of Novo-Aleksandrovskaia *stanitsa*. June 24, 1943, GARF, 7021/17/11, p. 28.

255 Teberda—54 children: Akt of the Commission of Teberda, July 5, 1943, GARF, 7021/17/7, p. 3.

256 Krasnodar – 1st case, 320 people, including non-Jews; 2nd case: unknown number: Akt of the Commission of Krasnodar, February 22, 1943, GARF, 7021/16/5, p. 5; Akt of the Commission of Krasnodar, January 21, 1944, GARF, 7021/16/462, p. 88.

257 Akt of the Commission of Krasnodar, February 22, 1943, GARF, 7021/16/5, p. 5; Akt of the Commission of Krasnodar, January 21, 1944, GARF, 7021/16/462, p. 88.

258 With the exception of Nal'chik and Stavropol': Akt no. 97 of the Commission of the Kabardino-Balkarsk Republic, GARF, 7021/7/109, p. 200; Belikov, *Okkupatsiia*, pp. 92-93.

medical workers did not differ from the one applied to other Jews: They were subjected to persecutions[259] and then killed altogether.[260] Nevertheless, the Germans appeared to recognize the prominent position of this group and the respect they enjoyed among their fellow Jews by assigning them to serve as members and heads of the *Judenräte* in many of the North Caucasian towns.[261]

4.2. Mixed couples

In the North Caucasus, more than one pattern of the German policy towards mixed couples and their offspring at the stages of their registration and assembly is observable. Sometimes the Germans declared their intentions immediately. In Stavropol', where the procedures of registration and assembly coincided, mixed couples were clearly mentioned in the first (and the only) German proclamation addressed to the Jews:

> These measures [the assembly order – KF] apply to the families in which the husband is Jewish, and the wife is non-Jewish. They do not apply to those families in which only the wife is Jewish.[262]

In contrast, in Kislovodsk, where the destruction was not immediate, various mixed families were exempted from the obligation to assemble.[263] In the villages, only non-Jewish spouses were exempted from the registration and assembly, whereas their

259 Essentuki: Statement of the doctor Sokol'skii, June 30, 1943, GARF, 7021/17/4, p. 57(?).

260 Stavropol', Teberda: Document of the Stavropol' Medical Institute, GARF, 7021/17/294, p. 7. List of 94 names of the employees of the Teberda resort who were shot on December 14, 1942. The report was drawn up no later than January 13, 1943, GARF, 7021/17/7, pp. 9-11.

261 Piatigorsk, Novorossiisk: Intelligence digest of NKVD administration of Ordzhonikidzevskii *krai*, December 17, 1942, in Vodolazhskaia, Krivneva, and Mel'nik, *Stavropol'e v period nemetsko-fashistskoi okkupatsii (avgust 1942-ianvar' 1943)*, p. 67; Akt of the Commission of Novorossiisk, October 18, 1943, GARF, 7021/16/11, p. 1.

262 Akt of the Commission of Stavropol', July 11, 1943, GARF, 7021/17/1, pp. 95-96; Statement of Klavdiia Korol'kova, July 2, 1943, GARF, 7021/17/1, p. 36.

263 *Dokumenty obviniaiut*, p. 142.

Jewish partners and children were registered and then assembled.[264] This arrangement was in place from the beginning in most of the Caucasian localities, but was later applied with some deviations.

Thus, non-Jewish spouses were excluded from the anti-Jewish policy during certain periods. Later, separate registration of all members of mixed families was conducted. In Essentuki, only one Jewish parent and his offspring were registered at the time of Jewish registration.[265] In different towns, separate registration of unregistered mixed families was conducted at times.[266] This step did not necessarily imply immediate destruction: Only some of those in mixed couples were selected and arrested. Just before their retreat, the Germans had to decide whether to exterminate mixed couples (and if so, just the Jewish ones or all members) or to grant them exemption. Their policies varied greatly from one area to another. In the towns of Stavropol'skii *krai*, the Germans were harsher. A possible explanation may be that the EG D Headquarters was stationed in Stavropol'. It appears that by the end of the occupation period, they decided to eliminate the mixed couples and their offspring in the towns of the *krai*. Fifteen such families in Essentuki were earmarked for arrest on the eve of the German retreat in January 1943,[267] but they went into hiding and survived until the liberation of the town.[268] In the neighboring town of Kislovodsk, the Germans arrested the mixed couples (including the non-Jewish spouses and their children) in January 1943; some of them were subsequently released while the others were killed.[269]

The German policies towards intermarried couples were also stiff in Novorossiisk (in Krasnodarskii *krai*). The distinctive feature of the killing of mixed couples in this town is that it was

264 Village of Vorontsovo-Aleksandrovskoe: Statement of Lidia Brailovskaia, 1943, GARF, 7021/17/10, p. 33.

265 Statement of Aleksandr Gontov, June 30 1943, GARF, 7021/17/4, p. 61.

266 More than one month later after the annihilation of the Jews on September 9, 1942 – October 20, 1943. Statement of Sokol'skii, June 30, 1943, GARF, 7021/17/4, p. 57 (?).

267 Ibid.

268 Letter by by the painter L. N. Tarabukin and his wife D. R. Gol'dshtein to the writer Iu. Kalugin, 1943, YVA, M.35/25, p. 86.

269 Statement of Polina Lipman, June 10, 1943, GARF, 7021/17/5, p. 6.

carried out simultaneously with the extermination of the whole Jewish community in October 1942. Thus, unlike in many other Caucasian towns, the mixed families in Novorossiisk did not have even minimal time to calculate their steps. The order issued in this town stipulated that:

> Jewish women married to Russians are to present themselves at the assembly points. Provided they have children, only they [the Jewish wives and the children – KF] must assemble. If a Jewish man is married to a Russian woman, the whole family must present itself.[270]

As a result, non-Jewish women married to Jews were executed with their children in Novorossiisk.[271] It is probable that the German stringency and promptness in annihilating the mixed couples and their offspring there had to do with the protracted and fierce warfare in the town itself, which was divided in half between the Soviets and the Germans. The Germans suspected, Soviet civilians of taking sides with the Red Army, and enacted especially harsh policies towards the local population. In apparent retaliation, the Germans got rid of a sizable group of Russians married to Jews in Novorossiisk under the pretext of completing the killing operation directed against the Jews.

In contrast, the German policy was more lenient in Krasnodar. Judging by the statements of the surviving non-Jewish spouses, some of the Jewish spouses were arrested during the large-scale action conducted in the town in August 1942.[272] The others had been arrested in October[273] and were apparently exterminated soon afterwards. Most significantly, the common offspring of the intermarried couples were spared.[274] Even if the children were

270 Questioning of Zoia Chernova, October 14, 1943, GARF, 7021/16/11, p. 118.

271 Questioning of Anna Silina (1910), October 16, 1943, GARF, 7021/16/11, p. 112.

272 Krasnodar: Statement of Valentina Merosidi, July 8, 1943, GARF, 7021/16/5, p. 32; Statement of Ksenia Dement'eva, June 30, 1943, GARF, 7021/16/5, p. 69.

273 Statement of Alexandra Nebel'son, August 6, 1943, YVA, M.33/301, p. 27.

274 Statement of Valentina Merosidi, July 8, 1943, GARF, 7021/16/5, p. 32;

initially arrested, they were released in the aftermath.[275] There exists no record that the non-Jewish spouses were annihilated in Krasnodar.[276]

It is difficult to draw general conclusions on the German policies concerning the mixed couples in small urban and rural localities. Sometimes, summary executions of both Jewish and non-Jewish spouses took place.[277] Overall, however, the Germans tended to kill solely the Jewish spouses, excluding their non-Jewish spouses and children from extermination, especially if some "Aryans" argued in their favor.[278] On occasion, it could even be their own spouses who did so, as was the case with a Jewish woman who had been already detained in the *Kommandatur* whose husband managed to persuade a Russian collaborator to release her.[279] In exceptional cases, even Jewish spouses benefitted from the fact that they had intermarried and were saved from annihilation, despite the fact that they had already gone through some stages preceding the destruction.[280] In other cases, however, the Germans killed mixed couples, including their children.[281]

4.3. Evacuees

As already mentioned, by the summer of 1942, evacuees constituted possibly the absolute majority of the Jewish population in the North

Statement of Alexandra Nebel'son, August 6, 1943, YVA, M.33/301, p. 27; Statement of Ekaterina Kalinskaia, July 1, 1943, GARF, 7021/16/5, p. 56.

275 Statement of Alexandra Nebel'son, August 6, 1943, YVA, M.33/301, p. 27.

276 Ibid., YVA, M.33/301, p. 27; Statement of Valentina Merosidi, July 8, 1943, GARF, 7021/16/5, p. 32; Statement of Ekaterina Kalinskaia, July 1, 1943, GARF, 7021/16/5, p. 56; Statement of Ksenia Dement'eva, June 30, 1943, GARF, 7021/16/5, p. 69.

277 Labinskaia *stanitsa*: Questioning of Raisa Niminskaia (1926), August 24, 1943, YVA, M.33/292, p. 106.

278 See Chapter 9, "The Local Population and the Holocaust in the North Caucasus."

279 Otradnenskaia *stanitsa*: Testimony of Roza Lipkin (1904), [no date], ICJ, TC 2860.

280 Mikoianshakhar: Testimony of Ida Nikeeva, July 29, 1943, GARF, 7021/17/10, p. 204.

281 Akt of the Commission of the Novo-Aleksandrovskaia *stanitsa*: June 24, 1943, GARF, 7021/17/11, p. 28.

Caucasus.[282] The Germans were well aware of this, but greatly exaggerated the dimensions of Jewish evacuation. To quote a German military document dated November 29, 1942: "The data on the 2.5 million Jews who are waiting there [at Makhachkala – KF] for the transportation are confirmed."[283] They occasionally dealt with the evacuated Jews as a separate group in their own right. During the destruction of the largest single Jewish community of Stavropol', the Germans issued two different assembly orders, first one for evacuees and then one for native Jews.[284] One can understand the large proportion of the Jewish evacuees verses the "native" Jews, in that 3,500 complied with the first order and only 500 with the second. In the town of Armavir, the relationship was more balanced: 176 native families of the town and some 200 evacuated families.[285]

In rural areas, the Germans and local collaborators often regarded all the evacuees collectively as Jews[286] and, furthermore, as those who were caught while attempting to escape from the Caucasus.[287] All evacuees had to either produce "Aryan" documents or immediately bring witnesses in order to prove their "flawless" origin. Otherwise, they ran the risk of being killed on the spot because of their allegedly Jewish ancestry.[288] The testimony of a Russian witness pertaining to the evacuation from "Rote Fahne" *kolkhoz* underscores the point:

282 Villages of Mikhailovka in Stavropol'skii *krai*, Khanskaia and Kuzhorskaia in Krasnodarskii *krai*: Akt of the Commission of Mikhailovka, June 29, 1943, GARF, 7021/17/10, p. 53; Akt of the Commission of Maikop, August 20, 1943, YVA, M.33/288, pp. 7-8.

283 3 Panzer-Division. Abt. 1c. Befragung von Zivilisten im Raum Nowo Poltawskaja. Ergebnis, November 29, 1942, YVA, JM/5605.

284 Akt of the Commission of Stavropol', July 11, 1943, GARF, 7021/17/1, pp. 95-96; Ibid., July 13, 1943, Ibid., p. 14; Statement of Isaak Lekhel, [no date], GARF, 7021/17/1, p. 65.

285 Akt of the Commission of Armavir, January 28, 1943, TsAMO RF, 51/958/52, pp. 91-92, courtesy of the USHMM.

286 Stavropol'skii *krai* – unidentified village: Testimony of Boris Chrol'nik, 1991, YVA, 0.3/6422, p. 7; Statement of Irina D'iakonova, 1943, GARF, 7021/17/11, p. 113.

287 Stavropol', village of Mikhailovskoe: File of Taisiia Mozgovaia and Ekaterina Vinnikova-Mozgovaia, 2000, YVA, M.31/9080; Akt of the Commission of Petrovskii *raion*, July 10, 1943, GARF, 7021/17/1, p. 107.

288 Testimony of Lidiia Pasternak, August 3, 1990, YVHN.

> The German advance unit cut off the [rescue] route. One of the armed persons pulled off my raincoat where my passport was kept. On our way, we came across groups of Jews removed from carts with crying old men and wailing children. Then, we were caught by the policemen from a concentration camp. "Are there communists? Are there Jews?" The [*kolkhoz*] team-leader (*brigadir*) told them: "On the first cart there are evacuees." The policemen asked me to produce my passport but I had none. They took me for Jewish and arrested me. But two Kamykiian witnesses confirmed that I was Russian, and I was released.[289]

At the stage of the takeover, the Germans occasionally singled out the Jewish evacuees for especially severe physical maltreatment.[290] They took the Jews' possessions, raped women,[291] and shot the Jewish evacuees indiscriminately.[292] Later on, after the beginning of the "orderly" occupation, the Germans demanded the local administration register the population and earmark all the evacuees,[293] which made survival for evacuated Jews in the region far more difficult.

Despite their numerical prevalence, the Germans clearly discriminated against the evacuated Jews while forming Jewish Councils in the North Caucasus. There is only one piece of evidence indicating that an evacuated Jew was appointed membership in the *Judenrat*.[294] One may assume that the Germans did not regard the evacuees as a monolithic homogeneous group deserving specific representation in the Jewish Councils.

289 Statement of the teacher Elena Mikhailova and housewife Karmen Mandzhieva, June 30, 1943, GARF, 7021/8/26, p. 123.

290 Village of Novo-Alekseevskoe: Interrogation of Stepan Bogoslavskii, August 28, 1943, GARF, 7021/16/12, p. 141.

291 Unidentified *stanitsy* in Krasnodarskii *krai*: File of Natal'ia Dudnik, 1997, YVA, M.31/7704.

292 Village of Zunda in Krasnodarskii *krai*: File of Ivan and Praskov'ia Palaguta, 2001, YVA, M.31/9385.

293 Villages of Izobil'noe and Troitskoe: Akt of the Commission of Izobil'nenskii *raion*, June 29, 1943, GARF, 7021/17/10, p. 121; Akt of the Commission of the village of Troitskoe, July 16, 1943, GARF, 7021/8/27, p. 54.

294 Essentuki: Testimony of Samuil Belenkov, August 10, 1943, GARF, 7021/17/4, p. 22.

A particular group of evacuees that merits attention is Jewish orphans who had been evacuated from the endangered regions of the Soviet Union, including the Crimea, and placed in children's homes.[295] German behavior towards this group resembled their treatment of Jewish patients in the Caucasian hospitals. At the time of the great actions[296] (or in some cases much later),[297] German representatives arrived at the orphanages. They then selected all the Jews among the children and personnel, took them away, and killed them by gassing.[298] This was done under the pretexts of "resettling them in underpopulated areas of Ukraine with the rest of the Jews"[299] or of needing to send them to a separate children's home.[300] In another case, the Germans detected the Jewish children by simply individually questioning them about their origin, without trying to convince them of alternative plans.[301] Almost all Jewish children placed in the children's homes in the Caucasus and the Jewish personnel – some dozens or even hundreds of persons – were murdered.[302]

295 Late August-September: Akt of the Commission of Kislovodsk, June 18, 1943, YVA, JM/10650; Akt of the Commission of Besskorbnaia *stanitsa*: December 12, 1943, GARF, 7021/16/435, p. 196.
November 1942, Teberda: Testimony of Vadim Maniker, April 1975, YVA, 0.3/4108, p. 3.

296 Late August-September: Akt of the Commission of Kislovodsk, June 18, 1943, YVA, JM/10650; Akt of the Commission of Besskorbnaia *stanitsa*, December 12, 1943, GARF, 7021/16/435, p. 196.

297 November 1942, Teberda: Testimony of Vadim Maniker, April 1975, YVA, 0.3/4108, p. 3.

298 Kislovodsk, Teberda, Besskorbnaia *stanitsa*: Akt of the Commission of Kislovodsk, June 18, 1943, YVA, JM/10650; List of names of the murdered children, Teberda, no later than January 13, 1943, GARF, 7021/17/7, pp. 17-18; Akt of the Commission of Besskorbnaia *stanitsa*, December 12, 1943, GARF, 7021/16/435, p. 196.

299 Akt signed by the workers of the children's house no. 18 in Kislovodsk, June 19, 1943, GARF, 7021/17/5, p. 18.

300 Akt of the Commission of Besskorbnaia *stanitsa*, December 12, 1943, GARF, 7021/16/435, p. 196.

301 Ibid., p. 196.

302 Kislovodsk, Teberda, Nizhniaia Teberda: Akt of the Commission of Kislovodsk, June 18, 1943, YVA, JM/10650; Testimony of Oleg Kurikhin in Frolov, *Znak sud'by*, pp. 140-141; Memorandum of the Committee of the VKP(b) of Karachaevskaia Autonomous *oblast'*, no later than June 24, 1943, GARF, 7021/17/8, pp. 2-3.

Considering the specific local circumstances in the North Caucasus (i.e., the very small number of Jews before the war and their visibility during the evacuation), evacuation became a theme of Nazi propaganda in the region for the Germans, the Jews, and the locals. References to Jewish evacuation included statements that their evacuation was made at the expense of the Soviet war effort,[303] or that the evacuated Jews were settled solely in the places in the region from which ethnic Germans had been previously deported (a point directed at the Germans whose worldview stipulated that Jews always benefitted at the expense of Germans). The propaganda focused particularly on the Russian-Jewish "encounter" during the evacuation. The article, published evidently as part of an editorial-sponsored contest for the "best" presentation of the Jewish topic, underscores the point by recalling how a "proud Cossack woman became a serf of the evacuated Jewess," and how the "Jews maltreated her, took the best of her two rooms, and the local authorities protected them."[304]

* * *

When assessing the number and internal structure of the Jewish population in the occupied North Caucasus, some basic assumptions must be made. First, it was made up predominantly of evacuees and refugees who came there after the outbreak of the war and outnumbered the small native Jewish population of the region.[305] Second, the native Jewish population was able to

303 B. Shyr, "Eshe odna podlost': Iz nedavnego proshlogo," *Stavropol'skoe slovo*, no. 16, August 30, 1942, State Archive of Stavropol'skii *Krai* (GASK), R-1052/5069; Editorial, "Znamental'nyi iubilei," *Kuban'*, no. 14, November 7, 1942, p. 1, TsDNIKK, courtesy of the USHMM.

304 N. Kapralova, "Khoziaika polozheniia," *Stavropol'skoe slovo*, no. 38, October 21, 1942, GASK, R-1052/5069, courtesy of the USHMM.

305 The case of Stavropol' underscores the point. In this town, the Germans initially demanded that the Jewish evacuees present themselves at the assembly points and some time later issued such an order regarding the native Jews of the town. Thus, Stavropol' constitutes one of very few cases in which it is possible to determine the numerical relationship between the two groups. According to

partly evacuate prior to the German conquest. The corollary to that argument is that one cannot make use of the prewar statistics concerning the North Caucasian Jewry and must rely on empirical evidence produced during the Holocaust in the region and its aftermath.

The assessment of the death toll in the region during the Holocaust should have in its consideration the available figures for the sizable Jewish urban communities – Krasnodar (thousands of people[306]), Stavropol' (4,000 people[307]), and Nal'chik (1,500 people[308]), but also in much smaller resort towns of Essentuki (2,000 people[309]), Kislovodsk (2,000 people[310]), Minvody (1,800 people[311]), and Piatigorsk (2,800 people[312]), as well as the important harbor town of Novorossiisk (at least 1,000 people, and probably much more[313]). According to the most cautious estimates, the rest of the towns hosted smaller Jewish communities comprised of less than 1,000 people.[314]

Soviet data, 3,500 Jews complied with the first order, and 500 with the second one. (Akt, July 16, 1943, GARF, 7021/17/1, p. 48). In other words, the evacuees constituted 87.5% of the entire Jewish population of the town.

306 Akt of the Commission of Krasnodar, June 30, 1943, GARF, 7021/16/5, pp. 11, 14; Krasnodar trial, Military court of the North Caucasian Front, July 14-17, 1943, in *Dokumenty obviniaiut*, p. 104.

307 Akt, July 16, 1943, GARF, 7021/17/1, p. 48.

308 "How Jews were Murdered" (Hebrew), *Ha-tsofe*, April 8, 1943, p. 1. See also, "Nazis' Atrocities" and Akt of the Commission of the Kabardino-Balkarsk Republic, October 1, 1943, GARF, 7021/7/103, p. 4.

309 Akt of the Commission of Essentuki, July 10, 1943, GARF, 7021/17/4, p. 1; Report of Moisei Evenson, Viktor Shklovskii, ed., [no date], YVA, P.21.2/1.

310 Akt, July 5, 1943, GARF, 7021/17/5, pp. 35-36.

311 Statement of Aleksei Sapunov, June 26, 1943, GARF, 7021/17/2, p. 11; Statement of Andrei Pavlov, June 26, 1943, GARF, 7021/17/2, p. 13.

312 Akt of the Commission of Piatigorsk, GARF, 7021/17/3, p. 8; Intelligence digest of the NKVD administration of Ordzhonikidzevskii *krai*, December 17, 1942, in Vodolazhskaia, Krivneva, and Mel'nik, *Stavropol'e v period nemetsko-fashistskoi okkupatsii (avgust 1942-ianvar' 1943)*, p. 67.

313 Akt of the Commission of Novorossiisk, October 18, 1943, GARF, 7021/16/11, p. 1: Memorandum of the command of the Krasnodar group [*kust*] of partisan detachments, October 1942 (?), TsDNIKK, 4373/1/35, pp. 62-66 in Beliaev and Bondar', *Kuban' v gody Velikoi Otechestvennoi voiny, 1941-1945*, p. 557.

314 To illustrate the point, there is no divergence of opinions concerning the number of the Holocaust victims in Cherkessk – 820 people: Akt of the Commission

The estimate of the dimensions of the Holocaust in numerous dispersed North Caucasian villages is compounded because of the absence of German sources and frequent transportation of the Jews from one locality to another. Therefore, Soviet sources often provide contradictory information concerning the numerical assessments of the Holocaust in rural areas and must be treated with caution. Besides, in a limited number of North Caucasian villages, Soviet authorities recorded extremely high numbers of "general" victims (by the standards of the "average" death toll for the area).[315] This gives rise to the possibility that for their own reasons Soviet authorities preferred to categorize them as non-Jews, despite the fact that these people were also killed because of being somehow related to the Jews. In the opinion of the author, it cannot be ruled out that the victims were, or stemmed from, Judaizers.[316] In at least one case, it is

of Cherkessk, July 13, 1943, GARF, 702/17/12, p. 69. Conversely, in certain cases the available data are contradictory, which has to do *inter alia* with the fact that the victims were referred to as "Soviet people," "peaceful citizens," etc. This was, for example, the case of Elista. On the one hand, there is proof that 300 Jews were destroyed there: Akt, January 5, 1943, "From the Bulletin no. 2 on the Facts of Beastly Actions of the German Fascist Scoundrels during the Period of the Occupation of Kalmytskaia ASSR," Political Department of the 28th Army, YVA, M.40.MAP/108, p. 1. However, other documents indicate a higher number of victims, i.e., "620 Jews, Russians, Ukrainians, and Kalmyks:" Akt on the destruction of the Jewish population of Elista, July 6, 1943, GARF, 7021/8/27, pp. 87-88.

315 That is, those who were referred to as "Soviet people" in contrast to otherwise frequent invocation of the Jewish victims in the Soviet documents dealing with the region – e.g., Labinskaia *stanitsa*, village of Belaia Glina: Akt of the Commission of Labinskaia *stanitsa*, July 5, 1943, GARF, 7021/16/15, p. 1; Akt of the Commission of the village of Belaia Glina, January 5, 1944, GARF, 7021/16/435, p. 265.

316 Judaizers: The term (in Russian – *zhydovstvuiushie*) covers a wide range of sects that embraced some, many, or all tenets of Orthodox Judaism: *subbotniki, gery, subbotniki-karaimity, subbotniki-molokane,* Christian *subbotniki.* A number of the adherents of these sects lived in the North Caucasus (*subbotniki, gery*). Itzhak Oren and Naftali Prat, eds., *Kratkaia evreiskaia entsiklopediia*, vol. 8 (Jerusalem: Keter, 1976-2005), pp. 635-639. On Judaizers in the North Caucasus, see Anatolii Kriukov, "Religioznye sekty na Kubani: stanovlenie, vnutrennee razvitie, vzaimootnosheniia s gosudarstvennymi i obshestvennymi institutami: 30-e gg. XIX v. -1917 g.," (PhD diss., Kubanskii gosudarstvennyi universitet kul'tury i iskusstv, 2004), pp. 59, 122-123.

known that Judaizers had dwelt in Labinskaia *stanitsa* prior to the Bolshevik Revolution.[317] If this is indeed the case, this may account for the Soviet reluctance to provide the explanation for the unusually brutal way that the Germans treated these North Caucasian villagers. Given all these reservations, it seems that the number of Holocaust victims in the region may fluctuate between 35,000 to 45,000 Ashkenazi Jews.

Since the Judaizers embraced some tenets of Judaism, the Germans could view them as "related to Jews/Judaism" and thus, subject to annihilation.

317 A. Simonova, "Gery i subbotniki v opisanii anonimnogo rostovskogo sionista (osen' 1917 g.)," *Vestnik Evreiskogo Universiteta v Moskve* 1, no. 17 (1998): p. 194.

Chapter Five

Food Conditions and the Holocaust in the Crimea and the North Caucasus[1]

During the war, some German decision-makers and strategists (particularly at the lower and middle levels) regarded the destruction of the Jewish population in the Soviet territories under their control as a measure necessary to get rid of "surplus mouths" in the regions, which had suffered from starvation and undernourishment. A report by Professor Peter-Heinz Seraphim, a Nazi expert in population politics in Eastern Europe, that he had forwarded to General Georg Thomas from the Wehrmacht Economic and Armament Department (*Amt für Wehrwirtschaft und Rüstung des OKW*) on December 2, 1941, is instructive:

> The creaming-off of agricultural surpluses from Ukraine as food supplies for the Reich is only conceivable if trade in Ukraine is pushed down to a minimum. Efforts to achieve this will be made by:
> 1. Eradicating surplus mouths (Jews, and the population of the large Ukrainian cities), which, like Kiev, will receive no quota of supplies.[2]

Some contemporary scholars reiterate the idea of the relationship between the necessity to supply the Reich and the Wehrmacht, on the

1 The subject is enlarged upon in Kiril Feferman, "Food Factor as a Possible Catalyst for the Holocaust-Related Decisions: The Crimea and North Caucasus," *War in History* 15, no. 1 (2008): pp. 72-91.

2 Report from an armament inspector in Ukraine forwarded to General Thomas personally. December 2, 1941, (Exhibit USA-290), *The Trial of German Major War Criminals*, pp. 73-75, in Michael Burgleich, *Germany Turns Eastwards: A Study of Ostforschung in the Third Reich* (New York and Cambridge: Cambridge University Press, 1988), p. 221.

one hand, and the worsening food situation in the territories under the German control, on the other. It is claimed that such a link led to the accelerated pace of the annihilation of the Jewish population:

> Facing a war which was claiming many victims, the National Socialist occupation authorities now confronted the question of whether foodstuffs should be placed at the disposition of the Jewish population… or rather go to the soldiers fighting at the front.[3]

The current section attempts to explore this relationship in the Crimea and the North Caucasus. Emphasis is laid on the elucidation of the following subjects: the food situation on the eve of the German takeover of the areas, as well as the Germans' preset concepts and their actual policy regarding the plunder, requisitioning, and distribution of food to the local population, including Jews. This is analyzed with an eye to the food situation in urban and rural areas in the Crimea and the North Caucasus.

1. The Crimea

1.1. Soviet period

One of the consequences of the German Blitzkrieg was that in the areas close to the border, the Soviets failed to evacuate up to 70% of their strategic (*mobilizatsionnye*) stocks and, thus, lost them to the Germans.[4] But the Crimean peninsula belonged to the regions

3 Christoph Dieckmann, "The War and the Killing of the Lithuanian Jews," in Ulrich Herbert, ed., *National Socialist Extermination Policy: Contemporary German Perspectives and Controversies* (New York and London: Berghahn Books, 2000), pp. 253-260. Christian Gerlach formulated this approach in the following fashion: "Economic interests and crises were by far more important influences on the tempo of the liquidation of the Jews, especially in the phases of acceleration. The various liquidation programs in Belorussia… were in large part responses to pressures related to food economics." Christian Gerlach, "German Economic Interests, Occupation Policy and the Murder of the Jews in Belorussia, 1941/43," ibid., p. 227.

4 Aleksandr Ogurechnikov, "Prodovol'stvennoe obespechenie v period Velikoi

captured at a relatively advanced stage of the war. As a result, the Soviets had sufficient time to remove their food resources from the Crimea. It should be clearly recognized that the removal of food stocks from the area later had a devastating effect on the remaining population.[5] In the meantime, the astronomical size of devaluation led to a sharp increase in the price of food.[6]

Nonetheless, as in the case of the evacuation of the population,[7] Soviet policies concerning the "relocation" of food were characterized by ambiguity. On the one hand, the harvest was collected and stockpiled in the Crimea well into September 1941.[8] This was the result of the Soviet resolution to hold the peninsula and to leave important food reserves there. On September 10, 1941, local Crimean authorities issued the directive to begin with the autumn sowing. On the other hand, characteristic of Soviet ambiguity towards their plans for the peninsula, this decision was not extended to *sovkhozy* of the People's Commissariat for Agriculture,[9] which were directly subordinate to the central Soviet government. In fact, these *sovkhozy* were already engaged in moving their food stocks away from the Crimea. Unfortunately, it is impossible to establish the precise proportion of the *kolkhozy/ sovkhozy* working for the "evacuation" of food and those ordered to continue the conventional agricultural programs. Thus, the dimensions of the relocation of food stocks from the peninsula cannot be assessed at this stage in the research.

Yet, as the front line was rapidly approaching the Crimea,

Otechestvennoi voiny (1941-1945 gg.)," *Voenno-istoricheskii arkhiv* 6, no. 21 (2001): p. 80.

5 Arnold, *Die Wehrmacht und die Besatzungspolitik in den besetzten Gebieten der Sowjetunion*, pp. 158-164.

6 Simferopol': Diary of Chrisanf Lashkevich, entry from November 22, 1941, State Archive of the Autonomous Republic of the Crimea (DAARK), P-156/1/31, pp. 56-57.

7 See Chapter 1, "Jews in the Crimea from the Beginning of the German-Soviet War (June 22, 1941) to the German Occupation (November 1941)."

8 Information of the Crimean District Committee of the VKP(b) on the work of *sovkhozy* and *kolkhozy* of the Crimea in the wartime conditions, September 10, 1941, in Kondranov and Stepanova, *Krym v period Velikoi Otechestvennoi voiny*, pp. 56-57.

9 Ibid., pp. 56-57.

talk of proceeding with the harvest plans ceased. By late October 1941, it was already clear that the Germans would soon enter the peninsula. Under these circumstances, the Soviet authorities urgently ordered all Crimean ministries and supply organizations to "sell all available food… in the storages of Simferopol'" on October 29.[10] The local inhabitants were supposed to act as "buyer." It is doubtful whether there was time to carry out this decision. However, it indicates that by the time of the German occupation, important food reserves were still available in Crimean storages.

The question "Who managed to take them over?" remains largely unanswered. At least part of these resources passed through the hands of local people, because on the eve of the Red Army's retreat from the Crimea the Soviets distributed food (either for payment or free of charge).[11] Local people looted Soviet food storages in the interim period before the entry of German troops, as recorded in the diary of a Russian witness in Simferopol':

> On October 31, November 1, and today, shops and storages were looted… People flocked to the plant and began to take sugar, tinned goods, jam. They took the foodstuffs throughout the day, but according to the accounts [of the fellow townsmen], the Germans were able to seize much more…[12]

Judging by a number of wartime sources, local inhabitants had sufficient food at their disposal during the first period of the German occupation of the Crimea.[13]

10 Decree of the [Crimean] committee of the VKP(b) on evacuation, October 29, 1941, in ibid., p. 53.

11 Memorandum "O rabote Krymskogo Obkoma VKP(b) po rukovodstvu partizanskim dvizheniem i podpol'noi rabotoi v Krymu," February 13, 1943, DAARK, P-1/1/2144a.

12 Diary of Chrisanf Lashkevich, entry from November 2, 1941, in Liubov' Kravtsova and Mikhail Tiaglyi, eds., *Peredaite det'iam nashim o nashei sud'be* (Simferopol': BETs "Khesed Shymon," 2001), p. 54. It was also the case in Feodosiia: Rozaliia Krichevskaia, *Dvadtsat' deviat' mesiatsev iz detstva* (Beer Sheva, 1997), pp. 10-11.

13 Diary of Chrisanf Lashkevich in Krichevskaia, *Peredaite detiam nashim o*

The situation was different in the places the Red Army had kept hold of in the peninsula in 1941-1942, namely Kerch and Sevastopol' and their adjacent areas. The fact that large-scale warfare was being conducted there led to the exhaustion of available food stocks. In addition, in Kerch, where the food conditions were better (the area was closer to the Soviet mainland and, therefore, easier to arrange the food supply), the Soviets declared their intention to destroy (and in all probability succeeded in doing so) the important portion of the remaining food reserves.[14] Soviet declarations that these stocks were first of all distributed to the local people and partisans were exaggerated.[15] In retrospect, the German breakthrough was too sudden for the Soviets to cope with a logistical task of such scope.

The food supply in Sevastopol' became graver as the Germans' siege slowly strangled sea communications with the Soviet mainland. Therefore, after the siege in November 1941, the "Sevastopol' fortified area" was forced to rely largely on its own modest food resources from then on:

> Food resources in the Sevastopol' area do not meet even current needs. The local food industry does not cope with the growing needs. Requests are lodged with the Crimean authorities and the Command of the Black Sea to allocate necessary resources. Slaughter of individual cattle is forbidden henceforth without special permission.[16]

nashei sud'be, pp. 51-53; Memoirs of Il'ia Sirota, February 16, 1945, DAARK, P-156/1/40, p. 112.

14 Andrei Pirogov, *Etogo zabyt nel'zia: Vospominaniia byvshego voennoplennogo* (Odessa: Odesskoe knizhnoe izdatel'stvo, 1961), pp. 6, 8.

15 Kerch area: Letter of the First Secretary of the Kerch Committee of the VKP(b) Vladimir Bulatov, which contained information on the resumption of normal life in the liberated Kerch and the areas of the Kerch peninsula, January 30, 1942, in Kondranov and Stepanova, *Krym v period Velikoi Otechestvennoi voiny*, pp. 91-92. See also Pirogov, *Etogo zabyt nel'zia*, p. 6.

16 Decree of Sevastopol' Municipal Committee of defense on the establishment of food stocks in the town, October 30, 1941, in ibid., p. 73.

Local industry was incapable of meeting the enhanced demands on the local food stocks. One should view Soviet demands to dispatch all people unnecessary for the defense of the Sevastopol' area from the city (i.e., in order to get rid of "surplus mouths") with this background in mind.[17] However, even on the eve of the fall of Sevastopol', civilians were still given a bread ration, albeit a modest 200 grams per person.[18] By the time of the German takeover in the areas around Kerch and Sevastopol', the food supply was even more strained. The local population, among them Jews, had difficulties in subsisting on their own, even in the short run.

1.2. German occupation period[19]

Already during the phase of the military planning for Operation Barbarossa, the Germans had been studying uses of the occupied Soviet hinterland for the German war effort.[20] Notions of "traditional" occupation policy based on the experience of the First World War, harsh as they were, such as showing consideration for the local population and promoting general economic reconstruction,[21] did not offer much advantage in terms

17 Decree of Sevastopol' Municipal Committee of the VKP(b) on the evacuation of the town's population, November 13, 1941, in ibid., p. 79.

18 Testimony of Vladimir Petrov in Gel'man and Glubochanskii, *Kholokost*, p. 102.

19 Norbert Kunz, *Die Krim unter deutscher Herrschaft*, pp. 139-155.

20 Alex J. Kay, "The Purpose of the Russian Campaign is the Decimation of the Slavic Population by Thirty Million," in Alex J. Kay, Jeff Rutherford, and David Stahel, eds., *Nazi Policy on the Eastern Front, 1941: Total War, Genocide, and Radicalization* (Rochester, NY: University of Rochester Press, 2012), pp. 191-129; Idem., *Exploitation, Resettlement, Mass Murder*, pp. 47-67, 133-138; idem., "Germany's Staatssekretär: Mass Starvation and the Meeting of 2 May 1941," *Journal of Contemporary History* 41, no. 4 (2006): pp. 685-700; Arnold, *Die Wehrmacht und die Besatzungspolitikin den besetzten Gebieten der Sowjetunion*, pp. 85-96, 101-109; Christian Gerlach, *Krieg, Ernährung, Völkermord: Forschungen zur deutschen Vernichtungspolitik im Zweiten Weltkrieg* (Hamburg: Hamburger Edition, 1998), pp. 167-258.

21 On the German population policies in the East during the First World War, see, for example, Christian Westerhoff, "'A kind of Siberia': German Labour and Occupation Policies in Poland and Lithuania during the First World War,"

of material support for the eastern army (i.e., mobilization of maximum resources to provide the fighting forces and homeland with urgently needed raw materials and foodstuffs). Given the expected exacerbation of shortages in the Reich in the fall of 1941, the Wehrmacht was supposed to occupy the Soviet wheat fields and maintain operations largely by living off the land.[22] This policy was reiterated on a number of occasions by the highest civil and military authorities of the Reich after the beginning of the war.[23]

Among the vast body of German documentation on this subject, the *Generalplan Ost* should be pointed out,[24] of which only one draft out of several remains. This plan envisaged the large-scale resettlement of Soviet Slavs, which would eventually make space for German settlers. Also, German planners designated northcentral Russia, with an emphasis on the biggest cities, such as Moscow and Leningrad, as a "food deficit" zone, whose population would have to be diminished by starvation. However, in this sense, both the Crimea and the North Caucasus were closer to or actually part of the "food surplus" zones of Ukraine and the Transcaucasus, with whose population the Germans had to deal more positively. The degree of connection between actual German policies and those of the *Generalplan Ost* in the East is debatable.

Despite the fact that, by and large, the Germans took over the Crimea when it had relatively satisfactory food conditions, the situation began to deteriorate in the first months of the

First World War Studies 4, no. 1 (2013): pp. 51-63; Wolfram Dornik and Peter Lieb, "Misconceived Realpolitik in a Failing State: The Political and Economic Fiasco of the Central Powers in Ukraine, 1918," *First World War Studies* 4, no. 1 (2013): pp. 111-124.

22 Rolf-Dieter Müller, "From Economic Alliance to a War of Colonial Exploitation," in Boog et al., *The Attack on the Soviet Union*, pp. 140-141.

23 Ibid., pp. 174-175; Pohl, *Die Herrschaft der Wehrmacht*, pp. 183-194; Karel Berkhoff, *Harvest of Despair: Life and Death in Ukraine Under Nazi Rule* (Cambridge, MA and London: Harvard University Press, 2004), pp. 164-186; Arnold, *Die Wehrmacht und die Besatzungspolitik in den besetzten Gebieten der Sowjetunion*, pp. 245-250; 254-258.

24 Kay, *Exploitation, Resettlement, Mass Murder*, pp. 99-101. See also Czesiaw Madajczyk, ed., *Vom Generalplan Ost zum Generalsiedlungsplan*, 'Einzelveroffentlichungen der Historischen Kommission zu Berlin', Bd. 80. Munich: K. G. Saur, 1994.

occupation.[25] In this respect, it is worth quoting postwar evidence produced in the West German court by a former German officer in the Crimea:

> The conditions in Simferopol' were not at all favorable for the Russian population. They suffered from extreme hunger because it was extraordinarily difficult to supply the town with food. It must also be acknowledged that the winter of 1941-1942 was particularly harsh, not only for the troops but also for the civilian population.[26]

The testimony recognizes the gravity of the problem, tends to account for it by "natural factors," and claims that everyone was in short supply of food, including the Wehrmacht itself.

Several factors may account for this change. The aforementioned general calculations, which dictated the German policy in most of the occupied Soviet territories (i.e., living off the land and providing supplies to the Reich, Wehrmacht, and, only afterwards, to those in the German service), were of paramount importance in the Crimea and were fully backed by the Commander of the 11th Army, General von Manstein. In the order signed on November 20, 1941, he claimed:

> The food situation in our Fatherland requires that the troops be supplied with food from local resources and, furthermore, that as much stocks as possible be put at the Fatherland's disposal… A considerable part of the population of the enemy's towns will have to starve.[27]

It is significant that as a result of the drastic German measures

25 Simferopol' and elsewhere: OSR USSR, no. 153, CSPSS, Berlin, January 9, 1942, Yad Vashem Archives (YVA), 0.51/165 II; Testimony of Efim Gopshtein, August 17, 1944, YVA, M.35/21, pp. 171-172.

26 "Strafsache gegen Walter Bierkamp, Erich G," Abschrift, April 13, 1967, YVA, TR.10/1147, p. 599.

27 Secret circular by the Commander of the 11th Army N 2379/41, November 20, 1941, translation into Russian, DAARK, P-156/1/24, p. 1.

to stop what they regarded as the looting and plunder of food stocks by the local people, the Germans seized a considerable part of the food reserves left by the Soviets.[28] The Germans did not perceive this as enough, and, in line with the general imperatives of their policies, they plundered food arbitrarily from the Jews.[29] They also placed demands on the local population to deliver any "food surplus to the municipal storages, in order to prevent the starvation of the population, which did not possess food stocks."[30]

In Kerch, the German policy was no less stringent. The German command demanded the local people to deliver all available food; in addition, in November 1941, the latter was ordered to register all domestic animals and prohibited from slaughtering cattle without the explicit permission of the Germans.[31] The order was rigidly enforced.[32] The Germans' lack of consideration for the local population found expression in the fact that in November-December 1941 mills and plants in Kerch did not run, nor were there any public places (e.g., grocery stores, cafeterias, etc.) where citizens could buy or obtain food.[33] This background shines light on the reasoning of the German military report from November 27, 1941, stating that "the liquidation of the Jews [in Kerch] will be accelerated, owing to the dangerous food situation in the town."[34] In all reality, it was the German authorities in this town who were consciously creating this "dangerous situation." The food access for Jews in Kerch deteriorated to such a point that as

28 Simferopol': ibid., p. 54.

29 Simferopol': Testimony of Efim Gopshtein, August 17, 1944, YVA, M.35/23, p. 53.

30 Simferopol': *Golos Kryma* (Simferopol'), December 21, 1941, in Volodimir Khurkovich, ed., *Okupatsiinyi rezhym v Krymu, 1941-1944 rr.: za materialamy presy okupatsiinykh vlastei* (Simferopol': Tavriia, 1996), pp. 5-7.

31 Akt of the Commission of Kerch, August 24, 1944, in Kondranov and Stepanova, *Krym v period Velikoi Otechestvennoi voiny*, p. 199.

32 Ibid., p. 199.

33 Letter of Vladimir Bulatov, January 30, 1942, in ibid., p. 90.

34 OK I(V)/287, "TB für die Zeit vom 23.-27.11.1941," Kerch, November 27, 1941, YVA, M.29.FR/41, p. 30.

soon as the Germans announced that the imprisoned Jews would be deported to work the fields, the latter readily leapt at this appeal.[35]

It should be emphasized that the German policy of starving the Jews was in no case a unique phenomenon characteristic of Kerch, but was also applied to other urban areas. This was also the case in Yalta, where conditions in the ghetto, to which the town's Jews had been confined in December 1941, made it easier for the Germans to subject the Jews to starvation.[36] In Dzhankoi, where the Jews were interned in a camp, the Germans also used the food argument in order to justify a speedy killing operation. According to a military report dated January 1, 1942, this time it did not reference the "welfare of the general population," but rather the rapidly deteriorating sanitary and food situation:

> ...creation of the "Jewish concentration camp" in Dzhankoi led to repeated negotiations between the SD, the 1c/AO, the *Feldgendarmerie*, and ourselves. According to a report by the *Ortskommandant* of Dzhankoi, hunger is rampant in the camp, and there is a danger of an epidemic, so the cleansing had to be carried out immediately.[37]

Using the dire food situation as an argument for the murder of Jews found its utmost expression in the postwar testimony of the Quartermaster of the 11th Army, the man who approved the execution of the *Aktion* in Simferopol'.[38] He mentioned it explicitly as the rationale behind the decision to exterminate the Jewish population in the town:

35 "Story of Iosef Vaingarten," (Yiddish), *Eynikayt*, July 15, 1942, p. 1; Report of Moisei Evenson, Viktor Shklovskii, ed., [no date], YVA, P.21.2/1.

36 Il'ia Erenburg, ed., *Murder of a People* (Yiddish), 2nd ed., (Moscow: Der Emes, 1945), p. 63; West, *In the Ropes of Destruction*, p. 141; Mangupli, *Kerosinovyi vkus detstva*, p. 13.

37 NOKW-1866, National Archives and Records Administration (NARA), T-501, roll 59, frame 291, courtesy of Dr. Martin Dean.

38 See Chapter 3, "Destruction of the Jewish Population in the Crimea."

> Based on the order of December 11, 1941, I authorised another raid. In this case, the step was carried out solely in the interests of the local population, in order to maintain orderly provisions, as was our task.[39]

The Commander of the 11th Army General von Manstein, did not refer to this line of reasoning in his postwar testimony at the Nuremberg Trial. Yet, he did say that there were severe difficulties in securing food provisions in the Crimea – even to the Wehrmacht, whose food supply had been reduced in the winter of 1941-42.[40]

It is noteworthy that the Soviet report drawn soon after Kerch was liberated in the late December 1941 had not viewed the food situation in the town under the German rule so grave, stating that: "When our units abandoned the area, flour and other products were allocated to the population, which considerably exceeded its current needs."[41] Despite the fact that there exist no similar assessments with respect to the rest of the Crimean towns, it is possible to infer from it the general food situation in the peninsula. This argument is substantiated by the lack of any indication of serious food shortages in other Crimean towns, most specifically Simferopol', throughout November-December 1941. By late December 1941, the Germans began to ration food out to the local population, albeit very modestly, and only to those registered at a job center (*birzha truda*).[42] Yet, most people seemed to subsist on their own stocks preserved from the Soviet period.[43]

On paper, Crimean Jews were entitled to food rations set at half of what was to be distributed to non-Jews. According to the directives of *Korück* 553, a Jewish adult was to receive 35 grams

39 "Strafsache gegen Walter Bierkamp, Vernehmungsniederschrift, S. (Oberst i.G. Oberquartiermeister der 11 Armee until September 1942), December 18, 1961, YVA, TR.10/1147, p. 188.

40 Testimony of Erich von Manstein, August 12, 1946, *PNWCT*, vol. 21.

41 Letter of Vladimir Bulatov, in Kondranov and Stepanova, *Krym v period Velikoi Otechestvennoi voiny*, pp. 91-92.

42 Simferopol': Diary of Chrisanf Lashkevich, January 1942, DAARK, P-156/1/31, p. 90.

43 Simferopol': Ibid.

of fats, 750 grams of bread, and 1 kilogram of potatoes per week.[44] But there is absolutely no evidence that Jews were ever fed during the first two months of the occupation of the peninsula. To put it otherwise, the dreadful reality of the Holocaust turned out even gloomier than army planners had envisaged.

After early 1942, by which time the bulk of the Jews in the Crimean towns had been killed, the Germans continued to assess the food conditions in the peninsula as very grave. By the end of December, the EG D estimated that the general mood was governed, as before, by the food shortages.[45] Given the predetermined German concepts analyzed above, the question arises as to how they attempted to solve the problem, as some sort of solution was imperative, considering the protracted warfare in the peninsula. One of the cost-free methods was to banish the locals from the starving towns to the countryside to allow them to look for the food on their own. Indeed, this was proposed and realized on a large scale in the Crimea.[46] However, the Germans sanctioned the movement of the population into the countryside only halfheartedly, as this ran counter to another component of the German policy: restricting the free movement of people around the peninsula on security grounds.

The food situation in the Crimean towns remained strained throughout the winter of 1941-42. According to the Germans' own estimates, the mortality rate in the peninsula rose in January 1942 by 100% (apparently in contrast to December 1941).[47] According to a Soviet wartime report, alarmed by the Soviet offensive, the Germans prohibited the beginning of sowing in the spring of 1942.[48] Evidently, as time passed, the situation did not improve, essentially as a result of the non-interventionist German policy. Gradually,

44 Oldenburg, *Ideologie und militärisches Kalkül*, p. 165.

45 OSR USSR, no. 150, CSPSS, Berlin, January 2, 1942, YVA, 0.51/165 II.

46 Simferopol' and other big towns: OSR USSR, no. 153, CSPSS, Berlin, January 9, 1942, YVA, 0.51/165 II. See also Arad, Krakowski, and Spektor, *The Einsatzgruppen Reports*, pp. 272-273; EM no. 184, March 23, 1942, Russian State Military Archive (RGVA), 500/1/773, p. 106.

47 EM no. 178, March 9, 1942, RGVA, 500/1/773, p. 41.

48 Memorandum "O rabote Krymskogo Obkoma VKP(b)," DAARK, P-1/1/2144a.

the Germans began to see the direct relationship between the improvements of the food conditions of the local people and their attitudes towards the German rule in the area. The EG D report from May 1, 1942, is instructive in this respect:

> Whereas in winter the attitudes of the population on the Crimean peninsula were affected in a very negative fashion by the very strained food situation, in April there was a positive turnabout… By and large, the very strained food conditions have improved somewhat.[49]

The Germans redressed the situation only partially when they began to allocate food rations to local people, which varied from simple bread rations (200 grams of bread in March 1942 in Feodosiia[50]) to those combined with meat dishes (March 1942 in Alushta[51]). By April 1942, daily bread rations for those living in the towns were increased and set at 300 grams for employed persons and 200 grams for unemployed ones.[52]

On the other hand, the plunder or requisitioning of what the German authorities referred to as "food surpluses" abated somewhat in 1942.[53] Over time, there had remained less and less food to confiscate from the local people. Besides, this also had to do with the more pragmatic German approach, which now envisaged the possibility of protracted warfare with the Soviet Union. Nevertheless, in the areas conquered in the previous period by the Wehrmacht in 1942 (Kerch and Sevastopol'), the former harsh policy was reiterated. That is, under threat of heavy reprisals, the locals were demanded to deliver every extra kilogram of food, were forbidden to trade, and were subject

49 "Allgemeine Lage und Stimmung auf der Halbinsel Krim," CSpSd, Kommandostab, MbOg, no. 1, Berlin, May 1, 1942, RGVA, 500/1/775, p. 77.

50 EM no. 184, March 23, 1942, RGVA, 500/1/773, p. 106.

51 "Allgemeine Lage und Ernährung," EM no. 184, March 23, 1942, RGVA, 500/1/773, p. 106.

52 EM no. 190, April 8, 1942, RGVA, 500/1/773, p. 241.

53 Fraidorfskii *raion*: OK I/742, FG, "TB für April 1942," Fraidorf. April 26, 1942, YVA, 0.51/185 II, p. 3.

to plundering, as indicated in the diary of one of Sevastopol'"s inhabitants:

> Upon the arrival of the German occupants in the town of Sevastopol' on July 1, 1942, they began to loot houses... Mass shootings and plunder multiplied from the time of the appearance of the Gestapo head in the town, who had made up his mind to plunder and to destroy the peaceful population. Possession of any extra kilogram of food products was punishable with execution. No trade was conducted whatsoever in the market; stores were empty.[54]

As for Soviet POWs, they suffered continuously from terrible malnourishment or insufficient water supply, as there was almost no change in the POW camps in the Crimea in 1941-1942.[55]

The Germans correctly assessed the food situation in the rural areas as more satisfactory.[56] Apart from the general observation that villagers possibly had more food at their disposal, it should also be borne in mind that fewer German troops were deployed in the rural areas. Therefore, plunder of the food reserves belonging to the inhabitants of rural areas was less systematic and thorough than in the towns. It is also arguable that as the Germans were in particular need of the support of local inhabitants in the struggle against the Soviet partisans, they restrained themselves somewhat in requisitioning food in rural areas.

While a considerable number of rural Jews were annihilated in November-early December 1941, those who survived were compelled to perform hard agricultural labor.[57] Their bread was also taken away,[58] and they were not provided with any food for

54 Diary of the priest Boris Pekarchuk, [no date], DAARK, R-1289/1/1a, pp. 3-4.

55 POW camps near Simferopol' and Armiansk: Testimony of Testimony of Zalman Uzikov, December 14, 1987, YVA, 0.3/4939, pp. 18, 22, 24.

56 EM no. 178, March 9, 1942, RGVA, 500/1/773, p. 41; EM no. 190, April 8, 1942, RGVA, 500/1/773, p. 241.

57 Villages of Pervomaiskoe and "Frunze": Interrogation of Stepan Beznos, May 27, 1944, State Archive of the Russian Federation (GARF), 7021/9/194, p. 89; Questioning of Mariia Rozhkovskaia, July 22, 1944, YVA, M.33/63, p. 28.

58 Villages of "Frunze" and Kalinskoe: Questioning of Mariia Rozhkovskaia, July

their work.[59] Local people were forbidden to give any food to Jews.[60] This was a policy of starvation. While the local population's suffering was supposedly to be alleviated under the Germans' amoral argument for Jewish annihilation, the Jews surviving after exterminations in Crimean villages fared worse.

Jews were able to attempt to find refuge in the partisan units scattered all over the peninsula. Yet, in the first phase of the partisan warfare, which coincided with the almost complete annihilation of the Jews in the Crimea in the winter of 1941-1942, a serious food crisis confronted the partisans.[61] This had to do with preset logistical problems: i.e., before the actual occupation of the Crimea, the Soviet partisan command had reckoned with the possibility that the Germans could eventually occupy the peninsula, but assumed that they would keep it only until May 1942 at the latest. As a result of this miscalculation, food reserves were stockpiled in the forests for only six months.[62] One partisan leader estimated, as is recorded in his postwar memoir, that "in the course of one hard winter, 250 partisans died of starvation [i.e., one-third of their total number, according to one estimate[63]]; the survivors were terribly exhausted."[64]

To sum up, the dimensions of the food crisis in the Crimea were apparently far from critical in the first months of the German occupation of the Crimea, except for Kerch and Sevastopol'. This appraisal reflects rather satisfactory provisions for the local people prior to the German takeover, as well as the Soviet failure to move

22, 1944, YVA, M.33/63, p. 28; Interrogation of Konstantin Zhukovskii, May 27, 1944, GARF, 7021/9/194, p. 87.

59 Village of "Frunze": Questioning of Mariia Rozhkovskaia, July 22, 1944, YVA, M.33/63, p. 28.

60 Villages of Pervomaiskoe and Topalovka: Interrogation of Stepan Beznos, May 27, 1944, GARF, 7021/9/194, p. 89. See also the account of D. I. Makarycheva, [no date], DAARK, P-156/1/36.

61 Genov, *Dnevnik partizana*, p. 169 (entry from March 19, 1942); Il'ia Vergasov, *V gorakh Tavrii* (Kiev: Izdatel'svo khudozhestvennoi literatury "Dnipro," 1969), pp. 35-37.

62 Ivan Kozlov, *V Krymskom podpol'ie*, p. 77; Genov, *Dnevnik partizana*, p. 62 (entry from November 7, 1941).

63 Untitled document, Russian State Archive of Social and Political History (RGASPI), 69/1/10, p. 146.

64 Kozlov, *V Krymskom podpol'ie*, p. 77.

away all the food they planned. Therefore, the local population subsisted on its own, at least in the first months of the occupation. The extermination of Jews in November-December 1941 did not affect the food conditions in the Crimea. However, the situation did deteriorate in the following months, as the Germans were reluctant to feed the local people at the expense of what was designated for the needs of the Reich and the Wehrmacht.

2. The North Caucasus

2.1. Soviet period

The North Caucasus, most specifically the vast territories of Krasnodar and Stavropol', counted as an important Soviet agricultural asset. As the Soviet Union lost Ukraine in 1941, which had up to that point served as the most important supplier of grain to the country, the significance of the North Caucasus only increased. Food conditions in the North Caucasus were better than in the rest of the Soviet regions, particularly those close to the front line, both in terms of food availability and price.[65] This was related to the generally favorable climatic conditions of the area, as well as the relative scarcity of population, especially in towns.

The Soviets made full use of Caucasian food resources by funneling them to other regions where the provisions were worse.[66] As the Caucasus had to cope with waves of refugees who had been sweeping in since the beginning of the war, Soviet authorities decided to ration the food. These were mainly such basic commodities as bread, sugar, and confectionary for the

65 Borovoi, *Vospominaniia*, p. 250.

66 Tula district in central Russia and besieged Leningrad: Decree of the Bureau of the Committee of the VKP(b) of [Stavropol'skii] *krai* on rendering assistance with seed and food grain to the population of Tula district, which suffered from the German Fascist occupiers, April 23, 1942, in Boiko, *Stavropol'e v Velikoi Otechestvennoi voine 1941-1945 gg.*, pp. 89-90. See also the decree of the Bureau of the Committee of the VKP(b) of [Stavropol'skii] *krai* on rendering assistance with seed and food grain to the working people of Leningrad, July 2, 1942, in ibid., p. 99.

civil population beginning September 1, 1941.[67] Despite logistical problems and temporary failures (like those that took place in Krasnodarskii *krai* in September 1941[68]), it seems that the food provisions with basic commodities remained satisfactory until the German takeover.[69] To illustrate the point, at that time, working men in Elista were distributed 800 grams of bread per day while non-working members of his family were given 500 grams. Besides, there were monthly allocations of sugar.[70] However, prices for other categories of food were high.[71]

With the front line rapidly approaching the borders of the North Caucasus in the summer of 1942, Soviet authorities faced a tight schedule for "solving" the food problem, which implied that no public food stocks should be left in the abandoned territory. The order of the Military Council of the North Caucasian Front, "On the preparation for elimination of reserves of bread, fuel, cattle and other articles of value provided their removal becomes impossible" was issued only on July 28, 1942.[72] Therefore, the removal of food reserves was increasingly replaced by their distribution to the local population and, in particular, by their physical destruction, as demonstrated by the excerpt related to Beloglinskii *raion*.[73]

One can make a general observation concerning the efficiency of the Soviet policy. Despite the logistical difficulties involved and

67 Beliaev and Bondar', *Kuban' v gody Velikoi Otechestvennoi voiny, 1941-1945*, pp. 53-54.

68 Baking of bread for army needs increased. This resulted in the shortage of bread available for the civil population. In mid-September 1941, food coupons for 15,000 tons of bread were not covered (*ne otovareny*). Enormous lines emerged. Ibid., pp. 99-100.

69 Village of Kursavka and Slavianskaia station in Krasnodarskii *krai*: Testimony of Testimony of Tsilia Gadleva, October 25, 1990, YVA, 0.3/4391, p. 9. See also the diary of Grigorii Ioffe, entry from November 9, 1941, DAARK, P-156/1/31, p. 31.

70 Poppe, *Reminiscences*, p. 158.

71 Krasnodar, Slavianskaia station: Diary of Grigorii Ioffe, entries from November, 10 and 14, 1941, DAARK, P-156/1/31, pp. 31, 32.

72 Beliaev and Bondar', *Kuban' v gody Velikoi Otechestvennoi voiny, 1941-1945*, pp. 315-316.

73 See p. 105 of this book.

the belatedness of the Soviet measures,[74] a considerable portion of the cattle and grain were duly removed from the area that would be occupied by the Germans:

> From July 20 until August 1, 1942, 206,700 heads of cattle, 411,300 sheep and goats, and more than 10,000 wagons of grain were moved from Krasnodarskii *krai* into the internal Soviet regions.[75]

> According to the preliminary data, as of August 5, 1942, some one million heads of cattle… 88,000 tons of grain were moved outside of the Terek River.[76]

According to the Soviet sources, a certain part of the food resources (mostly grain) was distributed to Soviet *kolkhozniki*.[77] Yet, there is no evidence that this was also done in the towns where local people looted the abandoned Soviet storages[78] and thus increased their own food resources. The Soviets destroyed considerable public stocks of food.[79] Nevertheless, the Germans were able to seize part of the cattle,[80] while there is no evidence that the grain was also captured. The bottom line is that by the time of the German occupation, the food conditions in Caucasian villages were better than in the towns. The latter still had enough provisions (mostly private-owned) for their citizens not to suffer from starvation in the short run. In the longer run, both the Germans and the local population benefitted from the collection of the 1942 fall harvest in this region.

74 Decree of the Bureau of the Committee of the VKP(b) of [Stavropol'skii] *krai* on the removal of cattle from the North areas of the *krai* to the area of Kizliar, July 27, 1942, in Boiko, *Stavropol'e*, pp. 102-103.

75 Grechko, *Bitva za Kavkaz* , p. 64.

76 Telegram sent by the Committee of the VKP(b) of [Stavropol'skii] *krai* on the measures taken in the *krai* in view of the military situation, September 8, 1942, in Boiko, *Stavropol'e*, pp. 109-110.

77 Ibid.; Grechko, *Bitva za Kavkaz*, p. 64.

78 Kislovodsk, Stavropol': Report of Moisei Evenson, Viktor Shklovskii, ed., [no date], YVA, P.21.2/1. See also Belikov, *Okkupatsiia*, pp. 50-51.

79 Grechko, *Bitva za Kavkaz*, p. 64.

80 Telegram sent by the Committee of the VKP(b) of [Stavropol'skii] *krai* in Boiko, *Stavropol'e*, pp. 109-110.

2.2. German occupation period

According to the EG D, in the Caucasus the Germans came to possess one of the richest Soviet agricultural assets:

> With the conquest of the Caucasian corn-growing steppe, one of Russia's most important agricultural surplus areas comes into the German power sphere. Most specifically, the area between Manytsch and Kuban' was a significant supply source of the Soviet Union.[81]

Although in a small number of industrial centers food conditions were unsatisfactory,[82] overall, the Germans did not view the food situation in the region as acute as in other Russian areas.[83] German strategists had no illusions regarding the source of this prosperity – i.e., more favorable climatic conditions and the prompt withdrawal of the Red Army – as well as the fact that the rural inhabitants plundered the public-owned food storages. Nevertheless, the most important task of providing the Wehrmacht and the local population with food in the short run could potentially be fulfilled.[84]

German food policy in North Caucasian towns varied from one locality to another. In a number of places, free trade in food commodities was encouraged.[85] To this end, movement restrictions were lifted, which led to significant improvements in the food conditions there. But even in these localities, the relief was only temporary, because the Germans traded with the food plundered from the Soviet stores, and there were natural limits to this "bounty," as indicated in a wartime testimony pertaining to Stavropol':

81 "Wirtschaftliche Lage im Operationsgebiet Nordkaukasien," CSpSd, Kommandostab, Berlin, MbOg, no. 28, Geheim, November 6, 1942, RGVA, 500/1/776, p. 25. See also Azamat Tatarov, "Sel'skokhoziaistvennye resursy Severnogo Kavkaza v ekonomicheskoi strategii Germanii v 1942-1944 gg.," *Nauchnyi zhyrnal KubGAU* 107 (2015): pp. 484-907.

82 Armavir, Maikop: Belikov, *Okkupatsiia*, pp. 92-93; CSpSd, Kommandostab, Berlin, MbOg, no. 28, Geheim, November 6, 1942, RGVA, 500/1/776, p. 26.

83 CSpSd, Kommandostab, Berlin, MbOg, no. 28, Geheim, November 6, 1942, RGVA, 500/1/776, p. 26.

84 Ibid.

85 Oldenburg, *Ideologie und militärisches Kalkül*, p. 275.

> There was an abundance in the Voroshilovsk [Stavropol' – KF] markets both of food and of consumer goods. For the most part, those were the goods plundered during the bombardment of the town on August 3, 1942, and the German entry to Voroshilovsk. At the same time, the German authorities did not prevent the delivery of agricultural productions to the town from the adjacent localities, which mainly resulted also from plundering food storehouses and seizing the abandoned property of *kolkhozy*.[86]

Yet, in other towns the stores were not reopened, and the result was a considerable increase in prices of food commodities.[87] Under such circumstances, local people were forced mainly to live off their stocks.[88] To cap it all, similar to the line adopted in most of the occupied Soviet territories, the Germans paid particular attention to the smooth arranging of food supplies to the Reich,[89] which took precedence over the provisions for the Army and the population. It is no wonder, therefore, that during the short period of German dominance in the Caucasus that the food situation in the region deteriorated markedly.[90] Significantly, however, it never reached the stage of starvation in any urban locality.

The generally moderate German policy in the region had sometimes found expression in its distribution of food to the local people since the beginning of the German occupation.[91] Yet, the

86 Belikov, *Okkupatsiia*, pp. 92-93.

87 Krasnodar: Intelligence survey no. 6 of the NKVD *krai* Administration, September 12, 1942, in Beliaev and Bondar', *Kuban' v gody Velikoi Otechestvennoi voiny, 1941-1945*, pp. 460-461.

88 Essentuki, Stavropol': Testimony of Raisa Kogan, April 29, 1943, GARF, 7021/17/4, p. 12; Belikov, *Okkupatsiia*, p. 99.

89 Stavropol'skii *krai*, Labinskaia *stanitsa*: Intelligence digest of the NKVD administration of Ordzhonikidzevskii *krai*: December 17, 1942, in Vodolazhskaia, Krivneva, and Mel'nik, *Stavropol'e v period nemetsko-fashistskoi okkupatsii (avgust 1942-ianvar' 1943)*, p. 71. Interrogation of traitors and henchmen, GARF, 7021/16/15, p. 14.

90 Krasnodarskii *krai*: Krinko, *Zhyzn' za liniei fronta*, p. 96.

91 Essentuki: Letter by the painter L. N. Tarabukin and his wife D. R. Gol'dshtein to the writer Iu. Kalugin. [1943] YVA, M.35/25, p. 85; "Massacre of the Caucasus

food rations allocated to the locals in some industrial centers did not suffice and caused the opposite results – i.e., the initially pro-German attitudes gave way to apathy, as admitted in a German post-occupation report:

> The bread allocations in the cities and entire districts, such as Cherkessk, Maikop, Novorossiisk, etc., were too small for subsistence. After a short time, the friendly pro-German mood gave way to cold indifference.[92]

Furthermore, in many towns there was no food distribution at all, at least during the first period of the occupation.[93] In the last months of the German occupation, the bread provisions in Krasnodar were set at the very low level of 200 grams for working people, while the rest were denied any provision at all.[94] Thus, German food policies were instrumental in further alienating the local population.[95]

German policy during the initial phase (the first four to six weeks) of the occupation in the towns is of particular importance because it is largely within this time span and in these localities that the Jews were exterminated in the North Caucasus. Most of the Jews in the region were evacuees or refugees, and as such were the first to run short of food reserves.[96] They were denied food rations at all stages – first as ordinary inhabitants of the

Jews" (Hebrew), [Jewish Anti-Fascist Committee, source: letters from the local inhabitants], *Ha-tsofe* (Tel Aviv), no. 1702, August 4, 1943.

92 "Gedanken über die Möglichkeit einer stärkeren Einflußnahme des Reichsführer SS auf die Verhältnisse in den militärisch besetzten und geführten Gebieten," March 15, 1942 [Apparently, there is a mistake in the date. 1943 is more appropriate – KF], RGVA, 1323/2/267, p. 7.

93 Krasnodar, Piatigorsk: Intelligence survey no 6, in Beliaev and Bondar', *Kuban' v gody Velikoi Otechestvennoi voiny, 1941-1945*, pp. 460-461; Intelligence digest of the NKVD administration of Ordzhonikidzevskii *krai*, December 17, 1942, in Vodolazhskaia, Krivneva, and Mel'nik, *Stavropol'e v period nemetsko-fashistskoi okkupatsii (avgust 1942-ianvar' 1943)*, pp. 68-69.

94 Konstantin M. Simonov, *Raznye dni voiny: Dnevnik pisatel'ia*, [no date], available from http://militera.lib.ru/db/simonov_km/2_08.html.

95 Oldenburg, *Ideologie und militärisches Kalkül*, pp. 275-280.

96 As compared to the native residents. Essentuki: Testimony of Raisa Kogan, April 29, 1943, GARF, 7021/17/4, p. 12.

towns,[97] then as forced laborers,[98] and finally as prisoners before their execution.[99] Sometimes this was done publicly, such as by pasting signs reading "No bread for Jews" in the bread store fronts.[100] In the vast Caucasian region, there is only one example of food distribution for Jews within towns. In the town of Teberda, food was extended to the Jews in the town's orphanage – this single occurrence of distribution was carried out only during the time when the Romanians controlled the town.[101]

In rural areas, Jews were occasionally provided with food rations, albeit inadequately.[102] The German authorities reduced the food rations for the small number of Jews who had survived the first wave of killing operations by half, as compared to the non-Jewish population.[103] During hours of forced labor, many Jews were not given any food at all.[104] The Jews were always denied food while detained together prior to their execution[105] or during

97 Essentuki: Akt of the Commission of Essentuki, July 10, 1943, GARF, 7021/17/4, p. 1. Letter by the painter L. N. Tarabukin and his wife D. R. Gol'dshtein to the writer Iu. Kalugin, [1943], YVA, M.35/25, p. 85.

98 Nal'chik, Mikoianshakhar: Testimony of Raisa Shamilova, August 19, 1998, in Danilova, *Iskhod gorskikh evreev*, p. 26; Testimony of Ida Nikeeva, July 29, 1943, GARF, 7021/17/10, p. 204.

99 Elista, Teberda: Report of the ESC on the atrocities of the German Fascist occupiers in the occupied *ulusy* and town Elista, [no later than September 10, 1943], GARF, 7021/8/26, pp. 10-11; Akt on Teberda, July 5, 1943, GARF, 7021/17/7, pp. 4-5.

100 Essentuki: Letter by the painter L. N. Tarabukin and his wife D. R. Gol'dshtein to the writer Iu. Kalugin. [1943]. YVA, M.35/25, p. 85. See also "Massacre of the Caucasus Jews" (Hebrew), [Jewish Anti-Fascist Committee, source: letters from the local inhabitants], *Ha-tsofe* (Tel Aviv), no. 1702, August 4, 1943., p. 3.

101 Testimony of Vadim Maniker, April 1975, YVA, 0.3/4108, p. 3.

102 "4th GKKK" *kolkhoz* in Krasnodarskii *krai*," testimony of the doctor Antonina Sitnikova, July 12, 1943, YVA, M.33/301, p. 156; Akt of the Commission of "4th GKKK" *kolkhoz*, July 12, 1943, YVA, M.33/301, p. 152.

103 Untitled document, BA-MA, RW 46/630, TBM/Qu Br.B.Nr. 426/42 (1.9.1942) in Oldenburg, *Ideologie und militärisches Kalkül*, p. 303.

104 Akt of the Commission of the village of Menzhynskoe, June 27, 1943, GARF, 7021/17/10, pp. 155-156.

105 Stavropol'skii *krai*, village of Izobil'noe, Egorlykskii *raion*: Akt of the Commission of Izobil'nenskii *raion*, June 29, 1943, GARF, 7021/17/10, pp. 121-122; Akt of the Commission of Egorlykskii *raion*, GARF, 7021/17/10, p. 86.

their transport from one area to another.[106] There is at least one case where there is a record of starvation among the Jews as the local people were forbidden to give them food – but this was a rather rare exception to the rule.[107] As the food conditions in the countryside were, in general, more satisfactory, the German policy did not have such a devastating effect on the Jews' prospects for survival there.

In summarizing the relationship between the food factor and the Holocaust in the North Caucasus, it is illuminating that in wartime and postwar sources, the Germans never gave food considerations as the rationale behind their decision to kill the Jews in the region, in contrast to the Crimea. The generally favorable climatic conditions of the Caucasus and its status as the recognized Soviet agricultural reservoir rendered the food argument hardly compatible with the profile of the region. The majority of the Jews in the North Caucasus were killed under conditions in which the local inhabitants had sufficient food stocks they could have traded with Jews for money or goods. Even while some Jews remained alive when the food situation in the region deteriorated in the course of the occupation, the Germans never raised the food argument as a pretext for getting rid of the Jews.

106 Akt of the Commission of Otradnenskaia *stanitsa*, GARF, 7021/16/464, p. 16.

107 Bekeshevskaia *stanitsa*: Akt of the Commission of Suvorovskii *raion*, GARF, 7021/17/12, p. 3. The author is unaware of other cases of malnourishment of Jews in Caucasian villages.

Chapter Six

The Fate of Karaites and Krymchaks in the Crimea and Mountain Jews in the North Caucasus during the Holocaust

1. German Attitudes Towards "Special Jewish Groups" prior to the Seizure of the Crimea and the Caucasus

The Germans did not view Karaites, Krymchaks, and Mountain Jews as one unit, but preferred to deal with them separately. Nevertheless, there were many common features in the German approaches towards these groups that enable the exploration of their fate during the Holocaust in the Crimea and the Caucasus within the framework of one chapter. For the purposes of this study, they are dubbed "special Jewish groups."

The common features of these groups of Jews include: a) insufficient German knowledge of these groups with respect to their connections to the Jews and Judaism; b) German suspicions voiced before, during, and even after the German occupation of the Crimea and the North Caucasus that these groups shared certain common religious or racial characteristics with the Jews and, thus, may deserve the same treatment as the latter, i.e. total annihilation; c) involvement of established German academia, new Nazi "scholarship," as well as interactive on-ground investigations in the Crimea and the North Caucasus conducted in the attempt to establish the degree of Jewishness of these groups; d) German policies towards these groups that differed from the standard Nazi approach to the Jews (i.e., exemption from the standard cleansing of all Jews in the territories under German rule) and varied from partial annihilation, complete extermination (but as a rule, separately from and later than that of the Ashkenazi Jews), and recognition as non-Jews; and e) attempts by all these groups to present themselves as different from Jews and, thus, to secure their exemption from anti-Jewish decrees.

By the time the Germans invaded the Soviet Union, they had already faced the problem of 18 Karaites living in the Reich itself. After the Nuremberg laws were passed, the Karaites pleaded with the German authorities for an exemption from the discriminatory anti-Jewish legislation.[1] Consequently, the latter consulted experts from the German scholarly community for their views on the topic. Most of the contemporary German experts viewed the Karaites as a Jewish sect. In a May 1938 report from the Foreign University of Berlin's Russia Institute, the experts reached no definitive conclusion, but strongly implied that the Karaites were "racial Jews," based on a mixture of cultural evidence. Prior to the October Revolution, the report noted, the Karaites had primarily engaged in trade "and typically Jewish crafts," such as jewelry making, shoemaking, and tailoring. Although they did not recognize the authority of the Talmud, they claimed to descend from Jews. Thus, it was decided that due to their "extremely strong familial seclusion… a strong mixing of the Karaites with Tatars or Russians is not to be accepted."[2]

Professor Lothar Löffler[3] of the University of Königsberg's

1 Shmuel Spektor, "The Karaites in German-Dominated Europe in the Light of the German Documents" (Hebrew), *Peamim* 29 (1986): p. 91.

2 "Rußland-Institut der Auslandhochschule Berlin, 19.5.1938," contained in memo, v. Ulmenstein to RMdI, June 17, 1938, in Eric Ehrenreich, *The Nazi Ancestral Proof: Genealogy, Racial Science, and the Final Solution* (Bloomington and Indianapolis: Indiana University Press, 2007), pp. 12-13.
Nazi Germany's handling of "special Jewish groups" is indicative of close links between the Nazi regime and scholarship and the close involvement of the latter in the "Final Solution of Jewish Question." On this subject, see Alan E. Steinweis, *Studying the Jew: Scholarly Antisemitism in Nazi Germany* (Cambridge, MA: Harvard University Press, 2006).

3 Lothar Löffler (1901-1983): Worked at the Kaiser Wilhelm Institute for Anthropology in 1927; served as a member of the NSDAP and the SA in 1932;

Racial Biological Institute was less circumspect. The Karaites, wrote Löffler in 1939, liked to portray themselves as "opponents of the Jews," but:

> … in fact, it has now turned out that they are a camouflaged Jewish organization that earlier was supposed to ease the then politically obstructed way for the Jews to [St.] Petersburg… Therefore, in the absence of proof to the contrary, it is to be assumed that any such sects contain racially foreign blood.[4]

This was also the conclusion drawn by anonymous authors of a memorandum compiled for the *Judenreferat*[5] of the SS in the summer of 1938. They looked through all the available literature on Karaites, including Jewish sources, and examined the whole history of the emergence of the Karaite movement, emphasizing the status of Karaites in Tsarist Russia. Although Karaites had been equal to Russians in terms of civil rights, it was still stressed in the report that the Tsarist administration viewed them as a Judaic sect. The conclusion was clear: "The Karaites are to be considered as Jews."[6]

Nevertheless, the decision reached in early 1939 by the Reich Genealogical Office (*Reichsstelle für Sippenforschung*) under the Nazi Party and the Ministry of Interior, the highest party and state authority to rule in racial matters,[7] overlooked the stance of

served as chair and director of the Racial Biological Institute at the University of Königsberg in 1934; became regional head of the Racial Political Department of the NSDAP in 1934; became chair of the Genetics and Racial Biology Department in Vienna in 1942; detained by authorities due to his links to the Nazi regime until October 1945 and thereupon banned from his profession; worked at Niedersachsen Health Office in 1952; taught social biology at the Technical Institute at Hannover in 1954; received the *Bundesverdienskreuz I. Klasse* in 1956; taught at the Medical Institute at Hannover from 1968-1972.

4 Gutachten, Prof. Dr. Lothar Löffler, Rassenbiologischen Instituts der Universität Königsberg/Pr. November 2, 1939, in Ehrenreich, *The Nazi Ancestral Proof*, p. 113.

5 Department in charge of Jewish affairs.

6 Correspondence of the SD on the question of the Karaites, Russian State Military Archive (RGVA), 500/1/187, pp. 27-30.

7 On this agency, see the aforementioned book by Eric Ehrenreich.

the experts and the SS. This agency took a moderate approach by contending that:

> The statement that the Karaites have ancient connections to the Jews may, however, not be inferred, because the racial composition of a person is not based on whether or not he belongs to a specific people but, rather, it is always based on his personal ancestral relations and biological traits.[8]

Later, some 200 Karaites in occupied France also interceded with the German occupation authorities.[9] They enlisted the support of the White Russian circles and claimed that they were of Tatar-Turkish origin and that their religion was independent from Judaism. Their important argument was that in Tsarist Russia the Karaites had not been placed on the same footing as Jews, and were considered a separate religious group in their own right. Over the course of protracted inquiry conducted by the central authorities in Berlin, it was decided that the "French" Karaites were to be exempted from anti-Jewish measures. Furthermore, in due time, Nazi Germany even asked Vichy France (which had long adhered to a more extreme stance than the Germans by equating the Karaites with the Jews in the non-occupied zone[10]) to exclude Karaites from anti-Jewish measures there, too.

In occupied France, the Germans also encountered hundreds of Jews of Georgian,[11] as well as Bukharian, Iranian, and Afghan descent.[12] Initially, some of them complied with anti-Jewish

8 "Der Leiter der Reichsstelle für Sippenforschung," Berlin, January 5, 1939, RGVA, 500/1/263, p. 5.

9 Emanuela T. Semi, "L'oscillation ethnique: Le cas des Caraites pendant la Seconde Guerre Mondiale," *Revue de l'Histoire des Religions* 206, no. 4 (October-December 1989): pp. 377-398.

10 Emanuela T. Semi, "The Image of the Karaites in Nazi and Vichy France Documents," *Jewish Journal of Sociology* 32, no. 2 (1990): pp. 81-93.

11 [No first name] Eligulashvili, "How the Jews of Gruziia in Occupied France were Saved," *Yad Vashem Studies* 6 (1967): pp. 251-254.

12 Asaf Atchildi, "Rescue of Jews of Bukharan, Iranian and Afghan Origin in Occupied France (1940-1944)," *Yad Vashem Studies* 6 (1967): pp. 257-281. See also Warren Green, "The Fate of Oriental Jews in Vichy France," *Wiener Library Bulletin* 32, no. 49-50 (1979): pp. 40-50.

measures and, thus, became subjected to various restrictions. However, they soon appealed to the German authorities for recognition as non-Jews. Importantly, these groups were aware that the cases of the Karaites and Georgian Jews had already been positively solved.[13] Influential émigré and diplomatic circles interceded with the Germans on their behalf. In consequence, they also received recognition as non-Jews by the central authorities in Berlin.

Nazi Germany's policies were rather restrained towards the members of non-Ashkenazi groups professing Judaism who lived outside of the Soviet Union. However, it could be anticipated that German policies would be far more stringent towards Soviet Jews and people related to them. This had to do with the Nazi worldview, according to which Soviet Jews, in particular those living within the Soviet Union's "old borders" (i.e., before World War II), were considered the cornerstone of the Bolshevik regime and subject to prompt annihilation.[14]

Nazi Germany was aware of the existence of "special Jewish groups" living in the southern part of the Soviet Union. Most German efforts aimed at the exploration of the "special Jewish groups" were made as a part of the *Ostforschung* (research on the Eastern Europe).[15] In 1939-1942, some German research institutes, such as the *Auslandsinstitut, Institut für Grenz- und Auslandstudien* and the *Wansee-Institut*, produced semi-classified studies usually categorized as "*Nur für den Dienstgebrauch*" (for official use only) and made under the auspice of the SS.[16] This

13 Atchildi, "Rescue of Jews of Bukharan, Iranian and Afghan Origin in Occupied France (1940-1944)," pp. 259-260.

14 Altshuler, "The Unique Features of the Holocaust in the Soviet Union," p. 173.

15 On the *Ostforschung* in Nazi Germany, see Dietrich Beyrau and Mark Keck-Szajbel, "Eastern Europe as a "Sub-Germanic Space": Scholarship on Eastern Europe under National Socialism," *Kritika: Explorations in Russian and Eurasian History* 13, no. 3 (Summer 2012): pp. 685-723; Ingo Haar, "Deutsche 'Ostforschung' und Antisemitismus," *Zeitschrift für Geschichtswissenschaft* 48, no. 6 (2000): pp. 485-508; and Burgleich, *Germany Turns Eastwards.*

16 Gerhard Teich and Hanz Ruebel, Institut für Grenz- und Auslandstudien, Reichsführer-SS, Rasseamt, eds., *Verzeichnis der Völker, Volksgruppen und Volksstämme auf Gebiet der ehemaligen UdSSR: Geschichte, Verbreitung, Rasse, Bekenntnis* (Berlin: Steglitz, 1941); *Die Völker des Kaukasus und seiner*

"research" (which must be taken with a grain of salt, as it was conducted in the spirit of aiming to prove Nazi racial dogma) relied on the factual data from official Soviet publications, existing theoretical knowledge in German scholarship, and revelations from Nazi Germany's contacts with the émigrés (via both general interaction with the public and individual personal contacts) who had left Soviet Russia. The importance of these studies in defining Nazi Germany's approach towards "special Jewish groups" is significant, particularly when they also reflected the views of the SS, which was in charge of the "Solution of the Jewish Question" on Soviet territory.

This research traced the origin of the non-Ashkenazi Jewish groups and established their degree of Jewishness. In the Nazi mindset, this meant gauging how similar they were to the Ashkenazi Jews whom the Germans had gotten accustomed to seeing around. The studies focused on a number of points, with stress on the possibility of common ancestry with the Ashkenazi Jews. There was no unanimity in the German scholarly community on the Karaites' racial origin and language, with both Jewish and non-Jewish versions suggested. Regarding the Karaites' origin, it was only stated that Chazar link could be ruled out,[17] while their language was said to belong either to the Turko-Tatar group,[18] or to contain elements of Tatar and Hebrew.[19] The only research the Germans made concerning Krymchaks was related to their language, which they declared to be Crimean Tatar.[20] However, there was ambiguity regarding Mountain Jews. They were said to have originated in Persia, afterwards intermingling with the

Vorländer (Berlin und Stuttgart: Deutsches Ausland-Institut, 1941), and Nationalsozialistische Deutsche Arbeiter-Partei (NSDAP), Schutzstaffel, Reichssicherheitshauptamt, *Kaukasus*, Hrsg. vom Chef der Sicherheitspolizei und des SD (Berlin: Wannsee-Institut, 1942).

17 Reinhart Maurach, "Die Karaimen in der russischen Gesetzgebung," *Zeitschrift für Rassenkunde* 10, nos. 2-3 (1939): pp. 163-164.

18 Ibid., p. 59.

19 Reinhart Maurach, "Die Karaimen in der russischen Gesetzgebung," pp. 163-164.

20 Teich and Ruebel, *Verzeichnis der Völker, Volksgruppen und Volksstämme auf Gebiet der ehemaligen UdSSR*, p. 60.

Iranians. They had lived in the Caucasus since the 8th century AD.[21] Another study also advocated a non-Jewish version of the group's origin, claiming that the Mountain Jews were a "mixture of the Oriental race and other Asian and Indian races."[22] Yet, another study maintained that they were a "Jewish tribe that migrated to Dagestan."[23] Likewise, there was no certainty regarding the Mountain Jews' language, but all accounts regarded it as a mixture of other languages. But if in one "study" it contained elements of Yiddish, Tatar, Azerbaijani-Turkish, or Georgian;[24] in another one it had elements of only Tat and Turkish.[25]

Another racial characteristic of all groups included external appearance (with implications for possible intermarriage with local people, or, alternatively, "bearing traces of links" to Jews). German studies had information only with respect to the Karaites, who were described as possessing a non-Jewish appearance, "like Tatars."[26]

The religion (an important albeit poorly-defined characteristic in Nazi theory and policies[27]) practiced by all three groups was declared to be Jewish or Mosaic, with the stipulation that the Karaites did not recognize the Talmud.[28]

Finally, the Germans also inquired into the status enjoyed by these groups in the Russian Empire (although they assumed that Russian policies were informed by non-racial approaches[29]). Of

21 *Die Völker des Kaukasus und seiner Vorländer.*

22 Teich and Ruebel, *Verzeichnis der Völker, Volksgruppen und Volksstämme auf Gebiet der ehemaligen UdSSR*, pp. 60-61.

23 Ibid.

24 Ibid.

25 *Die Völker des Kaukasus und seiner Vorländer.*

26 Ibid., pp. 163-164.

27 On this topic see, for example, Dan Michman, "Jewish Religious Life under Nazi Domination: Nazi Attitudes and Jewish Problems," *Studies in Religion/Sciences Religieuses* 22, no. 2 (June 1993): pp. 147-165.

28 Teich and Ruebel, *Verzeichnis der Völker, Volksgruppen und Volksstämme auf Gebiet der ehemaligen UdSSR*, pp. 59-61.

29 This is increasingly questioned by contemporary scholarship, at least regarding the late imperial period. See Eugene M. Avrutin, "Racial Categories and the Politics of (Jewish) Difference in Late Imperial Russia," *Kritika: Explorations in Russian and Eurasian History* 8, no. 1 (Winter 2007): pp. 13-40;

particular importance for the German researchers was whether or not these groups were given the same treatment as Ashkenazi Jews (most specifically, whether a ban was imposed on their ownership of land). Again, the information was available only for the Karaites. They learned that the Karaites had possessed a privileged status in the Russian Empire that was distinct from the Jews: Since 1862, the Karaites had been equal to Russians. Yet, the Germans expressed the significant reservation that the Russian decision was made on grounds of the Karaites' social usefulness instead of according to racial criteria.[30]

The studies arrived at different conclusions as to how much Jewish blood was in the Karaites, Krymchaks, and Mountain Jews. Hence, the ensuing policy recommendations towards these groups also varied. Regarding the Karaites, the conclusions were rather positive: It was stated that the claim that they belonged to the ancient Jewry could not be substantiated.[31] Another study maintained that they were racially close to Crimean Tatars and were to be regarded as non-Jews.[32] There were no recommendations concerning the Krymchaks (obviously, for want of information about them). With respect to the Mountain Jews, it was recommended that they be regarded as a foreign body in the Caucasus — but what that actually meant was open to interpretation.[33]

Finally, of note is the way the "special Jewish groups" were semantically referred to in German correspondence. When these studies employed the term "*Jude*," this had obvious implications on the proposed German policies towards them. The names used for the Krymchaks and Mountain Jews contained a "Jewish" element ('*Krim-Juden*' / '*Krimtschaken*';[34]

Eli Weinerman, "Racism, Racial Prejudice and Jews in Late Imperial Russia," *Ethnic and Racial Studies* 17, no. 3 (1994): pp. 442-495.

30 Maurach, "Die Karaimen in der russischen Gesetzgebung," p. 172.

31 "Der Leiter der Reichsstelle für Sippenforschung," Berlin, January 5, 1939, RGVA, 500/1/263, p. 5.

32 Teich and Ruebel, *Verzeichnis der Völker, Volksgruppen und Volksstämme auf Gebiet der ehemaligen UdSSR*, p. 59.

33 Nationalsozialistische Deutsche Arbeiter-Partei et al., *Kaukasus*, p. 64.

34 Ibid., p. 60.

and '*Bergjuden*'/'*kaukasische Juden*',[35] respectively), while those regarding Karaites did not ('*Krim-Karaeer*'/'*Karaiten*'/'*Karaim*'[36]).

Thus, prior to their invasion of the areas populated by the non-Ashkenazi Jewish groups, the Germans did possess some knowledge concerning most of them. However, this information was often abrupt and self-contradictory and contained numerous loopholes or more than one version, especially concerning critical points. This left the possibility for various approaches to be applied to these groups if new relevant findings were gleaned on the spot and/or political considerations necessitated clear-cut decisions. In line with this view, their studies refrained from policy recommendations for Nazi Germany regarding the "special Jewish groups." There were also other *Ostforschung* studies published in Nazi Germany during this critical period (1939-1942) that presented an in-depth analysis of the developments in the regions, yet entirely disregarded the presence of "special Jewish groups" there.[37]

The inquiry into the question of whether or not Karaites should be regarded as Jews was continued in the summer of 1941 after the Wehrmacht took over Soviet Lithuania, which had a small Karaite community in the area of Trokai.[38] Over the course of the Jewish-Karaite dispute[39] and questioning of Jewish scholars

35 *Die Völker des Kaukasus und seiner Vorländer*; NSDAP, *Kaukasus*, p. 64.

36 Teich and Ruebel, *Verzeichnis der Völker, Volksgruppen und Volksstämme auf Gebiet der ehemaligen UdSSR*, p. 59.

37 Alexander Nikuradse, *Kaukasien, Nordkaukasien, Aserbeidschan, Armenien, Georgien: Geschichtlicher Umriß* (München: Hoheneichen-Verlag, 1942). There is no reference to Mountain Jews in any part of this otherwise very detailed review of the Caucasian population.

38 The analysis of the Karaites in Lithuania follows the notions invoked in Burgleich, *Germany Turns Eastwards*; Mikhail Kizilov, *The Sons of Scripture. The Karaites in Poland and Lithuania in the Twentieth Century* (Berlin: De Gruyter, 2015), pp. 321-365; ibid., *The Karaites of Galicia: An Ethnoreligious Minority among the Ashkenazim, the Turks, and the Slavs, 1772-1945* (Leiden and Boston: Brill, 2009), pp. 294-302; Kiril Feferman, "Nazi Germany and the Karaites in 1938-44: Between Racial Theory and Realpolitik," *Nationalities Papers* 39, no. 2 (March 2011): pp. 277-294.

39 Philip Friedman, "The Karaites under Nazi Rule," in Max Beloff, ed., *On the Track*

on the origin of the Karaites,[40] it was established that the Karaites "practiced a religion containing elements of Judaism, Islam, and Christianity, and spoke an old form of Turkish or Russian devoid of [Yiddish] jargon." The supposedly "scientific" racial criteria in this report did not betray any similarity to the Jews:

> Judging by their appearance, the Karaites make an overwhelmingly Tatar-Near Asiatic impression: dark, with wide brown eyes, prominent cheekbones, and partly armenoid" extended skulls, and smooth Near Asian noses. Neither their gestures nor their appearance make a Jewish impression.[41]

The decision was finalized in Alfred Rosenberg's *Ostministerium*, which stated that since the Karaites farmed and were not engaged in Jewish "parasitic" activities, they were not to be handled as Jews. This meant that "all unnecessary harshness" was to be avoided, lest this were to produce unfortunate political consequences in the Orient.[42] The invocation of foreign political considerations represents one of the very few examples when the Germans clarified what was likely their most important rationale behind their privileged treatment of one of the "special Jewish groups."

of Tyranny: Essays presented by the Wiener Library to Leonard G. Montefiore, O.B.E., on the occasion of his seventieth birthday (London: The Wiener Library, 1960), p. 110.

40 Ibid., p. 111.

41 Der Generalkomissar in Kauen, "Karaimenfrage in Litauen: Nichteinordnung als Juden," September 1, 1941, Yad Vashem Archives (YVA), JM/528.4.

42 RMfdOg, Berlin, Dr. Wetzel, "Stellung der Karaimen," Geheim, May 7, 1943, YVA, JM/5626.

2. Karaites in the Crimea[43]

2.1. General concerns

The Karaite community residing in the Crimean peninsula was the biggest in Eastern Europe.[44] According to the data of the 1926 Soviet census, 8,324 Karaites were registered in the region.[45] Like Ashkenazi Jews and other communities of a similar socio-economic profile, their number was slightly on the decrease on the eve of World War II (to some 6,500 people[46]) – but they were still visible. They were an ancient community, whose origin can hardly be elucidated with any degree of certainty, but they certainly belonged

43 On the fate of Karaites during the Second World War, see Kizilov, *The Sons of Scripture*, pp. 293-368; Hannelore Müller, *Religionswissenschaftliche Minoritätenforschung: Zur religionshistorischen Dynamik der Karäer im Osten Europas* (Wiesbaden: Harrassowitz, 2010), pp. 131-162; Yosef Algamil, *The Karaite Jews in the Eastern Europe in the Past and in the Present* (Hebrew) (Ramle: National Council of the Karaite Jews in Israel, 2000), pp. 163-209; Nathan Schur, *History of the Karaites* (Franfurt am Main and New York: Peter Lang, 1992), pp. 123-125; Shmuel Spektor, "The Karaites in German-Dominated Europe," pp. 90-108; Warren Paul Green, "The Nazi Racial Policy towards the Karaites," *Soviet Jewish Affaires* 8, no. 2 (1978): pp. 35-45; Friedman, "The Karaites under Nazi Rule," pp. 97-123.
For some literature on the Karaites in Russian, see Aleksandr Fuki, *Karaimy – synov'ia i docheri Rossii: Rasskazy i ocherki ob uchastii v boiakh ot Krymskoi voiny do Velikoi Otechestvennoi* (Moscow: "Interprint," 1995); Valentin Kefeli, *Karaimy* (Moscow: Rossiiskaia akademiia nauk, Institut eetnologii i antropologii im. N. N. Miklukho-Maklaia, 1992); Iurii Polkanov, *Karai – krymskie tatary – tiurki: Istoriia, etnografiia, kultura* (Simferopol': Assotsiatsiia krymskikh karaimov, 1997).

44 On the pre-Soviet history of the Crimean Karaites, see for example, Mikhail Kizilov, "Slaves, Money Lenders, and Prisoner Guards: The Jews and the Trade in Slaves and Captives in the Crimean Khanate," *Journal of Jewish Studies* 58, no. 2 (2007): pp. 189-210 and idem., "The Crimean Karaites in the Portrayal of the 19th Century Polish Travelers," *Studia Orientalia* 95 (2003): pp. 93-108; Mark Kupovetsky, "Dinamika chislennosti i rasseleniia karaimov i krymchakov za poslednie dvesti let," in Igor' Krupnik, ed., *Geografiia i kul'tura etnograficheskikh grupp tatar v SSSR* (Moscow: GO SSSR, 1983), pp. 76-93.

45 Warren Paul Green, "The Fate of the Crimean Jewish Community: Askenazim, Krimchaks, and Karaites," *Jewish Social Studies* 46, no. 2 (1984): p. 175.

46 Spektor, "The Karaites in German-Dominated Europe," p. 90; See also Table 14, "Krymchak and Karaite population in the Crimea as of 1930".

to one of the earliest groups that populated the peninsula.[47]

Under Russian rule, the Karaites were able to secure certain legal and economical privileges at first and then, in 1862, full equality in rights. Needless to say, the Ashkenazi Jews were never able to achieve such a level of emancipation in the Empire. Evidence, albeit scarce, indicates the strained relations between the Karaites and the Rabbinical Jews[48] (including Krymchaks) up to the Bolshevik Revolution in 1917.[49] Their social standing was relatively high. Some of the Karaites participated in the Civil War in Russia on the White side, later fleeing to Europe.[50] However, it seems that the more than 20 years of Soviet power in the Crimea resulted in easing centuries-old religious tensions between the two groups, as may be inferred, among other things, from intermarriages between Rabbanites and Karaites during this period.[51]

After the outbreak of Soviet-German hostilities, many of the conscript-age Karaite men were drafted into the Red Army.[52] Some

47 Tapani Harviainen, "The Karaites in Eastern Europe and the Crimea: An Overview," in Meira Polliack, ed., *Karaite Judaism; A Guide to Its History and Literary Sources* (Leiden: Brill, 2003), pp. 633-655.

48 Rabbinical Jews, or Rabbanites, are the adherents of Rabbinic Judaism, the mainstream form of Judaism since the 6th century, after the codification of the Talmud. Rabbinic Judaism gained predominance within the Jewish diasporas between the first and sixth centuries, with the development of the Talmud to control the interpretation of Jewish scripture and to encourage the practice of Judaism in the absence of Temple sacrifice.

49 Zionist Organisation, *Die Judenpogrome in Rußland*, p. 173.

50 Spektor, "The Karaites in German-Dominated Europe," p. 90. See also, Polkanov, *Karai — krymskie tatary — tiurki*, pp. 81-82.

51 I made this observation on the basis of analysis of the testimonies submitted in the collection of the Hall of Names in Yad Vashem, Jerusalem that dealt with the Holocaust in the Crimea. A growing share of mixed marriages between the Karaites and non-Karaites is mentioned in Polkanov, *Karai — krymskie tatary — tiurki*, pp. 83-84, 79-80; Algamil, *The Karaite Jews in the Eastern Europe in the Past and in the Present*, pp. 184-185; V.S. Kropotov, *Voennye traditsii krymskikh karaimov* (Simferopol', 2004), pp. 94-95.
On the relations between Karaites in Jews in interwar Evpatoriia, see Testimony of Revekka Flat, July 3, 2000, in Rivkina and Tiaglyi, *Vospominaniia zhitelei evreiskikh poselenii v Krymu*, p. 122.

52 Polkanov, *Karai — krymskie tatary — tiurki*, pp. 83-84. See also, Algamil, *The Karaite Jews in the Eastern Europe in the Past and in the Present*, pp. 184-185 and Kropotov, *Voennye traditsii krymskikh karaimov*, pp. 94-95.

Karaites later joined the partisan movement in the peninsula.[53] Overall, given their socio-economic profile (i.e., highly urbanized with a high level of literacy), the Karaites were in a relatively good position to learn of Nazi Germany's persecutions of the Jews. The available statistical data for the Karaites of Simferopol' (some 900-1,000 before the war and then 800 people registered in the 1942 and 1943 censuses[54]) and for the whole peninsula after the Soviet liberation (6,357 people as of July 1944,[55] in contrast to a slightly higher number on the eve of the war) imply that the great majority of the Crimean Karaites remained in the peninsula. This may indicate, in turn, that the Crimean Karaites did not envisage the possibility of being treated like Jews (of whom up to 40% were evacuated from the Crimea[56]) – perhaps because they did not regard themselves as belonging one way or another to the Jewish people.

The Crimean Karaites' saga began to draw the attention of the scholarly community in the 1960s.[57] They started to understand it better as scholars began to take notice of wartime German documents and the recently disclosed proceedings of trials conducted against Nazi criminals in Western Germany,[58] which presented the official wartime Nazi version of the events. It is noteworthy that, despite these findings, the theme of Karaite-German relations is mainly overlooked in the war accounts

53 Fuki, *Karaimy – synov'ia i docheri Rossii*. See also, Polkanov, *Karai – krymskie tatary – tiurki*, pp. 85-89 and Algamil, *The Karaite Jews in the Eastern Europe in the Past and in the Present*, p. 184.

54 Composition of the population of Simferopol' as of January 1, 1942, State Archive of the Autonomous Republic of the Crimea (DAARK), R-1302/1 (additional)/9, p. 8; Composition of the population of Simferopol' as of January 19, 1943, DAARK, R-1302/1 (additional)/9, p. 1.

55 Memorandum of the Commissar of Interior of the Crimean ASSR Vasilii Sergienko, March 24, 1945, in Vsevolod Vikhnovich, "Massovye etnicheskie deportatsii iz Kryma v 1944-1945 gg. i krymskie karaimy," *Paralleli* 4-5 (2004): pp. 89-90. My thanks are extended to Dr. Mikhail Kizilov for drawing my attention to and sharing the latter source with me.

56 Arad, *The Holocaust in the Soviet Union*, p. 374.

57 Friedman, "The Karaites under Nazi Rule," pp. 97-123.

58 Arad, *The History of the Holocaust*, pp. 374-376; Schur, *History of the Karaites*, pp. 123-125; Spektor, "The Karaites in German-Dominated Europe," pp. 90-108; Green, "The Fate of the Crimean Jewish Community," pp. 169-176; and Green, "The Nazi Racial Policy towards the Karaites," pp. 35-45.

presented by the Karaites themselves in Hebrew[59] and Russian.[60] In all probability, the Soviets were unaware of the Karaite-German relations[61] and, therefore, their sources do not deal with the topic. German reports seem to be the most reliable source, primarily because they were the only ones complied at the time the events occurred and not *a posteriori*.

2.2. German policy towards the Crimean Karaites

The EG D, which operated in the southern part of the Soviet Union, first faced the small groups of Karaites outside of the Crimea (in Kherson, Nikolaev, and Odessa[62]). It seems that the EG D refrained from making binding decisions, but did not treat them as Jews (i.e., in Odessa[63]). Many more Karaites lived on the peninsula, however, and the EG D Leader Otto Ohlendorf was reluctant to make a decision concerning them. He sensed that the problem of whether or not they must be "equated" to Jews (that is, to be annihilated) was beyond his competence. Ohlendorf likely considered granting an exemption from the Jewish status to such a large group to be the exclusive prerogative of the highest Reich authorities. One way or another, Ohlendorf requested clarification and conveyed the matter to Berlin.

In the meantime, the *Einsatzgruppe* command took initiative and exempted the Karaites from the anti-Jewish measures. Nevertheless, their registration alongside the Ashkenazi Jews proceeded unimpeded. This left all options open in the event

59 Yosef Algamil, *The Karaite Jews in the Eastern Europe in the Past and in the Present*, pp. 163-209. See also, Algamil, *The History of the Karaite Jewry* (Hebrew), vol. 1 (Ramle: National Council of the Karaite Jews in Israel, 1979), pp. 198-200.

60 Fuki, *Karaimy — synov'ia i docheri Rossii*. See also Kefeli, Karaimy; Polkanov, *Karai — krymskie tatary — tiurki*; and Kropotov, *Voennye traditsii krymskikh karaimov*, pp. 82-97, 125-126.

61 Vikhnovich, "Massovye etnicheskie deportatsii iz Kryma," pp. 89-93.

62 Angrick, *Besatzungspolitik und Massenmord*, p. 326.

63 Testimony of Polina Shtil'vasser (1924), [no date], YVA, 0.3/5218, p. 3; also available from the Central State Archive of the Public Organizations of Ukraine (Kiev), 1/23/1062, pp. 86-87, in Al'tman, *Zhertvy nenavisti*, p. 423; Liusia Kalika, "2.5 goda, provedennye v Odesse, okkupirovannoi fashistami i 3 mesiatsa v podzemel'e," manuscript, 2004, p. 11, courtesy of Mr. Vadim Altskan.

Berlin were to order the Karaites to be killed. In the town of Feodosiia, the local *Ortskommandatur* had registered them while adding its own short explanation of this group – "Jews without the Talmud."[64] Apparently this did not bode well for the Karaites, given the ongoing investigation of whether or not they were Jewish, as it meant some degree of association with a group earmarked initially for discrimination and eventually for destruction. However, it was not the army that made the decisions in such matters.

The *Einsatzgruppe* in the Crimea did not contend itself with simply bringing the matter before Berlin, but also performed its own logistical work on site. The result was the report compiled by the EG D on the historical background of the Krymchaks and Karaites published in the Situational Reports (*Ereignismeldungen*) series. For this purpose, Alfred Karasek, a "researcher" identified with the Nazi Party and various German security services, made use of the resources in Crimean libraries.[65] The report findings pertaining to the Karaites were as follows:

> During the registration of the Jews, the question concerning non-Jewish inhabitants of Jewish faith had to be clarified when the question of the Karaites... was dealt with. The following facts were established:
>
> According to their own testimony, the Karaites have nothing in common with the Jews apart from their religion. They are said to originate from a group of Mongols who lived in former times around the Black Sea. The Karaites had, contrary to the Jews, full citizens' rights during the time of the Tsar, of which they are proud to this day.[66]

64 OK I (V)/287, "TB für die Zeit bis 12.11.1941," Feodosiia, November 12, 1941, YVA, M.29.FR/41, p. 21.

65 Testimony of Efim Gopshtein, August 17, 1944, YVA, M.35/23, p. 59. See also, Aleksandr Ivanovich Polkanov, *Krymskie karaimy* (Simferopol', 1995), p. 5 and Polkanov, *Karai – krymskie tatary – tiurki*, p. 119. My thanks are extended to Dr. Mikhail Kizilov for drawing my attention to and sharing with me the latter two sources.

66 OSR USSR no. 142, CSPSS, Berlin, December 5, 1941, in Arad, Krakowski, and Spektor, *The Einsatzgruppen Reports*, p. 250.

In this respect, some points must be highlighted. First, the Karaites were referred to as "non-Jewish inhabitants of Jewish faith," which means that the EG D considered them to be, racially, non-Jews. Second, according to the report, the only problem with the Karaites was that the group practiced the Jewish religion, while nothing was said about the singularity of its religious practice. The difference between the Jews and the Karaites was also emphasized. The report combined some categorical remarks like "nothing in common with the Jews" with reservations, such as "according to their own testimony." Finally, while being positively disposed towards the Karaites, the report still tended (quite in line with the aforementioned *Ostforschung* reports) to refrain from giving any recommendations as to the further treatment of this group.

Of particular interest to the concerns of the chapter is the recently disclosed declaration made by the former Deputy Mayor of Sevastopol' under the German rule, Viktor Beletskii. After the war, Beletskii was arrested and tried by the Soviet authorities in 1947. Before, during, and after his trials, he claimed that he contributed to the survival of the Karaites in the town of Evpatoriia (where the largest Karaite community lived). His testimony deserves to be quoted at length:

> In November 1941… I was summoned to the SD, and after the conversation about who were Karaites and whether they and Jews were the same, I was proposed to compile a written note about them.
>
> In Evpatoriia, the annihilation of the Jews by the Germans was known, as well as the fact that the Karaites were worried about their fate and that they were [trying to] prove that they were not Jews.
>
> In view of the proposal given to me, I understood that the Germans wanted to have a document on the Karaites, which did not come from the Karaites who were in this case an interested party, but from a neutral party.

According to Beletskii's statements, he had written that:

> The Tsarist government did not deem the Karaites as Jews and did not discriminate against them… they were not subjected to limitations as Jews… there exists a religious rivalry between the Karaites and the Jews, there existed a ban on intermarriage between them and the Jews.[67]

Beletskii completed his declaration by a statement, which, according to his own confession, could not be directly inferred from his note. He wrote that "ethnographically and judging by their anthropological features, the Karaites constituted an independent people who had nothing in common with the Jews." Given the fact that it is difficult to assume that Beletskii somehow knew the content of the EG D report, which quotes his arguments almost in their entirety, his statement seems to be rather plausible, and, therefore, sheds more light on the German policy regarding the Karaite question.

This decision on the fate of the Karaites was made by Himmler himself, partly on the basis of the EG D reports and partly on that of the work conducted by Department VII of the RSHA, headed by Dr. Franz Six.[68] The decision was positive for the Crimean Karaites

67 Letter by Viktor Beletskii to the Prosecutor of Iaroslavskaia *oblast'*, April 22, 1955 and complaint by Viktor Beletskii forwarded to the Chief Prosecutor of the USSR, July 1955, USHMMA, RG-31.018M, reel 10, pp. 283-285, 297-299.

68 Angrick, *Besatzungspolitik und Massenmord*, pp. 327-328.
Franz Six (1906-1975): Became a member of the NSDAP in 1930; became a member of the SS and Chief of Department II (Internal security - *Inland*) of the SD Main Administration in 1935; became Professor of Journalistic Studies at the University of Königsberg in 1938; became Chief of Department VII (research of adversaries) of the RSHA in 1939; became Chair and President of the German Institute of International Studies at the University of Berlin; served as *Führer* of the *Vorkommando Moskau* (of the *Einsatzgruppe* B) from June-August 1941; became head of the Cultural-Political Department in the Foreign Office in June 1942; became SS-*Brigadeführer* in 1945; arrested in January 1946; sentenced to 20 years in the *Einsatzgruppen* Trial on April 10, 1948; pardoned by the US High Commissioner for Germany and released on October 3, 1952; later worked for "Organization Gehlen"; became a lecturer at the Höhn's Academy of Leadership in Economics at Bad Harzburg. On Franz Six, see Carl Tighe, "Six, Franz Alfred: A Career in the Shadows," *Journal of European Studies* 37, no. 1 (2007): pp. 5-50.

and reflected the German policy towards them applied elsewhere: They were neither to be treated as Jews nor to be executed like them.[69] It is unknown whether Himmler provided any explanation for his order, but it seems that the influence of external political factors (such as the alleged link between the Karaites and the Crimean Tatars[70]) cannot be ruled out. The *Reichsführer*-SS made his decision between December 5 and 8, 1941.[71]

The Germans did not specially announce to the Karaites that their matter had been solved positively. They were only exempted from the obligation to gather during the great *Aktionen* conducted in the first half of December 1941. As the Karaites became aware of what had happened to the Jews, they became extremely anxious about their own future under the new rule. For example, in Evpatoriia, the Karaites collected gold and deposited it with the local EG D leader.[72] As the report by the EG D admits, the Karaites had hoped that this donation would prevent them from being deported. The EG D leader accepted the donation, but his gesture would have proven meaningless if the previous arrangement order had been cancelled.

The Karaites were able to calm their fears rather quickly. According to the aforementioned testimony by Beletskii, around late December 1941, *Völkischer Beobachter*, the most important German newspaper at that time, published a small article of the Crimea regarding the recently conquered peoples in the peninsula. The article read that the "Karaites were a small people, often confused with the Jews. But actually it was established that they

69 "Strafsache gegen the EG D Leader Walter Bierkamp," München, July 16, 1959, YVA, TR.10/1147, pp. 18-19.

70 The presence of such a link from the first stage of the Nazi treatment of the Karaites in the USSR is implied by a number of researchers, among them a German scholar, Patrik von zur Mühlen: Zur Mühlen, *Zwischen Hakenkreuz und Sowjetstern*, p. 50.

71 The aforementioned report by the EG D was sent on December 5, 1941, and on December 8-10 the assembly was proclaimed for all Jewish groups of Simferopol' (Ashkenazim and Krymchaks), while the Karaites were granted an exemption from this order.

72 OSR USSR, no. 157, CSPSS, Berlin, January 19, 1942, in Arad, Krakowski, and Spektor, *The Einsatzgruppen Reports*, pp. 284-286.

were not Jews and, therefore, they are extended protection of the German Army like the rest of the peoples of the Crimea." One of the Germans soon made the content of the article known to the Karaites.[73]

However, the Germans occasionally maltreated Crimean Karaites. Such incidents usually occurred when the Germans retaliated against Soviet civilians. Between 60 and 120 Karaite victims of the German occupation were recorded in Evpatoriia.[74] Some Karaites were deported to perform forced labor in Germany[75] while others were arrested from time to time, evidently because they had Jewish relatives.[76] Likely influenced by such reports and unaware of the Karaite-German connections, the Soviets included the Karaites in the collective Soviet victims of the German occupation, alongside Jews and Krymchaks.[77]

It is noteworthy that even after Himmler's decision to treat the Karaites as non-Jews was made in Berlin and carried out in the Crimea, the *Einsatzgruppe* did not stop its investigation of the Karaites. The EG D created the most thorough study and distributed it in May 1942 as part of the series of the *Meldungen aus den besetzten Ostgebieten.* New insight provided by the report reflected political considerations. The reports were derived from the recent history of the Karaites, namely their allegedly high standing in Tsarist Russia and their support of the White Movement during the Civil War in Russia. More importantly, it was claimed

73 Complaint by Viktor Beletskii forwarded to the Chief Prosecutor of the USSR, July 1955, USHMMA, RG-31.018M, reel 10, p. 299.

74 Commission of Evpatoriia, list of victims (including their nationality), October 31, 1944, YVA, M.33/57, pp. 4-23.

75 Act of the Commission of the town of Evpatoriia, October 31, 1944, YVA, M.33/57, pp. 13-40.

76 Feodosiia: Questioning of Mark Al'ianaki, June 20, 1944, State Archive of the Russian Federation (GARF), 7021/9/58, p. 34.

77 Akt of the Municipal Commission on Reporting and Investigating the Atrocities of the German Fascist Occupants in Kerch, August 24, 1944, in Kondranov and Stepanova, *Krym v period Velikoi Otechestvennoi voiny,* p. 201. See also, Memorandum of Bogdan Kobulov and Ivan Serov submitted to Lavrentii Beriia, June 22, 1944, GARF, R-9479/1/284, p. 1, in Nikolai Bugai, ed., *Deportatsiia narodov Kryma: Dokumenty, fakty, kommentarii* (Moscow: INSAN, 2002), p. 54.

that "in recent years there took place a rapprochement between the Karaites and the Crimean Tatars furthered by the common anti-Bolshevik stance."[78]

The rest of the *Einsatzgruppe* argumentation involved pseudo-historical and racial criteria, which the Nazis had already used in their research on the Karaites. They repeatedly claimed that the group was problematic, as their religion was considered in many cases as belonging to the Jewish faith.[79] Furthermore, a new claim was put forth that "they have some Jewish blood." The Karaites had reason to perceive this as dangerous. However, as an apparent justification for the already made decision concerning the Karaites, it was mentioned that "with respect to their language and ancestry, they belong to the Turko-Tatar people" and, importantly, they are "in many other respects opposed to Judaism."[80]

In April 1942, the Germans' positive view towards the Crimean Karaites, along the lines of those mentioned in the EG D report, was confirmed in the book compiled by Alfred Frauenfeld, a future head of the German civil administration in the peninsula.[81] In addition to the EG D arguments, Frauenfeld emphasized the Karaites' aloofness from the Jews as he declared them Jew-haters.

Nazi discussion of the Karaites did not abate even during the years of the German hold of the Crimea. No new investigation was launched, but rather the already known points were reiterated. On October 6, 1942, the Ministry for the Occupied Territories issued a letter on the status of the Karaites to the *Reichskomissar für die Ukraine* in Rovno (on whose territory the Crimean Karaites lived). Again it was stated that, in terms of religion, they were not Jews. As for their racial origin, it stated that "the research conducted hitherto supports the point that they were not be viewed as Jews." The order, which came from Rosenberg's Ministry, was based on the regulation issued by Rosenberg himself in 1941 (which referred

78 CSpSd, Kommandostab, MbOg no. 1, Berlin, May 1, 1942, RGVA, 500/1/775, p. 78.

79 CSpSd, Kommandostab, MbOg no. 4, Berlin, May 2, *1942,* in Arad, Krakowski, and Spektor, *The Einsatzgruppen Reports*, pp. 344-345.

80 Arad, Krakowski, and Spektor, *The Einsatzgruppen Reports,* pp. 344-345.

81 Frauenfeld, *Die Krim*, p. 10.

solely to Lithuania and ostensibly did not affect the behavior of the EG D in the Crimea).[82]

Another document worth mentioning in this respect is the memorandum on the Karaites written within Rosenberg's Ministry in May 1943. It was conveyed *inter alia* to the *Reichskomissariat Ukraine*. The report traced the whole process of Nazi Germany's treatment of the Karaite question back to the prewar decision by the *Reichsstelle für Sippenforschung* from 1939. In terms of faith, the Germans did not consider the Karaites as Jews, whereas with respect to their racial origin, the decision was pending. They noted their singular language (which was of no link to the Jewish languages) and circumcision practices (they were like other 'Orientals' and not like the Jews). They also noted that their "appearance [was] racially different from the Jews," that they did not mix with Jews but rather maintained a close relationship with Crimean Tatars, and that "culturally Karaites are much higher than the East European Jews of the same area." Predictably, the conclusion was favorable for the Karaites: "Any comparison between Jews and Karaites is out of question. Karaites have to be treated as other Turk-Tatar peoples."[83] The last remark is most significant because it draws a connection between Karaites and Muslim Tatars. The link between the Karaite question and the Tatars and, more generally, Soviet Muslims, however vague in 1941, became more visible and even more so as the German reliance on and its desire to capitalize on the Muslim factor became more pronounced.[84]

82 RMfdOg, Dr. Leibbrandt, "Stellung der Karaimen," October 6, 1942, YVA, JM/5626.

83 RMfdOg, Berlin, Dr. Wetzel, "Stellung der Karaimen," Geheim, May 7, 1943, YVA, JM/5626.

84 As, starting from early 1943, the German situation in the war started to deteriorate and its previous staunch allies began to look for other options, Nazi leaders tried desperately to consolidate German alliance with various Islamic forces. On the importance of the Islamic factor in the German war strategy in the Soviet Union, see David Motadel, "Islam and Germany's War in the Soviet Borderlands, 1941–5," *Journal of Contemporary History* 48, no. 4 (October 2013): pp. 784-820. On the importance of Islamic factor in the German general war strategy, see for example, Gerhard Höpp, "Der Koran als 'Geheime Reichssache': Bruchstücke deutscher Islampolitik zwischen 1938 und 1945," in Holger Preißler and Hubert Seiwert, eds., *Gnosisforschung und Religionsgeschichte* (Marburg: Diagonal-Verlag, 1994), pp. 435-446.

It seems that most of the Karaites who collaborated with the Germans (both military and civil) were allowed to abandon the peninsula as the Germans withdrew their own forces from the Crimea in the first four months of 1944.[85] According to the German documents, some 500-600 Karaites served in the Wehrmacht and Waffen-SS.[86] Their fate has already been sufficiently studied in WWII scholarship.[87] However, the important point to be reiterated is that although Nazi research did not contain a clear-cut conclusion concerning the racial origin of the Karaites, they were left alive in the interim period. Its length was nominally contingent upon the lack of sufficient data to complete the study of the Karaites. However, it was more related to the Germans' growing dependence on the Turkish peoples and, more generally, on the Muslim factor.

2.3. From the Karaites' perspective

As mentioned above, upon their entry into the Crimea the Germans were hesitant regarding their approach towards the Karaites. According to the diary of a Russian inhabitant of Simferopol', the Karaites "began to keep themselves apart from the Jews, showed the Germans the Jewish dwellings, in conversations with Russians criticized Jews strongly."[88] In November 1941, Karaite representatives approached the Germans and attempted to persuade them that the Karaites had nothing in common with the Jews.[89] After a local collaborator filed a denunciation with the Germans claiming that the Karaites were of Jewish origin, the former asked a worker in the Crimean local museum to gather materials about the Karaites and to express his own opinion on the subject. Fortunately for the Karaites, the worker, Aleksandr Ivanovich Polkanov, was himself a Karaite (this fact was unknown

85 See the next section.

86 Untitled source compiled by Dr. Klopfer (NSDAP, Partei-Kanzlei), Dr. Klopfer (NSDAP, Partei-Kanzlei) and SS-*Standartenführer* Brandt (Persönlicher Stab, RFSS), September 27, 1944, YVA, JM/4473.

87 Spektor, "The Karaites in German-Dominated Europe," pp. 101-105.

88 Diary of Chrisanf Lashkevich, entry from December 7, 1941, DAARK, P-156/1/31, p. 73.

89 Ibid.

to the Germans) and succeeded in presenting the Karaites as a non-Jewish group. Apparently, all these sources (alongside the aforementioned report by Beletskii) were summarized in the EG D reports, which stated that the Karaites presented an account of their own history, emphasizing the non-Jewish origin of their group.[90]

The Germans had officially decided to exempt the Karaites from extermination in the Crimea, but after that, rather few details are known about the conditions of these people. They were allowed to serve in the local administrations and occasionally occupied key positions. According to a non-Jewish wartime testimony, they were able to become accountants in the Simferopol' municipal authority,[91] obviously due to their high education level.[92] A contemporary Karaite testimony maintains that in May 1942, one Karaite was even proposed the position of mayor in Evpatoriia – the highest appointment a local resident could hope to obtain in the German-occupied Soviet territories.[93] However, according to the same testimony, he refused to accept it and, as a result, he was executed with his family. Some other Karaites elsewhere in the Crimea did collaborate with the occupation authorities. For example, one citizen acted as an informer for the local police,[94] while another was given the position of landlord (*komendant dvora*), with turning in Jews to the Germans being part of his official duties.[95]

It is difficult to evaluate the relationship between the Karaites and the Jews in the German-occupied Crimea. To begin with, one

90 OSR USSR, no. 142, CSPSS, Berlin, December 5, 1941, in Arad, Krakowski, and Spektor, *The Einsatzgruppen Reports*, p. 250.

91 Diary of Chrisanf Lashkevich, entry from August 8, 1942, DAARK, P-156/1/31, p. 102.

92 After the evacuation of Soviet professionals and evacuation or extermination of Jews, the problem of the lack of professionals was felt everywhere in the German-seized areas.

93 This was S. M. Hodzha: Polkanov, *Karai – krymskie tatary – tiurki*,, p. 84. See also, Algamil, *The Karaite Jews in the Eastern Europe in the Past and in the Present*, p. 186.

94 Sevastopol': Trial in Sevastopol', interrogation of Giul'nara Khalilova, USHMMA, RG-31.018M, p. 62.

95 Simferopol': Testimony of Bella Goland, November 1, 1999, in Tiaglyi and Rivkina, *Vospominaniia zhitelei evreiskikh poselenii v Krymu*, p. 137.

cannot speak about the Karaites' behavior as an organized group, as they lacked their spiritual and secular leaders. Contradictory findings, which have come overwhelmingly from the Jewish side, present a complex picture. Jews knew that Karaites were not persecuted and sometimes attempted to pose as them, which could potentially involve a denunciation of a Jew by his Karaite neighbor.[96] At the same time, some Karaites offered Jews aid, which was crucial for their survival. Whether it included providing Jews with shelter[97] or giving them their own IDs,[98] such actions implied a mortal danger for the Karaites themselves.

Such lines of behavior were more pronounced in mixed Karaite-Jewish families. On the whole, in such families, Karaite parents made every effort to save their children. In Evpatoriia, one account tells of a Karaite mother (whose Jewish husband had been drafted into the Red Army) who:

> refused to allow their 17-year-old daughter Valeriia to go to the assembly point, sending her to her sister's in Saki instead. For over seven months, Sof'ia Pastak succeeded in hiding Valeriia and her [Jewish – KF] friend, Vera Redkina, 18, in her house. Early in July, Anna could no longer bear being away from her only daughter and walked from Evpatoriia to Saki in order to see her. Some Russian neighbors reported to the Gestapo that Pastak was hiding Jews. When the Gestapo arrested Valeriia and Vera, two Karaite women, Anna Briskina and Sof'ia Pastak, also went to their death. This was in Saki on July 3, 1942.[99]

96 Dzhankoi: Story of Purevich in Vasilii Grossman and Il'ia Erenburg, eds., *The Complete Black Book of Russian Jewry* (New Brunswick and London: Transaction Publishers, 2002), pp. 231-232.

97 Simferopol': Diary of Chrisanf Lashkevich, entry from December [?] 26, 1941, DAARK, P-156/1/31, p. 84. See also, Kropotkov, *Voennye traditsii krymskikh karaimov*, p. 91.

98 Evpatoriia: Letter by Mina Fishgoit, [no date], YVA, P.21.2/9.

99 Gubenko, *The Book of Sorrows*, pp. 43-44. A slightly different version is presented in Kropotkov, *Voennye traditsii krymskikh karaimov*, p. 91. According to this account, Sof'ia Pastak went willingly to the execution "in order to accompany scared Jewish children who were killed by the Fascists."

In some cases, Karaite families or spouses took care of their Jewish relatives by urging them not to comply with the German orders,[100] providing them with shelter in their own houses,[101] intervening on behalf of the arrested Jewish spouse,[102] or by simply refusing to part.[103] There was even a unique case, in which Karaites provided temporary shelter to a mixed Karaite-Jewish family not related to it.[104]

* * *

Over the course of the German occupation of the Crimea, the Karaites were fortunate to be recognized by the Germans as a group distinct from Jews. It seems that their main problem stemmed not from their ethnic origin (the Nazis tended to regard them as a Turkish people), but rather from their unique religion, which by all accounts contained elements of Judaism. Nevertheless, a combination of foreign political considerations and the desire to appease Crimean Tatars created conditions favorable for the Crimean Karaites. The result was the decision from Berlin to spare them from the annihilation. Despite this ruling, however, throughout their occupation of the Crimea, the Germans never reached a definitive conclusion about how to treat them because of the ambiguity of their Jewishness and the changing character of the Karaites' alliances.[105]

In the meantime, the Crimean Karaites occupied a unique place in the hierarchy of the Crimean peoples under the German rule. The Karaites' status was elevated above that of the Jews, which meant their survival in the German-occupied peninsula. It even

100 Evpatoriia: Story of Gita Gushanskaia, [no date], ibid., pp. 43-44.

101 Evpatoriia: ibid.

102 Feodosiia: Questioning of Mark Al'ianaki, June 20, 1944, GARF, 7021/9/58, p. 34.

103 Feodosiia and Dzhankoi: Interview with Savelii Al'ianaki (1932), March 30, 2004, author's archive.

104 Dzhankoiskii *raion*: ibid.

105 It must be mentioned that another scholar contends that by 1943 the Karaite question was finally positively solved by Nazi Germany: Polkanov, *Karai — krymskie tatary — tiurki*, p. 120. However, this assumption overlooks the continuous discussion of the Jewishness of the Karaites that took place in 1943-5.

exceeded that of Russians, who could, among other things, go on living, work for the German-sponsored local administration, and pursue their cultural and religious activities. Unlike Russians, however, the Karaites were mainly spared from deportations to Germany for "labor conscription." Hundreds of Karaites were given the possibility to leave with the retreating Wehrmacht, and to serve later on the German side.[106] However, the Karaites were subject to maltreatment once the Germans retaliated against the civilian population, and some were underprivileged on account of their Jewish relatives. The Karaites' status did not reach that of the Crimean Tatars, who were the Germans' closest allies in the region. The Tatars could live, work for the Germans, and pursue their cultural and religious activities, but they also fought on the German side in large numbers and were spared during German "reprisals."

3. Krymchaks in the Crimea[107]

3.1. General concerns

Like the Karaites of the Crimea, the Krymchaks were one of the most ancient inhabitants of the peninsula.[108] Jews had first arrived there in ancient times, while in the medieval ages Jewish emigrants from the Mediterranean basin reinforced the community. These colonies were partly strengthened by the arrival of Ashkenazi

106 Vikhnovich, "Massovye etnicheskie deportatsii iz Kryma," p. 88.

107 On the fate of the Krymchaks during WWII, see Igor' Achkinazi, *Krymchaki: Istoriko-etnograficheskii ocherk* (Simferopol': Dar, 2000), pp. 121-123; Anatolii Khazanov, *The Krymchaks: A Vanishing Group in the Soviet Union* (Jerusalem: The Hebrew University of Jerusalem, The Marjorie Mayrock Center for Soviet and East European Research, 1989), pp. 20-23; Spektor, "The Holocaust of the Krymchak Jews during the Nazi Occupation," pp. 18-27; Ben Tsvi Itshak, *The Outcasts of Yisrael* (Hebrew), Tel Aviv: N. Tabarski, 1953, pp. 90-97; and Rudolf Loewenthal, "The Extinction of the Krymchaks in World War II," *The American Slavic and East European Review* 10, no. 2 (1951): pp. 130-136.

108 Mark Kupovetsky, "K etnicheskoi istorii krymchakov," in Igor' Krupnik, ed., *Etnokontaktnye zony v evropeiskoi chasti SSSR* (Moscow: MFGO, 1989), pp. 53-69; ibid., "Dinamika chislennosti i rasseleniia karaimov i krymchakov," pp. 76-93; Wolf Moskovicz and Boris Tukan, "Krymchak Community: Their History, Culture, and Language" (Hebrew), *Peamim* 14 (1982): pp. 6-7.

Jews into the Crimea. Thus, in terms of ethnic origin, Krymchaks stemmed from the Jewish people, while in terms of religious belonging, they professed full-fledged rabbinical Judaism. They adopted one of the local Tatar dialects, but retained Hebrew for sacral needs.

Under Russian rule, the Krymchaks' standing was generally equal to that of the Ashkenazi Jews.[109] But until the 20th century, Krymchaks did not intermarry with Ashkenazi Jews.[110] According to the available data, the educational level of Krymchaks was rather low.[111] In terms of occupation, most of them were craftsmen, engaged in small trade.[112] Twenty years of Bolshevik rule brought about a certain blurring of the Krymchaks' ethnic, language, and religious differences, and somewhat lessened their segregation.[113] Intermarriages not only with Ashkenazi Jews but also with the linguistically close Crimean Tatars were registered, and the educational level rose somewhat (although it still remained relatively low).[114] The social stratification of the Krymchaks also underwent transformation, and only a small number continued to work in petty crafts.[115] Their absolute number decreased during the first half of the 20th century, from 7,500 in 1912 to 6,383 in 1926,[116] and continued to do so until 1939.[117]

109 Yet, it is claimed sometimes that local Russian authorities treated them better that the Ashkenazim and even secured certain privileges for them: Max Rosenthal, "Krimchaks," in Isidore Singler and Cyrus Adler, eds., *Jewish Encyclopedia*, vol. 7 (New York and London: Funk & Wagnalls, 1904), p. 575 and Loewenthal, "The Extinction of the Krimchaks in World War II," p. 131.

110 Avrahm Yarmolisky, "Crimea," in *The Universal Jewish Encyclopedia*, vol. 3 (New York: The Universal Jewish Encyclopedia, Inc., 1941), p. 414, accessed in Loewenthal, "The Extinction of the Krymchaks in World War II," p. 131.

111 Achkinazi, *Krymchaki*, p. 120. See also Michael Zand, "Notes on the Culture of the Non-Ashkenazi Jewish Communities under Soviet Rule," in Yaacov Ro'i and Avi Beker, eds., *Jewish Culture and Identity in the Soviet Union* (New York, London: New York University Press, 1991), pp. 378-444.

112 Achkinazi. *Krymchaki*, p. 115.

113 Zand, "Notes on the Culture of the Non-Ashkenazi Jewish Communities under Soviet Rule," pp. 391-396.

114 Achkinazi, *Krymchaki*, p. 115.

115 Ibid., p. 119.

116 Khazanov, *The Krymchaks*, p. 19.

117 Yarmolisky, "Crimea," p. 414, accessed in Loewenthal, "The Extinction of the

There exists only scarce evidence of the Krymchaks' behavior during the period from the beginning of the war until the German takeover. Arguably, the Soviet enlistment program affected the Krymchaks in the same manner as the rest of the population.[118] In due time, some other Krymchaks made their way to partisans.[119] There is no available information concerning their evacuation, but some observations can be made. The concentration of a considerable number of Krymchaks in remote places, such as Karasubazar, situated off important evacuation routes, negatively impacted their ability to obtain information about the Nazis' persecution and annihilation of Jews. On the other hand, many Krymchaks dwelt in towns situated on the sea coast, through which the evacuation was carried out. Thus, they could have been exposed to the importance and expediency of escape. The question that remains largely unanswered is to what extent the Krymchaks identified themselves with the Ashkenazi Jews, and whether or not they realized that they might also become targets of the Nazi policies towards the Jews.

3.2. German policy towards the Krymchaks

Soon after the Germans' entry into the Crimea, the Krymchaks became the object of their keen interest, as the group was suspected of being Jewish. In the meantime, however, they were exempted from anti-Jewish measures. In Feodosiia, the local *Ortskommandatur* regarded the Krymchaks as having nothing in common with the Jews, but was circumspect about any future steps towards them:

Krymchaks in World War II," pp. 132-133; see also Table 14, "Krymchak and Karaite population in the Crimea as of 1930."

118 Testimony of Feodosiia Fuksman, May 11, 1996, YVHN. On the Krymchaks' participation in the war against the Germans, see V. K. Garagulia and N. V. Nikolaenko, eds., *Gor'kaia pamiat' voiny: Krym v Velikoi Otechestvennoi voine* (Simferopol': Krymskaia Akademiia gumanitarnykh nauk, Krymskii respublikanskii kraevedcheskii muzei, 1995), pp. 156-158.

119 Interview with Professor David Borokhov (1933), March-April 2004, author's archive. See also E.I. Peisakh, *Soobschenie v redaktsiiu Bolshoi Sovetskoi Entsiklopedii o narodnosti Krimchaki (k stat'e dlia BSE),* Leningrad, 1970, manuscript, p. 173, in Khazanov, *The Krymchaks*, p. 76f.

> Jewry was required by the SD to register… The order did not apply to Krymchaks, who are racially flawless and will be treated specially.[120]

Other German authorities in the peninsula admitted some link between the Jews and the Krymchaks by referring to them as a "Jewish mixture" (*jüdische Mischlinge*),[121] or as "Mohammedan Jews."[122]

Again, as in the case of the Karaites, the EG D conducted research on the Jewish background of the Krymchaks. Its conclusions, published in early December 1941 in the series of the Operational Situation Reports, were as follows:

> According to the statement of the Jews, the Krymchaks are Jews who emigrated from Italy some 400 years ago. They arrived in the Crimea and adopted the Tatar language as their everyday vernacular. The Krymchaks themselves maintain that they are a branch of Tatar people. It can be assumed that both are right. They are Jewish emigrants from Italy who, in the course of the centuries, intermarried with the Tatars, whose language they adopted. They kept their faith, however.[123]

This EG D report offers several observations. It is the only instance in the Crimea that the *Einsatzgruppe* invoked the "statements of [Ashkenazi] Jews" to support the claim that the Krymchaks were explicitly Jewish, in terms of ethnic origin. However, the Krymchaks' own standpoint that they were a "branch of Tatar people" was also quoted. The EG D conclusion regarding the Krymchaks' racial origin was not too promising: They were said to have originated

120 OK I/287, "TB für die Zeit vom 13.-16.11.1941," Feodosia, November 16, 1941, YVA, M.29.FR/41, p. 25.

121 *The Trial of German Major War Criminals*, p. 274; "Strafsache gegen Walter Bierkamp," München, July 16, 1959, YVA, TR.10/1147, pp. 18-19.

122 OK I(V)/287, "TB für die Zeit bis 12.11.1941," Feodosia, November 12, 1941, YVA, M.29.FR/41, p. 21.

123 OSR USSR, no. 142, CSPSS, Berlin, December 5, 1941, in Arad, Krakowski, Spektor, *The Einsatzgruppen Reports*, p. 250.

from the Jews and to have preserved their faith (which, however, was not referred to as Jewish). The report compilers regarded the Krymchaks' alleged intermarriages with the Tatars as the only thing in their favor. Nevertheless, the report left sufficient grounds for any verdict by the decision-makers in Berlin.

Sometime from December 5 to either December 8-9, 1941, Himmler's directive sealing the fate of the Krymchaks arrived: They were to be exterminated. In order to assuage the Krymchaks' fears that they would be killed as the Ashkenazi Jews had already been, the Germans occasionally spread rumors that clarification had arrived from Berlin not to shoot the Krymchaks.[124] It is noteworthy that the degree of the Krymchaks' Jewishness continued to preoccupy the Nazis even after the actions. Of course, by then no more fluctuation was allowed, and German reports served to justify their previously made decision, namely, by highlighting the group's Jewish roots. The EG D report from May 1, 1942 states:

> The question of the Krymchaks is singular. Unlike the Karaites, the Krymchkas can be found only in the Crimea. Their number is estimated at 6,000. By their religion, they are genuine Jews, and speak Tatar with an element of Hebrew; in terms of origin, this is doubtless an ethnic group originated primarily from Jewry. Under the Tsarist rule, they were equated to the Jews (ban on land possession, etc.). However, in contrast to the rest of the Jews, they were passive towards Bolshevism. The Tatars and Karaites hold them in utter contempt.[125]

Some points deserve attention. The religious factor, namely the fact that the Krymchaks practiced full-fledged Judaism, is again emphasized. In terms of ethnicity, the origin of the group was declared to be doubtlessly predominantly Jewish. In addition, the

124 Feodosiia: Vol'fson, *Krovavye zlodeianiia nemtsev v Krymu*, DAARK, P-156/1/34.

125 CSpSd, Kommandostab, MbOg, no. 1, Berlin, May 1, 1942, RGVA, 500/1/775, pp. 76-80.

report engaged two political considerations from the contemporary history of the time: the low status of the Krymchaks in the Tsarist Russia, similar to that of the Ashkenazi Jews, and the allegedly strained relations between the Tatars and the Krymchaks. The only argument in the Krymchaks' favor was their passivity towards the Bolshevik Revolution. It seems that the political concerns outweighed the strictly racial ones in the report's justification of the German decision to annihilate the Krymchaks. By the same token, another report drawn up by the EG D in January 1942 "proved" their Jewish roots by invoking local factors in stating that "The identical treatment for Jews and Krymchaks is viewed as natural, because the Krymchaks are generally regarded as Jews."[126]

Some oblique postwar evidence indicates that the *Einsatzgruppe* officers did not understand why Krymchaks were equated to Jews, because they did not resemble the latter.[127] However, the decision to murder the Krymchaks was carried out without any deliberations[128] everywhere.[129] Sometimes, these operations were carried out in the first ten days of December 1941, soon after the *Aktionen* against the Ashkenazi Jews.[130] In these cases, the whole procedure of registering, assembling, and then exterminating Krymchaks did not differ from what was applied to the Crimean Ashkenazim. The only slight exception

126 OSR USSR, no. 157, CSPSS, Berlin, January 19, 1942, in Arad, Krakowski, and Spektor, *The Einsatzgruppen Reports*, pp. 284-286.

127 "Strafsache gegen Johannes Schlupper," der Untersuchungsrichter 115 Ks 6a-c/71, Vernehmung des Angeschuldigten Rudolf E., December 21, 1971, YVA, TR.10/1081, p. 91.

128 Testimony of Otto Ohlendorf, *The Trial of German Major War Criminals*, pp. 6653-6654, in Lowenthal, "The Extinction of the Krymchaks in World War II," p. 135.

129 Feodosiia, Yalta: Moshe Gutovich, "From the conversation with Moshe Gutovich, Jewish refugee from Feodosiia" (Hebrew), *Ha-tsofe* (Tel Aviv), no. 1685, July 13, 1943. See also Vol'fson, *Krovavye zlodeianiia nemtsev v Krymu*, DAARK, P-156/1/34, p. 19 and Report of the Crimean Commission on the Conclusion of the Investigation of the Outcome of the German Occupation of the Crimea, December 16, 1941, DAARK, P-156/1/32, p. 15.

130 Usually within a few days – Simferopol', Yalta, and Evpatoriia: Testimony of Efim Gopshtein, D. Brichinskii, ed., August 16, 1944, YVA, M.35/23, pp. 59-60. See also Report of the Crimean Commission, DAARK, P-156/1/32, p. 15 and Akt of the Commission of Evpatoriia, May 9, 1944, GARF, 7021/9/57, p. 30.

to the established patterns of extermination involved a round-up,[131] or taking the Krymchaks straight from their houses,[132] once the group became small enough and the Germans did not experience any problem of manpower shortage to accomplish the task. The rate of survival among the Krymchaks in such *Aktionen* was low.[133] However, in other cases, the assembly for Krymchaks was proclaimed after a lengthier stretch of time (Feodosiia – 12 days,[134] Karasubazar – up to 45 days,[135] Kerch – 35 days[136]), which left more time for them to learn what had happened to the previously "resettled" Ashkenazi Jews. The longer interval between the assembly of Jews and Krymchaks may be accounted for by a shortage of German manpower, as well as a protracted investigation into the Krymchak question in the wake of the intercessions made by the Krymchaks in Kerch.[137]

In 1942, the pursuit and extermination of the Krymchaks also proceeded in rural areas[138] and the POW camps.[139] During the final wave of the large-scale extermination operations conducted by the Germans after the seizure of the remaining Soviet enclaves of Kerch (May 1942) and Sevastopol' (July 1942), all traces of a singular German treatment of the Krymchaks in contrast to the Ashkenazi Jews faded. In the German and Soviet documents pertaining to

131 Akt of the Commission of Evpatoriia, 1944, YVA, M.33/57, pp. 50-51.

132 Yalta: Report of Margarita Frolova-Meltsyna, [no date], YVA, 0.33/626, p. 6.

133 Memoirs of Gudzhi in Achkinazi, *Krymchaki*, pp. 121-122; untitled document, DAARK, R-1458/1/3, p. 2. See also FK (V) 810, Feodosia, "TB," December 20, 1941, YVA, 0.51/185 I, p. 4.

134 Untitled document, DAARK, P-1458/1/3, p. 2.

135 Commission on the History of the Great Patriotic War, DAARK, P-156/1/34, p. 19.

136 Crimean District Committee of the VKP(b), *Zverstva nemetskikh fashistov v Kerchi: Sbornik rasskazov postradavshikh i ochevidtsev* (Sukhumi: Krasnyi Krym, 1943), p. 18.

137 See further on in the chapter.

138 Villages of Karagoz and Tiumen: Interrogation of Vasilisa Genova, May 27, 1944, DAARK, R-1289/1/6, p. 131; 3 FG Abt. (mot.) 683, "TB für die Zeit vom 9.-25.5.1942," YVA, 0.51/185 I, p. 8.

139 Near Evpatoriia (?): "Strafsache gegen Johannes Schlupper," der Untersuchungsrichter 115 Ks 6a-c/71, Vernehmung des Angeschuldigten Rudolf E., December 21, 1971, YVA, TR.10/1081, p. 91.

that period, Krymchaks and Jews are mentioned alongside one another: the remaining members of both groups were summoned or revealed together at the assembly points and then and killed together at the same time at the same sites.[140] A German military report from Kerchenskii *raion* dated June 30, 1942, underscores the point:

> With respect to the Jews and Krymchaks, the *Feldgendarmerie* has taken necessary steps. In almost all cases, Jews, and in many cases Krymchaks, were issued false papers. In many cases, these people went so far that German surveillance bodies could not find out their identity when in possession of the false papers. Almost every day, hiding places are detected in which Jews and Krymchaks hide whose papers look well. All those arrested are transferred to the *Sk* stationed here for further treatment.[141]

It is of note that that despite the generally uncompromised policy, the Germans still granted few Krymchaks exemption from assembly. When the local municipality in Feodosiia appealed to the Germans and complained of the severe shortage of skilled manpower in the wake of the killing operations, the Germans honored the request and exempted nine Krymchak craftsmen from extermination.[142] Of special importance is the German behavior towards two Krymchak families in Simferopol'. According to one uncorroborated postwar testimony, which comes from the Krymchak side, these two families were spared because they held Iranian citizenship.[143] If taken for granted,

140 OSR USSR, no. 190, CSPSS, Berlin, April 8, 1942, in Arad, Krakowski, and Spektor, *The Einsatzgruppen Reports,* pp. 325-326; Kerch: Memoirs of Z. Ia. Borokhov in Achkinazi, *Krymchaki*, p. 123; Sevastopol': "Tragic End of the Jewry in the Western Russia" (Hebrew), *Ha-boker* no. 2691, September 6, 1944, p. 2 from *Izvestiia*, July 2, 1944.

141 OK I(V)/287, FG, "TB für die Zeit vom 15.-30.6.1942," Kerch, June 30, 1942, YVA, 0.51/185 II, p. 10.

142 Vol'fson, *Krovavye zlodeianiia nemtsev v Krymu*, DAARK, P-156/1/34.

143 In the past, their parents had emigrated from the Crimea; however, they returned in the 1920s: Khazanov, *The Krymchaks*, pp. 20-21.

this evidence indicates that even in the already "sealed" case of Krymchaks who were declared by Berlin to be ethnically Jews, the Germans sometimes considered foreign political considerations, and exempted individual Krymchaks from imminent annihilation.

3.3. From the Krymchaks' perspective

Insofar as organized activity on the part of the whole Krymchak group in a given locality is concerned, the available documents enable the reconstruction of developments only in Kerch. The Krymchak inhabitants of the town were exempted from the special Jewish registration in mid-November 1941. The order was reversed by late November, when it was declared that "All inhabitants of the town of Kerch and its vicinities who have the inscription "Krymchak" in paragraph 5 of their passports must appear in the department of German Police on November 28, 1941, from 8:00 am to 2:00 pm for registration. All those failing to appear will be made answerable."[144] Eight hundred and twenty-six people complied with the order.[145]

By that time, the local German commanders of the EG D and the Wehrmacht had already received the order to kill the Krymchaks in Kerch, in line with the policy applied to this group elsewhere in the peninsula at this time. Logistical difficulties, mostly manpower shortages, were likely the only things preventing the Germans from accomplishing the extermination of the Krymchaks in the area. The Ashkenazi Jews of Kerch were exterminated in early December, of which the Krymchaks soon learned.[146] What happened in the meantime was recorded in the postwar testimonies offered mainly by some surviving Krymchaks. One of them suffices to underscore the situation:

144 Nemetskaia politsiia bezopasnosti, November 26, 1941, copy, Order No. 3, DAARK, P-156/1/24, pp. 9, 13.

145 Achkinazi, *Krymchaki*, p. 123.

146 Testimony of Abraham Wein, August 3, 1988, YVA, 0.3/4822, p. 12; Interview with Professor David Borokhov, March-April 2004, author's archive.

> Macabre rumors circulated. Probably they brought us to engage in activity. Namely, five Krymchaks decided to gather at the apartment of A. S. Mizrachi. At the meeting [on November 25-26], it was decided to present the authorities published materials and the hand-written article by I. S. Kaia, "Krymchaks." The next day, the article was presented to the authorities. Upon reading it they gave it back and announced that head of the job center would be instructed to register the Krymchaks like the rest of the citizens.[147]

As a result, the local German command suspended the discriminatory steps directed against the Krymchaks of Kerch, and forwarded the inquiry to Berlin. This renewed investigation lasted some weeks, but by the end of December 1941 it became clear that the old policy towards the Krymchaks would be reiterated. They were demanded to assemble on January 3 or 4, 1942, obviously to be executed.[148] However, in late December 1941, Soviet marines landed in the area and liberated the town. Thus, hundreds of the Krymchaks living in the town were spared from annihilation. This turned out to be only a temporary respite. Only between 200 and 300 Krymchaks were able to evacuate, whereas the rest stayed in Kerch and were murdered when the Germans seized the town anew in May 1942.[149]

In retrospect, the renewed investigation of the Krymchak question initiated by the "Kerch group" did not only contribute to the survival of many Krymchaks who lived in the town and its

147 Memoirs of Z. Ia. Borokhov in Achkinazi, *Krymchaki*, p. 122. Testimony of Anbol, in *Sotsialisticheskii vestnik* 2 (605), (February 28, 1948) in West, *In the Ropes of Destruction*, pp. 138-140.

148 *Zverstva nemetskikh fashistov v Kerchi*, p. 18.

149 Interview with Professor David Borokhov, March-April 2004, author's archive; Khazanov, *The Krymchaks*, p. 21; Memoirs of Z. Ia. Borokhov, in Achkinazi, *Krymchaki*, p. 123; Mangupli, *Kerosinovyi vkus detstva*, pp. 19-21.
The minor evacuation of the Krymchak population from the besieged enclave of Kerch from January to May 1942 is to be ascribed primarily to the reluctance of the Soviet authorities to allow a large-scale evacuation of the civilians from the town. See Chapter 1, "Jews in the Crimea from the Beginning of the German-Soviet War (June 22, 1941) to the German Occupation (November 1941)."

vicinities, but also to those living in some other areas where the Krymchaks had not yet been exterminated. The Germans suspended its annihilation of the large Krymchak community in Karasubazar until January 17-18, 1942. The killing operation here was carried out relatively late, given the rapid pace of the EG D activities in the Crimea. All 468 Krymchaks of Karasubazar were killed.[150]

In areas with mixed Jewish-Krymchak populations, the interaction between the two groups was apparently higher. In many aspects, the individual responses of the Krymchaks to the Germans' persecutions resembled those of the Ashkenazi Jews. German orders caused turmoil for them everywhere. In Simferopol', where "resettlement" of the Krymchaks preceded that of the Ashkenazi Jews, many Krymchaks took the German promises for granted and prepared for evacuation. Old people were often more inclined to obey to German orders than the younger generations.[151] In Feodosiia, the Ashkenazi Jews had already disappeared by the time of the assembly order for the Krymchaks, and half of the latter went into hiding instead of going to the assembly point. Others, however, believed the rumors disseminated by the Germans that no harm would be done to them and presented themselves in "their best national clothes," apparently ready to evacuate.[152] When the area in question was temporarily seized by the Red Army, the Krymchaks attempted to evacuate.[153] Later, under German rule, they attempted to assume a non-Krymchak identity.[154] There also exists some record of military resistance waged by Krymchaks either as individuals[155] or as Crimean partisans.[156]

150 Vol'fson, *Krovavye zlodeianiia nemtsev v Krymu*, DAARK, P-156/1/34, p. 19. In the closed Krymchak community of this town, the author is unaware of any attempt to evade the imminent assembly.

151 Account of D. I. Makarycheva, [no date], subsection "Krymchaks," DAARK, P-156/1/36.

152 Vol'fson, *Krovavye zlodeianiia nemtsev v Krymu*, DAARK, P-156/1/34.

153 Feodosiia: Achkinazi, *Krymchaki*, p. 122.

154 Feodosiia, Kerch: Questioning of Anna Ashkinazi, June 20, 1944, GARF, 7021/9/58, p. 29; OK I(V)/287, FG, "TB für die Zeit vom 15.-30.6.1942," Kerch, June 30, 1942, YVA, 0.51/185 II, p. 10.

155 Simferopol': Khazanov, *The Krymchaks*, pp. 20-21.

156 Near Kerch: Interview with Professor David Borokhov, March-April 2004, author's archive.

The fact that the Krymchaks were rather traditional underlies the singularity of their responses to the Holocaust. In the last moments of their lives, as they faced the German execution squads near Feodosiia, the assembled Krymchaks "sat on land and began to sing their ancient songs."[157] The Krymchaks were native inhabitants of the Crimea and knew the local ways. Most of them were proficient in the Tatar language, and their own mother tongue constituted one of the dialects of the Tatar language.[158] In their external appearance they often resembled other native groups of the region. The positive aspects of the Krymchak-Tatar connections are reflected in a number of the testimonies recently offered by the Krymchak survivors and their children. According to them, such links could come to the fore in an intermarried family, when a Tatar husband appealed successfully to the Germans on behalf of his Krymchak wife by claiming that she was a Tatar and not a Krymchak.[159] In other cases, Krymchak children and small families were given permanent or temporary shelter in Tatar villages.[160] On the other hand, there also exists a wartime testimony that a Tatar husband denounced his Krymchak wife.[161]

* * *

The great majority of the Krymchaks of the Crimea perished during the German occupation of the peninsula. According to the calculations made by the Krymchaks themselves, more than 5,500 Krymchaks were killed by the Germans. Since the Crimea was the main reservoir of the Krymchaks, it means that more than 70% of their prewar number was exterminated in 1941-

157 Vol'fson, *Krovavye zlodeianiia nemtsev v Krymu*, DAARK, P-156/1/34.

158 74.1% of the Krymchaks still identified Crimean Tatar as their mother tongue in 1926: Khazanov, *The Krymchaks*, p. 4.

159 Simferopol': Interview with Vladimir Peisakh (1933?), March 22, 2004, author's archive.

160 Near Simferopol' (?), near Sevastopol' (?): Khazanov, *The Krymchaks*, pp. 20-21; Interview with Andrei Gordeev (1960), August 2004, author's archive.

161 Karasubazar: Questioning of Bekir Smolskii, February 4, 1944, YVA, M.33/82, p. 33.

1944.[162] A Soviet source mentions the higher figure of 7,000.[163] The destruction did not pass over a single town in the Crimea.[164] Thus, the Germans delivered a mortal blow to one of the most ancient Jewish communities. In 1945, the number of the Krymchaks was estimated only at 2,500 people.[165]

4. Mountain Jews in the North Caucasus[166]

4.1. General concerns

Mountain Jews have dwelt in the Caucasian areas from ancient times. Their distant forefathers once lived in the southwestern part of present-day Iran. In the Caucasus[167], their biggest settlements were situated in north Azerbaijan and southern Dagestan, from where they migrated all over the region.[168] In the course of the

162 According to calculations by E. I. Peisakh and Isaak Kaia: *Soobshenie v redaktsiiu Bolshoi Sovetskoi Entsiklopedii*, p. 173 in Khazanov, *The Krymchaks*, p. 23. See also Table 7, "Annihilation of the Jewish (Ashekenazi and Krymchak) population in the Crimea in 1941-1942."

163 Vol'fson, *Krovavye zlodeianiia nemtsev v Krymu*, DAARK, P-156/1/34.

164 One can find statistical data pertaining to the dimensions of the annihilation of the Krymchaks in various Crimean towns in the folowing sources: Kerch – Some 500 Krymchaks: Private letter from Kerch, June 22, 1945. The author of the letter returned to Kerch after the war: West, *In the Ropes of Destruction*, p. 145. Yalta – 200 Krymchaks: Report of the Crimean Commission, DAARK, P-156/1/32, p. 15. Evpatoriia – 150 Krymchaks: Akt of the Commission of Evpatoriia, July 5, 1944, GARF, 7021/9/57, p. 19.

165 Peisakh and Kaia, *Soobshenie v redaktsiiu Bolshoi Sovetskoi Entsiklopedii*, p. 173 in Khazanov, *The Krymchaks*, p. 16.

166 This subject is enlarged upon in Kiril Feferman, "Nazi Germany and the Mountain Jews: Was There a Policy?" *Holocaust and Genocide Studies* 21, no. 1 (2007): pp. 96-114.
On the prewar history of the Mountain Jews, see Zand, "Notes on the Culture of the Non-Ashkenazi Jewish Communities," pp. 408-416.

167 The first paragraph deals with the entire Caucasian region, i.e., the North Caucasus and the Transcaucasus. Therefore, when reference is made to the North Caucasus it is explicitly mentioned as such. After the first paragraph, the book returns to the convention whereby the terms "North Caucasus" and "Caucasus" are used interchangeably to denote the North Caucasus.

168 Mark Kupovestky, "Sotsiokul'turnyi analiz formirovaniia kollektivnoi pamiati i mifologem o proiskhozhdenii gorskikh evreev Vostochnogo Kavkaza do 80-kh godov XIX veka," *Etnograficheskoe obozrenie* 6 (2009), pp. 58-73; Bulgakova,

1920s, antisemitism in the North Caucasus intensified, and in 1926, pogroms directed against Mountain Jews broke out in Makhachkala (Dagestan), as well as in some other localities in the region.[169] According to various estimates, the total number of the Mountain Jews in the Soviet Union on the eve of the German invasion ranged from 34,300 to 35,800 people.[170] They spoke a local language containing some elements of Hebrew but resembled local people in all other aspects of life, with the exception of religion. However, there is uncertainty regarding the level of their religious observance by the time of the war.

From the beginning of the hostilities between Nazi Germany and the Soviet Union in June 1941, Mountain Jews had been affected by the war like other Soviet citizens. Many men were drafted and enlisted in the Red Army. The fact that the Caucasus was seized one year after the outbreak of the war indicates that there was a large-scale enrollment of Mountain Jews into the army prior to the German occupation of the North Caucasus. In 1941, mainly younger men enrolled;[171] in 1942, it was the older generation's turn.[172]

A number of factors concerning both the organized evacuation arranged by the authorities and individual escape attempts should be taken into consideration. The first has to do with the large time span of one year from the beginning of the war until the German takeover, during which the Germans exterminated hundreds of thousands of the Jews in the Soviet Union. Viewed from this standpoint, Mountain Jews were in an advantageous position to learn

"Sel'skoe naselenie Stavropol'ia," p. 78. Altshuler, *Jews of the Eastern Caucasus*, pp. 32-56.

169 Liudmila Gatagova, "Caucasian Phobias and the Rise of Antisemitism in the North Caucasus in the 1920s," *The Soviet and Post-Soviet Review* 36 (2009): pp. 42-57.

170 Altshuler, *Jews of the Eastern Caucasus*, pp. 151-152.

171 Testimony of Nikolai Shamilov, [no date], Institute of Contemporary Jewry (ICJ), TC 2647 (not transcribed); Testimony of Noshum Shamilov, October 11, 1988, YVA, 0.3/5157, p. 9.

172 Testimony of Raisa Shamilova, August 19, 1998, in Danilova, *Iskhod gorskikh evreev*, p. 70; Testimony of Khanukaev family, December 4, 1973, ICJ, 10 (106), p. 10.

about the impending danger. Nevertheless, the available evidence suggests that unlike Ashkenazi Jews, who had lived permanently in the Caucasus prior to the German entry yet who had evacuated in large numbers, the Mountain Jews tended to evacuate on a smaller scale.[173] There are some possible explanations of this phenomenon. The Mountain Jews interviewed in the postwar period point out economic hardships[174] or lack of time[175] that influenced their decisions whether or not to evacuate. As the North Caucasus was occupied at an advanced stage of warfare, one should also consider the lack of men (or often of any adults) drafted into the army in many Mountain Jewish families. As men traditionally held enhanced positions in the family, their absence was often an important obstacle for the remaining family's evacuation.[176] To this, the conventional reasons, which also prevented Jews elsewhere from escaping, such as the logistical difficulties involved,[177] vain anticipation for the official sanction to go,[178] and fear of the unknown[179] must be added.

Before the war, the Mountain Jews' knowledge of the German persecution of Jews was limited to a tiny stratum of educated people,[180] while most Mountain Jews seemed to be unaware of it.[181]

173 Village of Bogdanovka, Nal'chik: Testimony of Ilisho Ashurova (1918), January 8, 1998, in Danilova, *Iskhod gorskikh evreev*, p. 90; Testimony of Noshum Shamilov, October 11, 1988, YVA, 0.3/5157, p. 12.

174 Nal'chik: Testimony of Liviia Digilova (1936), August 19, 1999, in Danilova, *Iskhod gorskikh evreev*, p. 45; Testimony of Noshum Shamilov, October 11, 1988, YVA, 0.3/5157, p. 12.

175 Nal'chik: Testimony of Dina Pinkhasova (Kulent), January 1, 1973, ICJ, 4 (106), p. 13.

176 Nal'chik: Testimony of Besirit Ashurova, January 7, 1998, in Danilova, *Iskhod gorskikh evreev*, p. 39; Testimony of Moshe Moshiakh (1931), 1990, YVA, 0.3/6879, pp. 2, 3; Testimony of Khanukaev family, December 4, 1973, ICJ, 10 (106), p. 12.

177 Nal'chik: Testimony of Noshum Shamilov, October 11, 1988, YVA, 0.3/5157, p. 12.

178 Nal'chik — "No one proposed our family to evacuate": Ibid., p. 13.

179 Nal'chik: Ibid.

180 Village of Khamidia in Kabardino-Balkariia; apparently Nal'chik: Testimony of Raisa Shamilova, August 19, 1998, in Danilova, *Iskhod gorskikh evreev*, p. 72; Testimony of Noshum Shamilov, October 11, 1988, YVA, 0.3/5157, p. 9.

181 Nal'chik: Testimony of Besirit Ashurova, January 7, 1998, in Danilova, *Iskhod*

After the outbreak of the war, the scope of the contacts between the "foreign" Ashkenazi Jews who escaped through the area and the Mountain Jews was rather limited.[182] The Mountain Jews' exposure to the impending danger grew following the meeting of the Mountain Jewish population in Nal'chik organized by the Soviet authorities on October 9, 1941. The meeting's official goal was to promote the collection of warm clothes for the Red Army. Concomitantly, the authorities let the 70-year-old Mountain Jewish speaker, Shamilov, declare at the meeting that a special danger jeopardized the existence of the Mountain Jews:

> Our Jewish brethren have become Hitler's victims; it is ordered to kill, to plunder, or to bury them in the earth... The hangman desires to destroy all Soviet Jews and to enserf Slavs. This won't happen! Alongside the Russians, the sons of the Jewish people will destroy the Fascists.[183]

Nevertheless, it appears that the factual information that could potentially have encouraged the Mountain Jews to opt for evacuation remained unclear. The result was that a belated decision to escape, which could not be accomplished due to insurmountable logistical problems, could occur:

> Prior to the war in Nal'chik, we considered evacuation. One of our relatives was a Communist. He said that the Germans maltreated girls and killed children. He asked at least to take the girls with him. Yet, Father said that he could not let the

gorskikh evreev, p. 38. See also Testimony of Raisa Shamilova, August 19, 1998, in ibid., p. 25.

182 Nal'chik, Mozdok: Testimony of Lena Simakhova, January 10, 1998, in Danilova, *Iskhod gorskikh evreev*, p. 109; Testimony of Noshum Shamilov, October 11, 1988, YVA, 0.3/5157, p. 9.

183 M. Shekichacheva and D. Shabaev, eds., *Kabardino-Balkariia v gody Velikoi Otechestvennoi voiny: Sbornik dokumentov* (Nal'chik: El'brus, 1975), p. 31, quoted in Avsentii Driaev, "Rol' natsional'nogo i religioznogo faktorov na Severnom Kavkaze v gody Velikoi Otechestvennoi voiny, 1941-1945 gg.," (PhD diss., Vladikavkaz: Severo-Osetinskii gosudarstvennyi universitet im. K. L. Khetagurova, 2009), p. 72.

children go. When the war approached, Father finally decided to evacuate. We loaded our possessions onto a carriage, but soon the horse fell ill. We stayed in the Kabardin village of Argudan, where my grandmother worked.[184]

4.2. German policies towards the Mountain Jews

The first case of annihilation of the Mountain Jews took place outside of the North Caucasus. It occurred in "Shaumian" *kolkhoz* situated in Evpatoriiskii *raion* of the Crimea.[185] Mountain Jews appeared to constitute the majority of the population of the *kolkhoz*, which was established in the early 1930s. In January-February 1942, the Germans killed all the Ashkenazi inhabitants of the *raion*, and the Mountain Jews remained the only Jews left in the whole area.[186] In March 1942, one of the local inhabitants reported to the German authorities that there was a Jewish settlement there. Immediately thereupon, the EG D, aided by the *Feldgendarmerie* and local collaborators, arrested and executed all 114 Mountain Jews who lived in the *kolkhoz*.[187] Quite predictably, there were no combat-age men among the victims.[188] The murder of the Mountain Jews in the Crimea was conducted by the members of the same EG D that later handled the "Mountain Jewish Question" in the North Caucasus.

German wartime documentation and testimonies offered in the postwar trials demonstrate that the Wehrmacht and SS forces were fully aware that they victimized Mountain Jews.[189] The EG D did not seek prior authorization from Berlin to sanction the murder of the Mountain Jews. Significantly, the execution of the Mountain

184 Testimony of Lena Simakhova, January 10, 1998, in Danilova, *Iskhod gorskikh evreev*, p. 110.

185 FK (V) 810, "TB für die Zeit vom 1.-15.3.1942," March 16, 1942, YVA, M.29. FR/40, p. 20.

186 Mina Fishgoit's report, [no date], YVA, P.21.2/9.

187 Akt of the Commission of Evpatoriiskii *raion*, June 26, 1944, GARF, 7021/9/79, p. 10.

188 "Urteil gegen Karl R. Pallmann, Paul H. Lorenz, Hans H. Jakob, Erich Buballa, Otto Dolezych, Josef Kappl, Carl Friedrich M. Berherns wegen Mordes," July 22, 1971, YVA, TR.10/724, pp. 89-90.

189 FK (V) 810, "TB für die Zeit vom 1.-15.3.1942," March 16, 1942, YVA, M.29. FR/40, p. 20; FK 810, "TB für die Zeit vom 27.2-13.3.1942," YVA, M.29.FR/40, p. 28.

Jews as such was mentioned in the respective military report[190] but was not mentioned in the *Ereignismeldung* compiled by the SD. Hence, it seems that the decision by the EG D to exterminate the Mountain Jews in the Crimea was likely considered under local circumstances. Otherwise, given the fact that the *Ereignismeldungen* series was drawn up in Berlin, the reference to the murder of the Mountain Jews by the EG D would evidently imply at least Berlin's tacit approval of this step. According to the German military report dated March 16, 1942, Mountain Jews who lived in the Crimea were said to have participated in the effort of world Jewry, made under the auspices of the Soviet authorities, to settle in the Crimea. Such a conclusion may be derived from the special emphasis that the German report laid on the fact that the Mountain Jews "were settled in the area with the aid of the American Jewish money."[191]

As a result of the summer-fall campaign of 1942, the Germans came to control territory containing some settlements of the Mountain Jews. But significantly, most of them were never conquered. Out of the total population of Mountain Jews registered in the Soviet Union in 1939 (35,000 people[192]), it seems that some 3,000 Mountain Jews remained in the occupied territories of the North Caucasus.[193] Most of them resided in the Nal'chik area, but some lived in the Mozdok area, as well as in Jewish *kolkhozy* in Stavropol'skii *krai*.

Another important factor for understanding the course of the "Final Solution" as it pertained to the Mountain Jews in the Caucasus was the length of time the specific settlement was under occupation. Of the areas in the Caucasus seized by the Germans, the area of Nal'chik, occupied for 65 days from late October 1942 until early January 1943, should be emphasized. The rest of the relevant places, namely the town of Mozdok, as well as the rural

190 FK (V) 810, "TB für die Zeit vom 1.-15.3.1942," March 16, 1942, YVA, M.29. FR/40, p. 20.

191 Ibid.

192 Altshuler, *Jews of the Eastern Caucasus*, pp. 151-152.

193 Dr. Yitzhak Arad estimates the number of surviving Mountain Jews in the occupied area to be about 5,000: Arad, *The History of the Holocaust*, p. 535. I am inclined to estimate their number at about 3,000 maximum.

settlements where the Mountain Jews constituted the weighty part of the population (such as the villages of Bogdanovka and Menzhynskoe in Stavropol'skii *krai*), were occupied for almost five months (from early August 1942 until early January 1943).

The available German documentation indicates that they did not expect to find the Mountain Jews in the areas of the North Caucasus under their control, but rather assumed that that their settlements were located to the east and south of the occupied region.[194] It is possible that such notions led to a delay in the formulation of the German policies towards the Mountain Jews in the Caucasus. Alternatively, the Germans' ignorance of the existence of the Mountain Jews in the region under their control might have resulted in the Germans' treating all the Jews in the mixed Ashkenazi-Mountain Jewish settlements in the same way.

The first places in which the Germans faced Mountain Jews in the Caucasus were the aforementioned villages of Bogdanovka and Menzhynskoe.[195] This area was occupied towards late August 1942. The Mountain Jews constituted an important segment of the Jewish population of both the *kolkhozy*, which was estimated at some 850 persons. In Bogdanovka, numerous incidents of property plunder and depredations of the Jewish inhabitants, including physical assault, were recorded.[196] There is no evidence that the Germans even momentarily considered treating Mountain and Ashkenazi Jews in these *kolkhozy* differently. Conceivably, the very fact that both groups lived together in the same *kolkhoz* resulted in the Germans assuming that there was no distinction between

194 Teich and Ruebel, *Verzeichnis der Völker, Volksgruppen und Volksstämme auf Gebiet der ehemaligen UdSSR*, pp. 60-61.

195 Until recently, it was thought that this was also the case in the village of Ganshtakovka in the North Ossetiian ASSR, with the number of victims in the midst of Mountain Jews fluctuating between 300 to 1,400 (*Al'tman, Zhertvy nenavisti*, p. 284 and Elena Voitenko, "Kholokost na iuge Rossii v period Velikoi Otechestvennoi Voiny (1941-1943 gg.)," p. 176). However, a recent study has convincingly proved that the village of Ganshtakovka and *kolkhoz* (village) of Menzhynskoe analyzed in this book is actually the same place (Pavel Polian, *Mezhdu Aushvitsem i Bab'em Yarom. Razmyshleniia i issledovaniia* (Moscow: ROSSPEN, 2010), pp. 140-141).

196 Akt of the Commission of the village of Bogdanovka, June 29, 1943, GARF, 7021/17/10, p. 158.

any Jewish inhabitants of the two *kolkhozy*, and, therefore, all of them were annihilated. Finally, dozens of the Mountain Jewish families who remained in Bogdanovka and Menzhynskoe were shot on September 20 and October 19, 1942, respectively.[197] The total number of the victims was approximately 850 people,[198] of whom the Mountain Jews constituted the absolute majority.[199]

It cannot be established with certainty which German forces were responsible for the mass murder of the Jews in these two *kolkhozy*. In principle, the area was handled by the Ek 12. However, a Soviet wartime report compiled immediately after the liberation of the region mentions that a 600-strong Wehrmacht unit was stationed in Bogdanovka, which handled the Jews in the village until the very end.[200] Such being the case, the German Army might be directly involved in the annihilation of the Jews in the *kolkhoz*. Therefore, one should broach the possibility that the Germans (especially in the case of Bogdanovka) were unaware that there was a "special Jewish group" there. Otherwise, the army or the *Einsatzgruppe* could have needed more time to formulate their policies towards Mountain Jews, as compared to the case

197 Akt of the Commission of the village of Menzhynskoe, June 27, 1943, GARF, 7021/17/10, pp. 155-156; Akt of the Commission of Bogdanovka, June 29, 1943, GARF, 7021/17/10, p. 158.

198 Minutes of the Plenary meeting of the Ordzhonikidze District Committee of the VKP(b) on the terror of the occupiers in the occupied territory and their plans to use lands of *kolkhozy* and *sovkhozy*, March 9, 1943, in Vodolazhskaia, Krivneva, and Mel'nik, *Stavropol'e v period nemetsko-fashistskoi okkupatsii (avgust 1942-ianvar' 1943)*, p. 81. See also Akt of the Commission of the 10th Guard of the Kuban Cossack Chivalry Corps, copy, North Caucasian Front, January 4, 1943, Central Archive of the Ministry of Defense of the Russian Federation (TsAMO RF), 51/958/52, p. 32 (?), courtesy of the USHMM.

199 This conclusion is made on the basis of the analysis of the victims' surnames and family names: Akt of the Commission of Menzhynskoe, June 27, 1943, GARF, 7021/17/10, pp. 155-156; Akt of the Commission of Bogdanovka, June 29, 1943, GARF, 7021/17/10, p. 158.

200 Akt of the Commission of Bogdanovka, June 29, 1943, GARF, 7021/17/10, p. 158. According to a Jewish memoir, at least one local policeman was involved in the shootings of Jews in Bogdanovka. Prizov Yuri, "The Reminiscences of a Young Holocaust Survivor," [no date], United States Holocaust Memorial Museum Collection: 2011.337.1. I am grateful to Crispin Brooks from the USC VHA for sharing this source with me.

in question when in all likelihood, there was no special German discussion on this issue and the whole matter was resolved as if the villages had solely Ashkenazi Jewish population.

The developments in Mozdok, captured in early August 1942, unfolded in a different way.[201] Overall, the situation in the town under German rule is unclear. The area was handled by the *Sonderkommando* 10b (subordinated to the EG D). According to the only relevant German report, small *Teilkommandos* were sent in the "neighboring places" of the headquarters of the unit stationed until November-December 1942 in the town of Prokhladnyi in North Ossetiia.[202] Contradictory testimonies of the Mountain Jewish survivors and lack of the precise German documentation concerning the situation in Mozdok resulted in conflicting assessments and explanations regarding the German policies towards the Mountain Jews there. To begin with, the reports of the Soviet Extraordinary Commission do not contain any statement of mass murder of Jews or any Soviet citizens in Mozdok.[203] Secondly, other Soviet findings and testimonies of the Mountain Jews substantiate this claim, but contend that the Mountain Jews underwent some stages that usually preceded the physical annihilation, such as registration[204] and forced labor.[205] Some of them were killed.[206] Concomitantly, there are some indirect indications in German wartime documents, as well as in postwar testimonies, that the Jews of the town were executed, whereas it is stated nowhere that the victims were Jews.[207] The juxtaposition of these sources suggests that maltreatment of the

201 1,714 Jews lived in North Ossetiian ASSR as of 1939 (Altshuler, *Distribution of the Jewish Population of the USSR*, pp. 9-11, 13-15) and it is suggested that a significant number of them were Mountain Jews residing in the republic's second largest city, Mozdok.

202 CSpSd, Kommandostab, MbOg, no. 26, Berlin, October 23, 1942, YVA, JM/4539. In November-December 1942, its headquarters were transferred to Nal'chik: Angrick, *Besatzungspolitik und Massenmord*, pp. 622-623

203 Akt of the Commission of Mozdok, July 27, 1943, GARF, 7021/17/10.

204 Testimony of Aleksandr Raziev (1932), January 13, 1998, in Danilova, *Iskhod gorskikh evreev*, pp. 163-164.

205 Statement of Mountain Jews, residents of Mozdok, April 24, 1944, YVA, JM/24670.

206 Testimony of Rotsel Arzakhanov, June 12, 1990 (?), YVHN.

207 Angrick, *Besatzungspolitik und Massenmord*, pp. 622-623.

Mountain Jews in Mozdok, including their extermination, indeed took place, albeit on a relatively small scale.

One cannot account for such a contention by suggesting that "the town was situated close to the front line and, therefore, the forces of the *Einsatzgruppe* did not arrive there"[208] because, during a certain period, a *Teilkommando* of the *Sonderkommando* 10b was stationed there.[209] Rather, this development may be explained by the beginning of the internal German discussion concerning their attitudes towards the Mountain Jews. It is conceivable that while implementing the preliminary stages of their *Judenpolitik*, which usually culminated in the annihilation of all the Jews, the Germans realized that there was a group that should be treated differently from the European Jews.

Thus, German policy towards the Mountain Jews in various regions was multi-faceted by October 1942, when they occupied Nal'chik and faced the large settlement of this group, numbering some 1,000-1,500 people. The Germans plundered the property of the Mountain Jews on a particularly large scale[210] (as compared to their non-Jewish neighbors[211]), and sent them to perform humiliating forced labor inside the area with no food supply.[212] The German orders concerning the forced labor were not strictly enforced, and some of the Mountain Jews were able to evade them,[213] while others, such as mothers with small children, were

208 Arad, *The History of the Holocaust*, 2004, p. 532.

209 Angrick, *Besatzungspolitik und Massenmord*, p. 622.

210 Testimony of Raisa Shamilova, August 19, 1998, in Danilova, *Iskhod gorskikh evreev*, pp. 27, 30.

211 I was able to draw such a conclusion after a careful investigation of declarations of the inhabitants of the area, which dealt with the loss caused to their property during the period of the German occupation. These declarations were submitted to the Soviet authorities after the liberation of the area. They are preserved in GARF, collection 7021, catalog 7.

212 Testimony of Noshum Shamilov, October 11, 1988, YVA, 0.3/5157, p. 19; Testimony of Zhenia Biazrova, January 9, 1998, in Danilova, *Iskhod gorskikh evreev*, p. 48.

213 Testimony of Elizaveta Nazarova (1917), January 6, 1998, in Danilova, *Iskhod gorskikh evreev*, p. 134; Testimony of Guchi Motaeva (1929), January 6, 1998, in ibid., pp. 122-123.

legally exempted from the forced labor.[214] The laborers bore special signs, but only during working hours.[215] In a certain neighborhood of Nal'chik, all the Mountain Jews were detained and placed in a camp with no provisions supplied.[216] Sometimes members of this group were beaten,[217] while in a number of cases the maltreatment climaxed in the murder of Mountain Jews, almost exclusively men.[218]

On the face of it, the overall tough policy applied to the Mountain Jews in Nal'chik left no place for compromise. Nonetheless, in the course of November-December 1942, no decision regarding them was rendered in Berlin. During this period, the authorities in Berlin were asked to express their views on the subject, possibly because there was a controversy between the army and the SD on this matter.[219] During this time, the German discussion about whether and/or to what extent the Mountain Jews were indeed Jews resumed anew.[220] Alongside the existing researchers, other scholars (both Germans and local specialists) were also involved.[221] Furthermore, the subject even reached the Office for Genealogical Affairs.[222] During this period, officers of the *Einsatzgruppe* visited the houses of the Mountain Jews and even attended their ceremonies, such as weddings.[223]

214 Testimony of Elizaveta Nazarova, January 6, 1998, in ibid., p. 134.

215 Ibid., pp. 132, 134.

216 Testimony of Dina Pinkhasova (Kulent), January 1, 1973, ICJ, 4 (106), pp. 15-16.

217 Akt of the Commission of the Kabardino-Balkar Republic, 1943, GARF, 7021/7/109, p. 200; Testimony of Moshe Moshiakh, 1990, YVA, 0.3/6879, p. 4.

218 Testimony of Raisa Shamilova, August 19, 1998, in Danilova, *Iskhod gorskikh evreev*, pp. 28, 29; Testimony of Noshum Shamilov, October 11, 1988, YVA, 0.3/5157, pp. 19-20; Testimony of Vladimir Shamilov, June 22, 1995, YVHN; Testimony of Dina Pinkhasova (Kulent), January 1, 1973, ICJ, 4 (106), p. 14; Testimony of Iakov Alkhasov (1925), November 1973, ICJ, 6 (106), p. 9.

219 It is admitted solely in a piece of postwar evidence: Poppe, *Reminiscences*, p. 166.

220 Mordechai Altshuler, "Nazi Attitudes towards the Jewishness of the Mountain Jews and Other Oriental Communities" (Hebrew), *Peamim* 27 (1986): pp. 9-10.

221 Poppe, *Reminiscences*, p. 166.

222 Altshuler, "Nazi Attitudes", pp. 9-10.

223 Testimony of Raisa Shamilova, August 19, 1998, in *Iskhod gorskikh evreev*, p. 30; Testimony of Zhenia Biazrova, January 9, 1998, ibid., p. 48.

They investigated the lives of witnesses in the group[224] and questioned members of the other nations about the Mountain Jews.[225] Two preliminary conclusions on the Mountain Jews made by the Germans figured prominently: 1) They did not look like the Jews; and 2) they had many wives.[226] Of particular importance is the fact that the *Einsatzgruppe* commander, Walter Bierkamp, regarded the latter fact a result of the influence of Islam on Mountain Jews.[227] By late December 1942, the EG D ruled that the Mountain Jews had nothing to do with Jews and that they had to be referred to as a Tat people.[228]

The problem of the Mountain Jews was never touched upon in the Reports from the Occupied Eastern Territories. Otherwise, it is plausible that the leadership in Berlin would have had to express its view and promptly decide how to deal with them.[229] One can hardly presume that the decision-makers in Berlin were unaware of the developments on site. Rather, the solution of the problem by "scholarly" means points out the unwillingness of the German authorities to take precipitate steps and their tendency to adhere to

224 Testimony of Aleksandr Simakhov, January 8, 1998, ibid., p. 172; Testimony of Raisa Shamilova, August 19, 1998, ibid., p. 30.

225 Testimony of Noshum Shamilov, October 11, 1988, YVA, 0.3/5157, p. 18; Testimony of Elizaveta Nazarova, January 6, 1998, in Danilova, *Iskhod gorskikh evreev*, p. 130; Testimony of Zhenia Biazrova, January 9, 1998, ibid., p. 48.

226 "Strafsache gegen Walter Bierkamp," Bayer, Landeskriminalamt, Z. Zt. (deleted), March 26, 1962, Vernehmungsniederschrift, H. Friedrich (member of Ek 10a of Persterer), YVA, TR.10/1147, p. 495.

227 Bev. D. RmfdbOg beim Ob. Kdo., der Heeresgruppe A Min.Dirig., Dr. Bräutigam an RmfdbOg., "Bergjuden," December 26, 1942, YVA, JM/5640.

228 Ibid. See also Otto Bräutigam, *So hat es sich zugetragen: Ein Leben als Soldat und Diplomat* (Würzburg: Holzner Verlag), 1968, p. 535f and Poppe, *Reminiscences*, p. 166.

229 This line of reasoning may be implicitly supported by the way the Krymchak-Karaite topic was handled in the *Ereignismeldungen* series of the EG D in November-December 1941, when the fate of each group was decided upon approximately within two-three weeks afterwards. The relevant German report written previously in the series of the *Ereignismeldungen von den besetzten Ostgebieten* was composed in Berlin on December 5, 1941, while the *Aktionen* directed against the Krymchaks were conducted within 4-6 days after this date: OSR USSR, no. 142, CSPSS, Berlin, December 5, 1941, in Arad, Krakowski, and Spektor, *The Einsatzgruppen Reports*, p. 250

whatever stance was most convenient regarding the Mountain Jews. Characteristically, in postwar testimonies many attempted to claim credit for the rescue of Mountain Jews, including the Kabardin national leader, Selim Shadov, installed by the Germans;[230] the Soviet professor of German origin Nicholas Poppe, who defected to the Germans;[231] Otto von Bräutigam, an influential employee of Rosenberg's Ministry;[232] Theodor Oberländer, German military commandant of Nal'chik;[233] and even some members of the EG D.[234]

For its part, Soviet intelligence claimed to have left a spy, codenamed "P," in August-September 1942, whom they had assigned to work in the collaboration administration the Germans were due to establish. According to the doctoral dissertation of a

230 Altshuler, *Jews of the Eastern Caucasus*, pp. 122-124; Untitled document from personal library of Professor Alexander Dallin.

231 Nicholas Poppe (1897-1991) was an important Soviet Turkologist. From 1932 he was the Corresponding Member of the USSR Academy of Sciences. During the war he found himself in the North Caucasus occupied by the Wehrmacht, where he was benevolently received due to his German origin. He left the area with the retreating German Army in 1943 and finally made his way to the United States, where he eventually obtained a teaching position at the University of Washington. In 1983, he published his memoirs, in which he claims to have played an important role in the rescue of Mountain Jews in the occupied North Caucasus. According to his statement, upon having learnt that he, Poppe, was in the area under the German control, the German authorities asked him to express his opinion on the Jewishness of Mountain Jews. He stated in no uncertain terms that the latter was not a Jewish group. Poppe, *Reminiscences*, p. 165.

232 Otto von Bräutigam (1895-1992): Began service as an expert on Russia in the German Foreign Office in 1920; became a member of the NSDAP in 1939; became Consul General in Batum in the Caucasus in 1940; became a representative of the Ministry of the Occupied Eastern Territories in the Supreme Command of the ground forces (OKW) in July 1941; chaired the conference in the RmdbOg on the definition of the term "Jew" in the occupied territories on January 29, 1942; interned by the US Army in 1945; began service as advisor in East European affairs for the US secret services in 1947; charged with multiple murders in *Nürnberg-Fürth* in 1950 but found not guilty; became head of the Department East in the Ministry of Foreign Affairs of the Federal Republic of Germany in 1953; served as Consul-General in Hong Kong from 1958-1960; awarded the *Bundesverdienstkreuz* (Federal Cross of Merit) in 1959. Bräutigam, *So hat es sich zugetragen*, p. 535f.

233 Polian, *Mezhdu Aushvitsem i Bab'em Yarom*, pp. 141-142.

234 "Strafsache gegen Walter Bierkamp," Erster Staatsanwalt (deleted), Vernehmungsniederschrift, Dr. Johannes L. Leiter der Abteilung III der EG D im Kaukasus, November 21, 1966, YVA, TR.10/1147, p. 563.

former Soviet intelligence worker who had access to the otherwise inaccessible archive of the FSB Administration for Kabardino-Balkariia, "it is mainly thanks to 'P' that the Mountain Jewish population of the republic was spared from the genocide during its occupation by the German Fascists."[235] One way or another, it appears that by the time the Wehrmacht withdrew from the North Caucasus, a preliminary decision had been reached not to treat the Mountain Jews as Jews.

4.3. From the Mountain Jews' perspective

According to some evidence, from time to time Mountain Jews in Nal'chik were able to maintain their conventional routine of life even in the conditions of occupation, such as their religious observance[236] (including the burial ceremony[237]), employment,[238] and even their rendering of aid to the persecuted Ashkenazi Jews.[239] Apart from that, it stands to reason that the total annihilation of the Ashkenazi Jews, as well as the German hardline policies initially pursued towards the Mountain Jews, facilitated their rapidly increasing awareness of Nazi Germany's persecution and annihilation of Jews.[240] The result was that some of them chose not to abide by the registration order, but to stay in their homes and go nowhere.[241] Many attempted to hide in the anti-tank trenches, which served also as a shelter from the air attacks that were quite widespread in this region close to the

235 Aslan Kazakov, "Deiatel'nost' organov gosudarstvennoi bezopasnosti Kabardino-Balkarii po neitralizatsii podryvnykh aktsii emigrantskikh organizatsii v 20-kh-50-kh gg 20 veka," (PhD diss., Akademiia FSB Rossii, 2005), p. 105 (Source: Archive of the Federal Security Service for Kabardino-Balkariia, 10/1/4 and 10/1/6).

236 Testimony of Nikolai Shamilov, [no date], ICJ, TC 2647.

237 Testimony of Elizaveta Nazarova, January 6, 1998, in Danilova, *Iskhod gorskikh evreev*, p. 133.

238 Testimony of Nikolai Shamilov, [no date], ICJ, TC 2647.

239 Testimony of Besirit Ashurova, January 7, 1998, in Danilova, *Iskhod gorskikh evreev*, p. 38.

240 Testimony of Nikolai Shamilov, [no date], ICJ, TC 2647; Testimony of Moshe Moshiakh, 1990, YVA, 0.3/6879, p. 5.

241 Nal'chik: Testimony of Aleksandr Raziev (1932), January 13, 1998, in Danilova, *Iskhod gorskikh evreev*, p. 162.

front line.[242] Conversely, others opted to escape to distant non-Russian villages.[243] Some of them went even further by burning all identification papers[244] or by making it to the Russian side of the front.[245] Occasionally, such behavior was the result of a spontaneous reaction rather than a well-calculated move, as some of the Mountain Jews did not know what was happening even in their own hometowns.[246] To quote just one testimony pertaining to Nal'chik: "They did not go out of the houses, since they were scared. They learned the news from rumors, fellow-workers, and neighbors."[247]

During and shortly after the extermination of the Ashkenazi Jews, a sort of window of opportunities was opened for the Mountain Jews living in Nal'chik. They were allowed to voice their arguments vis-à-vis the Germans. But, most importantly, they pulled all the strings they could in an attempt to appeal to the Germans not to treat them as Jews. The Mountain Jews had no illusions about what this equation meant. They were aware of the fate of the Ashkenazi Jews of Nal'chik, who had been exterminated as early as in the first phase of the German occupation.[248] As mentioned above, many Mountain Jews became themselves subject to the German discriminatory policies.

The Mountain Jews devised a multi-faceted strategy involving both the demand (usually made by their non-Jewish neighbors) to resume the investigation of the group and the attempt to persuade the local German authorities to believe that they had nothing in common with the Ashkenazi Jews. The effort to capitalize on the

242 Nal'chik: Testimony of Iakov Shamilov (1930), January 11, 1998, ibid., p. 99; Testimony of Guchi Motaeva, January 6, 1998, ibid., p. 120; Testimony of Besirit Ashurova, January 7, 1998, ibid., p. 39

243 Unknown Kabardin village, near Nal'chik: Testimony of Raisa Shamilova, August 19, 1998, ibid., p. 72; Testimony of Dvora Khanukaeva (1904), November 1973, ICJ, 8 (106), p. 10.

244 Unknown Kabardin village: Testimony of Raisa Shamilova, August 19, 1998, in Danilova, *Iskhod gorskih evreev*, p. 73.

245 Testimony of Zhenia Biazrova, January 9, 1998, ibid., p. 48.

246 Nal'chik: Testimony of Raisa Shamilova, August 19, 1998, ibid., p. 74.

247 Ibid., pp. 28-29.

248 Akt no. 98 of the Commission of the Kabardino-Balkarsk Republic, February 15, 1943, GARF, 7021/7/109, p. 202.

intercession of the Kabardin neighbors was especially effective. The Kabardins appealed to the Germans, saying that the Mountain Jews were "our people, we live many years with them, they have nothing in common with Jews, they are Tats, they cannot be touched, they are ours."[249] Of smaller scope were the attempts made by educated people among the Mountain Jews, themselves, to persuade the Germans that they were Tats and not Jews.[250] When faced with the necessity of receiving the German officers in their houses, all Mountain Jews, in particular the elders, made every effort to show the Germans that their customs differed from those of the European Jews and resembled those of their Kabardin neighbors.[251] It is worth mentioning that some Mountain Jews resisted German rule while fighting in the ranks of the partisan movement.[252] But such a method could hardly serve a rescue route for the masses of Mountain Jews made up of elderly people, women, and children.

* * *

The retreat of the Wehrmacht from the North Caucasus occurred before the Germans reached a final conclusion on how to treat the Mountain Jews. During and before the first stage of their occupation of the region, the Germans encountered villages where the Mountain Jews were living together with the Ashkenazi Jews. It is suggested that such joint settlement led the Germans to regard both groups as one. As a result, the Mountain Jews were exterminated in all places where they were not recognized as a separate group. Therefore, there was no need in elucidating the degree of their Jewishness. It may be cautiously estimated that about 1,100-1,500 Mountain Jews were murdered in the

249 Testimony of Noshum Shamilov, October 11, 1988, YVA, 0.3/5157, p. 18; Testimony of Elizaveta Nazarova, January 6, 1998, in Danilova, *Iskhod gorskikh evreev*, p. 130; Testimony of Alexandr Simakhov, January 8, 1998, ibid., p. 172.

250 Testimony of Noshum Shamilov, October 11, 1988, YVA, 0.3/5157, p. 18.

251 Testimony of Raisa Shamilova, August 19, 1998, in Danilova, *Iskhod gorskikh evreev*, p. 30; Testimony of Zhenia Biazrova, January 9, 1998, ibid., p. 48; Testimony of Khanukaeva, November 1973, ICJ, 8 (106), p. 8.

252 Testimony of Alexandr Simakhov, January 8, 1998, in Danilova, *Iskhod gorskikh evreev*, p. 173.

Holocaust,[253] which constituted some 25-30% of their number in the area under German control.

During the same time frame and even later, German policy towards most Mountain Jews who lived in the large centers of Mozdok and Nal'chik functioned at an intermediate stage. The Germans did not vigorously enforce their orders, such as forced labor, on this group. It appears that at a certain point, the German policies were suspended, or at least became more bearable. It is likely that this was related to the Germans' debates about the Mountain Jews' degree of Jewishness that had been developing since approximately late October 1942. As this question appeared to have been resolved by the time of the German drive into the region, it is tempting to view this alteration in the German policy as a reconsideration of the geopolitical factors inside and outside of the North Caucasus. It cannot be ruled out that the shift took place under some pressure from the local population and/or moderate elements within the German administration in the Caucasus.[254] It is difficult to guess what final decision the Germans would have reached concerning the Mountain Jews if it had not been contingent upon numerous changing factors. In any case, by January 1943, when the Germans were forced to withdraw their troops from the North Caucasus, they exempted Mountain Jews from the "Jewish decrees."[255]

253 Arad, *The History of the Holocaust*, p. 535; Altshuler, *Jews of the Eastern Caucasus*, p. 151; Polian, *Mezhdu Aushvitsem i Bab'em Yarom*, p. 143.

254 Altshuler, *Jews of the Eastern Caucasus*, pp. 124, 126.

255 German policies continued to evolve towards recognition of Mountain Jews as non-Jews at least until April 1943: Auswärtiges Amt, April 29, 1943, YVA, TR.3/322.

Chapter Seven

Jewish Responses to the Holocaust[1] in the Crimea

Introduction: Jewish Reactions to the Holocaust in the Occupied Soviet Territories[2]

In contrast to other German-occupied areas elsewhere in Europe, Jewish responses during the Holocaust in the Soviet territories were frequently influenced by the relatively short time span between the onset of the German occupation and the destruction of the Jewish population. Dina Porat's remarks on the Holocaust of the Lithuanian Jewry are also of relevance to the Soviet Jews who lived within the country's "old" borders (i.e., those that formed part of the country prior to the outbreak of World War II):

> The decisive majority of Lithuanian Jews, about 80%, did not undergo the preliminary stages that characterized German policy against the Jews in western, southern, and

1 On the Jewish reactions to the Holocaust, see, for example, Dan Michman, "Jewish Resistance during the Holocaust and its Implications: Theoretical Notes" (Hebrew), *Dapim le-heker ha-Shoa* 14 (1997): pp. 7-42; Michael R. Marrus, "Types of Jewish Resistance: Categories and Comparison from the Historiographical Standpoint," in Israel Gutman, ed., *Major Changes Within the Jewish People in the Wake of the Holocaust: Proceedings of the Ninth Yad Vashem International Historical Conference held in Jerusalem in June 1993* (Jerusalem: Yad Vashem, 1996), pp. 257-288.

2 Within the borders existing before the outbreak of the Second World War, unless otherwise stated.

> central Europe. They did not experience the two or two-and-a-half years of ghetto life before the deportations to the death camps started, as the Jews in the Polish ghettos of the Generalgouvernment did. They were not even killed in the two waves of extermination...[3]

Many stages preceding the physical destruction of the Jews were often skipped over in the occupied Soviet territories. In any case, they took place in a more accelerated fashion as compared to the rest of occupied Europe. The Crimea and the North Caucasus, where the bulk of the Jewish population was exterminated within one month of the beginning of the German occupation, are clearly characteristic in this respect.[4]

Another principal feature of the Jewish responses in the occupied Soviet territories was the absence of Jewish organizational, communal, and religious structures operating prior to the German conquest. This situation was especially pronounced in the old Soviet territories,[5] to which both the Crimea and the North Caucasus belonged. This proved seriously to undermine the sense of Jewish solidarity.[6] Furthermore, the Germans appointed people to leadership positions in the emerging Jewish communities who were often only casual figures who did not enjoy the support of ordinary Jews.[7]

3 Dina Porat, "The Holocaust in Lithuania: Some Unique Aspects," in Cesarani, *The Final Solution*, p. 161. See also Altshuler, "The Unique Features of the Holocaust in the Soviet Union," pp. 181-185.

4 Serbia seems to be the area which most resembles many of the occupied Soviet territories in terms of the amount of time between the beginning of the German occupation and the destruction of the Jewish population. In Serbia, the Jewish male population was killed within six months of the onset of the occupation. Twelve months after the appearance of the Germans there remained no more Jews in Serbia. Walter Manoschek, "'Coming Along to Shoot Some Jews?': The Destruction of the Jews in Serbia," in Heer and Naumann, *War of Extermination*, pp. 39, 44-49, 50-51.

5 In the "new" areas, some remnants of the established Jewish leadership were still available. In the wake of the German occupation, the newly appointed heads of the Judenräte were often recruited among them. See, for example, Tikva Fatal-Kna'ani, "Grodno: Attempts to Resist, Escape and Rescue" (Hebrew), *Dapim le-heker ha-Shoa* 14 (1997): pp. 51-52.

6 Altshuler, "The Unique Features of the Holocaust in the Soviet Union," p. 184.

7 Arad, *The History of the Holocaust*, p. 251; Al'tman, *Zhertvy nenavisti*, pp. 115-119.

Under these circumstances, the pursuit of religious and cultural activities characteristic of Jewish responses in many other occupied countries became increasingly more complicated, if it was managed at all.[8] The Caucasian case is particularly illuminating, as the large-scale relocation of the Jewish population caused by the war meant that most of the Jews residing in the region on the eve of its occupation were strangers to the area. Specific local conditions, such as the attitudes of the local population and the partisans towards the Jews, the German occupation policy, and the composition of the Jewish population, among others, were also instrumental in forging the patterns of the Jewish responses.

Jewish reactions to the Holocaust in the occupied Soviet territories should also be examined against the background of the peculiarities of the war between Nazi Germany and the Soviet Union. Most European countries fell victim to the German aggression. Unlike them, in spite of serious setbacks in the initial period of the warfare that involved immense human and territorial losses, the Red Army was able to evade the decisive blow of the Wehrmacht. What is especially important to the central concern of this chapter is that regardless of whether the Red Army's retreat was characterized by organized redeployment or flight at all costs, this process created the networks of the underground and partisan movements.[9]

The various Jewish populations were affected differently by

8 Michman, "Jewish Religious Life under Nazi Domination,": pp. 147-165; Isaiah Trunk, *Jewish Responses to Nazi Persecution: Collective and Individual Behavior in Extremis* (New York: Stein and Day, 1979), pp. 21-25, 26-32.

9 For its part, the Soviet leadership urged the establishment of actively-operating partisan and other underground networks from the beginning of the war. According to the following evidence, "In the areas occupied by the enemy, partisan detachments and sabotage units were designated to combat the enemy's troops, to stir up partisan warfare wherever possible, to blast bridges and roads, to damage telegraph and telephone lines, to burn down the storages, etc. This activity is to be promoted in a timely fashion by the First Secretaries of *oblast'* and *raion* [Party] committees." Directive of the SNK SSSR and the TsK VKP(b) to the Party's and the Soviet organizations of the front areas, no. P509, June 29, 1941, in Vladimir Zolotarev, ed., *Velikaia Otechestvennaia voina 1941-1945*, pp. 500-501.

the policies in the territories expected to be abandoned by the Red Army.[10] It is natural that in the border regions swept by the initial German offensive, these measures were implemented only partially, if at all. However, the Crimea and the North Caucasus were captured by the Germans at a relatively advanced stage of the war, and it is, therefore, reasonable to suggest that more Jews could to be affected by these policies. For the purposes of this study, Jewish participation in warfare in the ranks of the Red Army and the partisan movement is referred to as "armed resistance."[11]

It should be also emphasized that in some of the occupied Soviet territories, patterns of Jewish resistance evolved independently of the Soviet-dominated underground network. This was especially the case in the areas with considerable Jewish populations, such as Lithuania and Belorussia, where the Germans had tolerated a more protracted Jewish existence. In such areas, there were both Jewish partisan detachments[12] and underground forces in ghettos with a multitude of resistance activities.[13] In contrast, in the areas with relatively small Jewish populations where the pace of annihilation was quick, such as the Crimea and the North Caucasus, the scope of Jewish armed resistance was more limited.

* * *

10 For some literature on the Jewish participation in the partisan warfare elsewhere in the occupied Soviet territories, see Yitzhak Arad, "The Armed Jewish resistance in Eastern Europe," in Michael Berenbaum and Abraham J. Peck, eds., *The Holocaust and History: The Known, the Unknown, the Disputed, and the Reexamined* (Bloomington and Indianapolis: Indiana University Press, 2002), pp. 591-600.

11 For general literature on Jewish resistance in the occupied Soviet territories, see Gershon Shapiro and Semeon L. Averbukh, eds., *Ocherki evreiskovo geroizma*, vols. 2-3 (Kiev: Kniga, 1994-1997).

12 Semeon Shveibish, "Evreiskii semeinyi partizanskii otriad Sh. Zorina," *Vestnik Evreiskovo Universiteta v Moskve* 13 (1996): pp. 88-109.

13 Yitzhak Arad, "Jewish Fighting Underground in the East European Ghettos: Ideology and Reality" (Hebrew), in Israel Gutman, ed., *Major Changes Within the Jewish People in the Wake of the Holocaust*, pp. 325-344; Shmuel Spektor, "Mass Flight and their Connection with the Jewish Uprising" (Hebrew), in ibid., pp. 357-362.

The Crimea

1. Before the Killing Operations

1.1. General concerns

Prior to the *Aktionen*, Jews in the Crimea had to adapt themselves promptly to their intensified maltreatment and rapid impoverishment (owing to the continuous plunder of their property and the necessity to live off whatever stocks were available), as well as to the sporadic physical assaults against them. At the same time, they were forced to define their attitudes towards the obligations to register, to bear the six-pointed star, and to perform forced labor. German policies caused a growing strain among the Jewish public in the Crimea. As Jewish communal institutions were weak from their inception, an exploration of the more basic structures of their lives, such as family, provides insight into how Jews functioned amidst the constantly deteriorating life conditions before the killing operations.

Jewish responses to the Germans' persecutions largely depended on family composition. In mixed families, there was a non-Jewish member that, other conditions being equal, potentially exhibited special patterns of behavior that either varied from or influenced those of his or her circle of relatives and acquaintances. The gender factor was also important, in that there was a relatively large number of women in the Crimean Jewish population whom, for operative reasons, the partisans were less eager to accept than men, as the partisan command expected women to be more of a burden than an asset under the specific conditions of the Crimean partisan movement. The objective reasons for this included inadequate food provision, poor sanitary conditions, and a high amount of physical pressure – a more subjective factor was the gender bias of male commanders who considered women as a source of unnecessary friction in the homogeneous male units.[14]

14 On the involvement of Jewish women in the Soviet partisan movement, see, for example, Tamara Vershitskaia, "Jewish Women Partisans in Belarus," *Journal of Ecumenical Studies* 46, no. 4 (2011): pp. 567-572.

These considerations combined to contribute to lower numbers of Jews in the resistance. Joining the partisans was the only possibility of armed resistance left for the Jews in the peninsula. At the same time, women were able to wander more freely than Jewish men, who could be revealed on account of their circumcision.

General factors such as geography, climatic conditions, and food availability also affected Jewish responses to the Nazi measures. It should additionally be borne in mind that most Crimean Jews had lived in the peninsula prior to the German occupation, which meant that they had friends and acquaintances there and knew the local customs and geography. Some of them were proficient in other local languages, aside from Russian, such as Ukrainian or Tatar. In terms of geography, the peninsula was a rather small stretch of land surrounded by sea from almost all sides. In medium-sized Crimean towns, let alone smaller localities, Jews were easily identifiable. The Crimean landscape (i.e., vast steppe, small forests, and difficult-to-access mountains) was not favorable for escape or hiding. Another factor detrimental for Jewish survival was the fact that the extermination actions and ensuing relentless persecution of Jews in the Crimea began in the late fall to early winter of 1941 under severe weather conditions.[15] This was exacerbated by the strict German movement policy, residence restrictions, and inadequate food provisions, particularly during the first period of the occupation. Jewish behavior was also influenced by the extent of knowledge they possessed concerning the Nazis' antisemitic ideology and practices, as well as their annihilation of the Jewish people.

During the period of Jewish legal existence under German rule, which often ended in the assembly order, Jewish families faced enormous pressure. The majority of families complied with all the orders, but a small minority defied some or all of them. Initially, there were potentially different reactions to the German regulations within one family. In Simferopol', for example, a Jewish

15 OSR USSR, no. 145, CSPSS, Berlin, December 12, 1941, Yad Vashem Archives (YVA), 0.51/165 II. See also Arad, Krakowski, and Spektor, *The Einsatzgruppen Reports*, p. 256, and Genov, *Dnevnik partizana*, p. 57 (entry from November 28, 1941).

man and his family did not bear the required stars, except for his son-in law, who did and was beaten by the Germans.[16] Sometimes married couples parted to overcome current hardships with the understanding that they would reunite later, as was the case with a Jew in Simferopol' who left his wife on December 11, 1941, and later found shelter at different sites in the town.[17] In the same town, a Jewish couple refused to go to the registration center, whereas the rest of their large family registered and was eventually executed.[18] Moreover, this couple joined a partisan unit, which constituted not only a defiance of the German regulations but also a further step on the road to resistance.

Occasionally, however, families failed to reach a consensus, and the result was detrimental to all. In Kerch, two adult daughters were eager to escape but their aging mother refused to allow them to leave, on the grounds that their escape would certainly lead to German retaliation. What follows is the testimony offered by a Soviet underground agent:

> But they cannot do anything wrong to us," Polia's sister tried to convince herself. "They will just evacuate us. You see... provisions for three days." I offered to find a shelter for them one by one, [and] promised to procure new passports with various nationalities and family names inscribed in them. Polia and her sister agreed, but the old mother declined categorically. "You want them to hang us, don't you?" she said with fervor. "We don't need to run away and hide. We are no criminals. I am an old woman. Throughout my whole life I didn't hurt a fly. Why do they have to hurt me? The same holds true for my girls. Who may have anything

16 Memoirs of Il'ia Sirota, February 16, 1945, State Archive of the Autonomous Republic of the Crimea (DAARK), P-156/1/40, p. 113. This was also the case with a few members of a Jewish family in Feodosiia: Rozaliia Krichevskaia, *Dvadtsat' deviat' mesiatsev iz detstva* (Beer Sheva, 1997), pp. 12-13.

17 Testimony of Lev Iurovskii, recorded by Lev Kvitko, 1944, YVA, M.35/14, p. 81.

18 Story of Aleksandra (Sarah) Gershtein, in Gubenko, *The Book of Sorrows*, pp. 58-61.

> against them? They are modest and quiet [girls] and know to get on well with people. Who would come to hurt them and why? Just think about it! Why do we have to go into hiding? Thousands of Jews are to be deported, not only us. Where everyone is present we shall also be. But we are not going to hide like fugitives." However hard we tried, we did not succeed in dissuading her. She also would not agree to let Polia go. She began to cry and complain that she was old and helpless, and never thought that Polia could abandon her in her old age.[19]

There were other Jews who did not believe in the Germans' promises, but for various reasons were reluctant or unable to escape. Some were seized by panic to such a point that they declared their intention to commit suicide.[20] Significantly, some occasionally considered such measures even before the calamities began to strike the Jewish community. When the Germans entered Simferopol', one witness's sister shouted at him, "You worked for such a long time [in a pharmacy] and could not get some poison?!"[21] Nevertheless, before the killing operations only few Jews committed suicide.[22] This may indicate that at this point, most Jews still had hope for survival. Yet, in the areas where the assembly order was being rigidly enforced, more Jews attempted or actually committed suicide.[23]

Of interest is the behavior of intermarried Jews who distanced themselves from the mainstream Jewish public. It turns out that these Jews were inclined to make their decisions under pressure

19 Story of Polia Govardovskaia and her sister and mother in Kozlov, *V Krymskom podpol'ie*, pp. 45-46, 49-50.

20 Kerch: Interview with Professor David Borokhov (1933), March-April 2004, author's archive.

21 Memoirs of Il'ia Sirota, February 16, 1945, DAARK, P-156/1/40, p. 112.

22 Feodosiia, Simferopol': Questioning of Liudmila Novikova, June 21, 1944, State Archive of the Russian Federation (GARF), 7021/9/58, p. 7; Conversation with the doctor, Mariia Borodina, 1945 (?), DAARK, P-156/1/37.

23 Simferopol', Yalta: Akt of the Commission of Simferopol', October 4, 1944, YVA, M.33/70, p. 6; Report of Margarita Frolova-Meltsyna, [no date], YVA, 0.33/626, p. 6.

from their non-Jewish spouses, who often assessed the situation realistically and held no illusions regarding the German plans for the Jews. Jewish members of mixed families were also less exposed to the mindset of other Jews, as it was offset to some extent by the outlook of the non-Jewish population, to which Jewish spouses were more exposed by virtue of their family links. In Evpatoriia, for example, the Russian husband of a Jewish woman refused to let his wife go to the assembly site. Instead, he dug a small chamber under the floor and hid her.[24] In the same town, the Karaite father-in-law of a Jewish woman neither allowed her to register nor to sew a star on her clothes.[25]

With respect to captured Soviet Jewish soldiers, there exists some record that upon having gained knowledge of the Germans' treatment of Jews, a certain number of them attempted to commit suicide before being taken prisoner.[26] Others, however, in full cognizance of what the Germans were doing to the Jews, adapted non-Jewish identities upon capture by changing their obviously Jewish personal data, such as father's name (*otchestvo*) and nationality, to non-Jewish versions.[27] Those who were captured had to reinvent themselves immediately by fully or partly changing their biographies. Many Jews tried to survive under false "Aryan" identities, posing as Russians[28] and, particularly, as Tatars[29] or other Muslims.[30] Knowledge of the respective languages was absolutely necessary in this case. Although in the first months of the German occupation the majority of the Soviet POWs in the Crimea refrained from

24 Story of Gorovits in Gubenko, *The Book of Sorrows*, pp. 41-43.

25 Story of Gushanskaia in ibid., pp. 43-44.

26 "Tragic End of the Jewry in Western Russia"; Aharon Shneer, *Plen*, vol. 2 (Jerusalem: Noi, 2003), pp. 129, 327.

27 Testimony of Anatolii Zhukov, [no date], in Polian and Shneer, *Obrechennye pogibnut'*, pp. 176-177.

28 Ibid., p. 177. See also Gel'man and Glubochanskii, *Kholokost*, p. 59.

29 Gel'man and Glubochanskii, *Kholokost*, p. 69; Story of Zacharii Zengin in Shneer, *Plen*, vol. 2, p. 238.

30 Testimony of Anatolii Zhukov, in Polian and Shneer, *Obrechennye pogibnut'*, p. 177. See also testimony of Sof'ia Frenkel', no date, YVHN and testimony of Zalman Uzikov, December 14, 1987, YVA, 0.3/4939, pp. 15-22.

attempting to escape,[31] some Jewish POWs still opted for escape from German captivity.[32]

1.2. Responses to the registration order

The first German comprehensive measure demanding the entire Jewish population to register already entailed mortal danger for the Jews. Indeed, the notorious Soviet passport system, according to which Jews permanently residing in the peninsula could easily be detected,[33] fell into the German hands. However, owing to a certain degree of population relocation in the Crimea, by the time of the German conquest, refugees arriving in the peninsula were not covered by the Soviet passport system to which the Germans had access. By complying with the order to register, however, Jews in this category lost their important advantage over the Germans. That is, as long as the Jews were unregistered, the Germans were unaware of their precise location in the Crimea because it was not listed on their passports – registration compromised this advantage. In other respects, however, the refugees were especially vulnerable, as they were detached from their native area and their knowledge of the Crimea, its people, and their habits was not adequate enough to ensure survival. This feeling of estrangement was exacerbated in the course of the hysterical antisemitic campaign orchestrated by the Germans from the beginning of the occupation.[34]

The fact that Jews were singled out for registration created an uproar among the Jewish populations.[35] The question regarding profession misled many of them into thinking that the Germans

31 OSR USSR, no. 153, CSPSS, Berlin, January 9, 1942, YVA, 0.51/165 II; Arad, Krakowski, and Spektor, *The Einsatzgruppen Reports*, pp. 272-273.

32 OK II/915, FG, "TB für die Zeit vom 21.-29.11.1941," O.U., November 29, 1941, YVA, M.29.FR/41, p. 34; Story of Semeon Sotnikov, in Shneer, *Plen*, vol. 2, p. 188.

33 It should be remembered that under Soviet rule, unlike town dwellers, inhabitants of rural areas did not have passports.

34 Testimony of Efim Gopshtein, August 16, 1944, YVA, M.35/21, pp. 172-173; CSpSd, Kommandostab, MbOg, no. 14, Berlin, July 31, 1942, Russian State Military Archive (RGVA), 500/1/775, pp. 377-379.

35 Yalta: Statement of Aleksandr Ponomarev, June 30, 1944, YVA, M.33/368, p. 52.

intended to utilize Jewish manpower.[36] Nevertheless, in Kerch, where the German authorities did not ask Jews about their professions but contented themselves with only the registration of their personal data and addresses,[37] the registration created no major turmoil among the Jews. Arguably, this had to do with the fact that at this point Jews had not yet been singled out for maltreatment, and the German administration had threatened every inhabitant of Kerch, regardless of ethnicity, with capital punishment for failure to acquiesce to its numerous regulations.[38] Besides, the registration of the Jews in the town was preceded by the registration of the whole population, and before then by the same procedure regarding laborers, regular employees, and engineers. In light of this, Jews in Kerch could have regarded their registration as just another listing of a specific group of population.

Only a minority of Jews in the Crimea refused to comply with the registration order.[39] A German report from February 1942 estimated the number of those in Simferopol' who defied it at 300 people.[40] Initially, German measures to enforce registration were rather mild but soon became much more intense, as, once revealed, the unregistered Jews were publicly hanged.[41] As a result, not everyone who initially evaded registration was able to continue doing so. At this stage, there were only few "transgressors," who had already made up their minds to escape from their native homes.[42]

36 Simferopol': Testimony of Efim Gopshtein, August 16, 1944, YVA, M.35/23, p. 56.

37 Kozlov, *V Krymskom podpol'ie*, p. 45.

38 Ibid., pp. 42-43. Apparently, the Germans feared that Kerch could be easily infiltrated with enemy agents.

39 Feodosiia, Simferopol', Sevastopol', Yalta: Interview with Savelii Al'ianaki (1932), March 30, 2004, author's archive; OSR USSR, no. 170, CSPSS, Berlin, February 18, 1942, in Arad, Krakowski, and Spektor, *The Einsatzgruppen Reports*, p. 296; Story of Anna Sal'nik-Korsakina, in Gel'man and Glubochanskii, *Kholokost*, p. 123; File of Mariia Frolova, Porfirii Kulik, and Anton and Elena Artemis, 2003, YVA, M.31/9983.

40 OSR USSR, no. 170, CSPSS, Berlin, February 18, 1942, in Arad, Krakowski, and Spektor, *The Einsatzgruppen Reports*, p. 296.

41 Simferopol': Testimony of Max Solomin from Simferopol', Recorded by Lev Kvitko, 1944, YVA, M.35/14, p. 87.

42 Simferopol': Testimony of Lev Iurovskii, recorded by Lev Kvitko, 1944,

In a few cases, registration was followed by the order to resettle in a camp or in a ghetto.[43] At this point, masses of Jews were subjected to especially hard conditions and depredations during the first phase of the German occupation. In areas where this happened, their reactions reflected the despair that other Crimean Jews sensed only on the eve of their physical annihilation. Such was the case in Yalta's ghetto, where a rumor circulated that "rich American Jews would provide redemption for those placed in the ghetto and that soon they would be moved to Palestine."[44] According to another source, most of Yalta's Jews were confident of hard days to come – they thought that they would be sent to a battlefield near Sevastopol', but they did not believe they faced imminent death.[45] On the other hand, a small minority of the ghetto inmates viewed the situation realistically and tried to escape from ghettos and camps.[46]

1.3. Responses to the assembly order

Despite the fact that the killing operations were not orchestrated simultaneously throughout the peninsula, overall, the Germans succeeded in keeping their programs secret from most Jews until the moment when the *Aktionen* were actually carried out. Most Jews complied with the assembly order, eagerly hoping for the better. Even if it was rumored that the Germans had killed Jews elsewhere, many Jews refused to believe it.[47] After the order was proclaimed, they gave their possessions to Russians "for safekeeping" and prepared food and their most valuable possessions to take for

YVA, M.35/14, p. 80. See also Story of Aleksandra Gershtein in Gubenko, *The Book of Sorrows*, pp. 58-61.

43 Dzhankoi, Yalta: See Chapter 3, "The Destruction of the Jewish Population in the Crimea."

44 Statement of Aleksandr Ponomarev, [no date], GARF, 7021/9/59, p. 84(?).

45 Letter of P. Nesterenko, July 5, 1944, YVA, P.21.2/8.

46 Dzhankoi, Yalta: Testimony of Mark Al'ianaki, no later than July 4, 1944, GARF, 7021/9/5, p. 76. See also Diary of Shargorodskaia, entry from January 2, 1942, DAARK, P-156/1/31, p. 160.

47 Sevastopol': Story of Sal'nik-Korsakina, in Gel'man and Glubochanskii, *Kholokost*, p. 123.

the "evacuation announced in the German order."[48] Some Jewish doctors took their medical equipment with them to the assembly point,[49] while others demanded from the Germans a receipt for their "deposited" possessions.[50]

Some Jews in possession of reliable information concerning the *Aktionen* tended to refrain from conveying it to those Jews residing in the localities where the killing of Jews had not yet occurred (for fear of being identified as Jews or for other reasons). Such being the case, their behavior reinforced the atmosphere of ignorance favorable for the implementation of German plans. The following testimonial excerpt illustrates the situation described above:

> Lev Iurovskii went around the villages towards Melitopol'. He arrived there on December 31, 1941. On his way there, he came by the Crimean Jewish [agricultural] colonies. They did not know anything about what was going on, but had a presentiment and were terribly anxious. Lev Iurovskii made up his mind not to inform them of the occurrences in Simferopol' and of what awaited them, and went away.[51]

Even when those Jews aware of the German atrocities against them recommended to other Jews not to comply with the assembly order, they did not explicitly state what the assembly meant but remained rather vague. Therefore, the Jews who refrained from fulfilling the assembly order did not take the necessary precautions and, thus, became exposed to immediate arrests in their own apartments in the wake of the killing operations. The story of an elderly Jewish man whom a witness came across in Simferopol' underscores the point:

48 Simferopol': Diary of Chrisanf Lashkevich, entry from December 7, 1941, DAARK, P-156/1/31, p. 73.

49 Feodosiia: Questioning of Ol'ga Korchagina, May 10, 1944, GARF, 7021/9/58, p. 103.

50 Simferopol': Conversation with the inhabitant of Simferopol' Il'ia Sirota, February 16, 1945, DAARK, P-156/1/40.

51 Ibid., p. 369.

> An elderly man from a neighboring courtyard came to us for advice on whether he should go to the camp. He heard that the order did not apply to people over 80 years of age. We advised him not to go. I felt like hugging this helpless old man. Two days later the Gestapo took him away.[52]

The main source of the rumors seemed to emanate from an in-depth assessment of the reality rather than from information leaks. Yet, deficiencies occurred in the German extermination mechanism, which could affect Jewish behavior:

> In Simferopol' a non-Jewish wife was let go from the assembly point. She noticed that those detained inside were terribly maltreated. She stated with confidence that no one would be resettled but killed.[53]

In some cases, Ashkenazi Jews who faced the assembly order and its unclear consequences were not the first group earmarked for "resettlement." Occasionally, similar orders had already been issued for Krymchaks and Gypsies, and their deportation had already taken place. This was the case in Simferopol':

> On December 11, 1941, Lev Iurovskii and his wife decided to go to the assembly point, despite bad presentiments. On their way, they came across a Russian woman who urged them not to go there. She had met a disguised Gypsy man. Gypsies had been "evacuated" some days ago, and he had managed to escape from the execution.[54]

52 Mina Fishgoit's report, [no date], YVA, P.21.2/9.

53 Memoirs of A. F. Peganova, November 9, 1944, DAARK, P-156/1/40, p. 43.

54 Testimony of Lev Iurovskii, 1944, YVA, M.35/14, p. 81.
On the extermination of Crimean Gypsies, see, for example, Martin Holler, "Extending the Genocidal Program: Did Otto Ohlendorf Initiate the Systematic Extermination of Soviet "Gypsies?" in Kay, Rutherford and Stahel, *Nazi Policy on the Eastern Front, 1941*, pp. 267-288 and Mikhail Tiaglyi, "Were the 'Chingené' Victims of the Holocaust? Nazi Policy toward the Crimean Roma, 1941-1944," *Holocaust and Genocide Studies* 23, no. 1 (2009): pp. 26-53.

Such information potentially provided the Jews with important life-and-death knowledge in due time so that they could calculate their further steps.[55]

Pessimistic forecasts had begun to prevail among the Jewish community in Simferopol' by the time the assembly order was issued. According to the diary of a Jewish witness, at this point they ranged from estimates that Jews would be 1) "sent to march in front of the German Army advancing to Sevastopol' to serve as a buffer"; 2) "sent to work in Bessarabia"; 3) "sent to work in the agricultural colonies of Fraidorfskii *raion* and Larindorfskii *raion*"; 4) "sent over to the USSR beyond the front line"; to 5) "destroyed altogether."[56] Such rumors considering the possibility of physical annihilation of the Jews in no uncertain terms reflected the constantly deteriorating conditions of the Jews. Some of them grasped what was going on, and accepted the inevitable. There is striking evidence that one Jewish man in Simferopol' organized a funeral banquet (*pominki*), in accordance with Russian customs, for himself on the eve of the assembly day because he felt that it was the end.[57] Others plunged into constant prayer.[58]

Immediately prior to the great *Aktion* in Simferopol', the Germans began to act politely and quietly towards the Jews.[59] Such policy reflected a noticeable shift in their behavior and had a soothing effect on the Jews. According to postwar German evidence, the general situation in Simferopol' (especially food conditions) was so grave that some Jews even reacted enthusiastically to their alleged departure to Germany:

> One fooled the victims, saying they would be resettled to Germany so that in this way they were led to get on the truck.

55 Feodosiia: Moshe Gutovich, "From the Horrors of the Massacre in Feodosiia" (Hebrew), [From the conversation with Moshe Gutovich, Jewish refugee from Feodosiia, source: *Eynikayt*], *Ha-tsofe* (Tel Aviv), no. 1685, July 13, 1943, p. 3.

56 Testimony of Efim Gopshtein, August 16, 1944, YVA, M.35/23, pp. 60-61.

57 Memoirs of Il'ia Sirota, February 16, 1945, DAARK, P-156/1/40, p. 114.

58 Sevastopol': Story of Sal'nik-Korsakina, in Gel'man and Glubochanskii, *Kholokost*, p. 124.

59 Testimony of Lev Iurovskii, 1944, YVA, M.35/14, p. 81.

> As a matter of fact, the situation evolved in such a way that the victims were duped to such an extent that they were glad to get out of Simferopol'. They even sang upon their departure.[60]

Jews in Kerch were also inclined to believe that all would turn out well in the end. According to a wartime Jewish testimony, after spending more than a day in the town's prison they jumped readily at the explanation provided by the German commander of the prison. He approached them and said politely: "Citizens! Sleep, have a rest. Tomorrow we'll take you to *sovkhozy*, you'll get two kilograms of bread per day."[61] The ensuing reactions of the Jews were as follows:

> People calmed down and began to make arrangements in order to work in the same village. The next day, upon the arrival of the trucks, there emerged a large crowd. It was very difficult to reach the trucks, as everyone wished to get out of the prison and get to the village. Only the strongest were able to push their way to the trucks, and the rest of the people stayed, though the trucks came and went the whole day.[62]

In other towns, however, Jews often avoided pessimistic dispositions, losing hope only at the last moment. Some even made commercial arrangements for their property, as they believed it was still possible that they would survive. In Feodosiia, for example, some Jews made deals with their Russian neighbors stipulating that if they should safely return, they would equally divide their property between the Jewish owners and their non-Jewish Russian neighbors.[63]

In a number of towns, the direct relationship between the

60 "Strafsache gegen Walter Bierkamp," Erich G., Abschrift, April 13, 1967, YVA, TR.10/1147, p. 599.

61 Lev Kvitko, "The man who rose from his grave," (Yiddish), *Eynikayt*, October 25, 1942, p. 2.

62 Report of Moisei Evenson, Viktor Shklovskii, ed., YVA, P.21.2/1. See also Kvitko, "The man who rose from his grave," p. 2.

63 Interview with Savelii Al'ianaki, March 30, 2004, author's archive.

particularly harsh German treatment of the Jews and desperate mood of the Jewish population at the time of the assembly order is observable.[64] However, even in these places, that despair was not common. The description of what took place at the time the assembly order was issued for the inmates of Yalta's ghetto underscores the point:

> Every Jew thought that nothing good would come out of it. Nevertheless, it was thought that probably there would be no executions but that the Jews would be sent over to specially designated areas beyond Simferopol' as the German officers warned... Other Jews said that we would probably be sent to the front line. One recalled the Soviet radio broadcasts [which claimed] that if the Germans were short of manpower in some sectors of the front, they brought there women, children, and old men. At the same time, Jews were strongly seized by the fear of execution.[65]

Some Jews attempted legally to defy the assembly order. Such law-abiding behavior had to do with the hope that the German assault against them would eventually take on some orderly form. Besides, these people assumed correctly that the assembly was fraught with danger. In Yalta, a Jewish man presented himself to the Gestapo and announced that he was not a Jew but was only brought up in a Jewish family and that the circumcision was made on medical grounds.[66] Others did not deny their Jewishness, but claimed an exemption from the assembly on the grounds that they were married to non-Jews[67] or that one of their parents was a non-Jew.[68]

64 Simferopol', Yalta: Testimony of Efim Gopshtein, August 16, 1944, YVA, M.35/23, p. 61; Mina Fishgoit's report, [no date], YVA, P.21.2/9.

65 Report of Margarita Frolova-Meltsyna, [no date], YVA, 0.33/626, p. 6.

66 Memoirs of A. M. Berliand, November 1944, DAARK, P-156/1/37, pp. 27-33.

67 Simferopol': Memoirs of A. F. Peganova, November 9, 1944, DAARK, P-156/1/40, pp. 34-45.

68 Sevastopol': File of Boris Korchminov (Nekrasov) and Valentina Gornostai (Nekrasova), Interrogation of Anna Sechnaia, December 12, 1950, USHMMA, RG-31.018M, reel 7.

Unlike them, other Jews failed to grasp the all-encompassing nature of the German onslaught against Jews. These Jews bought one of the main arguments of the Nazi's antisemitic propaganda by subscribing to the view that the Germans maltreated Jews solely because the latter formed a cornerstone of the Soviet regime. Therefore, they claimed an exemption from the assembly order on the grounds that they had nothing to do with the Soviet ruling elite. In Feodosiia, for example, a Jewish woman submitted the following request to the German authorities:

> My husband is mentally ill. He is 51 years old and incapable of performing physical work. Our family has worked at a tobacco plant from the age of 10. I have never been the member of any party. I request you to consider it and to leave us [alone].[69]

Her request was not honored, as the Germans killed all the Jews regardless of their status in the Soviet state.

In a number of cases, 12- to 14-year-old children adopted independent behavior. In apparent defiance of their parents, who did comply with the German regulations, these children did not present themselves at the assembly points, instead going into hiding.[70] Some Jews were desperate enough to leave their children with non-Jewish acquaintances after the assembly order was proclaimed,[71] sometimes for payment.[72] Such behavior reflected some parents' acknowledgement that the assembly order implied physical annihilation.

Once assembled, the Jews were seized with panic. Absorbed

69 Request submitted by Katz Margol Izrailevna in Feodosiia, "V mezzanine vo dvore Gestapo," essay by Lazar' Lagin [1945], in Rubinstein and Altman, *The Unknown Black Book*, p. 370.

70 Story of Izia Gofman (7th-grade schoolboy in Kerch), in Gubenko, *The Book of Sorrows*, p. 75; Story of Mosia Gol'dshtein (5th-grade schoolboy in Kerch) in ibid., pp. 75-76.

71 Feodosiia, village of Saragol': Interview with Savelii Al'ianaki, March 30, 2004, author's archive; "Alla-Roza Brazgol," Lev Kvitko, ed., [no date], YVA, M.35/14, p. 90.

72 "Peretsfel'd" *kolkhoz*: Testimony of Rachel Horowitz, March 20, 1988, YVA, 0.3/4875, p. 9.

entirely by the anticipation of impending disaster, they accepted the inevitable.[73] Yet, some Jews displayed the presence of mind even under such extreme circumstances to either escape themselves[74] or allow and/or help their relatives to flee.[75] The following episode pertaining to Evpatoriia describes one Jewish woman's self-composure and escape:

> A Jewish woman with good knowledge of German heard the Germans talking to each other: "We have already executed one group of Jews. Now we'll do it with the next group." So she wrote a note in German as if the *Kommandant* had permitted her to leave.[76]

However, most non-compliance was overt. Small children in a village in Fraidorfskii *raion* declined to accompany their parents to the execution point and escaped on their own.[77] In Evpatoriia, an adult Jewish woman fled the camp on the eve of the execution.[78] Such instances were cases of a few fortunate Jews who managed to escape death during the actions and then somehow go into hiding.[79] There exists almost no record of resistance by the Jews at this stage of the Holocaust in the Crimea, i.e., during the killing operations of 1941 and 1942, with the exception of one case in Feodosiia, where: "At the end of December 1941, when groups of prisoners in Feodosiia were transported, the butcher Aaron

73 Simferopol', Yalta: Testimony of Anbol, *Sotsialisticheskii vestnik*, 2 (605), February 28, 1948, in West, *In the Ropes of Destruction*, p. 140; Akt of the Commission of Yalta, May 13, 1944, DAARK, R-1289/1/11, pp. 6-7.

74 Sevastopol': Story of Sal'nik-Korsakina, in Gel'man and Glubochanskii, *Kholokost*, p. 124. See also Testimony of Aza Tumbinskaia, in ibid., p. 138.

75 Karasubazar: File of Sofia Leonidi and Venera Dinishaeva, [no date], YVA, M.31/8955.

76 Testimony of Rachel Horowitz, March 20, 1988, YVA, 0.3/4875, p. 7.

77 Fraidorfskii *raion*: Story of Mina Fishgoit, YVA, P.21.2/9; See also West, *In the Ropes of Destruction*, p. 140.

78 Evpatoriia: West, *In the Ropes of Destruction*, p. 140.

79 Simferopol', Dzhankoi, and Kerch: Interrogation of Il'ia Sirota, GARF, 7021/9/194, pp. 155-157; Lev Kvitko, "The man who rose from his grave," (Yiddish), *Eynikayt*, October 25, 1942, p. 2.

killed one guard and injured the other. He managed to escape."[80]

It is significant that the actions, in particular the first great wave, were not synchronized throughout the region. Therefore, the Germans relied on a ramified system of movement restrictions, which *inter alia* were to prevent Jews and non-Jews from spreading information concerning the details of their persecution and annihilation of Jews. Despite the fact that this method was efficient overall, there were some exceptions to the rule, as explicitly acknowledged in the EG D report from January 2, 1942: "Rumors about executions in other areas complicated the action in Simferopol.'"[81] This also happened with large groups of Krymchaks in Feodosiia and Kerch. The Krymchaks were left alive for many days after the Ashkenazi Jews in the respective towns were killed; during this time, information about their murder had somehow leaked, becoming known to the Krymchaks.[82]

2. After the Killing Operations

2.1. General concerns

Jews discovered after the extermination actions had no chance for survival, apart from some cases in which a combination of resourcefulness and domestic circumstances made it possible, at least in the short run. According to a piece of postwar Jewish testimony, upon the Germans' revelation of a Jewish man and his wife in the farm (*khutor*) of Burycha:

> The Germans were loath to deal with him as he said that he was ill with a venereal disease. The Germans were very afraid

80 Excerpts from the book *Kem byl Gitler v deistvitelnosti*, 1982, YVA, 0.32/62, p. 7. See also Questioning of Liudmila Novikova, June 21, 1944, GARF, 7021/9/58, p. 6.

81 OSR USSR, no. 150, CSPSS, Berlin, January 2, 1942, in Arad, Krakowski, and Spektor, *The Einsatzgruppen Reports, pp. 266-267.*

82 Feodosiia, Kerch: Questioning of Ol'ga Korchagina, May 10, 1944, GARF, 7021/9/58, p. 103; Interview with David Borokhov, March-April 2004, author's archive.

> of it. He was deported to a remote house and left there to die of starvation.[83]

In order to survive long term in the occupied Crimea, it was highly necessary for a Jew to have a non-Jewish appearance,[84] speak fluent Russian without any traces of a Yiddish accent, be proficient in the local language, such as Ukrainian[85] or Tatar,[86] and be acquainted with reliable "Aryan" friends.[87] In the towns where security checks were especially tight, these factors played a relatively minor role. It was dangerous for persecuted Jews to stay in their native towns; there are only few recorded cases of survival in such conditions, primarily in shelters made in apartments[88] or, as with mixed couples, in the apartments of their non-Jewish relatives.[89] At times, the continual German pressure and resulting atmosphere could prove so unbearable that Jews surrendered themselves to the authorities.[90] If Jews were unable to find safe shelter and provisions anywhere in the Crimea, they tended to move away from the peninsula.[91] In order to do so, they had to pass through numerous German or Romanian posts set up at the narrow entry into the

83 Zuiaskii *raion*: Testimony of Musia Leikin (Iofin), December 27, 2000, YVA, 0.33.C/6428.

84 Villages of Autka and Burycha, Memoirs of A. M. Berliand, November 1944, DAARK, P-156/1/37, pp. 27-33; Testimony of Musia Leikin (Iofin), December 27, 2000, YVA, 0.33.C/6428.

85 Village of Topalovka: Testimony of D. I. Makarycheva, [no date], DAARK, P-156/1/36, p. 90.

86 Near Sevastopol': Gel'man and Glubochanskii, *Kholokost*, p. 59.

87 Sevastopol', Simferopol': Story of Sal'nik-Korsakina, in ibid., p. 124. See also Memoirs of Il'ia Sirota, February 16, 1945, DAARK, P-156/1/40, p. 116.

88 Simferopol': Testimony of Efim Gopshtein, August 16-17, 1944, DAARK, P-156/1/37, pp. 71-106; Statement of Elena Grammatik. June 9, 1944, GARF, 7021/9/95, p. 130.

89 Evpatoriia, near Staryi Krym: Story of Gushanskaia in Gubenko, *The Book of Sorrows*, pp. 43-44; Testimony of Khanania Kurzon, August 3, 2000, YVHN.

90 Simferopol', Kerch: File of Ekaterina Kolesnikova. 1993, YVA, M.31/5541; See also Diary of Chrisanf Lashkevich, entry from December (?) 26, 1941, DAARK, P-156/1/31, p. 84.

91 Letter by Mina Fishgoit, [no date], YVA, P.21.2/9; Testimony of Lev Iurovskii, 1944, YVA, M.35/14, p. 82.

Crimea. Southern Ukraine was a much more vast region than the Crimea, with better food supplies and a different population composition that, ostensibly, entailed more possibilities for rescue.

2.2. Between towns and the countryside

The Crimean towns and countryside presented different conditions for the survival of Jews in the post-extermination period. In this respect, towns had no clear-cut disadvantages over the rural areas, and visa-versa. To mention just several factors, it was easier for a Jew to "get lost" in a town by assuming a new identity, especially if the town was large enough. Yet, under German rule, inhabitants of the towns were in a state of permanent undernourishment to the point of starvation. Therefore, Jews who had been living in towns and who had survived the extermination operations often faced conditions necessitating their flight to rural areas. Jews who managed to survive the operations and hide in the Crimean towns also faced recurring round-ups. It was dangerous for the Jews to revisit their old apartments, which were constantly supervised by the Germans, as well as the Russian police.[92] In Simferopol', a Jew hid at his friends' place until December 23, 1941, then returned to his sister's apartment, only to be captured there.[93] Jews could risk staying for a short period in their native towns only if they had a reliable "Aryan" friend who could provide them with shelter and accommodation.[94] Attempts to hide in one's own house by relying upon an "Aryan" spouse could be easily frustrated by the short-term arrest of the "Aryan" spouse.[95]

There is almost no record of hiding in one permanent site throughout the occupation period, as non-stop German searches[96]

92 Simferopol': Staboffz. der FG, "TB als Anlage zum KTB für die Zeit vom 1.-31.1.42," February 2, 1942, YVA, M.29.FR/60, p. 7.

93 Diary of Chrisanf Lashkevich, entry from December 26, 1941, DAARK, P-156/1/31, p. 82.

94 Kerch, Sevastopol': "Story of Iosef Vaingarten," (Yiddish), *Eynikayt*, July 15, 1942, p. 1; Story of Sal'nik-Korsakina, in Gel'man and Glubochanksii, *Kholokost*, p. 124.

95 Simferopol': Memoirs of Il'ia Sirota, February 16, 1945, DAARK, P-156/1/40, p. 118.

96 In particular in Simferopol': OSR USSR, no. 170, CSPSS, Berlin, February 18, 1942, in Arad, Krakowski, and Spektor, *The Einsatzgruppen Reports*, p. 296.

and fear of denunciations[97] led Jews constantly to seek new places to hide. Sooner or later, either their hosts or the Jews themselves could no longer bear the pressure, and Jews fled the towns in pursuit of a safer place.[98] Possession of new "Aryan" IDs brought only temporary alleviation; ultimately, survival was dependent upon escape from one's native area.[99] The following postwar Soviet evidence, however dubious, also underscores the point:

> In Simferopol', two officers of the German army settled in an apartment of a Jewish engineer. The officers advised the engineer to choose an area where he was not known. Some days later, they took him and his wife in their vehicle dressed in ordinary warm clothes to Dzhankoi.[100]

Consequently, the aforementioned considerations led the Jews to wander around the Crimea in search of safety. In most cases, they tried to settle in villages or small localities in order to be as far from their native towns as possible.[101] The important criteria Jews considered in settling in a new place included whether Germans were there[102] and, perhaps more significantly, whether they would be recognized by anyone.[103] The latter

97 Karasubazar, Sevastopol': OK II/937/V, "TB für die Zeit vom 1.-15.2.42," Karasubazar, February 14, 1942, YVA, M.29.FR/40, p. 3. See also, "Tragic End of the Jewry in Western Russia."

98 Jews, Simferopol': Testimony of Lev Iurovskii, 1944, YVA, M.35/14, p. 82; Hosts, Simferopol': Memoirs of Il'ia Sirota, February 16, 1945, DAARK, P-156/1/40, p. 119; Testimony of Musia Leikin (Iofin), December 27, 2000, YVA, 0.33.C/6428.

99 Simferopol', Evpatoriia: Testimony Musia Leikin (Iofin), December 27, 2000, YVA, 0.33.C/6428. See also file of Mikhail and Tat'iana Gur'ianov, [no date], YVA, M.31/8796.

100 Il'ia Vergasov, *Krymskie tetradi* (Moscow: Sovetskii pisatel', 1971), p. 100, in YVA, 0.51/185 II.

101 Around the peninsula, Ak-Mechet': Interrogation of Il'ia Sirota, GARF, 7021/9/194, p. 157; Mina Fishgoit's report, [no date], YVA, P.21.2/9; File of Mikhail and Tat'iana Gur'ianov, [no date], YVA, M.31/8796.

102 Simferopol', Evpatoriia: Story of Aleksandra Gershtein in Gubenko, *The Book of Sorrows*, pp. 58-61; Mina Fishgoit's report, [no date], YVA, P.21.2/9.

103 Dzhankoi, Evpatoriia: Story of Grigorii Purevich, ed., Lev Kvitko, [no date] in Grossman and Erenburg, *Chernaia kniga*, pp. 291-294; Mina Fishgoit's report, [no date], YVA, P.21.2/9.

factor sometimes encouraged the Crimean Jews to apply for forced labor in Germany for the sole purpose of getting out of the peninsula.[104] In contrast, some mixed-marriage couples and their offspring did have specific places in the Crimea where they could go and hide, such as the areas where their non-Jewish relatives lived.[105] By the same token, those Jews who enjoyed the protection of non-Jews, most specifically Jewish children given over by their parents on the eve of an assembly, also had one or more addresses in which they could find shelter.[106]

Apart from a desire to find a safe place, Jews persecuted in the Crimea were driven by the grave food situation. In the harsh winter of 1941-1942, food rationing in the Crimean towns was scarce, if it existed at all, and the civilian population suffered from serious under-nourishment. Conversely, the food situation in the rural settlements was better.[107] Viewed from this perspective, Jewish flight from towns into rural areas of the peninsula also reflected the additional dimension of escape from starvation.

2.3. In pursuit of "Aryan" documents

Possession of an "Aryan" ID offered the strongest survival potential for the persecuted Jews.[108] Such possession was critical, given the strict residence and movement restrictions imposed in

104 Story of Iakov and Son'ia Bedrin in Mark Goldenberg, "Tragediia evreiskoi obschiny Feodosii," in *Problemy Kholokosta v Ukraine: Tezisy dokladov i soobshenii Mezhdunarodnoi nauchnoi konferentsii (Dnepropetrovsk, 2002)* (Zaporozh'e: Premier, 2003), p. 60.

105 Saki, Simferopol': Story of Briskina, in Gubenko, *The Book of Sorrows*, pp. 43-44; Statement of Arsenii Podymov, before November 1944, YVA, M.33/70, p. 106.

106 Villages of Kirmachi and Takhtaba in Dzhankoiskii *raion*, Simferopol': Interview with Savelii Al'ianaki, March 30, 2004, author's archive; Story of Sal'nik-Korsakina in Gel'man and Glubochanksii, *Kholokost*, pp. 124-5.

107 See section 4A, "Food Conditions and the Holocaust in the Crimea and the Caucasus."

108 Villages of Autka and Topalovka: Memoirs of A. M. Berliand, November 1944, DAARK, P-156/1/37, pp. 27-33; Account of D. I. Makarycheva, [no date], DAARK, P-156/1/36.

the Crimea, expressed *inter alia* in the following German order, dated April 1942:

> Heads of all localities have to draw lists of all inhabitants… and a list of all aliens (*Fremderregister*). These lists will include all the persons who settled in this locality after June 22, 1941. [The latter] list will include also Jews registered with the letter "E." Crossing the border of the locality is forbidden.[109]

Not only did the ID have to be "Aryan," often it also had to be properly stamped by the German authorities or by the local administration established by the Germans.[110] The stamps also needed to be updated from time to time after they expired. It was desirable, and sometimes absolutely necessary, to be provided with other documents of the occupation regime, such as food stamps. Because of the harsh German identification policy, even non-Jews (in particular, conscription-aged men) detected without valid IDs could be sent to transition camps, where they faced terrible conditions in anticipation of a security check.[111]

In the Crimea, Jews could obtain an "Aryan" ID along the lines of the following examples. In one exceptional case, a Jewish relative with connections in the local Soviet administration was provided with a Greek passport in the final days before the German takeover.[112] Complete strangers occasionally offered or sold their own IDs to Jews[113] or offered those of other people,

109 Directive to the heads of localities in the Crimea: DAARK, P-156/1/24, p. 37. See also residence regulations in the towns and villages of the Crimea, report of the Commander of the North Caucasian Front Semeon Budennyi, July 1942, Russian State Archive of Social and Political History (RGASPI), 69/1/622, p. 9.

110 Mina Fishgoit's report, [no date], YVA, P.21.2/9; See also Testimony of Musia Leikin (Iofin), December 27, 2000, YVA, 0.33.C/6428.

111 POW camp near Simferopol': Testimony of Zalman Uzikov, December 14, 1987, YVA, 0.3/4939, p. 18.

112 Simferopol': Testimony of Musia Leikin (Iofin), December 27, 2000, YVA, 0.33.C/6428.

113 Simferopol': Testimonies of Liusia Rabin and Miriam Paver, recorded by Lev Kvitko, 1944, YVA, M.35/7, p. 32; Conversation with Il'ia Sirota, February 16, 1945, DAARK, P-156/1/40. Their testimony is also presented in Rubenstein and Altman, *The Unknown Black Book*, pp. 365-368.

particularly IDs belonging to those whose identity could not be easily validated.[114] Good friends of the Jews sometimes gave them their own documents or procured other people's passports.[115] Occasionally, people in the local administration and even the Germans themselves transferred such documents to the Jews, contributing to their survival.[116] The following uncorroborated postwar Soviet evidence illustrates an instance in which Jews received help from Germans:

> In Feodosiia, some women who spoke German made the acquaintance of the German prison guards. As the former book-keeper of the Financial Department, Ashkenadze, recalled for the author, these women began to fetch forged certificates and documents for Communists and Jewish acquaintances. In such a way, dozens of people were released from the prisons, including Ashkenadze himself.[117]

In exceptional cases, Jews established dangerous contacts with local collaborators, and through them procured "Aryan" IDs.[118]

Jews in the peninsula rarely forged their passports.[119] They largely preferred to exist without any identifying documents than with Jewish documents.[120] There were many non-Jews who traveled throughout the Crimea in pursuit of food, and, therefore, Jewish travelers could also potentially claim a non-Jewish identity:

114 For example, the ID of a husband who served in the Red Army, Simferopol': Testimony of Lev Iurovskii, 1944, YVA, M.35/14, p. 82 and that of the sister who perished during the bombardments of Evpatoriia: Mina Fishgoit's report, [no date], YVA, P.21.2/9.

115 Simferopol', Evpatoriia: Story of Margolina, in Gubenko, *The Book of Sorrows*, pp. 55-57; Mina Fishgoit's report, [no date] YVA, P.21.2/9.

116 Bakhchisarai: Story of Sal'nik-Korsakina, in Gel'man and Glubochanskii, *Kholokost*, p. 127.

117 Vergasov, *Krymskie tetradi*, YVA, 0.32/62, p. 16, in YVA, 0.51/185 II.

118 Karasubazarskii *raion* (?): Gitel' Gubenko, *Kniga pechali* (Simferopol': Redotel' Krymskogo Upravleniia po pechati, 1991), p. 34.

119 Simferopol': Story of Aleksandra Gershtein in Gubenko, *The Book of Sorrows*, pp. 58-61; Diary of Chrisanf Lashkevich, entry from 27 July 1942, DAARK, P-156/1/31, p. 69.

120 Area of Staryi Krym: Gubenko, *Kniga pechali*, pp. 36-37.

German,[121] Chechen, Russian, Ukrainian,[122] Karaite,[123] or Tatar.[124] The underground industry of falsifying IDs of which the persecuted Jews could take advantage did not develop fully in the peninsula until the summer of 1942. Soviet authorities in the remaining Soviet enclaves of the Crimea seemed to have played a role in the emergence of this industry. Otherwise, it is difficult to account for the sharp increase of Jewish refugees from the fallen Soviet stronghold of Kerch who, according to a wartime German report, had almost perfect "Aryan" IDs.[125] Yet, by this time, the Germans had apparently become aware of the widespread phenomenon of fraudulent IDs and, therefore, took special precautions for authenticating the identity of their bearers. As was the case, the Germans revealed many Jews despite the fact that they had possessed perfectly forged passports.[126]

2.4. Jewish responses to the Holocaust in rural areas

The Jewish rural population in the Crimea appeared to be in an especially precarious position in the unfolding of the Holocaust. The fact that some of these people were well-connected with those around them paled into insignificance, as they were visible and easily identifiable by virtue of their residence in small localities. Jews living in villages, particularly the inhabitants of the Jewish agricultural regions, tended to communicate primarily in Yiddish, which gave them away, as many of them spoke Russian with a Yiddish accent.

121 Feodosiia: OR I (V) 287, "TB für die Zeit vom 1.-15.3.1942," Feodosiia, March 15, 1942, YVA, M.29.FR/40, p. 30.

122 Village of Kambary and Yalta: OK I/853, "TB für die Zeit vom 16.-30.9.1942," Simferopol', September 30, 1942, YVA, 0.51/185 II, p. 7; File of File of Mariia Frolova, Porfirii Kulik, and Anton and Elena Artemis, 2003, YVA, M.31/9983.

123 Dzhankoi: Story of Grigorii Purevich, in Grossman and Erenburg, *The Complete Black Book of Russian Jewry*, pp. 231-232.

124 Simferopol': Testimony of Serafima Babina, January 6, 2004, author's archive.

125 FG der OK I (V)/287, "TB für die Zeit vom 15.-30.6.1942," Kerch, June 30, 1942, YVA, 0.51/185 II, p. 10.

126 FG der OK I (V)/287, "TB für die Zeit vom 1.-14.8.1942," Kerch, August 14, 1942, YVA, 0.51/185 I, p. 13.

Jewish *kolkhozniki* were also usually less informed about the possibility of the Germans' future persecutions and murder of Jews in their areas, as they had less contact with the greater Jewish population, particularly the evacuees who had settled or escaped through the towns.[127] Therefore, the cases when rural Jews took steps in explicit response to the Holocaust-related information in the towns were a clear exception to the trend. One such response concerning a 13-year-old Jewish girl in "Voroshilov" *kolkhoz* is as follows:

> When the Germans occupied the Crimea and news of their atrocities reached the village, the aunt and the uncle went to the village headman with all their money and the only gold jewelry they had and begged him to save Esfir'. The headman spoke to the priest who agreed to baptize her. Her new name was Frosia. When they got home from the priest's home they reached a decision – they would not wait for the Germans to kill them. The same day they hanged themselves.[128]

The extermination actions in the villages were usually not preceded by registration or the order to bear six-pointed stars. As a result, it was difficult for the Jews in rural areas to foresee such a rapid pace of the Germans' violence towards them and, hence, to take the precautions necessary for survival. Therefore, there exists no record of survival in the killing operations conducted in the rural areas at the beginning of the German occupation (November-December 1941), the time when the majority of the Jewish *kolkhozniki* in the Crimea were destroyed. Although some rural Jews refused to comply with the German orders prior to and during the *Aktionen*, these attempts were overwhelmingly unsuccessful.[129] Other Jews managed to evade the extermination for some months by hiding in nearby areas. Yet, they were usually

127 Unidentified Crimean Jewish agricultural colonies in late December 1941: Testimony of Lev Iurovskii, 1944, YVA, M.35/14, p. 82.

128 Tel'manskii *raion*: Story of Esfir' (Esther) Vaikhanskaia in Gubenko, *The Book of Sorrows*, pp. 101-102.

129 "Molotov" *kolkhoz*, village of Naibrot: *Gubenko, Kniga pechali, pp. 39*, 42.

detected by local collaborators and turned in to the Germans, as it was impossible to lead an autonomous existence without aid from the villagers.[130] The following excerpt from an EG D report correctly assessed the possibility for the Jews to survive under these circumstances:

> Except for small groups, which occasionally show up in the northern Crimea, there are no more Jews, Krymchaks, or Gypsies. As experiences of the past weeks have proven, wherever they have been able to hide their identity with false documents, etc., they will be recognized anyway sooner or later.[131]

There exist some examples when the German allowed a more protracted Jewish existence in the rural settlements in the peninsula. In these places, Jews were obliged to register, bear distinctive signs, and deliver all valuable possessions to the German authorities.[132] In these settings, patterns of Jewish reactions were similar to those in the Crimean towns. Attempts were made to obtain "Aryan" IDs and to relocate to another area in the countryside.[133] In a new locality, it was extremely difficult to hide without aid of the locals, even without open denunciations.[134] There were some cases of suicides of Jews who perceived their conditions as desperate or unbearable.[135]

130 Fraidorfskii *raion*, "Molotov" *kolkhoz*: 3./ Feldgend., Abt. (mot) 683, "TB des im Freidorfer Gebiet eingesetzten Zuges," O. U., February 11, 1942, YVA, M.29. FR/40, p. 5; Gubenko, *Kniga pechali, p. 39.*

131 OSR USSR, no. 190, CSPSS, Berlin, April 8, 1942, YVA, 0.51/184, p. 19; Arad, Krakowski, and Spektor, *The Einsatzgruppen Reports*, pp. 325-326.

132 Village of Kamenka: Akt of the Commission of Larindorfskii *raion*, October 16, 1944, DAARK, R-1289/1/13, pp. 8-9.

133 From the village of Nagaichi into the village of Nem-Adargin; into a remote *kolkhoz*: Gubenko, *Kniga pechali*, p. 46; Testimony of Rachel Horowitz, March 20, 1988, YVA, 0.3/4875, p. 7.

134 Village of Budenovka: Questioning of Efrosiniia Dozenko, July 21, 1944, YVA, M.33/63, p. 30.

135 "Novaia Zaria" and "Voroshilov" *kolkhozy*: ibid., p. 44; Story of Vaikhanskaia in Gubenko, *The Book of Sorrows*, pp. 101-102; General Akt of the Commission of Tel'manskii *raion*, October 25, 1944, YVA, M.33/75, p. 71.

In an exceptional case in Kolaiskii *raion*, no intensification of the anti-Jewish policy took place after the Germans had first plundered Jewish property. Furthermore, after the Germans had taken all cows, sheep, pigs, and bread from the Jews, they began to provide them with food rations. This somewhat assuaged Jewish fears. The relatively stable situation, which did not replicate itself in other Crimean villages, led Jews and non-Jews alike to conclude that the Germans would spare the Jews.[136] However, the Jews were killed in mid-February 1942 in the course of a comprehensive *Aktion*, and there exists no record of the Jews' escape from this village or any other form of non-compliance with the German regulations.

3. Jewish Resistance to the Holocaust in the Crimea

3.1. General concerns

As was presented above, Jewish reactions to the Holocaust in the Crimea confined themselves primarily to acquiescence to German policies. Only isolated cases of non-compliance were recorded, and none of armed resistance. The reasons for such behavior were analyzed at the beginning of the chapter. It deserves to be restated, however, that this pattern of responses was in no way unique in the Crimea. It should also be borne in mind that prior to the great *Aktionen*, the dimensions of the immediate physical assault on the Jews' lives were limited.

There appears to be only one recorded incident of a German attack on Jews prior to the actions in the Crimea that triggered active Jewish resistance.[137] Apart from its immediate outcome, the incident made an impression on the inner circle of Jews who learned of it. According to the wartime testimony of a male Jewish survivor, he gathered some 50 acquaintances and recalled the tragedy. He suggested that a thousand-or-so strong group of

136 Village of Baigonchik: Story of the chairman of "Oktiabr'" *kolkhoz*, DAARK, P-156/1/37, p. 135.

137 Story of the book-keeper Peckerman in the current study (pp. 128-129).

"our people will gather and attack the Germans. Many people will perish during the operation, but hundreds of people will obtain weapons and will be able to go to mountains or forests." However, an objection was raised that it would be impossible to destroy the population of 15,000-20,000 people. Other people were calmed as the Germans began to behave less vehemently in the streets, and were polite and refrained from beating people.[138] Another witness describing the way the Jews were transported to the extermination site near Simferopol' expressed similar deliberations.[139] Other testimonies, however, pass in silence over the possibility of resisting the Germans. It is perhaps this silence that speaks most loudly about the Jews' lack of opportunities for resistance.

For their part, the Germans did not expect any armed Jewish resistance, only envisaging the possibility of Jews going into hiding.[140] Although apartments belonging to Jews were occasionally searched for weapons prior to the actions,[141] this was rather an isolated episode in comparison with the all-out German effort aimed against partisans and scattered units of the Red Army. The juxtaposition of Jewish and German sources indicates that the possibility of armed Jewish non-compliance, whether as group or as individuals, was considered only theoretically; it was never weighed as a serious option. Therefore, in the Crimean peninsula, Jewish armed resistance was solely reliant upon the opportunities offered by the Soviet networks of underground and partisan movements.

138 Testimony of Max Solomin, 1944, YVA, M.35/14, pp. 86-87.

139 Memoirs of Il'ia Sirota, February 16, 1945, DAARK, P-156/1/40, p. 115.

140 Evpatoriia: OK I (V)/277, "TB für die Zeit vom 11.-20.12.1941," Evpatoriia, December 21, 1941, YVA, M.29.FR/41, p. 40.

141 Simferopol': FG der OK II/915, "TB für die Zeit vom 21.-29.11.1941," Simferopol', November 29, 1941, YVA, M.29.FR/41, p. 33

3.2. Underground and partisan movement[142]

Although the Soviet underground movement possessed no proven information concerning the German intentions towards the Crimean Jews, it generally assumed that the Germans singled out Jews for maltreatment.[143] At first, the Soviet underground in the Crimea recruited some Jews[144] and occasionally helped others by issuing them "Aryan" IDs[145] or effecting the rescue of a Jewish child, for example.[146] Nevertheless, overall its attitude towards maintaining contacts with Jews and employing them in clandestine activity remained problematic, because they were considered a security risk.

The case of Ivan Kozlov, the head of the Soviet underground network in Kerch, is instructive. According to his own postwar memoir, Kozlov went to great lengths to save the already-registered Jewish teenager Polia Govardovskaia[147] (previously employed by the Soviet underground) and her sister. He proposed to provide them with "Aryan" IDs and to arrange their relocation to another area, with an eye to employing Polia in secret activity because he evidently thought that the Jewish girl would be useful for the Soviet underground. Kozlov's evidence is quoted at length:

142 On the partisan and underground movement in the Crimea during World War II, see Oleg Roman'ko, *Krym v period nemetskoi okkupatsii: natsional'nye otnosheniia, kollaboratsionizm i partizanskoe dvizhenie, 1941-1944* (Moscow: Tsentrpoligraf, 2014), pp. 320-328; Mark Goldenberg, "Evrei v krymskom partizanskom dvizhenii i podpol'e 1941-1944 gg.," in Viktoriia Mochalova, et al., eds., *Materialy Odinnadtatoi Ezhegodnoi Mezhdistsiplinarnoi konferentsii po iudaike* (Moscow: Sefer and Institut Slavianovedeniia RAN, 2004), pp. 388-392; Vergasov, *Krymskie tetradi*, in YVA, 0.32/62; Vergasov, *V gorakh Tavrii*; Genov, *Dnevnik partizana*.

143 Kozlov, *V Krymskom podpol'ie*, pp. 45-49.

144 Southern Crimea, Karasubazar: EG D report, February-March 1942, DAARK, P-849/1/198. See also file of Mariia and Aleksandra Chumasova, 2004, YVA, M.31/9912.

145 Yalta: Testimony of Nelli Tektonidi, file of Peotr, Mariia, Natal'ia and Tat'iana Petrov, 2001, YVA, M.31/9381.

146 Simferopol': File of Tat'iana Zelenskaia and Pavel Chariuta, 1995, YVA, M.31/6800.

147 On Polia Govardovskaia's story, see also p. 317.

> Polia Govardovskaia had insisted that I leave her in the occupied town. However, I objected on the grounds that she was Jewish. She claimed: "I was brought up under the Soviet power and have never felt any difference between Jew and Russian. Now, when it comes to defend the Motherland you are talking about it. It is painful." I reminded [her] that the Hitlerites treated the Jews in a particularly cruel fashion. – "And I think that they maltreat all Soviet people in the same fashion."[148]

Kozlov yielded to Polia's request. In appearance, she bore more resemblance to an Armenian. Kozlov promised to procure her an Armenian ID. The still-acting Soviet authorities provided her with a job in a new place as a sailor. She was also given a new apartment. No one suspected her of being Jewish. However, after her mother intervened, this plan did not materialize.

Later, when the dimensions of the anti-Jewish atrocities became clearer, the Soviet underground tended not to employ Jews,[149] although there were exceptions to the rule.[150] Occasionally, however, Soviet clandestine networks in the Crimea were instrumental in rescuing some Jews by sheltering them[151] and/or smuggling them to the partisans.[152] The following testimony from Yalta suffices to underscore the point:

148 Kozlov, *V Krymskom podpol'ie*, pp. 26-27.

149 Such a conclusion was made as a result of the analysis of the collection of the Crimean underground groups preserved in the DAARK (P-849/1, 3) and presently available but still not catalogued in the USHMMA.

150 According to the German documents, Jews participated in the clandestine networks in Feodosiia, Yalta and Evpatoriia; then, they were found and executed. Goldenberg, "Evrei v krymskom partizanskom dvizhenii i podpol'e," pp. 390-391.

151 Report of the Secretary of the Simferopol' Underground City Committee of the VKP(b) for the period October 1943-April 1944, in Mikhail Tiaglyi, "Protivostoianie Katastrofe evreev Kryma," in idem., ed., *Evreiskii opyr v Ukraini v period Golokostu* (Dnipropetrovsk, Zaporozhi: Ukrainska biblioteka Golokostu, 2004).

152 From Simferopol' into a partisan unit in March 1944: File of Ekaterina Kolesnikova, 1993, YVA, M.31/5541.

> As I wandered around the rural areas of the Crimea, I came to the village of "Krasnyi Pakhar." One family agreed to let me stay with them, provided I would look after their child and give them some possessions, and that the village headman would agree to this arrangement. I gave them a clock. The headman gave his consent, though I was not registered with the Germans. He turned out to be the member of the Soviet underground network. But the situation deteriorated, as during the registration of passports in the village I was revealed by a *registratory*[153] who came from Evpatoriia. I had to run away, and the headman provided me with some papers.[154]

By the time of the German entry to the Crimea, the Soviets had made important preparations for the deployment of a large-scale partisan movement all over the peninsula. Like elsewhere in the Soviet Union, their nucleus was made up of male members of "extermination battalions" (*istrebitel'nye bataliony*). Future partisans were initially scrutinized by the Party authorities, and were selected from ideologically reliable persons,[155] sometimes almost entirely from the members of the Party.[156] Among them there were also Jews.[157] Soviet sources maintain that by the beginning of the German occupation, 3,134 people were recruited for partisan warfare in the peninsula.[158]

Unlike in other occupied Soviet territories, the partisan movement in the Crimea became active in the first weeks of the German occupation, and occasionally inflicted losses on the German troops.[159] Yet, following German anti-partisan operations

153 Those who registered the population.

154 Mina Fishgoit's report, [no date], YVA, P.21.2/9.

155 Ekaterina N. Shamko, *Partizanskoe dvizhenie v Krymu v 1941-1944 gg.* (Simferopol': Krymizdat, 1959), pp. 10-11.

156 Yalta: Vergasov, *Krymskie tetradi*, YVA, 0.32/62, p. 18.

157 Village of Ikor: Testimony of Bronia Volovik, July 31, 1990, YVHN.

158 Note of the Crimean District Committee of the VKP(b) on the situation of the partisan movement in the Crimea, December 18, 1942, in Kondranov and Stepanova, *Krym v period Velikoi Otechestvennoi voiny,* p. 252.

159 Area of Alushta: OSR USSR, no. 156, CSPSS, Berlin, January 16, 1942, in Arad, Krakowski, and Spektor, *The Einsatzgruppen Reports*, p. 283.

and the general shift in the balance of forces in the peninsula away from their favor, the Soviet partisan movement suffered heavy setbacks in 1941 and the first half of 1942,[160] and its numerical strength decreased drastically (to 760 people as of January 1, 1942[161]). However, even in their worst moments, the partisans continued to cause a serious military hindrance to the German troops in the Crimea.[162]

Jews fought in the Crimea as commanders and commissars of detachments,[163] as well as doctors[164] and ordinary partisans.[165] Many Jewish partisans excelled in the operations against the Germans and local collaborators.[166] Scouts soon informed the partisans of the extermination of the Jewish population in the Crimea,[167] which apparently affected the zeal of the Jewish partisans. Partisan activity in the Crimea unfolded under conditions of an extremely sparse food situation, which, combined with the high mortality rate from fierce warfare, caused more than half of the initially recruited partisans to perish by the end of 1942.[168] It stands to reason that

160 Area of Simferopol' and elsewhere: Wehrmachtsdienststelle, Gr. GFP 647, *Kommando* Simferopol', "TB für die Zeit vom 2.-11.11.1941," November 11, 1941, YVA, M.29.FR/120, p. 3; Information on the conditions of the partisan warfare in the Crimea prepared by the Crimean District Committee of the VKP(b), July 7, 1942, in Kondranov and Stepanova, *Krym v period Velikoi Otechestvennoi voiny*, p. 230.

161 Untitled document, RGASPI, 69/1/10, p. 146.

162 Bidermann, *In Deadly Combat*, pp. 121-122.

163 Genov, *Dnevnik partizana*, pp. 44, 176. See also Gubenko, *Kniga pechali*, p. 48 and list of partisan units operating in the Crimea from 1941 to 1944, April 25, 1989, DAARK, P-849/1/492.

164 Genov, *Dnevnik partizana*, p. 44. See also Gubenko, *Kniga pechali*, p. 48.

165 Genov, *Dnevnik partizana*, pp. 59, 67, 206. See also Gubenko, *Kniga pechali*, p. 48 and West, *In the Ropes of Destruction*, p. 145.

166 Genov, *Dnevnik partizana*, pp. 65, 69, 83, 161, 173, 174, 191.

167 Ibid., pp. 84, 87.

168 By the beginning of the partisan warfare in the Crimean forests, there were 3,134 partisans. Since then, the human losses can be broken down into several categories: dead owing to starvation – 450, deserters and missing in action – 400, and killed in action – 848. Furthermore, 556 sick, injured and exhausted persons were sent away [to the Soviet zone] but 150 were selected to be sent to forests. Of the 556 of those sent away there are 230 civilians. Note of the Crimean District Committee of the VKP(b), in Kondranov and Stepanova, *Krym v period Velikoi Otechestvennoi voiny*, p. 252.

the respective figures for the Jewish victims among the partisans were in line with this general trend.[169]

It must be emphasized that on the eve of the German entry into the Crimea, the high command of the Crimean partisan movement envisaged the possibility of a large-scale escape of civilians into the forests.[170] The newcomers were supposed to undergo a security check, while politically dubious elements were not to be allowed into the forests, and the rest would be sent to separate detachments. To counter this problem, necessary preparations were ordered. Nevertheless, although the partisan command generally welcomed the arrival of the civilian population into the forests, the local population remained ignorant of this possibility. One way or another, the rapid German advance into the Crimea thwarted this intention of the partisan command.

As for the Jewish population, inhabitants of towns were especially hindered from joining the partisans, due to stringent German movement regulations and the fact that partisan bases were located in difficult-to-access areas. These premises, combined with the increasing paucity of food reserves available to the partisans in the winter of 1941-42, curtailed the possibility of masses of Jews making their way into the partisan-dominated areas of the Crimea.[171] Given the numerical prevalence of the Jews living in the towns (72.3% of the total Jewish population as of 1939[172]), relatively few of them joined the partisans.[173] In contrast, many

169 Genov, *Dnevnik partizana*, p. 206; Testimony of Roza Perelman, June 29, 1999, YVHN.
Mark Goldenberg estimates that 145 Jewish partisans died in the course of 1941-42. Goldenberg, "Evrei v krymskom partizanskom dvizhenii i podpol'e 1941-1944 gg.," p. 389.

170 Order no. 1 of the commander of the partisan movement in the Crimea A. V. Mokrousov on the appointment of commanders of areas and tasks of detachments and areas, October 31, 1941, in Kondranov and Stepanova, *Krym v period Velikoi Otechestvennoi voiny*, pp. 210-211.

171 Testimony of Zinaida Zhitomirskaia, April 30, 1992, YVHN.

172 Altshuler, *Distribution of the Jewish Population of the USSR* , pp. 9-11, 63-65.

173 In particular, inhabitants of larger towns, above all from Simferopol': Testimony of Peotr Meilman, February 1991, YVHN; Testimony of Boris Nepomniashii, December 5, 1994, YVHN. To a much lesser extent, Feodosiia and Kerch: Testimony of Il'ia Dolzhanskii, October 2, 1991, YVHN; Interview with David

Jewish residents of the Crimean rural areas did join the partisan ranks.[174] It is of note that partisan units formed in Fraidorfskii and Larindorfskii *raiony* – i.e., "Jewish National Regions" – were unable to make their way to the forests. Instead, they withdrew towards Sevastopol' and apparently fought against the Germans there.[175] The Jewish partisans consisted of many men and women around the age of 30,[176] but there were few Jewish men and women above 50.[177] Only rarely did whole Jewish families, including children, make their way to the Crimean partisans.[178]

The partisan movement served as a rescue channel for hundreds of Crimean Jews.[179] This applied in particular to Jews in rural areas, whose proximity to partisan bases made it easier for them to venture there.[180] It should be emphasized that the leadership

Borokhov, March-April 2004, author's archive.

174 For the "Jewish National Regions", see testimony of Shor, [no date], YVHN; Testimony of Evgeniia Tsirkina, December 28, 1995, YVHN. For other areas with a noticeable Jewish presence, see Karasubazar and Kolai: Story of Aleksandra Gershtein in Gubenko, *The Book of Sorrows,* pp. 58-61; Testimony of Ul'k Khatison, July 28, 1995, YVHN; Testimony of Tsilia Khaikina, August 2, 1996, YVHN. Smaller urban localities of Alushta and Bakhchisarai: Testimony of Nata Maibiurova, April 18, 1993, YVHN; Testimony of Svetlana Shmukler, February 14, 1993, YVHN.

175 Goldenberg, "Evrei v krymskom partizanskom dvizhenii i podpol'e," p. 388.

176 Peisakh Uritskii: Testimony of Shor, [no date], YVHN; Eva Vol'kovich: Testimony of Evsei Fel'dman, [no date], YVHN; Mikhail Magidov: Testimony of Iakov Magidov, December 13, 1994, YVHN; Testimony of Rakhel' Razumova, August 29, 1995, YVHN; Efim Pevzner: Testimony of Vladimir Khinin, June 26, 1988, YVHN.

177 Women: Testimony of Evsei Fel'dman, [no date], YVHN; Testimony of Peotr Meilman, February 1991, YVHN; Men: Testimony of Grigorii Tsivkin, June 8, 1995, YVHN; Testimony of Il'ia Dolzhanskii, October 2, 1991, YVHN.

178 Vergasov, *Krymskie tetradi*, YVA, 0.32/62, p. 16; Testimony of Rakhel' Razumova, [no date], YVHN.

179 The Crimean researcher Mark Goldenberg calculated that in 1941-1944, "233 Jews and Krymchaks" fought among the ranks of the Crimean partisan units. In 1941, Jews made up 6.5% of the total number of the Crimean partisans. The author relies upon the data of the Crimean HQ of the Partisan Movement (DAARK, P-151). Goldenberg, "Evrei v krymskom partizanskom dvizhenii i podpol'e," p. 388.

180 Unlike some other occupied territories. See Nechama Tec, "Jewish Resistance in Belorussian Forests: Fighting and the Rescue of Jews by Jews," in Ruby Rohrlich, ed., *Resisting the Holocaust* (Oxford: Berg, 1998), pp. 77-94.

Drawing of partisans in the Crimea, by the painter Garbovietzki. Courtesy: YVA

of the Crimean partisan movement was initially positively disposed towards accepting civilians in its ranks. Nevertheless, the Jews' prospects for surviving the German occupation in partisan units were not high. This was the result of logistical shortcomings of Soviet planning in partisan warfare in the Crimea as well as harsh conditions (most specifically, lack of food provisions) and the incessant German hunt for partisans — which was most intense during the period in which the partisan units could still have sheltered many Jews (December 1941-July 1942).

Chapter Eight

Jewish Responses to the Holocaust in the North Caucasus

1. Before the Killing Operations

1.1. General concerns

Responses of the Jewish population to the German persecutions in the North Caucasus reflected its status and composition, peculiar conditions of the region, and the unique features of the German occupation. All this should be seen in the context of Holocaust-related information presumably available to the Jews. Although difficult to document, it may be suggested that, on the whole, Jews under the German occupation of the Caucasus in 1942 were well aware of the Holocaust. This assumption has to do with two major interwoven factors. First, the war between Nazi Germany and the Soviet Union had already been going on for a year, and information had gradually leaked about the Germans' annihilation of Soviet Jews during this period. Second, refugees constituting the essential part of the Jewish population had previously escaped into the North Caucasus ahead of the approaching German armies because they knew or feared what awaited them under German rule. The large-scale flight of the Jews from the Caucasus in the summer of 1942, however belated, is instructive in this respect.

In terms of gender and age, the Jewish population in the Caucasus consisted mostly of women (relatively many men had already been drafted into the army), elderly people, and small children. This predominance of women and elderly people among the Jewish population was undesirable for the Caucasian partisan movement. By and large, the Jewish population profile reflected that of the local non-Jewish population. Yet, if there was a discrepancy between them (for example, if there were young or middle-aged Jewish men among the evacuees whereas their non-Jewish counterparts were serving in the army), it was striking and certainly detrimental for those who stood out.

Of particular importance was the fact that the majority of the Jews in the North Caucasus were displaced persons with little or no knowledge of local customs. Perhaps their aloofness was also a factor in their responses to the Holocaust, although this is equivocal. The large majority of them complied with German orders and were killed, sharing the same responses and fate as the "local" Jews. However, it may be anticipated that those Jewish evacuees who considered the possibility of defying German orders had more limited options at their disposal, as compared to the native Caucasian Jews. This largely had to do with the disadvantage of the former group's position as newcomers into the region. They were overwhelmingly ignorant of specific local conditions and geography. They also did not know where they could go or whom they could ask for help; neither were they aware of the shortest way to escape, including the whereabouts of partisans. Unlike them, the local Caucasian Jews could potentially rely upon a circle of their friends and acquaintances for survival.[1]

On the other hand, sometimes the position of the Jewish evacuees was advantageous. The local people's Jewish origin was often no secret to their neighbors,[2] making local Jews' positions

1 "Good people," Essentuki: Statement of Aleksandr Gontov, June 30 1943, State Archive of the Russian Federation (GARF), 7021/17/4, pp. 60-64; Friends-neighbors, Essentuki: Testimony of Samuil Belenkov, August 10, 1943, GARF, 7021/17/4, p. 25; "a friend in another town," from Kislovodsk to Minvody: Interrogation of Mikhail Fingerut (1880), June 25, 1943, GARF, 7021/17/5, p. 31.

2 Kislovodsk: Testimony of Rimma Zikhlinskaia (1930), June 16, 1988, Yad Vashem Archives (YVA), 0.3/4927, p. 3.

vulnerable throughout the occupation period. The Native Caucasian Jews could indeed have had friends and acquaintances in the region who could have potentially helped them during the Holocaust – but they might also have had enemies for whom the German occupation presented a propitious moment to settle accounts with certain Jews. In contrast, the fact the newcomers were strangers in the Caucasus could have been favorable for them, as they likely would not have had any personal enemies in the region, including in the local administration. As the Jewish refugees were not already well-known in the Caucasus, they could potentially have survived by claiming that they were not Jews, provided they did not possess an unmistakably Jewish appearance.

The newcomers were recognizable in the Caucasian towns by their manners, good clothes, and even their hairstyle.[3] The refugees had to carry all their valuables with them, with basically no place to conceal them. As a result, the Jewish refugees were frequently vulnerable to robbery by the local population under the threat of turning them in.[4] The Jewish evacuees also had limited food resources and, despite the general availability of food in the North Caucasus, sometimes suffered from starvation due to the Germans denying them food rations.[5]

Their connections among the local population were considerably low, compared to those of the native Caucasian Jews. Jewish newcomers tended to communicate with and seek help from people in their own circle, particularly those evacuated from the same institute or laboratory.[6] Many of these were Jews themselves, which further narrowed their circle of potential

3 Stavropol': Belikov, *Okkupatsiia*, p. 66.

4 Village of Dzhiginka in Krasnodarskii *krai*; village of Novozavedennoe: Testimony of Ol'ga Polonskaia, May 1, 1962, YVA, 0.3/2246, p. 7; Statement of Anna Shlaen, 1943, GARF, 7021/17/11, p. 114.

5 Essentuki, Bekeshevskaia *stanitsa* in Stavropol'skii *krai*: Testimony of Raisa Kogan, April 29, 1943, GARF, 7021/17/4, p. 12; Akt of the Commission of Suvorovskskii *raion*, July 26, 1943, GARF, 7021/17/12, p. 3.

6 Essentuki (?), Krasnodar: Letter by the painter L. N. Tarabukin and his wife D. R. Gol'dshtein to the writer Iu. Kalugin, [1943], YVA, M.35/166; Testimony of Mina Horowitz (1908), August 1, 1973, YVA, 0.3/3682, pp. 7-9.

rescuers during the Holocaust. By the time of the German takeover, a significant number of the Jewish newcomers were unemployed, and thus had limited connections outside their families and/or residences.[7] Even those who were employed found it difficult to establish long-standing connections, as they had arrived in the area some 9-10 months at the earliest prior to the German occupation. The estrangement from the general population and feeling of misplacement grew in smaller towns and villages; in large cities, this alienation was less pronounced.

In the post-action period, the refugees refrained from asking unfamiliar local people for help, preferring to manage on their own. Jewish survivors among the evacuees tended to wander around the region, hiding in the cold steppe. They would not ask anyone for food or accommodation, and appealed to non-Jews for help only as a last resort.[8] For example, a young Jewish woman named Ida Sirota and her two small children were released from a group of detained evacuees because she had claimed that she was not a Jew. Yet, she knew no one in the area and, hence, had nowhere to go. Their only acquaintance in the region was a Russian family that had warmly accommodated them at the time of the evacuation in one of the villages in the Rostov district. In order to reach their home, Ida Sirota and her children had to walk for two months in order to avoid entering towns and villages.[9]

Geographically, the region was made up of a relatively small number of medium-sized towns and a large number of dispersed villages. The distance between them was long, but those situated in valleys were presumably reachable by foot. As the annihilation of Jews in the Caucasus commenced in the late summer of 1942 and reached its peak in early fall, the weather conditions were more or less favorable for those Jews who decided to escape. This time frame was also advantageous for the persecuted Jews, as in

7 See Chapter 2, "Jews in the North Caucasus from the Beginning of the German-Soviet War (June 22, 1941) to the German Occupation (August 1942)."

8 File of Anna and Evdokiia Karnaukh, 2000, YVA, M.31/8964.

9 File of Taisiia Mozgovaia and Ekaterina Vinnikova-Mozgovaia, 2000, YVA, M.31/9080.

the Caucasus they could find fruits and vegetables in fields and gardens. Thus, certain "natural" possibilities presented themselves for surviving Jews.

General aspects of the German policies in the Caucasus affected the responses of Jews to their persecution. As Nazi Germany regarded the population of the region to be disposed towards it, authorities introduced important alleviations of the occupation regime in the North Caucasus as compared to other occupied Soviet territories. The considerable easing of residence and movement regulations should be emphasized. According to wartime and postwar sources, prior to the killing operations, Jews could move relatively freely from one locality to another.[10] German measures aimed at capturing Jews and other "enemies of the Reich" were relatively rare at the initial stages of the occupation of the North Caucasus.[11] However, the various anti-Jewish steps preceding the Jews' annihilation, such as the imposition of yellow badges,[12] which did occur were not orchestrated simultaneously — and the Germans did not succeed in keeping these measures hidden from the Jews living nearby. Sometimes rumors of the atrocities reached the Jewish public and affected their behavior. In Essentuki, for example, a rumor circulated that the Germans had already killed the Jews of the neighboring towns of Piatigorsk and Kislovodsk; consequently, some people attempted to escape from Essentuki.[13]

German officials and those in their service regarded these rumors seriously and did their best to refute them. The case of Novorossiisk is especially interesting, as in this town the Germans took care to publish in their first appeal to the Jewish population:

10 Some dozens of kilometers away from each other. From Piatigorsk to Kislovodsk and from Nal'chik to Piatigorsk: Testimony of Tsilia Gadleva (1917), October 25, 1990, YVA, 0.3/4391, p. 10. See also Testimony of Elizaveta Nazarova (1917), January 6, 1998 in Danilova, *Iskhod gorskikh evreev*, p. 135.

11 Gul'kevichi *stanitsa*: Interrogation of Marfa Tokareva, May 16, 1944, YVA, M.33/303, p. 83.

12 Essentuki: Testimony of Samuil Belenkov, August 10, 1943, GARF, 7021/17/4, p. 24.

13 Testimony of Raisa Kogan, April 29, 1943, GARF, 7021/17/4, p. 13.

> The rumors that the Germans killed Jews are false. The German command is willing to grant a shelter for the Jews as the town is temporarily bombarded.[14]

The appeal took into consideration specific local conditions, which gave it more credibility. Novorossiisk was only partly seized by the Wehrmacht and was subjected to permanent bombardment by the Soviet forces.

In another case, when it became known in Essentuki that in neighboring Piatigorsk it was obligatory to bear the six-pointed stars, the local *Kommandant* von Beck assured the Jewish Committee that nothing of the kind would happen in Essentuki.[15] Individual soldiers of the German Army occasionally employed such methods of camouflage, which probably gave more weight and plausibility to their declarations.[16] It appears that in most cases, the explanations provided by the Germans had a mollifying effect on the Jews.

1.2. Responses to the registration order

One of the first German measures of the Jewish policy in the Caucasus was the required registration of the entire Jewish population. Many Jews sensed the danger this involved, and escaped from Caucasian urban and rural centers but remained elsewhere in the German-controlled region.[17] Sometimes Jews were aware of the maltreatment practiced by the Germans and their allies towards the Jews in other places, prompting them to go into hiding. This was the case of all the Jews in Dzhiginka *stanitsa*. However, the Germans issued a calming announcement, which was reinforced by the words of a Russian inhabitant, who said that no harm would be done to Jews. Upon hearing this, the

14 Questioning of Zoia Chernova, October 14, 1943, GARF, 7021/16/11, p. 118.

15 Testimony of Samuil Belenkov, August 10, 1943, GARF, 7021/17/4, p. 24.

16 Village of Naturbovo: Interrogation of Klavdiia Parshikova, August 12, 1942, YVA, M.33/291, pp. 98-99.

17 Village of Dovsun: Akt of the Commission of the Dovsun country council, GARF, 7021/17/10, p. 15.

Jews reappeared from their hiding places.[18] The following evidence denotes a similar situation in Kislovodsk:

> Initially the Germans endeavored to "encourage" the Jews, most of whom escaped towards the mountains or took the refuge with Georgian or Russian families, to return to their places of residence. Almost every day the German occupation authorities pasted announcements, which warned Jewish inhabitants not to believe the "false rumors" that the Nazis intended to annihilate the Jewish people. Their only intention was to separate them from the "Aryan" population by means of marking the clothes, but they were ready to guarantee their existence "in respect and quiet." Gradually Jews were influenced by this propaganda and left the shelters places for their houses.[19]

Sooner or later, most Jews in the Caucasus complied with the registration order. The reason stated by a survivor in Kislovodsk for doing so was that it was impossible to avoid registration in the town as it was small and that if "you do not comply with the order it becomes common knowledge."[20] This phrase reveals that in smaller towns, Jews were unable to forego registration. Needless to say, most of the Jews in the North Caucasus found themselves in precisely such small towns. These people sensed the inherent danger in the German order, but assumed that non-compliance with a specific German regulation entailed a more concrete peril. The role of the Jewish Council members in enforcing the German order is illuminating in this respect. According to one male Jewish survivor's wartime evidence, he had failed to register in Essentuki on account of being ill and:

> On August 22, 1942, the last day of the registration, the Chairman of the Jewish Committee, Shats, and his deputy,

18 Interrogation of Aleksandr Chebanenko, January 25, 1944, YVA, M.33/304, p. 7.

19 West, *In the Ropes of Destruction*, pp. 108-109.

20 Testimony of Rimma Zikhlinskaia, June 16, 1988, YVA, 0.3/4927, p. 3.

> Iudovich, came to me to propose that I register immediately. According to their statements, they were informed that I was Jewish and that I had not presented myself at the registration. They explained to me that the Committee could not bear responsibility for me, and that in his capacity of the chairman, he [Shats] was unwilling to expose himself to the danger of being executed.[21]

In Krasnodar, the head of the *Judenrat*, Professor Naum Vilik, was threatened and "persuaded" to sign the "Appeal to the Jewish Population," which called upon the Jews not to be afraid and to assemble voluntarily.[22]

The reasons that led one ordinary Jew in Krasnodar to comply with the registration order were completely different. Rather than being scared or threatened into registering, he assumed he could obtain a job due to his profession (pharmaceutical chemist) and, therefore, registered immediately.[23] This was a rational line of reasoning, which had fostered out of the widespread belief (encouraged by the Germans) that Jewish specialists would be given preferential treatment in terms of employment, and even that they would likely be spared in the end. Conversely, non-compliance was largely a sporadic phenomenon. There were individual Jews[24] and whole families[25] who failed to register, but the available reports do not reveal what motivated them to do so.

Almost immediately upon registration, Jews were required to bear six-pointed stars, to perform forced labor, and often to collect huge amount of valuables for the Germans. Jews rarely evaded

21 Statement of Aleksandr Gontov, June 30, 1943, GARF, 7021/17/4, pp. 60-64.

22 Statement of Anna Sokolitskaia-Vasser, January 11, 1944, GARF, 7021/16/462, p. 204.

23 Krasnodar: Statement of Aleksandra Bronshtein, January 11, 1944, GARF, 7021/16/462, p. 211; Questioning of Aleksandra Bronshtein, January 11, 1944, GARF, 7021/16/462, p. 212.

24 Krasnodar, Novorossiisk: Akt of the Commission of Krasnodar, 1943, GARF, 7021/16/435, p. 73; Questioning of Anna Silina (1910), October 16, 1943, GARF, 7021/16/11, p. 112.

25 Mozdok: Testimony of Aleksandr Raziev, January 13, 1998, in Danilova, *Iskhod gorskikh evreev*, p. 162.

these regulations.[26] Most Jews complied with these orders because of two interwoven reasons. The first was fear. For example, the family of a Jewish witness in Essentuki was scared that they would be seized immediately and killed. But the witness heard that Jews were only sent to work. Disillusioned, he believed that the Germans were content only with sending Jews to perform forced labor. Therefore, the next day the Jewish witness presented himself at the *Kommandatur*.[27] The second reason was the possibility that Jews could save themselves by bribing German officials, a proposition formulated by the elder of the Jewish community in Kislovodsk, who reportedly said that [by depositing valuables] the Jews would be able to redeem themselves (*vykupitsia*).[28] As a result of this emotional appeal, the Jews delivered huge amount of valuables and commodities.[29] As for the forced labor, the Jews made every effort to apply themselves. In the village of Naturbovo, "they worked harder in agriculture than their non-Jewish neighbors accustomed to this kind of work, in order not to let Germans find any fault with them."[30] Occasionally, unaware of the true aim of the German policy, some Jews tried to circumvent legally the forced labor order by procuring medical certificates. In Zheleznovodsk, two Jewish doctors applied to the out-patients department because they were seriously ill. The department issued certificates stating that they were unable to carry out physical work.[31] But the Germans disregarded these documents, and the Jews were sent to work nevertheless. This attempt to evade fulfilling the orders involved both legalist behavior and naiveté.

26 Akt of the Commission of Essentuki: July 10, 1943, GARF, 7021/17/4, p. 1.

27 Testimony of Samuil Belenkov, August 10, 1943, GARF, 7021/17/4, p. 22.

28 Testimony of Fania Skliar, September 1975, YVA, 0.3/3934, p. 7. According to another version, he said: "Jews! If you wish to save the lives of your children, bring the goods." Testimony of Rimma Zikhlinskaia, June 16, 1988, YVA, 0.3/4927, p. 5.

29 Testimony of Rimma Zikhlinskaia, June 16, 1988, YVA, 0.3/4927, p. 4; Statement of Boris Khshive, July 3, 1943, GARF, 7021/17/5, p. 48.

30 Interrogation of Klavdiia Parshikova, August 12, 1942, YVA, M.33/291, pp. 98-99.

31 Statement of the doctor K. T. Gavrilova, 1943, GARF, 7021/17/6, p. 25.

Welfare institutions of the Jewish community, such as a hospital and hostel for homeless and sick Jews in Essentuki (the only case of this sort in the region), were also established during the interim period.[32] Aside from the fact that the policy of misleading the Jewish public against the Germans' real intentions apparently proved effective, it is illuminating that the Jews in Essentuki were able to establish active welfare institutions within such a short span of time.[33] This reaction may testify to the desire of some Jews to find *modus vivendi* with the German authorities, in hopes that sooner or later the arbitrary maltreatment of Jews would end and be replaced by at least some orderly form of discrimination.

Of special interest is the group reaction to maltreatment, in general, which is exemplified by the Mountain Jews' behavior in the village of Bogdanovka. According to the evidence (which is the only of this sort), Mountain Jews lodged frequent complaints to the German military *Kommandant* on the plunder of their property by the German soldiers (some 600 of them were stationed in the village).[34] This indicates an organized attempt, likely by the leadership of the Jewish public, to negotiate with the Germans the terms under which the Jews could lead some sort of normal life. Characteristically, the complaints of the Mountain Jews were disregarded as, in accordance with the German schemes, the arbitrary maltreatment of the Jews was a necessary step prior to their annihilation. The fact that this conduct was recorded in a wartime Soviet official report relying on the testimonies of (apparently non-biased) non-Jewish inhabitants of the village makes it more plausible. On the other hand, it is possible that the document implies that the Jews were ready to risk their own lives in order to save their property.

1.3. Responses to the assembly order

Jewish responses to the announcement to assemble were not uniform, ranging from dismissal of serious danger to foreseeing

32 Testimony of Samuil Belenkov, August 10, 1943, GARF, 7021/17/4, p. 24.

33 Ibid., p. 24.

34 Akt of the Commission of Bogdanovka, GARF, 7021/17/10, p. 158.

extermination.[35] On the day of the German proclamation on October 7, 1942 that the assembly was due to take place in Essentuki, many Jews present in the building of the Jewish Committee "took the bread designated for the working Jews."[36] These people appeared to have taken the German assembly-resettlement-evacuation order at face value, and for them every additional piece of bread became indispensable in the case of evacuation. Also in Essentuki, two Jewish sisters decided to distribute all their possessions among their friends upon having heard the announcement.[37] While desperation could have motivated this decision, it is also likely that the sisters believed that the assembly order involved merely evacuation and that, therefore, they would no longer need their possessions.

The strained atmosphere caused by the assembly order led some Jewish families to part. Some family members, usually young women with or without children (although it was physically easier for those without) chose to defy the assembly order.[38] The older members tended to be more compliant, or felt physically unable to challenge the order.[39] Some Jews were desperate enough to attempt to conceal their children with non-Jewish acquaintances,[40] implying that the Jews anticipated the worst possible scenario to materialize. The unique letter written by a Jewish woman named Roza Golub in the city of Maikop on August 28, 1942, one day before the assembly took place, is characteristic of this group of Jews. She wrote the letter to her Russian husband, who was fighting in the Red Army, and left it with his mother, who preserved it. Her testimony is quoted at length:

35 Issued usually some 3-4 weeks after the beginning of the German occupation.

36 Statement of Aleksandr Gontov, June 30, 1943, GARF, 7021/17/4, p. 62.

37 Letter by the painter L. N. Tarabukin and his wife D. R. Gol'dshtein to the writer Iu. Kalugin, [1943] YVA, M.35/166; Yitzhak Arad and Il'ia Al'tman, eds., *Neizvestnaia chernaia kniga* (Jerusalem, Moscow: Tekst, 1993), p. 389.

38 Essentuki, Kislovodsk: Testimony of Faina Gulianskaia, July 2, 1943, GARF, 7021/17/4, p. 17; Testimony of Zinaida Shuster, [no later than June 26, 1943], GARF, 7021/17/206, p. 54.

39 Essentuki: Testimony of Faina Gulianskaia, July 2, 1943, GARF, 7021/17/4, p. 17.

40 Essentuki: Testimony of Agripina Chekinovskaia as invoked in the statement of Aleksandr Gontov, June 30 1943, GARF, 7021/17/4, p. 63.

> Today I am parting the family and so, leaving my lovely children Lil'ia and Zhenia apparently forever. Probably I will survive, but I am not sure of it; no one is sure. It is terribly painful for me. I am writing this letter and weeping floods of tears. Yes! I have lived only twenty-five years, and it is truly little… Be a good father to our orphan children. I hope that if you find a wife, and this is quite probable, you will keep [her] to take care of the children… This is my last night at home. Tomorrow, on August 29, 1942, we will be relocated (*nas otpravliaiut*)… The last night! What happens then I don't know.[41]

Here is almost the complete realization of what the assembly order meant, showing the agony of a young Jewish woman facing the inevitable. Unwilling to let her children share her fate, she pleaded with her husband to take care of them. Another case, this time that of a physically disabled Jewish woman from Essentuki, also highlights the growing desperation:

> While in a bad physical condition, the inhabitant of Essentuki Raisa Ovrutskaia rejected the request of her friends to go to a *stanitsa* and hide there. She did not wish to expose anyone to danger because of herself. She was unwilling to take possessions to the assembly point, as she evidently understood what its purpose was.[42]

Even under such extreme circumstances, only a few Jews considered circumventing the German decrees by converting to Orthodox Christianity. However, once discouraged from doing so, either by priests or by the mere speed of events, they acknowledged defeat and complied with the assembly order.[43] The testimony offered by a

41 Al'tman and Terushkin, *Sokhrani moi pis'ma*, p. 143.

42 Statement of Vyrabova, approximately 1943, GARF, 7021/17/4, p. 37.

43 Krasnodar, Stavropol': Krasnodar trial, testimony of Kirill Il'iashev, June 28, 1943, Archive of the Federal Security Service of the Russian Federation (AFSB RF), H-16708, p. 927, courtesy of the USHMM; Belikov, *Okkupatsiia*, p. 67. See also section 9A, "The Responses of Orthodox Christianity and Islam in the Crimea and the North Caucasus to the Holocaust."

priest's son from Stavropol' on behalf of his father is instructive in this regard. After the priest explained to a Jewish woman that the Germans forbade baptizing Jews, he said:

> I recommended to her not to tell anyone that she was a Jewess. But she did not listen to my advice. Sometime later, she came and said that she had decided to share the fate of her people and would present herself at the assembly point. The only thing that she asked me for was to bring her [there], as she was terribly scared.[44]

The question arises as to why the majority of the Jewish population in the North Caucasus, which was arguably knowledgeable of, or at least fearful of, what awaited them, complied with the assembly order. General explanations refer to similar patterns of behavior of the Jews elsewhere in occupied Europe and in many other occupied areas of the Soviet Union.[45] Thus, the majority of the Jews in the North Caucasus complied with the assembly order as they had with previous German decrees. Although some Jews persistently hesitated, German tactics of deception largely had a soothing effect on them – often by assurances that the alleged aim of the resettlement was simply to send the Jews elsewhere.[46] By the same token, in Essentuki a Jew was permitted to go home from the assembly point so that he could retrieve a sewing machine to service the Jewish population.[47] As a result, many Jews believed that they were being deported to work, or to say the least, they were unaware of what awaited them.[48] In line with such interpretations,

44 Belikov, *Okkupatsiia*, p. 67.

45 Raul Hilberg, *The Destruction of the European Jews*, revised and definitive ed. (New York: Holmes & Meier, 1985), pp. 1030-1044; Idem., *Perpetrators, Victims, Bystanders: The Jewish Catastrophe 1933-1945* (New York: Aaron Asher Books, 1992), pp. 16, 178.

46 Cherkessk, Essentuki: Akt of the Commission of Cherkessk, July 13, 1943, GARF, 702/17/12, pp. 68-69; Statement of Matvei Makogonenko, August 13, 1943, GARF, 7021/17/2, pp. 14-15.

47 Testimony of Samuil Belenkov, August 10, 1943, GARF, 7021/17/4, p. 25.

48 Essentuki: Letter of S. Boris Aisenberg to Il'ia Erenburg, June 1943, in Altshuler, Arad, and Krakowski, *Sovetskie evrei pishut Il'ie Erenburgu*, p. 125.

in the same town a Jewish dentist took her dental instruments and medicines to the assembly point.[49]

Moreover, one should take into account that, overall, prior to the *Aktionen*, the German *Judenpolitik* in the Caucasus had been relatively moderate by the standards of the German occupation of the Soviet Union, and had not employed overt terror. This apparently influenced many Jews to heed the assembly orders. The evidence on Cherkessk underscores the point. According to postwar German evidence, an EG D officer came in the mayor's office and:

> said to the Jews who resided there that they have nothing to fear. But he needed the list of the Cherkessk Jews [claiming that they were to receive food and tobacco provision as well as medical service]. It was announced to the Jews at the mayor's office when they would have to present themselves at the railway station. By means of his machinations... [he] created the situation whereby none of the Jews fled; everyone appeared voluntarily.[50]

It may be suggested that the Jews assumed that the assembly and the ensuing "resettlement" constituted another step in German anti-Jewish policies, but was not fraught with immediate danger. On the contrary, some believed that only strict obedience with the assembly order could be instrumental in the rescue of Jews. In Krasnodar, the non-Jewish neighbors of the quarter urged a "grandmother Anna Grauerman" and her relatives not to present themselves at the assembly; however, she "did it for her granddaughter, daughter, and herself."[51] At times, even when the Jews learned from a local collaborator what awaited them, some chose not to escape.[52]

49 Testimony of Samuil Belenkov, August 10, 1943, GARF, 7021/17/4, p. 25.

50 "Urteil gegen Johannes Schlupper, Heinrich Winterstein, Rudi Eschenbach," Landesgericht München I, July 24, 1974, YVA, TR.10/956, pp. 34-35, 61.

51 Interrogation of Lidiia Ivanova, January 6, 1944, GARF, 7021/16/462, p. 24.

52 Village of Menzhynskoe: Testimony of Shmuel Matbaev, [no date], YVA, 0.3/4879, p. 7; See also testimony of Alexander Guseev, after 1976, YVA, 0.3/6970, p. 3.

Finally, in a number of localities where the Germans did employ terror, Jews lived in a state of permanent fear during the period preceding their annihilation. This was the case in Mikoianshakhar, where more than 60 Jews were confined to the ghetto until early December 1942. According to a wartime testimony of a Jewish survivor, the Jews knew what awaited them, as the Jews of the neighboring town of Cherkessk had been killed in late September 1942.[53] No attempt to escape from this confinement took place until early December 1942, when the ghetto in Mikoianshakhar was liquidated. There are some possible explanations of this phenomenon: German terror, terrible conditions in the ghetto, fear of the unknown future, and the hope that the Germans would leave specific people alive on account of their value as workers.

The fact that numerous Jewish medical personnel remained in the occupied Caucasus contributed to the emergence of the widespread phenomenon of several suicide attempts committed by Jewish doctors[54] and their families.[55] This phenomenon was perhaps unique to the region. Suicide attempts became especially widespread once the assembly order was proclaimed.[56] As for other groups of the Jewish population, the cases of suicides among them were most limited, and seemed to be a reaction to particularly cruel maltreatment by the Germans.[57]

The minority of Jews who did not present themselves at

53 Testimony of Ida Nikeeva, July 29, 1943, GARF, 7021/17/10, p. 204.

54 Akt of the Commission of Essentuki, July 10, 1943, GARF, 7021/17/4, p. 2; Akt of the Commission of Novorossiisk, October 18, 1943, GARF, 7021/16/11, p. 8.

55 Piatigorsk, Zheleznovodsk: Memoirs of Liubov' Guzman on the fate of her aunt, Ella Frank, July 1997, YVA, 0.33/6139, p. 7; Statement of the doctor K. T. Gavrilova, 1943, GARF, 7021/17/6, p. 25.

56 Kislovodsk, Novorossiisk: Akt signed by the workers of the hospital no. 5404 of Kislovodsk, May 20, 1943, GARF, 7021/17/5, p. 16; Testimony of Fania Skliar, September 1975, YVA, 0.3/3934, p. 13; Akt of the Commission of Novorossiisk, October 18, 1943, GARF, 7021/16/11, p. 8.

57 Akt of the Commission of Aleksandriiskaia *stanitsa*, January 25, 1943, GARF, 7021/17/9, p. 12.

the assembly points were guided by the fear that they would be arrested and killed. Sometimes, the decision to defy the German order was made spontaneously, without any prior preparation. In Kislovodsk, for example, a Jewish woman had complied with the order and arrived at the railway station for departure but did not know its destination. Then, according to her own wartime testimony, she felt that the "train was heading for a destruction" and escaped with her children.[58] At times, Jews figured out what was happening due to the tough German policy applied to them, personally, and resorted to escape. Also in Kislovodsk, after the Germans seized most of the valuable possessions of a Jewish witness, telling her that they would send her to a new place of residence, she understood "what was going on" and escaped with her child.[59] Information leaks concerning German plans and their actual policies towards the Jews that somehow stemmed from the Germans themselves, also potentially contributed a gradual change of mind among Jews.[60] Some Jews took the next step in defying the German regulations and immediately went into hiding,[61] while the others tried to procure "Aryan" documents.[62] Nevertheless, even after defying the assembly order, some Jews were not determined to challenge completely the German orders at this stage. In one example, the SS visited a Jewish man's apartment and issued strong admonishments to his Russian wife.[63] Such instances could prompt Jews to change their minds and report to the Gestapo, as this Jewish man did.

Jewish behavior during the killing operations should be seen in the broader context of the Jews' reactions up to that point. It

58 Testimony of Zinaida Shuster, [no later than June 26, 1943], GARF, 7021/17/206, p. 54.

59 Testimony of Rozaliia Grin, [no later than June 26, 1943], GARF, 7021/17/206, p. 31.

60 Kislovodsk: Testimony of Fania Skliar, September 1975, YVA, 0.3/3934, p. 7; Testimony of Tsilia Gadleva, October 25, 1990, YVA, 0.3/4391, p. 11.

61 Kislovodsk, Krasnodar: Testimony of Rimma Zikhlinskaia, June 16, 1988, YVA, 0.3/4927, p. 5. See also statement of Aleksandra Bronshtein, January 11, 1944, GARF, 7021/16/462, p. 211.

62 Essentuki: Testimony of Raisa Kogan, April 29, 1943, GARF, 7021/17/4, p. 14.

63 Ibid., p. 211.

seems that the level of non-compliance with the German orders at this stage did not substantially increase. The majority of the Jews in North Caucasian towns obeyed the orders. Yet, there is a noticeable record of escape attempts made during the extermination actions. Occasionally these attempts failed, and the Jews were caught and killed.[64] However, in other cases Jews did succeed in escaping during the *Aktionen*.[65]

2. After the Killing Operations

2.1. General concerns

Extermination actions marked the most significant watershed in Jewish existence under German rule in the North Caucasus. In order to survive in the aftermath, Jews had to either go into hiding in their home localities, move away to other towns and villages, procure false documents or change existent ones, or use their connections among the local population.

Jewish behavior after the *Aktionen* in the North Caucasus was peculiar in comparison to other regions. Given the unique composition of the North Caucasian population, having a non-Jewish appearance and lack of a specifically Yiddish accent, rather than possessing impeccable "Aryan" documents, were the major factors contributing to Jewish survival. Prior to the actions, there were incidents when "people with a Semitic appearance were driven away from the lines in the market."[66] After the action in Kislovodsk, a house-owner suspected a male witness who had been renting a room of being Jewish (although the latter possessed "Aryan" documents), and required that he immediately abandon her apartment.[67] These

64 Kislovodsk, Minvody: Testimony of Nikolai Mikheev, July 8, 1943, GARF, 7021/17/2, p. 16; Testimony of Fedor Lisitsin, February 8, 1943, GARF, 7021/17/2, p. 17.

65 Essentuki, Tikhoretsk: Letter of L. N. Rubanenko to Il'ia Erenburg, October 6, 1944, YVA, P.21.3/41; Akt of the Commission of Tikhoretsk, February 3, 1943, YVA, M.33/289, p. 3.

66 Essentuki: Testimony of Ia. Talianskii, [no date], GARF, 7021/17/4, p. 30.

67 Interrogation of Mikhail Fingerut, June 25, 1943, GARF, 7021/17/5, p. 31.

instances reflected persecution based on Jewish appearance, but a Jewish girl with a light-complexioned face and brown hair had survived in her native town of Piatigorsk (albeit in a different neighborhood) for many months of the German occupation.[68]

Furthermore, in the ethnically heterogeneous North Caucasus, when faced with a suspect who had a non-Russian appearance, the authorities had to consider the possibility that he belonged to one of the non-Slavic Caucasian groups. Some Jews were able successfully to claim Caucasian identities in order to account for their Semitic appearance, circumcision, and/or lack of necessary documents. For example, in the village of Vorontsovka, a Jewish girl claimed that she was an Armenian,[69] while in Mikoianshakhar a Jewish woman asserted that she was an Armenian married to a Russian.[70] Survival under Slavic identities in the Caucasus was less widespread and limited solely to women, as men needed to account for their circumcision.[71] In one example, a male Jewish survivor invented the story that his father had been Tatar (explaining his circumcision) and that his mother had been Russian but that he had been placed in an orphanage at the age of one, which explained why he did not know his father (and, hence, was ignorant of the Tatar language).[72]

The Jewish population's limited connections among the local population in the North Caucasus influenced their behavior in the post-action period. The postwar testimony of a Jewish witness concerning her experiences in Krasnodar illustrates this notion.

68 Memoirs of Memoirs of Liubov' Guzman on the fate of her aunt, Ella Frank, July 1997, YVA, 0.33/6139, p. 6.

69 Stavropol'skii *krai*: Statement of Anna Shlaen, 1943, GARF, 7021/17/11, p. 116.

70 Testimony of Tsitsilia Tsirul'nik, 1943, GARF, 7021/17/10, pp. 201-202. Another case of survival of a Jewish woman in Mikoianshakhar who claimed an Armenian identity is recorded in Yuri Prizov, "The Reminiscences of a Young Holocaust Survivor," [no date], United States Holocaust Memorial Museum Collection: 2011.337.1.

71 Near Tikhoretsk – as a Ukrainian; village of Krasnaia Poliana – as a Pole: Testimony of Lea Wilderman, April 1990, YVA, 0.3/5676, p. 11; Testimony of Gicia Lejzerowicz (1914), May 31, 1947, YVA, M.49.E/2439, p. 2.

72 Armavirskii *raion* (?): Testimony of Iakov Vinokurov, October 19, 1999, YVA, VT/2489.

She had escaped to the region from Ukraine in 1941 and was in occupied Krasnodar by the late summer of 1942:

> I worked as a field worker and supervisor in a laboratory. The Gestapo required that all the inhabitants of the town register at the police. I could find no trustworthy person.... I did not risk escape because I had no warm clothes, did not know the area, and could not count on the assistance of the local population. The escape would certainly have betrayed the fact that I was Jewish. I needed someone in whom to place my confidence. My choice fell upon Sof'ia Krasnova at the laboratory. I disclosed my secret to Sof'ia Krasnova, and [she] took care of me, calmed me down, and let me stay with her.[73]

As long as there remained the slightest possibility to do so, the Jews refrained from asking unfamiliar local people for help, preferring to survive on their own. As a result, they applied to non-Jews for help only as a last resort.

2.2. Between towns and countryside

As already mentioned, the Germans imposed only minor residence and movement restrictions in the occupied North Caucasus.[74] The practical outcome of this policy for a Jew who survived the action was that few combing operations were conducted in Caucasian towns and villages. Besides, the registration of the local population had been carried out at the advanced stage of the occupation.[75] Yet, it may be suggested that local German-installed headmen did not rigidly enforce this directive in the villages, as they became sensitive to the changes of the war in the Soviets' favor. This was the

73 Testimony of Mina Horowitz, August 1, 1973, YVA, 0.3/3682, pp. 6-9.

74 See Chapter 4, "Destruction of the Jewish Population in the North Caucasus."

75 Local headmen were required to record all the residents with a special emphasis on the newcomers and evacuees in towns by October 1942 (Service instruction of Dr. Mantel) and in villages by December 1942 (Directive of the *starosta* of the village of Medvezh'e in Vodolazhskaia, Krivneva, and Mel'nik, *Stavropol'e v period nemetsko-fashistskoi okkupatsii (avgust 1942-ianvar' 1943*, p. 56.

case in the village of Arzyr, where there was no need to produce an ID in order to register.[76] The situation replicated itself on a smaller scale in the towns, whose larger size offered more opportunities for Jews to conceal themselves. The extent to which the movement and residence restrictions were enforced in the North Caucasus was limited, compared to the Crimea and other German-occupied areas on Soviet territory. Despite the Germans' tough declarations aimed at restricting the population's freedom of movement,[77] there were apparently no large-scale arrests of those who did not comply with such regulations.

The options that a Jewish survivor of the extermination actions had at his disposal in the Caucasus were varied. First, he could run the risk of staying in his home locality. This step could prove viable in a large town, where the person could potentially conceal himself even among people with whom he was not acquainted. Still, this was a locality one knew, and one faced fewer chances of coming across the Germans and local denouncers the less one ventured around town. Hiding appeared far riskier for those Jews eager to leave their home localities for a small town or village, where it was easier to detect the presence of any newcomer.

Middle-sized resort towns (Essentuki, Kislovodsk, etc.) were evidently not large enough for a Jew to remain unrecognized there. It was only possible to secure a hiding place if one had a good friend upon whom to rely for shelter.[78] In these towns, Jews who managed to survive did so only during the killing operations and then just a short time in the aftermath, unless they fled elsewhere.[79] In Essentuki, for example, a Jewish woman and her six-year-old son succeeded in concealing themselves during the first 10 days after the action only because

76 Stavropol'skii *krai*: File of Pelageia and Polina Karnaukh, 2000, YVA, M.31/8964.

77 Essentuki, Stavropol': Statement of Aleksandr Gontov, June 30, 1943, GARF, 7021/17/4, pp. 63-64; Belikov, *Okkupatsiia*, pp. 92-93.

78 Essentuki: Statement of Aleksandr Gontov, June 30, 1943, GARF, 7021/17/4, pp. 60-64.

79 Kislovodsk: Interrogation of Mikhail Fingerut, June 25, 1943, GARF, 7021/17/5, p. 31; Statement of Boris Khshive, July 3, 1943, GARF, 7021/17/5, pp. 48, 50.

she was cautious enough to hide in other peoples' apartments; her own apartment was searched several times.[80] The pressure she and those who gave her refuge faced was insurmountable, and, therefore, she fled into neighboring Piatigorsk. In another example from Kislovodsk, a Jewish woman decided to leave her small daughter with a Russian neighbor, reasoning, and justly so, that it would be too dangerous for her to wander around with a child.[81] It is clear, however, that even in large towns it was mortally dangerous to stay in one's own apartment or even to revisit it from time to time.[82] A 61-year-old Jew named Mikhail Fingerut fled his own resort town for refuge in another.[83] He left Kislovodsk and arrived in the neighboring town of Minvody. He then obtained an "Aryan" passport, with which he managed to go to Armavir. He finally found short-term employment in the large city of Krasnodar. Traveling alone and being of old age was an advantage for Fingerut. However, a young large Jewish family also trying to flee Essentuki did not succeed. In spite of being in possession of "Aryan" IDs, this family was caught and killed somewhere on their way out of Essentuki, with the husband's combat age (36) drawing attention to the family.[84] Yet, it should be emphasized that this case likely constitutes the only documented evidence of an unsuccessful attempt to move from one area to another in the Caucasus.

Significantly, Jews escaped to towns, and not villages, in the majority of the recorded cases.[85] This reflects two main factors: the small size of the villages with the ensuing inability of Jewish refugees to find safe shelter, and the more pronounced anti-Jewish sentiments among rural inhabitants of the North Caucasus. Once in a village, possession of an "Aryan" ID was critical in securing

80 Testimony of Faina Gulianskaia, July 2, 1943, GARF, 7021/17/4, p. 17.

81 File of Anna Popova and Ol'ga Pyl'neva, 1998, YVA, M.31/7816.

82 Krasnodar: Krasnodar trial, interrogation of Tat'iana Kostigova, March 20, 1943, AFSB RF, H-16708, p. 878, courtesy of the USHMM.

83 Interrogation of Mikhail Fingerut, June 25, 1943, GARF, 7021/17/5, p. 31.

84 Testimony of Raisa Kogan, April 29, 1943, GARF, 7021/17/4, p. 14: Ages: father (36), daughter (18), second daughter (3), mother (70), nephew (5).

85 See further on in the chapter.

a Jew's future.[86] Otherwise, Jewish refugees usually fell victim to denunciations[87] or extortions[88] by the locals.

A final possibility entailed wandering around the region without permanently settling anywhere. In the initial phase of the German occupation (August 1942), the advancing German troops tended to regard almost all movement within the region as attempts of Jews to escape.[89] However, following the consolidation of the German hold in the Caucasus (September-November 1942), the persecuted Jews were sometimes able to go from one town to another relatively unimpeded.[90] This picture did not change considerably until the end of the German occupation, although the movement restrictions worsened somewhat by the final weeks of 1942.

2.3. In pursuit of "Aryan" documents

As already indicated, possession of "Aryan" IDs was frequently instrumental in the survival of Jews in the North Caucasus. In many cases, this was a major factor influencing the decision of the German and collaborationist authorities concerning the fate of the Jews. Jews were prepared to pay a high sum of money to procure such documents if they had the means to do so.[91] In addition to purchasing the documents from non-Jews, Jews could

86 Such as the Jewish woman who escaped from Novorossiisk to the village of Tonel'naia in Krasnodarskii *krai*: Questioning of Emma Mitel'man (1912), October 15, 1943, GARF, 7021/16/11, p. 48.

87 Farm "Privolnyi" and then on the *sovkhoz* no. 30: Testimony of Samuil Belenkov, August 10, 1943, GARF, 7021/17/4, p. 25.

88 Krasno-Vostochnyi *aul*, village of Dzhiginka: Testimony of A. S. Bagiennovskaia, [no later than June 26, 1943], GARF, 7021/17/206, pp. 72-73; Testimony of Ol'ga Polonskaia, May 1, 1962, YVA, 0.3/2246, p. 7.

89 Villages of Petrovskoe and Bashanta: Akt of the Commission of Petrovskii *raion*, GARF, 7021/17/1, p. 107; Akt of the Commission of Bashanta, GARF, 7021/8/26, pp. 39-40. See also section on evacuees in chapter 4, "Destruction of the Jewish Population in the North Caucasus."

90 From Kislovodsk to Kabardino-Balkariia and from Essentuki into a steppe: from Kamennomostskaia *stanitsa* to Abadzekhovskaia *stanitsa* and around the region: Testimony of Tsilia Gadleva, October 25, 1990, YVA, 0.3/4391, p. 11; Testimony of Raisa Kogan, April 29, 1943, GARF, 7021/17/4, p. 13; File of Klavdiia Sysoeva, Agripina Dedova and others, [no date], YVA, M.31/8884.

91 75,000 rubles for five family members in Essentuki: Testimony of Raisa Kogan, April 29, 1943, p. 14.

also obtain "Aryan" IDs from their friends who gave them their own documents.[92] Jews in possession of other people's "Aryan" IDs sometimes adapted them to fit their needs.[93]

The wartime testimony, quoted at length below, of a Jewish woman named Anna Shlaen constitutes evidence of how one resourceful Jew endeavored to survive and attempted to help other Jews survive despite the sometimes terrible options accorded with procuring "Aryan" IDs. The witness had been evacuated from the Ukrainian town of Zaporozh'e to the village of Novozavedennoe (Stavropol'skii *krai*). In the village she came across another Jewish family, the Tseitlins (mother, daughter, and 10-year-old son), who had been evacuated from Leningrad. After Russian police took away their valuables on September 11 or 15, 1942, the Tseitlins seem to have been doomed. However, when the census was conducted again, the testimony states:

> We [i.e. Shlaen and the mother – KF] decided to record mother Mariia Il'inichna Tseitlin and her son Alik as Jews; daughter Tsilia was to be recorded as a Russian who had allegedly lost sight of her relatives in the train and a Jewish woman looked after her until the arrival of her mother. This was done. When 10-year-old Alik learned that his sister would remain alive, he began wailing and pleaded with his mother: "Tsilia will live, and I want to live, too." I witnessed this conversation. When I came home, I told my mother and brother that we had to buy Russian documents. [In the meantime] we decided to take Mother's passport and change the nationality from Jewish to Russian. But it was all too visible, and they buried the passport in the earth. I had the union card (*soiuznyi bilet*) with a stamp and a picture. Yet,

92 Minvody, Kamennomostskaia *stanitsa*: Interrogation of Mikhail Fingerut, June 25, 1943, GARF, 7021/17/5, p. 31; File of File of Klavdiia Sysoeva, Agripina Dedova and others, [no date], YVA, M.31/8884.

93 For example, a Jewish woman in Novorossiisk changed the newly obtained documents to correspond to her Russian husband's family name (he was drafted into the Red Army). Questioning of Emma Mitel'man, October 15, 1943, GARF, 7021/16/11, p. 46.

> nothing was recorded concerning my nationality. I chose the proper ink and inscribed "Russian."[94]

Some Caucasian Jews who remained in their home localities refrained from forging passports, as they were easily recognizable. For example, the mother of a Jewish witness in Kislovodsk refused her Russian neighbor's proposal to forge her passport on the grounds that "her father was known all over the town; we were also well known."[95] Rather, it made sense for them to obtain "Aryan" passports in other towns, and to this end they were prepared to risk the trip to a neighboring place.[96] Nevertheless, in a number of cases procuring "Aryan" documents was to no avail, as the authorities demanded the Jews produce further proof of their "flawless" origin.[97]

The looser character of the German occupation in the North Caucasus, with its absence of strict residence and movement restrictions at the initial stages of the occupation, somewhat diminished the role of the "Aryan" IDs. Occasionally, Jews who wandered around the region managed to survive without any documents whatsoever.[98] Jews facing document checks could claim that their passport was lost. Significantly, such an explanation could suffice for the authorities in the short-run, provided the person was a complete newcomer and no one knew that he or she was Jewish. The following example of a Jewish evacuee in an unidentified village is instructive in this regard:

Until September 8, he hid in the house. No one knew about

94 Soldatsko-Aleksandrovskii *raion*, Stavropol'skii *krai*: Statement of Anna Shlaen, 1943, GARF, 7021/17/11, p. 115. All the Jews mentioned in the document were ultimately saved.

95 Testimony of Fania Skliar, September 1975, YVA, 0.3/3934, p. 8.

96 From Essentuki to Piatigorsk and from Novorossiisk to the village of Tonelnaia: Testimony of Faina Gulianskaia, July 2, 1943, GARF, 7021/17/4, p. 17. See also the questioning of Emma Mitel'man, October 15, 1943, GARF, 7021/16/11, pp. 46-48.

97 Essentuki: Testimony of Ia. Tal'ianskii, [no date], GARF, 7021/17/4, p. 30.

98 From Essentuki outside; from Piatigorsk to Kislovodsk: Testimony of Raisa Kogan, April 29, 1943, GARF, 7021/17/4, p. 14; Testimony of Tsilia Gadleva, October 25, 1990, YVA, 0.3/4391, p. 10.

> him. Previously, an order had been issued in the *kolkhoz* to present to the Gestapo a list of the evacuees. So the search was being conducted for the evacuees. On September 8, a check-up of the documents was carried out in the house. [Balaban] said that the documents were lost, and that he was Romanian.[99]

As long as a Jew neither possessed a typical "Semitic appearance" nor had any "Aryan" documents, he or she still ran the risk of being detained as an ordinary suspect, but was not exterminated immediately on account of being Jewish. This happened with a young Jew arrested because he was a "combat-age man without documents"; he managed to survive in the camp as his true identity was never revealed.[100]

If a person was denounced on the charge that he was a Jew, possessing an "Aryan" ID was not sufficient grounds for making his or her case. In such an event, the Jew's fate depended on evidence established by German or local "specialists in the Jewish Question" who scrutinized the suspect thoroughly, as is exhibited by the testimony of a Russian man in Krasnodar:

> The [German] officer began interrogation, while charging me with being Jewish. I denied it and produced the available documents, which stated that I was Russian by nationality. Initially, he did not believe me and punched me in the teeth. Then, he began examining my hands. Thereupon, the officer said: "I am the representative of the authority and order you to take off your clothes." I complied with this order. Upon having ascertained that I was not Jewish, the officer ordered me however to recite the prayer *Otche nash* [*Pater Noster* – KF] and cross myself. I read the prayer and crossed myself. Then, the officer began to inquire whether there were Jews among my ancestors. I replied by saying that I did not know whether there were Jews among my ancestors.

99 Soldatsko-Aleksandrovskii *raion*: Statement of Irina D'iakonova, 1943, GARF, 7021/17/11, p. 113.

100 Testimony of Iakov Vinokurov, October 19, 1999, YVA, VT/2489.

It is evident that only a small number of Jews could have possessed such a knowledge of "Pater Noster" learned by heart. Therefore, it was extremely difficult for them to survive such interrogations.

Some Jews who felt or knew what the German anti-Jewish steps meant destroyed their documents and claimed a non-Jewish identity.[101] Such behavior could bring about rescue only if no one in the area had known them previously. This was the case with one female Polish Jew, a complete foreigner in the Caucasian region, who had experienced three months in German-occupied Poland. In "Krasnaia poliana" *kolkhoz* in Stavropol'skii *krai*, she had destroyed all her documents except for the craftsman certificate of her husband [enlisted in the Red Army – KF] testifying that he was of Polish origin.[102] Another Jewish newcomer had heard rumors about the Germans' maltreatment of Jews, and tore up his passport before setting off to wander around the region.[103]

4. Jewish Resistance during the Holocaust in the North Caucasus[104]

Before the retreat of the Red Army, Soviet authorities had set up a nucleus of an underground network consisting primarily of ideologically reliable Communist and *Komsomol* cadres, who had to be in good health, inconspicuous, and able to withstand the anticipated German persecutions.[105] Besides the low efficiency

101 Dzhiginka: File of Pelageia and Polina Karnaukh, 2000, YVA, M.31/8964.

102 Testimony of Gicia Lejzerowicz, May 31, 1947, YVA, M.49.E/2439, p. 2.

103 Armavir: Testimony of Iakov Vinokurov, October 19, 1999, YVA, VT/2489.

104 For a general survey of the Soviet underground and partisan movements in the region, see Linets, *Severnyi Kavkaz nakanune i v period nemetsko-fashistskoi okkupatsii*, pp. 412-474 (partisans) and 475-512 (underground); Krinko, *Zhyzn' za liniei fronta*, pp. 155-186.

105 Untitled document, State Archive of Krasnodarskii *Krai* (GAKK), R-1255/1/1, p. 3, in Krinko, *Zhyzn' za liniei fronta*, p. 104. See also Aleksandr Linets, "Partizanskoe dvizhenie v Stavropol'skom krae v period nemetsko-fashistskoi okkupatsii," (PhD diss., Piatigorskii gosudarstvennyi lingvisticheskii universitet, 2003), p. 29.

of these clandestine networks and their painful failures,[106] Jewish representation in their ranks was insignificant. Still, some Jews did work for them, including a Jew in Essentuki who was able to save his own life after being duly warned about the forthcoming arrests of the Communists and provided with "getaway" addresses in Caucasian Muslim villages.[107]

A number of young Jews joined the ranks of the pro-Soviet underground operating in Stavropol'. They participated primarily in propaganda activities directed at the Russian population of the town. According to a wartime source:

> A small group of Jewish youngsters joined their Russian friends, who were acting in a clandestine fashion. Thus they saved their lives and contributed [to the underground's success]... In particular, a Jewish girl, Hanna, appeared all of a sudden in the midst of the railway workers and distributed leaflets on the Patriotic War of the Red Army.[108]

The activities of partisans in the North Caucasus were characterized by a number of specific features that affected the possibilities for Jews to join their ranks and, by association, to save their lives. Based on the documents of local partisan movements, general patterns may be inferred, meaning that the Soviets likely succeeded in deploying a ramified network of well-supplied partisan units across the region in due time. As of August 1, 1942, there were 130 partisan detachments deployed in

106 Untitled document, Central Archive of the Ministry of Defense of the Russian Federation (TsAMO RF), 38663/1/41, p. 42, in Movsur Ibragimov, *Vlast' i obschestvo*, pp. 299-300. See also Maksim Andrienko, "Naselenie Stavropol'skogo kraia v gody Velikoi Otechestvennoi voiny: otsenka povedencheskikh motivov," (PhD diss., Piatigorskii gosudarstvennyi lingvisticheskii universitet, 2005), p. 76.

107 Essentuki: Statement of Lazar' Iudin, approximately 1943, GARF, 7021/17/4, p. 47 (?)

108 And This is the First News... What the Nazis are Doing with the Jewish Population before their Retreat in Russia" (Hebrew), *Davar*, no. 5366, February 24, 1943, p. 1 (source: Moscow, special telegram to *Davar* dated February 22, 1943).

Krasnodarskii *krai* alone, with a total number of 5,049 fighters.[109] By the beginning of the German occupation, 40 partisan units were deployed in the neighboring Stavropol'skii *krai*, which had numbered approximately 2,000 people.[110] Both Kabardino-Balkariia and North Ossetiia had 14 partisan units each.[111] In addition to the Soviet-run partisan units in a number of areas dominated by Mountain peoples, there were also active local insurgents,[112] although there is no evidence concerning Jewish participation in the ranks of these units.

In the first months of the occupation, the partisan movement in the North Caucasus was only a small hindrance to the German presence in the region.[113] The small increase in its activities throughout September-October was followed by a German crackdown.[114] However, by December 1942, the partisans' activities were again on the rise, reaching their peak at the time of the German withdrawal.[115] For a variety of reasons, the partisan detachments in the region did not suffer considerable casualties, and the great majority of the partisans serving in the Caucasus survived the German occupation.[116]

109 Beliaev and Bondar', *Kuban' v gody Velikoi Otechestvennoi voiny, 1941-1945*, p. 350. The figures were slightly different according to another source: 75 partisan detachments, which were made up of 5,742 people. Untitled document, Russian State Archive of Social and Political History (RGASPI), 69/1/128, p. 103.

110 Untitled document, RGASPI, 69/1/128, p. 113.

111 Untitled document, RGASPI: 69/1/784, p. 105.

112 Kabardino-Balkariia, Karachaevskaia *oblast'*: Ibragimov, *Vlast' i obschestvo*, pp. 299-300.

113 Linets, *Severnyi Kavkaz nakanune i v period nemetsko-fashistskoi okkupatsii*, p. 58.

114 Krasnodarskii *krai*: In November 1942, there was recorded a decline in the partisan activity for a number of reasons: 1) The number of the partisan units diminished; 2) their food bases were reduced; 3) German retaliation measures increased; 4) during active warfare it was difficult to cross the front line. Beliaev and Bondar', *Kuban' v gody Velikoi Otechestvennoi voiny, 1941-1945*, pp. 584-585. See also Pohl, *Die Herrschaft der Wehrmacht*, p. 302.

115 CSpSd, Kommandostab, Berlin, MbOg, no. 28, Geheim, November 6, 1942, YVA, JM/4539; CSpSd, Kommandostab, Berlin, MbOg, no. 33, Geheim, December 11, 1942, ibid.

116 By late November 1942, there were 5,512 partisans in Krasnodarskii *krai*: Beliaev and Bondar', *Kuban' v gody Velikoi Otechestvennoi voiny*, 1941-1945, p.

By and large, there is scarce evidence of Jewish participation in the partisan units operating in the North Caucasus, as well as the role of the partisans in rescuing Jews. Most sources pass entirely in silence over the subject for a number of reasons.[117] Partisan units operated in the region only after the majority of the Jews had already been annihilated and, thus, could hardly be instrumental in rescuing them. Furthermore, from the beginning of the German occupation, those in charge of the partisan movement in the Caucasus did not deem it as a possible channel of rescue for civilians. Rather, these units were formed on the basis of the existent extermination battalions,[118] which, in turn, were raised from the most reliable elements of the local population of the North Caucasus, mostly conscript-aged men. Thus, the composition and the character of the Jewish population in the region (i.e., predominance of refugees, few men of combat age among them) were hardly compatible with the aforementioned requirements of the partisan leadership. It is no small wonder, therefore, that only 20 Jews fought in the ranks of the partisan movement in Stavropol'skii *krai*, alongside 1,704 Russians.[119] The respective figures for Krasnodarskii *krai* are 39 Jews (0.6%) alongside 5,775 Russians,[120] which were only slightly higher than the share of Jews in region's population as of 1939.

Nevertheless, a few Jews were involved in the partisans' activities in the region.[121] Some Mountain Jews offered shelter to

588. To put it otherwise, the number of the partisans in the territory remained almost unchanged during August-November 1942.

117 Ibid., pp. 441-448; 493-505; 538-556.

118 Plan of organization of partisan movement on the territory of [Stavropol'skii] *krai*, July 22, 1942, in Boiko, *Stavropol'e v Velikoi Otechestvennoi voine 1941-1945 gg.*, p. 142.

119 Andrienko, "Naselenie Stavropol'skogo kraia v gody Velikoi Otechestvennoi voiny," p. 70.

120 Iurii Evtushenko, "Partizanskoe dvizhenie na Kubani v period Velikoi Otechestvennoi voiny," (PhD diss., Kubanskii gosudarstvennyi universitet, 2005), p. 135.

121 Stavropol', Kabardino-Balkariia: Conversation of the member (G. N. Anpilogov) of the Commission for Complying with the Chronicle of the Great Patriotic War with the Secretary of the District Committee of the VKP(b) (V. V. Vorontsov) on the activities of the Stavropol' partisans, September 20, 1945, in

partisans in their houses.[122] Others escaped, determined to join the partisans somewhere in the Caucasus, but could not reach them,[123] indicative of a more general phenomenon: there is no record that the Jews in the Caucasus were ever able to make their way to partisan detachments. The reason was that the partisans were deployed in such a fashion that not only the Germans, who were willing to reveal them, but also those civilians, who were eager to join them, had difficulty doing so.

Vodolazhskaia, Krivneva, and Mel'nik, *Stavropol'e v period nemetsko-fashistskoi okkupatsii (avgust 1942-ianvar' 1943)*, p. 157; Testimony of Avgosh Shamilova, January 8, 1998, in Danilova, *Iskhod gorskikh evreev*, pp. 30-31; Testimony of Elizaveta Nazarov, January 6, 1998, ibid., p. 135.

122 Nal'chik: Testimony of Sarra Golman, July-August 1974, YVA, 0.3/6039, p. 3.

123 A Jewish woman and five more Jewish men, evacuees from the Air College: Testimony of Tsilia Gadleva, October 25, 1990, YVA, 0.3/4391, pp. 10-11.

Chapter Nine

The Local Population and the Holocaust in the Crimea

1. German Population Policy in the Crimea[1]

1.1. Towards the Russian population[2]

As already mentioned, the Crimea occupied a special place in German population policies. Acknowledging its unique strategic position, Hitler announced his intention to include the peninsula in the Reich at a conference held on July 16, 1941, at the Führer Headquarters at the "Wolf's Lair" (*Wolfsschanze*).[3] This was

1 Roman'ko, *Krym v period nemetskoi okkupatsii*, pp. 11-52; ibid., *Krym pod piatoi Gitlera: nemetskaia okkupatsionnaia politika v Krymu (1941-1944)* (Moscow: Veche, 2011); ibid., *Nemetskaia okkupatsionnaia politika na territorii Kryma i natsional'nyi vopros* (Simferopol: Antikva, 2009); Norbert Kunz, *Die Krim unter deutscher Herrschaft*, pp. 295-224; Angrick, *Besatzungspolitik und Massenmord*, pp. 467-484.

2 In the Crimean context, the terms "Russians," "Slavs," "Christians," or "Orthodox Christians" refer basically to the same group of the local population, which encompassed Russians and, to a lesser extent, Ukrainians. Other ethnic groups that practiced Orthodox Christianity (Greeks, Bulgarians and Armenians) were numerically negligible. In any case, when the latter groups are meant, the text explicitly refers to them. On the involvement of Russians and Ukrainians in the Holocaust during the Soviet-German war, see, for example, Iurii Radchenko, "'We emptied our magazines into them': The Ukrainian Auxiliary Police and the Holocaust in Generalbezirk Charkow, 1941-1943," *Yad Vashem Studies* 41, no. 1 (2013): pp. 63-98; Dmitrii Zhukov and Ivan Kovtun, *1-aia russkaia brigada SS "Druzhina"* (Moscow: Veche, 2010), pp. 45, 79, 81.

3 Kay, *Exploitation, Resettlement, Mass Murder*, p. 181. See also Garagulia,

supposed to involve serious population relocation in the Crimea; most specifically, the new settlement of Germans and the removal of a considerable part of the local population. Immediately upon the successful completion of the Battle of the Crimea in July 1942, Hitler issued an executive order requiring the forceful deportation of all Crimean residents, with the exception of Tatars.[4] Various German agencies had conducted research investigating this possibility at the first stage of the occupation in 1941-1942[5] and later in 1943.[6] Furthermore, it is obvious that *Reichsführer*-SS Heinrich Himmler's visit to the Crimea from October 27-31, 1942[7] (although prompted by increasing partisan activities in the peninsula) can be also seen within the framework of the possible Germanizing of the Crimea, given the fact that "population policies" was the SS field of specialization in the Nazi state. Yet, apparently due to the perpetually loose German control of the peninsula, these plans never materialized, and the decision was formally postponed until the final victory in the Eastern campaign.

Kondranov, and Kravtsova, *Krym v Velikoi Otechestvennoi voine*, p. 55; Adolf Hitler, *Monologe im Führerhauptquartier 1941-1944*, pp. 39, 48, 63-64, 90, 124, 128, entries from July 5-6, July 27, August 18, September 18, November 5, 1941; Dallin, *Deutsche Herrschaft in Rußland 1941-1945*, pp. 266-269; Picker, *Hitlers Tischgespräche im Führer-Hauptquartier, 1941-1942* (, pp. 272 (entry from May 8, 1942), 290-291 (entry from May 13, 1942), and Trevor-Roper, *Hitler's Secret Conversations, 1914-1941*, pp. 16 (entry from July 27, 1941), 68, 70 (entry from October 17, 1941).

4 Pohl, *Die Herrschaft der Wehrmacht*, pp. 298-299.

5 "Bericht über der Siedlungsmöglichkeiten in der Nogaischen Steppe (Taurien) und der Halbinsel Krim durch OKVR Donner und Major Seifert," March 10, 1942, BA-MA, film 44423, Bl., 646-669, in Angrick, *Besatzungspolitik und Massenmord*, p. 328. See also Erhard Wetzel's Memorandum on Generalplan Ost, April 7, 1942, Nuremberg Document NG-2325 and *Der Dienstkalender Heinrich Himmlers*, p. 356.

6 Report of the RMfdbO submitted to Alfred Rosenberg, March 1943, in Ryszard Torzecki, "Die Rolle der Zusammenarbeit mit der deutschen Besatzungsmacht in der Ukraine für der Okkupationspolitik," in Werner Röhr, ed., *Okkupation und Kollaboration (1938-1945): Beiträge zu Konzepten und Praxis der Kollaboration in der deutschen Okkupationspolitik* (Berlin and Heidelberg: Huethig Verlagsgemeischaft, 1994), p. 263.

7 Witte, *Der Dienstkalender Heinrich Himmlers*, pp. 600-602.

The new power took a tough stance towards the majority of the local population that was no different than from what the Germans had done in the other areas where ethnic Russians were predominate.[8] Two basic factors contributed to the continuity of German policy in this respect. First, the German occupations of the aforementioned areas and the Crimea were accomplished approximately within the same period. Second, the 11th Army, which occupied the peninsula, was part of and subordinated to the Army Group South that had been assigned to the conquest of southern and eastern Ukraine (which had a similar ethnic structure, with the exception of the Tatars). The Crimea neither possessed important industrial facilities that the Germans were interested in restarting, nor did it have mineral resources worthy of German exploit.[9] The Germans' strategy provided for minimal investment into such areas, including the establishment of an orderly administration.[10] The continual warfare in the peninsula until July 1942 had served as a convenient pretext for the Germans to refrain from "excessive expenditure" in caring for the Crimean population.

Despite some exceptions, the initial period of the German occupation (November-December 1941) was characterized by harsh measures periodically applied to the local Russian population. According to a piece of wartime evidence from Jews and partisans, after the seizure of Feodosiia the Germans "arrested 50 hostages, and from then on they resorted to executing 50 local inhabitants every day,"[11] apparently in response to increasing partisan activity in the area. In the first days of December 1941, the Germans shot some 300 people in Simferopol' for "plunder"; one week later,

8 Truman O. Anderson, "Germans, Ukrainians and Jews: Ethnic Politics in Heersgebiet Süd, June-December 1941," *War in History* 7, no. 3 (2000): pp. 325-352.

9 On the Crimea's economy in the German calculations, see Kunz, *Die Krim unter deutscher Herrschaft*, pp. 34-41.

10 Müller, "From Economic Alliance to a War of Colonial Exploitation," pp. 174-175.

11 Moshe Gutovich, "From the Horrors of the Massacre in Feodosiia" (Hebrew), [From the conversation with Moshe Gutovich, Jewish refugee from Feodosiia, source: *Eynikayt*], *Ha-tsofe* (Tel Aviv), no. 1685, July 13, 1943, p. 3.

18 people were hung in the town for the murder of a German soldier.[12] In Yalta, some teenagers were hung for "plunder" in early December of the same year.[13] As so it went on.

German policy radicalized as hostilities resumed in the peninsula at the end of 1941. The Wehrmacht command concluded (apparently not without foundation) that the local population had lent support to the Red Army troops landing on the southern coast of the Crimea.[14] Consequently, the Germans began collectively to treat the local people in these towns as actual Soviet accomplices. Thousands of civilians, mainly Russians and Ukrainians, were decimated by the Germans on such grounds in Feodosiia and Evpatoriia.[15] In other areas of the peninsula under German control, what the Germans considered as preventive steps (such as heavy residence and movement restrictions,[16] large-scale resettlement of civilians,[17] curfews,[18] and "mopping-up" operations)[19] were widely applied.

1.2. Towards the Crimean Tatars

Prior to their entry into the peninsula, the Germans had certain ideas for dealing with the Crimean Tatars that were distinct from those concerning the Slavic population, but had not yet devised any definite plans. After the German takeover, the Crimean Tatars

12 Genov, *Dnevnik partizana*, p. 87 (entry from December 27, 1941).

13 Vergasov, *Krymskie tetradi*, p. 48.

14 "Strafsache gegen Walter Bierkamp," Bayerisches Landeskriminalamt IIIa/SK, München, October 31, 1965, Beschuldigen Vernehmung, Werner Karl R. Major i. Generalstab, Yad Vashem Archives (YVA), TR.10/1147, p. 515.

15 OSR USSR, no. 184, CSPSS, Berlin, March 23, 1942, in Arad, Krakowski, and Spektor, *The Einsatzgruppen Reports*, pp. 317-318; Akt of the Commission of the town of Evpatoriia, July 5, 1944, State Archive of the Russian Federation (GARF), 7021/9/57, p. 20.

16 Genov, *Dnevnik partizana*, p. 195 (entry from April 26, 1942).

17 From Yalta to the countryside near Simferopol': Akt of the Commission of Yalta, August 19, 1944, GARF, 7021/9/59, p. 183.

18 Simferopol', Yalta: Staboffz. der FG, "TB als Anlage zum K," "TB für die Zeit vom 1.-30.11.1941," December 2, 1941, YVA, M.29.FR/118, p. 6; Statement of Elena Levitskaia, July 5, 1944, YVA, M.33/368, p. 138.

19 Feodosiia, Simferopol': OK I (V)/287, "TB für die Zeit vom 1.-15.3.1942," Feodosia, March 15, 1942, YVA, M.29.FR/40, p. 30; Testimony of Efim Gopshtein, August 16, 1944, YVA, M.35/21, p. 162.

gave the Germans a warm and enthusiastic reception all over the peninsula,[20] setting the stage for future cooperation between the Tatars and the emerging German power. As a singular development in the peninsula at any given point, the German authorities sanctioned autonomous Tatar national activity in the cultural and educational domains under the so-called Muslim Committees (*muskomy – Musul'man komiteleri*), so long as they did not assume a political character.[21] School instruction was allowed in the Tatar language; newspapers, theater, and journals were also permitted to operate in Tatar.[22] In due time, Crimean Tatars also received unique economic privileges (i.e., material assistance, help in ensuring trips to Ukraine to procure bread, permission to engage in private trade, etc.).[23] The Tatars were exempted from the Germans' harsh *Vergeltungsmassnahmen* ("retaliation measures"), including civilian executions.[24] The Germans persecuted neither Tatar Communist Party nor *Komsomol* members.[25]

In December 1941-January 1942, the Germans decided to initiate the mass enlistment of Tatars into the units established by

20 OSR USSR, no. 153, CSPSS, Berlin, January 9, 1942, YVA, 0.51/165 II; OSR USSR, no. 157, CSPSS, Berlin, January 19, 1942, in Arad, Krakowski, and Spektor, *The Einsatzgruppen Reports*, pp. 284-286. See also Frauenfeld, *Die Krim*, p. 74.

21 "Predatel'skaia rol' tatarskogo naseleniia v period okkupatsii Kryma," 1944, State Archive of the Autonomous Republic of the Crimea (DAARK), P-156/1/41; Kirimal Edige, *Der Nationale Kampf Der Krimtürken - mit besonderer Berücksichtigung der Jahre 1917-1918* (Emsdetten/Wesfalen: Verlag Lechte, 1952), p. 307.

22 Zur Mühlen, *Zwinschen Hakenkreuz und Sowjetstern*, pp. 184-5; Torzecki, "Die Rolle der Zusammenarbeit mit der deutschen Besatzungsmacht in der Ukraine für der Okkupationspolitik," p. 263.

23 Report "O razvedyvatel'noi rabote v Krymu po sostoianiiu na 1 iiulia 1943 g." by the Representative of the Headquarters of the Partisan Movement Vladimir Bulatov, July 28, 1943, YVA, M.40.RCM/11, p. 1.

24 Evpatoriia: Interrogation of Ul'ian Kravchik, June 30, 1944, YVA, M.33/57, p. 47.

25 Memorandum "O rabote Krymskogo Obkoma VKP(b) po rukovodstvu partisanskim dvizheniem i podpo'noi rabotoi v Krymu," February 13, 1943, DAARK, P-1/1/2144a.

the EG D;[26] the German Army was not yet ready to sanction the formation of auxiliary units raised from Soviet nationals. It should be remembered that at this juncture, no other group among the Soviet people had been allowed to join its military units – Crimean Tatars were the first. The *Einsatzgruppe*'s patronage enhanced the status of the Tatars among all other groups in the peninsula.

The growing German reliance on the Crimean Tatars in 1941-42 resulted in a unique development not replicated anywhere else in the occupied Soviet territories. In an apparent reversal of previous intentions, the Germans approved the plans to resettle 25,000 Crimean Tatars from other areas back in the Crimea.[27] Regardless of whether or not it was only a German tactical maneuver to appease the Tatars, this step (in light of the Germans' own prospects for the colonization of the peninsula and their general sights on Eastern space) highlighted the special character of the relationship between Nazi Germany and the Crimean Tatars. As the Germans had willingly subscribed to the extreme Tatar circles' stance that the "Jewish settlement in the peninsula had been made possible solely at the expense of the Tatars and ethnic Germans," these Tatar newcomers were likely to be settled on Jewish property.[28]

The Germans maintained these policies at least throughout 1941-1942; that is, during the period when the bulk of Crimean Jewry was annihilated. After that, the relations between the Crimean Tatars and the Germans gradually transformed. Due to a change in the general balance of forces in the Soviets' favor and the growing activity of Crimean partisans, a slightly increasing number of Tatars began to side with the Soviet partisans.[29] Furthermore, other ethnic groups, such as Ukrainians and Bulgarians, were later given

26 Andrej Angrick, "Die Einsatzgruppe D und die Kollaboration," in Kaiser, *Täter im Vernichtungskrieg*, p. 78; Joachim Hoffmann, *Die Ostlegionen 1941-43: Turkotataren, Kaukasier und Wolgafinnen im deutschen Herr* (Freiburg: Rombach Verlag, 1981), p. 43.

27 Zur Mühlen, *Zwinschen Hakenkreuz und Sowjetstern*, p. 125.

28 CSpSd, Kommandostab, MbOg, no. 4, Berlin, May 22, 1942, in Arad, Krakowski, and Spektor, *The Einsatzgruppen Reports*, pp. 344-345.

29 Kirimal, *Der Nationale Kampf Der Krimtürken*, p. 316.

preferential treatment, as the Germans sought to broaden their basis of support in the Crimea.[30] However, overall, the Germans viewed the Crimean Tatars as their most reliable allies in the region throughout the entire occupation period, and treated them accordingly.

1.3. Annihilation of Jews as a message to the local population

The impact of the Holocaust on the local population should be viewed against the backdrop of prospective German dominance in the peninsula. The case of the main town of the Crimea, Simferopol', is well documented and is representative of what took place elsewhere in the peninsula. Those responsible for carrying out the extermination of the Simferopol' Jews (*Einsatzkommando* 11b) took precautions to conceal their preparations and implementation of the killing operation, which they conducted outside of the town. Neither Russian nor Tatar police forces took part in the execution of the Jews; they participated solely in the preliminary stages, such as combing neighborhoods in pursuit of Jews and taking them out of their houses to the assembly point.[31] The German authorities issued no written order for the Jews to assemble – the relevant announcement was made by an oral directive from the *Judenrat*.[32]

Rumors that Simferopol''s Jews were to be killed surfaced before the killing operation. On December 7, 1941, a non-Jewish inhabitant of the town recorded in his diary:

> There are rumors spreading in the midst of the population that all the Jews will be shot down. An acquaintance frequented by the Germans states that they say that the Jews will be shot.[33]

Following the extermination of the Jews and the Krymchaks in Simferopol', information about what had happened soon spread.

30 Report by the Head of the Southern Headquarters of the Partisan Movement, December 29, 1942, YVA, M.40.RCM/18, p. 1.

31 Testimony of Efim Gopshtein, August 16, 1944, YVA, M.35/23, p. 64.

32 Ibid., p. 60.

33 Diary of Chrisanf Lashkevich, entry from December 7, 1942, DAARK, P-156/1/31, p. 72.

The EG D itself admitted that an information leak had occurred soon after the operation was conducted. In reports submitted in January and February 1942, all the blame for the leaked information was put on "fleeing Jews, Russians, and also… the loose talk of German soldiers."[34] An analysis of the possible sources of this leak and the German reaction to it is instrumental for understanding the underlying German motives behind their treatment of the local population in the Crimea.

As for the Wehrmacht soldiers, it should be emphasized that only "selected" forces were assigned to participate in the action. Nonetheless, the forthcoming operation appeared to be no secret to the German rank-and-files stationed in the Crimea.[35] Nor was it kept secret from other German military agencies in the town long before the action had taken place. As the report of the *Ortskommandatur* I/853 of Simferopol' explicitly mentioned as early as November 14, 1941:

> [The population of Simferopol'] was some 156,000 inhabitants; some 120,000 remained in the city, among them 20,000 Jews... The SD will execute the remaining 11,000 Jews.[36]

The representative of the German Ministry of Foreign Affairs at AOK 11, Werner Otto von Hentig, knew the exact number of Jews killed near Simferopol' several days after having returned to the Crimea in April 1942 (after having been absent for the duration of five months).[37]

34 OSR USSR, no. 150 (January 2, 1942), 157 (January 19, 1942), 170 (February 18, 1942), Berlin, CSPSS in Arad, Krakowski, and Spektor, *The Einsatzgruppen Reports,* pp. 266-267, 284-286, 296.

35 Diary of Chrisanf Lashkevich, entry from December 7, 1942, DAARK, P-156/1/31, p. 72.

36 OK I/853, "TB für die Zeit vom 5.-15.11.1941," Simferopol, November 14, 1941, YVA, M.29.FR/41, p. 23.

37 Hürter, *Hitlers Heerführer*, pp. 292-293; idem., "Nachrichten aus dem 'Zweiten Krimkrieg' (1941/42)," in ibid.; Otto Werner, "Hentig als Vertreter des Auswärtigen Amtes bei der 11. Armee," in Wolfgang Elz and Sönke Neitzel, eds., *Internationale Beziehungen im 19. und 20. Jahrhundert* (Paderborn: Schöningh, 2003), pp. 361-387.

However, the scope of contact between the German soldiers and the local population in the second part of December 1941 had remained limited.[38] In addition, it is doubtful whether even a small number of Wehrmacht soldiers (almost all of whom came from the Gendarmerie, which was in charge of maintaining secrecy), let alone the EG D men, who possessed inside information, could have leaked away relevant information on a large scale only a few days after the *Aktion* had been carried out. Therefore, even though important, the Wehrmacht played only a minor role in disseminating the information on the mass murder of Jews in Simferopol', if at all.

Hence, there are other possible channels by which the information on the Simferopol' *Aktion* could have funneled. The possibility that such information could have emanated from "fleeing Jews" seems to be an exaggeration. Very few Jews who were eyewitnesses to the murder survived. They were most concerned with concealing their identities and keeping a low profile in the aftermath. There is evidence that a Jew who knew with certainty about the massacre near Simferopol' chose neither to identify as a Jew nor to convey this information to the Jews residing in rural areas, which illustrates this point.[39]

After exterminating the Jews, the Germans quickly seized their personal possessions and dwellings.[40] Most of what the Germans took in the wake of the actions, such as their valuables, was not made available to the local people. In the short run, a few locals benefited from dispossession of the Jews, such as those involved in selling the clothes of Holocaust victims on the black

38 Testimony of Efim Gopshtein, August 16, 1944, YVA, M.35/21, p. 165.

39 Testimony of Lev Iurovskii, 1944, YVA, M.35/14, p. 82

40 On the German dispossession of Soviet Jews during the Holocaust, see, for example, Martin Dean, *Robbing the Jews: The Confiscation of Jewish Property in the Holocaust* (New York: Cambridge University Press, 2008), pp. 173-221; ibid., "Seizure of Jewish Property and Inter-Agency Rivalry in the Reich and in the Occupied Soviet Territory," in Feldman and Seibel, *Networks of Nazi Persecution*, pp. 88-102 and Yitzhak Arad, "Plunder of Jewish Property in the Nazi-Occupied Areas of the Soviet Union," *Yad Vashem Studies* 29 (2001): pp. 109-148.

market.[41] According to a postwar report of a Russian witness, in the village of Bagerovo (Kerchenskii *raion*), the local headman had plundered so much Jewish property that he was executed by the Germans.[42] Only later did authorities allocate houses and apartments formerly owned by Jews to some locals who had been loyal to the German administration – this was probably the most precious reward that the Germans were ever ready to offer the inhabitants of the Crimea for their service. Thus, the circle of those among the local people who benefited from the Jews' annihilation was somewhat expanded. Despite German efforts to arrange the orderly takeover of Jewish property, a number of Jewish apartments were nevertheless "illegally" plundered by the locals.[43] From the second part of 1942, when the Germans expressed more readiness to operate industrial, trade, cultural, and other facilities in the peninsula, more non-Jews took jobs previously occupied by the Jews.

On the whole, given the way in which the annihilation of the Jewish population had been carried out in Simferopol', it was quite difficult to conceal this killing operation. The preparations for it were such that the local population had witnessed the Germans' intensified maltreatment of the Jews for more than a month. In this respect, it should be remembered that the largest Jewish community in Simferopol' was not confined to a ghetto, nor were ghettos set up anywhere in the Crimea (with a couple of exceptions). Thus, the local people could easily observe the maltreatment of the Jews.

Important German directives, such as the first German order directed at the Jews in the town, had been publically displayed, which enabled the locals to learn of the precarious position of the Jews. The Germans frequently practiced "informal" maltreatment

41 Simferopol': "Strafsache gegen Walter Bierkamp," Erich G., Abschrift, April 13, 1967, YVA, TR.10/1147, p. 599.

42 Statement of Vera Kluge, August 2, 1949, DAARK, P-849/1/239.

43 Simferopol': *Golos Kryma* (Simferopol'), January 29, 1942, in Khurkovich, *Okupatsiinyi rezhym v Krymu, 1941-1944 rr.*, p. 15.

of the Jews in Simferopol' (i.e., beating,[44] raping,[45] plunder of property[46]), which was likely even more illuminating of their attitudes towards the Jews. There exists one testimony stating that the Germans drove local women from the nearby houses and forced them to deepen the anti-tank trenches into which the corpses of the Jews were then dropped.[47] According to a diary of an inhabitant of the town, after the killing operation the Germans refrained from discussing the fate of the Jews with the local people, even in private conversation,[48] which only confirmed the latter's worst fears. Thus, it stands to reason that local population in Simferopol' served as the main, albeit not the only, channel for transferring the information on the fate of the Jews.

The important point is that the *Einsatzgruppe* did not feel uneasy about this information leak. It was only alarmed that the local population had projected the extermination of Jews onto their own fate, as the locals assumed that the Germans were going to conduct an ethnic cleansing of all Crimean inhabitants. The reports by the EG D noted this change of mind but viewed it as a transparent phenomenon, a point which the following excerpt from an EG D report dated January 2, 1942, underscores:

> The attitude towards Jews has been confirmed. In general, the shooting of Jews has been positively received after the initial fear of similar treatment for the rest of the population subsided.[49]

44 Diary of Chrisanf Lashkevich, entry from November 22, 1941, DAARK, P-156/1/31, p. 69; memoirs of Il'ia Sirota, February 16, 1945, DAARK, P-156/1/40, p. 113.

45 Memoirs of A. F. Peganova, November 9, 1944, DAARK, P-156/1/40, p. 44.

46 Testimony of Musia Leikin (Iofin), December 27, 2000, YVA, 0.33.C/6428.

47 Testimony of Katherina Danova in L. Aizenshtat and I. Baburina, eds., *Kniga zhivykh, Vospominaniia evreev-frontovikov, uznikov getto i kontslagerei, boitsov partizanskikh otriadov, zhytelei blokadnogo Leningrada* (St. Petersburg: Akropol', 1995), p. 125.

48 Testimony of Efim Gopshtein, August 16, 1944, YVA, M.35/21, p. 165.

49 OSR USSR, no. 150, CSPSS, Berlin, January 2, 1942, in Arad, Krakowski, and Spektor, *The Einsatzgruppen Reports*, pp. 266-267.

The representative of the German Foreign Ministry at the AOK 11 confirmed that the local population was affected by the executions of Crimean Jews (most specifically, by those of Simferopol').[50] This suggests that this "by-product" of the *Aktion* in Simferopol' and, more generally, of the Holocaust in the Crimea, served the Germans in instilling an atmosphere of terror among the local population (mainly on its Russian segment). The importance of this motive grew after the short term of reasonable relations between the Germans and local population ended in the wake of the Soviet landings at the turn of 1941 and ensuing German reprisals against the civil population. It became fully manifest in the second half of 1942 in the recently captured Sevastopol', as indicated in a wartime testimony of a Russian inhabitant of the town:

> The gendarme who drove me to work threatened that if we did not obey the German authorities we should face the same fate as the Jews at the 8th station.[51]

Thus, the important goal of securing the German occupation of the Crimea at a minimum "maintenance" cost was attained. The German policy had a double effect on the local citizens' efforts and chances to rescue Jews. On the one hand, the frightened local population seriously weighed the possibility of German retaliations. On the other hand, the already noticeable sentiment of a "common fate"[52] seemed to be reinforced and potentially gave hope for the Jews in finding shelter among the local people.

50 Hürter, *Hitlers Heerführer*, p. 293; idem., "Nachrichten aus dem 'Zweiten Krimkrieg' (1941/42)," pp. 361-387.

51 Sevastopol': Testimony of K. I. Shevchenko, June 26, 1944, GARF, 7021/9/46, p. 83.

52 OSR USSR, no. 157, CSPSS, Berlin, January 19, 1942, in Arad, Krakowski, and Spektor, *The Einsatzgruppen Reports,* pp. 284-286.

2. The Responses of the Local Population to the Holocaust[53]

From the beginning of the war until the German seizure of the peninsula, the composition of the non-Jewish population changed slightly (provided the enlistment in the Red Army affected all groups of the population in a similar fashion). The most important development in this change was the deportation of more than 50,000-60,000 ethnic Germans conducted in August 1941.[54] Thus, this otherwise significant segment of population, which often helped intensify the Holocaust in other parts of the Soviet Union,[55] played a very limited role in the extermination of the Jews in the Crimea.[56]

2.1. Russians

2.1.1. General concerns

The attitudes of the local Russian population towards the German power in the peninsula were influenced by the fact that hostilities in the German-Soviet front deeply affected the well-being of the

53 On this subject, see, for example, Yitzhak Arad, "The Local Population in the German-Occupied Territories of the Soviet Union and its Attitude toward the Murder of the Jews," in David Bankier and Israel Gutman, eds., *Nazi Europe and the Final Solution* (Jerusalem: Yad Vashem, 2003), pp. 233-248 and Daniel Romanovsky, "The Soviet Person as a Bystander of the Holocaust: The Case of Eastern Belorussia," in Bankier and Gutman, *Nazi Europe and the Final Solution*, pp. 276-306.

54 In 1941, some 62,000 the Germans were deported from the Crimea. GARF, 8/31/69, p. 11, in Garagulia, Kondranov, and Kravtsova, *Krym v Velikoi Otechestvennoi voine*, p. 7. According to the data of the Crimean archives, the number of the deported Germans exceeded 52,000 people.

55 Eric C. Steinhart, *The Holocaust and the Germanization of Ukraine* (New York: Cambridge University Press in association with the United States Holocaust Memorial Museum and German Historical Institute, Washington, D.C., 2015.), pp. 207-230; Doris L. Bergen, "The Nazi concept of 'Volksdeutsche' and the exacerbation of antisemitism in Eastern Europe, 1939-45," *Journal of Contemporary History* 29, no. 4 (1994): pp. 569-582.

56 There are some testimonies that imply that the remaining Crimean Germans carried out the rescue of Jews: Memoirs of Il'ia Sirota, February 16, 1945, DAARK, P-156/1/40, p. 119; Story of Sal'nik-Korsakina, in Gel'man and Glubochanskii, *Kholokost*, pp. 125-6.

civilians in the Crimea. Many able-bodied men had been enlisted in the Red Army since the beginning of the war. Thus, agriculture and industry lacked working hands in the summer and fall of 1941. The accelerated evacuation and rapid approach of the war paralyzed the economy of the peninsula. Thus, the economic situation of the local people seriously deteriorated because of the war, and it is suggested that some of them blamed the Germans for the grievances they had to endure. However, with the exception of the Sevastopol' area, there was no large-scale fighting in the Crimea at the time of the German conquest in October-November 1941. As a result, the civil population managed the German takeover relatively smoothly.

The German occupation did not lead to any visible improvement in the economic standing of the Russian population. This was particularly true in November-December 1941, when the Germans employed the tactics of living off the land most overtly: few organizations and plants were reopened, with only a small number of people recruited into their staff and provided with the most essential currency of that time — food coupons. The Russian population had maintained largely neutral attitudes towards the Germans, but this period was characterized by a gradual change of mood from positive to more negative. Even so, there was no clear change until the large-scale executions of the local Jews and combing operations in towns conducted after January 1942. The following observation made in the EG D report from January 9, 1942, which applied mainly to POWs and people on the German payroll, states:

> The attitude towards [the] German occupation continues to be positive. A larger part of the population is afraid of the Russians' return. 7,000 prisoners from Feodosiia on the march via Simferopol' [to] Dzhankoi, partly under guard, [made] no attempt to go over to the Russians.[57]

57 OSR USSR, no. 153, CSPSS, Berlin, January 9, 1942, in Arad, Krakowski, and Spektor, *The Einsatzgruppen Reports*, pp. 272-273.

The drastic steps the Germans took against the non-Jewish civilian population and the annihilation of the Jews deeply affected the local people. As a result, the enthusiasm or indifference that considerable segments of the population had initially displayed at the arrival of the Germans[58] soon gave way to more pronounced anti-German sentiments. It was within this period (from late December 1941 onwards), that Soviet[59] and German[60] sources recorded a growing sympathy by the Russian and Ukrainian (and to a lesser extent Greek) populations towards the partisans. This shift was exacerbated further by the worsening food situation.[61] After the German reprisals against the Crimean civilian population had taken place, the number of active supporters of the new order in the peninsula diminished drastically. Importantly, the Red Army and Soviet partisans' constant incursions into the Crimea from the first half of 1942 had prevented the Russians from collaborating with the Germans on a large scale. Furthermore, the enhancement in the status of other groups in the German-controlled peninsula (primarily Tatars) was negatively perceived by the Russian majority. Considered from this perspective, relatively many among the local Russian population potentially viewed the Jewish plight with compassion.

58 Testimony of Efim Gopshtein, August 16, 1944, DAARK, P-156/1/37, pp. 71-72; Diary of Igor' Nosenko, member of the Simferopol' underground organization, DAARK, P-156/1/31, pp. 166-170; OSR USSR, no. 145, CSPSS, Berlin, December 12, 1941, in Arad, Krakowski, and Spektor, *The Einsatzgruppen Reports*, p. 256, also in YVA, 0.51/165 II.

59 Kozlov, *V Krymskom podpol'ie*, p. 77; Genov, *Dnevnik partizana*, p. 87 (entry from December 27, 1941); Report of the Commander of the North Caucasian Front Semeon Budennyi, July 1942, Russian State Archive of Social and Political History (RGASPI), 69/1/622, p. 10.

60 OSR USSR, no. 157, CSPSS, Berlin, January 19, 1942, in Arad, Krakowski, and Spektor, *The Einsatzgruppen Reports*, pp. 284-286.

61 See section 4A, "Food Conditions and the Holocaust in the Crimea and the Caucasus."

2.1.2. Collaborators[62]

Like elsewhere in occupied Europe, for want of their own forces, the Germans needed local collaborators to ensure that the "Final Solution" would be smoothly implemented. In the Crimean peninsula, where the annihilation of Jews took place largely within one month from the beginning of the occupation, the Germans needed collaborators in two major fields. The first involved an auxiliary administration and police in charge of overseeing the registered Jews, detecting those who were not registered, and guarding the killing operations. This depended on the availability of the Germans' own police and security formations in every given Crimean locality. In the post-*Aktion* phase, the detection of Jews in hiding was the main task of the local administration/police concerning Jewish matters. The second field in which the Germans needed local collaborators was propaganda, which also came to the fore during this period. As the Germans had already killed all registered Jews by this period, the main task of the local propaganda was to convince the population that the German policy to murder Jews had been in their best interest (which was never explicitly mentioned but only implied).

The Germans had set up collaboration administrations in the Russian-dominated towns of the Crimean peninsula from the very beginning of the occupation. Initially, these consisted of undermanned municipal authorities, as well as auxiliary police and a ramified network of secret agents (subordinated directly to the Germans), in which the largest number of collaborators were employed. The activity of these forces had the most direct bearing on the unfolding of the Holocaust and, thus, constitutes the core of the current section.

The Germans established Russian police soon after their

62 On collaboration in the occupied Soviet territories, see, for example, Ol'ga Baranova, "Nationalism, Anti-Bolshevism or the Will to Survive? Collaboration in Belarus under the Nazi Occupation of 1941-1944," *European Review of History: Revue Europeenne d'Histoire* 15, no. 2 (2008): pp. 113-128; Boris Kovalev, *Natsistskaia okkupatsiia i kollaboratsionizm v Rossii, 1941-1944* (Moscow: AST, 2004).

takeover.[63] These forces were not numerous, as the occupying power likely did not place much confidence in Russian collaborators in the peninsula. Prior to the extermination actions, the Germans limited the police force's activity primarily to surveillance and supervision insofar as the solution to the "Jewish Question" was concerned.[64] At this stage, Russian policemen were rarely involved in actively enforcing the anti-Jewish policies.[65] However, after the killing operations, their involvement grew. In 1941-1942, Russian policemen, representatives of the local administration and members of their families, and, in particular, secret agents of SD and GFP, were frequently involved in revealing Jews in hiding and handing them over to the Germans.[66] In a final account, the involvement of the local Russian police (or, the extent to which the Germans allowed its involvement) in the anti-Jewish policies in the Crimean towns remained rather limited when compared to many other occupied territories of the Soviet Union.[67] Furthermore, in exceptional cases guided by compassion, romance, or neighborly feelings, Crimean Russians and Ukrainians acting in official capacities in

63 In Simferopol' it was established by November 9, i.e., one week after the entry of the Germans. Wehrmachtsdienststelle, Gr., GFP 647, Kommando Simferopol, "TB für die Zeit vom 2.-11.11.1941," November 11, 1941, YVA, M.29.FR/120, p. 4.

64 Sevastopol', Simferopol', Evpatoriia: Sevastopol' trial, interrogation of Ernst Schrewe, 1947, RG-06.02505; "Strafsache gegen Persterer," Bayerisches Landeskriminalamt IIIa/1, Vernehmungsniederschrift, Ernst Heirich D., Ek 11b, April 18, 1959, YVA, TR.10/1158, p. 7; Interrogation of Ul'ian Kravchik, June 30, 1944, YVA, M.33/57, p. 48.

65 Arrests of Jews in their houses in a neighborhood of Simferopol': Testimony of Efim Gopshtein, August 16, 1944, YVA, M.35/23, p. 64.

66 Kerch, Simferopol', Evpatoriia: Gubenko, *The Book of Sorrows*, pp. 75-76. See also the file of Saltykova (Simonenko, D'iachikhina), State Archive of the Security Service of the Republic of the Crimea (ASBU RK), no. 11319; File of Aleksandr Pashkov, 1947, ASBU RK, no. 10131, pp. 8-114, courtesy of the USHMM; "Urteil gegen Johannes Schlupper, Heinrich Winterstein, Rudi Eschenbach," Landesgericht München I, July 24, 1974, YVA, TR.10/956, p. 32.

67 Radchenko, ""We emptied our magazines into them"; Martin Dean, "The German 'Gendarmerie,' the Ukrainian 'Schutzmannschaft' and the 'Second Wave' of Jewish Killings in Occupied Ukraine: German Policing at the Local Level in the Zhitomir Region, 1941-1944," *German History* 14, no. 2 (1996): pp. 168-192.

towns helped the Jews during the Holocaust. This was the case with a few policemen in Feodosiia,[68] as well as a Russian manager of the camp in Dzhankoi, who secretly supported Jewish and non-Jewish inmates by bringing them food.[69]

In the aforementioned cases, support to Jews was clandestine for obvious reasons. In contrast, what occurred in Feodosiia is of particular interest, as it stands out as the only case in which the collaboration administration or some of its representatives in the Crimea dared to speak out openly in favor of Jews. The German-appointed municipal administration of this town pleaded with the Germans on behalf of the elderly Jewish doctor Mikhail Fidlov.[70] Possible rationales behind this behavior of the administration included concern for the sanitary conditions in Feodosiia, the fact that this Jewish doctor was one of the most respectable people in the town, or, to a smaller extent, personal concern for the fate of a specific Jew. Regardless of the reasoning behind the decision, the case is unique.

It is noteworthy that in closed institutions such as orphanages, no responsible functionaries could be denounced by outsiders, as the latter did not know what was going on within its walls. Therefore, relatively large-scale rescues of all Jews in such institutions could sometimes occur. The workers in them were eager and able to help Jews on the rare occasions they could manage to do so. This was the case with the rescue of 25 (36, according to another source[71]) Jewish children, saved by the director and personnel of the Mamak orphanage near Simferopol'.[72] The children, including those who had managed to escape from the extermination actions and return to the orphanage, were then given clean "Aryan" passports (with their age often reduced in order to avoid their deportation to forced labor in

68 Goldenberg, "Tragediia evreiskoi obschiny Feodosii," p. 60.

69 Account edited by Lev Kvitko in Grossman and Erenburg, *Chernaia kniga*, pp. 291-294. According to the testimony, he was betrayed by one of the camp inmates and severely beaten by the Germans: Story of Grigorii Purevich in idem., *The Complete Black Book of Russian Jewry*, p. 232.

70 West, *In the Ropes of Destruction*, pp. 142-143.

71 Account of D. I. Makarycheva, [no date], DAARK, P-156/1/36, pp. 28-40.

72 List of names of Jewish children saved by M. S. Pruss (director) and the personnel of the Mamak orphanage, no later than 1943, DAARK, P-156/1/40, p. 84.

Germany) and later transferred to Slavic families, who adopted them.[73] The following evidence is indicative of what was described above:

> 14-year-old Pavel Polatnik was not finished off during the action in Simferopol'. He came back to the orphanage directed by Maria Stanislavovna Gruz. A man of confidence in the registration department issued an "Aryan" ID for him; his age was reduced from 14 to 12. By the same token (including provision with "Aryan" IDs), 36 Jewish children were saved, including Viktor Zel'tsman (his age was reduced from 16 to 12) and Bella Kaplan (5 years old).[74]

During the Holocaust, a certain number of Jews found themselves in Russian, Russian-Ukrainian, and, to a lesser extent, Bulgarian, Greek, or Armenian villages in the Crimea. Some had lived there prior to the outbreak of the war, but most moved there after the killing operations. In the villages, the Jews were totally dependent on the good will of the village headmen (*starosty*), whom the occupation authorities had appointed to these positions, and sometimes on Russian policemen raised from the local inhabitants.[75] German policy in the Crimea created masters of life and death out of these headmen in their localities. The headmen were solely responsible for sanctioning strangers' stays in his settlement and, according to German regulations, had to report any Jewish presence immediately to the nearest German or Romanian authorities.

Headmen usually treated the Jews in accordance with the German orders, often out of fear of German reprisals.[76] This was

73 Thank-you letter of M. I. Rimmer to M. S. Pruss, director of the Mamak orphanage, for the rescue of children in the orphanage during the occupation, no earlier than April 14, 1944, DAARK, P-156/1/40, p. 83.

74 Account of D. I. Makarycheva, [no date], DAARK, P-156/1/36, pp. 28-40.

75 "Urteil gegen Karl R. Pallmann, Paul H. Lorenz, Hans H. Jakob, Erich Buballa, Otto Dolezych, Josef Kappl, Carl Friedrich M. Berherns wegen Mordes," July 22, 1971, YVA, TR.10/724, p. 55.

76 Near Staryi Krym, unidentified area, Kerchenskii *raion*, testimony of Khanania Kurzon, August 3, 2000, YVHN; FK 810, "TB für die Zeit vom 27.2-13.3.1942," March 13, 1942, YVA, M.29.FR/40, p. 28 in Gubenko, *Kniga pechali*, p. 28.

particularly so during the first months of the German occupation, when the German successes had loomed large compared to partisan activities and their possible repercussions. Fear of denunciation by other villagers and a high prize (up to 100 Reichsmarks) offered by the Germans for the extradition of hidden Jews created a special momentum.[77] Then, according to German wartime reports, local collaborators in the Russian villages "expressed readiness to kill the Jews on their own."[78] A Soviet wartime source indeed confirms that the personal involvement of Russian headmen and policemen in the extermination of Jews was not an uncommon phenomenon, mostly at the initial stages of the German conquest. Headmen and policemen were involved in several stages of the active anti-Jewish measures, such as turning Jews in hiding over to the Germans,[79] guarding them at assembly points,[80] and assisting the Germans in conducting the executions.[81] They even reached the point of leading the hunt for Jews, as it was the case in "Molotov" *kolkhoz*:

> In December 1941, the Germans and local policemen conducted a round-up and execution of the Jews. 21 people escaped in the steppe and hid in a ditch... They came to get bread in the village. The starosta assembled men and conducted an ambush. Thus, those who came to get bread at the house of kolkhoznik Bereziuk were caught. They were locked in the office and guarded by the policemen.[82]

77 Feodosiiskii *raion*, North Crimea: *Kem byl Gitler v deistvitelnosti?* (Moskva, 1982), YVA, 0.32/62, p. 7; Account of D. I. Makarycheva, [no date], DAARK, P-156/1/36, p. 90.

78 OSR USSR, no. 145, CSPSS, Berlin, December 12, 1941, YVA, 0.51/165 II.

79 Unknown locality, village of Nagaichi: Decree of Ganon, the military investigator of the Military Prosecutor's Office, June 19, 1944, GARF, 7021/9/84, p. 42; Gubenko, *Kniga pechali*, p. 46.

80 Ichkinskii *raion*, interrogation of Georgii Moskotov, May 13, 1946, USHMMA, RG-74.001/16.

81 Villages of Friling, Lekkert, and Rottenshtadt: Questioning of Evgeniia Padaia, July 23, 1944, YVA, M.33/63, p. 35; Memorandum "O zverstvakh nemetsko-fashistskikh okkupantov i ikh prispeshnikov v Krymskoi ASSR," May 21, 1944, GARF, 7021/9/194, p. 121.

82 Akt of the Commission of "Molotov" *kolkhoz*, Evpatoriiskii *raion*: June 24, 1944, GARF, 7021/9/79, p. 27.

In November 1941-June 1942, the Wehrmacht often deployed its troops around Crimean villages. Particularly strict residence and movement regulations were introduced in the area, which almost entirely curtailed the possibility that a *starosta* would act positively towards the Jews. The following evidence from a partisan source about the village of Ablesh-Nemetskii illustrates the role of the *starosta*:

> It was very difficult [for the liaison man of the partisan movement] to stay here due to the following strict regulation. The head of every family was obliged to place a list of his family members on the door of his house. The list had to be confirmed by the *starosta*. If it was revealed during a security check that more people were present in the house than recorded on the list, the whole family was shot. [The local] population terrorized by the Germans fears to offer accommodation even to close relatives.[83]

The testimony points to the *starosta*'s apparent omnipotence in determining the fate of the strangers in his village, among them persecuted Jews who wandered around the Crimean peninsula. At the same time, it is also indicative of the *starosta*'s own life being at stake if he violated German directives. Such being the case, he was left to the mercy of his fellow villagemen, who potentially could have denounced him, especially if there were Germans in the area. Therefore, in such locations it was virtually impossible for the village headman to support the Jews.[84]

However, in the event that there were no German troops in the area, the headmen enjoyed a certain amount of freedom with respect to enabling Jews to stay in his locality. At such times, their behavior was less stringent. Furthermore, despite the fact that the Germans appointed the *starosta* from carefully screened

83 Genov, *Dnevnik partizana*, p. 195 (entry from April 26, 1942).

84 Village of Topalovka: Account of D. I. Makarycheva, [no date], DAARK, P-156/1/36, p. 92.

people who appeared sympathetic to German rule,[85] the Soviet underground succeeded in planting its own people as headmen in some villages.[86] Some findings indicate that these small islands of Soviet influence turned into a real shelter for Jews in the German-occupied Crimea,[87] even though headmen sometimes compelled the Jews to work in return.[88]

Other headmen were unwilling to run the risk of allowing the Jews into their villages. Yet, they turned them away without reporting these cases to the Germans, although this also entailed danger for the *starosta* himself.[89] Headmen rarely went further in assisting the Jews, as they did not wish to compromise their positions. However, one headman did extend a semblance of help, although he still urged the Jew to abandon his village:

> When Max Solomin arrived at a certain village, its headman told him that he would not be able to stay in the village because his Jewish accent betrayed him. Max Solomin proposed to pose as a deaf-and-mute. The headman approved of the idea and made an inscription in his passport to this effect, but refused to let him stay in the village.[90]

85 "Urteil gegen Karl R. Pallmann, Paul H. Lorenz, Hans H. Jakob, Erich Buballa, Otto Dolezych, Josef Kappl, Carl Friedrich M. Berherns wegen Mordes," July 22, 1971, YVA, TR.10/724, p. 55.

86 By the end of 1942, the Soviet authorities had recorded eight cases in which the German-appointed headmen worked for the Crimean partisan movement. "The following headmen work for us: Seitlerskii *raion*, village of Burnash – deputy regional headman (*raionnyi starosta*); Ichkinskii *raion* – regional *starosta*; Zuevskii *raion*, village of Baraskhan; Starokrymskii *raion* – regional headman; Starokrymskii *raion*, village of Chernyi Kosh; Starokrymskii *raion*, village Kresty; Kolaiskii *raion* – regional headman." Note of Committee of the VKP(b) on the situation of the partisan movement in the Crimea, December 18, 1942, in Kondranov and Stepanova, *Krym v period Velikoi Otechestvennoi voiny* p. 253.

87 "Krasnyi Pakhar'" *kolkhoz*; village of Turmanovka, Dzhankoiskii *raion*: Mina Fishgoit's report, [no date], YVA, P.21.2/9; File of Varvara and Nikolai Linichenko, Ivan Radov and Vera Kudritskaia, Efrosinia and Gavriil Smirnov, 2003, YVA, M.31/10159.

88 "Krasnyi Pakhar'" *kolkhoz*: Mina Fishgoit's report, [no date], YVA, P.21.2/9.

89 Unidentified villages: Mina Fishgoit's report, [no date], YVA, P.21.2/9.

90 Unidentified village: Testimony of Max Solomin, [1944], YVA, M.35/14, p. 88.

Few headmen authorized Jews to stay in their villages without valid IDs.[91] Only in a small number of sources is it explicitly claimed that greed outweighed the *starosta*'s fear of being denounced to the Germans. In such cases, the headmen either capitalized on the situation of the Jews by taking a bribe,[92] overtly exploiting and plundering them,[93] or even "employing" them semi-officially in distant areas for many months after the first killing operations.[94] Sometimes if a headman suspected a person of being Jewish, he did his best to get rid of him or her in a "humane" fashion, i.e., something besides turning the Jew into the Germans, which would have certainly resulted in execution. In one example, the headman accelerated the suspect's deportation to perform forced labor in Germany.[95] Apparently in this case, the *starosta* had concluded that the profit he could gain from exploiting the suspect was not worth it if it turned out that the latter was Jewish.

It is noteworthy that on some occasions, headmen or Russian policemen who were otherwise noted for their indifferent, if not hostile, attitudes towards "other" Jews helped those with whom they had connections. For example, some kept their Jewish wives[96] or gave protection to Jews who were more distant relatives. The Ukrainian headman of the village of Topalovka was known for his vigorous persecution of "other" Jews, but the following evidence indicates that he tried to help a Jewish family member:

91 Dzhankoiskii and Evpatoriiskii *raiony*: Account edited by Lev Kvitko in Grosmman and Erenburg, *Chernaia kniga*, p. 294; Gubenko, *Kniga pechali*, p. 13.

92 "Voroshilov" *kolkhoz*, all their money and the only gold jewelry the family had: Story of Esfir' (Esther) Vaikhanskaia in Gubenko, *The Book of Sorrows*, pp. 101-102.

93 Village of Topalovka: Account of D. I. Makarycheva, [no date], DAARK, P-156/1/36, p. 91.

94 Village of Sivashskoe: FK 774 (Abt. VII), "Lagebericht für April-Mai 1942," May 17, 1942, YVA, 0.51/185 I, p. 12.

95 Village of Bakhcheli: Story of Fania Margolina in Gubenko, *The Book of Sorrows*, pp. 55-57.

96 Villages of Dos-Dzhurchili and Naibrot: OK I/742 in Freidorf, FG, "TB für April 1942," April 26, 1942, YVA, 0.51/185 II, p. 3; OK I(V)/742, "TB für die Zeit vom 10.-26.5.1942," Fraidorf, May 26, 1942, YVA, M.29.FR/37, p. 39.

> Magarov protected a Jewish woman with two children because she was his brother's wife. The brother had been drafted into the Army. However, this woman and her children were denounced and executed.[97]

The last remark from the above testimony sheds light on long-term prospects of Jewish survival in the Russian villages in the Crimea: even Jews who enjoyed the protection of the most powerful man in the village could be denounced and handed over to the Germans.

From the very onset of the occupation, despite their general reluctance to invest heavily in administering the Crimea, German authorities allocated special budgets to spread antisemitic propaganda throughout the peninsula.[98] Analysis of the most widespread Crimean newspaper at the time, *Golos Kryma*, published in Simferopol' in Russian,[99] as well as the content of radio broadcasts,[100] reveals the considerable scope of virulent and vulgar antisemitic propaganda.[101] The overall efficiency of this propaganda effort is difficult to assess, but the research conducted by Mikhail Tiaglyi suggests that its continuous operation had a profound effect on at least some segments of the Crimean population.[102]

97 Account of D. I. Makarycheva, [no date], DAARK, P-156/1/36, p. 95.

98 On the German-instigated antisemitic propaganda in the occupied Soviet territories, see Robert E. Herzstein, "Anti-Jewish Propaganda in the Orel Region of Great Russia, 1942-1943: The German Army and its Nazi Collaborators," *Simon Wiesenthal Center Annual* 6 (1989): pp. 33-56.

99 A. A. Kokhan, "Gazeta "Golos Kryma" v strukture organov nemetskoi propagandy: 1941-1944 gg.," *Istorichni i politologichni doslidzhennia* 3-4 (45-46) (2010): pp. 230-236; Tiaglyi, "The Role of Antisemitic Doctrine in German Propaganda in the Crimea, 1941–1944": pp. 421-459.

100 Crimean Collection of materials of the Department of Propaganda of the German Propaganda Staff in the Crimea on ideological influence on the population, *Radiovestnik*, nos. 1, 5, 7-9, 12, DAARK, P-156/1/27.

101 Testimony of Efim Gopshtein, August 16, 1944, YVA, M.35/21, pp. 172-173; Tiaglyi, "The Role of Antisemitic Doctrine in German Propaganda in the Crimea, 1941–1944": p. 425.

102 Ibid., pp. 445-448.
On the extent of antisemitism among local collaborators, see Vladimir Solonari, "Hating Soviets—Killing Jews: How Antisemitic Were Local Perpetrators in Southern Ukraine, 1941–42?" *Kritika: Explorations in Russian and Eurasian History* 15, no. 3 (Summer 2014): pp. 505-533.

2.1.3. Ordinary people

The predominantly Russian and Ukrainian population of the Crimean towns displayed various patterns of behavior towards the Jewish plight.[103] According to the diary of a Russian inhabitant of Simferopol', the Slavic population displayed sympathy towards the Jews *en masse* and even helped them. In the entry written just a couple of days before the killing operation, he noted that:

> During last five weeks, Russian people… continue to maintain relations with Jews, none of them refuse to meet them, Russians refuse to show the Germans apartments of "*iudy*"[104] on the pretext that they know none, they hasten to warn the Jews on the arrival of German plunderers, and take Jewish possessions for keeping. In the streets I see Russians walking together with Jews who bear stars all the time. Russian children continue to play with Jewish ones, and the adults never forbade it.[105]

On the other hand, diametrically opposed attitudes of the local Russian population towards the Jews were expressed in an EG D report from January 19, 1942, which noted that the Slavic population[106] positively received news of the shooting of Jews and Krymchaks. The report is as follows:

> The deportation of the Jews, Krymchaks, and Gypsies… is generally welcomed. This again proves the general rejection of Jewry on the part of the population in the countryside, as well as in the towns.[107]

103 The population of all Crimean towns, except Bakhchisarai, Dzhankoi, and Karasubazar, had a Russian-Ukrainian majority.

104 i.e., Jews. The way the word is spelled here and was frequently pronounced by the Germans has an additional pejorative connotation in Russian because it closely resembles the Biblical Judas.

105 Diary of Chrisanf Lashkevich, entry from December 7, 1942, DAARK, P-156/1/31, p. 72.

106 When the Crimean Tatars are meant in the EG D reports, they are explicitly referred to.

107 OSR USSR, no. 157, CSPSS, Berlin, January 19, 1942, in Arad, Krakowski, and Spektor, *The Einsatzgruppen Reports*, pp. 284-286.

There is no contradiction between these two sources. Initially, the dominant attitude of the Crimean Russians towards the Jews was compassion and solidarity on the one hand, and aloofness on the other.[108] The German report, however, was written after the killing operation and "retaliations" against the Crimean Russians, when the mood of the local Russians was already strongly characterized by fear. To this one must add the fear of German punishment for failure to denounce Jews (punishable by death).[109] Aside from this sentiment, antisemitism tracing back to the prewar period was another factor affecting the behavior of some ordinary Russians and Ukrainians towards Jews. The Russian wife of a Jew in Sevastopol' stated:

> Though my husband was in possession of [a] Russian passport and certificate of baptism from 1919, he was arrested due to denunciation... Prior to the arrival of the Germans, the informer who led to my husband's arrest had threatened me. She knocked at my door and said "Wait!" The Germans will come and then we'll show you!"[110]

Unfortunately, almost no documental evidence was preserved concerning the informers and their motives. For a variety of political reasons, Soviet post-liberation reports downplayed the subject as far as Russians and Ukrainians were concerned, and rarely went into details. For their part, the Germans contended themselves with general observations, such as "The Crimean population is anti-Jewish and occasionally brings Jews to the *Kommando* for liquidation."[111]

At the same time, there exists abundant evidence from Jewish and Soviet sides of sympathetic behavior displayed by Crimean Russians towards Jews. The dimensions of such behavior

108 Simferopol': Conversation with Mariia Borodina, 1945 (?), DAARK, P-156/1/37.

109 Kerch: Order no. 5 of the German Security Police, [no date], USHMMA, RG-31.030M, reel 1.

110 Statement of N. V. Mendel'son, May 27, 1944, YVA, M.33/66, p. 20.

111 OSR USSR, no. 145, CSPSS, Berlin, December 12, 1941, YVA, 0.51/165 II.

may be consciously accentuated in both types of the sources due to the need to highlight the so-called "brotherhood of nations" and other political reasons. Still, this is important evidence, and in most cases it may be relied upon, albeit with a due degree of caution. Among the various non-Jewish responses sympathetic to the Jews, attempts to save Jewish children stand out.[112] In most cases, this behavior apparently stemmed from humanitarian concerns and the desire of childless couples to have children of their own. The occurrences in Simferopol' are illuminating in this respect:

> In a number of cases, the Russians crowded up in front of the building in Simferopol' where Jews were gathered and brought food and possessions. The Russians also wrote requests to receive Jewish children, stating that they were ready to adopt and baptize them.[113]

Occasionally, Russians living in rural areas were willing to save Jewish children. In one case, however, the headman of the village of Pervomaiskoe, whom the Germans held personally responsible for eliminating all the Jews in his locality, did not allow the local Russians to do so. He stated in no uncertain terms that the case would be regarded as providing shelter to the Jews, with obvious implications to the villagers: "If you don't turn them in you're going in there with them!"[114] Those who adopted Jewish children ran the risk of being persecuted and murdered themselves, and in order to counter this danger they tended to move away from their native localities.[115] Sometimes people who had initially adopted Jewish children were unable to bear

112 Kerch, Simferopol': "Story of Iosef Vaingarten" (Yiddish), *Eynikayt*, July 15, 1942, p. 1; File of Kolesnikova, 1993, YVA, M.31/5541; File of Mikhail and Tat'iana Gur'ianov, 2000, YVA, M.31/8796.

113 Testimony of Efim Gopshtein, August 16, 1944, entry from December 12, 1941, DAARK, P-156/1/31, p. 79.

114 Story of Israel' Smol'ianskii in Gubenko, *The Book of Sorrows*, p. 92.

115 From Kerch to a *kolkhoz* near Dzhankoi: Story of Vaingarten in Grossman and Erenburg, *Chernaia kniga*, p. 283.

the burden, and got rid of them by bringing them to the authorities.[116]

Some Russians and Ukrainians did assist Jewish survivors of the killing operations. This consisted of providing them with shelter,[117] bare essentials,[118] and/or medical assistance. The following testimony is from Kerch in November-December 1941:

> After surviving the execution near Kerch, I returned to a clinic in the town because my medical condition had deteriorated gravely. Despite the fact that I did not have any ID or money, the clinic's manager arranged my treatment in the clinic for two weeks until I got better.[119]

A number of people gave the Jews "Aryan" IDs free of charge while others sold them. Such people ran the risk of being denounced, revealed, and/or killed for rendering aid to Jews. Given the fact that the quantity of the evidence indicating rescue activity on the part of the Crimean Russians is rather limited, it must be emphasized that it is quite possible that sooner or later the Germans detected and killed most of them, leaving almost no trace of their deeds.

In villages, the behavior of ordinary inhabitants must be seen against the background of that of their headmen. It appears that for the most part, the locals complied with the anti-Jewish policies of their *starosta*.[120] Occasionally, ordinary villagers followed their

116 Village Saragol': "Alla-Roza Brazgol," Lev Kvitko, ed., [no date], YVA, M.35/14, p. 90.

117 Armenians in Sevastopol'; Greeks in Karasubazar and Yalta: File of Leonidi et al., YVA, M.31/8955; Story of Sal'nik-Korsakina in Gel'man and Glubochanskii, *Kholokost*, pp. 124-5, 128.

118 Village near Kerch: Story of Iosif Vaingarten in Grossman and Erenburg, *Chernaia kniga*, p. 283.

119 Ibid.

120 Village of Topalovka: Account of D. I. Makarycheva, [no date], DAARK, P-156/1/36.
Rarely were ordinary peasants more zealous then their headmen in persecuting Jews. In the village of Kangil (Karasubazarskii *raion*), the *starosta* allowed a number of Jews to stay overnight. But the next day, his nephew, suspecting that they were Jewish, turned them in to the Romanian HQ. Story of Aleksandra Gershtein in Gubenko, *The Book of Sorrows*, pp. 58-61.

headmen in persecuting Jews themselves.[121] However, there is also evidence that rural citizens helped Jews in defiance of the headmen's orders. In November-December 1941, Russian inhabitants of the village of Frunze consistently brought food during the night to five Jewish families.[122] Sometimes, Russian peasants provided Jews with essential goods.[123] If there were no Germans or Romanians in the area, they sometimes even went further by giving the Jews a permanent shelter.[124] It is of note that unlike in the towns, there is no record that "transgressors" were ever punished for rendering aid to Jews in villages. The headmen preferred to solve such problems within their villages so as to avoid giving the Germans pretext to meddle in their affairs.

Of importance are the attitudes of the non-Jewish sides in mixed families towards their spouses and children. Some non-Jews handed their Jewish spouses over to the Germans;[125] in contrast, others risked grieving publicly over their spouses who went to the assembly points.[126] In Karasubazar, a husband turned in his wife but managed to save their four children.[127] Others were able to save some children, while the rest were arrested and killed;[128] some managed to keep all their children alive.[129] Non-Jewish parents were sometimes unaware of the

121 Village of Novyi Karagurt: File of Danil Kamchenko, 1944, ASBU RK, No 6567, pp. 117-121, courtesy of the USHMM.

122 Questioning of Mariia Rozhkovskaia, July 22, 1944, YVA, M.33/63, p. 28.

123 Near Kerch: Story of Khaimovich, in the report of the Metropolitan Nikolai (member of the ESC), "From Day to Day" (Yiddish), *Eynikeyt*, March 17, 1945, p. 2.

124 Armenians in the village of Baruncha; Russians and Ukrainians in the villages of Dobrushino and Opan': Story of Aleksandra Gershtein in Gubenko, *The Book of Sorrows*, pp. 58-61; File of Dar'ia Striletskaia, Vera Voronina, and Liubov' Cherletskaia, 2001, YVA, M.31/9500.

125 Karasubazar: Questioning of Bekir Smolskii, February 4, 1944, YVA, M.33/82, p. 33.

126 Simferopol': Diary of Chrisanf Lashkevich, entry from December 12, 1941, DAARK, P-156/1/31, p. 86.

127 Ibid.

128 Simferopol': Interrogation of Ekaterina Sirota (1897), June 22, 1944, GARF, 7021/9/194, p. 162.

129 Simferopol', Yalta: Statement of Vera Sigalenko, August 3, 1944, YVA, M.33/68, p. 163; File of Mariia Frolova, Porfirii Kulik, and Anton and Elena Artemis, 2003, YVA, M.31/9983.

final verdict, and learned that they were exempted from the fate of the Jews only upon arrival at the assembly point.[130] In Yalta, some officially registered non-Jewish spouses continued visiting their Jewish husbands and wives up until the last days of the ghetto, at which time they were prevented from doing so.[131]

Once revealed, non-Jewish parents in hiding were usually given a choice. In some cases, mothers followed their children,[132] or non-Jewish husbands voluntarily followed their Jewish wives and children when the latter were arrested.[133] For example, this was the case of a Russian man in the Artek pioneer camp. As the Germans were about to take his Jewish wife, he took her by hand and said, "Well, I am also coming. We are the same (*my odinakovye liudi*)," and they were executed together.[134] A semi-official Soviet postwar testimony (written by a former Crimean partisan) claimed that all Russian spouses refused to part with their Jewish wives and husbands when the German officers offered them the opportunity to do so on the eve of the killing operation in Yalta,[135] but this may very well have been another Soviet attempt to present the "brotherhood of nations."

130 Simferopol': Memoirs of A. F. Peganova, November 9, 1944, DAARK, P-156/1/40, p. 43.

131 Report of Margarita Frolova-Meltsyna, [no date], YVA, 0.33/626, p. 6; Statement of Aleksandr Ponomarev, GARF, 7021/9/59, p. 84 (?).

132 Simferopol', village of Uchkui-Tarkhan: "Strafsache gegen Walter Bierkamp," Bayerisches Landeskriminalamt, Vernehmungniederschrift, W. Max Wilhelm, May 22, 1964, YVA, TR.10/1147, pp. 426-427; Gubenko, *The Book of Sorrows*, p. 96.

133 Sevastopol' and Simferopol': Report of the Metropolitan Nikolai, "From Day to Day" (Yiddish), *Eynikeyt,* March 17, 1945, p. 2; Diary of Chrisanf Lashkevich, entry from July 28, 1942, DAARK, P-156/1/31, p. 50.

134 Leonid Sobolev, *Dorogami pobedy: Odessa, Krym, Sevastopol'* (Moscow: Khudozhestvennaia literatura, 1944).

135 Vergasov, *Krymskie tetradi*, p. 49.

2.2. Crimean Tatars[136]

2.2.1. General concerns

Soviet sources indicate the mass desertion of Crimean Tatars from the Red Army[137] and their disclosure of partisan food basements to the Germans,[138] although it is evident that the dimensions of these developments and their comprehensiveness were deliberately accentuated in Soviet documents in order to conceal the failures of the Soviet command. Wartime and postwar evidence also demonstrate that from the beginning of the occupation, the Crimean Tatars had favored the German rule.[139] Significantly, they had emerged as a reliable pro-German force in the peninsula as early as November-December 1941, which coincided with the most comprehensive wave of killing operations against Jews.

This was an unparalleled development in the Crimea, especially given the fact that the fighting was still under way and the Germans had not subdued sizable parts of the peninsula. Among other things, it meant that while the impending outcome of the warfare in the Crimea was still unclear, many of the Crimean

136 Alexander Statiev, "The Nature of Anti-Soviet Armed Resistance, 1942-44: The North Caucasus, the Kalmyk Autonomous Republic, and the Crimea," *Kritika: Explorations in Russian and Euroasian History* 6, no. 2 (Spring 2005): pp. 306-314; Brian G. Williams, "The Hidden Cleansing of Muslims in the Soviet Union: The Exile and Repatriation of the Crimean Tatars," *Journal of Contemporary History* 37, no. 3 (2002): pp. 323-348.

137 "The overwhelming majority of the deserters are Tatars. Appointed commanders and commissars for the most part came over to German service." Report "O polozhenii i deiatel'nosti partizanskikh chastei v Krymu" by the Political Department of the Maritime Army, May 14, 1942, YVA, M.37/378, p. 7; "Predatel'skaia rol' tatarskogo naseleniia v period okkupatsii Kryma," 1944, DAARK, P-156/1/41.

138 "The food was placed primarily by means of the Tatar guides, and when the Germans came they plundered these storages with the guides-betrayers." Vergasov, *V gorakh Tavrii*, p. 37; Kozlov, *V Krymskom podpol'ie*, p. 77; "Predatel'skaia rol' tatarskogo naseleniia v period okkupatsii Kryma," 1944, DAARK, P-156/1/41.

139 CSpSd, Kommandostab, MbOg, no. 1, Berlin, May 1, 1942, RGVA, 500/1/775, pp. 77-78; OK II/937/V, "TB für die Zeit vom 1.-15.2.1942," Karasubazar, February 14, 1942, YVA, M.29.FR/40, p. 3; Bidermann, *In Deadly Combat*, p. 120.

Tatars pinned their hopes on a German victory – at least on the local scale, as indicated in the EG D report from January 1942:

> The Tatars, who freely offered their services to the Germans, declared that they can only accept existence under German protection. They rightly assume that they would be totally exterminated if the Reds return.[140]

During the Soviet counter-offensive in late December 1941-January 1942, masses of the Crimean Tatars aligned themselves with the Germans, ending the possibility of supporting the Soviet side. In retrospect, this constituted a point of no return for them: as a group, as the Soviets never forgot this.

As indicated in "The Crimea and the North Caucasus: Historical Background," the seeds of the Tatars' discontent with the Soviet regime had been sown long before the entry of the German troops into the peninsula in October-November 1941. It seems that a considerable number of Tatars, mostly among the intellectual elite and religious traditionalists, continued to view themselves as the Crimea's leading nation. For them, the Tatars' gradual loss of cultural and political autonomy during the interwar period, as well as the Soviet crackdown on religion, was another step in robbing them of their rulership and land in the peninsula, first by Imperial Russian and then by Soviet colonization. For those Crimean Tatars, the Germans appeared as a convenient tool for restoring historical justice and reinstalling their ancient rights in the peninsula.

2.2.2. Collaborators

According to statistical estimates, from early December 1941, thousands of Crimean Tatars served in German-trained military formations. Some 10,000 Tatars had been drafted into the Red Army,[141] but the number of Crimean Tatars who fought on the

140 OSR USSR, no. 157, CSPSS, Berlin, January 19, 1942, in Arad, Krakowski, and Spektor, *The Einsatzgruppen Reports,* pp. 284-286.

141 Valentin Bojzow, "Aspekte der miltärischen Kollaboration in der UdSSR von 1941-1944," in Röhr, *Okkupation und Kollaboration (1938-1945)*, p. 306; Hoffmann, *Die Ostlegionen 1941-43*, p. 44.

German side amounts to 20,000 people.[142] All Tatar POWs were released from the camps.[143] By February 1942, the EG D alone had recruited 5,451 Tatars, and not every candidate was accepted.[144] These figures should be considered with the following facts in mind: Conscription into the Red Army was obligatory, and covered the best (in terms of combat ability) age groups. In contrast, enlistment in the German-sponsored formations was more voluntary, and encompassed the remaining age groups; thus, to some extent, it served as a litmus test of the Tatars' attitudes towards the German occupation.

Many Crimean Tatars (recruited primarily from the POWs) were attached to regular Wehrmacht units, and engaged in warfare around the Crimea;[145] there is no record of their participation in the persecution of Jews. Others were placed in a special detachment, the so-called "Tatar" or "Caucasian" company, trained and guided solely by the EG D men.[146] This unit was engaged in a variety of the *Einsatzgruppe* activities, such as arresting those suspected of being either Soviet activists or Jews,[147] performing round-ups, and participating in anti-partisan warfare.[148] Other sources document

142 Bojzow, "Aspekte der miltärischen Kollaboration," p. 306; Zur Mühlen, *Zwinschen Hakenkreuz und Sowjetstern*, p. 184.

143 Bojzow, "Aspekte der miltärischen Kollaboration," p. 306; Kirimal, *Der Nationale Kampf der Krimtürken*, p. 305.

144 Angrick, "Die Einsatzgruppe D und die Kollaboration," p. 78; Nationalsozialistische Deutsche Arbeiter-Partei, Schutzstaffel, Sicherheitspolizei, *Die Einsatzgruppen in der bezetzten Sowjetunion 1941/42*, pp. 397-398.

145 Interrogation of Amed Isliamov, May 31, 1944, GARF, 7021/9/194, p. 246. See also "Predatel'skaia rol' tatarskogo naseleniia v period okkupatsii Kryma," 1944, DAARK, P-156/1/41.

146 Hoffmann, *Die Ostlegionen 1941-43*, p. 43.

147 Bakhchisaraiskii *raion*, Simferopol': "Strafsache gegen Walter Bierkamp," Staatsanwaltschaft, München, Berlin, Herr Fritz U., Vernehmungsniederschrift, December 6, 1962, YVA, TR.10/1147, p. 377; File of Chakai Kurtvab, 1944, ASBU RK, No 13759, pp. 9-27; File of Musa Musaev, 1944, ASBU RK, no. 15614, pp. 15-38, courtesy of the USHMM.

148 Simferopol', unidentified areas: Files of Kurtvab and Musaev, files of Bekir Usein Abibulaev, Seit Khalil Abliaev, Asan Ali Dabla, Seit Memet Bekirov, Il'mi Dzhemilev, Ismail Izedinov, Memet Izmailov, Aiza Memetov, Belial'Memetov, Ibraim Chki, Isan Shernazarov, Refat Useinov, and Ismail Beretdin, 1944, ASBU RK, No 6941, courtesy of the USHMM.

the "revealing, arrests, and execution of the Jewish and Gypsy population"[149] and "cleansing a prison of its Jewish and other inmates."[150] What follows is the statement of a former Tatar soldier of this company during the course of his interrogation in 1950:

> In February 1942, I guarded the detained Jews… marched [them] out for execution outside of the town Dzhankoi. We prepared those detained for the execution… The Germans shot them. We dug [the graves of] those executed.[151]

For obvious reasons, the soldier kept his silence regarding the involvement of the company soldiers, including his own share in the killing operation itself. Yet, it is known that in other occupied Soviet areas, the SS resorted widely to binding its recruits raised in among the local population and POWs "by blood," i.e., by having them participate in murderous activities.[152] Consequently, it is quite possible that the company soldiers executed Jews in such *Aktionen.*

The Tatars serving in these units were given the property of the executed Jews, including Jewish apartments, as remuneration for their services.[153] All this took place after the recruitment of the Tatars was enabled in January 1942; therefore, they could not have participated in the initial killing operations conducted in November-December 1941 but only in those conducted in the "post-action" period. It is difficult to regard the behavior of the Tatars who enrolled in these units and their attitudes towards the Jews as a free expression of specifically Tatar national aspirations, as there is no certainty regarding what led the Tatar POWs to join them. On the one hand, they were released from POW camps

149 Unidentified areas since July 1942: Interrogation of Edem Khalilev, May 27, 1944, GARF, 7021/9/194, p. 240. See also Sevastopol': Interrogation of Giul'nara Khalilova (Seidova), April 7, 1947, USHMMA, RG-31.018M, reel 7 and Simferopol': Dean, "Examination of KGB Trial Files," pp. 17-19,

150 Simferopol': "Urteil in der Strafsache gegen Walther Kehrer und Max Drexler," September 17, 1975, YVA, TR.10/865, p. 34.

151 Interrogation of Suleiman Fizlos, March 9, 1950, USHMMA, RG-74.001/12.

152 For example, Kovalev, *Natsistskaia okkupatsiia i kollaboratsionizm*, p. 65.

153 Interrogation of Amed Dinshaev, May 31, 1944, GARF, 7021/9/194, p. 243.

following the German decision to favor Crimean Tatars — i.e., they were excluded from Germany's discriminatory policies towards other Soviet POWs. Their enlistment in this unit appeared to be voluntary; those selected by the EG D were not sent back to camps, but eventually released to serve in other German-sponsored formations. On the other hand, it is assumed that the EG D recruited those Crimean Tatar POWs who were "healthy, robust, and ready to perform any duty,"[154] but there is no information about their convictions for joining.

Larger numbers of Tatars voluntarily enrolled in local militias (*Schutzmanschaften*), established primarily in Tatar villages and designed to deal with specifically local security tasks.[155] They were subordinated to the commander of German police in the Crimea.[156] German influence on these forces was lower, and confined mainly to draft and combat instruction. The activity of these troops was mostly in the context of a distinctively Tatar national movement. However, the data available concerning these formations are scarce, and come mainly from the biased partisan or other Soviet wartime sources as the following report demonstrates: "The local [rural] Tatar population detains all those passing and brings them to Gestapo."[157] Soviet security reports maintained that the Tatar militiamen were paid salaries and given lands and property taken from other ethnic groups, mainly Russians and Greeks. They also received various tax preferences.[158] Other Soviet reports are more detailed with respect to the participation of Tatars in anti-partisan warfare,[159]

154 Dean, "Examination of KGB Trial Files," p. 16,

155 Kirimal, *Der Nationale Kampf Der Krimtürken*, p. 305.

156 Angrick, "Die Einsatzgruppe D und die Kollaboration," p. 79.

157 Referring to the data that the author possesses. Affidavit of the Deputy Head of the Special Section of the Headquarters' Main Directorate of the Partisan Movement of the Crimea Popov given in the Political Department of the Maritime Army, June 6, 1942, RGASPI, 69/1/621, p. 34.

158 Boris Kovalev, *Povsedenevnaia zhizn' Rossii v period natsistskoi okkupatsii* (Moscow: Molodaia gvardiia, 2011), pp. 218-219.

159 Akt of the 4th partisan detachment, February 1942 (?), DAARK, P-151/1/392; Information on the struggle of Crimean partisans in the Germans' rear, July 7, 1942, DAARK, P-1/1/2144a.

but, again, there is almost no record of their involvement in the Holocaust. It must be emphasized that the research regarding on-spot developments is greatly impeded by the fact that the Soviets deported the entire Crimean Tatar population from the Crimea in the spring-summer of 1944,[160] and there simply remained no one to question on site immediately after the war. The complete lack of other wartime survival testimonies of Ashkenazi Jews in the Tatar villages also perhaps suggests that Crimean Tatars tended to extradite those who entered their localities in pursuit of a safe shelter.[161]

There is more information concerning the Holocaust-related activity of the Tatar militias in the towns. German sources state explicitly that Tatars played an important role in the intelligence network created by the SD, and contributed to the exposure of hiding Jews.[162] Abundant evidence from various sources demonstrates that Tatar militiamen were involved in combing operations,[163] surveillance of the Jewish camp in Dzhankoi,[164] detecting arrested Jews[165] (including Jewish POWs[166]) and then

160 Dinara Khavadzhi, "Pravove reguluivannia natsionalnoi deportatsii z Krims'koi ARSR ta repatriatsii do Avtonomnoi Respubliki Krim u skladi Ukraini (1941-1996 rr.): istoriko-pravove doslidzhenia" (PhD diss., Natsyonal'nii universitet vnutrishnikh sprav, 2002); Greta Uehling, "Having a Homeland: Recalling the Deportation, Exile, and Repatriation of the Crimean Tatars to their Historic Homeland" (PhD diss., University of Michigan, 2000).

161 On the Tatars' attitudes towards the Krymchaks, see Chapter 5, "Fate of Karaites and Krymchaks in the Crimea and Mountain Jews in the North Caucasus during the Holocaust" and further on in the current chapter (section "Ordinary people").

162 Simferopol': OSR USSR, no. 157, CSPSS, Berlin, January 19, 1942, in Arad, Krakowski, and Spektor, *The Einsatzgruppen Reports,* pp. 284-286. See also the testimony of Serafima Babina, January 6, 2004, author's archive.

163 Simferopol': Staboffz., der FG, "TB als Anlage zum K," "TB für die Zeit vom 1.-31.1.1942," February 2, 1942, YVA, M.29.FR/60, p. 9, also in YVA, M.29. FR/118, p. 18.

164 Dzhankoi: OK II/939, "TB für die Zeit vom 11.-20.12.1941," Dzhankoi, December 20, 1941, YVA, M.29.FR/41, p. 50.

165 Simferopol': Diary of Chrisanf Lashkevich, entry from July 21, 1942, DAARK, P-156/1/31, p. 48.

166 Memoirs of Semeon Kriger, [no date], in Polian and Shneer, *Obrechennye pogibnut'*, p. 327. See also the statement of V. N. Romanova-Petrova, 1947, GARF, 7021/9/46, pp. 71-72.

guarding them,[167] and even in safeguarding the *Aktion* itself.[168] There also exists wartime and postwar evidence that Tatar units or individual policemen participated in killing the Jews.[169] Another wartime testimony mentions that Tatar forces were given a free hand in revealing and killing Jews hiding in Sevastopol':

> After the mass deportation of Jews took place Tatars... in the service of Gendarmerie were permitted to conduct arrests. They detected sick Jews, took them, and eliminated them themselves.[170]

A Soviet postwar investigation from 1947 supported the claim that the Tatars working for the local SD were actively involved in denouncing the Jews in Sevastopol'.[171]

One cannot fail to notice the wide spectrum of Tatar involvement in the persecution of Jews (from intelligence activity to participation in killings), which indicates that the Germans had great confidence in these forces. In rural areas, the Germans relied almost completely on the Tatar *Schutzmanschaften*, due to the paucity of the German troops there. Importantly, the Tatar local militias were raised from the first stage of the occupation and, thus, were occasionally

167 Simferopol': The testimony refers to *'kaukasischen Hilfswilligen'*. In the opinion of the author, in consideration of place and time, this is a clear implication of the Crimean Tatars. "Nachtragsanklageschrift in der Strafsache gegen Walter Kehrer," October 28, 1970, YVA, TR.10/802, pp. 3-4.

168 Dzhankoi and Evpatoriia: Interrogation of Dmitrii Pankeev, July 14, 1944, DAARK, R-1289/1/16, p. 24 and in GARF, 7021/9/193, p. 17; Report of the Crimean Commission on the Conclusion of the Investigation of the Outcome of the German Occupation of the Crimea, December 16, 1941, DAARK, P-156/1/32, p. 15.

169 Dzhankoi, Simferopol', POW camp near Sevastopol': DAARK, R-1289/1/16, p. 24; "Strafsache gegen Walter Bierkamp," Auswertung der Vernehmungsprotokolle russischer Zeugen von Bl. 1/92-65/40 d., Akte. Bl, 7, Iwan D., Ab Okt. 41 bei der Tataren-Komp, YVA, TR.10/1147, p. 576; Statement of V. N. Romanova-Petrova, 1947, GARF, 7021/9/46, pp. 71-72.

170 Statement of Aleksandra Ru(a)dzak, June 22, 1944, YVA, M.33/66, p. 23.

171 Interrogation of Giul'nara Khalilova (Seidova), April 7, 1947, USHMMA, RG-31.018M.

involved in carrying out various phases of the persecution of Jews, including their extermination.[172]

Some words should be said with respect to the political and ideological collaboration between the Crimean Tatars and Nazi Germany, and its repercussions on the unfolding Holocaust in the peninsula. A wartime Soviet report explicitly accused the Tatar national leadership of initiating the process of the mass enlistment of the Tatars for the German cause.[173] During the interrogations of former Tatar soldiers of the EG D unit conducted in 1944, it was claimed that Tatar politicians from the Simferopol' Muslim Committee had worked actively to convince the Tatar POWs to fight for the Germans.[174] However, given the fact that the deportation of Crimean Tatars was being conducted at this time precisely under this pretext, such findings must be approached with caution.

Secular aspects of anti-Jewish propaganda of the Crimean Tatars found their utmost expression in the publication of the organ of the Simferopol' Muslim Committee *Azat Krim* (Liberated Crimea) newspaper, published in the Tatar language twice a week from January 11, 1942.[175] Its circulation rose from 10,000 copies in 1942[176] to 15,000 in 1943.[177] *Azat Krim* adopted the Nazi antisemitic rhetoric, including the identification of Jews with Bolshevism.[178] The following excerpt from an article published in March 1942 is instructive:

172 "Gorkii" *kolkhoz*: Interrogation of Anna Popova, May 27, 1944, GARF, 7021/9/194, p. 97.

173 Report of the Secretary of the Crimean District Committee of the VKP(b) Vladimir Bulatov, December 20, 1941, in Bugai, *Deportatsiia narodov Kryma*, p. 56.

174 Interrogation of Edem Khalilev, May 27, 1944, GARF, 7021/9/194, p. 240; Interrogation of Amed Isliamov, May 31, 1944, GARF, 7021/9/194, p. 246.

175 Mikhail Tiaglyi, "Antisemitic doctrine in the Tatar Newspaper 'Azat Kirim' (1942-1944)," *Dapim: Studies on the Shoah* 25, no. 1 (2011): pp. 161-182.

176 Kirimal, *Der Nationale Kampf Der Krimtürken*, p. 307.

177 Oleg Roman'ko, *Musul'manskie legiony vo Vtoroi mirovoi voine* (Moscow: AST, 2004), p. 159.

178 Editorial "Europe at work (in Crimean Tatar)," *Azat Krim*, January 23, 1943; HQ of the Partisan Movement of the Crimea, report on the content of materials published in *Azat Krim* compiled by the Secretary of TsK VLKSM I. Iromashektov, June 28, 1943, DAARK, 151/1/388; Editorial, *Azat Krim*, April 6, 1943.

> If this was not a Jewish but indeed a worker and peasant state, how could it have been that all power was gathered in the hands of the Jews; that the Jews enjoyed all wealth, high awards, positions and profitable workplaces, spacious homes, the most fertile plots of land and other such things, all in Jewish hands?… If that state were truly the state of workers and farmers, why did the Jews and commissars have all the high positions?… One can pose thousands of such questions, but there is just one answer: this country was not the state of workers and farmers; it was a state in the hands of one group – it was a Jewish state.[179]

***

The aforementioned notions of a large-scale involvement in the "Final Solution" may characterize the Crimean Tatars as a group insofar as such a generalization is admissible. Yet, like every other people, individual Tatars who worked for the German administration or who were somehow connected to it displayed various patterns of behavior towards the Jews. On the one hand, there is evidence that Tatars denounced or otherwise persecuted Jews, even sometimes killing them. On the other hand, there is evidence of Tatars' attempts to rescue Jews to various degrees. However, such evidence does suffer from the problem of authenticity, resulting from the impossibility to substantiate many of the claims from the wartime sources. The following testimony, in which a Crimean Tatar working for the collaborationist administration in Karasubazar claimed to have made a number of rescue attempts, illustrates this notion:

> From those who survived the atrocities in Karasubazar I know: Piastro, Zhanna, whom I personally issued a Russian passport… and Gornogolovina, Nadezhda Grigor'evna, who escaped from Simferopol' when the action was under

179 *Azat Krim,* March 20, 1942, in Tiaglyi, "Antisemitic doctrine in the Tatar newspaper 'Azat Kirim,'" pp. 169-170.

> way there. I arranged for her an apartment in Karasubazar and provided her with a work as a secretary. I managed to save [the] three-year-old girl Vakulenko, Alla, daughter of a Russian father, employee of the NKVD, and a Jewish mother.[180]

Significantly, this man produced this testimony when he was interrogated by a Soviet security officer in 1944. It seems that by highlighting his successful efforts to save the lives of the Jews, he was trying to diminish his own involvement in the collaborationist administration (which could have included participation in various officially-sanctioned anti-Jewish measures). Yet, the personal data of the Jews he had apparently rescued and the fact that the events occurred in a small town give more plausibility to the account.

2.2.3. Ordinary people

As already mentioned, there is no evidence characterizing the behavior of the Tatar inhabitants of rural areas towards the Ashkenazi Jews. However, according to a number of recently produced testimonies, "rural" Tatars rescued some Krymchaks and mixed Karaite-Jewish families. In all the cases, the latter resembled the Tatars in their appearance and were proficient in the Tatar language.[181] Yet, all of these testimonies were produced decades after the events had allegedly taken place. The statements made in 2001 by two Krymchak women who claimed to be saved by a Tatar family in the village of Aiman-Kui in Kerchenskii *raion* in December 1941[182] are examples of such testimonies.

Tatars living in towns left a few more traces of their behavior towards the Jews, compared to the rural citizens. German military reports from December 1941 and February 1942 emphasized the especially "comfortable atmosphere" in the Tatar-dominated towns, where the population had a friendly disposition towards

180 Ibid.

181 Sevastopol'skii *raion* (?), Simferopol'skii *raion*: Interview with Andrei Gordeev (1960), August 2004, author's archive; Interview with Vladimir Peisakh, March 22, 2004, author's archive.

182 File of Adzhykadir and Aishe Kurtiev, 2001, YVA, M.31/8487.

the Germans and actively denounced Jews.[183] The testimony of a Jewish survivor also supports this claim.[184] According to a wartime Soviet testimony, Tatars instilled an atmosphere of terror among the Jews in Yalta,[185] but there are no concrete examples of what this really meant. The recently published memoirs of a Jewish survivor in Feodosiia reveal the various forms of the Tatars' maltreatment of Jews. According to her testimony, after the action (which her mixed Ukrainian-Jewish family had legally survived), Tatar children used to stone her and her brother by crying "*Zhidy*!"[186] At the same time, there is evidence that Tatars saved Jews in the towns with mixed populations,[187] or at least refrained from informing on the Jews in Tatar-dominated towns.[188]

Provided the testimonies of Tatars saving the Krymchaks and the mixed Jewish-Karaite families are authentic, this may suggest that the Tatars were more willing to save "their" Jews, that is, those with whom they had lived side by side for centuries. In contrast, "European" Jews were considered foreigners and deserved, at best, neutral treatment. At worst, they were deemed as invaders who had made incursions into the ancient Tatar land under the protection of first the Russian and then the Soviet state. In such cases, they were treated as enemies, and were either done away with in the villages or (apparently more frequently) handed over to the Germans.

183 Bakhchisarai, Karasubazar: OK Bachtschisaray, "TB," December 14, 1941, YVA, M.29.FR/41, p. 48; OK II/937/V, "TB für die Zeit vom 1.-15.2.1942," Karasubazar, February 14, 1942, YVA, M.29.FR/40, p. 3.

184 Bakhchisarai: Story of Sal'nik-Korsakina, in Gel'man and Glubochanskii, *Kholokost*, p. 123.

185 Statement of Aleksandr Ponomarev, June 30, 1944, YVA, M.33/368, p. 52.

186 Rozalia Krichevskaia, *Dvadtsat' deviat' mesiatsev iz detstva* (Beer Sheva, 1997), pp. 32-33.

187 Sevastopol' and Simferopol': "Tragic End of the Jewry in the Western Russia." See also the memoirs of Il'ia Sirota, February 16, 1945, DAARK, P-156/1/40, p. 116; Interview with Vladimir Peisakh, March 22, 2004, author's archive; Account of D. I. Makarycheva, [no date], DAARK, P-156/1/36.

188 Karasubazar: File of Sof'ia Leonidi and Venera Dinishaeva, [no date], YVA, M.31/8955.

Chapter Ten

The Local Population and the Holocaust in the North Caucasus[1]

1. German Population Policy in the Caucasus[2]

1.1. Towards the Russian[3] population

Unlike most territories that Germany hoped to seize in the East, according to Nazi plans, the Caucasus was eventually to be awarded to Turkey. Furthermore, the Transcaucasus (comprising of Georgia, Armenia, and Azerbaijan) was to be spared the horrors of the German *Hungerpolitik*, enjoying a relatively satisfactory food supply under

1 For a general survey of the local population in the North Caucasus during the German occupation, see Jeronim Perović, *Der Nordkaukasus unter russischer Herrschaft: Geschichte einer Vielvölkerregion zwischen Rebellion und Anspassung*, Köln: Böhlau, 2015, pp. 430-441; Dieter Pohl, "Deutsche Militärverwaltung: Die bessere Besatzung? Das Beispiel Kaukasus 1942/43," *Mitteilungen der Gemeinsamen Kommission für die Erforschung der jüngeren Geschichte der deutsch-russischen Beziehungen* 2 (2005): pp. 51-59; Linets, *Severnyi Kavkaz nakanune i v period nemetsko-fashistskoi okkupatsii*, pp. 375-391; Khadzhi Imbragimbejli, "Krakh gitlerovskogo okkupatsionnogo rezhima na Kavkaze," in Basov and Kumanev, *Narodnyi podvig v bitve za Kavkaz*, pp. 265-285.

2 This section refers to the term "Caucasus" comprising both the North Caucasus and the Transcaucasus. Therefore, when the North Caucasus is implied it is referred to explicitly.
On this subject, see Alexander M. Nekrich, *Nakazannye narody* (New York: Khronika, 1978), pp. 41-63 (North Caucasus), 64-79 (Kalmykiia); Angrick, *Besatzungspolitik und Massenmord*, pp. 590-610 (the entire region).

3 In the chapter, the terms Russian, Russian-Ukrainian, and Slav are used interchangeably and refer essentially to the same population group, unless otherwise stated.

German rule by virtue of its being the most important Soviet oil reservoir. The question arises whether and to what extent these factors affected actual German policies towards the population of the North Caucasus, which was the only part of the Caucasian region seized by the Wehrmacht. Furthermore, the North Caucasus also bordered Ukraine, the "food surplus" territory that Nazi Germany ruthlessly exploited, and the southern part of central Russia, which in the Nazi mindset belonged to the dead zone of starvation.

At any rate, by the beginning of the German invasion, the Nazi leadership did not consider the North Caucasus to possess any value in its own right. In accordance with the decisions made at the conference at the Führer's Headquarters on July 16, 1941, it was decided that its territory would be divided between the *Reichskommisariaten* of Ukraine and the Caucasus.[4] However, by the summer of 1942, the changing course of the war dictated an adjustment in the projected German policies towards the population of the North Caucasus. First, from a tactical standpoint, there was no major fighting within the region to potentially trigger German retaliations against the civilians. Second, the German conquest of the North Caucasus in the second half of 1942 took place within the general context of some moderation in the harsh policies to which the Germans had adhered in most of the Soviet-occupied areas.[5] Third, it is claimed, with some justification, that the German military administration in the North Caucasus (similar to military administrations established in other areas close to the front line[6] and dissimilar to civil governments established in the regions poised far away from the front line[7]) was prepared

4 Kay, *Exploitation, Resettlement, Mass Murder*, p. 185.

5 For the analysis of reforms in *Reichskommissariat Ukraine* and *Reichskommissariat Ostland*, see Timothy Patrick Mulligan, *The Politics of Illusion and Empire: German Occupation Policy in the Soviet Union, 1942-1943* (New York: Praeger, 1988), pp. 61-76, 77-92.

6 For example, Pohl, *Die Herrschaft der Wehrmacht*, pp. 87-116; Arnold, *Die Wehrmacht und die Besatzungspolitik in den besetzten Gebieten der Sowjetunion*, pp. 109-123.

7 For example, Stephen A. Connor, "Golden Pheasants and Eastern Kings: The German District Administration in the Occupied Soviet Union, 1941-1944," (PhD diss., Wilfried Laurier University, 2007); Jonathan Steinberg, "The Third

to alleviate further the conditions of the local population.[8]

All of this created the situation whereby German policies towards the local Russian population turned out to be milder in the North Caucasus than elsewhere towards this group in the occupied territories of the Soviet Union. In the North Caucasus, the Germans assumed that the Russian-Ukrainian majority resented Soviet rule,[9] but regarded their attitudes towards the German occupation as affected by fear and intimidation from the Bolshevik regime.[10] The Wehrmacht was thus required to behave with caution towards the Russian population, particularly in the towns.[11] Among the Slavic population, the Germans singled out Cossacks, who were considered particularly hostile to the Soviet regime and, therefore, friendly to the German presence.[12] The Cossacks were the only Russian group in the Caucasus awarded autonomy, with the autonomous Cossack region and its population of some 160,000 people established in the lower Kuban' area.[13]

The following episode is indicative of the milder atmosphere of the German occupation in the region. According to a Soviet report, in the village of Naturbovo:

> On the night of October 22, 1942, [the Germans] arrested all Party members and some non-affiliated persons (*bespartiinye*). This made a painful impression on the village. Until then, the

Reich Reflected: German Civil Administration in the Occupied Soviet Union, 1941-4," *The English Historical Review* 110, no. 437 (June 1995): pp. 620-651.

8 Arnold, *Die Wehrmacht und die Besatzungspolitik in den besetzten Gebieten der Sowjetunion*, pp. 123-136.

9 Gendarmerie Zug 33, "Tätigkeits- und Lagebericht für die Zeit 1.-15.11.1942," O.U., November 16, 1942, Russian State Military Archive (RGVA), 1358/1/9, p. 86.

10 CSpSd, Kommandostab, Berlin, MbOg, no. 28, Geheim, November 6, 1942, Yad Vashem Archives (YVA), JM/4539.

11 "Merkblatt für das Verhalten gegenüber kaukasischen Völkern," [no date], RGVA, 1323/2/263, p. 219.

12 "Anlage zu II./Pol.Rgt. Einsatz- und TB des Batallions für die Zeit vom 1.-31.8.1942," (Auszug aus dem KTB), September 12, 1942, RGVA, 1358/1/9, p. 106.

13 Bugai, *Kazachestvo Rossii*, pp. 66-67; Krinko, *Zhizn' za liniei fronta*, p. 78.

> Germans had been behaving in a friendly fashion, joking easily, playing with children, and displaying all signs of favor towards the Russian population. After the arrest, appeals were immediately made to the effect that those arrested be released. All members of the *kolkhoz* with the exception of two signed the appeals. Two days later, all those arrested were released, while the Gestapo gave them instructions to work honestly. They were to present themselves daily to the police.[14]

The evidence implies that the Russian population sometimes could influence German policy at the local level. It also testifies to the Germans' receptiveness to the demands of the local population. Furthermore, the dimensions of these phenomena could have been broader, as neither Germans nor Soviets were interested in highlighting such incidents. However, from time to time, increasing partisan activities that caused casualties on the German side led the German command to resort to the "proven" retaliation methods against the civilian population, which ran counter to the declared policy of unique administration of the North Caucasus.[15] In such cases, they imposed curfews,[16] took and executed hostages,[17] or arbitrarily killed civilians.[18] Some (or at times, even entire) parts of the population in specific localities were sometimes forcefully evacuated.[19] On the whole, however, those were rare incidents, limited almost exclusively to Russian non-Cossack settlements.

14 Interrogation of Klavdiia Parshikova, August 12, 1943, YVA, M.33/291, pp. 100-102.

15 Oldenburg, *Ideologie und militärisches Kalkül*, p. 282.

16 Village of Levokumskoe: Memoirs of Peotr Belokurov, November 13, 2002, YVA, 0.33/6783, pp. 3-5.

17 Akt of the Commission of Novorossiisk, October 18, 1943, YVA, M.33/306, p. 57.

18 Villages of Kuzhorskaia and Bogulov: Akt of the Commission of Maikop, August 20, 1943, YVA, M.33/288, p. 8; Akt of the Commission of the North Caucasian Front, January 7, 1943, Central Archive of the Ministry of Defense of the Russian Federation (TsAMO RF) 51/958/52, p. 51, courtesy of the USHMM.

19 Village of Krasnaia Batareia and Novorossiisk: Testimony of Ol'ga Polonskaia, May 1, 1962, YVA, 0.3/2246, p. 7; Akt of the Commission of Novorossiisk, October 18, 1943, YVA, M.33/306, p. 57.

1.2. Towards the non-Slavic population

The Germans were aware that numerous small non-Russian minorities populated the North Caucasus, and the Wehrmacht command sought to preserve the delicate balance among them.[20] This was because the Germans estimated that their exclusive reliance on one specific people would have a devastating effect on the attitudes of other Caucasian groups towards the German rule[21] and, thus, would be detrimental to their tasks in the Caucasus. Therefore, the Germans adhered to the policy not to favor any minority in the region.[22] The complicated mosaic structure of the Caucasian population led German strategists to conclude that one of their main tasks should be to assuage the local peoples' fears that their autonomy (already promised by declarations during the Germans' entry into the territory) might be affected.[23] The Germans took notice of widespread anti-Russian sentiments among the non-Russian peoples in the Caucasus, and prepared to capitalize upon them.[24]

The Germans worked out special arrangements to preserve the popularity of the occupation regime among the "mountain peoples" (*Bergvölker*), the term they used to refer to the non-Russian population in the North Caucasus. The rationale behind

20 RMfdOg, "Richtlinien für die Behandlung der Ostvölker Kaukasien," Geheim, August 20, 1942, Bundesarchiv (BA), R 6/66.

21 Letter to the RSHA by the Head of Communication in the Ministry of the Occupied Eastern Territories Siefers, "Podrobnosti formirovaniia vspomogatel'nykh voisk iz chisla Tatarskikh i kavkazskikh narodov," no. 1020/42, translation into Russian, June 10, 1942 (another version March 20, 1942), State Archive of the Autonomous Republic of the Crimea (DAARK), P-849/3/315.

22 Natalia Doronina, "Natsistkaia propaganda na okkupirovannykh territoriakh Stavropol'ia i Kubani v 1942-1943 gg.: tseli, osobennosti, krakh" (PhD diss., Stavropol'skii gosudarstvennyi universitet, 2005), pp. 52-53.

23 Prior to this point, the Germans limited themselves to vague declarations – for example, about a common German-Caucasian enemy or about the freedom of religion that the Germans granted to the Caucasians. See, for example, the leaflet "Völker Kaukasiens! Nur im Kaukasus verbreiten!," YVA, JM/5716, 5637.

24 *Die Völker des Kaukasus und seiner Vorländer* (Berlin und Stuttgart: Deutsches Ausland-Institut, 1941), RGVA, 1323/1/54, p. 27. See also "Strafsache gegen Theodor Oberländer, Kerrar Gaidar-Ogly Aleskerow," Vernehmungsprotokoll, Moscow, February 16, 1960, YVA, TR.10/2147, p. 522.

this policy was the German assumption that the Caucasian peoples generally resented the Soviet rule and, therefore, enthusiastically welcomed German conquest.[25] Particular attention was paid to granting complete religious freedom to the peoples of the region.[26] Among other aspects of the German policy, it is worth mentioning several measures that reflected the special position of the Caucasian peoples under German rule. Capital punishment was to be exercised against Caucasians only in exceptional cases.[27] The Germans were to observe the property rights of the mountain people and the honor of Caucasian women.[28] The latter part of the order was apparently largely observed. [29] The Germans also established local governments in charge of Caucasian cultural, religious, and domestic affairs, as well as local militias.[30] Certainly, the absence of German garrisons stationed in many villages – as the Germans relied on local militias in coping with the local security tasks[31] – was a weighty factor in the German policy of trying to win over the native Caucasians. As was manifested in a Soviet intelligence report, however biased, pertaining to autonomous

25 CSpSd, Kommandostab, Berlin, MbOg, no. 28, Geheim, October 30, 1942, YVA, JM/4539.

26 See section 9A, "The Responses of Orthodox Christianity and Islam in the Crimea and the North Caucasus to the Holocaust."

27 "Todestrafe gegen Kaukasier," H.Gr.A an AOK 17, no. 1583/42, g.Kdos., November 3, 1942 (v. Greiffenberg), Anwendung der Todesstrafe gegen Zivilpersonen im Bereich der H.Gr.A, H.Gr.A, OQu/Qu2/VII, no. 1981/43 geh., March 1, 1943 (v. Kleist) in Hoffmann, *Die Ostlegionen 1941-43*, p. 440.

28 CSpSd, Kommandostab, Berlin, MbOg, no. 28, Geheim, October 30, 1942, YVA, JM/4539. See also Doronina, "Natsistkaia propaganda na okkupirovannykh territoriakh Stavropol'ia i Kubani…", pp. 54, 57-58.

29 Although Soviet reports recorded a number of rapes in the North Caucasus, all of them were Russian and Ukrainian women. Galina Kameneva, "Zhenshiny Severnogo Kavkaza v gody Velikoi Otechestvennoi voiny 1941-1945 gg," (PhD diss., Stavropol'skii gosudarstvennyi universitet, 2004), p. 76.

30 3 Panzer-Division, Abt. 1c. "Propaganda in den Feind," Dem XXXX Panzerkorps, September 26, 1942, YVA, JM/5605.

31 Adygea: Vokasu Khalitov, "Obespechenie Krasnoi Armii liudskimi resursami i voenno-patrioticheskaia podgotovka sovetskikh voisk nakanune i v gody Velikoi Otechestvennoi voiny: Na materialakh respublik Severnogo Kavkaza: 1939-1945 gg.," (PhD diss., Chechenskii gosudarstvennyi pedagogicheskii institut, 2004), p. 140.

Adygeiskaia *oblast'* (Krasnodarskii *krai*), the Germans supported the conservative, traditional segment of the local non-Russian population, and refrained from interfering into specifically local problems:

> In the national *raion* of Adygea, the Germans adhere to an extremely "peaceful" policy of making advances to the national segment [i.e., *Adygeitsy* – KF]. They support old traditions, and give "honorable elders" the right to solve the matters of local and internal importance.[32]

2. The Responses of the Local Population to the Holocaust

2.1. Slavic population

2.1.1. General concerns

One German military report had recorded positive attitudes of the Russian population towards the new rule as early as in the first phase of the occupation:

> Also the local Russian population is not hostile to the German presence and owing to the Bolsheviks' atrocities... and the good conduct of German soldiers, [it] is strongly disposed against Bolsheviks.[33]

Additionally, the EG D report from early November 1942 mentioned that:

> The most recent reports from the areas of Voroshilovsk [Stavropol' – KF], Maikop, Krasnodar, Piatigorsk, Elista, etc.,

32 Intelligence survey of the NKVD Administration, December 1942, in Beliaev and Bondar', *Kuban' v gody Velikoi Otechestvennoi voiny, 1941-1945*, p. 647.

33 Abschrift, Dienststelle F. P., no. 39, 180, Btl.-Gef., Std., Bericht vom 25.8-17.9.1942, September 17, 1942, YVA, JM/5640.

> indicate and confirm that after initial reservation, the [local] population displayed openness towards German troops... The locals' disgust of the Jews is manifest everywhere.[34]

According to this source, the Germans' persecution of Jews was a heavy factor in the gradual change of the disposition of the local population towards the German presence, from cool to more positive.

Characteristically, the *Einsatzgruppe* did not go into any details regarding the local population's attitudes towards Jews, other than general observations. Nor did Soviet reports touch much upon this topic. At most, they contended themselves with references to certain events, such as what occurred in the village of Nini, where "at the meeting [*skhodka*], it was announced that the annihilation of Jews was imperative."[35] It is unclear who arranged the meeting or how the public reacted upon this announcement, or indeed whether the Jews in the village were assaulted or arrested as a result.

Therefore, a discussion of local Russian views towards the Jews in the North Caucasus before the German occupation is necessary. Prewar developments contributed to some of the resentment towards the Jews, particularly among the Cossacks. Of special importance and peculiar relevance to the region, though, is the period from the beginning of the war until the German occupation. Thousands of refugees, among them many Jews, flocked into the region, and a number of them settled there. Soviet authorities forced the Russian and Ukrainian inhabitants of Caucasian towns and villages to accommodate the numerous newcomers. This contact resulted in an increase in antisemitic feelings among the locals within the evacuation period, with the Slavic population, including the Cossacks, behaving in a hostile manner towards the Jewish refugees.[36]

34 CSpSd, Kommandostab, Berlin, MbOg, no. 28, Geheim, November 6, 1942, YVA, JM/4539.

35 Akt of the Commission of Archangel'skii *raion*, July 20, 1943, State Archive of the Russian Federation (GARF), 7021/17/9, p. 50.

36 Elista, Krasnodar: Testimony of Liudmila Bradichevskii, May 13, 1996, Institute

2.1.2. Collaborators

The anti-Jewish crusade unleashed by the Germans immediately upon their conquest of the Caucasus in leaflets[37] and Russian-language newspapers[38] was the most efficient way of conveying Nazi messages to the local people.[39] As it so happened, the local Russian population took an interest in their ominous work. Antisemitic propaganda in the Russian language newspapers zeroed in on a number of topics, most of which repeated the same messages transmitted elsewhere in the German-occupied Soviet territories.[40] One of the most popular notions was the complete identification of Jews with the Soviet regime and the Russian people's ensuing rejection of Jews, as demonstrated in the following excerpt from *Stavropol'skoe slovo* from September 17, 1942:

> But strange enough, the results of the hysterical outbursts of *Sovinformburo*, the propaganda department of the Red Army, and especially of the Jewish meeting,[41] were entirely different. To their surprise, Russian people did not explode with resentment over the "atrocities" towards the Jews... What is

of Contemporary Jewry (ICJ), (217) 183, p. 3; Saul Borovoi, *Vospominaniia*, pp. 249-250, 252, 254; Kiril Feferman, "A Soviet Humanitarian Action?: Centre, Periphery and the Evacuation of Refugees to the North Caucasus, 1941-1942," *Europe-Asia Studies* 61, no. 5 (2009): pp. 819-821.

37 Untitled document, BA-MA, RH 23/51; "Propagandamaterial des Korück 550," (September-October?) 1942, in Oldenburg, *Ideologie und militärisches Kalkül*, pp. 300-301.

38 The newspaper clippings, on which the current section is based, were provided to the author courtesy of the USHMM.

39 To illustrate the point, the newspaper *Kuban'* (Krasnodar) was circulated in 5,000 copies, which is a huge number for such a relatively underpopulated area.

40 See for, example, Kovalev, *Povsedenevnaia zhizn' Rossii*, pp. 200, 206-209; Robert E. Herzstein, "Anti-Jewish Propaganda in the Orel Region of Great Russia, 1942-1943: The German Army and its Nazi Collaborators," *Simon Wiesenthal Center Annual* 6 (1989): pp. 33-55.

41 Meetings of the representatives of the Jewish people were part of the massive Soviet propaganda campaign aimed at rallying world Jewry around the Soviet cause. There were several such meetings, closely supervised by the authorities. Here it seems that the article is making reference to the second radio meeting held in Moscow on May 24, 1942.

> the reason of this indifference, who is to blame? The answer is laconic: Jews themselves. Who was in our days the actual master of the country? Jews. Who are these *Kaganovichi*,[42] *Maiskie*,[43] *Erenburgi*,[44] *Oistrakhi*[45] and others and others? Jews. The whole life from the beginning to the end was in their satanic hands.[46]

However, it is likely that the theme of Jewish prominence in the Soviet apparatus did not appeal in particular to North Caucasian Russians, who had not witnessed this phenomenon in their region. Therefore, this idea was sometimes given specific Caucasian traits and artificially adjusted to local developments, such as the persecution of Cossacks.[47] In another example, Maikop's newspaper published a letter written allegedly by the person who in 1936 had accused a local Jew of cheating and was condemned

42 This is a plural form of "Kaganovich," and the implication here is Lazar' Kaganovich, one of the most prominent Soviet leaders under Stalin and the only Jew in Stalin's inner circle throughout his entire rule. On Kaganovich, see E. A. Rees, *"Iron Lazar": A Political Biography of Lazar Kaganovich* (London; New York, NY: Anthem Press, 2012).

43 This is a plural form of "Maiskii," and the implication here is Ivan Maiski, an important Bolshevik and Soviet ambassador to the UK during the Second World War. Ivan Maiksii was born a Pole as Jan Lachowiecki.

44 This is a plural form of "Erenburg," and the implication here is Il'ia Erenburg, one of the most important Soviet propagandists and writers. He was of Jewish origin. Erenburg played a prominent role in the Soviet anti-Nazi propaganda during the Second World War. On Erenburg, see for example, Katerina Clark, "Ehrenburg and Grossman: Two Cosmopolitan Jewish Writers Reflect on Nazi Germany at War," *Kritika: Explorations in Russian and Eurasian History* 10, no. 3 (Summer 2009): pp. 607-628.

45 This is a plural form of "Oistrakh," and the implication here is David Oistrakh, a great Soviet violinist of Jewish origin.

46 "Nekotorye priemy bol'shevistskoi propagandy," *Stavropol'skoe slovo*, no. 27, September 17, 1942, State Archive of Stavropol'skii *krai* (GASK), R-1052/5069.

47 "Kazachestvo vozrodit rodnuiu Kuban," *Osvobozhdennyi Maikop*, no. 18, October 18, 1942, Center of Documentation of the Contemporary History of Krasnodarskii *krai* (TsDNIKK). See also "Staryi kubanskii kozak: Dorogie brat'ia, syny Kubani," *Osvobozhdennyi Maikop*, no. 22, November 1, 1942, TsDNIKK.

to a three-year term in a gulag for antisemitism.[48] Of note are also the several public attacks in the newspapers on the Judaizers, the group associated with the Jews and Judaism in the North Caucasus, which reflected the unique conditions of the region.[49]

The modification of Nazi-sponsored propaganda with an eye to a specifically local agenda in the North Caucasus was most prominent when it concerned the theme of evacuation. References to Jewish evacuation included statements that their evacuation was made at the expense of the Soviet war effort,[50] that the evacuated Jews were settled solely in those places in the region from which ethnic Germans had been previously deported, and, in particular, that Russians had suffered in the Russian-Jewish "encounter" during the evacuation. The Russian population was especially sensitive to the latter notion. One article from *Stavropol'skoe slovo*, evidently published as a part of the editorial-sponsored contest for the "best" presentation of the Jewish topic, underscores the point. The article recalls how a "proud Cossack woman became a serf of the evacuated Jewess [and how] Jews maltreated her, took the best of her two rooms, and the local authorities protected them."[51]

With respect to the actual persecution of Jews in the North Caucasus, it appears that propaganda in newspapers shifted its message for how the local population should regard the Jews, i.e., from hostile indifference to a much more negative line calling for more tangible action. Certainly, in no way could it be compassion, which was, according to *Stavropol'skoe slovo*, the response of some Russians towards the plight of the Jews. Prior to the *Aktionen*, the advice was as follows:

48 "Rasskazy maikopchan: Gospodin V. – sluzhashii," *Osvobozhdennyi Maikop*, no. 1, August 24, 1942, TsDNIKK.

49 N. Polibin (Mayor of Maikop): *Kuban'*, no. 15, November 11, 1942, TsDNIKK. See also "Ostalos' ikh eshe nemalo," *Osvobozhdennyi Maikop*, no. 12, September 30, 1942, TsDNIKK.

50 B. Shyr, "Eshe odna podlost' (Iz nedavnego proshlogo)," *Stavropol'skoe slovo*, no. 16, August 30, 1942, GASK, R-1052/5069; Editorial "Znamenatelnyi iubilei," *Kuban'*, no. 14, November 7, 1942, p. 1, TsDNIKK.

51 N. Kapralova, "Khoziaiika polozheniia," *Stavropol'skoe slovo*, no. 38, October 21, 1942, GASK, R-1052/5069.

> Although we have the right to take revenge on you, to pay you in your own coin… we shall be fairer towards you… Jews: we shall simply take no notice of you.[52]

The order of the day certainly changed after the killing operations. The local inhabitants were called upon to denounce Jews who had managed to survive under Russian identities.[53] The local people could easily gauge from the articles in Russian newspapers that no Jews remained (or were supposed to remain) in the Caucasus under German rule.[54]

Local administrations and police forces were established soon after the German takeover.[55] Although the activity of collaborators often had a direct impact upon the fate of the Jews, their role was subordinate. They could neither initiate nor stop the implementation of the "Final Solution" on their own. Nevertheless, some sources indicate that in a number of cases, they did play an important role in either curbing or enhancing some aspects of the persecution of Jews. In particular, in Essentuki, Mayor Rostovtsev took an active stand concerning the "Jewish Problem." According to a wartime testimony of a local inhabitant, he (as well as the local police chief) sanctioned that on the evening of the assembly day, "Jewish children might be given over to Russians."[56] To put it otherwise, Jewish parents willing to hand their children over to Russians could do so and, thus, save them. In this case, the mayor's policy was more lenient than that of the Germans. In another case, Essentuki's mayor also overruled the German decision, but with

52 I. Solskii, "Mozhno li ikh zhalet'?" *Stavropol'skoe slovo*, no. 17, September 2, 1942, GASK, R-1052/5069.

53 Valentina, "Nashy osvoboditeli," *Osvobozhdennyi Maikop*, no. 6, September 16, 1942, TsDNIKK. See also "Ostalos' ikh eshe nemalo," *Osvobozhdennyi Maikop*, no. 12, September 30, 1942, TsDNIKK.

54 "Chastushki," *Kuban'*, no. 15, November 11, 1942, TsDNIKK. See also the editorial "Pochemu?," *Kuban'*, no. 6, January 15, 1943, TsDNIKK.

55 Piatigorsk: Testimony of the Ek 12 man P. Pffeifer during the trial in Piatigorsk, 1968, in Arad, *Unichtozhenie evreev SSSR v gody okkupatsii (1941-1944)*, p. 241.

56 Statement of the advocate Aleksandr Gontov, June 30, 1943, GARF, 7021/17/4, p. 63.

a policy that was more stringent than the original German one. According to the testimony of a Jewish wife in a mixed family:

> I was entitled to forego [the registration], because the announcement read that the mixed marriages would remain, but Mayor Rostovtsev forbade me to stay since my husband was absent [he was serving in the Red Army – KF]. There were 10-15 such mixed marriages, but all of them were required to assemble in the school.[57]

Provided these testimonies are taken for granted, and they seem authentic, then the mayor's steps ran counter to the German policies applied elsewhere in the occupied territories and may be seen as a certain deviation – once as an alleviation and once as a stringency – from the established pattern of the solution of the "Jewish Question." It is clear that such decisions could not be made without German approval, and there is no indication that in either case they overruled the mayor's decision. It may be speculated, therefore, that the Germans were ready to tolerate the local Russian authorities' independent steps in the *Judenpolitik* as long as they did not contradict the basic principles of the persecution of Jews. Such toleration may be seen as gesture of goodwill towards the local Russians and the Russian administrations, whose cooperative attitude was crucial to German interests in the area.

The testimony is also instructive in another respect. That is, in many cases the German orders were unclearly formatted, leaving room for interpretation. The local administration was the only authority empowered to interpret the German orders. Therefore, deprived of the possibility to plead their case directly before the Germans, Jews had to apply to the local authorities (typically the headman or police chief), who thus had the final say in their cases.[58]

On other occasions, representatives of the collaboration administration were somewhat more restrained in their behavior, demonstrating an unwillingness to take responsibility in making

57 Testimony of Raisa Kogan, April 29, 1943, GARF, 7021/17/4, p. 12.

58 Essentuki, Kislovodsk: ibid. See also, *Dokumenty obviniaiut*, p. 142.

decisions. In one case in Essentuki, the local administration postponed the final verdict that demanded the suspect produce further proof of his non-Jewish origin. According to the testimony of the Jewish witness:

> I produced my Soviet passport and military card to the Police head Gavrilov. But he said: "We do not believe Soviet documents. Give [me] your birth certificate." I had none. I said that I had been born in Piatigorsk and can produce live witnesses of my nationality from there. I was released for 24 hours.[59]

Such situations provided only temporary respite, but resourceful Jews could avail themselves of the opportunity and try to escape.

Restraint could sometimes mean the eagerness to contend oneself with only little proof of "Aryan" origin. In Mikoianshakhar, a Jewish woman and her four children were summoned for interrogation on August 24, 1942. She claimed that her husband was a Russian and that she was an Armenian. The authorities believed and released her.[60] By the same token, after a brief interrogation, a Jewish woman was legally registered as non-Jewish in late December 1942 in Krasnodar as she produced photo, written request, and CV.[61] In another case, restraint meant the reluctance to arrest the suspect. This was the case in Krasnodar, where, in the final phase of the occupation, the chief of the neighborhood (*burgomistr raiona*) revealed that the passport of the Jewish witness was a fraud and "denied his application for registration," yet did not denounce him.[62] Investigation into the allegedly Jewish origin of a person could drag on for a long time, but he or she was not arrested in the meantime. The testimony of Anna Shlaen provides an example:

> On December 15, 1942, it was the last time that we were summoned one-by-one to the *Kommandatur* for

59 Testimony of Ia. Talianskii, [no date], GARF, 7021/17/4, p. 30.

60 Testimony of Tsitsilia Tsirul'nik, 1943, GARF, 7021/17/10, pp. 201-202.

61 Testimony of Mina Horowitz, August 1, 1973, YVA, 0.3/3682, pp. 9-10.

62 Interrogation of Mikhail Fingerut, June 25, 1943, GARF, 7021/17/5, p. 31.

> interrogation, during which we were asked about our personal data and family history, and the demand was made to say whether we were Jews (*iudy*). The interrogation was terminated without reaching a clear-cut conclusion.[63]

Nonetheless, it should be taken into account that these notions are based on the testimonies of those who survived because the authorities were undecided in their cases. With all due importance of this phenomenon, it still constituted a deviation from the established pattern: as a rule, Jews who did not possess "Aryan" documents were murdered in the North Caucasus like elsewhere in the occupied Soviet territories. With some rare exceptions, no one survived to testify in these cases.

In Caucasian towns, collaboration administrations were involved in various measures directed against the Jews, such as verifying their documents,[64] communicating German orders to the Jewish population if there was no specific Jewish agency (such as the *Judenrat*) to serve this purpose,[65] and exploiting Jews for forced labor.[66] The local police was also employed in searching for and denouncing Jews.[67] In the apparently exceptional case of Piatigorsk, the Germans also established Russian security police that were subordinated to the *Einsatzkommando* 12; in addition to the aforementioned competence of auxiliary police, the extermination of Jews and Communists was also under the Piatigorsk security police's authority.[68] In all other cases, there exists no record that Russian policemen were employed in safeguarding

63 Statement of Anna Shlaen, 1943, GARF, 7021/17/11, p. 116.

64 Essentuki: Testimony of Ia. Talianskii, [no date], GARF, 7021/17/4, p. 30.

65 Cherkessk and Tikhoretsk: "Strafsache gegen Johannes Schlupper," der Untersuchungsrichter 115 Ks 6a-c/71, Vernehmungsniderschrift, Schlupper, December 14, 1971, YVA, TR.10/1081, p. 56; Beliaev and Bondar', *Kuban' v gody Velikoi Otechestvennoi voiny, 1941-1945*, pp. 464-465.

66 Akt of the Commission of Cherkessk: July 13, 1943, GARF, 702/17/12, pp. 68-69.

67 Essentuki and Krasnodar: Testimony of Faina Gulianskaia, July 2, 1943, GARF, 7021/17/4, p. 17; Krasnodar trial, interrogation of the defendant Tishenko, 1943, Archive of the Federal Security Service of the Russian Federation (AFSB RF), H-16708, vols. 4-5, p. 115, courtesy of the USHMM.

68 Khalitov, *Obespechenie Krasnoi Armii*, p. 145.

the killing operations, let alone their participation in them. This was primarily because in non-Cossack localities, that is, mainly in towns, the Germans did not identify the local Russians as a sufficiently reliable group. After the *Aktionen*, the collaborators were sometimes awarded Jewish property.[69]

The situation was different in the Caucasian rural areas, where local collaborators were employed in a wide range of anti-Jewish policies. Like elsewhere, they were involved in summoning Jews to the assembly points,[70] as well as searching for Jews in hiding[71] and denouncing them.[72] Unlike in towns, however, they participated in small-scale killing operations.[73] Russian collaborators in villages also robbed Jews of their property.[74]

Evgenii Zhuravlev, a North Caucasian historian well-acquainted with the content of investigations conducted by the Soviets after their return in 1943 (these files continue to be inaccessible to most researchers), claims that the collaborators were led mainly by their fear of the Bolsheviks, as well as by financial motives; also, they came from the ranks of the "former" (*byvshye*), i.e., members of the former ruling classes in the Tsarist

69 Essentuki and Piatigorsk: Testimony of Samuil Belenkov, August 10, 1943, GARF, 7021/17/4, p. 26; Testimonies of the schoolchildren V. Rubtsov, N. Beletzkii, G. Kruglenko, B. Sorokin, A. Kuznetsov, and A. Zimin in Arad, *Unichtozhenie evreev SSSR v gody okkupatsii (1941-1944)*, p. 244; Khalitov, *Obespechenie Krasnoi Armii*, p. 143.

70 Villages of Soldatsko-Aleksandrovskoe and Labdanka in Stavropol'skii *krai*: Akt of the Commission of Soldatsko-Aleksandrovskii *raion*, GARF, 7021/17/11, p. 112; Account of Isser Klubok, September 28, 1943, YVA, P.21.2/3.

71 Villages of Izmailovo and Labdanka *stanitsa*: Account of Isser Klubok, September 28, 1943, YVA, P.21.2/3; Testimony of Iakov Vinokurov, October 19, 1999, YVA, VT/2489.

72 Village of Orlovka: Akt of the Commission of Budennovsk, July 25, 1943, GARF, 7021/7/1, p. 122.

73 Stavropol'skii *krai* – villages of Zhuravskoe and Novozavedennoe: Akt of the Commission of Zhuravskoe, August 18, 1943, GARF, 7021/17/11, p. 47; Statement of Anna Shlaen, 1943, GARF, 7021/17/11, p. 114.

74 Village of Apsheronskaia: Report "O massovykh ubiistvakh, nasilii i izdevatel'svakh nemetskikh fashistov v okkupirovannykh raionakh," Intelligence Department of the Southern Headquarter of the Partisan Movement, December 4, 1942, Russian State Archive of Social and Political History, RGASPI, 69/1/1048, p. 8.

Empire, whose privileged position was ended by the Bolsheviks who perceived them as class enemies and persecuted them.[75] Another North Caucasian scholar, Vokasu Khalitov, adds to this list criminal elements previously persecuted by the Soviets; those who believed in Nazi Germany's victory and wished to align themselves with the winning party; and those who regarded service on the German side as an alternative to being deported for forced labor in Germany.[76] To these groups we should also add ideologically-driven collaborators, who did not belong to any of the aforementioned groups.[77]

2.1.3. Ordinary people

The report written by the EG D in the fall of 1942 estimated that anti-Jewish sentiments were widespread among the local people:

> The reports that arrive from the operational area signal that for the most part there is a general aversion for the Jews. The population has experienced itself how the Jews, who occupy mainly the most important positions, learned to profit from the war, and the resulting deprivations by forcing up prices and engaging in the black market. The population demonstrates understanding, and receives enthusiastically the steps that are being taken against the Jews, such as their removal from all the positions, marking, and forced labor… Influential circles among the local population view the measures taken hitherto against the Jews as insufficient, and require to apply a harsher policy.[78]

The report reflected a wishful attempt to present the entire local Slavic population as an active supporter of the German persecution

75 Zhuravlev, *Kollaboratsionizm na iuge Rossii*, pp. 116-117.

76 Khalitov, *Obespechenie Krasnoi Armii*, pp. 141-143.

77 On this kind of collaborationism, see Oleg Budnitskii and Galina Zelenina, eds., *Svershilos': Prishli nemtsy! Ideinyi kollaboratsyonizm v SSSR v period Velikoi Otechestvennoi voiny* (Moscow: ROSSPEN, 2012).

78 CSpSd, Kommandostab, Berlin, MbOg, no. 28, Geheim, October 30, 1942, YVA, JM/4539.

of Jews. Yet, despite being a generalization, the report does appear to point out the widespread antisemitic attitudes among the local Slavic population.

To begin with, it is noteworthy that in almost all the towns and villages, the local Russian population served as eyewitnesses to some of the stages preceding the physical annihilation of the Jews. This was the case in Stavropol', where a detailed order to the Jewish population was published on the first page of a local newspaper[79] and disseminated by the Germans all over the town.[80] In towns, it was quite visible that Jews were being sent to perform forced labor or suffering from other forms of persecution.[81] In Essentuki, for example, the Jews were the only category of the population publicly denied the bread distribution.[82] Furthermore, the local population was able to witness the overt public plundering of Jewish property, occurring usually just before the Jews were sent to be killed.[83] Just as the local population was able to witness pre-*Aktion* persecution, some of them also inevitably witnessed the killings (or at least knew they were happening). Although this was rare, local people were sometimes present at mass killing operations against Jews,[84] or at public executions of individual Jews.[85]

79 This was an order that specified several things: the establishment of a Jewish Committee of Elders; attendance at an assembly for all the Jews on August 12; a ban on Jews leaving the town; and punishment for non-compliance with the order. *Russkaia pravda*, no. 2, August 5, 1942, in Al'tman, *Zhertvy nenavisti*, p. 59.

80 Akt of the Commission of Stavropol', July 11, 1943, GARF, 7021/17/1, pp. 95-96.

81 Essentuki and Kislovodsk: Akt of the Commission of Essentuki, July 10, 1943, GARF, 7021/17/4, p. 1; "Massacre of Caucasus Jews" (Hebrew), [Jewish Anti-Fascist Committee, source: letters from the local inhabitants], *Ha-tsofe* (Tel Aviv), no. 1702, August 4, 1943, p. 3.

82 "Massacre of Caucasus Jews" (Hebrew), *Ha-tsofe*, August 4, 1943, p. 3.

83 Essentuki and Novorossiisk: Testimony of Samuil Belenkov, August 10, 1943, GARF, 7021/17/4, p. 25; Questioning of Nadezhda Al'chenko, September 16, 1943, GARF, 7021/16/11, p. 114.

84 Stavropol': "Strafsache gegen Walter Bierkamp," Bayerisches Landeskriminalamt, Vernehmungsniederschrift, K. Walter, April 22, 1970, YVA, TR.10/1147, p. 613.

85 Stavropol': "And This is the First News… What the Nazis are Doing with the Jewish Population before their Retreat in Russia" (Hebrew), *Davar*, no. 5366, February 24, 1943, p. 1 (source: Moscow, special telegram to *Davar* dated February 22, 1943).

For the most part, however, Germans annihilated Jews from the towns in relative secrecy. Even Soviet agents often did not know for sure what had happened to the assembled Jews.[86] Thus, the local people were in such a position that they potentially could have learned about the precarious condition of the Jews but, arguably, were largely unaware of it or unable to believe that they had indeed been murdered. For example, according to evidence from a 1943 Soviet investigation in Krasnodar, in a friendly conversation conducted during the occupation, a Russian policeman recalled how he had participated in the executions of the Jewish population in Krasnodar. His interlocutor interrupted him by exclaiming that:

> That's impossible! It was the Jewish representative who assembled the Jews in order to send them to work. He guaranteed them security![87]

With respect to property matters, at times the Germans allowed the local population to take part in the distribution of plundered Jewish property, either by selling it to them or by encouraging the local authorities to distribute it to special target groups, potentially broadening the German base of support.[88] For example, in the following instruction of the collaboration administration forwarded to the headman of the village of Spitsevka:

> As a *starosta* of the village, you are in charge of Jewish possessions and of distributing them as an aid to former

86 Maikop — the Jewish population of the town was moved away to an unknown destination: Intelligence survey of the [Krasnodar] NKVD Administration, September 1942, in Beliaev and Bondar', *Kuban' v gody Velikoi Otechestvennoi voiny*, 1941-1945, pp. 510-511; Novorossiisk — "Then, 2,000-2,500 people were evacuated in order to be resettled in the area specially designated for them": Memorandum of the command of Krasnodar group [*kust*] of partisan detachments, October 1942 (?), in ibid., p. 557.

87 Interrogation of Tat'iana Kostigova, March 20, 1943, AFSB RF, H-16708, vols. 4-5, pp. 877-878.

88 Essentuki: Testimony of Samuil Belenkov, August 10, 1943, GARF, 7021/17/4, p. 25.

political prisoners, to the poorest populations, and to those who suffered under the Bolsheviks.[89]

Occasionally, the local Slavic population rendered essential assistance to Jews in the North Caucasus. Shelter was usually provided to the Jews a short time before the Germans retreated from the region.[90] Timing was a critical factor in the rationale behind the Russians' behavior. Arguably, some of them perhaps desired "to gain points" for when the Soviet interrogators eventually confronted them about their activity under German rule. Yet, humanitarian motives should not be entirely discarded. It should also be taken into account that there is no evidence that the Germans intimidated the Caucasian urban population to the effect that its members would not have rendered any assistance to the Jews. The Yad Vashem Collection of Righteous Among the Nations relies mainly on recently submitted testimonies of Jewish survivors; according to these sources, from the onset of the occupation, some Russians in predominately rural areas of the Caucasus had sheltered Jews.[91] Most of them did so out of compassion. At the same time, in many of these cases, the survivors were small children without parents, while their rescuers had no children of their own. Hence, the rescuers' behavior may have been the result of their desire to "obtain" children.[92]

On rare occasions, Russians or Ukrainians provided Jews with

89 Stavropol'skii *krai*: Clarification of the *Oberburgmistr* in Vodolazhskaia, Krivneva, and Mel'nik, *Stavropol'e v period nemetsko-fashistskoi okkupatsii (avgust 1942-ianvar' 1943)*, p. 48. The author is unaware of the true dimensions of this phenomenon in other localities nor of the response of local people to these German overtures. However, in this way, large numbers of the local Russians in the region could potentially have become beneficiaries of the Holocaust.

90 Krasnodar and Stavropol'(?): Interrogation of Mikhail Fingerut, June 25, 1943, GARF, 7021/17/5, p. 31; "And This is the First News...," (Hebrew), *Davar*, no. 5366, February 24, 1943, p. 1.

91 E.g., "Nezaimenka" Farm and Brykhovetskaia *stanitsa* in Krasnodarskii *krai*, village of Arzgir: File of Vera Buriachok, 1996, YVA, M.31/7789; File of Natal'ia Dudnik, 1997, YVA, M.31/7704.

92 File of Vera Buriachok, 1996, YVA, M.31/7789; File of Ivan and Praskov'ia Palaguta, 2001, YVA, M.31/9385; File of Boik, [no date], YVA, M.31/4839.

temporary shelter in the first stage of the occupation.[93] Of emphasis is the role of some Russian evacuees from Leningrad, whose positive attitudes and help were crucial for the survival of a few Jews.[94] In another case in Armavir, during the preliminary bureaucratic correspondence between the personnel of an orphanage and the municipal administration, the former succeeded in reducing the officially recorded number of the Jewish children by half from 28 to 14.[95] This meant that 14 Jewish children were rescued, while 14 others were killed.

During the first stages of the occupation, Jews could hope for other means of potential help, which arguably were not fraught with such a high risk for the rescuer. For example, one person proposed to help a Jew fake his passport for that of a different nationality, and gave him prior warning of the Germans' arrival.[96] Yet, if a non-Jew were to give a Jew his or her own ID, this would then jeopardize his or her own position during the German occupation, as one case has shown.[97] There were times when Russians and Ukrainians would deny Jews the right to stay in their houses but, even so, would not denounce them.[98] According to mainly non-Jewish wartime testimonies, some Russians were friendly towards the Jews – even if their behavior sometimes rendered no practical aid. This ranged from advising Jews not to go to the assembly point[99] (important at a critical moment of disorientation for the

93 Kislovodsk: Lev Sheinin, *Literaturnaia gazeta*, October 29, 1957; Report of Moisei Evenson, Viktor Shklovskii, ed., [no date], YVA, P.21.2/1.

94 Kislovodsk, Peredovaia *stanitsa*: Report of Moisei Evenson, Viktor Shklovskii, ed., [no date], YVA, P.21.2/1; Memoirs of Mikhail Bugakov, 2005, YVA, 0.33/7074.

95 Questioning of Vera Ol'shevskaia (1906), August 13, 1943, YVA, M.33/286, pp. 7-9.

96 Kislovodsk: Testimony of Fania Skliar, September 1975, YVA, 0.3/3934, pp. 8, 10.

97 Kislovodsk: Interrogation of Mikhail Fingerut, June 25, 1943, GARF, 7021/17/5, p. 31.

98 Kislovodsk: Testimony of Tsilia Gadleva (1917), October 25, 1990, YVA, 0.3/4391, p. 11.

99 Kislovodsk and Krasnodar: Statement of Boris Khshive, July 3, 1943, GARF, 7021/17/5, p. 50; Interrogation of Lidiia Ivanova, January 6, 1944, GARF, 7021/16/462, p. 24.

Jews but safe for the advisor), to accompanying them if they did,[100] and offering free food to those detained (largely symbolic acts of solidarity but visible and, hence, dangerous for the advisors and helpers).[101] More tangible aid included supplying Jews with food in a clandestine manner (critical but presumably unobserved by outsiders and, hence, relatively safe for the helper).[102]

Some record of public manifestations of friendship, or even solidarity, with the Jews deserves particular attention. This is especially remarkable, given the generally pro-German or indifferent stance of the majority of the local population. Although the Germans generally did not punish such steps, one still had to reckon with the possibility of a German crackdown. In Kislovodsk, for example, a Jewish survivor reported that the Germans dispersed the "crowd of Russians who came to see off the Jews."[103] The evidence pertaining to the city of Krasnodar given by a Soviet intelligence agent acting in the occupied city is even more impressive:

> On the day when the Jews were to be dispatched from the city of Krasnodar, many Russian inhabitants gathered to protest near the building of the former court at Krasnaia Street. All of them were dispersed by the police.[104]

Regardless of whether the demonstrators had family connections with the Krasnodar Jews, this testimony constitutes one of the most striking indications of public protest over the German maltreatment of Jews demonstrated by Russian inhabitants, not only in the North Caucasus but also in all the occupied Soviet territories. It

100 Kislovodsk and Krasnodar: Statement of Boris Khshive, July 3, 1943, GARF, 7021/17/5, p. 50; Statement of K. M. Stepaniuk, [no date], GARF, 7021/16/462, p. 10.

101 Kislovodsk: Confirmation by Klavdiia Filipenko, July 29, 1943, GARF, 7021/17/5, p. 67.

102 Krasnodar: Interrogation of Lidiia Ivanova, January 6, 1944, GARF, 7021/16/462, p. 24.

103 Statement of Boris Khshive, July 3, 1943, GARF, 7021/17/5, p. 50.

104 Intelligence survey no. 21 of the NKVD Administration, October 6, 1942, in Beliaev and Bondar', *Kuban' v gody Velikoi Otechestvennoi voiny, 1941-1945*, p. 461.

is significant that the available documents do not indicate that the demonstrators were punished. Nor is there any record of German persecution of those who expressed their sympathy with the Jews, with the notable exception of one woman, who was arrested and killed "for expressing solidarity with the Jewish family."[105]

Also illuminating is the wartime testimony concerning Zhukovskii *khutor* (farm). The witness was a Jewish woman who had lived there with her mother and children:

> The police arrived while I was at work. They made sure that I was Jewish and took me to the village of Padchinka, and then to the village of Novoselitsk. There I was required to produce documents, but I had none. I expected immediate execution. But Zhukovskii's people hastily produced a paper, in which they stated that I consistently worked well and did no harm to anyone. Then, by the order of the *Kommandant*, my family and I were released and sent to the same village to be placed under police surveillance.[106]

It is of note that the locals did not state that she was not Jewish but rather only mentioned her merits as a good person and hard worker. Although the Germans were at times sympathetic to the demands of the local Russian population in other matters, their acquiescence in this instance concerning the witness's Jewishness (even as a clear exception to the rule) is still impressive. If this story is indeed authentic, it may imply that in exceptional cases in the North Caucasus (apparently only in remote localities), a sizable group of Russians pleading a Jew's case could bear fruit, and even lead to a reversal of the clear-cut German *Judenpolitik*.

At the same time, however, many inhabitants of the North Caucasus collaborated with the German anti-Jewish decrees. This ranged from denunciations of Jews (active collaboration, presumably initiated by the denouncers and likely the most

105 Krasnodar: Statement of Konstantin Shepelev, no later than August 1, 1943, GARF, 7021/16/5, p. 54.

106 Novoselitskii *raion*, Stavropol'skii *krai*: Statement of Mariia Shakhniuk, 1943, GARF, 7021/17/11, p. 70.

dangerous form of collaboration for the persecuted Jews)[107] to the involvement of orphanage personnel in the selection of children (less active collaboration, resulting from compliance with the German orders yet apparently equally perilous for the Jews)[108] to the refusal by local inhabitants to shelter in their homes the sole Jewish child among all the children from the evacuated orphanage (less active collaboration leaving some rescue chances for the Jews).[109] Unfortunately, there is no record of the collaborators' motives, but it may be suggested that in most cases, in addition to their antisemitism, some feared the Germans. Others desired to gain financial profit from their actions, and robbed the Jews under the threat of turning them over to the Germans[110] or denounced them.[111] For their part, the Germans, of course, encouraged local people to turn in Jews. In Peredovaia *stanitsa*, for example, they gave the citizens a couple of sheep or a steer in return for their denunciations.[112]

Of particular attention is the behavior of non-Jewish spouses in mixed families. They were mostly spared from extermination. Non-Jewish "Aryan" spouses could legally approach the local administration and try to argue that there were no problems, at least insofar as their own Jewish links or their common children with the Jewish spouse were concerned.[113] There is evidence that these pleas were sometimes successful.[114] In other cases, the non-

107 Nal'chik, Peredovaia *stanitsa*: Testimony of Lena Simakhova, January 10, 1998, in Danilova, *Iskhod gorskikh evreev*, p. 114; Memoirs of Mikhail Bugakov, 2005, YVA, 0.33/7074.

108 Kislovodsk: Akt signed by the workers of the children's house no. 18, June 19, 1943, GARF, 7021/17/5, p. 18.

109 Krasnodarskii *krai*: Memoirs of Mikhail Bugakov, 2005, YVA, 0.33/7074.

110 Villages of Dzhiginka and Novozavedennoe: Testimony of Ol'ga Polonskaia, May 1, 1962, YVA, 0.3/2246, p. 7; Statement of Anna Shlaen, 1943, GARF, 7021/17/11, p. 114.

111 *Sovkhoz* no. 30: Testimony of Samuil Belenkov, August 10, 1943, GARF, 7021/17/4, p. 25.

112 Memoirs of Mikhail Bugakov, 2005, YVA, 0.33/7074.

113 Essentuki: Statement of the advocate Aleksandr Gontov, June 30, 1943, GARF, 7021/17/4, pp. 63-64.

114 Krasnodar, Otradnenskaia *stanitsa*: Statement of Ekaterina Kalinskaia, July 1, 1943, GARF, 7021/16/5, p. 56; Testimony of Roza Lipkin (1904), [no date], ICJ, TC 2860.

Jewish spouses became subject to persecution on account of their Jewish connections. In such instances, they could be thrown out from their apartments[115] or have their possessions confiscated by the German or local policemen.[116] When faced with German persecutions, some non-Jewish people chose to go with their Jewish family members to the very end (i.e., assembly and extermination),[117] while others went into hiding with their children.[118]

2.1.4. The Cossacks[119]

In the North Caucasus, the German armies faced a large Cossack population. Despite being ethnically (Russians and Ukrainians) and religiously (Orthodox Christian) identical with the Slavic majority, the Cossacks nevertheless differed from them for a variety of historical reasons. In this respect, of emphasis is their political and religious conservatism, as well as their strong military tradition in the pre-Soviet era, as well as their choice to fight on the White side in the Russian Civil War and their subsequent ruthless persecution by the triumphant Reds during the 1920s and 1930s. Their prewar attitudes towards the Jews were perhaps also different, namely more stringent and less tolerant.[120] Their pre-existing negative disposition towards Jews had the potential to become more directly manifest after the beginning of the war, when the Caucasian Cossacks came into contact with masses of Jews (i.e., those who had been evacuated

115 Krasnodar: Statement of Ekaterina Kalinskaia, July 1, 1943, GARF, 7021/16/5, p. 56.

116 Belorechenskaia *stanitsa* in Krasnodarskii *krai*: Questioning of Elena Eftaf'eva, August 20, 1943, GARF, 7021/16/12, p. 15.

117 Stavropol': Testimony of Dina Usatenko in Belikov, *Okkupatsiia*, p. 68; Piatigorsk: Testimony of Lazar' Lazarev in Zinovii Tsukerman, ed., *Katastrofa: Poslednie svideteli: Vtoraia kniga vospominanii* (Moscow: Dom evreiskoi knigi, 2008), p. 180.

118 Stavropol': Statement of Liudmila Klimiuk, July 1, 1943, GARF, 7021/17/1, p. 8.

119 On the Cossacks during the Second World War, see Zhuravlev, *Kollaboratsionizm na iuge Rossii*, pp. 101-109; Peotr Krikunov, *Kazaki: mezhdu Gitlerom i Stalinym: Krestovyi pokhod protiv bol'shevizma* (Moscow: "Iuza" and "EXMO," 2005).

120 Krasnodar: Testimony of Natal'ia Krechetovich (1931), August 29, 1999, YVA, 0.33.C/5961.

and resettled in the area), apparently for the first time in their history.[121]

When the Germans occupied the region, it appeared that the Cossacks were the only group among the Russian population who had given them a welcome reception.[122] This was reciprocated by the German policy of granting special privileges to the Cossacks, which, according to the Soviet report written after the occupation, strengthened the Cossacks' already positive view of the new rule.[123] One of the most important results of these attitudes were the ultimate fighting of 11,000 Caucasian Cossacks on the German side,[124] many of whom fought vigorously against the Red Army,[125] and eventual retreat of even more Cossacks (80,000) with the Wehrmacht.[126]

As the Germans paid particular attention to the enrollment of the Cossacks in various German-sponsored units, they initiated a concrete propaganda effort to this effect. This effort contained general antisemitic motives borrowed from the instruments of classic Nazi propaganda, as well as those applied in the areas

121 Uspenskaia *stanitsa* in Krasnodarskii *krai* on August, 3-19, 1941; then, the city of Krasnodar from August 24 to November 24, 1941: Borovoi, *Vospominaniia*, p. 252.

122 Oberkommando der Heeresgruppe A — Abt. VII (Militärverwaltung), Tgb., no. 182/42, H. Qu., Abschrift, Betr.: Kosaken, August 25, 1942, YVA, JM/5605.

123 Krasnodarskii *krai*: Memorandum of Committee of the All-Union Lenin Communist Union of Youth (*Komsomol*) of Krasnodarskii *krai* on the training of youth to serve in partisan units and underground groups, [no date], in Beliaev and Bondar', *Kuban' v gody Velikoi Otechestvennoi voiny, 1941-1945*, p. 568.

124 On the collaboration between the German occupation authority and the Cossacks as seen from the latter side in the North Caucasus, see, for example, P. N. Donskov, *Don, Kuban' i Terek vo vtoroi mirovoi voine: Istoricheskaia povest' o vtoroi voine kazachestva s bolshevikami (1941-1945 gg.)* (New York, 1960). Although written apologetically, this book provides an important insight into the scope of resentment against the Soviet rule among the Cossacks. And although any reference to the Jewish question was tactfully omitted and limited solely to the invocation of Lazar' Kaganovich's role, it seems to have played no small role in the Cossacks' agenda during the German occupation.

125 Krikunov, *Kazaki: mezhdu Gitlerom i Stalinym,* pp. 207-235; Doronina, "Natsistkaia propaganda na okkupirovannykh territoriakh Stavropol'ia i Kubani…", p. 80.

126 Bugai, *Kazachestvo Rossii*, pp. 66-67.

with a predominantly Russian population. In addition, in the Cossacks' case, the Germans placed an emphasis on both the allegedly irreconcilable interests of Cossackdom (often regarded as a separate entity) and the fact that Jewry was typically identified with the Bolshevik regime.[127] These notions were expressed for example, in Maikop's newspaper *Maikopskaia zhizn'* on October 10, 1942: "The German army liberated Kuban' from the *Zhido*-Communist oppression; the bright star of revival has risen for our Cossackdom."[128]

It is against this background that the attitudes of the local Cossack population towards the Jews during the German occupation of the North Caucasus in the second half of 1942 should be analyzed. In the Cossack settlements, the ordinary inhabitants frequently carried out denunciations,[129] and there were even incidents of lynchings of Jews.[130] Local police and village headmen arrested Jews,[131] supervised those who were detained,[132] and sometimes participated in the killing actions.[133] A Wehrmacht unit comprised predominantly of Cossacks (part of the Cavalry

127 "Dobrodetel'nyi podvizhnik prep. Sergii Radonezhskii," *Kuban'*, no. 20, November 27, 1942, TsDNIKK; "Vozrodim slavu kubanskikh kazakov!" *Osvobozhdennyi Maikop*, no. 31, December 6, 1942, TsDNIKK. See also Dmitrii Zhukov and Ivan Kovtun, *Antisemitskaia propaganda na okkupirovannykh territoriiakh RSFSR* (Rostov-na-Donu: "Feniks", 2015), pp. 113-114.

128 *Maikopskaia zhyzn'*, October 10, 1942, quoted in Natal'ia Garazha, "Deiatelnost' organov vlasti po mobilizatsii rabochego klassa na pobedu v gody Velikoi Otechestvennoi voiny 1941-1945 gg.: Na materialakh Krasnodarskogo kraia," (PhD diss., Adygeiskii gosudarstvennyi universitet, 2005), p. 157.

129 Mozdok, Otradnenskaia *stanitsa*: Testimony of Semeon Rechister, December 20, 1991, YVHN; Testimony of Roza Lipkin (1904), [no date], ICJ, TC 2860.

130 Village of Dzhiginka: Interrogation of Aleksandr Chebanenko, January 25, 1944, YVA, M.33/304, p. 7.

131 Grigoripolinskaia *stanitsa*: Akt of the Commission of Novo-Aleksandrovskaia, June 24, 1943, GARF, 7021/17/11, p. 28.

132 Krasnodar Trial, interrogation of Margarita Ivanova, March 19, 1943, AFSB RF, H-16708, vols. 4-5, p. 847, courtesy of the USHMM.

133 Village of Urozhainoe, Kotliarevskaia *stanitsa*: Report on the partisan activities by the Secretary of the Committee of the VKP(b) of [Stavropol'skii] *krai* Mikhail Suslov, top secret, October 25, 1942, RGASPI, 69/1/619, page illegible; Akt no. 75 of the Commission of the Kabardino-Balkar Republic, June 24, 1943, GARF, 7021/7/109, p. 171.

Nazi propaganda leaflet, written in verse: "Hasten, Cossack, it's time to rescue a family and a Motherland! Enough to carry on your shoulders an onerous burden with disgrace!" Courtesy: RHCA

Regiment led by Major Fürst von Urach) killed Jews in the North Caucasus in August 1942.[134]

Yet, the involvement of the Cossack officials in implementing the "Final Solution" was not confined to their personal participation in the persecution and murder of Jews. The entire Cossack autonomous administration was mobilized to ensure the smooth functioning of the killing machine. The following Soviet wartime document relating to one of the Cossack areas of Krasnodarskii *krai* underscores the point:

134 BA-MA, RH 23/14, Korück 531/Qu an Kav. Regt. Major Fürst von Urach (20.8.1942), betr., Erschießungen, in Oldenburg, *Ideologie und militärisches Kalkül*, p. 306.

> Region Head [*ataman raiona*] Rykov Georgii wrote strict ordinances to the headmen of the *kolkhozy* to the effect that Jews be brought to the police department [*uprava*] of the region. He stipulated that those who gave shelter to the Jews would be handed to the German authorities.[135]

Local and regional Cossack officials were also involved in the "final screening" of Jews, the process by which it was decided who would be killed.[136] Sometimes this "verification" was carried out solely by Cossack officials without any German control,[137] which testifies to the high level of confidence the Germans had in their Cossack collaborators for their involvement in the "Final Solution." Occasionally, autonomous Cossack units participated in the killing operations against Jews.[138] Guided by the *Feldgendarmerie*, they supervised the local population, and the seizure of Jews was part of their duties.[139] However, it should be remembered that, for the most part, these troops were raised at a relatively advanced stage of the German occupation, when the bulk of Caucasian Jewry had already been annihilated.

However, even in the depressing atmosphere of the time, some ordinary Cossacks diverted from the patterns discussed above and rendered aid to the Jews, sometimes even saving them from murder.[140] The circumstances for Jewish survival were in

135 Akt of the Commission of Kalnibolotskaia *stanista*: November 30, 1943, YVA, M.33/301, p. 120.

136 Akt of the Commission of Novo-Aleksandrovskaia *stanitsa*: June 24, 1943, GARF, 7021/17/11, p. 28.

137 Village of Grigoripolinskaia: ibid.

138 Unidentified locality apparently in Krasnodarskii *krai*, village of Levokumskoe in Stavropol'skii *krai*: Krasnodar trial, interrogation of Margarita Ivanova, April 13, 1943, AFSB RF, H-16708, vols. 4-5, p. 847, courtesy of the USHMM; Testimony of Philip Tenebaum, December 27, 2007, author's archive.

139 BA-MA, RH 23/40, Korück 550/Qu, "Befehl nu. 14 für Einsatz der Ordnungsdienste (14.8.1942)," in Oldenburg, *Ideologie und militärisches Kalkül*, p. 289.

140 Unidentified *stanitsa* in Krasnodarskii *krai* and Akhmetovskaia *stanitsa* in Krasnodarskii *krai*: Gordon, "On the Jewish settlements in the Crimea" *Eynikayt*, August 16, 1945, p. 3; File of Praskovia Bondarenko et al., [no date], YVA, M.31/8088.

line with those invoked in the previous sections of this chapter; namely, that those of mixed families had greater chances to survive. For example, in one case in Belorechenskaia *stanitsa*, when the execution of Jewish children from mixed families was taking place, one of the local inhabitants approached the German officer in charge and pleaded with him to set the Jews free.[141] In another case recorded by a Jewish survivor immediately after liberation, a Cossack woman argued with a German officer in Labinskaia *stanitsa* in order to convince him to free a female Jew. According to the testimony, she prudently employed a semi-racial argumentation as she "pleaded with the policeman [on the witness's behalf] and claimed that the witness's father was Russian and she belonged predominantly to the Russian nation."[142] It appears that the few documented cases of the survival of Jews in the Cossack settlements were actually "legally" arranged and, thus, incurred less risk for the people who rescued Jews.

2.2 Non-Slavic population[143]

2.2.1. General concerns

It is important to bear in mind that there were many national and religious ethnicities in the region that can be distinguished by various backgrounds and behavior during the Holocaust. Their difference from the Russian-Ukrainian majority was apparent for all sides involved: Germans, Soviets, and Jews. This study deals with these peoples as a whole, and, therefore, the term "Caucasian non-Russian population" is used collectively to denote all non-Russian minorities who resided in the German-occupied portion of the region. Nevertheless, whenever necessary, the reference is made to the specific ethnic affiliation of the person involved.

The reasons for the behavior of non-Russian minorities in the North Caucasus during the war can be traced back to the prewar

141 Belorechenskaia *stanitsa*: Statement of Evdokiia Voskovoinikova, August 20, 1943, GARF, 7021/16/12, p. 6.

142 Questioning of Raisa Niminskaia (1926), August 24, 1943, YVA, M.33/292, p. 106.

143 Statiev, "The Nature of Anti-Soviet Armed Resistance, 1942-44," pp. 288-306.

developments in the region.[144] From the onset of the war, these peoples' increasing dissatisfaction with Soviet rule was expressed *inter alia* in their reluctance to fight[145] and in their growing defection from the Red Army.[146] After the withdrawal of the Soviet forces from the Caucasus, anti-Soviet forces occasionally emerged, consisting entirely of non-Russian inhabitants.[147] In a number of places, they seized abandoned Soviet cities and retained them until the entry of the German troops. In the meantime, they persecuted Soviet activists, put almost a complete halt to the movement of civilians away from these areas, and destroyed Soviet evacuation convoys while killing all the evacuees.[148] This had a detrimental effect on the chances of Jews to escape, although there is no indication that it was directed specifically against the Jews.

Testimonies of Jewish survivors, as well as Soviet and German reports, suggest that the non-Russian population frequently welcomed the entry of German forces into the Caucasus.[149] A Soviet post-occupation report claimed highly improbable figures of local collaborators.[150] For their part, the German documents were also

144 See section A, "The Crimea and the Caucasus prior to the Holocaust."

145 "Dlia nikh voevat' za Stalina ili Gitlera byl odin chert: Nikto iz nikh ne khotel voevat"," testimony of Avsei Shvartsberg on the 409 Rifle Division, September 22, 2006, available from http://www.iremember.ru/content/view/395/75/lang.ru.

146 Reports of the Political Administration of the Transcaucasian Front, October 1942, in Valentin Bojzow, "Aspekte der miltärischen Kollaboration in der UdSSR von 1941-1944," in Röhr, *Okkupation und Kollaboration (1938-1945*, p. 307; Poppe, *Reminiscences*, p. 160.
For its part, the Soviet regime did not place much confidence in non-Russian Caucasians, excluding a significant part of them from the draft. Bezugol'nyi, "Narody Kavkaza," pp. 45-46.

147 For example, the untitled document of the Central Archive of the Defense ministry of the Russian Federation (TsAMO RF), 38663/1/41, p. 42 and 38663/1/44, pp. 4-5, quoted in Ibragimov, *Vlast' i obschestvo*, pp. 299-300.

148 Kislovodsk and Mikoianshakhar: Testimony of Fania Skliar, September 1975, YVA, 0.3/3934, p. 4; Poppe, *Reminiscences*, p. 160; Testimony of Vadim Maniker, April 1975, YVA, 0.3/4108, p. 2.

149 Kislovodsk and Kalmykiia: Testimony of Rimma Zikhlinskaia (1930), June 16, 1988, YVA, 0.3/4927, p. 3; CSpSd, Kommandostab, Berlin, MbOg, no. 28, Geheim, October 30, 1942, YVA, JM/4539.

150 "Some 2,000 Balkars out of the total population of 40,000 supported directly or indirectly the German Fascist occupiers", in Nikolai Bugai, ed., *'Soglasno Vashemu ukazaniiu!': O deportatsii narodov SSSR v 20-40 e gg.* (Moscow:

biased, as was the case with the report from the Kabardin village of Deiskoe dated November 22, 1942, depicting exclamations of gratitude by the local people to the Germans:

> "You liberated us, Kabardins." This was the greeting of the elders. "You liberated us from forced labor in *kolkhozy*. You returned to us the freedom of belief. We can now work our own fields, our children will be free and not the slaves of the Bolshevik despots. For all this we are sincerely thankful to you."[151]

In most cases, the sympathy of the non-Russian inhabitants of the North Caucasus towards German rule did not disappear, and even sometimes increased throughout the whole occupation period.[152] Nevertheless, as a result of the gradual change of the strategic situation on the Soviet-German front, the local non-Russian inhabitants became somewhat more reserved in their enthusiasm towards German rule.[153] By the end of the occupation, many local people were enlisted in the German-raised units[154] or had left the region with the retreating Wehrmacht,[155] which is indicative of their pro-German and/or anti-Soviet sentiments.

These observations notwithstanding, the point must be

AIRO-XX, 1995), p. 6. It should be kept in mind that this was written after the deportations of some local people from the region, and definitely was supposed to justify these Soviet measures.

151 Feindnachrichtenblatt vom 10.12.1942, Gen.Kdo., LII.A.K., Ic., December 10, 1942, in Hoffmann, *Die Ostlegionen 1941-43*, p. 444.

152 Karachaevo district, Kabardino-Balkariia: Korück 531, KTB, S. 35, 10.10.1942, "Besuch des Uraza Bairam Festes in Kislowodsk am 11.10.1942,"Bev., D., RMfdbO Min.Dirig., Dr. Bräutigam, Abschrift, BA, R 6/65.

153 In particular, since November 1942: Kom.Gen. D. Sich.Tr. u. Befh. H.Geb. A an H.Gr. A, Monatsbericht, 1.-31.10.1942, no. 1123/42 geh., 8.11.1942 (v. Roques), Archiv des Verf Hoffmann in Hoffman, *Die Ostlegionen 1941-43*, p. 443.

154 Chivalry Corps in Kalmykiia: Gerhard von Mende, "Die Kalmücken," *Zeitschrift für Geopolitik* 22, no. 7 (1951): p. 445.

155 3,000 in Kabardino-Balkariia alone: Report of the Commission of the Party Control of the VKP(b), August 1944, in Khadzhi-Murat Sabanchiev, *Byli soslany navechno: deportatsiia i reabilitatsiia balkarskogo naroda* (Nal'chik: El'brus, 2004), p. 9.

made that the various Caucasian minorities demonstrated different extents of pro-German sentiments. The juxtaposition of wartime German and Soviet reports indicates that they were most pronounced among the Karachaevo people and least among the Adygeans, Cherkesses, Kalmyks, Kabardins, and Balkars.[156] The remaining groups do no figure prominently in the relevant reports, and it is therefore impossible to draw any conclusions regarding them.

The position of these peoples regarding the "Jewish Question" is difficult to determine (if such a generalization is possible at all). The subject was largely foreign to them, and played no substantial role in their daily life or political discourse. The memoirs of a Jewish woman evacuated through the region in May 1942 are instructive in this respect. On her way, she came across a number of non-Russian villages to the west of Minvody whose inhabitants:

> ... pitied us, though of course they traded at the rates favorable for them; yet, there emanated no belligerence from them, but rather curiosity. At one stop, my brother and I took water from the water-tower. A local woman asked us: "Where is the train with the Jews? I'd like to have a look at them!"[157]

Yet, one should not idealize the picture. Even in such remote places where the Jews had not been known prior to the war, the seeds of antisemitism had sometimes already been sown by the evacuation period.

Although often supportive of German war aims in and around the region,[158] these ethnic groups sometimes pursued a separate domestic agenda, partly reflective of but not entirely identical with German ideas concerning the region. The following

156 CSpSd, Kommandostab, Berlin, MbOg, no. 28, Geheim, November 6, 1942, RGVA, 500/1/776, pp. 15-16; "Besuch des Uraza Bairam Festes in Kislowodsk am 11.10.1942," Bev. D. RMfdbO Min.Dirig. Dr. Bräutigam, Abschrift, BA, R 6/65.

157 Testimony of Anfisa Kalnitskaia (1926), [no date], ICJ, TC 2759.

158 CSpSd, Kommandostab, Berlin, MbOg, no. 28, Geheim, November 6, 1942, RGVA, 500/1/776.

piece of postwar Soviet evidence could be fabricated by Soviet security agencies willing to provide *a posteriori* justification of charges of mass collaboration leveled by the Soviets against several Caucasian nations and collectively deported from the region after Soviet return. As such, it must be approached with caution. Yet, it could be also authentic, indicating the readiness of Caucasian nationalists to forge an alliance with Nazi Germany and to embrace its anti-Jewish policies, and as such it is worth mentioning:[159]

> Among the main goals of the "Special Party of Caucasian Brethren," which was active in the North Caucasus during the Great Patriotic War, it was stated: to precipitate the destruction of Bolshevism in the Caucasus in the name of Russia's defeat in its fight against Germany; the establishment of a free federative republic in the Caucasus to enjoy the mandate of the German Reich; [and] the deportation of Russians and Jews from the region.[160]

Sometimes these groups formed their own guerilla formations (evidently with some German support), which operated independently in the Caucasus.[161] Unfortunately, the actual attitudes and behavior of these groups towards the Jews cannot be clarified due to a lack of sources. Needless to say, the ruthless Soviet persecution of these groups after the liberation of the region and the deportation of many Caucasian minorities[162] present a serious impediment to a thorough elucidation of the topic.

159 Again, it is significant that the report was drawn up after the deportations, and was doubtlessly supposed to justify in retrospect the Soviet punitive measures.

160 Amanzholova, et al., *Natsional'naia politika Rossii*, p. 317.

161 Kabardino-Balkariia: Untitled document, TsAMO RF, 38663/1/41, p. 42 in Ibragimov, *Vlast' i obschestvo*, pp. 299-300.

162 For example, Elza-Bair Guchinova, "Deportation of the Kalmyks (1943-1956): Stigmatized Ethnicity," in Uyama Tomohiko, ed., *Empire, Islam, and Politics in Central Eurasia: Slavic Eurasian Studies* (Sapporo: Slavic Research Center, Hokkaido University, 2007), pp. 187-220.

2.2.2. Collaborators

The Jewish theme did not figure prominently in propaganda activities in the occupied non-Russian areas of the North Caucasus. There are only scarce references to the subject, such as the following one mentioned in the declaration of the autonomous government of Kabardino-Balkariia ("Appeal to the Kabardin and Balkar Peoples") from November 1942:

> The German army liberated us from *Zhido*-Bolshevik dominion. Upon having received from Germany's hands this great and sacred gift freedom, the Kabardin and Balkar People now became the master of its own fate.[163]

It is tempting to regard this simply as lip-service to the Germans. Nonetheless, other conditions being equal, the higher extent of rallying on the German side implied the growing embrace of all Nazi slogans and policies, including their fixed ideas concerning the Jews and actual implementation of the "Final Solution."

Furthermore, local collaborators serving as policemen participated in the killing operations directed against the Ashkenazi Jewish population.[164] Sometimes, they were brought as reinforcement to Russian policemen who exterminated Jews in Russian localities.[165] Occasionally, non-Russian policemen were remunerated with the possessions of exterminated Jews or simply grabbed them on their own.[166] In light of the relatively small record of the involvement of the non-Russian policemen in various phases of the Holocaust (which may be accounted for by the limited presence of Ashkenazi Jews in non-Russian localities), the few cases in which they rendered

163 Untitled document, [no date], GARF, 7021/148/406.

164 Village of Novo-Osetinskaia, "Vazhnyi" *khutor*: Akt of the Commission of Mozdok, July 27, 1943, GARF, 7021/17/10, p. 238; Interrogation of Patiia Erkemova, June 12, 1948, USHMMA, RG-74.001/22.

165 Akt of the Commission of Dubovo-Balkavskoe, July 10, 1943, GARF, 7021/17/10, p. 149.

166 Kislovodsk and "Vazhnyi" *khutor*: Testimony of Fania Skliar, September 1975, YVA, 0.3/3934, p. 11; Interrogation of Ali Abzaliev, July 13, 1948, USHMMA, RG-74.001*47 (Fiche #22); Interrogation of Patiia Erkemova, June 12, 1948, ibid.

aid and even saved Ashkenazi Jews may be given more weight in the research than would usually be warranted.[167]

Some local non-Russian inhabitants of the region persecuted Jews while serving in the so-called "Tatar" or "Caucasian" Company (*Kaukasier-Kompanie*), which operated under the EG D.[168] At least part of its members were raised from Soviet POWs prior to the German drive into the Caucasus,[169] but there is no information concerning the enlistment of the rest of the soldiers into this unit. The question of ethnic and religious belonging of most of its some 200 members remains largely unanswered, but some sources claim it was made up of Crimean Tatars, Armenians, Azerbaijanis, Georgians,[170] and "Caucasians" (that is, inhabitants of the North Caucasus),[171] primarily the Karachaev people.[172] It may be deemed as an established fact that the non-German members of this unit complied with the orders (including those concerning Jews) of their German commanders, and sometimes even operated independently without any German surveillance.[173]

This Caucasian unit of the EG D also participated in a variety of the murderous *Einsatzgruppe* activities directed against Jews. Originally, it was stationed in Stavropol' and then divided into Gruppen (smaller teams) and dispatched, together with the SD-*Kommandos*, into various towns and villages of the vast North Caucasian region.[174] The available testimonies

167 Kislovodsk: Testimony of Fania Skliar, September 1975, YVA, 0.3/3934, pp. 9, 12.

168 On its activity in the Crimea, see Chapter 8, "The Local Population and the Holocaust in the Crimea."

169 "Strafsache gegen Walter Bierkamp," Auswertung der Vernehmungsprotokolle russischer Zeugen von Bl. 1/92-65/40 d. Akte, Alfons G. Dolmetscher bei der EG D, Bl. 3, W(oroschilowsk), K(uberer), [no date], YVA, TR.10/1147, p. 575.

170 Ibid., p. 575.

171 "Strafsache gegen Walter Bierkamp," Auswertung der Vernehmungsprotokolle russischer Zeugen von Bl. 1/92-65/40 d. Akte, B. 7-8, Iwan D. ab Okt. 41 bei der Tataren-Komp, Woroschilowsk – K, [no date], YVA, TR.10/1147, p. 576.

172 Interrogation of Mikhail Fingerut, June 25, 1943, GARF, 7021/17/5, p. 31.

173 Village of Suadag in North Ossetiia: Document no. 215, "O peresechenii linii fronta," February 13, 1943, GARF, 7021/12/66, pp. 12-13.

174 "Strafsache gegen Walter Bierkamp," Auswertung der Vernehmungsprotokolle

point out to this unit's involvement in round-ups,[175] the murder of Jews in a gas van,[176] the arrest and execution of Jews,[177] and killing operations.[178] Soldiers of the unit were duly remunerated for their work. According to the proceedings of the Krasnodar trial, after the killing operation in the town, every soldier of the Caucasian Company was allowed to take some of the personal possessions of the Jewish victims, as well as their seven-day food supply.[179]

The attitudes of the Caucasian collaborators towards the Mountain Jews deserve special attention. The sources from which this subject may be elucidated are rather singular. On the one hand, there is an important interview offered soon after the war by Selim Shadov, Head of the National Council of Kabardino-Balkariia.[180] According to his evidence, after a delegation of anxious Mountain Jews had visited him, he approached *Feldmarschall* von Kleist and succeeded in persuading him that Mountain Jews were not to be treated as Jews, but rather as a native people. This

russischer Zeugen von Bl. 1/92-65/40 d. Akte, Islam G. Buerger d. UdSSR, [no date], YVA, TR.10/1147, p. 582. See also Dean, "Examination of KGB Trial Files", p. 20.

175 Stavropol': "Strafsache gegen Walter Bierkamp," Auswertung der Vernehmungsprotokolle russischer Zeugen von Bl. 1/92-65/40 d. Akte, B. 7-8, Iwan D. ab Okt. 41 bei der Tataren-Komp, Woroschilowsk – K, [no date], YVA, TR.10/1147, p. 576. However, another German, who testified in this trial, assumed that the unit was not active in Stavropol'. "Strafsache gegen Walter Bierkamp," Auswertung der Vernehmungsprotokolle russischer Zeugen von Bl. 1/92-65/40 d. Akte, Islam G. Buerger d. UdSSR, [no date], YVA, TR.10/1147, p. 582.

176 Stavropol': "Nachtragsanklageschrift in der Strafsache gegen Kehrer," YVA, TR.10/802, p. 5. See also Dean, "Gutachten in dem Verfahren gegen Alfons Götzfried," pp. 19-20.

177 Armavir: "Strafsache gegen Walter Bierkamp," Staatsanwaltschaft, München, Berlin, Vernehmungsniederschrift, Herr Fritz U., December 6, 1962, YVA, TR.10/1147, p. 381.

178 Kislovodsk, Krasnodar: Interrogation of Mikhail Fingerut, June 25, 1943, GARF, 7021/17/5, p. 31; Krasnodar trial, interrogation of Nikolai Pushkarev, June 17, 1943, AFSB RF, H-16708, vol. 1, p. 189, courtesy of the USHMM.

179 Krasnodar trial, interrogation of Nikolai Pushkarev, June 17, 1943, AFSB RF, H-16708, vol. 1, p. 66, courtesy of the USHMM.

180 Altshuler, *Jews of the Eastern Caucasus*, pp. 122-124 (untitled document from the personal library of Professor Alexander Dallin).

interview has already been analyzed in the scholarship,[181] but some points, nevertheless, should be highlighted. Shadov's interview is inaccurate in the description of some details. It apparently contains an exaggeration of Shadov's own role in the rescue of Jews, and, most importantly, no wartime evidence substantiates his words. Nor, equally significant, is it supported by any postwar German evidence.[182] At the same time, some testimonies that Mountain Jews offered dozens of years after the war are supportive of his version.[183] If taken for granted in its most important details, this intercession constitutes a prominent act of pleading on behalf of the Jews in the region, and presents the leadership of the German-picked Kabadino-Balkar administration in a positive light.

In the last decade, the surviving Mountain Jews have produced testimonies that shed more light on the behavior of other non-Russian officials in the German service towards them. This behavior was largely restrained, especially in Nal'chik,[184] and was apparently limited, at most, to extortions, which could have also involved threats of extradition to the Germans.[185] In rural localities, though, this behavior might have included denunciations.[186]

2.2.3. Ordinary people

What little evidence hitherto preserved concerning the attitudes of ordinary non-Russian people towards the Jews during the German occupation of the North Caucasus hardly suffices to paint a clear picture of what really occurred there. Again, it should be stressed that there were relatively few Jews (especially Ashkenazi) in these areas. A large number of Caucasian

181 Ibid., pp. 124-125.

182 These sources, quite predictably, highlight the role of the Germans themselves in the rescue of the Mountain Jews: Poppe, *Reminiscences*, p. 166; Polian, *Mezhdu Aushvitsem i Bab'em Yarom*, pp. 141-142.

183 Testimony of Besirit Ashurova, January 7, 1998, in Danilova, *Iskhod gorskikh evreev*, p. 40; Testimony of Aleksandr Simakhov, January 8, 1998, in ibid., p. 173.

184 Testimony of Guchi Motaeva (1929), January 6, 1998, in ibid, p. 123.

185 Testimony of Ilisho Ashurova (1918), January 8, 1998, in ibid., p. 86.

186 Village of Bogdanovka: Testimony of Sergei Amiramov, January 1, 1998, in ibid., p. 146.

minorities were deported after the return of the Soviets. Unless they had committed crimes punishable by Soviet laws,[187] there exists almost no record that could resolve the question. In fact, the only source of information (however deficient) left are the testimonies submitted by the Jews either during the war or more recently.

Quite predictably, an exploration of the available sources suggests that ordinary Caucasians behaved differently towards various groups of the Jews. As already stated elsewhere, they tended to identify the majority of Ashkenazi Jewish refugees as newcomers who did not belong to the established order in the region. Even if largely devoid of religiously motivated antisemitism,[188] the attitudes of the local population towards the Ashkenazi Jews were still affected by a complex set of factors. Some of them were favorable for the Jews – i.e., traditional welcoming receptions as guests or solidarity with the oppressed and other minorities. The geopolitical factors, however, such as the German presence and the sympathy of non-Russian minorities towards it, were detrimental for the Jews. In the non-Russian towns and villages (*auly*), the local inhabitants occasionally exploited the precarious conditions of the Jews in hiding, and extorted their possessions under the threat of extradition to the Germans.[189] Sometimes, after there was nothing left to take they turned the Jews in to the Germans,[190] although this was not always the case.[191] There was also an instance in which a Karachai family sheltered

187 That is, in "our" case they actively assisted the Germans in killing the Jews, and were condemned thereupon, so that one can learn about their activity from the Soviet trial documentation.

188 See section 9A, "The Responses of Orthodox Christianity and Islam in the Crimea and the North Caucasus to the Holocaust."

189 Krasno-Vostochnyi *aul*, unidentified *aul* in Stavropol'skii *krai*: Testimony of A. S. Bagiennovskaia, no later than June 26, 1943, GARF, 7021/17/206, pp. 72-73; Testimony of L. S. and R. L. Prazement, [no date], GARF, 7021/17/206, pp. 104-105.

190 Krasno-Vostochnyi: Testimony of A. S. Bagiennovskaia, [no later than June 26, 1943], GARF, 7021/17/206, pp. 72-73.

191 Unidentified *aul* in Stavropol'skii *krai*: Testimony of L. S. and R. L. Prazement, [no date], GARF, 7021/17/206, pp. 104-105.

Jews in their house for the duration of five months.[192] The actual situation in this Karachai village and that of this specific family, including its ethnic and religious make-up, as well whether or not German troops were present in the village or in its vicinity, is unknown. In another case, a Karachai family in Mikoianshakhar provided a Jewish family with a shelter for only one night. This was, however, critical, because that night a round-up of Jews was conducted. The family then directed the Jews to a getaway route.[193] Therefore, more direct conclusions cannot yet be drawn, but it does suggest that the non-Russian minorities were sometimes willing to shelter or potentially otherwise help Jews.

With respect to the Mountain Jews, the local non-Russian people seemed not to view them as foreigners, but rather as another local group suddenly singled out by an external power for maltreatment. It should be noted that all relevant testimonies elucidating the subject were given by Mountain Jews several decades after the war. Thus, this only source of information should be viewed with special caution. Besides, many Mountain Jewish witnesses were still living in these places at the time of the testimony, which could further impair their integrity. According to this evidence, ordinary Caucasians frequently rendered aid to the Mountain Jews, including providing them with shelter[194] (active aid, fraught with mortal danger for the helper), refraining from denouncing them[195] (passive aid, which apparently carried less risk for the helper), or giving prior warning not to gather at the assembly site before the

192 Teberda: File of Shamail, Ferdaus, Sultan and Muchtar Khalamliev, 1994, YVA, M.31/6228.

193 Prizov Yuri, "The Reminiscences of a Young Holocaust Survivor," [no date], United States Holocaust Memorial Museum Collection: 2011.337.1.

194 Nal'chik – numerous cases; Volnyi *aul* in Kabardino-Balkariia: Testimony of Raisa Shamilova, August 19, 1998, in Danilova, *Iskhod gorskikh evreev*, p. 30; Testimony of Lena Simakhova, January 10, 1998, in ibid., p. 112; Testimony of Guchi Motaeva, January 6, 1998, in ibid., p. 123; Testimony of Ilisho Ashurova, January 8, 1998, in ibid., p. 39.

195 Village of Staryi Leken in Kabardino-Balkariia: Testimony of Raisa Shamilova, August 19, 1998, in ibid., p. 73.

Aktion[196] (important advice with no risk for the advisor). There were also personal attempts to persuade the Germans that the Mountain Jews were not actually Jews but rather Tats, a local tribe[197] (important initiatives, but relatively safe for non-Jews in the Caucasus). The number of denunciations was relatively low, which supports these claims to a certain extent.[198]

196 Near Bogdanovka: Testimony of Ilisho Ashurova, January 8, 1998, in ibid., p. 87.

197 Nal'chik: Testimony of Lena Simakhova, January 10, 1998, in ibid., p. 172; Testimony of Liviia Digilova, August 19, 1999, in ibid., p. 56.

198 Village of Menzhynskoe and unidentified village in Kabardino-Balkariia: Testimony of Ilisho Ashurova, January 8, 1998, in ibid., p. 85; Testimony of Noshum Shamilov, October 11, 1988, YVA, 0.3/5157, pp. 17-18.

CHAPTER ELEVEN

Responses of Orthodox Christianity and Islam in the Crimea and the North Caucasus to the Holocaust[1]

1. Background

1.1. THE CRIMEA

In the Crimean peninsula, there was a close relationship between Islam and the only large ethnic group that practiced it, Crimean Tatars. It is sometimes difficult to distinguish between specifically Tatar national activities and those bearing religious character. Over the course of the 19th century and the era of religious enlightenment, the Crimean Tatars had emerged as one of the leading Islamic communities of the Russian Empire.[2] Later, during the Soviet period, continuous

1 Kalmyks, most of whom professed Buddhism, constituted the only group in the region that practiced this religion. It is not analyzed, however, in this study as a separate religion because of the actual lack of sources. On German attitudes towards the Kalmyks, see, for example, Mende, "Bericht von Sachbearbeiter Dr. Himpel," (RMfdO?), "Richtlinien für die Behandlung der Ostvölker," Kaukasien, December 11, 1942, Yad Vashem Archives (YVA), JM/5716; CSpSd, Kommandostab, Berlin, MbOg, no. 28, Geheim, November 6, 1942, YVA, JM/4539. For some literature on Kalmyks, see Joachim Hoffmann, *Deutsche und Kalmyken, 1942 bis 1945* (Freiburg: Rombach, 1986).

2 Paul Robert Magocsi, *This Blessed Land: Crimea and the Crimean Tatars* (Toronto, Ontario: University of Toronto Press, 2014), especially chapter 5 "Crimea in the Russian Empire"; Hakan Kirimli, *National Movements and National Identity among the Crimean Tatars, 1905-1916* (Leiden and New York: E. J. Brill, 1996). On Tsarist policies towards Islam, see, for example, Robert D. Crews, *For Prophet and Tsar: Islam and Empire in Russia and Central Asia* (Cambridge, MA: Harvard University Press, 2006; Elena I. Campbell, "The Autocracy and the Muslim Clergy in the Russian Empire (1850s-1917)," *Russian Studies in History* 44, no. 2 (Fall 2005): pp. 8-29.

and ever-increasing anti-religious pressure[3] elicited a multitude of responses among the Tatars.[4] It seems that resentment over these policies was stronger in the traditionally-minded rural settlements. In the towns and larger localities, however, secularization among the Tatars was more widespread, both in those dominated by Tatars as well as in those that were predominantly non-Tatar. For them, the employment and cultural opportunities the Soviets provided largely made up for the Bolshevik assault on Islam. In contrast to some other Islam-dominated areas of the Soviet Union, this assault had caused no armed resistance on the part of the Tatars during the interwar period.

Numerous settlers arrived in the peninsula during the 19th century, most of whom (Russians and Ukrainians) practiced Orthodox Christianity. By the end of the 19th century, Orthodox Christian Russians and Ukrainians constituted the largest group in the religiously heterogeneous Crimea, and their populations were reinforced by the native Crimean Greeks and Bulgarians. Some other Christian denominations were also represented in the peninsula, such as the Protestant Church established by Germans[5] and the Armenian Church by Armenians. Like elsewhere in the Russian Empire, Orthodox Christianity enjoyed a privileged status and the support of the state.[6] In the peninsula, however,

3 E. M. Khairuddinova, "Osobennosti vzaimootnoshenii Sovetskoi vlasti i musul'man v Krymskoi ASSR (nachalo 20-kh – konets 30-kh gg. XX veka," *Istoricheskie nauki* 24 (63), no. 2 (2011): pp. 134-139.
On Soviet policies towards Islam during the prewar period, see, for example, Shoshana Keller, *To Moscow, not Mecca: The Soviet Campaign against Islam in Central Asia, 1917-1941* (Westport, CT: Praeger, 2001); Frank Nesemann, "Der Sowjetstaat und der Islam 1917-1941," in Christoph Gassenschmidt and Ralph Tuchtenhagen, eds., *Politik und Religion in der Sowjetunion 1917-1941* (Wiesbaden: Harrassowitz, 2001), pp. 207-235.

4 Williams, *The Crimean Tatars*, pp. 356, 359-60.

5 L. P. Kravtsova and E. V. Karpach, eds., *Nemetskoe naselenie Tavricheskoi gubernii* (Odessa: Astroprint, 2000).

6 Mara V. Kozelsky, "Christianizing Crimea: Church Scholarship, "Russian Athos," and Religious Patriotism of the Crimean War," (PhD diss., University of Rochester, 2004).
On Tsarist policies towards Orthodox Christianity, see, for example, Heater J. Coleman, ed., *Orthodox Christianity in Imperial Russia: A Source Book on Lived Religion* (Bloomington and Indianapolis: Indiana University Press, 2014); Vera

this process had been partly offset by the special recognition granted by the Imperial authorities to Muslim clergy, as well as the extremely heterogeneous make-up of the Crimean Christian population. During the Soviet period (until 1939), the Orthodox clergy had been subjected to aggressive persecution by the state, an unrestrained anti-religious campaign, the mass arrests of priests, and the confiscation of Church property.[7]

1.2. The North Caucasus

In dealing with Orthodox Christianity in the North Caucasus, a distinction should be drawn between the "native" peoples (such as Ossetiians), who professed it, and the Slavs. The former belonged to the unique "pre-Russian" ethno-religious mosaic of the region, and in many aspects, including indifference or ignorance of Jews, were closer to their Muslim neighbors than to the religiously similar Slavs. In turn, regarding the Slavs, a distinction should be made between the Cossacks and the "proper" ethnic Russians. In terms of religious conservatism, contemporary scholarship suggests that the Cossacks remained the more traditional of the two and the more reserved in its attitudes towards non-Christians, with particular cautious and even hostile behavior displayed towards the Jews.[8]

Both the Cossacks and the native Caucasian Christians were numerically overshadowed by Orthodox Christians, most specifically the ethnic Russians and Ukrainians who had been arriving in the Caucasus since the second part of the 19th century.

Shevzov, *Russian Orthodoxy on the Eve of Revolution* (Oxford: Oxford University Press, 2004).

7 Iurii Katunin, "Pravoslavnaia tserkov' i gosudarstvo: problema vzaimootnoshenii v 1917-1939 gg. (na primere Kryma)," (PhD diss., Tavricheskii universitet im. Vernadskogo, 2003), pp. 221-412.
On Soviet policies towards Orthodox Christianity during the prewar period, see, for example, Hiroaki Kuromiya, "Why the Destruction of Orthodox Priests in the Soviet Union in 1937-38?" *Jahrbücher für Geschichte Osteuropas* 55, no. 1 (2007): pp. 86-93; Anna Dickinson, "Quantifying Religious Oppression: Russian Orthodox Church Closures and Repression of Priests 1917–41," *Religion, State and Society* 28, no. 4 (2000): pp. 327-335.

8 Norkina, "The Origins of Anti-Jewish Policy," pp. 62-76; Paul E. Heineman, "In Defense of an Anachronism: The Cossack Question on the Don, 1861-1914," (PhD diss., Georgetown University, 1999), pp. 307-346.

Arguably, in terms of religious behavior, the latter were less strict then the local Christians, and it may be very cautiously suggested that the newcomers were less inclined than the Cossacks to define their attitudes towards the Jews (whose number was very small in the region) in religious terms. In the North Caucasus Orthodox Christianity was persecuted by the Bolsheviks throughout the entire prewar period.[9]

The long history of Islam in the region developed alongside that of Orthodox Christianity. Over the course of centuries, the penetration of Islam had been stopped, although the region remained mostly dominated by Islamic realms (Ottoman Turkey, Persia). Yet, their influence was counterbalanced by the neighboring Russian state.[10] During its penetration into the region in the late 18th and early 19th centuries, Russia faced powerful resistance, primarily by the Muslim inhabitants of the North Caucasus.[11] As a singular development, which did not replicate itself later, the latter managed to overcome their ethnic heterogeneity and establish a state according to the strict Muslim laws. Russia's final victory in the 1860s put an end to this unique experiment, and was followed by the emigration of many Islamic peoples into Ottoman Turkey.[12]

Significantly, the North Caucasian Muslims had maintained their own agenda both during the Russian Civil War and the interwar period. Muslim insurgents fought vigorously against what they perceived as an encroachment on Islam and their autonomy by the Reds and the Whites. For the most part, this struggle was confined to group and clan resistance, with no emergence of a

9 E.g., Nataliia Serdiukova, "Gosudarstvennaia politika v oblasti religii v 1920-e gg.: Na materialakh Severnogo Kavkaza" (Moscow: Moskovskii pedagogicheskii gosudarstvennyi universitet, 2006).

10 Michael Khodarkovsky, "Of Christianity, Enlightenment, and Colonialism: Russia in the North Caucasus, 1550-1800," *The Journal of Modern History* 71, no. 2 (June 1999): pp. 394-430.

11 Sean Pollock, "*Empire by Invitation*?: *Russian Empire-building in the Caucasus in the Reign of Catherine II*," (PhD diss., Harvard University, 2006); Gammer, *Muslim Resistance to the Tsar*.

12 Walter Richmond, *The Northwest Caucasus: Past, Present, Future* (London: Routledge, 2008), pp. 74-80; McCarthy, *Death and Exile*, pp. 34, 53f.

pan-Islamic movement in the North Caucasus.[13] Throughout the interwar period, this trend essentially remained unchanged, despite the discontent and resentment brewing from the rigorous anti-religious measures that the Soviet authorities had actively promoted in the region (especially in the 1930s),[14] creating the potential for resistance on the part of the local Muslims.[15] It is noteworthy that there is no indication that the Muslim struggle had antisemitic features; it seemed to follow a mostly domestic agenda.

2. During the War

2.1. Orthodox Christianity[16]

2.1.1. General concerns

After their invasion of the Soviet Union, the Germans were keen on capitalizing on the public discontent within some circles of the Soviet population over the Soviet persecution of the Orthodox Church.[17] German policies in church matters should be seen in

13 Pavel Aptekar', "Voina bez kraia i kontsa," *Rodina* 1-2 (2001), available from http://www.istrodina.com/2000_01_02/warnend.htm; Movsur Ibragimov, *Narody Severnogo Kavkaza v period Velikoi Otechestvennoi voiny 1941-1945 gg.* (Moscow: Moskovskii pedagogicheskii univesitet, 1997), pp. 37-42; Fanny E. Bryan, "Anti-religious activity in the Chechen-Ingush republic of the USSR and the survival of Islam," *Central Asian Survey* 3, no. 2 (1984): pp. 99-115.

14 The following data illustrate the dimensions of this policy. In 1936, 56% of the prayer buildings were closed in Kabardino-Balkariia as compared to the situation as of 1917. Untitled document, State Archive of the Russian Federation (GARF), 5263/1/97, pp. 4-5, in Ibragimov, *Vlast' i obschestvo*, p. 385.

15 As was the case of some of Caucasian peoples who resorted to armed resistance against the Soviet power from the beginning of the German invasion of the USSR. V. B. Veprintsev and I. A. Mochalin, "Bandity stremilis'... sokhranit' fashistskii poriadok," *Voenno-Istoricheskii Zhurnal* 5 (1996): pp. 83-89.

16 Al'tman, *Opfer des Hasses: Der Holocaust in der UdSSR 1941-1945*, pp 494-502; Mikhail Shkarovskii, "O podderzhke Pravoslavnoi tserkvi ne mozhet byt' i rechi': Tserkovnaia politika Natsistskoi Germanii na okkupirovannykh territoriiakh SSSR, 1941-1945 gg," *Istochnik* 6 (2001): pp. 74-96; Hans-Heinrich Wilhelm, "Der SD und die Kirchen in den besetzten Ostgebieten 1941/42," *Militärgeschichtliche Mitteilungen* 29, no. 1 (1981): pp. 55-99.

17 Karel Berkhoff, "Was there a Religious Revival in Soviet Ukraine under

this light. However restrictive, they crafted their policies so as to gain the support of wide circles among the local population – particularly during the first phase of the occupation, which was often crucial with respect to the Holocaust.

In dealing with the Orthodox Church in the occupied Soviet areas, the Germans noticed a possible link to the "Solution of the Jewish Question." A directive of the RSHA [*Reichssicherheitshauptamt* (Reich Main Security Office)] from October 31, 1941, stated:

> … under no circumstances should the masses receive teaching about God that is rooted in Judaism and borrows its understanding of religion from Jewish ideas… It is clear that the confinement of "God's chosen people" to ghettos and the eradication of this people… are compulsory measures that will further the cause of liberating the eastern regions of Europe. It is also clear that under no circumstances should the clergy be allowed to interfere with these measures, particularly in the regions infected by the Jews, where, on the basis of the Orthodox teaching, they are preaching that the healing of the world begins with the Jews. It is clear from the above that… the solution of the Church question in the occupied eastern regions… if skillfully handled, could be wonderfully resolved in favor of a religion free from Jewish influence.[18]

In contrast to German-occupied Europe, the possibilities of the Orthodox clergy to interfere in the implementation of the "Final Solution" in the Soviet Union on behalf of the Jews were far more limited. Because priests were not in control of large land possessions

the Nazi Regime?" *Slavonic and East European Review* 78, no. 3 (July 2000): pp. 536-567; Wilhelm, "Der SD und die Kirchen in den besetzten Ostgebieten 1941/42," pp. 55-94.

18 Mikhail Shkarovski, "The Attitude of the Russian Orthodox Church and the Ukrainian Greek Catholic Church to the Holocaust during World War II," in John K. Roth and Elisabeth Maxwell-Meynard, eds., *Ethics and Religion*, vol. 2 of *Remembering for the Future: The Holocaust in an Age of Genocide* (New York: Palgrave, 2001), p. 487.

and/or monasteries, but merely of small churches, they were unable to provide mass shelter. Additionally, the occupation authorities controlled the content of the priests' sermons and even the process of their appointments. One of few things that the clerics could do for the sake of the Jews was to grant them baptism certificates. Whether or not the Germans recognized them is analyzed in the following sections.

It must be pointed out that only in an extremely limited number of exceptions is it possible to speak about one cohesive voice of the Orthodox Church in its reaction to the Holocaust at the time – or even about those of a few individuals. In the occupied Soviet areas, the Germans were cautious enough to refrain from establishing one centralized institution in charge of church affairs.[19] Thus, eventually every priest was left to himself in addressing the plight of the Jews. The great majority of them adopted the conformist view, which was, in practice, tantamount to the tacit approbation of the German policy. Other segments of the clergy even adjusted to the language and spirit of the German antisemitic propaganda, propagating it to the laymen.

2.1.2. The Crimea

In the initial period of the German occupation, there were cases in which Jews converted to Orthodox Christianity. The principal and likely sole motive behind their decisions was the desire legally to evade the harsh German policies towards Jews. As the Crimean Jews were rather secularized, it is not surprising that there is no record of their families or friends opposing this move on religious grounds. However, there were apparently no conversions among the Krymchaks. Some Jews had opted for conversion prior to the extermination actions,[20] while

19 The only exception was the "Orthodox Mission in the Liberated Areas of Russia" with its center in Pskov, which was given ecclesiastical authority over the northwestern areas of Russia. Kovalev, *Povsedenevnaia zhizn' Rossii*, pp. 476-479.

20 Feodosiia, Simferopol', "Voroshilov" *kolkhoz*: Note of baptism of Boris Nudel'man, November 20, 1941, Feodosiia municipal archive (*uprava*), State Archive of the Autonomous Republic of the Crimea (DAARK), P-1458; Statement of Leon Vatman, not later than October 1944, YVA, M.33/68, p. 166.

others resorted to it only thereafter.[21] The decision to embrace Christianity by some Jews incarcerated in the Feodosiia prison evidently occurred in the interim period.[22]

The Germans did not acknowledge these conversions, however, and annihilated the fresh converts like the rest of the Jews.[23] They also exterminated those Jews who had converted to Christianity even prior to the German occupation.[24] In addition, the Germans took harsh measures against the priests who issued the baptism certificates. Some of them were executed,[25] while others were imprisoned for a long time.[26] The Orthodox priests who gave shelter to Jews were killed like ordinary laymen.[27] Thus, the phenomenon of Jewish conversion to Orthodox Christianity in the Crimea under the German occupation was promptly ended. It is worth mentioning that despite the large-scale involvement of the Romanian Orthodox clergy that had accompanied the Romanian troops in the peninsula, regarding their conversion activities there is no record of how they behaved towards Jews in the region.[28]

21 Simferopol': Memoirs of A. F. Peganova, November 9, 1944, DAARK, P-156/1/40, pp. 44-45; Diary of Chrisanf Lashkevich, entry from December (?) 21, 1941, DAARK, P-156/1/31, pp. 87-89.

22 Questioning of Liudmila Novikova, June 21, 1944, GARF, 7021/9/58, p. 6.

23 Simferopol': Memoirs of A. F. Peganova, November 9, 1944, DAARK, P-156/1/40, pp. 44-45; Statement of Leon Vatman, [no later than October 1944], YVA, M.33/68, p. 166.

24 Karasubazar and Sevastopol': Gubenko, *The Book of Sorrows*, p. 86; Statement of N. V. Mendelson, May 27, 1944, YVA, M.33/66, p. 20.

25 Alupka and Simferopol': Report of the Metropolitan Nikolai, (member of the ESC), "From Day to Day" (Yiddish), *Eynikeyt*, March 17, 1945, p. 2; Memoirs of A. F. Peganova, November 9, 1944, DAARK, P-156/1/40, pp. 44-45.

26 Simferopol': Diary of Chrisanf Lashkevich, entry from January 1942, DAARK, P-156/1/31, p. 87.

27 Alupka: Report of the Metropolitan Nikolai, (member of the ESC), "From Day to Day" (Yiddish), *Eynikeyt*, March 17, 1945, p. 2.

28 Until December 12, 1941, the Romanians baptized 200,000 people in the Crimea. Mikhail Shkarovskii, *Natsistkaia Germaniia i Pravoslavnaia tserkov': Natsistskaia politika v otnoshenii Pravoslavnoi Tserkvi i religioznoe vozrozhdenie na okkupirovannoi territorii SSSR* (Moscow: Krutitskoe patriarshege podvor'e, Obshestvo liubitelei tserkovnoi istorii, 2002), p. 403. See also Vadim Iakunin, *Russkaia Pravoslavnaia tserkov' na okupirovannykh territoriiakh SSSR v gody Velikoi Otechestvennoi voiny 1941-1945 gg.* (Samara: Samarskii gosudarstvennyi universitet, 2001), pp. 205-206.

The sources provide some information about the clergy who helped Jews (e.g., by baptizing them or providing shelter, etc.), as well as the rationales behind their decisions. The available documents indicate that these priests occupied minor positions in the church hierarchy.[29] The only possible exception to this trend is the oblique postwar statement concerning an archpriest,[30] against whom "the accusation was brought… that he baptized Jews."[31] If this statement is to be believed, it can be interpreted (besides its direct meaning that the archbishop helped Jews) that some people in church hierarchy denounced the archpriest: if it were proven that he rendered aid to Jews he would have been fired at best and imprisoned or shot at worst. At any rate, this was a sure recipe to get rid of him. This in turn implies that the "Jewish weapon" was made use of in the inter-church struggle for power in the German-controlled Crimea. Another possible conclusion is that the low-ranking clergyman accused of rendering aid to Jews were handled by the Germans on par with ordinary Christians, but the Germans were cautious enough not to extend this treatment to high-ranking priests, in order to avoid alienating the Church too much.

With respect the clergy's motives for baptizing the Jews, it may be suggested (although it is never explicitly invoked in the reports) that in a number of cases the clergymen were guided by compassion for the persecuted Jews, in addition to the eternal Christian motive to convert them. Yet, in other cases it is clearly mentioned that the conversion of Jews involved the payment of money (sometimes huge sums) even though, for the most part, it could not be established whether the money was paid to priests or to mediators.[32]

29 Simferopol' – the priest in charge of the cemetery and a priest of another small church; Alupka – church priest: Diary of Chrisanf Lashkevich, entry from January 1942, DAARK, P-156/1/31, p. 87; Report of the Metropolitan Nikolai, (member of the ESC), "From Day to Day" (Yiddish), *Eynikeyt*, March 17, 1945, p. 2.

30 Apparently the archbishop.

31 The record indicates that he was the archpriest of Simferopol': Iakunin, *Russkaia Pravoslavnaia tserkov' na okupirovannykh territoriiakh SSSR*, p. 224.

32 Feodosiia: Questioning of Liudmila Novikova, June 21, 1944, GARF,

It is also of note that almost all the references to baptism and sheltering Jews refer to town priests, predominantly in Simferopol'.[33]

The paucity of relevant sources precludes the ability to draw precise conclusions concerning the extent of the repercussions of the German church policies in the Crimea on the Holocaust. Nevertheless, it appears that the church policies here did not differ substantially from what was being realized in other predominately Russian-populated regions during 1941-42.[34] Like elsewhere, the Orthodox clergy in the peninsula was placed under the strict control of the occupation authorities, who also largely controlled the content of their sermons (including perpetuating the anathema on "Judeo-Bolshevism").[35] Occasionally secular propaganda tools, such as newspapers, contributed to spreading traditional Christian anti-Jewish accusations.[36] The Germans gave permission to open churches on a large scale; in the initial phase of the occupation, 70 churches were opened in the peninsula.[37] Just as happened everywhere, this aroused the local people's sympathy for the Germans, particularly in 1941. However, there is no evidence that the Crimean Christians were overly enthusiastic over this development. German gestures in the ecclesiastical domain were overshadowed by their rigid policies in other fields (e.g., decreasing the food supply, and executing civilians as retaliation).

2.1.3. The North Caucasus

The nature of the Germans' relationship with Orthodox Christianity in the North Caucasus was a peculiar phenomenon,

7021/9/58, p. 6. See also "Story of Vaikhanskaia," in Gubenko, *The Book of Sorrows*, pp. 101-102.

33 Diary of Chrisanf Lashkevich, entry from December (?) 21, 1941, DAARK, P-156/1/31, pp. 87-89; Memoirs of A. F. Peganova, November 9, 1944, DAARK, P-156/1/40, pp. 44-45; Testimony of Lev Iurovskii, 1944, YVA, M.35/14, p. 82; Statement of Leon Vatman, [no later than October 1944], YVA, M.33/68, p. 166.

34 Kovalev, *Natsistskaia okkupatsiia i kollaboratsionizm*, pp. 431-478.

35 Ibid., pp. 205-206.

36 Tiaglyi, "The Role of Antisemitic Doctrine in German Propaganda in the Crimea, 1941–1944": pp. 428-429.

37 Iakunin, *Russkaia Pravoslavnaia tserkov' na okupirovannykh territoriiakh SSSR*, pp. 205-206.

compared to the rest of the Russian Orthodox space. The generally more liberal character of German rule in the Caucasus in relation to that in the other German-occupied Soviet territories was also manifest in the church policies.[38] Like elsewhere in the occupied territories, Germans permitted churches to be opened in the Caucasus.[39] However, in the Caucasus their policies were much more benevolent with respect to the church, its adherents, and the clergy. Apart from the churches, they also allowed Sunday Schools to be opened for training priests.[40] In addition, they made religious instruction obligatory in private schools,[41] and forbade working on Orthodox holidays. They also granted privileges to those observing the religious rituals, such as baptism.[42] German officers and the representatives of the local administration attended church services,[43] and their presence certainly influenced the character of the sermons.

The Germans largely refrained from interfering in day-to-day church affairs.[44] It is particularly interesting that the Caucasus was the only region in which they tolerated the activities of the so-called "Revivalist" (*Obnovlentsy-Tikhonovtsy*) wing of the Orthodox Church[45] (considered to be pro-Soviet). At the same

38 Evgenii Zhuravlev, "Nemetskii okkupatsyonnyi rezhym i religioznyi vopros na yuge Rossii v gody Velikoi Otechestvennoi voiny," *Nauchnye problem gumanitarnykh issledovanii* 4 (2009): pp. 25-32.

39 Krasnodarskii *krai*, Stavropol': Beliaev and Bondar', *Kuban' v gody Velikoi Otechestvennoi voiny, 1941-1945*, p. 611 (footnote 1); Belikov, *Okkupatsiia*, pp. 108-109.

40 Stavropol'skii *krai*: Intelligence digest of the NKVD administration of Ordzhonikidzevskii *krai*, December 17, 1942, in Vodolazhskaia, Krivneva, and Mel'nik, *Stavropol'e v period nemetsko-fashistskoi okkupatsii (avgust 1942-ianvar' 1943)*, p. 69.

41 Maikop: Memorandum of Sluzhava in Beliaev and Bondar', *Kuban' v gody Velikoi Otechestvennoi voiny, 1941-1945*, p. 602; Zhuravlev, *Kollaboratsionizm na iuge Rossii*, p. 119.

42 For example, the right to grind white flour in Krasnodarskii *krai*. Krinko, *Zhizn' za liniei fronta*, pp. 80-81.

43 Novocherkassk: Iakunin, *Russkaia Pravoslavnaia tserkov' na okupirovannykh territoriiakh SSSR*, p. 200.

44 Beliaev and Bondar', *Kuban' v gody Velikoi Otechestvennoi voiny, 1941-1945*, p. 611f.

45 Shkarovskii, *Natsistkaia Germaniia i Pravoslavnaia tserkov'*, p. 403. On this

time, the Germans did interfere in those church matters that affected (or potentially could have) their Jewish policy or the means for conveying their message to the Christian laity. They relentlessly persecuted and killed even those Jews who had long since converted to Christianity.[46] They imposed a ban on baptizing Jews from the very first days of their arrival in the region.[47] German policy also included appointments of clergy, as well as assignments for certain priests to deliver sermons invoking explicit attacks on Jews. According to the following evidence from the Aleksandro-Nevskaia Church in Maikop, on October 11, 1942:

> A requiem (*panikhida*) was served for the "Christians killed and tortured to death in prisons and camps." Before the service, Father Peotr gave the sermon on "the horrors of terror by means of which *Zhidy* and Communists were tormenting our Fatherland."[48]

The impact of such sermons on individual Christians cannot be ascertained precisely, but a number of wartime and postwar sources indicate a rather enthusiastic response on the part of the Christian population. In Krasnodar, for example, a special public prayer was offered in the Dmitrievskaia Church "to honor the liberators."[49] In Kislovodsk, the local people gave bread and salt to the representatives of the German administration as a token of thanks for opening the churches.[50] The Armenian Gregorian clergy in the Caucasus was also supportive of the German rule, due to

topic, see also Alexandr Pantiukhin, "*Obnovlencheskoe dvizhenie Russkoi pravoslavnoi tserkvi v 20-40 gg. XX v. (na materialakh Stavropol'ia i Tereka*," (PhD diss., Iuizhnyi federal'nyi universitet, 2013), especially chapter 3.2.

46 Kislovodsk and Krasnodar: *Dokumenty obviniaiut*, p. 142; Statement of Vera Fenster, June 24, 1943, GARF, 7021/16/5, p. 50.

47 Stavropol': Account of the priest's son Leonid Polevoi in Belikov, *Okkupatsiia*, p. 67.

48 Krasnodarskii *krai*: Krinko, *Zhizn' za liniei fronta*, pp. 80-81.

49 *Kuban'* (Krasnodar), September 26, 1942, in Khalitov, "Obespechenie Krasnoi Armii," p. 163s.

50 Iakunin, *Russkaia Pravoslavnaia tserkov' na okupirovannykh territoriiakh SSSR*, p. 201.

their recently acquired religious freedom.[51] In such an atmosphere, it is not surprising that no record of any kind of assistance to Jews exists. Most specifically, there is no indication that the Orthodox clergy rendered baptism certificates to Jews in the German-occupied North Caucasus.

It is noteworthy that Christian motives were in no way absent from the antisemitic propaganda launched by the Russian-language newspapers during the occupation. The excerpt from an article published in Krasnodar's main newspaper in late November 1942 underscores the point:

> Russian people intimidated or deceived by *Zhidy* abandon the Red Army of the Bolsheviks. Russian volunteer units are already being established… and in the struggle with the Jewish (*zhidovskie*) hordes of Satan's servants, God's grace will again give the triumph to the Fatherland's loyal sons.[52]

In another article, the local newspaper from Piatigorsk, *Piatigorskoe ekho*, explained to its readers why the Bolsheviks had cracked down on Christianity. According to the newspaper, the answer was simple: i.e., it was because of the allegedly Jewish roots of the founder of the Soviet state, Vladimir Lenin, who was in the same vein upbraided as the "Anti-Christ."[53] On the whole, the scope of this kind of antisemitic rhetoric in the Caucasus remained limited, and the degree of its efficiency, especially in large cities, is questionable.

When the Christian factor is juxtaposed with other aspects of the North Caucasian realities (including the entrenched conservatism of the local people, German gestures vis-à-vis them, and the fact that many Jews were alien to the region), it seems that

51 Somova, "Kul'turnye i religioznye uchrezhdeniia Stavropol'skogo kraia," p. 97; Khalitov, *Obespechenie Krasnoi Armii*, p. 175.

52 "Dobrodetel'nyi podvizhnik prep. Sergii Radonezhskii," *Kuban'* (Krasnodar), no. 20, November 27, 1942, p. 2, Center of Documentation of the Contemporary History of Krasnodarskii *krai* (TsDNIKK), 1774-R/2.

53 Beldeninov, "Antikhrist," *Piatigorskoe echo*, no. 61, November 6, 1942, p. 3, in Khalitov, *Obespechenie Krasnoi Armii*, p. 167.

Orthodox Christianity played an important role in enlisting the support of the population for the German cause. The significance of antisemitic motives in this campaign was in no way negligible. It should be emphasized that these notions pertain to the Russian and Ukrainian Orthodox believers, as the information concerning non-Slavic Christians in the Caucasus (i.e., the Mountaineers) is insufficient to draw any conclusion.

2.2. Islam

2.2.1. General concerns[54]

Regarding the attitudes of people practicing Islam in the occupied Soviet territories towards the persecution and killing of Jews, the following factors should be borne in mind. Prior to the outbreak of hostilities, the number of Jews who had lived in Muslim-dominated rural localities was very small. During the war, some Jews were resettled in these places by the Soviet authorities within the framework of the evacuation program, or made their way there on their own in pursuit of a safe shelter. The number of Jews (Ashkenazi or otherwise) who had embraced Islam in the region prior to the war was negligible, if there were any at all. Nor is there any record of Jewish conversion to Islam during the Holocaust.[55] Accordingly, the widespread route of "Christian" rescue of Jews, namely the issuance of conversion certificates to them, was non-present in the case of Islam.

An additional factor that should be considered was the insignificant German military and security presence in Muslim-dominated rural localities, stemming from inadequate German

54 Motadel, "Islam and Germany's War in the Soviet Borderlands, 1941–5," pp. 784-820; A. A. Nurullaev, "Musul'mane Sovetskogo Soiuza v Velikoi Otechestvennoi voine," in Nikolai Trofimchuk, ed., *Religioznye organizatsii Sovetskogo Soyuza v gody Velikoi Otechestvennoi voiny 1941-1945 gg. Materialy "Kruglogo stola"* (Moscow: RAGS, 1995), pp. 57-69.

55 The case of mixed couples, of which one spouse was Jewish and the other Muslim, is analyzed in the sections dealing with mixed couples and the respective groups of the local people.

manpower but particularly from the fact that, overall, the Germans were more confident in the Muslim population. The practical consequence of such deployment of the Wehrmacht was the absence of what had been occurring occasionally in the rest of the rural localities: i.e., round-ups, security checks, and, most importantly, arrests and executions of civilians, including Jews. It stands to reason that most of the "suspects" were handed over to the Germans and perished thereupon, but there is almost no record of this. Thus, it is difficult to gauge the scope of interpersonal contact between the Muslims and the Jews in the North Caucasus, but it remained most limited before and during the Holocaust. In addition, the examination of the few available sources is greatly impaired by the fact that very many Muslim inhabitants of the region were deported by the Soviets. Thus, analysis of the policy practiced by the adherents of Islam concerning the persecution and annihilation of the Jews is limited to the exploration of the content of prayers, declarations, and newspaper articles.[56]

It appears that the presence of anti-Jewish slogans in these sources was relatively modest. They were sometimes promoted in conjunction with the Nazi notions of "Judeo-Bolshevism." However, explicit references to Jews are almost non-existent in the aforementioned evidence. This may be indicative of the small place they occupied in the Nazi Islamic propaganda campaign in the Soviet Union and its potentially low appeal to the Soviet Muslims, a conclusion drawn from an analysis of the general aspects of the Nazi propaganda aimed at the Caucasian Muslims. The adherents of Islam in the Caucasus held generally positive attitudes towards Nazi Germany, regarding it as the "liberator from the godless Bolsheviks." This benefited Germany's *Judenpolitik* as a part of a "package deal" – even though the subject appeared to be foreign and incomprehensible to most Soviet Muslims.

The Crimea and the North Caucasus were the only regions of the Soviet Union in which the Germans encountered a mass

56 I am grateful to Mr. Vadim Altskan of the United States Holocaust Memorial Museum (USHMM) who permitted me to explore the still unprocessed collection of newspapers published in the North Caucasus during the occupation.

presence of peoples who practiced Islam. Yet, with all the importance of the Crimea and the North Caucasus, the Germans regarded this advance into the region only as the first part of their general drive towards the Muslim East. It is in light of these considerations that the German policy-makers calculated their steps towards the Crimean Tatars in 1941 when a "lightening war" against the Soviet Union still seemed feasible. In 1942, the possibilities of a further German drive towards the Muslim East were almost entirely curtailed. As a result, the newly conquered areas of the North Caucasus and the already "pacified" Crimea then acquired a quality in their own right as important in the German Islamic strategy. The broad German vision of the "Islamic factor" in the regions in question did not disappear completely, but rather underwent a transformation. It became more localized and mindful of a specifically domestic agenda. With respect to the ethnically and religiously heterogeneous Caucasus (which had no large, single Islamic people, but did have a considerable Christian population), the strategy shifted primarily towards maintaining the delicate and easy-to-upset balance between various power groups among the local population.

The position of adherents of Islam in the Soviet-occupied areas in relation to the Holocaust should be examined with respect to the following factors. First and foremost, from the fall of 1941 the German "Muslim" policies had been gravitating towards enlisting the support of the Islamic peoples of the Soviet Union. Gradually, the Germans became increasingly ready to go to great lengths to demonstrate their particularly benevolent attitudes towards Islam and its adherents. Mosques were opened, and Muslim POWs were given privileged treatment (involving better conditions in the camps and their further release).[57] High-ranking German officials participated in Muslim festivals,[58] which became a manifestation

57 This is in sharp contrast to the period stretching from June to November 1941 when masses of Soviet Muslim POWs in German captivity were exterminated. Iskander Giliazov, *Na drugoi storone: kollaboratsionisty iz povolzhsko-priural'skikh tatar v gody Vtoroi Mirovoi voiny* (Kazan': Izd-vo "Master Lain," 1998), pp. 65-72.

58 Karachaevskii *raion*, Kabardino-Balkariia: Korück 531, KTB, S. 35, October

of the Nazi-Muslim alliance.[59] It seems that, by and large, the Germans were confident of the pro-German stance of the Muslim clergy and, therefore, let them function relatively freely.

It is difficult to evaluate the impact of strictly religious motives in the behavior of ordinary Soviet Muslims. It seems that the extent of secularization was profound in the areas under review. Nevertheless, each person had his or her own personal background, which had to do *inter alia* with his or her own origin, personal attitudes vis-à-vis Islam, and other factors that are not easy to pinpoint. Overall, it may be very cautiously suggested that religious motivations did somewhat play a role the Soviet Muslims' interactions with the Jews and Germans, as compared to Orthodox Christians, despite the generally high level of secularization in the region. Such being the case, they could potentially fall more sensitive to the Soviet anti-religious crusade and the Nazi propaganda's ensuing linkage between the "Judeo-Bolsheviks" and the Soviet attacks on Islam. On the other hand, insufficient familiarity with Islamic religious dogma among ordinary Soviet Muslims and their effective and continuous rupture from the world centers of Islam were detrimental to the German attempts to mobilize them under pan-Islamic slogans.

2.2.2. The Crimea[60]

In the prewar period, the vigorous Soviet anti-religious policy deeply affected the position of Islam in the Crimea. This campaign

10, 1942, "Besuch des Uraza Bairam Festes in Kislowodsk am 11.10.1942," Bev. D. RMfdbO, Min.Dirig. Dr. Bräutigam, Abschrift, BA, R 6/ 65; "Bericht über das Kurmanfest in Naltschik," Bev. D. RmfdbOg Min.Dirig. Dr. Bräutigam an RmfdbOg, December 18, 1942, Ibid.

59 Azamat Tatarov, "Musul'manskie prazdniki v politike Tret'iego Reikha sredi gortsev Severnogo Kavkaza v 1942-1944 gg.," *Nauchnyi zhyrnal KubGAU* 110 (2015): pp. 595-600.

60 David Motadel, *Islam and Nazi Germany's War* (Cambridge, Mass.; London, England: The Belknap Press of Harvard University Press, 2014), pp. 150-160; E. Bakhrevskii, A. Efimov, and D. Zonlotarev, "Islam v Krymu: istoriia, sovremennost', perspektivy," *Rossiia i musul'manskii mir* 6 (2000): pp. 60-66; M. Amirkhanov, "Islam in Tatar National Ideology and Policy," in Jorgen S. Nielsen, ed., *The Christian-Muslim frontier: Chaos, Clash, or Dialogue?* (London: I.B. Tauris, 1998), pp. 67-82.

involved the nationalization of *Waqf*[61] estates and property, the closing and demolition of still-functioning mosques, the arrests and executions of mullahs, the cutting off of connections with the foreign Islamic world, and the initiation of measures making it impossible to participate in the pilgrimage to Mecca.[62] As a result, on the eve of the German invasion, Islam in the Crimea was in a state of crisis and decay.[63] The German occupation brought about a revival of religious life in the peninsula, a process that was presided over by the local Muslim committees. Mosques were reconstructed, and religious traditions began to reignite. At least 50 mosques were opened in the peninsula.[64]

The peculiar Crimean development, insofar as Islam was concerned, corresponded to the activities of the newspaper *Azat Krim* (Liberated Crimea). The newspaper took up the slogan of "unity in language, thought, and faith," which in all likelihood appealed to the Germans propagating pan-Islamic ideas. Its authors discussed *inter alia* the subject of liberation of the Oriental peoples based on the wide front of a Muslim unity embracing the Arab world, Afghanistan, Iran, Turkey, Azerbaijan, and the Crimea.[65] The Islamic propaganda in this newspaper eagerly presented the war between Nazi Germany and Soviet Union in the context of a religious conflict concerning the liberation of Muslims from the "Soviet godless

61 Islamic religious endowment.

62 Yaacov Ro'i, *Islam in the CIS: A Threat to Stability?* (London: Royal Institute of International Affairs, Russia and Eurasia Programme, 2001), pp. 63-64; Kirimal, *Der nationale Kampf der Krimtürken*, p. 295.

63 Svetlana Chervonnaia, "Islamskii faktor v natsional'nom i pravozashitnom dvizhenii krymskikh tatar (1990-e gg.)," in idem., ed., *Islam v Evroazii: Sovremennie etnicheskie i esteticheskie kontseptsii sunnitskogo islama, ikh transformatsiia v massovom soznanii i virazhenie v iskusstve musulmanskikh narodov* (Moscow: "Progress-Traditsiia," 2001), p. 306; Katunin, Pravoslavnaia tserkov' i gosudarstvo, pp. 359, 388.

64 Zur Mühlen, *Zwinschen Hakenkreuz und Sowjetstern*, p. 184; Kirimal, *Der nationale Kampf der Krimtürken*, p. 307; Frauenfeld, *Die Krim*, p. 74.

65 M. Kurtiev, *Azat Krim*, no. 26, April 21, 1942, p. 3 in Chervonnaia, "Islamskii faktor v natsional'nom i pravozashitnom dvizhenii krymskikh tatar (1990-e gg.)," p. 307.

regime."[66] Such motives were also repeatedly expressed during public prayers.

The extent of anti-Jewish themes in Islamic propaganda in the Crimea occasionally varied, but, on the whole, it was on the rise. On January 3, 1942, a prayer was offered in Simferopol' for Hitler and the Wehrmacht.[67] During the public prayer of more than 500 Muslims in the town of Karasubazar in April 1942, the following solemn message was conveyed to Hitler: "Your victory is the triumph of the Muslims of the whole world."[68] In February-March 1942, 2,000 Tatars of the village of Kokkozi offered a public prayer dedicated to the "German warriors": "We, Tatars, swear to combat the herd of Jews and Bolsheviks together with the German warriors."[69] Most important is the fact that this propaganda was not confined solely to local prayers. but was also spread on a large scale by the newspaper *Azat Krim*. Typical Nazi clichés of the alleged linkage between the Jews and Bolshevik regime were smoothly inserted into semi-religious slogans like "crusade of Bolshevik and Jewish liars against religion."[70] The following excerpt from an article published in April 1942 underscores the point:

> To the Liberator of the Oppressed Peoples, Son of the German Nation Adolf Hitler. Since the arrival of the brave sons of the great Germany to the Crimea we, Muslims, have stood shoulder-to-shoulder with the German people, have taken weapons in arms and have begun to fight until the last drop of blood for the great all-human ideas promoted

66 HQ of the Partisan Movement of the Crimea, report on the content of materials published in *Azat Krim* compiled by the Secrteary of Central Committee of the All-Union Lenin Communist Union of Youth I. Iromashektov, June 28, 1943, DAARK, 151/1/388.

67 Valentin Bojzow, "Aspekte der miltärischen Kollaboration in der UdSSR von 1941-1944," in Röhr, *Okkupation und Kollaboration (1938-1945)*, p. 305.

68 *Azat Krim*, April 10, 1942, in Amanzholova, et al., *Natsional'naia politika Rossii*, p. 319 and in DAARK, 151/1/390.

69 Bakhchisaraiskii *raion*: Bojzow, "Aspekte der miltärischen Kollaboration," p. 319.

70 A. Ibraim, "Neskol'ko slov o religioznykh shkolakh," *Azat Krim*, May 18, 1943; Report on the content of materials, [no date], DAARK, 151/1/388.

> by you – the complete and definite destruction of the Red Jewish [*zhidovsko*]-Bolshevik plague.[71]

For their part, the Germans were impressed by recurrent manifestations of specifically religious support, mainly in the form of the mass prayers they received from the Crimean Tatars. In April 1942, the report of the EG D deviated from its typically dry style of exposition and noted with satisfaction that:

> The especially positive attitudes of the Tatars in the Crimea towards Germany found again its clear expression on the Führer's birthday. The Tatars offered prayers for the well-being of the Führer.[72]

2.2.3. The North Caucasus[73]

Soviet policies had an equally devastating effect on the conditions of Islam in the North Caucasus. In 1940, only seven mosques functioned in Stavropol'skii *krai*, as compared to 68 before 1917.[74] The German occupation led to a renaissance of Islamic religious life in the region, which had found its utmost expression in the opening and reopening of mosques. Sixty mosques were reopened in 1942 under the Germans in Stavropol'skii *krai* alone; 52 of them were in Cherkesskaia Autonomous *oblast'*.[75] In every locality of the Kabardin Republic, two or three mosques were opened,[76] as well in

71 Ibid., p. 320.

72 CSpSd, Kommandostab, MbOg, no. 1, Berlin, May 1, 1942, Russian State Military Archive (RGVA), 500/1/775, p. 77.

73 Motadel, *Islam and Nazi Germany's War*, pp. 134-150; I. Sh. Aliskerov, "Vliianie religioznykh i etnicheskykh faktorov na voenno-politicheskuiu obstanovku na Severnom Kavkaze v gody Velikoi Otechestvennoi voiny 1941-1945 gg.," in Trofimchuk, *Religioznye organizatsii Sovetskogo Soyuza v gody Velikoi Otechestvennoi voiny 1941-1945 gg.*, pp. 78-94.

74 Statement of Vladimir V. Bulatov, representative of the Council for Religious Affairs (CRA) for Stavropol'skii *krai*, minutes of the instructional meeting no. 17, December 20-22, 1950, GARF, 6991/3/66, p. 123, in Ro'i, *Islam in the CIS*, pp. 63-64f.

75 Statement of Vladimir Bulatov in ibid., pp. 63-64.

76 Representative of the CRA, [no date], GARF, 6991/3c/560, p. 21, in Vladimir Degtiariov, *Pobezhdaia smert': Vospominaniia* (Rostov-na-Donu: Oblknigizdat, 1962), p. 131.

the Muslim villages (*auly*) of Adygeiskaia Autonomous *oblast'* in Krasnodarskii *krai*.[77]

From the beginning of the German entry into the North Caucasus, German policy had involved the benevolent treatment of Islam and its adherents. Apart from granting religious freedom to all religions, it stipulated the demand to display "special care for Muslim woman and Muslim festivals."[78] The Germans declared Friday to be a day off in the Muslim localities,[79] and distributed numerous copies of the Quran in the Arabic language.[80] They did not confine themselves to declarations and gestures alone, but also granted unique privileges to the Islamic clergy in the North Caucasus. Not only did the Germans grant the freedom for the positions of mullahs and senior mullahs to be established in Muslim areas, but they also placed Islamic clerics on the same footing, in terms of authority and salary, as the heads of administration in towns and smaller localities.[81] Islamic themes were promoted in the newspaper *Gazavat* (Holy War) printed in Germany and disseminated in the North Caucasus.[82]

According to the report of the EG D, Caucasian Muslims were enthusiastic about the religious freedom granted under the German rule.[83] The report of the High Police and SS Leader in the Caucasus pertaining to an unknown rural locality near the Balkar village of Bakssantal illustrates the way in which the villagers expressed their gratitude to the Germans:

77 Intelligence survey of the Southern Headquarters of the Partisan Movement, November 1942 (?), in Beliaev and Bondar', *Kuban' v gody Velikoi Otechestvennoi voiny, 1941-1945*, p. 607.

78 "Aktennotiz über Besprechung zwischen OKW," Abwehr 2, Berlin, January 29, 1942, BA, R6/66.

79 CSpSd, Kommandostab, MbOg, no. 34, Geheim, December 18, 1942, YVA, JM/4539.

80 Poppe, *Reminiscences*, p. 164.

81 Aliskerov, "Vliianie religioznykh i etnicheskykh faktorov," p. 91.

82 Doronina, "Natsistkaia propaganda na okkupirovannykh territoriakh Stavropol'ia i Kubani...", p. 61.

83 CSpSd, Kommandostab, MbOg, no. 34, Geheim, December 18, 1942, YVA, JM/4539.

> I permitted the inhabitants of another locality to open anew their "mosque" [sic] that had been closed for many years. For the opening ceremony, I dispatched an officer who participated in the ceremony as a representative of the German Reich. The Council of Elders solemnly presented him with an original Mohammeddan fur cape with a hood and a scarf (worth 40,000 rubles).[84]

The Soviet report on the Kabardino-Balkar Republic, however biased, is one of few relevant sources and sheds some light onto the behavior of the Islamic clerics on spot:

> Part of the Muslim clergy was ill-disposed to the Soviet power. When the Germans came, they came over to serve them. In Kabardino-Balkariia, the Germans restored and opened… mosques. *Kadi* of Kabardino-Balkariia Khadzhi Koze Kotekov signed an "Appeal to the Muslims." In November 1942, printed leaflets in Kabardin and Balkar villages, as well as in Nal'chik, appeared, in which people were urged to pray to Allah for the German victory.[85]

In such appeals, the German propaganda made a special point to emphasize that "Judeo (*zhido*)-Bolsheviks" were to blame for trampling on Islam, that the Wehrmacht had liberated them region from "Judeo-Bolshevik rule," and local Muslims were called to restore their religion.[86]

The special relationship between Nazi Germany and Islam in the Caucasus was brought into light as representatives of the Islamic clergy in the region conferred on Hitler the title of the

84 "Verhältnisse, Sitten und Gebräuche im Einsatzgebiet," "Kampfgruppe Marx" an HSSPF Kaukasien, December 9, 1942, RGVA, 1358/1/9, p. 98.

85 Balikoev, *Narody Severnogo Kavkaza v gody Velikoi Otechestvennoi voiny (1941-1945)*, p. 96.

86 Appeal to the Kabardin and Balkar People, Nal'chik, November 1942, GARF, R-7021/148/405, p. 29, in Zhukov and Kovtun, *Antisemitskaia propaganda na okkupirovannykh territoriiakh RSFSR*, p. 16.

"Great Imam of the whole Caucasus."[87] The following piece of evidence is from one of the very few sources regarding the way that the Islamic clerics used their newly acquired powers:

> *Kadi* of Nagornyi and Kuvinskii *raiony* of the Kabardino-Balkar Republic forbade Kabardins and Balkars from now on to marry women who practiced another religion. All the marriages registered during the years of the Soviet power were declared invalid and subjected immediately to a renewed registration in accordance with the religious laws.[88]

At least in their everyday activities, it seems that the Islamic clerics focused on merely internal religious matters.

* * *

There remains the question of whether and to what extent the Crimean and the Caucasian Christians and Muslims differed in their exposure and susceptibility to the anti-Jewish religious propaganda in their encounter with persecuted and hiding Jews. It seems that explicitly pro-German and anti-Jewish appeals affected ordinary Christians and Muslims more in the Crimea than in the North Caucasus, where the German occupation was short-lived. This was especially the case with the Crimean Tatars, whose Islamic religion was particularly favored by the German occupation authorities and who frequently reciprocated by presenting publicly the fight for Germany as a struggle for the Islamic cause. However, it seems that beyond the intellectual and religious circles, specifically religious appeals to the populations in the Crimea and the Caucasus, urging them to embrace the notions of Jew-hatred allegedly embedded in their religions, could produce only meager results during the German occupation.

87 Aliskerov, "Vliianie religioznykh i etnicheskikh faktorov," p. 84; Khadzhi Ibragimbejli, "Krakh gitlerovskogo okkupatsionnogo rezhyma na Kavkaze," in Basov and Kumanev, *Narodnyi podvig v bitve za Kavkaz*, p. 272.

88 Balikoev, *Narody Severnogo Kavkaza v gody Velikoi Otechestvennoi voiny (1941-1945)*, p. 97.

Within two-and-a-half years in the Crimea and five months in the Caucasus, it was simply too difficult for the Germans to undo the results of decades-long and thorough Soviet secularization. In the exceptional case of ordinary Crimean Muslims, many of them were grateful to Nazi Germany for its overall positive treatment of this group, including in their religious policy, and were therefore ready to struggle for its cause (at least, in their home areas from 1941-1942). Yet, even their religious motivation remained limited, as expressed in the letter of a Tatar soldier who fought in the ranks of the Wehrmacht:

> The mosque is again open, and everyone goes to pray. We live once again as we did in earlier times. Allah has again blessed us.[89]

The statement of the representative of the German Ministry of Foreign Affairs attached to the 11th Army concerning his experience of the propaganda activities among the Caucasian POWs conducted apparently in 1941-1942 is also illustrative in this respect:

> Religious questions did not captivate the audience too much, because the Muslims know little about their religion. Although they condemned persecution of religion and clergy in the USSR, none of them had any personal experience, none of them personally felt painful regarding it.[90]

The lack of evidence prevents the drawing of any clear-cut conclusions. If this was the case of Crimean and Caucasian Muslims, the religious groups that were mostly favored and mostly benefitted from the German occupation regime, all the

89 Letter by Ablamit Metschit (Field Post no. 00462, recon. bat. 132) in the German service, which was checked by the field-post censor available in Bidermann, *In Deadly Combat*, p. 120.

90 Giliazov, *Na drugoi storone*, p. 195; Hürter, "Nachrichten aus dem 'Zweiten Krimkrieg' (1941/42)," in Elz and Neitzel, *Internationale Beziehungen im 19. und 20. Jahrhundert*, pp. 361-387.

more so was it the case of Crimean and Caucasian Christians, who were less favored by the Germans but still benefitted from their religious policies. It may be suggested that on the ground, each Crimean or Caucasian approached the subject of the persecution and annihilation of Jews individually on the grounds of his or her personal circumstances vis-à-vis the Soviets, the Germans, and the Jew in question. Arguably, the religious factor did play a role in these calculations, but its significance should not be overestimated, especially in dealing with a people of whom many had experienced no prewar contact with Jews.

CONCLUSION:

The Holocaust in the Crimea and the North Caucasus in a Comparative Perspective

1. The Destruction of Ashkenazi Jews

The Wehrmacht engaged in intensive warfare in a relatively small territory of the Crimea precisely during the period when the mass murder of the Jews occurred. Following the German offensive in October-November 1941, large Soviet armies disintegrated and dispersed throughout the peninsula. The German command was determined to crash the remaining pockets of Soviet resistance, and therefore sanctioned large-scale mopping-up and combing operations in the Crimea. Against this background, German authorities regarded the local Jewish population as a pro-Soviet force to be liquidated immediately. Their measures involved severe movement and residence restrictions, especially in militarily unstable areas where Soviet incursions, whether by the Red Army or partisans, took place or were expected (this included almost the entire Crimean peninsula) that were detrimental to the chances for Jewish survival.

In this respect, the North Caucasus was distinct in almost every aspect. The region was a vast area where Soviet armies had retreated but were not encircled during the German offensive in the summer of 1942. The partisans kept a low profile throughout most of the German occupation. Consequently, the Germans had no need to maintain large forces there, nor did they conduct any combing operations, mop-ups, or round-ups in the region. Viewed from this angle, the situation in the Caucasus fostered more favorable conditions for the persecuted Jews. Importantly, following the smooth character of the German takeover of the North Caucasus, the actual absence of serious Soviet military resistance, and low-key partisan activity, the Germans refrained from leaping at the pretext of "military necessity" to justify their prompt extermination of the Jews in the region.

Of particular importance is the duration of the Wehrmacht and the EG D presence in the areas. In the Crimea, most of the units of the EG D and regular troops of the 11th Army were stationed there from November 1941 until July 1942. Given the fact that the peninsula was a relatively small stretch of land surrounded by sea from almost all sides, such a massive presence of German troops, particularly the EG D, was disastrous for the Crimean Jews. On the other hand, in the vast Caucasian region, the number of German forces (both the Wehrmacht and the EG D) were inadequate and unable to cope with security tasks (among which the "Solution of the Jewish Problem" figured prominently). Almost the whole *Einsatzgruppe* was deployed in the Caucasus throughout the short period of the German occupation. Although it managed to carry out extermination actions in every locality, its strength was entirely insufficient to comb the whole area. Because of this — and also for political reasons — there were almost no mop-ups in the Caucasus. Such being the case, in order to seize the Jews, the Germans would have needed to rely mainly on the network denouncers in the long run. Given the relatively short period of the German occupation, this left the Jews more chances to survive.

As for the involvement of Romanian troops in the extermination of Jews in the Crimea and the North Caucasus, it must be remembered that they had been subordinated to the Wehrmacht command in both regions. However, when there was no German presence, leaving the Romanians as the sole Axis representation, their actions may be considered as rather independent of the local German orders in some areas. In both the Crimea and the North Caucasus, Romanian troops participated in an "unorganized" plunder of property of the Jews who were still alive at that point, and committed rapes and other maltreatment against the Jewish population. However, regarding the killing of Jews in the areas under the Romanian control, in the Crimea the Romanians were actively involved in the seizure and murder of Jews while in the North Caucasus this record is noticeably shorter. This change in the behavior of Romanians may perhaps be ascribed to internal Romanian developments, and possibly war-weariness.[1]

Time was another significant factor. The Holocaust in the Crimea corresponds mainly to 1941 (the Blitzkrieg) and the first wave of the extermination of Soviet Jewry. During this time, a final German victory in the war against the Soviets had seemed close. Therefore, the annihilation of the Jews, particularly within the "old" Soviet territories (of which the Crimea and the Caucasus formed part), where Jews were considered to be particularly "dangerous," was deemed one of the most urgent tasks of Nazi Germany. In contrast, developments in the Caucasus should be seen against the background of what had occurred in 1942: "Operation Reinhardt" against European Jewry,[2] on the one hand, and the gradual moderation of German policies in the occupied Soviet areas resulting from the failure of the lightening war, on the other. This could potentially have benefitted some non-Ashkenazi groups, but there was no change in the policy applied to Ashkenazim.

As the annihilation of Jews was conducted by the same EG D in both regions, the patterns of extermination were similar, including a relatively short period (an average of one month or so) before the killing operations. In almost all urban localities, Jews were registered and then compelled to bear six-pointed stars and perform forced labor, but camps and ghettos were rarely established. Usually, only one *Aktion* was conducted — but it was comprehensive. As a singular development in the Caucasus, of note are the monetary indemnities the Germans frequently imposed on the Jews, which was likely related to the notion that the evacuated Jews were considered well-off by the Soviet standards.

Both subjective factors, such as the stance of the military

1 Dennis Deletant, *Hitler's Forgotten Ally: Ion Antonescu and His Regime, Romania 1940-44* (New York: Palgrave Macmillan, 2006), pp. 205-229.

2 Bogdan Musial, "The Origins of 'Operation Reinhard': The Decision-Making Process for the Mass Murder of the Jews in the 'Generalgouvernement,'" *Yad Vashem Studies* 28 (2000): pp. 113-153.

command and the personal relations between army commanders and the EG D, and the "natural" factors, such as geography, weather, and food availability, were different in all areas of the two regions. In this light, the attitudes of the supreme Wehrmacht commanders in the two regions warrant particular attention. There is evidence that General von Manstein approved of the Nazi genocide of the Jews and cooperated closely with the EG D. This was reflected not only in what he said but, most importantly, in what he did – particularly by the way in which he guided his troops. Much less is known about General von Kleist's attitudes, but the little available evidence indicates that he was fairly uncooperative with the *Einsatzgruppe*, insofar as the extermination of Jews was concerned. Furthermore, some testimonies suggest that he was opposed to it.

In the Crimea, the Jewish population was exterminated rapidly, even at a considerable price to the Wehrmacht, as it had to allocate necessary logistic resources in doing so that were in short supply for the 11th Army itself. It may even be claimed that given the serious military challenges in the Crimea, it should have been hardly possible for the *Einsatzgruppe* to destroy the bulk of the Crimean Jews as quickly as it actually did. It is significant that one of the simultaneous consequences of the Holocaust in the Crimea was the atmosphere of terror that the Germans deliberately fostered against the local population. The importance of instilling terror only grew after the short "honeymoon" period in the relations between the Germans and local population ended.

In this respect, it should be noted that annihilation of the Jewish population in the North Caucasus was conducted under different circumstances. The army involvement was relatively marginal as compared to the Crimea. This is indicative of a situation in which the local people were more positively disposed towards German rule in the North Caucasus in comparison with the Crimea, and, as a result, the Germans had almost no need to resort to terror. Furthermore, it may be cautiously stated that the undermanned EG D managed to overcome its logistical shortcomings in carrying out the extermination of the Jews mainly by employing local collaborators, particularly in the expansive rural areas.

There was no noticeable difference between the Germans' treatment of Jewish POWs and their ensuing fate in either the Crimea or the North Caucasus. The prisoners experienced no improvement in the Germans' attitudes towards the Soviet POWs in 1942. Once revealed as Jewish, such soldiers were killed. The discrepancy is in numbers: in the Crimea, where the fighting was fierce, relatively many Soviet soldiers fell into German captivity, among them numerous Jews. In contrast, in the North Caucasus the Germans did not succeed in bagging Soviet armies, captivated fewer Soviet troops, and the absolute number of Jews among them was insignificant.

The behavior of both the persecuted Jews and the Germans was significantly affected by the "natural" factors of geography, weather, and food availability. This was directly related to whether and to what extent persecuted Jews should contact local people in pursuit of shelter from unbearable weather conditions, food, or other bare essentials, such as medicines. The trend was the same everywhere: In order to survive, the Jews chose to wander around in a wild countryside where no one lived. Jews turned to the local people only when survival by other means became impossible. In this respect, the Crimea was a small, underpopulated area with almost no large towns. Its landscape consisted of many difficult-to-access mountains and few forests. Most importantly, it was surrounded by water from nearly all sides, and the only exit was effectively controlled by the Germans. The Crimea turned out to be a trap for persecuted Jews, who moved around it in pursuit of a safe place. In contrast, the part of the North Caucasus that had been occupied by the Germans was largely a vast flat area with almost no forests. It had many medium-size towns and scattered villages, with few large cities. Therefore, the region was conducive for wandering around in search of a shelter, but proved difficult if one needed to hide permanently.

Weather conditions during the period following the mass extermination of the Jewish population exacerbated the geographic ones, and had a direct bearing on the survival chances for those Jews who found no shelter in the towns and villages. In the Crimea, the destruction first took place in the cold winter of

1941, and continued intensively throughout the early cold part of 1942. In order to survive during winter, one needed, among other things, access to the woods and warm clothes. From time to time, it was necessary to have at least a temporary shelter from cold. All this necessitated contact with the local people, which could have disastrous consequences for the Jews. Thus, the weather conditions critically decreased chances for Jews to survive in the Crimea. In contrast, the North Caucasus had a relatively warmer climate, and the killing operations took place in the late summer-fall of 1942. In this respect, Jews could survive in the region for a longer period of time without needing to rely upon the local population. Therefore, in terms of weather conditions, the North Caucasus was by far the more expedient place for Jewish survival.

Availability of food was another factor that affected the unfolding of the Holocaust in the regions under review. In the Crimea, the Germans claimed that they had to precipitate the extermination of the Jews due to the severe food shortage. As the food crisis was not so serious in the first phase of the German occupation – when they killed the great majority of Jews – their claim was unfounded. In fact, the food problem was the result of the Germans' reluctance to provide for the Crimean civilian population. The situation was different in the North Caucasus, however. Initially, there was simply more food available for everyone, including the German occupying power, the local population, and the Jews. As a result, Jews had more chances to survive the German occupation in the Caucasus than in the Crimea when food was the defining issue. Needless to say, however, the abundance of food in the North Caucasus did not deter the Germans from annihilating the Jews.

2. The Fate of the Krymchaks, Karaites, and Mountain Jews

In the Crimea and the North Caucasus, the Krymchaks, Karaites, and Mountain Jews attempted to obtain German recognition as ethnicities distinct from Ashkenazi Jewry. Consequently, the Germans agreed to deal with most members of these groups separately, and scrutinized each group's connections with the Jews and Judaism. It should be stressed, however, that at the same time in various places in the regions the Germans did not always extend such recognition to a minority of these groups, regarding them predominantly as Jews. As a result, these people were killed.

The guiding German policy toward these groups seems to have been related to regional differences, and probably even more, to time. To begin with, the Germans' decisions on the degree of Jewishness of these groups stemmed solely from quasi-"scholarly" considerations. In all of the cases, an investigation was launched in which both German scholars in the Reich itself and local "scientists" or public figures acting under the auspice of the EG D produced their conclusions. Thereupon, the final decision was made in Berlin. In 1941, Heinrich Himmler personally ruled the decision concerning the Karaites and the Krymchaks. In contrast, it is unknown whether there was any involvement of SS central authorities concerning the Mountain Jews in 1942, which was handled by the Reich Genealogical Office.

This is the formal side of the picture. However, there is a multitude of subjective notions that may be drawn from the factors in the German decision-making. First of all, purely "theoretical" considerations, namely the "degree of Jewishness of these groups whether in terms of race or religion" (as Nazi Germany viewed it), did play a role in all of these cases. However, the timing of the German occupation of the Crimea (November 1941) was also significant. This was the time when the Wehrmacht was at the gates of Moscow, and an overall victory in the Eastern campaign appeared close. It is no wonder, therefore, that under such circumstances the Germans dealt with the Karaite-Krymchak question in a clear-cut manner within a short span of time, possibly regardless of the local Crimean agenda. Thus, German decision-making in this case was primarily an internal German development. Yet, later on, internal factors, namely the alleged proximity between the Karaites and the Crimean Tatars, influenced the Germans' approach towards the former group.

The story was different in the North Caucasus. However, the way in which the extermination of Mountain Jews in the Crimea in March 1942 and in Caucasian villages in September-October 1942 began to unfold resembled the way in which the Germans handled the Karaite-Krymchak issue: i.e., those Mountain Jews were speedily killed without any prior investigation of whether they constituted a special group. When such an investigation was launched in November 1942, local factors, namely the German desire to appease the local patrons of the Mountain Jews, played an increasingly important role. The result was that, unlike in the Crimea, most of the Mountain Jews in the North Caucasus were left untouched. This could have been the result of either a compromise, or alternatively, the lack of any decision on the subject. Thus, the case of the Mountain Jews, whose status remained unclear until the German withdrawal from the region, falls between the cases of the Crimean Karaites, who were given recognition (albeit temporary, but it was in effect throughout the entire war) as non-Jews, and the Krymchaks, who were equated to Ashkenazi Jews and exterminated.

3. Jewish Responses to the Holocaust

The timing of the German occupation was of great significance in defining the Jewish reactions to the German persecution. The Crimean peninsula was occupied in 1941, and, although it occurred more than four months after the beginning of the German invasion of the Soviet Union, it is suggested that ignorance of what awaited them under German rule was an important rationale behind the behavior of many Crimean Jews. By comparison, as the North Caucasus was seized in the course of the second year of the war, many Jews knew about the Nazis' persecution and annihilation of their people and calculated their steps accordingly – particularly those evacuees whose escape into the Caucasus was often initiated by the information they had received about the German persecution of Jews. This may account for the high share of suicides committed by the Caucasian Jewish refugees before the killing operations, whereas this phenomenon was largely non-existent in the Crimea.

As the pace of the Holocaust in the Crimea and the North Caucasus was quick (the annihilation of the Jewish population was, as a rule, carried out about one month after the beginning of the German occupation), the majority of the Jews in both regions were unable to assess correctly what was happening to them and what lay ahead. They complied with the German orders, assuming that only complete obedience would ensure their survival. Only a small minority chose to defy them. In this sense, both regions presented a similar pattern of Jewish reactions, compared to what took place elsewhere in the occupied Soviet territories.

Jewish responses differed in the Crimea and the Caucasus, as the Holocaust had unfolded in a different fashion in each region. In the Crimea, anti-Jewish measures were orchestrated simultaneously in every area. German measures involved *inter alia* severe movement restrictions that made it difficult for the Crimean Jews to learn about the persecution and annihilation in neighboring areas and then to take necessary measures. The situation was different in the North Caucasus, where the movement restrictions were not severe and where, more generally, the Germans were not so strict in carrying out the anti-Jewish policy at the same pace in the various places. Viewed from this angle, more opportunities to learn and to escape presented themselves for the Jews in the North Caucasus.

The profile of the Jewish population that remained in the regions also varied, creating important repercussions on the Jews' reactions. In the Crimea, there were more combat-age men, as not everyone had been drafted into the army. Hence, Jewish armed resistance (i.e., joining partisans) was much more widespread. It was also easier to join the resistance from the numerous Jewish rural settlements scattered across the Crimea. That was not true with the Caucasus. There, there were many fewer Jewish men, especially of combat age, on the eve of the German occupation: By 1942, most of them had already been enlisted in the Red Army. The remaining Jewish public in the Caucasus consisted mostly of women, often accompanied by elderly persons and children, and Soviet partisans in the Caucasus were not interested in such reinforcements. A minority of the Jews who resided in villages were mainly strangers to the area and, therefore, could not make their way to the partisans. To this must be added the desire of the Crimean partisan leadership to allow civilians to join their ranks, and the reluctance of the Caucasian partisan commanders to let the civil population join the partisans. All this combined turned the Crimea into a place where relatively many Jews (chiefly from rural areas) fought in the ranks of the powerful partisan movement, while there was almost a complete absence of Jews in the more passive Caucasian partisan units.

The distinctive feature of the Jewish population in the North Caucasus was related to their prevalence among the larger group of evacuees into the region. The Jewish evacuees were a foreign element in the region, hardly integrated into the local population. Largely ignorant of local conditions and geography, they knew neither where to go nor whom to ask for help, nor even the shortest and the most secure way to escape. The Jewish newcomers socialized mostly with the people with whom they had evacuated. Evidently, most of the Jewish refugees remained unemployed throughout the whole evacuation period, and, therefore, did not establish any work-related connections, which could have been helpful at the time of the German occupation.

On the other side, the fact they were strangers in the Caucasus could sometimes act in their favor. The newcomers had no personal enemies in the region, for whom the German occupation could have presented a propitious moment to settle old accounts with the Jews. Besides, the refugees were unknown in the Caucasus, and, provided they did not possess an unmistakably Jewish appearance, they could sometimes manage to survive simply under a non-Russian identity. Furthermore, the presence of numerous non-Slavic ethnic groups in both the Crimea and the North Caucasus made it possible for the Jews to assume their identities in order to account for their own non-Slavic appearance, Yiddish accent, and circumcision.

The peculiar character of the German occupation in every region also left its mark on the Jewish responses to the persecution. In the Crimea, the possession of "Aryan" documents was critical because of the incessant round-ups and security checks. The local population was registered from the beginning of the occupation, and, generally speaking, the German presence was visible. As a result, the search for "Aryan" documents became a widespread Jewish response in the Crimea. It is evident that the Jews' chances for survival in such conditions were limited. In the Caucasus, the situation was different in that it was certainly beneficial to possess "Aryan" documents, but doing so was frequently inconsequential in influencing the authorities' attitudes towards a person suspected of being Jewish. In the Caucasus, a Jew could sometimes manage to survive without any ID, as there were few security checks, and the registration of population began only at the end of the German rule.

Finally, once Jews realized they needed to disappear from their places of residence, a comparison of the areas in the two regions to which the Jews tried to escape is in order. In the Crimea, they went from towns to villages because of the availability of food in rural areas and the large German presence in the Crimean towns. However, when it was no longer possible to hide in the villages, the Crimean Jews tended to move outside of the peninsula. In comparison, the main direction of Jewish escapees in the Caucasus was from villages into towns, which was primarily the result of the strong anti-Jewish feelings in the mainly Cossack villages. Smaller residence and, particularly, movement restrictions in the North Caucasus made it easier for the Jews to move unimpeded from one area into another. It is of note that food concerns did not play a substantial role in deciding where to go, as the food conditions were satisfactory all over the Caucasus.

4. The Legacy of the Holocaust in the Crimea and the North Caucasus

Despite serious differences between the two places, the Holocaust was carried out similarly in the Crimea and the North Caucasus. At the same time, the Holocaust in these two regions was different from how it happened in other areas occupied by the Germans. Both of them are situated on Russia's ethnic frontier where, for centuries, a complex interethnic fabric comprising Slavs (mostly

Russians) and non-Slavs (mostly groups professing Islam) had been molding. Jews, Ashkenazi and non-Ashkenazi, who found themselves in the Crimea and the North Caucasus met not harmony but charged relations, which sometimes exploded with Jews as targets. Under heavy-handed Soviet rule, these tensions appeared to vanish, but in fact remained just beneath the surface.

They resurfaced again with the German onslaught into the Crimea and the North Caucasus, during which the Germans played various ethnic groups against each other while favoring those among them viewed as underprivileged under Russian and Soviet rule. By that time, the extermination of the Jews was the major pillar of Nazi ideology and policy – and they were adamant in pursuing this line to the end. As the history of the Holocaust in other places in Nazi-dominated Europe demonstrates, a deviation, whether temporary or more permanent, from this genocidal pattern could only take place if the Germans were confronted with pressures from elements in local governments or populations whose support was vital for Nazi Germany. In the Crimea and the North Caucasus there were no influential privileged groups or players willing to extend protection to the Ashkenazi Jews, and thus the latter were doomed. In contrast, smaller groups of Karaites and Mountain Jews succeeded in gaining protection from the local Islamic groups, which proved instrumental in preventing the Germans from murdering these groups, too. German reasoning was certainly theorized and cloaked in official Nazi phraseology, as these two groups were declared racially and religiously non-Jewish. Another small group, the Krymchaks, attempted to play the same game, but garnered little support from the local forces. Unlike the Karaites and Mountain Jews, the Krymchaks were declared Jewish and annihilated.

To understand the Holocaust in these regions, it is also important to consider specific Soviet circumstances, whatever they entailed. On the whole, it seems that the local population was more sympathetic to the Soviet cause in the Crimea than in the Caucasus. Jews, partly as a result of Nazi propaganda and partly due to real developments that took place on the ground, were frequently identified by the local people with the Bolsheviks and their rule. Therefore, the local people were more eager to lend support to the Jews because of general pro-Soviet sentiments in the Crimea than in the North Caucasus. Another dimension involves the extent of Soviet political, military, or social dynamics on the impact on the Holocaust in these regions. As everywhere on Soviet territory, the Soviet leaders refrained from announcing to the Jews that they were singled out by the Germans for extermination and, thus, missed the opportunity to save masses of local Jews. However, they did contribute in a certain way to the rescue of Jews by allowing them to join the Red Army, partisan troops, or underground resistance groups. In contrast to defenseless Jewish civilians who, by and large, could hope only for the mercy of the local people, those serving in these Soviet formations could fight and defend their lives, although their survival during the Holocaust was by no means guaranteed. The Jews' chances for acceptance into these units were higher in the Crimea than in the North Caucasus.

Finally, while although this subject falls beyond the purview of the current study, it should be remembered that both these regions were the only ones in the liberated Soviet territories to be cleansed of those ethnic groups accused of having collaborated with the Germans. This factor is of paramount importance for the study of the Holocaust legacy in these places, as it considerably complicated proper investigation of Nazi crimes there and also created additional or competing grievances and memories,[3] which for many local people were — and remain today — on a par with the Holocaust of the Jews. Yet, this will be a topic for other researchers.

3 See, for example, Uehling, "Having a Homeland: Recalling the Deportation, Exile, and Repatriation of the Crimean Tatars to their Historic Homeland."

Tables

Table 1. Jewish Population by Republic, *Krai* and *Oblast'* (Urban and Rural) and Sex, 1939

	Number	% of Total	Male (%)	Female (%)
Crimean ASSR	65,452	5.8	46.4	53.6
Ordzhonikidzevskii *krai*	7,791	0.4	53.3	46.7
Krasnodarskii *krai*	7,351	0.2	54.9	45.1
Adygeiskaia AO	302	0.1	54.0	46.0
Kabardino-Balkar ASSR	3,414	1.0	49.4	50.6
North Ossetiian ASSR	1,714	0.5	53.0	47.0
Kamykiian ASSR	1,355	0.2	71.1	28.9

Source: Mordechai Altshuler, *Distribution of the Jewish Population of the USSR, 1939* (Jerusalem: The Hebrew University, Center for the Research of East European Jewry, 1993), pp. 9-11, 13-15.

Table 2. Jewish Urban Population by City and Town in the North Caucasus[1] (Jewish Population + 100), 1939

	Number of Jews	% of the total
Krasnodarskii *krai*	6,040	0.77
Adygeiskaia AO	222	0.40
Unspecified	5,818	0.80
Ordzhonikidzevskii *krai*	5,577	1.41
Kabardino-Balkar ASSR	3,113	3.68
Nal'chik	3,007	6.27
Other (3)	106	0.29
North Ossetiian ASSR	1,569	1.01
Ordzhonikidze	1,517	1.16
Other (3)	52	0.21
Kamykiian ASSR[2]	344	0.21

Source: Altshuler, *Distribution of the Jewish Population of the USSR*, 1939, pp. 35-38.

1 All the tables dealing with this region refer only to the due-to-be-occupied areas of the North Caucasus.

2 Including the data for the Autonomous Soviet Socialist Republic of the Volga Germans (*Avtonomnaia sovetskaia sotsialitsicheskaia respublika Nemtsev Povolzh'ia*).

Table 3. Rural Jewish Population in the Crimea and the North Caucasus, 1939

	Number	% of Total
Crimean ASSR	18,065	3.34
Larindorfskii *raion*	3,492	24.35
Fraidorfskii *raion*	2,200	15.31
Orzhonikidzevskii *krai*	2,214	0.14
Krasnodarskii *krai*	1,311	0.05
Adygeiskaia AO	80	0.04
Kabardino-Balkar ASSR	301	0.11
North Ossetiian ASSR	145	0.08
Kamykiian ASSR[3]	99	0.22

Source: Altshuler, *Distribution of the Jewish Population of the USSR,* 1939, pp. 63-65, 66-69.

3 Including the data for the Autonomous Soviet Socialist Republic of the Volga Germans (*Avtonomnaia sovetskaia sotsialitsicheskaia respublika Nemtsev Povolzh'ia*).

Table 4. National Composition of the Population of the North Caucasus According to the 1939 census (in thousands)

	Kabardino-Balkariia	North Ossetiia	Krasnodarskii *krai*	Incl. Adygea	Stavropol'skii *krai*	Incl. Karachaevo-Cherkessia
Russians	127.1	156.1	2,748.8	203.7	1,465.7	124.0
Ukrainians	11.0	9.6	149.7	7.7	40.8	4.3
Georgians	1.2	6.9	4.3	0.2	3.0	0.1
Armenians	1.1	10.9	60.4	2.1	24.5	0.9
Tatars	3.0	1.3	6.4	1.7	6.1	0.9
Germans	4.7	4.3	34.2	0.8	43.0	0.6
Kabardintsy	150.3	4.1	0.2	0.1	4.3	1.6
Balkary	39.0	-	-	-	1.8	0.2
Ossetiians	4.3	168.4	0.6	-	8.9	3.9
Adygeitsy	0.3	0.2	60.4	55.8	17.1	15.8
Karachaevtsy	0.1	-	0.1	-	73.5	67.8
Gypsies	0.1	0.3	-	-	-	-
Greeks	0.1	2.0	42.5	1.7	9.4	1.5
Jews	4.6	2.1	7.6	0.3	7.1	0.3

Source: Vladimir Kabuzan, *Naselenie Severnogo Kavkaza v 19-20 vekakh: etnostatisticheskoe issledovanie* (St. Petersburg: Izd-vo "Russko-Baltiiskii informatsionnyi tsentr BLITZ," 1996), p. 209.

Table 5. Course of the Holocaust in Crimean Towns

Town	Number of Jews[4] in 1939	Number of Jewish victims	German units involved	Romanian troops involved	Local administration involved	Stars, forced labor, indemnities	*Judenrat, starosta,* camp, ghetto	Date of destruction
Alushta	251	280[5]						24.11.1941 and early 12.1941
Armiansk	107	14						26.11.1941
Bakhchis-arai	228	90	Sk 11a; OK II/576	-	-	-	-	13.12.1941
Dzhankoi	1,397	443-720 or more	Sk 10b; SD (*Gruppenstab*); OK II/939; FG	-	Tatars, Russian police; *Burgormistr*	Forced labor, summary executions	Provisional ghetto; general camp served as a Jewish camp	30.12. 1941
Evpatoriia	4,249	800-900+150[6]	Sk 11a; Sk 11b; OK I(V)/277	-	Tatars, Russians	Stars, forced labor, collection of gold and valuables	*Judenrat*	23.11.1941

4 Including Krymchaks.
5 Including inhabitants of Alushtinskii *raion*.
6 In the first killing operation, Ashkenazi Jews were murdered; in the second – Krymchaks.

Table 5 Continued

Town	Number of Jews[4] in 1939	Number of Jewish victims	German units involved	Romanian troops involved	Local administration involved	Stars, forced labor, indemnities	*Judenrat, starosta,* camp, ghetto	Date of destruction
Feodosiia	2,922	1,052-1,300[7]	Ek 10b; FK 810; OK I(V)/287; OK II/915	-	Police rounding-up the Krymchaks	Stars, forced labor	*Starosta*, Prison	Early (4?) 12.1941
Karasub-azar	429	76+468[8]	Sk 11b; OK II/937	+	Tatars[9]	-	*Starosta*	10. 12.1941;17-18.1.1942
Kerch	5,573	3,000-7,500-11,600	Sk 10b; OK I (V)/287	+	-	Stars	Prison	Early 12.1941 and 05.1942
Simferopol'	22,791	11,000 -17,000	Sk 11a; Sk 11b; OK I/853; FG; GFP 647	-	+	Stars, forced labor	*Judenrat*	10-11.12. 1941
Sevastopol'	5,988	1,200-4,200	Sk 11a; *Kommandatur*; FG; OK I/290	-	Russians, Tatars	Stars, forced labor	*Judenrat*	12.07.1942

7 Including 245 Krymchaks. Sources distinct from the ESC give the number of Jewish victims in Feodosiia, which fluctuate considerably: 1) 3,000 people. Moshe Gutovich, "From the conversation with Moshe Gutovich" (Hebrew), originally in *Eynikayt*, "Jewish refugee from Feodosiia," *Ha-tsofe* (Tel Aviv), no. 1685, July 13, 1943; 2) 738 Jews. Il'ia Erenburg, "The Hangmen of the Jewish People Were Punished by the Court," (Yiddish), *Eynikayt*, December 27, 1942, p. 3.

8 In the first killing operation, Ashkenazi Jews were murdered; in the second – Krymchaks.

9 In the annihilation of Krymchaks.

Table 5 Continued

Town	Number of Jews[4] in 1939	Number of Jewish victims	German units involved	Romanian troops involved	Local administration involved	Stars, forced labor, indemnities	*Judenrat, starosta,* camp, ghetto	Date of destruction
Staryi Krym	133	105[10]						12.1941-2.1942
Sudak	79[11]	25 75						13.2.1942 1-4.1944
Yalta	2,060	800 – 2,000	Sk 11a; OK II/662	+	Tatars	Stars	*Judenrat,* ghetto	18.12.1941

Sources: State Archive of the Russian Federation (GARF), 7021/9/1-2, 38-40, 42, 44-50, 56-60; Yad Vashem Archive (YVA), M.33/55-56, 60-61, 65-70, 76-77, 82, 87, 368, 369, 1189; Il'ia Al'tman, ed., *Kholokost na territorii SSSR: Entsiklopediia* (Moscow: ROSSPEN, 2009); Mikhail Tiaglyi, *Mesta massovogo unichtozheniya evreev Kryma v period natsistskoi okkupatsii poluostrova (1941-1944): Spravochnik* (Simferopol': BETs "Chesed Shymon," 2005); Manfred Oldenburg, *Ideologie und militärisches Kalkül: Die Besatzungspolitik der Wehrmacht in der Sowjetunion 1942* (Köln: Böhlau Verlag, 2005), pp. 182-196; Yitzhak Arad, *The History of the Holocaust: Soviet Union and the Annexed Territories* (Hebrew) (Jerusalem: Yad Vashem, 2004), pp. 376-383; Andrej Angrick, *Besatzungspolitik und Massenmord: Die Einsatzgruppe D in der südlichen Sowjetunion 1941-1943* (Hamburg: Hamburger Edition, 2003), pp. 294-361; Altshuler, *Distribution of the Jewish Population of the USSR 1939*, pp. 30-31, 63-65, 66-69; Mark Goldenberg, "K voprosu o chisle zhertv sredi mirnogo naseleniia Kryma v period natsistskoi okkupatsii (1941-1944 gg.)," *Buleten: 'Golokost i suchasnist'* 3, no. 4 (9, 10) (2003).

10 Including Krymchaks and those brought from the neighboring villages of Karagoz and Koktebel'.
11 The data refer to the Jewish population residing in both the town of Sudak and the adjacent rural raion.

Table 6. Course of the Holocaust in the Crimean countryside, by *raiony* and Villages

Raion	Village (*selo* or *derevnia*) or *kolkhoz*	Number of Jews in 1939	Number of Jewish victims	German units involved	Local administration involved	Stars, forced labor, ghetto, maltreatment	Dates of destruction
Ak-Mechetskii		121	85[12]				Spring 1942
Ak-Sheikhevskii	Smidovichi		31				27.12.1941 or Spring 1942
Biukon-larskii		470	202				
Dzhankoiskii		1,213	5,182				
Fraidorfskii	The entire *raion*	2,200	829-854	EG D; OK I/277; OK I/742; FK 810	*Starosty*, police		11-12 1941, 2.1942
Fraidorfskii	Fraidorf	450	64				21.11.1941
Fraidorfskii	Amancha		188	EG			23.11.1941
Fraidorfskii	Kari		131 (136)	+			11-12.1941
Fraidorfskii	Minus-Evreiski		104	+			23.11.1941
Fraidorfskii	Peretsfeld		92-103				15.11.1941
Fraidorfskii	Naibrot		26				23.11.1941
Evpatoriiskii	The entire *raion*	1,174	500	EG, FK	*Starosty*, police		12.1941, 3.1942
Evpatoriiskii	Ikor		58	+			
Evpatoriiskii	Naidorf		41	+	*Starosta*, police		16.12.1941
Evpatoriiskii	No. 106		300-500[13]				

12 The data refer to all Soviet citizens killed in the respective area.

13 The estimate is based on Gordon, "On the Jewish settlements in the Crimea" (Yiddish), *Eynikayt*, August 16, 1945, p. 3.

Table 6 Continued

Raion	Village (*selo* or *derevnia*) or *kolkhoz*	Number of Jews in 1939	Number of Jewish victims	German units involved	Local administration involved	Stars, forced labor, ghetto, maltreatment	Dates of destruction
Evpatoriiskii	"Shaumian"	114	113[14]	EG, FK	Police		1.3.1942
Evpatoriiskii	Voikovstat	200-300	-		Romanians	Ghetto	-
Ialtinskii		337	32				
Ichkinskii	The entire *raion*	623	105[15]				Late 1941-early 1942
Ichkinskii	Ichki	77	26				
Ichkinskii	Varvarovka		40				
Ichkinskii	Cheirus		36				
Kolaiskii	Maifel'd[16]		More than 1,000	FK 608	Police	No food supply	1.1942
Kolaiskii	Alach		29				4.1942
Larindorfskii	The entire *raion*	3,492	370				
Larindorfskii	Kamenka		61	+	*Starosty*, police	Stars	1.1942
Larindorfskii	(Der) Emes		24				28.2.1942
Larindorfskii	Lekkert		47	+	*Starosta*	Rapes	2.1942
Larindorfskii	Sverdlovskoe		99	+		Stars	7.12.1941

14 Mountain Jews.

15 Including Krymchaks.

16 Gathered from all over Kolaiskii *raion*.

Table 6 Continued

Raion	Village (*selo* or *derevnia*) or *kolkhoz*	Number of Jews in 1939	Number of Jewish victims	German units involved	Local administration involved	Stars, forced labor, ghetto, maltreatment	Dates of destruction
Larindorfskii	Kalinindorf		36				
Larindorfskii	Voroshilovo		24				24.11.1941
Larindorfskii	Iudendorf		20				
Larindorfskii	Frunze		17				2.1942
Leninskii	The entire *raion*	349	312				
Maiak-Salynskii		174	36				
Sakskii	The entire *raion*	1,854	530				
Sakskii	Buzul-Montanai		138	+			7.12.1941
Sakskii	Staryi Karagurt		57				2.1942
Sakskii	Novyi Karagurt		More than 60				4.3.1942
Sakskii	Novoselovka		200				Late 1941
Sakskii	"Molotov" *kolkhoz*		15	EG			3.1942
Sakskii	Kambar		13	SD, OK I/853			9.1942
Seitlerskii	Seitler	179	53				Late 1941
Simferopol'skii	The entire *raion*	728	890	EG			
Simferopol'skii	"Gorky" *kolkhoz*	80	78	Sk 11b	*Starosta*		22.1.1942
Simferopol'skii	Kalinovka		54	Sk 11b			22.1.1942

Table 6 Continued

Raion	Village (*selo* or *derevnia*) or *kolkhoz*	Number of Jews in 1939	Number of Jewish victims	German units involved	Local administration involved	Stars, forced labor, ghetto, maltreatment	Dates of destruction
Simferopol'skii	Pervomaiskoe		61	Sk 11b		Stars, Jewish houses marked, forced labor	21.1.1942
Tel'manskii	The entire *raion*	1,910	418				
Tel'manskii	Kurman-Kemel'chi	211	57				17.2.1942
Tel'manskii	Rottenshtat		222	+	*Starosta*, police		1.1942
Zuia	Eni-Krymchak		17[17]				2,4.1942

Sources: GARF, 7021/9/30-37, 41, 43, 52-55, 59, 61-62, 79-84, 193; YVA, M.33/55-59, 62-64, 71-75, 78-85, 88; DAARK, R-1289/1/40; Al'tman, *Kholokost na territorii SSSR*; Tiaglyi, *Mesta massovogo unichtozheniya evreev Kryma*; Oldenburg, *Ideologie und militärisches Kalkül*, pp. 176-182; Arad, *The History of the Holocaust*, pp. 383-388; Angrick, *Besatzungspolitik und Massenmord*, pp. 294-361; Altshuler, *Distribution of the Jewish Population of the USSR 1939*, pp. 30-31, 63-65, 66-69; Goldenberg, "K voprosu o chisle zhertv sredi mirnogo naseleniia Kryma."

17 Krymchaks.

Table 7. Annihilation of the Jewish (Ashkenazi and Krymchak) Population in the Crimea in 1941-1942

	12.12	16.11-15.12	09.01	01.01-15.01	15.01-31.01	01.02-15.02	16.02-28.02	23.03	15.03-31.03	1.07-15.07
Ashkenazim	2,910	17,645	3,176	685	3,286	920	729	678	588	1,029
Krymchaks	-	2,504	-		-	-	-	-	-	18

Sources: Tiaglyi, *Mesta massovogo unichtozheniya evreev Kryma*; Yitzhak Arad, Shmuel Krakowski, and Shmuel Spektor, eds., *The Einsatzgruppen Reports: Selection from the Dispatches of the Nazis' Death Squads Campaign against the Jews (July 1941- January 1943)* (New York: Holocaust Library, 1989); GARF, 7021/9/1-84.

Table 8. Course of the Holocaust in North Caucasian Towns

Town	Number of Jews in 1939	Number of Jewish victims	German units involved	Romanian troops involved	Local administ-ration involved	Stars, forced labor, indemnity	*Judenrat*, camp, ghetto	Date of destruction
Armavir	323	525-1,000	Ek 11 (TK Schulz and others); OK I/289			Stars, forced labor	*Judenrat*; partly within the POW camp	9.1942
Budennovsk	41	300-3,000	Ek 12 (TK Strochschneiden)					
Cherkessk	400	820	Ek 11 (TK Schlupper); OK I/920	-	-	Stars, forced labor	*Judenrat* (?), *starosta*	28.9. 1942
Elista	344	300	Sk Astrakhan; OK I/649; soldiers of the 16th Army			Stars, forced labor	-	9.9. 1942
Essentuki	581	2,007[18]	OK II/ 915	-	-	Stars, forced labor	*Judenrat*	9.9. 1942
Georgievsk	116	700-1,100	Ek 12 (Caucasian unit); OK					27.8; 8.9; 25.10. 1942

18 According to uncorroborated evidence, after more than one month of internment in a sort of ghetto, one more group was executed on October 29, 1942. If this evidence is to be believed, then the total number of Jewish victims in Essentuki reachs 2,483 people. Elena Voitenko, “Kholokost na iuge Rossii v period Velikoi Otechestvennoi Voiny (1941-1943 gg.),” (PhD diss., Stavropol’skii gosudarstvennyi universitet, 2005), p. 158.

Table 8 Continued

Town	Number of Jews in 1939	Number of Jewish victims	German units involved	Romanian troops involved	Local administ-ration involved	Stars, forced labor, indemnity	*Judenrat*, camp, ghetto	Date of destruction
Kislovodsk	766	2,000	Ek 12; OK II/ 915	-	-	Stars, forced labor, indemnity	*Judenrat*	9.9. 1942
Krasnodar	1,931	1,800- 3,000	Sk 10a, GFP	-	-		*Judenrat, starosta*	8.1942
Kropotkin	109	Up to 700	Ek 11					8-9.1942
Maikop	595[19]	200	Ek 11 (TK Kubjak); OK I/921		*Burgomistr*			8-9. 1942
Mikoi-anshakhar	49	60+67	FG			Ghetto, forced labor		18.9.1942; 9.12.1942
Minvody	98	1,800	Ek 12; OK II/ 915; GFP	-	-	Stars		9.9.1942
Mozdok	306	-			Local police			
Nal'chik	3,007	600-1,500	Sk 10b; FG	-	+	Stars, forced labor		11-12. 1942
Nevinnomyssk	65	100 or 510						8.1942
Novorossiisk	1,595	More than 1,000	Sk 10a (TK)	-	+		*Judenrat, starosta*	13.9 or 22.9.1942
Piatigorsk	1,139	2,800-3,000	OK; Ek 12	-	+	Stars, forced labor	*Judenrat*	6.9.1942
Prokhladnyi		Up to 700						

19. As of 1926

Table 8 Continued

Town	Number of Jews in 1939	Number of Jewish victims	German units involved	Romanian troops involved	Local administ-ration involved	Stars, forced labor, indemnity	*Judenrat*, camp, ghetto	Date of destruction
Stavropol'	3,500	4,000	Ek 12; FK 676	-	+		*Judenrat*	12, 14.8. 1942
Tikhoretsk		316			*Burgomistr*	Stars, forced labor		
Zheleznovodsk	105	More than 100	*Kommandant*					8.1942

Sources: GARF, 7021/7/109; 8/26-27; 12/1, 62; 16/2-15, 422, 435, 436, 460-466; 17/1-17, 294; 116/11, 149, 172 ; YVA, M.33/286, 290, 293, 301, 303; Central Archive of the Ministry of Defense of the Russian Federation (TsAMO RF), 51/958/52; Proceedings of Krasnodar trial, 1943, Archive of the Federal Security Service of the Russian Federation, (AFSB RF), H-16708, courtesy of the United States Holocaust Memorial Museum (USHMM); Al'tman, *Kholokost na territorii SSSR*; Oldenburg, *Ideologie und militärisches Kalkül*, pp. 304-306; Arad, *The History of the Holocaus*, pp. 525-530; Angrick, *Besatzungspolitik und Massenmord*, pp. 545-670.

Table 9. Course of the Holocaust in Rural Areas of Krasnodarskii *krai*,[20] by *raiony* and Villages

Raion	**Village (*derevnia, selo*) or *stanitsa* (stn.)**	**Number of Jews in 1939**	**Number of victims**	**Stars, forced labor, maltreatment**	**German units involved**	**Local administration involved**	**Date of destruction**
Anapskii	Dzhiginka		72				9.1942
Anapskii	Apsheronskaia		1,000		+	Police	
Archangel'skii	Otradnaia		64				8.1942
Armavirskii	Stn. Kuzhorskaia		36				8.1942
Beloglinskii	Belaia Glina	4	Up to 3,500				8.1942
Beloglinskii	Bezlesnyi		75				
(?)	Stn. Dondukovskaia		100				10.1942
Gul'kevichskii	Stn. Gul'kevichi	2	131-150	Stars			8.1942
Il'inskskii	Turkin		47				
Ivanovskii	Naturbovo		Up to 40				Late 8.1942
Kaganovicheski			64				
Kalnibolotskii	Stn. Kalnibolotskaia		48		+		Late 9. 1942
Koktebeil'skii	The whole *raion* plus stn. Dinskaia		50				9.1942
Korenovskii	Stn. Korenovskaia	16	120				10.1942
Kurganenskii			Up to 3,000				9.1942

20 The following *raiony* of Krasnodarskii *krai* were not occupied: Adler-Gelendzhevskii, Tuapsinskii, Shapsugskii. The following *raiony* were occupied only partly: Armianskii, Tul'skii. Aleksandr Beliaev and Irina Bondar', eds., *Kuban' v gody Velikoi Otechestvennoi voiny*, 1941-1945, p. 480.

Table 9 Continued

Raion	Village (*derevnia, selo*) or *stanitsa* (stn.)	Number of Jews in 1939	Number of victims	Stars, forced labor, maltreatment	German units involved	Local administration involved	Date of destruction
Kurganenskii	Stn. Labinskaia	27	1,500-2,500	Stars, forced labor	Ek 11	Police	28.8; 9; 12.1942
Kurganenskii	Stn. Mikhailovskaia	6	19 or 420				8 or 9. 1942
Ladozhskii	Stn. Ladozhskaia		More than 3,000	Rapes, severe maltreatment		Police	12.1942
Ladozhskii	Stn. Otradnenskaia		483	No food supply	+		Early 10.1942
Ladozhskii	Severnoe, Sheremet'evka, Stn. Tbilisskaia, Vannovka		213	Maltreatment; throwing people in the Kuban' River	+		8.1942
Leningradskii	Stn. Leningradskaia	14	600				10.1942
Novo-Aleksandrovskii	Stn. Novo-Aleksand-rovskaia		480[21] or 541	Forced labor in agriculture			09.1942
(?)	Stn. Novo-Derevian-skaia		42	Dispossession	SS unit		10.1942
(?)	Stn. Novo-Minskaia		42				11.1942
(?)	Stn. Novo-Sherbin-skaia, Abinskaia and Belorechenskaia		200				9.1942

21 In this *stanitsa* all the Jews from the area were assembled.

Table 9 Continued

Raion	Village (*derevnia, selo*) or *stanitsa* (stn.)	Number of Jews in 1939	Number of victims	Stars, forced labor, maltreatment	German units involved	Local administration involved	Date of destruction
(?)	Stn. Sergievskaia		92				8.1942
Novo-Alekseevskoe	Grigoripolisskaia		150				10.1942
Novopokrovskii	Stn. Il'inskaia		460-494				8.1942
Sovetskii	Stn. Sovetskaia		30	Forced labor	-	Police	30.12.1942
Staro-Sherbinovskii	Staro-Sherbinovskaia		200		*Kommandant*, head of Gestapo	-	15.9.1942
Starominskii	Stn. Starominskaia		63		+		19.9.1942
Temergoevskii	Stn. Temirgoevskaia		3,000[22]				9.1942
(?)	Stn. Tikhoretskaia		316				8.1942
Timashevskii	Stn. Dneprovskaia						
Udobnenskii	Udobnenskaia		369-453		EG D		14.10.1942
Uspenskii	Uspenskoe		131	Imprisonment			29.8, 3.9.1942
Uspenskii	Stn. Ust'-Labinskaia		387		Gendarmerie	Police	15.12.1942
Varennikovskii	Stn. Dzhiginka		78	Stars, torture	*Kommandant*	Inhabitants	9.1942
(?)	Stn. Iaroslavskaia		29				11.1942

Source: GARF, 7021/16/4, 6-20, 460-466; YVA, M.33/286-287, 291, 300, 302; TsAMO RF, 51/958/52; Al'tman, *Kholokost na territorii SSSR*.

22 In this *stanitsa* all the Jews from the area were assembled.

Table 10. Course of the Holocaust in Rural areas of Stavropol'skii *krai*, by *raiony* and Villages

Raion	Village (*derevnia*, *selo*), *stanitsa* (stn.) or *kolkhoz*	Number of Jews in 1939	Number of Jewish victims	German units involved	Local administration involved	Date of destruction
Adygeiskii	Stn. Giaginskaia		67 or 150			
Adygeiskii	Stn. Shevchen-kovskaia		11			
Aleksandriisko-Obilenskii	Stn. Alexandriis-kaia		54			8.1942
Apanasenkovskii	Divnoe		300 or 360			9.1942
Apolonskii	Stn. Martinskaia		41			8.1942
Arkhangel'skii	Arkhangel'sk		48 or 70			7.9.1941
(?)	Starodubka		70			4.9.1942
Arkhangelskii	Nini		61			
Arzgirskii	Arzgir	3	150 or 675	Ek 12, *Kommandatur*		9.1942
Blagodarnenskii	Blagodarnoe	13	169+1			9-11.1942
Blagodarnenskii	Alekseevskoe		26			8.1942
Blagodarnenskii	Ipatovo	8	54+86			8,9.1942
Georgievskii	Stn. Alexandrovskaia		55			9.1942
Georgievskii	Stn. Nezlobnaia	9	Up to 508			9-10.1942
Giaginskii	Dondukovskaia		97			Early 10.1942
Egorlyksii	Stn. Novo-Troitskaia	1	240+319			26.9, 20.10.1942
Izobil'nenskii	Izobil'noe	15	Up to 300			8.1942

Table 10 Continued

Raion	Village (*derevnia*, *selo*), *stanitsa* (stn.) or *kolkhoz*	Number of Jews in 1939	Number of Jewish victims	German units involved	Local administration involved	Date of destruction
Izobilnenskii	Moskovskoe	At least 94	118	EG, local police		29.8.1942
Karachaevskii	Nizhnii Arkhyz		20			12.1942
Krasnog-vardeiskii	Dmitrievskoe		185+150			8,12.1942
Kurskii	Bogdanovka	550	452	*Kommandant*, 600 soldiers stationed		24.9.1942
Kurskii	Stn. Kurskaia		250			19.10.1942
Kurskii	Menzhynskoe		218	+	*Burgomistr*	19.10.1942
Levokumskii	Levokumskoe		286		Cossacks	2.10.1942
Levokumskii	Urozhainoe		30	-	Police	14.9.1942
Libkhnetovskii	Rozhdestvenskoe		433			27.9.1942
Novo-Aleksandrovskii	Stn. Novo-Aleksandrovskaia		541			Late 9.1942
Novo-Aleksandrovskii	Stn. Grigoripolin-skaia		150	+	Police and *ataman*	13.10.1942
Petrovskii	Petrovskoe	21	Up to 500[23]			9-11.1942
Petrovskii	Stn. Mikhailovki		600-800	+		9, 10.1942
Piatigorskii	Stn. Goryachev-odskaia		185+150			8,12.1942
Piatigorskii	Zelenokumsk		200			9.1942
Shpakovskii[24]	Blagodatnoe		74 or 94			7.11.1942
Soldatsko-Aleksandrovskii	Soldatsko-Aleksandrovskoe		Up to 270		Police	9.1942

23 Brought from the entire *raion*.

24 In the whole area 149 Jews were killed. Akt of the Commission of Shpakovskii *raion*. GARF, 7021/17/12, p. 55.

Table 10 Continued

Raion	Village (*derevnia*, *selo*), *stanitsa* (stn.) or *kolkhoz*	Number of Jews in 1939	Number of Jewish victims	German units involved	Local administration involved	Date of destruction
Soldatsko-Aleksandrovskii	"Molotov" *kolkhoz*		269	+	+	9.1942
Soldatsko-Aleksandrovskii	Novozavedennoe		No less than 100			26.8.1942
Soldatsko-Aleksandrovskii	Gor'kaia Balka		48	+	Police	
Spitsevskii	Spitsevka		174			19.12.1942
Staro-Mar'evskii	Staro-Mar'evka		150			9.1942
Stepnovskii	Stepnoe		480	+		19.9.1942
Stepnovskii	Solominka		39			12.1942
Suvorovskii	Stn. Suvorovskaia		70	*Kommandant*		Early 10.1942
Suvorovskii	Stn. Bekeshev-skaia		72			12.12.1942
Suvorovskii	Borguevskii Council		170			26.8.1942
Teberdinskii		341	EG	+		14, 22.12. 1942
Trunovskii	Trurnovka		48			25.11.1942
Trunovskii	Bezopasnoe	1	161+9			9, 11.1942
Trunovskii	Donskoe		112+161			25.8, 9.1942
Turkmenskii	Letniaia Stavka		156			9.1942

25 It is not clear whether the rural areas in question were occupied in August or October 1942.

Table 10 Continued

Raion	Village (*derevnia*, *selo*), *stanitsa* (stn.) or *kolkhoz*	Number of Jews in 1939	Number of Jewish victims	German units involved	Local administration involved	Date of destruction
Vorontsovo-Aleksandrovskii	Vorontsovo-Aleksandrovskoe	8	200			7..9.1942
Vorontsovo-Aleksandrovskii	Novo-Krest'ian-skoe		62			9.1942
Vorontsovo-Aleksandrovskii	Novo-Grigor'evskoe		50			5..9.1942
Vorontsovo-Aleksandrovskii	Novo-Kislianov-skoe		62			
Voroshilovskii	Mikhailovka		13+52			8, 9.1942
(?)	Stn. Zelenchuk-skaia		180			12.1942

Source: GARF, 7021/17/8-17; TsAMO RF, 51/958/52. Al'tman, *Kholokost na territorii SSSR*.

Table 11. Course of the Holocaust in Rural Areas of the Kabardino-Balkar Autonomous Republic,[25] by *raiony* and Villages

Raion	Village (*selo*)	Number of Jews in 1939	Number of Jewish victims	Stars, forced labor, maltreatment	German units involved	Local police or authorities involved	Date of destruction
Zol'skii	Zol'skoe		48	Stars, forced labor	Sk 10a		14.12.1942

Source: GARF, 7021/7/103, 109.

Table 12. Course of the Holocaust in Rural Areas of the North Ossetiian Autonomous Republic, by *raiony* and Villages

Raion	Village or stanitsa	Number of Jews in 1939	Number of Jewish victims	Stars, forced labor, maltreatment	German units involved	Local administration involved	Date of destruction
Mozdokskii	Stn. Novo-Osetinskaia		11		-	Police	11.9.1942

Source: GARF, 7021/17/10. TsAMO RF, 51/958/52.

Table 13. Course of the Holocaust in Rural Areas of the the Kamykiian Autonomous Republic, by Regions - *ulusy* or *raiony* and Villages

Raion	Village (*selo*) or *kolkhoz*	Number of Jewish victims	Stars, forced labor, maltreatment	German units involved	Local administration involved	Date of destruction
Troitskii	Troitskoe	29	Forced labor		*Starosta*	10.1942
Zapadnyi	"Dimitrov" *kolkhoz*	19		*Kommandatur*		9.1942
	"Rote Fahne" *kolkhoz*	9				8-9.1942
	Plodovitoe	50 families				10.1942

Source: GARF, 7021/8/26-27; Al'tman, *Kholokost na territorii SSSR.*

Table 14. Krymchak and Karaite Population in the Crimea as of 1930

Town/*raion*	Krymchaks	Karaites
Bakhchisarai	5	150
Dzhankoi	75	10
Evpatoriia	250	990
Feodosiia	560	790
Karasubazar	1,050	-
Kerch	560	790
Sevastopol’	830	800
Simferopol’	2,500	940
Simferopol’skii *raion*	25	130
Karasubazarskii *raion*	100	-
Yalta	50	150
Total in the Crimea	6,080	4,170

Source: Report “O kul’turnom stroitel’stve sredi natsmenshinstv” presented by the People’s Commissariat for Education at the 1st All-Crimean Conference of national minorities dedicated to the problems of the national policy carried out by the Party and the Soviet authorities and to current tasks of the national construction in the Crimea, in Igor’ Achkinazi, *Krymchaki: Istoriko-etnograficheskii ocherk* (Simferopol’: DAR, 2000), pp. 117-118.

Table 15. Evacuation of Children's Homes and Medical Institutions from the Crimea into the North Caucasus as of 1942

Into Krasnodarskii *krai*

No.	Institution	Evacuated from	Number of children or patients	Brought into
1	Children's home	Dzhankoi	61	Nadezhnaia station into Spokoinskii *raion*
2	Children's home No 2	Simferopol'	82	Razdol'naia station into Korenovskii *raion*

Into Stavropol'skii *krai*

No	Institution	Evacuated from	Number of children or patients	Brought into
1	Children's home	Alushta	59	Erken-Shakhar into Cherkesskaia *oblast'*
2	Lenin children's home	Kerch	87	Erken-Shakhar into Cherkesskaia *oblast'*
3	Kim children's home	Kerch	83	Erken-Shakhar into Cherkesskaia *oblast'*
4	Children's home	Bakhchisarai	56	Erken-Shakhar into Cherkesskaia *oblast'*
5	Voikov children's home	Kerch	116	Piatigorsk
6	Medical Tubercular Sanatorium No 30	Southern Coast of the Crimea	75	Teberda
6	Medical Tubercular Sanatorium No 28	Southern Coast of the Crimea	75	Teberda
6	Medical Tubercular Sanatorium I. T.	Southern Coast of the Crimea	21	Teberda

6	Bobrov Medical Tubercular Sanatorium	Southern Coast of the Crimea	230	Teberda
6	Ada Eshel Medical Tubercular Sanatorium	Southern Coast of the Crimea	233	Teberda
7	Infants' home [*dom mladentsa*]	Kerch	73	Cherkessk
8	"Proletarii" Osseous-Tubercular Sanatorium	Evpatoriia	285	Teberda
9	Krupskaia Osseous-Tubercular Sanatorium	Evpatoriia	260	Teberda
10	"Krasnyi partizan" Osseous-Tubercular Sanatorium	Evpatoriia	148	Teberda
11	"Pioner" Osseous-Tubercular Sanatorium	Evpatoriia	158	Teberda
12	Osseous-Tubercular Sanatorium	Evpatoriia	118	Teberda
13	Children's home	Yalta	105	Station A-Obilenskaia

Statistical data of the Department of Statistics of the RSFSR on the number of people evacuated into autonomous republics, territories, and districts in the course of 1942. Department of the Council of People's Commissars of the RSFSR for the Economic Arrangement of the Evacuated Population, 1942, YVA, JM/24.745.

The table is also based on the information of the Medical Department of [Stavropol'skii] *krai*.

List of Archives and Journals

BA — Federal Archives (Berlin, Germany)
AFSB RF — Archive of the Federal Security Service of the Russian Federation (Moscow, Russia)
ASBU RK — State Archive of the Security Service of the Republic of the Crimea (Simferopol', Ukraine)
AUFSB KK — Archive of the Administration of the Federal Security Service of Krasnodarskii *krai* (Krasnodar, Russia)
DAARK — State Archive of the Autonomous Republic of the Crimea (Simferopol', Ukraine)
GAKK — State Archive of Krasnodarskii *krai* (Krasnodar, Russia)
GASK — State Archive of Stavropol'skii *krai* (Stavropol', Russia)
GARF — State Archive of the Russian Federation (Moscow, Russia)
HGS — Holocaust and Genocide Studies
ICJ, DOH — The Hebrew University of Jerusalem, Institute of Contemporary Jewry, Department of Oral History
JSS — Jewish Social Studies
RGASPI — Russian State Archive of Social and Political History (Moscow, Russia)
RGVA — Russian State Military Archive (Moscow, Russia)
RHCA - Russian Holocaust Center Archive (Moscow, Russia)
TsAMO RF — Central Archive of the Ministry of Defense of the Russian Federation (Podol'sk, Russia)
TsDNIKK — Center of Documentation of the Contemporary History of Krasnodarskii *krai* (Krasnodar, Russia)
TsDNISK — Center of Documentation of the Contemporary History of Stavropol'skii *krai* (Stavropol', Russia)

TsK VKP(b) – Central Committee of the All-Union Communist Party (Bolsheviks)

USHMMA – United States Holocaust Memorial Museum Archive (Washington, D.C., USA)

YVA – Yad Vashem Archive (Jerusalem, Israel)

YVHN – Yad Vashem, Hall of Names (Jerusalem, Israel)

YVS – Yad Vashem Studies

Bibliography

Archival sources

Jerusalem, Israel

The Hebrew University of Jerusalem, Institute of Contemporary Jewry, Department of Oral History (ICJ)

Collection of oral testimonies

Yad Vashem Archive (YVA)

Collection TR.2 NOKW, Nuremberg Documents

Collection TR.2, Nuremberg Trial

Collection TR.3, Eichmann trial

Collection TR.10, Trials of Nazi criminals in Western Germany. Provenance: Z/s Ludwigsburg

Collection O.3, Testimonies of the Holocaust survivors

Collection O.51, SS documentation and Selected Records from "Osobyi" Archive in Moscow

Collection M.29FR, Selected records from Miltärarchiv-Bunderarchiv in Freiburg, Germany

Collection M.31, Righteous Among the Nations

Collection M.33, Extraordinary State Commission. Provenance: Moscow, Russia.

Collection M.35, Jewish Anti-Fascist Committee

Collection M.37, Selected records from the Ukrainian Archives

Collection M.40, Selected records from the Russian Archives

Collection P.21, Archive of Ilya Ehrenburg (Il'ia Erenburg)

Yad Vashem Hall of Names (YVHN)

Moscow, Russia

Gosudarstvennyi arkhiv Rossiiskoi Federatsii (GARF). State Archive of the Russian Federation

Fond 7021, *Chrezvychainaia Gosudarstvennaia Kommissiia po ustanovleniia i rassledovaniiu zlodeianii nemetsko-fashiskikh zakhvatchikov i ikh soobshnikov i prichinennogo imi usherba grazhdanam, kolkhozam, obshestvennym organizatsiiam i uchrezhdeniiam* (Extraordinary State Commission on Reporting and Investigating the Atrocities of the German Fascist Occupants and their Henchmen and the Damages inflicted by them to Citizens, *Kolkhozy*, Public Organizations, and Institutions), 1943-1945

Rossiiskii gosudarstvennyi arkhiv sotsial'no-politicheskoi istorii (RGASPI). Russian State Archive of Social and Political History

Fond 69, *Tsentralnyi Shtab Partizanskogo Dvizheniia pri Stavke Verkhovnogo Glavnokomanduiushego* (Central Headquarter of the Partisan Movement under the Headquarter of the Supreme Commander), 1942-1944

Rossiiskii gosudarstvennyi voennyi arkhiv (RGVA). Russian State Military Archive

Fond 1323, *Politseiskie i administrativnye organy Germanii i territorii vremenno okkupirovannykh ei* (Police and administrative institutions of Germany and of the territories temporarily occupied by it), 1936-1944

Simferopol', Ukraine

Derzhavnyi arkhiv Avtonomnoi Respubliki Krym (DAARK). State Archive of the Autonomous Republic of the Crimea

Fond P-156, *Komissiia po istorii Velikoi Otechestvennoi Voiny* (Commission on the History of the Great Patriotic War), 1944-1947

Fond P-1289, *Krymskaia respublikanskaia po ustanovleniia i rassledovaniiu zlodeianii nemetsko-fashiskikh zakhvatchikov i ikh soobshnikov i prichinennogo imi usherba grazhdanam, kolkhozam, obshestvennym organizatsiiam i uchrezhdeniiam KrASSR* (Crimean Republican Commission on Reporting and Investigating the Atrocities of the German Fascist

Occupants and their Henchmen and the Damages inflicted by them on Citizens, *Kolkhozy*, Public Organizations, and Institutions of the Crimean ASSR), 1944

Fond P-1457, *Kerchenskaia gorodskaia uprava* (Kerch Municipal Administration), 1941

Fond P-1458, *Feodosiiskaia gorodskaia uprava* (Feodosiia Municipal Administration), 1941-1942

Fond P-1465, *Kantseliariia nemetskogo komendanta Kerchenskogo porta* (Office of the Commandant of the Kerch Harbor), 1941

Washington, D. C., U.S.A.

United States Holocaust Memorial Museum Archive (USHMMA)

Record Group 11.001M.13. Miscellaneous German Military Records from the Reichsarchiv (and/or Heeresarchiv), Potsdam, Germany

Record Group 06.025. Selected Central Records of the Federal Security Service (FSB) of the Russian Federation (Moscow, Russia) Relating to War Crimes Investigations and Trials in the Soviet Union

Record Group 31.018M. Postwar War Crimes Trials Related to the Holocaust. Provenance: State Archive of the Security Service of the Republic of the Crimea. Simferopol', Ukraine

Record Group 74.001. Selected records from the war trial cases of the Nazi collaborators tried in the Kazakh SSR, 1943-1950. Provenance: Archive of the Committee for the National Security of the Republic of Kazakhstan

Selected Records from the Archives the Autonomous Republic of the Crimea, Ukraine

Selected Records from the Russian State Archive of the Ministry of Defense. Podol'sk, Russia

Party archive of the Crimean District Committee of the Communist Party of Ukraine. Simferopol', Ukraine

Headquarters of the Partisan Movement of the Crimea. Simferopol', Ukraine

Berlin, Germany
Bundesarchiv (BA)
R 6. *Reichsministerium für den besetzten Ostgebieten*

Primary sources

Al'tman, Il'ia and Terushkin, Leonid, eds. *Sokhrani moi pis'ma: Sbornik pisem i dnevnikov evreev perioda Velikoi Otechestvennoi voiny.* Moscow: Tsentr i Fond "Kholokost," izdatel'stvo "MIK," 2007.

Arad, Yitzhak, Krakowski, Shmuel, and Spektor, Shmuel, eds. *The Einsatzgruppen Reports: Selection from the Dispatches of the Nazis' Death Squads Campaign against the Jews (July 1941-January 1943).* New York: Holocaust Library, 1989.

Arad, Yitzhak. *Unichtozhenie evreev SSSR v gody okkupatsii (1941-1944): Sbornik dokumentov i materialov.* Jerusalem: Yad Vashem, 1991.

Ashkhotova, Raisa, ed. *Liki voiny: Sbornik dokumentov po istorii Kabardino-Balkarii v gody Velikoi Otechestvennoi voiny (1941-1945 gg.).* Nal'chik: El'brus, 1996.

Beliaev, Aleksandr and Bondar', Irina, eds. *Kuban' v gody Velikoi Otechestvennoi voiny, 1941-1945: Khronika sobytii.* Vol. 1. Krasnodar: Sov. Kuban', 2000.

Boiko, Stepan, ed. *Stavropol'e v Velikoi Otechestvennoi voine 1941-1945 gg.: Sbornik dokumentov i materialov.* Stavropol': Stavropol'skoe knizhnoe izdatel'stvo, 1962.

Bugai, Nikolai, ed. *Deportatsiia narodov Kryma: Dokumenty, fakty, kommentarii.* Moscow: INSAN, 2002.

———, ed. *'Soglasno Vashemu ukazaniiu!' O deportatsii narodov SSSR v 20-40 e gg.* Moscow: AIRO-XX, 1995.

Dokumenty obviniaiut: Sbornik materialov o chudovishnykh zverstvakh Germanskikh vlastei na vremenno okkupirovannykh Sovetskikh territoriiakh. Moscow: Gospolitizdat, 1st ed. 1943, 2nd ed. 1945.

Dziuban, Orest, Dashkevich, Iaroslav, and Kuk, Vasil', eds. *Ukrain'ske derzhavotvorennia: Akt 30 chervnia 1941: zbirnyk dokumentiv i materialiv.* Lviv-Kiev: Literaturna ahentsiia "Piramida," 2001.

Garagulia, Vadim, Kondranov, Ivan, and Kravtsova, Liubov', eds. *Krym v Velikoi Otechestvennoi voine, 1941-1945.* Simferopol': Tavriia, 1994.

Garagulia, Vadim and Nikolaenko, N. V., eds. *Gor'kaia pamiat' voiny: Krym v Velikoi Otechestvennoi voine.* Simferopol': Krymskaia Akademiia gumanitarnykh nauk, Krymskii respublikanskii kraevedcheskii muzei, 1995.

Gel'man, Boris and Glubochanskii, Aleksandr, eds. *Kholokost: Katastrofa v Krymu.* Simferopol': Predstavitel'stvo "Sokhnut-Ukraina," 2004.

Herasymov, Ivan, et al., eds. *Kniga skorbi Ukrainy: Avtonomnaia respublika Krym.* Simferopol': Tavrida, 2001.

Hurkovych, Volodymyr, ed. *Okupatsiinyi rezhym v Krymu, 1941-1944 rr.: Za materialamy presy okupatsiinykh vlastei.* Simferopol': Tavriia, 1996.

Kichikov, M., ed. *Kalmykiia v Velikoi Otechestvennoi Voine 1941-1945: Dokumenty i materialy.* Elista: Kalmytskii Institut iazyka, literatury i istorii pri Sovete Ministrov Kalmytskoi ASSR, Partiinyi arkhiv Kalmytskogo Obkoma KPSS, 1966.

Kommunisticheskaia Partiia Ukraini. Tsentralnyi Komitet. Institut Istorii Partii. *Nimetsko-fashistskii okupatziiony rezhim na Ukraini: Zbirnyk dokumentiv i materialiv.* Kiev: Derzhavnee vidavnitstvo politichnoi literaturi USSR, 1963.

Kondranov, Ivan. and Stepanova, A., eds. *Krym v period Velikoi Otechestvennoi voiny, 1941-1945: Sbornik dokumentov i materialov.* Simferopol': Tavriia, 1973.

Kravtsova, Liubov' and Tiaglyi, Mikhail, eds. *Peredaite detiam nashim o nashei sud'be.* Simferopol': BETs "Khesed Shimon," 2001.

Krymskii oblasnoi komitet VKP(b), ed. *Zverstva nemetskikh fashistov v Kerchi: Sbornik rasskazov postradavshikh i ochevidtsev.* Sukhumi: Krasnyi Krym, 1943.

Madajczyk, Czesiaw, ed. *Vom Generalplan Ost zum Generalsiedlungsplan*, 'Einzelveroffentlichungen der Historischen Kommission zu Berlin'. Bd. 80. Munich: K. G. Saur, 1994.

Shekichacheva, M. and Shabaev, D., eds. *Kabardino-Balkariia v gody Velikoi Otechestvennoi voiny: Sbornik dokumentov.* Nal'chik: El'brus, 1975.

The Trial of German Major War Criminals: Proceedings of the International Military Tribunal Sitting at Nuremberg, Germany. London: International Military Tribunal, 1946-51.

Tiaglyi, Mikhail, ed. *Kholokost v Krymu: Dokumentalnye svidetel'stva o genotsyde evreev Kryma v period natsistskoi okkupatsii Ukrainy (1941-1944)*. Simferopol': BETs "Khesed Shimon," 2002.

Vlasov, V. A., ed. *Zakonodatel'nye i administrativno-pravovye akty voennogo vremeni (s 22 iunia 1941 g. po 22 marta 1942 g.)*. Moscow: Iurizdat, 1942.

Vodolazhskaia, Valeriia, Krivneva, Mariia, and Mel'nik, Nelli, eds. *Stavropol'e v period nemetsko-fashistskoi okkupatsii (avgust 1942-ianvar' 1943): Dokumenty i materialy Komiteta po delam arkhivov Stavropol'skogo kraia, Gosudarstvennogo arkhiva Stavropol'skogo kraia, Tsentra dokumentatsii noveishei istorii Stavropol'skogo kraia*. Stavropol': Knizhnoe izdatel'stvo, 2000.

Witte, Peter, et al., eds. *Der Dienstkalender Heinrich Himmlers 1941/42*. Hamburg: Christians, 1999.

Secondary sources

Achkinazi, Igor'. *Krymchaki: Istoriko-etnograficheskii ocherk*. Simferopol': DAR, 2000.

Aizenshtat, L. and Baburina, I., eds. *Kniga zhivykh, Vospominaniia evreev-frontovikov, uznikov getto i kontslagerei, boitsov partizanskikh otriadov, zhytelei blokadnogo Leningrada*. St. Petersburg: Akropol', 1995.

Algamil, Yosef. *The Karaite Jews in the Eastern Europe in the Past and in the Present* (Hebrew). Ramle: National Council of the Karaite Jews in Israel, 2000.

———. *The History of the Karaite Jewry* (Hebrew). Vol. 1. Ramle: National Council of the Karaite Jews in Israel, 1979.

Al'tman, Il'ia, ed. *Kholokost na territorii SSSR. Entsiklopediia*. Moscow: ROSSPEN, 2009.

——— (Ilya Altman). *Opfer des Hasses: Der Holocaust in der UdSSR 1941-1945*. Translated by Ellen Greifer. Gleichen: Muster-Schmidt, 2008.

———. *Zhertvy nenavisti: Kholokost v SSSR, 1941-1945*. Moscow: Fond "Kovcheg," 2002.

Altshuler, Mordechai. *Distribution of the Jewish Population of the USSR, 1939*. Jerusalem: The Hebrew University of Jerusalem, Center for the Research of East European Jewry, 1993.

———. *Soviet Jewry on the Eve of the Holocaust*. Jerusalem: The Hebrew University of Jerusalem, Center for the Research of East European Jewry and Yad Vashem, 1998.

———. *Jews of the Eastern Caucasus: The History of the Mountain Jews from the Beginning of the 19th Century* (Hebrew). Jerusalem: Ben Zvi Institute for the Study of Jewish Communities in the East, Institute of Contemporary Jewry, The Hebrew University of Jerusalem, 1990.

Altshuler, Mordechai, Arad, Yitzhak, and Krakowski, Shmuel, eds. *Sovetskie evrei pishut Il'ie Erenburgu, 1943-1966*. Jerusalem: Yad Vashem and Center for Research and Documentation of East European Jewry, 1993.

Amanzholova, D. A. et al., eds. *Natsional'naia politika Rossii: Istoriia i sovremennost'*. Moscow: Informatsionno-izdatel'skoe agentstvo "Russkii mir," 1997.

Andrienko, Maksim. "Naselenie Stavropol'skogo kraia v gody Velikoi Otechestvennoi voiny: otsenka povedencheskikh motivov." PhD diss., Piatigorskii gosudarstvennyi lingvisticheskii universitet, 2005.

Angrick, Andrej. *Besatzungspolitik und Massenmord: Die Einsatzgruppe D in der südlichen Sowjetunion 1941-1943*. Hamburg: Hamburger Edition, 2003.

Arad, Yitzhak. *In the Shadow of the Red Banner: Soviet Jews in the War against Nazi Germany*. Jerusalem: Yad Vashem, The International Institute for Holocaust Research; Gefen, 2010.

———. *The Holocaust in the Soviet Union (Comprehensive History of the Holocaust)*. Jerusalem and Lincoln: Yad Vashem and University of Nebraska Press, 2009.

———. *The History of the Holocaust: Soviet Union and the Annexed Territories* (Hebrew). Jerusalem: Yad Vashem, 2004.

Arad, Yitzhak and Al'tman, Il'ia, eds. *Neizvestnaia chernaia kniga*. Jerusalem, Moscow: Tekst, 1993.

Arnold, Klaus J. *Die Wehrmacht und die Besatzungspolitik in den besetzten Gebieten der Sowjetunion: Kriegführung und Radikalisierung im Unternehmen Barbarossa*. Berlin: Dunker & Humboldt, 2004.

Astashkevich, Irina. "The Pogroms in Ukraine in 1917-1920: An Alternate Universe." PhD diss., Brandeis University, 2013.

Balikoev, Totraz. *Narody Severnogo Kavkaza v gody Velikoi Otechestvennoi voiny (1941-1945)*. Vladikavkaz: Severo-Osetinskii gosudastvennyi universitet im. K. L. Khetagurova, 2000.

Barrett, Thomas M. *At the Edge of the Empire: The Terek Cossacks and the North Caucasus Barrier, 1700-1860*. Boulder, CO: Westview Press, 1999.

Basov, Aleksei. *Krym v Velikoi Otechestvennoi Voine, 1941-1945*. Moscow: Nauka, 1987.

Belikov, German. *Okkupatsiia: Stavropol': Avgust 1942-ianvar' 1943*. Stavropol': Fond dukhovnogo prosvesheniia, 1998.

Belokon', V., Kolpikova, T., Kol'tsova, Ia., and Maznitsa, V., eds. *Stavropol'e: Pravda voennykh let: Velikaia Otechestvenaia v dokumentakh i issledovaniiakh*. Stavropol': Stavropol'skii gosudarstvennyi universitet, 2005.

Bennigsen, Alexandre and Wimbush, S. Enders. *Muslim National Communism in the Soviet Union: A Revolutionary Strategy for the Colonial World*. Chicago: University of Chicago Press, 1979.

Ben Tsvi, Itshak. *The Outcasts of Yisrael* (Hebrew). Tel Aviv: N. Tabarski, 1953.

Berkhoff, Karel. *Harvest of Despair: Life and Death in Ukraine under Nazi Rule*. Cambridge, MA and London: Harvard University Press, 2004.

Bezugol'nyi, Alexei. "Narody Kavkaza v Vooruzhennykh silakh SSSR v gody Velikoi Otechestvennoi Voiny 1941-1945 gg." PhD diss., Stavropol'skii gosudarstvennyi universitet, 2004.

Bidermann, Gottlob Herbert. *In Deadly Combat: A German Soldier's Memoir of the Eastern Front*. Lawrence, Kansas: University Press of Kansas, 2000.

Borovoi, Saul. *Vospominaniia: Pamiatniki evreiskoi istoricheskoi mysli*. Moscow: Evreiskii Universitet v Moskve, Jerusalem: Gesharim, 1993.

Bräutigam, Otto. *So hat es sich zugetragen: Ein Leben als Soldat und Diplomat*. Würzburg: Holzner Verlag, 1968.

Budnitskii, Oleg and Zelenina, Galina, eds. *Svershilos': Prishli nemtsy! Ideinyi kollaboratsyonizm v SSSR v period Velikoi Otechestvennoi voiny*. Moscow: ROSSPEN, 2012.

Bugai, Nikolai and Gonov, Askarbi. *Kavkaz – narody v eshelonakh: 20-60-e gody*. Moscow: INSAN, 1998.

Bugai, Nikolai, ed. *Deportatsiia narodov Kryma: Dokumenty, fakty, kommentarii*. Moscow: INSAN, 2002

———, ed. *Kazachestvo Rossii: ottorzhenie, priznanie, vozrozhdenie (1917-90 gody)*. Moscow: Mozhaisk-Terra, 2000.

———, ed. *'Soglasno Vashemu ukazaniiu!': O deportatsii narodov SSSR v 20-40 e gg*. Moscow: AIRO-XX, 1995.

Bulgakova, Natal'ia. "Sel'skoe naselenie Stavropol'ia vo vtoroi polovine 20-kh – nachale 30-kh godov 20 veka: Izmeneniia v demograficheskom, khoziaistvennom i kul'turnom oblike." PhD diss., Stavropol'skii gosudarstvennyi universitet, 2003.

Burgleich, Michael. *Germany Turns Eastwards: A Study of Ostforschung in the Third Reich*. New York and Cambridge: Cambridge University Press, 1988.

Chlenov, Michael. "Oriental Jewish Groups in the Former Soviet Union: Modern Trends and Development." The 21st Annual Rabbi L. Feinberg Memorial Lecture in Judaic Studies, University of Cincinnati, March 10, 1998.

Coleman, Heater J., ed. *Orthodox Christianity in Imperial Russia: A Source Book on Lived Religion*. Bloomington and Indianapolis: Indiana University Press, 2014.

Connor, Stephen A. "Golden Pheasants and Eastern Kings: The German District Administration in the Occupied Soviet Union, 1941-1944." PhD diss., Wilfried Laurier University, 2007.

Crews, Robert D. *For Prophet and Tsar: Islam and Empire in Russia and Central Asia*. Cambridge, MA: Harvard University Press, 2006.

Dallin, Alexander. *Deutsche Herrschaft in Rußland 1941-1945: Eine Studie über Besatzungspolitik*. Düsseldorf: Droste, 1958.

Danilova, Svetlana, ed. *Iskhod gorskikh evreev: razrushenie garmonii mirov*. Nal'chik: Poligrafservis I T, 2000.

Davies, Robert W. and Wheatcroft, Stephen. *The Years of Hunger; Soviet Agriculture, 1931-1933*. New York: Palgrave Macmillan, 2009.

Dean, Martin. *Robbing the Jews: The Confiscation of Jewish Property in the Holocaust*. New York: Cambridge University Press, 2008.

Degtiariov, Vladimir. *Pobezhdaia smert': Vospominaniia*. Rostov-na-Donu: Oblknigizdat, 1962.

Dekel-Chen, Jonathan. *Farming the Red Land: Jewish Agricultural Colonization and Local Soviet Power, 1924-1941*. New Haven: Yale University Press, 2005.

———. "Shopkeepers and Peddlers into Soviet Farmers: Jewish Agricultural Colonization in Crimea and Southern Ukraine, 1924-1941." PhD diss., Brandeis University, 2001.

Deletant, Dennis. *Hitler's Forgotten Ally: Ion Antonescu and His Regime, Romania 1940-44*. New York: Palgrave Macmillan, 2006.

Donskov, P. N. *Don, Kuban' i Terek vo vtoroi mirovoi voine: Istoricheskaia povest' o vtoroi voine kazachestva s bolshevikami (1941-1945 gg.)*. New York: Izd-vo imeni Pokhodnoho Atamana Pavloca, 1960.

Doronina, Natalia. "Natsystskaia propaganda na okkupirovannykh territoriakh Stavropol'ia i Kubani v 1942-1943 gg.: tseli, osobennosti, krakh." PhD diss., Stavropol'skii gosudarstvennyi universitet, 2005.

Driaev, Avsentii. "Rol' natsional'nogo i religioznogo faktorov na Severnom Kavkaze v gody Velikoi Otechestvennoi voiny, 1941-1945 gg." PhD diss., Severo-Osetinskii gosudarstvennyi universitet im. K. L. Khetagurova, 2009.

Dymshits, Valerii, ed. *Gorskie evrei: istoriia, etnografiia, kultura*. Jerusalem, Moscow: DAAT, 1999.

Dymshits, Veniamin. *Magnitka v soldatskoi shineli*. Moscow: Arkhitektura, 1995.

Dzidzoev, Valerii. *Belyi i krasnyi terror na Severnom Kavkaze v 1917-1918 gg*. Vladikavkaz: Alaniia, 2000.

Earl, Hilary. *The Nuremberg SS-Einsatzgruppen Trial, 1945-1958*. Cambridge: Cambridge University Press, 2009.

Ehrenburg, Ilya (Erenburg, Il'ia), ed. *Murder of a People*. (Yiddish). 2nd ed. Moscow: Der Emes, 1945.

Ehrenreich, Eric. *The Nazi Ancestral Proof: Genealogy, Racial Science, and the Final Solution*. Bloomington and Indianapolis: Indiana University Press, 2007.

Evtushenko, Iurii. "Partizanskoe dvizhenie na Kubani v period Velikoi Otechestvennoi voiny." PhD diss., Kubanskii gosudarstvennyi universitet, 2005.

Frauenfeld, Alfred Aduard. *Die Krim. Ein Handbuch*. Simferopol: Aufstab für den Generalbezirk Krim, 1942.

Fisch, Arnold G. Jr. "Field Marshal Wilhelm List and the "Hostages Case" at Nuremberg: An Historical Reassessment." PhD diss., Pennsylvania State University, 1975.

Fisher, Alan W. *The Crimean Tatars*. Stanford: Hoover Institution Press, 1978.

———. *The Russian Annexation of the Crimea*. Cambridge: Cambridge University Press, 1972.

Frolov, N.M. *Znak sud'by: Vospominaniia i tvorchestvo zhertv natsyzma*. Moscow: Mysl', 2001.

Fuki, Aleksandr. *Karaimy — synov'ia i docheri Rossii: Rasskazy i ocherki ob uchastii v boiakh ot Krymskoi voiny do Velikoi Otechestvennoi*. Moscow: "Interprint," 1995.

Gammer, Moshe. *Muslim Resistance to the Tsar: Shamil and the Conquest of Chechnia and Daghestan*. London: Frank Cass, 1994.

Galbraith, David R. "The Defence and Evacuation of the Kuban Bridgehead, January – October 1943." MA Thesis, National University of Ireland, Maynooth, 2014.

Garagulia, V. K. and Nikolaenko N. V., eds. *Gor'kaia pamiat' voiny: Krym v Velikoi Otechestvennoi*. Simferopol': Krymskaia Akademiia gumanitarnykh nauk, Krymskii respublikanskii kraevedcheskii muzei, 1995.

Garazha, Natal'ia. "Deiatelnost' organov vlasti po mobilizatsii rabochego klassa na pobedu v gody Velikoi Otechestvennoi voiny 1941-1945 gg.: Na materialakh Krasnodarskogo kraia." PhD diss., Adygeiskii gosudarstvennyi universitet, 2005.

Genov, Ivan. *Dnevnik partizana*. Simferopol': Krymizdat, 1963.

Gerlach, Christian. *Krieg, Ernährung, Völkermord: Forschungen zur deutschen Vernichtungspolitik im Zweiten Weltkrieg*. Hamburg: Hamburger Edition, 1998.

Gertsen, Aleksandr. *Evrei v Krymu: Kratkii ocherk istrorii iudeiskih obshin Kryma*. Simferopol': Tavriia-Plus, 1999.

Gesin, Michael. "Holocaust: The Reality of Genocide in Southern Ukraine." PhD diss., Brandeis University, 2003.

Giliazov, Iskander. *Na drugoi storone: kollaboratsionisty iz povolzhsko-priural'skikh tatar v gody Vtoroi Mirovoi voiny*. Kazan': Izd-vo "Master Lain," 1998.

Goebbels, Joseph. *Die Tagebücher von Joseph Goebbels*. Elke Fröhlich, ed. Vol. 6. Munich: Saur, 2004.

Gorny, Yosef. *Jewish Press and the Holocaust, 1939-1945: Palestine, Britain, the United States, and the Soviet Union*. New York: Cambridge University Press, 2012.

Grechko, Andrei. *Bitva za Kavkaz*. Moscow: Ministerstvo Oborony SSSR, 1971.

Grossman, Vasilii and Ehrenburg, Ilya (Erenburg, Il'ia), eds. *The Complete Black Book of Russian Jewry*. New Brunswick and London: Transaction Publishers, 2002.

———, eds. *Chernaia kniga o zlodeiskom povsemestnom ubiistve evreev nemetsko-fashistskimi zakhvatchikami vo vremenno-okkupirovannykh raionakh Sovetskogo Soiuza i v lageriakh unichtozheniia Pol´shi vo vremia voiny 1941-1945 gg*. Jerusalem: Tarbut, 1980.

Gubenko, Gitel'. *Kniga pechali*. Simferopol': Redotdel' Krymskogo Upravleniia po pechati, 1991.

———. *The Book of Sorrows*. New York: GStanislav Company, Inc., 2003.

Guttstadt, Corry. *Turkey, the Jews, and the Holocaust*. Cambridge: Cambridge University Press, 2013.

Hartmann, Christian. *Operation Barbarossa: Nazi Germany's War in the East, 1941–1945*. Oxford: Oxford University Press, 2013.

Hebert, Valerie. *Hitler's Generals on Trial: The Last War Crimes Tribunal at Nuremberg*. Lawrence: University Press of Kansas, 2010.

Heineman, Paul E. "In Defense of an Anachronism: The Cossack Question on the Don, 1861-1914." PhD diss., Georgetown University, 1999.

Hellbeck, Jochen. *Revolution on My Mind: Writing a Diary under Stalin*. Cambridge, MA: Harvard University Press, 2006.

Herasymov, Ivan, et al., eds. *Kniga skorbi Ukrainy: Avtonomnaia respublika Krym*. Simferopol': Tavrida, 2001.

Hebert, Valerie. *Hitler's Generals on Trial: The Last War Crimes Tribunal at Nuremberg*. Lawrence, KS: University of Kansas Press, 2010.

Hilberg, Raul. *Perpetrators, Victims, Bystanders: The Jewish Catastrophe 1933-1945*. New York: Aaron Asher Books, 1992.

———. *The Destruction of the European Jews*. Revised and definitive ed. New York: Holmes & Meier, 1985.

Hitler, Adolf. *Monologe im Führerhauptquartier 1941-1944*. In Werner

Jochman, ed. *Die Aufzeichnungen Heinrich Heims*. Hamburg: A. Knaus, 1980.

Hoffmann, Joachim. *Kaukasien, 1942-1943: Das deutsche Heer und die Orientvölken der Sowjetunion*. Freiburg: Rombach Verlag, 1991.

———. *Die Ostlegionen 1941-43: Turkotataren, Kaukasier und Wolgafinnen im deutschen Herr*. Freiburg: Rombach Verlag, 1981.

———. *Deutsche und Kalmüken 1942 bis 1945*. Freiburg: Rombach Verlag, 1974.

Hubatsch, Walther. *Hitlers Weisungen für die Kriegsführung*. Frankfurt am Main: Bernard und Greaffe Verlag für Wehrwesen, 1962.

Hürter, Johannes. *Hitlers Heerführer: Die deutschen Oberbefehlshaber im Krieg gegen die Sowjetunion 1941/42*. 2nd ed. Munich: R. Oldenbourg Verlag, 2007.

Iakunin, Vadim. *Russkaia Pravoslavnaia tserkov' na okupirovannykh territoriiakh SSSR v gody Velikoi Otechestvennoi voiny 1941-1945 gg*. Samara: Samarskii gosudarstvennyi universitet, 2001.

Ibragimov, Movsur. *Vlast' i obshestvo v gody Velikoi Otechestvennoi voiny na primere natsional'nykh respublik Severnogo Kavkaza*. Moscow: Moskovskii pedagogicheskii univesitet, 1998.

———. *Narody Severnogo Kavkaza v period Velikoi Otechestvennoi voiny 1941-1945 gg*. Moscow: Moskovskii pedagogicheskii univesitet, 1997.

Israpov, Aleksandr. "Gosudarstvennye organy upravleniia i narod v 1941-1945 gg.: Aspekty politicheskogo, ekonomicheskogo i organizatsionno-pravovogo vzaimodeistviia na materialalkh avtonomnykh respublik Severnogo Kavkaza." PhD diss., Dagestanskii nauchnyi tsentr Rossiiskoi Akademii nauk, 2004.

Iurchuk, Ilona. "Politika mestnykh vlastei Kubani po zashite detstva i ee prakticheskaia realizatsiia v gody Velikoi Otechestvennoi voiny (1941-1945 gg.)." PhD diss., Armavirskii institut sotsial'nogo obrazovaniia, 2008.

Jörg, Friedrich. *Das Gesetz des Krieges. Das deutsche Heer in Russland, 1941 bis 1945: Der Prozess gegen das Oberkommando der Wehrmacht*. Munich: Piper, 1993.

Kabuzan, Vladimir. *Naselenie Severnogo Kavkaza v 19-20 vekakh: etnostatisticheskoe issledovanie*. St. Petersburg: Izd-vo "Russko-Baltiiskiiinformatsionnyi tsentr BLITZ," 1996.

Kameneva, Galina. "Zhenschiny Severnogo Kavkaza v gody Velikoi Otechestvennoi voiny 1941-1945 gg." PhD diss., Stavropol'skii gosudarstvennyi universitet, 2004.

Katunin, Iurii. "Pravoslavnaia tserkov' i gosudarstvo: problema vzaimootnoshenii v 1917-1939 gg. (na primere Kryma)." PhD diss., Tavricheskii universitet im. Vernadskogo, 2003.

Kay, Alex J. *Exploitation, Resettlement, Mass Murder: Political and Economic Planning for German Occupation Policy in the Soviet Union, 1940-1941*. New York: Berghahn, 2006.

Kazakov, Aslan. "Deiatel'nost' organov gosudarstvennoi bezopasnosti Kabardino-Balkarii po neitralizatsii podryvnykh aktsii emigrantskikh organizatsii v 20-kh-50-kh gg 20 veka." PhD diss., Akademiia FSB Rossii, 2005.

Kefeli, Valentin. *Karaimy*. Moscow: Rossiiskaia akademiia nauk, Institut eetnologii i antropologii im. N. N. Miklukho-Maklaia, 1992.

Keller, Shoshana. *To Moscow, not Mecca: The Soviet Campaign against Islam in Central Asia, 1917-1941*. Westport, CT: Praeger, 2001.

Kenez, Peter. *Civil War in South Russia, 1919-1920: The Defeat of the Whites*. Berkeley: University of California, 1977.

Keren, Yehezkiel. *The Jewish Agricultural Settlements of the Crimea, 1922-1947* (Hebrew). Jerusalem: Zak & Co., 1973.

———. *Crimean Jewry from its Inception (Beginning) to the Holocaust* (Hebrew). Jerusalem: Reuven Mas, 1981.

Khachemizova, Elena. "Obshchestvo i vlast' v 30-e-40-e gody XX veka: politika repressii (na materialakh Krasnodarskogo kraia)." PhD diss., Adygeiskii gosudarstvennyi universitet, 2004.

Khalitov, Vokasu. "Obespechenie Krasnoi Armii liudskimi resursami i voenno-patrioticheskaia podgotovka sovetskikh voisk nakanune i v gody Velikoi Otechestvennoi voiny: Na materialakh respublik Severnogo Kavkaza: 1939-1945 gg." PhD diss., Chechenskii gosudarstvennyi pedagogicheskii institut, 2004.

Khavadzhi, Dinara. "Pravove reguluivannia natsionalnoi deportatsii z Krims'koi ARSR ta repatriatsii do Avtonomnoi Respubliki Krim u skladi Ukraini (1941-1996 rr.): istoriko-pravove doslidzhenia." PhD diss., Natsyonal'nii universitet vnutrishnikh sprav, 2002.

Khazanov, Anatolii. *The Krymchaks: A Vanishing Group in the Soviet Union*. Jerusalem: The Hebrew University of Jerusalem, the Marjorie Mayrock Center for Soviet and East European Research, 1989.

Kirimal, Edige Mustafa. *Der nationale Kampf der Krimtürken - mit besonderer Berucksichtigung der Jahre 1917-1918*. Emsdetten and Wesfalen: Verlag Lechte and Emsdetten (Westf.), 1952.

Kirimli, Hakan. *National Movements and National Identity among the Crimean Tatars, 1905-1916*. Leiden and New York: E. J. Brill, 1996.

Kizilov, Mikhail. *The Sons of Scripture. The Karaites in Poland and Lithuania in the Twentieth Century*. Berlin: De Gruyter, 2015.

———. *The Karaites of Galicia: An Ethnoreligious Minority among the Ashkenazim, the Turks, and the Slavs, 1772-1945*. Leiden and Boston: Brill, 2009.

Klychnikov, Iurii and Linets, Sergei. *Severokavkazskii uzel: osobennosti konfliktnogo potentsiala (istoricheskie ocherki)*. Piatigorsk: Reklamno-informatsionnoe agenstvo na KMV, 2006.

Kovalev, Boris. *Povsedenevnaia zhizn' Rossii v period natsistskoi okkupatsii*. Moscow: Molodaia gvardiia, 2011.

———. *Natsistskaia okkupatsiia i kollaboratsionizm v Rossii, 1941-1944*. Moscow: AST, 2004.

Krichevskaia, Rozaliia. *Dvadtsat' deviat' mesiatsev iz detstva*. Beer Sheva, 1997.

Kozelsky, Mara V. "Christianizing Crimea: Church Scholarship, "Russian Athos," and Religious Patriotism of the Crimean War." PhD diss., University of Rochester, 2004.

Kozlov, Ivan. *V Krymskom podpol'ie*. Moscow: Gospolitizdat, 1954.

Kravtsova, L. P. and Karpach, E. V., eds. *Nemetskoe naselenie Tavricheskoi gubernii*. Odessa: Astroprint, 2000.

Krikunov, Peotr. *Kazaki: mezhdu Gitlerom i Stalinym: Krestovyi pokhod protiv bol'shevizma*. Moscow: "Iauza" and "EXMO," 2005.

Krinko, Evgenii. *Zhizn' za liniei fronta: Kuban' v okkupatsii (1942-1943)*. Maikop: Adygeiskii gosudarstvennyi universitet, 2000.

Kriukov, Anatolii. "Religioznye sekty na Kubani: stanovlenie, vnutrennee razvitie, vzaimootnosheniia s gosudarstvennymi i obshestvennymi institutami: 30-e gg. XIX v. -1917 g." PhD diss., Kubanskii gosudarstvennyi universitet kul'tury i iskusstv, 2004.

Kropotov, V. S. *Voennye traditsii krymskikh karaimov*. Simferopol', 2004.

Kruchinin, Andrei. *Krymsko-tatarskie formirovaniia v Dobrovol'cheskoi armii: istoriia neudachnykh popytok*. Moscow: Voenno-istoricheskaia biblioteka "Voennoi byli," 1999.

Kunz, Norbert. *Die Krim unter deutscher Herrschaft 1941-1944: Germanisierungsutopie und Besatzungsrealität*. Darmschtadt: Wissentschaftliche Buchgesellschaft, 2005.

Levin, Eduard. *Sorok dnei do rasstrela*. Moscow: GPNTB Rossii, 2001.

Linets, Sergei. *Severnyi Kavkaz nakanune i v period nemetsko-fashistskoi okkupatsii: Sostoianie i osobennosti razvitiia (iiul' 1942-oktiabr' 1943 gg.)*. Rostov-na-Donu: Severo-Kavkazskii nauchnyi tsentr vysshei shkoly, 2003.

Linets, Aleksandr. "Partizanskoe dvizhenie v Stavropol'skom krae v period nemetsko-fashistskoi okkupatsii." PhD diss., Piatigorskii gosudarstvennyi lingvisticheskii universitet, 2003.

Littell, Jonathan. *The Kindly Ones: A Novel*. New York: Harper, 2009.

———. *Les bienveillantes: roman*. Paris: Gallimard, 2006.

Magocsi, Paul Robert. *This Blessed Land: Crimea and the Crimean Tatars*. Toronto, Ontario: University of Toronto Press, 2014.

Makarov, Vladimir and Khristoforov, Vasilii, eds. *Generaly i ofitsery Vermakhta rasskazyvaiut: Dokumenty iz sledstvennykh del nemetskikh voennoplennykh 1944-1951*. Moskva: MFD, 2009.

Mangupli, Larisa, *Kerosinovyi vkus detstva*. Kerch, 2003.

Manley, Rebecca. *To the Tashkent Station: Evacuation and Survival in the Soviet Union at War*. Ithaca: Cornell University Press, 2009.

Manstein von, Erick. *Verlorene Siege*. Bonn: Athenauem, 1957.

Martin, Terry. *The Affirmative Action Empire: Nations and Nationalism in the Soviet Union, 1923–1939*. Ithaca: Cornell University Press, 2001.

McCarthy, Justin. *Death and Exile: The Ethnic Cleansing of Ottoman Muslims, 1821-1922*. Princeton: Darwin Press, 1995.

Michman, Dan. *The Emergence of Jewish Ghettos during the Holocaust*. Translated by Lenn. J. Schramm. New York: Cambridge University Press, 2011.

Mikhailov, Igor'. *Okkupatsiia ili 160 dnei po germanskomu vremeni*. Stavropol': Servisshkola, 2007.

Molotov, Viacheslav. *Soviet Government Statements on Nazi Atrocities*. London: Hutchinson, 1946.

Motadel, David. *Islam and Nazi Germany's war*. Cambridge, Mass.; London, England: The Belknap Press of Harvard University Press, 2014.

Mühlen von zur, Patrick. *Zwinschen Hakenkreuz und Sowjetstern: Der Nationalismus der sowjetischen Orientvölker im Zweiten Weltkrieg.* Düsseldorf: Droste Verlag, 1971.

Müller, Hannelore. *Religionswissenschaftliche Minoritätenforschung: Zur religionshistorischen Dynamik der Karäer im Osten Europas.* Wiesbaden: Harrassowitz, 2010.

Mulligan, Timothy P. *The Politics of Illusion and Empire: German Occupation Policy in the Soviet Union, 1942-1943.* New York: Praeger, 1988.

Murphy, David E. *What Stalin Knew: The Enigma of Barbarossa.* New Haven, CT: Yale University Press, 2006.

Nationalsozialistische Deutsche Arbeiter-Partei. Schutzstaffel. Reichssicherheitshauptamt. *Kaukasus.* Hrsg. vom Chef der Sicherheitspolizei und des SD. Berlin: Wannsee-Institut, 1942.

Neitzel, Sönke, ed. *Tapping Hitler's Generals: Transcripts of Secret Conversations, 1942-1945.* St. Paul, MN: Frontline Books and MBI Publishing, 2007.

Nekrich, Alexander M. *Nakazannye narody.* New York: Khronika, 1978.

Nikulina, Elena. "Istrebitel'nye bataliony Stavropol'ia i Kubani v gody Velikoi Otechestvennoi voiny: 1941-1945 gg." PhD diss., Piatigorskskii gosudarstvennyi lingvisticheskii universitet, 2005.

Nikuradse, Alexander. *Kaukasien, Nordkaukasien, Aserbeidschan, Armenien, Georgien: Geschichtlicher Umriß.* München: Hoheneichen-Verlag, 1942.

Oldenburg, Manfred. *Ideologie und militärisches Kalkül: Die Besatzungspolitik der Wehrmacht in der Sowjetunion 1942.* Köln: Böhlau Verlag, 2005.

O'Neill, Kelly. "Between Subversion and Submission: The Integration of the Crimean Khanate into the Russian Empire, 1783-1853." PhD diss., Harvard University, 2006.

Oren, Itzhak and Prat, Naftali, eds. *Kratkaia evreiskaia entsiklopediia*, vol. 8. Jerusalem: Keter, 1976-2005.

Pandea, Adrian and Eftimie, Ardeleanu. *Românii în Crimeea, 1941-1944.* Bucharest: Editura Militară, 1995.

Pantiukhin, Alexandr. "Obnovlencheskoe dvizhenie Russkoi pravoslavnoi tserkvi v 20-40 gg. XX v. (na materialakh Stavropol'ia i Tereka." PhD diss., Iuizhnyi federal'nyi universitet, 2013.

Patel, Kiran Klaus. *Soldiers of Labor. Labor Service in Nazi Germany and New Deal America, 1933–1945*. New York: Cambridge University Press, 2005.

Perović, Jeronim. *Der Nordkaukasus unter russischer Herrschaft: Geschichte einer Vielvolkerregion zwischen Rebellion und Anpassung*. Köln: Böhlau, 2015.

Petersen, Hans-Christian. *Bevölkerungsökonomie – Ostforschung – Politik: eine biographische Studie zu Peter-Heinz Seraphim (1902–1979)*. Osnabrück: Fibre, 2007.

Petrenko, Tat'iana. "Evakuatsionnyi protsess na Stavropol'e letom 1942 goda: Uspekhi i trudnosti." PhD diss., Piatigorskii gosudarstvennyi tekhnologicheskii universitet, 2004.

Picker, Henry. *Hitlers Tischgespräche im Führer-Hauptquartier, 1941-1942*. Stuttgart: Seewald Verlag, 1963.

Pirogov, Andrei. *Etogo zabyt nel'zia: Vospominaniia byvshego voennoplennogo*. Odessa: Odesskoe knizhnoe izdatel'stvo, 1961.

Plokhy, Serhii. *The Cossack Myth: History and Nationhood in the Age of Empires*. Cambridge; New York: Cambridge University Press, 2012.

Pohl, Dieter. *Die Herrschaft der Wehrmacht: Deutsche Militärbesatzung und einheimische Bevölkerung in der Sowjetunion 1941-1944*. Munich: Oldenbourg, 2008.

Pohl, Otto. *Ethnic Cleansing in the USSR: 1937-1949*. London: Greenwood, 1999.

Polian, Pavel and Shneer, Aron, eds. *Obrechennye pogibnut': Sud'ba sovetskikh voennoplennykh-evreev vo Vtoroi mirovoi voine: Vospominaniia i dokumenty*. Moscow: Novoe izdatel'stvo, 2006.

Polian, Pavel. *Mezhdu Aushvitsem i Bab'em Yarom. Razmyshleniia i issledovaniia*. Moscow: ROSSPEN, 2010.

Polkanov, Aleksander. *Krymskie karaimy*. Simferopol', 1995.

Polkanov, Iurii. *Karai — krymskie tatary — tiurki: Istoriia, etnografiia, kultura*. Simferopol': Asotsiatsiia krymskikh karaimov, 1997.

Pollock, Sean. "Empire by Invitation?: Russian Empire-building in the Caucasus in the Reign of Catherine II." PhD diss., Harvard University, 2006.

Poppe, Nicholas. *Reminiscences.* Bellingham: Western Washington University, 1983.

Poulsen, Niels Bo. "The Soviet Extraordinary State Commission: An Analysis of the Commission's Investigative Work in War and Postwar Stalinist Society." PhD diss., Copenhagen University, 2005.

Puchenkov, Alexandr. *Ukraina i Krym v 1918-nachale 1919 goda. Ocherki politicheskoi istorii.* St. Petersburg: Nestor-Istoriia, 2013.

Rees, E. A. *"Iron Lazar": A Political Biography of Lazar Kaganovich.* London; New York, NY: Anthem Press, 2012.

Richmond, Walter. *The Northwest Caucasus: Past, Present, Future.* London: Routledge, 2008.

Rivkina, Elena and Tiaglyi, Mikhail, eds. *Vospominaniia zhitelei evreiskikh poselenii v Krymu.* Simferopol': BETS "Khesed Shimon," 2004.

Ro'i, Yaacov. *Islam in the CIS: A Threat to Stability?* London: Royal Institute of International Affairs, Russia and Eurasia Programme, 2001.

Roman'ko, Oleg. *Krym v period nemetskoi okkupatsii: natsional'nye otnosheniia, kollaboratsionizm i partizanskoe dvizhenie, 1941-1944.* Moscow: Tsentrpoligraf, 2014.

———. *Krym pod piatoi Gitlera: nemetskaia okkupatsionnaia politika v Krymu (1941-1944).* Moscow: Veche, 2011.

———. *Nemetskaia okkupatsionnaia politika na territorii Kryma i natsional'nyi vopros.* Simferopol: Antikva, 2009.

———. *Musul'manskie legiony vo Vtoroi mirovoi voine.* Moscow: AST, 2004.

Rotaru, Jipa, Teofil, Oroian, Vladimir, Zodian, and Moise, Leonida. *Hitler, Antonescu, Caucazul si Crimea: Sange romanesc si German pe frontul de Est.* Bucharest: Paideia, 1999.

Rubenstein, Joshua and Altman, Ilya (Al'tman, Il'ia), eds. *The Unknown Black Book: The Holocaust in the German-Occupied Soviet Territories.* Translated by Christopher Morris and Joshua Rubenstein. Bloomington: Indiana University Press, 2008. Published in association with the United States Holocaust Memorial Museum.

Sabanchiev, Khadzhi-Murat. *Byli soslany navechno: deportatsiia i reabilitatsiia balkarskogo naroda.* Nal'chik: El'brus, 2004.

Savochkin, Aleksandr. "Massovye repressii 30-40 kh gg. XX veka na Severnom Kavkaze kak sposob utverzhdeniia i podderzhaniia iskliuchitel'noi samosotoiatel'nosti gosudarstva." PhD diss., Vladimirskii iuridicheskii institut Federal'noi sluzhby ispolneniia nakazanii, 2008.

Schur, Nathan. *History of the Karaites*. Franfurt am Main and New York: Peter Lang, 1992.

Schwarz, Solomon. *Evrei v Sovetskom Soiuze s nachala vtoroi mirovoi voiny (1939-1965)*. New York: American Jewish Working Committee, 1966.

Serdiukova, Nataliia. "Gosudarstvennaia politika v oblasti religii v 1920-e gg.: Na materialakh Severnogo Kavkaza." Moscow: Moskovskii pedagogicheskii gosudarstvennyi universitet, 2006.

Shekhtman, Iosif. *Pogromy Dobrovol'cheskoi Armii na Ukraine: k istorii antisemitizma na Ukraine v 1919-1920 gg.* Berlin: Ostjüdisches Historisches Archiv, 1932.

Shamko, Ekaterina N. *Partizanskoe dvizhenie v Krymu v 1941-1944 gg*. Simferopol': Krymizdat, 1959.

———. *Podvigi krymskikh partizan*. Moscow: Voenizdat, 1964.

Shapiro, Gershon and Averbukh, Semeon L., eds. *Ocherki evreiskovo geroizma*. Vols. 2-3. Kiev: Kniga, 1994-1997.

Shevzov, Vera. *Russian Orthodoxy on the Eve of Revolution*. Oxford: Oxford University Press, 2004.

Shkarovskyii, Mikhail. *Natsistkaia Germaniia i Pravoslavnaia tserkov': Natsistskaia politika v otnoshenii Pravoslavnoi Tserkvi i religioznoe vozrozhdenie na okkupirovannoi territorii SSSR*. Moscow: Krutitskoe patriarshee podvor'e, Obshestvo liubitelei tserkovnoi istorii, 2002.

Shneer, Aron. *Plen: Sovetskie voennoplennye v Germanii, 1941-1945*. Jerusalem: Noi, 2003.

Shtoer, Hadas. "Neither Here, Nor There: *Mischlinge* under the Nazi Regime: Comparative Aspects" (Hebrew). MA Thesis: The Hebrew University of Jerusalem, 1999.

Simonov, Konstantin M. *Raznye dni voiny: Dnevnik pisatel'ia*. Moscow: Grifon, 2005.

Sirota, Naum. *Tak derzhalas' Kerch*. Simferopol': Krymizdat, 1961.

Sobolev, Leonid. *Dorogami pobedy: Odessa, Krym, Sevastopol'*. Moscow: Khudozhestvennaia literatura, 1944.

Somova, Inna. "Kul'turnye i religioznye uchrezhdeniia Stavropol'skogo kraia v period Velikoi Otechestvennoi voiny." PhD diss., Piatigorskii gosudarstvennyi lingvisticheskii universitet, 2004.

Stein, Marcel, ed. *Die 11. Armee und die „Endlösung" 1941/42: eine Dokumentensammlung mit Kommentaren*. Bissendorf: Biblio Verlag, 2006.

———. *Der Januskopf: Feldmarschall von Manstein; eine Neubewertung*. Bissendorf: Biblio Verlag, 2004.

Steinhart, Eric C. *The Holocaust and the Germanization of Ukraine*. New York: Cambridge University Press in association with the United States Holocaust Memorial Museum and German Historical Institute, Washington, D.C., 2015.

Steinweis, Alan E. *Studying the Jew: Scholarly Antisemitism in Nazi Germany*. Cambridge, MA: Harvard University Press, 2006.

Stepanenko, Sergei. *Deiatel'nost' Chrezvychainoi gosudarstvennoi komissii SSSR po vyiavleniiu voennykh prestuplenii fashystskoi Germanii na territorii Krasnodarskogo kraia*. PhD diss., Adygeiskii gosudarstvennyi universitet, 2010.

Streit, Christian. *Keine Kameraden: die Wehrmacht und die sowjetischen Kriegsgefangenen 1941-1945*. Stuttgart: Deutsche Verlags-Anstalt, 1978.

Teich, Gerhard and Heinz, Rübel, Institut für Grenz- und Auslandstudien. Reichsführer SS, Rasseamt, eds. *Verzeichnis der Völker, Volksgruppen und Volksstämme auf Gebiet der ehemaligen UdSSR: Geschichte, Verbreitung Rasse, Bekenntnis*. Berlin: Steglitz, 1941.

Teich, Gerhard and Heinz, Rübel, Nationalsozialistische Deutsche Arbeiter-Partei. Schutzstaffel. Rassenamt, eds. *Völker, Volksgruppen und Volksstämme auf dem ehemaligen Gebiet der UdSSR; Geschichte, Verbreitung, Rasse, Bekenntnis*. Leipzig: Schwarzhaupter Verlag, 1942.

Tiaglyi, Mikhail. *Mesta massovogo unichtozheniia evreev Kryma v period natsistskoi okkupatsii poluostrova (1941-1944): Spravochnik*. Simferopol: BETs "Khesed Shimon," 2005.

Trevor-Roper, Hugh. *Hitler's Secret Conversations, 1914-1941*. New York: Farrar, Strauss and Young, 1953.

Trunk, Isaiah. *Jewish Responses to Nazi Persecution: Collective and Individual Behavior in Extremis*. New York: Stein and Day, 1979.

Tsukerman, Zinovii, ed. *Katastrofa: Poslednie svideteli: Vtoraia kniga vospominanii*. Moscow: Dom evreiskoi knigi, 2008.

Ueberschär, Gerd R. and Wetter, Wolfram, eds. *Der deutsche Überfall auf der Sowjetunion: Unternehmen Barbarossa 1941*. Frankfurt am Main: Fischer Taschenbuch, 1991.

Uehling, Greta. "Having a Homeland: Recalling the Deportation, Exile, and Repatriation of the Crimean Tatars to their Historic Homeland." PhD diss., University of Michigan, 2000.

The Universal Jewish Encyclopedia. Vol. 3. New York: The Universal Jewish Encyclopedia, inc., 1941.

Vavilova, Novella. *Uroki razgnevannoi Klio*. Simferopol', 1998.

Vergasov, Il'ia. *Krymskie tetradi*. Moscow: Sovetskii pisatel', 1971.

———. *V gorakh Tavrii*. Kiev: Izdatel'stvo khudozhestvennoi literatury "Dnipro," 1969.

Voitenko, Elena. "Kholokost na iuge Rossii v period Velikoi Otechestvennoi Voiny (1941-1943 gg.)." PhD diss., Stavropol'skii gosudarstvennyi universitet, 2005.

Die Völker des Kaukasus und seiner Vorländer. Berlin und Stuttgart: Deutsches Ausland-Institut, 1941.

Die Völker des Ostraumes. Berlin: P. Stollberg, 1942.

Waddington, Lorna. *Hitler's Crusade: Bolshevism, the Jews and the Myth of Conspiracy*. Revised ed. New York: I. B. Tauris, distributed by Palgrave Macmillan, 2012.

Walter, Richmond. *The Northwest Caucasus: Past, Present, Future*. London: Routledge, 2008.

West, Benjamin. *In the Ropes of Destruction: Soviet Jews in the Nazi Holocaust, 1941-43* (Hebrew). Tel Aviv: Archion Ha-avoda, 1963.

Wildt, Michael. *Generation des Unbedingten: Das Führungskorps des Reichssicherheitshauptamtes*. Hamburg: Hamburger Edition, 2002.

Williams, Brian Glyn. *The Crimean Tatars: The Diaspora Experience and the Forging of a Nation*. Leiden: Brill, 2001.

Wir Erobern Die Krim: Soldaten der Krim-Armee Berichten. Berlin: Prälziche Verlagsantalt Neustadt and Weinstrasse, 1943.

Witte, Peter et al., eds. *Der Dienstkalender Heinrich Himmlers 1941/42*. Hamburg: Christians, 1999.

Wrochem von, Oliver. *Erich von Manstein: Vernichtungskrieg und Geschichtspolitik*. Paderborn: Ferdinand Schöningh Verlag, 2006.

Zellhuber, Andreas. *"Unsere Verwaltung treibt einer Katastrophe zu..."*

Das Reichsministerium für die besetzten Ostgebiete und die deutsche Besatzungsherrschaft in der Sowjetunion 1941-1945. München: Vögel, 2006.

Zhukov, Dmitrii and Kovtun, Ivan. *Antisemitskaia propaganda na okkupirovannykh territoriiakh RSFSR*. Rostov-na-Donu: "Feniks", 2015.

———. *1-aia russkaia brigada SS "Druzhina"*. Moscow: Veche, 2010.

Zhuravlev, Evgenii. *Kollaboratsionizm na iuge Rossii v gody Velikoi Otechestvennoi voiny (1941-1945 gg.)*. Rostov-na-Donu: Izdatel'stvo Rostovskogo universiteta, 2006.

Zionist Organisation. *Die Judenpogrome in Rußland*. Köln and Leizpzig: Jüdischer Verlag, 1910.

Zolotarev, Vladimir, ed. *Velikaia Otechestvennaia voina, 1941-1945*. Vol. 1. Moscow: Nauka, 1998.

Secondary works

Aliskerov, I. Sh. "Vliianie religioznykh i etnicheskikh faktorov na voenno-politicheskuiu obstanovku na Severnom Kavkaze v gody Velikoi Otechestvennoi voiny 1941-1945 gg.," in Nikolai Trofimchuk, ed. *Religioznye organizatsii Sovetskogo Soyuza v gody Velikoi Otechestvennoi voiny 1941-1945 gg. Materialy 'Kruglogo stola.'* Moscow: RAGS, 1995.

Altshuler, Mordechai. "The Unique Features of the Holocaust in the Soviet Union" in Yaakov Ro'i, ed. *Jews and Jewish Life in Russia and the Soviet Union*. Ilford, Essex: F. Cass, 1995.

———. "Intermarriage among Soviet Jews between the World Wars" (Hebrew). *Shvut* 13 (1988): pp. 31-40.

———. "Nazi Attitudes towards the Jewishness of the Mountain Jews and Other Oriental Communities" (Hebrew). *Peamim* 27 (1986): pp. 5-17.

———. "The Evacuation and Flight of Jews of Eastern Belorussia during the Holocaust: June-August 1941" (Hebrew). *Yahadut Zmanenu* 3 (1986): pp. 119-158.

Amirkhanov, M. "Islam in Tatar National Ideology and Policy," in Jorgen S. Nielsen, ed. *The Christian-Muslim Frontier: Chaos, Clash, or Dialogue?* London: I.B. Tauris, 1998.

Anderson, Truman O. "Germans, Ukrainians and Jews: Ethnic Politics in Heersgebiet Sued, June-December 1941." *War in History* 7, no. 3 (2000): pp. 325-352.

Angrick, Andrej. "Die Einsatzgruppe D und die Kollaboration," in Wolf Kaiser, ed. *Täter im Vernichtungskrieg: der Überfall auf der Sowjetunion und der Völkermord an den Juden.* Berlin: Propyläen, 2002.

———. "Die Eisatzgruppe D," in Peter Klein, ed. *Die Einsatzgruppen in der bezetzten Sowjetunion 1941/42: Die Tätigkeits- und Lagerberichte des Chefs der Sicherpolizei und des SD.* Berlin: Edition Hentrich, 1997.

Aptekar', Pavel. "Voina bez kraia i kontsa." *Rodina* 1-2 (2001).

Arad, Yitzhak. "The Armed Jewish resistance in Eastern Europe," in Michael Berenbaum and Abraham J. Peck, eds. *The Holocaust and History: The Known, the Unknown, the Disputed, and the Reexamined.* Bloomington and Indianapolis: Indiana University Press, 2002.

———. "White Stains in the Historiography of the Holocaust in Nazi-Occupied Territories of the Soviet Union," in Il'ia Altman, ed. *The Holocaust and the Case of the Jewish Anti-Fascist Committee: Proceedings of the Fourth International Conference "Lessons of the Holocaust in Contemporary Russia" held in Moscow on 1-2 October, 2002.* Moscow: Fond "Kholokost," 2002.

———. "Plunder of Jewish Property in the Nazi-Occupied Areas of the Soviet Union." *Yad Vashem Studies* 29 (2001): pp. 109-148.

———. "Jewish Fighting Underground in the East European Ghettos: Ideology and Reality" (Hebrew), in Israel Gutman, ed. *Major Changes within the Jewish People in the Wake of the Holocaust: Proceedings of the Ninth Yad Vashem International Historical Conference held in Jerusalem in June 1993.* Jerusalem: Yad Vashem, 1996.

Atchildi, Asaf. "Rescue of Jews of Bukharan, Iranian and Afghan Origin in Occupied France (1940-1944)." *Yad Vashem Studies* 6 (1967): pp. 257-281.

Avrutin, Eugene M. "Racial Categories and the Politics of (Jewish) Difference in Late Imperial Russia." *Kritika: Explorations in Russian and Eurasian History* 8, no. 1 (Winter 2007): pp. 13-40.

Bakhrevskii, E., Efimov, A., and Zonlotarev, D. "Islam v Krymu: istoriia, sovremennost', perspektivy." *Rossiia i musul'manskii mir* 6 (2000): pp. 60-66.

Baranova, Ol'ga. "Nationalism, Anti-Bolshevism or the Will to Survive? Collaboration in Belarus under the Nazi Occupation of 1941-1944." *European Review of History: Revue Europeenne d'Histoire* 15, no. 2 (2008): pp. 113-128.

Baskhaev, A. "Germanskaia okkupatsiia chasti territorii Kalmykii," in Kalmytskii institut gumanitarnykh issledovanii, Rossiiskaia akademiia nauk, eds. *Velikaia Otechestvennaia voina: sobytiia, liudi, istoriia.* Elista: Dzhangar, 2001.

Benoít, Lemay. "Le feld-maréchal Erich von Manstein: un instrument docile dans une entreprise criminelle." *Revue d'Histoire de la Shoah* 187 (2007): pp. 177-192.

Bergen, Doris L. "The Nazi concept of 'Volksdeutsche' and the Exacerbation of Antisemitism in Eastern Europe, 1939-45." *Journal of Contemporary History* 29, no. 4 (1994): pp. 569-582.

Berkhoff, Karel C. The "Russian" Prisoners of War in Nazi-Ruled Ukraine as Victims of Genocidal Massacre." *Holocaust and Genocide Studies* 15, no. 1 (2001): pp. 1-32.

———. "Was there a Religious Revival in Soviet Ukraine under the Nazi Regime?" *Slavonic and East European Review* 78, no. 3 (July 2000): pp. 536-567.

Beyrau, Dietrich and Keck-Szajbel, Mark. "Eastern Europe as a "Sub-Germanic Space": Scholarship on Eastern Europe under National Socialism." *Kritika: Explorations in Russian and Eurasian History* 13, no. 3 (Summer 2012): pp. 685-723.

Bezugol'nyi, Aleksei. "Ni mira, ni voiny: Polozhenie na sovetsko-turetskoi granitse i mery sovetskogo rukovodstva po predotvrashcheniiu turetskoi ugrozy v pervyi period Velikoi Otechestvennoi Voiny." *Voenno-Istoricheskii arkhiv* 5, no. 41 (2003): pp. 53-76.

Bidlack, Richard. "The Political Mood in Leningrad during the First Year of the Soviet-German War." *Russian Review* 59, no. 1 (2000): pp. 96-113.

Black, Peter. "Foot Soldiers of the Final Solution: The Trawniki Training Camp and Operation Reinhard." *Holocaust and Genocide Studies* 25, no. 1 (2011): pp. 1-99.

Boeck, Brian J. "Complicating the National Interpretation of the Famine: Reexamining the Case of Kuban." *Harvard Ukrainian Studies* 30, no. 1/4 (2008): pp. 31-48.

Bojzow, Valentin. "Aspekte der miltärischen Kollaboration in der UdSSR von 1941-1944," in Werner Röhr, ed. *Okkupation und Kollaboration (1938-1945): Beiträge zu Konzepten und Praxis der Kollaboration in der deutschen Okkupationspolitik*. Berlin, Heidelberg: Hüthig Verlagsgemeischaft, 1994.

Brown, Paul B. "The Senior Leadership of the Geheime Feldpolizei." *Holocaust and Genocide Studies* 17, no. 2 (2003): pp. 278-304.

Bryan, Fanny E. "Anti-religious Activity in the Chechen-Ingush Republic of the USSR and the Survival of Islam." *Central Asian Survey* 3, no. 2 (1984): pp. 99-115.

Campbell, Elena I. "The Autocracy and the Muslim Clergy in the Russian Empire (1850s-1917)." *Russian Studies in History* 44, no. 2 (Fall 2005): pp. 8-29.

Cantorovich, Irena and Cantorovich, Nati. "The Impact of the Holocaust and the State of Israel on Soviet Jewish Identity," in Yaacov Ro'i, ed. *The Jewish Movement in the Soviet Union*. New York: Woodrow Wilson Center Press, Johns Hopkins University Press, 2012.

Chervonnaia, Svetlana. "Islamskii faktor v natsional'nom i pravozashitnom dvizhenii krymskikh tatar (1990-e gg.)," in idem., ed. *Islam v Evroazii: Sovremennie etnicheskie i esteticheskie kontseptsii sunnitskogo islama, ikh transformatsiia v massovom soznanii i virazhenie v iskusstve musulmanskikh narodov*. Moscow: "Progress-Traditsiia," 2001.

Clark, Katerina. "Ehrenburg and Grossman: Two Cosmopolitan Jewish Writers Reflect on Nazi Germany at War." *Kritika: Explorations in Russian and Eurasian History* 10, no. 3 (Summer 2009): pp. 607-628.

Darabadi, Parvin. "Kavkaz i Kaspii v "Bol'shoi geostrategicheskoi igre" nakanune i v period Vtoroi Mirovoi voiny (geoistoricheskii ocherk)." *Kavkaz i globalizatsiia* 1 (2008): pp. 146-169.

Dean, Martin. "Crime and Comprehension, Punishment and Legal Attitudes: German and Local Perpetrators of the Holocaust in Domachevo, Belarus, in the Records of Soviet, Polish, German, and British War Crimes Investigations," in David Bankier and Dan Michman, eds. *Holocaust and Justice; Representation and Historiography of the Holocaust in Post-War Trials*. Jerusalem: Yad Vashem, 2010.

———. "Lebensbedingungen, Zwangsarbeit und Überlebenskampf in den kleinen Ghettos: Fallstudien aus den Generalkommissariaten Weissruthenien und Wolhynien-Podolien," in Christoph Dieckmann und Babette Quinkert, eds. *Im Ghetto 1939-1945; neue Forschungen zu Alltag und Umfeld*. Göttingen: Wallstein Verlag, 2009.

———. "Seizure of Jewish Property and Inter-Agency Rivalry in the Reich and in the Occupied Soviet Territory," in Gerald D. Feldman and Wolfgang Seibel, eds. *Networks of Nazi Persecution: Bureaucracy, Business, and the Organization of the Holocaust*. New York: Berghahn Books, 2005.

———. "The German 'Gendarmerie,' the Ukrainian 'Schutzmannschaft' and the 'Second Wave' of Jewish Killings in Occupied Ukraine: German Policing at the Local Level in the Zhitomir Region, 1941-1944." *German History* 14, no. 2 (1996): pp. 168-192.

Dekel-Chen, Jonathan. "Soviet-Jewish Agricultural Colonists, 1937-1945." *Jews in Eastern Europe* 3 [46] (Winter 2001): pp. 34-57.

Deletant, Dennis. "Transnistria and the Romanian Solution to the "Jewish Problem," in Ray Brandon and Wendy Lower, eds. *The Shoah in Ukraine; History, Testimony, Memorialization*. Bloomington: Indiana University Press in association with the United States Holocaust Memorial Museum, 2010.

Dickinson, Anna. "Quantifying Religious Oppression: Russian Orthodox Church Closures and Repression of Priests 1917–41." *Religion, State and Society* 28, no. 4 (2000): pp. 327-335.

Dieckmann, Christoph. "The War and the Killing of the Lithuanian Jews," in Ulrich Herbert, ed. *National Socialist Extermination Policy: Contemporary German Perspectives and Controversies*. New York and London: Berghahn Books, 2000.

Dornik, Wolfram and Lieb, Peter. "Misconceived Realpolitik in a Failing State: The Political and Economic Fiasco of the Central Powers in Ukraine, 1918." *First World War Studies* 4, no. 1 (2013): pp. 111-124.

Dubson, Vadim. "On the Problem of the Evacuation of Soviet Jews in 1941 (New Archival Sources)." *Jews in Eastern Europe* 3 [40] (1999): pp. 37-56.

Dufaud, Grégory. "The Establishment of Bolshevik Power in the Crimea and the Construction of a Multinational Soviet State: Organisation, Justification, Uncertainties." *Contemporary European History* 21, no. 2 (May 2012): pp. 257-272.

Dumitru, Diana. "An Analysis of Soviet Postwar Investigation and Trial Documents and Their Relevance for Holocaust Studies," in Michael David-Fox, Peter Holquist, and Alexander M. Martin, eds., *The Holocaust in the East: Local Perpetrators and Soviet Responses.* Pittsburgh, PA: University of Pittsburgh Press, 2013.

Eligulashvili. "How the Jews of Gruziia in Occupied France were Saved." *Yad Vashem Studies* 6 (1967): pp. 251-254.

Fatal-Kna'ani, Tikva. "Grodno: Attempts to Resist, Escape and Rescue" (Hebrew). *Dapim le-heker ha-Shoa* 14 (1997): pp. 51-75.

Feferman, Kiril. "Nazi Germany and the Karaites in 1938-44: Between Racial Theory and *Realpolitik*." *Nationalities Papers* 39, 2 (March 2011): 277-294

———. "Looking East or Looking South? Nazi Ethnic Policies in the Crimea and the Caucasus," in A. Weiss-Wendt, ed. *Eradicating Differences: The Treatment of Minorities in Nazi-Dominated Europe.* Newcastle: Cambridge Scholars Publishing, 2011.

———. "A Soviet Humanitarian Action?: Centre, Periphery and the Evacuation of Refugees to the North Caucasus, 1941-1942." *Europe-Asia Studies* 61, no. 5 (2009): pp. 813-831.

———. "Food factor as a Possible Catalyst for the Holocaust-Related Decisions: The Crimea and North Caucasus." *War in History* 15, no. 1 (2008): pp. 72-91.

———. "Nazi Germany and the Mountain Jews: Was There a Policy?" *Holocaust and Genocide Studies* 21, no. 1 (2007): pp. 96-114.

———. "Soviet Investigation of Nazi Crimes in the USSR: Documenting the Holocaust." *Journal of Genocide Research* 5, no. 4 (2003): pp. 587-602.

Förster, Jürgen. "Hitler's Decision in Favour of War against the Soviet Union." in Horst Boog et al., eds. *The Attack on the Soviet Union*, vol. 4 of *Germany and the Second World War*. Oxford: Oxford University Press, 1998.

———. "The Relation between Operation Barbarossa as an Ideological War of Extermination and the Final Solution," in David Cesarani, ed. *The Final Solution: Origins and Implementation*. London: Routledge, 1994.

Friedman, Philip. "The Karaites under Nazi Rule," in Max Beloff, ed. *On the Track of Tyranny. Essays presented by the Wiener Library to Leonard G. Montefiore, O.B.E., on the occasion of his seventieth birthday*. London: The Wiener Library, 1960.

Gatagova, Liudmila. "Caucasian Phobias and the Rise of Antisemitism in the North Caucasus in the 1920s." *The Soviet and Post-Soviet Review* 36 (2009): pp. 42-57.

Giliazov, Iskander. "Kollaboratsionizm tiurko-tatarskikh narodov SSSR v gody Velikoi Otechestvennoi voiny." *Ab Imperio* 1 (2000): pp. 107-128.

Gitelman, Zvi. "Internationalism, Patriotism, and Disillusion: Soviet Jewish Veterans Remember World War II and the Holocaust," in John K. Roth and Elizabeth Maxwell, eds. *Remembering for the Future*. Houndmills and New York: Palgrave, 2001.

Gerlach, Christian. "German Economic Interests, Occupation Policy and the Murder of the Jews in Belorussia, 1941/43," in Ulrich Herbert, ed. *National Socialist Extermination Policy: Contemporary German Perspectives and Controversies*. New York and London: Berghahn Books, 2000.

Gladkova, S. A. "Organizatsiia evakuatsii liudskikh i materialnykh resursov," in Kalmytskii institut gumanitarnykh issledovanii Rossiiskoi akademii nauk et al., eds. *Velikaia Otechestvennaia voina: sobitiia, liudi, istoriia*. Elista: Dzhangar, 2001.

Glantz, David M. "The Struggle for the Caucasus." *The Journal of Slavic Military Studies* 22, no. 4 (2009): pp. 588-711.

Goldenberg, Mark. "Evrei v krymskom partizanskom dvizhenii i podpol'e 1941-1944 gg.," in Viktoriia Mochalova, et al., eds. *Materialy Odinadtsatoi Ezhegodnoi Mezhdistsiplinarnoi konferentsii po iudaike*. Moscow: Tsentr nauchnykh i prepodavatelei iudaiki v vuzakh "Sefer," Institut Slavianovedeniia RAN, 2004.

———. "Kerchensko-Feodosiiskaia desantnaia operatsiia v sud'be evreev i krymchakov Vostochnogo Kryma." *Tkuma, Vestnik nauchno-prosvetitel'skogo tsentra "Tkuma" (Dnepropetrovsk, Ukraine)* 47-48, nos. 4-5 (2004).

———. "Tragediia evreiskoi obshchiny Feodosii." *Problemy Holokosta v Ukraine: Tezisy dokladov i soobschenii Mezhdunarodnoi nauchnoi konferentsii (Dnepropetrovsk, 2002)*. Zaporozh'e: Premier, 2003.

———. "K voprosu o chisle zhertv sredi mirnogo naseleniia Kryma v period natsystskoi okkupatsii (1941-1944 gg.)." *Buleten: 'Golokost i suchasnist'* 3, 4 (9, 10) (2003): pp. 4-6.

Green, Warren Paul. "The Fate of the Crimean Jewish Community: Askenazim, Krimchaks, and Karaites." *Jewish Social Studies* 46, no. 2 (1984): pp. 169-176.

———. "The Fate of Oriental Jews in Vichy France." *Wiener Library Bulletin* 32 (49-50) (1979): pp. 40-50.

———. "The Nazi Racial Policy towards the Karaites." *Soviet Jewish Affaires* 8, no. 2 (1978): pp. 35-45.

Greenspan, Henry. "'An Immediate and Violent Impulse:' Holocaust Survivor Testimony in the First Years after Liberation," in John K. Roth and Elizabeth Maxwell, eds. *Memory*. Vol. 3 of *Remembering for the Future: The Holocaust in an Age of Genocide*. Houndmills and New York: Palgrave, 2001.

Grimmer-Solem, Erik. "'Selbständiges verantwortliches Handeln' Generalleutnant Hans Graf von Sponeck (1888-1944) und das Schicksal der Juden in der Ukraine, Juni-Dezember 1941." *Militärgeschichtliche Zeitschrift* 72, no. 1 (2013): pp. 23-50.

Guchinova, Elza-Bair. "Deportation of the Kalmyks (1943-1956): Stigmatized Ethnicity," in Uyama Tomohiko, ed. *Empire, Islam, and Politics in Central Eurasia: Slavic Eurasian Studies*. Sapporo: Slavic Research Center, Hokkaido University, 2007.

Güçlü, Yücel. "The Uneasy Relationship: Turkey's Foreign Policy vis-à-vis the Soviet Union at the Outbreak of the Second World War." *Mediterranean Quarterly Summer* 13, no. 3 (2002): pp. 58-93.

Gurkin, V. V. and Kruglov, A. I. "Oborona Kavkaza: 1942 god." *Voenno-Istoricheskii Zhurnal* 10 (1992): pp. 11-18.

Haar, Ingo. "Deutsche 'Ostforschung' und Antisemitismus." *Zeitschrift für Geschichtswissenschaft* 48, no. 6 (2000): pp. 485-508.

Harviainen, Tapani. "The Karaites in Eastern Europe and the Crimea: An Overview," in Meira Polliack, ed. *Karaite Judaism; A Guide to Its History and Literary Sources*. Leiden: Brill, 2003.

Harward, Grant T. "First among Un-Equals: Challenging German

Stereotypes of the Romanian Army during the Second World War." *The Journal of Slavic Military Studies* 24, no. 3 (2011): pp. 439-480.

Hayward, Joel. "Too Little, Too Late: An Analysis of Hitler's Failure in August 1942 to Damage Soviet Oil." *The Journal of Military History* 64, no. 3 (July 2000): pp. 769-794.

———. "A Case Study in Early Joint Warfare: An Analysis of the Wehrmacht's Crimean Campaign of 1942." *Journal of Strategic Studies* 22, no. 4 (1999): pp. 103-130.

———. "Hitler's Quest for Oil: The Impact of Economic Considerations on Military Strategy, 1941-42." *Journal of Strategic Studies* 18, no. 4 (1995): pp. 94-135.

Heer, Hannes. "The Logic of the War of Extermination: The Wehrmacht and the Anti-Partisan War," in Hannes Heer and Klaus Naumann, eds. *War of Extermination: The German Military in World War II, 1941-1944*. New York and Oxford: Berghahn Books, 2000.

Henze, Paul B. "Fire and Sword in the Caucasus: The 19th Century Resistance of the North Caucasian Mountaineers." *Central Asian Studies* 2, no. 1 (1983): pp. 5-44.

Herzstein, Robert E. "Anti-Jewish Propaganda in the Orel Region of Great Russia, 1942-1943: The German Army and its Nazi Collaborators." *Simon Wiesenthal Center Annual* 6 (1989): pp. 33-55.

Hirschfeld, Yair. "Irans Bedeutung für die deutsche Kriegswirtschaft vom Beginn des Zweiten Weltkriegs bis zum anglo-russischem Besetzung Irans im August 1941." *Jahrbuch des Instituts für deutsche Geschichte* 7 (1978): pp. 421-446.

Holler, Martin. "Extending the Genocidal Program: Did Otto Ohlendorf Initiate the Systematic Extermination of Soviet "Gypsies?" in Alex J. Kay, Jeff Rutherford and David Stahel, eds. *Nazi Policy on the Eastern Front, 1941: Total War, Genocide, and Radicalization*. Rochester, NY: University of Rochester Press, 2012.

Höpp, Gerhard. "Der Koran als 'Geheime Reichssache': Bruchstücke deutscher Islampolitik zwischen 1938 und 1945," in Holger Preißler and Hubert Seiwert, eds. *Gnosisforschung und Religionsgeschichte*. Marburg: Diagonal-Verlag, 1994.

Hürter, Johannes. "Nachrichten aus dem 'Zweiten Krimkrieg' (1941/42): Werner Otto v. Hentig als Vertreter des Auswärtigen Amtes bei der 11. Armee," in Wolfgang Elz and Sönke Neitzel, eds. *Internationale Beziehungen im 19. und 20. Jahrhundert*. Paderborn: Schöningh, 2003.

Imbragimbejli, Khadzhi. "Krakh gitlerovskogo okkupatsionnogo rezhima na Kavkaze," in Aleksei Basov and Georgii Kumanev, eds. *Narodnyi podvig v bitve za Kavkaz: Sbornik statei*. Moscow: Nauka, 1981.

Kay, Alex J. "The Purpose of the Russian Campaign Is the Decimation of the Slavic Population by Thirty Million," in Alex J. Kay, Jeff Rutherford, and David Stahel, eds. *Nazi Policy on the Eastern Front, 1941: Total War, Genocide, and Radicalization*. Rochester, NY: University of Rochester Press, 2012.

———. "Germany's Staatssekretär: Mass Starvation and the Meeting of 2 May 1941." *Journal of Contemporary History* 41, no. 4 (2006): pp. 685-700.

Kerler, Dov-Ber. "The Soviet Yiddish Press: "Eynikayt" during the War, 1942-1945," in Robert Shapiro, ed. *Why Didn't the Press Shout? American and International Journalism during the Holocaust*. Jersey City, NJ: Yeshiva University Press, 2003.

Khairuddinova, E. M. "Osobennosti vzaimootnoshenii Sovetskoi vlasti i musul'man v Krymskoi ASSR (nachalo 20-kh – konets 30-kh gg. XX veka." *Istoricheskie nauki* 24 (63), no. 2 (2011): pp. 134-139.

Khodarkovsky, Michael. "Of Christianity, Enlightenment, and Colonialism: Russia in the North Caucasus, 1550-1800." *The Journal of Modern History* 71, no. 2 (June 1999): pp. 394-430.

Kisilitsyn, Sergei. "Raskazachivanie – strategicheskii kurs Bolshevistskoi politicheskoi elity v 20-kh gg," in *Vozrozhdenie kazachestva: istoriia i sovremennost'*. Novocherkassk: Novocherkasskii gosudarstvennyii universitet, 2001.

Kizilov, Mikhail. "Slaves, Money Lenders, and Prisoner Guards: The Jews and the Trade in Slaves and Captives in the Crimean Khanate." *Journal of Jewish Studies* 58, no. 2 (2007): pp. 189-210.

———. "The Crimean Karaites in the Portrayal of the 19th Century Polish Travelers." *Studia Orientalia* 95 (2003): pp. 93-108.

Klink, Ernst. "The Conduct of Operations," in Horst Boog et al. *The*

Attack on the Soviet Union. Vol. 4 of *Germany and the Second World War*. Oxford: Oxford University Press, 1998.

Kokhan, A. A. "Gazeta "Golos Kryma" v strukture organov nemetskoi propagandy: 1941-1944 gg." *Istorichni i politologichni doslidzhennia* 3-4 (45-46) (2010): pp. 230-236.

Kolesnik, Aleksandr. "Vedinom boevom stroiu: Moskovskoe narodnoe opolchenie v dokumentakh arkhiva Ministerstva Oborony SSSR, 1941-1945 gody." *Sovetskie Arkhivy* [USSR], 6 (1972): pp. 27-31.

Krinko, Evgenii. "Kollaboratsionizm na Kubani v gody Velikoi Otechestvennoi voiny." *Informatsionno-analitechskii vestnik Adygeiskogo respublikanskogo Instituta gumanitarnykh issledovanii (Maikop)* 3 (2002): pp. 221-232.

Kruglov, Aleksandr I. "German Sources on the Holocaust in the Territory of the Former USSR," in Il'ia Altman, ed. *The Holocaust and the Case of the Jewish Anti-Fascist Committee: Proceedings of the Fourth International Conference "Lessons of the Holocaust in Contemporary Russia" held in Moscow on 1-2 October, 2002*. Moscow: Fond "Kholokost," 2002.

———. "Unichtozhenie evreiskogo naseleniia v Krymu v 1941-1942." *Vestnik Evreiskogo Universiteta v Moskve* 15 (1997): pp. 216-232.

Kunz, Norbert. "Die Feld- und Ortskommandaturen auf der Krim und der Judenmord 1941/1942," in Wolf Kaiser, ed. *Täter im Vernichtungskrieg; der Überfall auf der Sowjetunion und der Völkermord an den Juden*. Berlin: Propyläen, 2002.

Kupovetsky, Mark. "Sotsiokul'turnyi analiz formirovaniia kollektivnoi pamiati i mifologem o proiskhozhdenii gorskikh evreev Vostochnogo Kavkaza do 80-kh godov XIX veka." *Etnograficheskoe obozrenie* 6 (2009), pp. 58-73.

———. "Ketnicheskoi istorii krymchakov," in Igor' Krupnik, ed. *Etnokontaktnye zony v evropeiskoi chasti SSSR*. Moscow: MFGO, 1989.

———. "Dinamika chislennosti i rasseleniia karaimov i krymchakov za poslednie dvesti let." *Geografiia i kul'tura etnograficheskikh grupp tatar v SSSR*. Moscow: GO SSSR, 1983.

Kuromiya, Hiroaki. "Why the Destruction of Orthodox Priests in the

Soviet Union in 1937-38?" *Jahrbücher für Geschichte Osteuropas* 55, no. 1 (2007): pp. 86-93.

Lasker, Daniel et al. "Karaites," in Michael Berenbaum and Fred Skolnik, eds. *Encyclopedia Judaica*. 2nd ed. Vol. 11. Detroit: Macmillian Reference USA, 2007.

Loewenthal, Rudolf. "The Extinction of the Krymchaks in World War II." *The American Slavic and East European Review* 10, no. 2 (1951): pp. 130-136.

———. "The Judeo-Tats in the Caucasus." *Historia Judaica* 15 (1952): pp. 51-62.

Lower, Wendy. "The 'reibungslose' Holocaust? The German Military and Civilian Implementation of the 'Final Solution' in Ukraine, 1941-1944," in Gerald D. Feldman and Wolfgang Seibel, eds. *Networks of Nazi Persecution: Bureaucracy, Business and the Organization of the Holocaust*. New York: Berghahn, 2005.

———. "Facilitating Genocide: Nazi Ghettoization Practices in Occupied Ukraine, 1941-1944," in Eric J. Sterling, ed. *Life in the Ghettos During the Holocaust*. Syracuse, N.Y.: Syracuse University Press, 2005.

Lübbers, Gert C. "Die 6. Armee und die Zivilbevölkerung von Stalingrad." *Vierteljahrshefte für Zeitgeschichte* 54, no. 1 (2006): pp. 87-123.

Maiorov, Nikolai. "Krasnodarskii protsess," in Mikhail Kardishev, ed. *Neotvratimoe vozmezdie: Po materialam sudebnykh protsessov nad izmennikami rodiny, fashistskimi palachami, i agentami imperialisticheskikh razvedok*. 2nd ed. Moscow: Voenizdat, 1987.

Mamoulia, Georges. "L'histoire du groupe Caucase (1934-1939)." *Cahiers du Monde russe* 48, no. 1 (Jan. - Mar., 2007): pp. 45-85.

Manoschek, Walter. "'Coming Along to Shoot Some Jews?': The Destruction of the Jews in Serbia," in Hannes Heer and Klaus Naumann, eds. *War of Extermination: The German Military in WWII*. New York and Oxford: Berghahn Books, 2000.

Marrus, Michael R. "Types of Jewish Resistance: Categories and Comparison from the Historiographical Standpoint," in Israel Gutman, ed. *Major Changes within the Jewish People in the Wake of the Holocaust: Proceedings of the Ninth Yad Vashem International*

Historical Conference held in Jerusalem in June 1993. Jerusalem: Yad Vashem, 1996.

Maurach, Reinhart. "Die Karaimen in der russischen Gesetzgebung." *Zeitschrift für Rassenkunde* 10, nos. 2-3 (1939): pp. 163-175.

Mende von, Gerhard. "Die Kalmücken." *Zeitschrift für Geopolitik* 22, no. 7 (1951): pp. 444-445.

Michman, Dan. "Jewish Resistance during the Holocaust and its Implications: Theoretical Notes." (Hebrew). *Dapim le-heker ha-Shoa* 14 (1997): pp. 7-42.

———. "Jewish Religious Life under Nazi Domination: Nazi Attitudes and Jewish Problems." *Studies in Religion/Sciences Religieuses* 22, no. 2 (June 1993): pp. 147-165.

Moldadossova, A. K. and Zharkinbaeva, R. S. "The Problem of Turkey's Neutrality during the Second World War in the Context of International Conferences." *The Journal of Slavic Military Studies* 28, no. 2 (2015): pp. 401-413.

Moskovicz, Wolf and Tukan, Boris. "Krymchak Community: Their History, Culture, and Language" (Hebrew). *Peamim* 14 (1982): pp. 5-31.

Motadel, David. "Islam and Germany's War in the Soviet Borderlands, 1941–5." *Journal of Contemporary History* 48, no. 4 (October 2013): pp. 784-820.

Musial, Bogdan. "The Origins of 'Operation Reinhard': The Decision-Making Process for the Mass Murder of the Jews in the 'Generalgouvernement.'" *Yad Vashem Studies* 28 (2000): pp. 113-153.

Müller, Rolf-Dieter. "From Economic Alliance to a War of Colonial Exploitation," in Horst Boog et al. *The Attack on the Soviet Union*. Vol. 4 of *Germany and the Second World War*. Oxford: Oxford University Press, 1998.

Nesemann, Frank. "Der Sowjetstaat und der Islam 1917-1941," in Christoph Gassenschmidt and Ralph Tuchtenhagen, eds. *Politik und Religion in der Sowjetunion 1917-1941*. Wiesbaden: Harrassowitz, 2001.

Neishtat, Mordekhai and Zand, Michael. "Mountain Jews," in Michael Berenbaum and Fred Skolnik, eds. *Encyclopedia Judaica*. 2nd ed. Vol. 14. Detroit: Macmillian Reference USA, 2007.

Norkina, Ekaterina. "The Origins of Anti-Jewish Policy in the Cossack

Regions of the Russian Empire, Late Nineteenth and Early Twentieth Century." *East European Jewish Affairs* 43, no. 1 (2013): pp. 62-76.

Nurullaev, A. A. "Musul'mane Sovetskogo Soiuza v Velikoi Otechestvennoi voine," in Nikolai Trofimchuk, ed. *Religioznye organizatsii Sovetskogo Soiuza v gody Velikoi Otechestvennoi voiny 1941-1945 gg.: Materialy 'Kruglogo stola.'* Moscow: RAGS, 1995.

Ogurechnikov, Aleksandr. "Prodovol'stvennoe obespechenie v period Velikoi Otechestvennoi voiny (1941-1945 gg.)." *Voenno-istoricheskii arkhiv* 6, no. 21 (2001): pp. 78-105.

Orishev, Aleksandr. "Politika Germanii v Irane nakanune Vtoroi mirovoi voiny." *Novaia i noveishaia istoriia* 6 (2002): pp. 25-36.

Pache, Jörg and Scharlau, Friederike. "Akteure der Vernichtung: Deutsche und sowjetische Täter - ein Vergleich." *Zeitschrift für Geschichtswissenschaft* 57, no. 12 (2009): pp. 973-985.

Pashchenia, Vladimir. "Puti zavoevaniia i uderzhaniia bol'shevikami vlasti v Krymu (1905-1945 gg.)." *Kul'tura narodov Prichernomor'ia* 90 (2006): pp. 118-179.

Patrakova, Valentina and Chernous, Viktor. "Russkie na Severnom Kavkaze: Istoricheskii ekskurs," in Viktor Chernous, ed. *Russkie na Severnom Kavkaze: Vyzovy XXI veka: Sbornik nauchnykh statei.* 2nd enl. ed. Rostov-na-Donu: Izdatel'stvo SKNTs VSh, 2002.

Penter, Tanja. "Collaborators on Trial: New Source Material on Soviet Postwar Trials against Collaborators." *Slavic Review* 64, no. 4 (2005): pp. 782-791.

Perović, Jeronim, "Highland Rebels: The North Caucasus during the Stalinist Collectivization Campaign." *Journal of Contemporary History* 0 (0), pp. 1-27.

Pieper, Henning. "SS-Oberscharführer Walter Kehrer und die 'Kaukasier-Kompanie': Eine Sondereinheit und ihre Rolle im Zweiten Weltkrieg 1942-1944." *Zeitschrift für Geschichtswissenschaft* 56, no. 3 (2008): pp. 197-221.

Pohl, Dieter. "The Murder of Ukraine's Jews under German Military Administration and in the Reich Commissariat Ukraine," in Ray Brandon and Wendy Lower, eds. *The Shoah in Ukraine; History, Testimony, Memorialization.* Bloomington: Indiana University Press in association with the United States Holocaust Memorial Museum, 2010.

———. "Deutsche Militärverwaltung: Die bessere Besatzung? Das Beispiel Kaukasus 1942/43." *Mitteilungen der Gemeinsamen Kommission für die Erforschung der jüngeren Geschichte der deutsch-russischen Beziehungen* 2 (2005).

Polian, Pavel. "First Victims of the Holocaust: Soviet-Jewish Prisoners of War in German Captivity." *Kritika: Explorations in Russian and Eurasian History* 6, no. 4 (2005): pp. 763-787.

Porat, Dina. "The Holocaust in Lithuania: Some Unique Aspects," in David Cesarani, ed. *The Final Solution: Origins and Implementation.* London: Routledge, 1994.

Poulsen, Niels Bo. "War Crime Investigation *po-sovetski*? Evaluating Material from the Extraordinary State Commission." *Kholocaust i suchasnost'* 1, no. 5 (2008): pp. 27-46.

Prusin, Alexander V. "Fascist Criminals to the Gallows!: The Holocaust and Soviet War Crimes Trials, December 1945–February 1946." *Holocaust and Genocide Studies* 17, no. 1 (2003): pp. 1-30.

Radchenko, Iurii. "'We emptied our magazines into them': The Ukrainian Auxiliary Police and the Holocaust in Generalbezirk Charkow, 1941-1943." *Yad Vashem Studies* 41, no. 1 (2013): pp. 63-98.

Rentrop, Petra. "Weißrussland," in Wolfgang Benz and Barbara Distel, eds. *Der Ort des Terrors: Geschichte der nationalsozialistischen Konzentrationslager, band 9.* Munich: C. H. Beck, 2009.

Robert, Geoffrey. "Stalin's Wartime Vision of Peace, 1939-1945," in Tymothy Snyder and Ray Brandon, eds. *Stalin and Europe: Imitation and Domination, 1928-1953.* Oxford; New York: Oxford University Press, 2014.

Romanovskii, Daniil. "The Soviet person as a bystander of the Holocaust: The case of Eastern Belorussia," in David Bankier and Israel Gutman, eds. *Nazi Europe and the Final Solution.* Jerusalem: Yad Vashem International Institute for Holocaust Research, 2003.

Roth, Karl Heinz. "Berlin-Ankara-Baghdad: Franz von Papen and German Near East Policy during the Second World War," in Wolfgang G. Schwanitz, ed. *Germany and the Middle East: 1871–1945.* Princeton, NJ: Max Wiener Publishers, 2004.

Semi, Emanuela T. "The Image of the Karaites in Nazi and Vichy France Documents." *Jewish Journal of Sociology* 32, no. 2 (1990): pp. 81-93.

———. "L'oscillation ethnique: Le cas des Caraites pendant la Seconde Guerre Mondiale." *Revue de l'Histoire des Religions* 206, no. 4 (October-December 1989): pp. 377-398.

Shaldanova, L. "Kholokost na territorii Kalmykii," in Kalmytskii institut gumanitarnykh issledovanii Rossiiskoi akademii nauk et al. , eds. *Velikaia Otechestvennaia voina: sobytiia, liudi, istoriia.* Elista: Dzhangar, 2001.

Shapira, Dan. "Some Notes on the History of the Crimean Jewry from the Ancient Times until the End of the 19th Century, with Emphasis on the Qrimçaq Jews in the First Half of the 19th Century," in Wolf Moskovich and Leonid Finberg, eds. *Jews and Slavs. Vol. 19: Jews, Ukrainians and Russians; Essays on Intercultural Relations.* Jerusalem: The Hebrew University of Jerusalem; Kyiv: Institute of Jewish Studies, 2008.

Shenderovich, Abram. "Zhyzn' i sud'ba." *Paralleli* 13-14 (2015): pp. 318-326.

Shkarovski, Mikhail. "The Attitude of the Russian Orthodox Church and the Ukrainian Greek Catholic Church to the Holocaust during World War II," in John K. Roth and Elisabeth Maxwell-Meynard, eds. *Ethics and Religion.* Vol. 2 of *Remembering for the Future: The Holocaust in an Age of Genocide.* New York: Palgrave, 2001.

———. "O podderzhke Pravoslavnoi tserkvi ne mozhet byt' i rechi': Tserkovnaia politika Natsistskoi Germanii na okkupirovannykh territoriiakh SSSR, 1941–1945 gg." *Istochnik* 6 (2001): pp. 74-96.

Schneppen, Heinz. "Generalkonsul a. D. Dr. Otto Bräutigam: Widerstand und Verstrickung: Eine quellenkritische Untersuchung." *Zeitschrift fur Geschichtswissenschaft* 60, 4 (2012): pp. 301-330.

Shtauber, Roni. "Cooperation between the Wehrmacht and the Einsatzgruppe D in the extermination of the Crimean Jews" (Hebrew). *Massuah* 15 (1987): pp. 212-221.

Shternshis, Anna. "Between Life and Death: Why Some Soviet Jews Decided to Leave and Others to Stay in 1941." *Kritika: Explorations in Russian and Eurasian History* 15, no. 3 (Summer 2014): pp. 477-504.

Shveibish, Semeon. "Evakuatsiia i sovetskie evrei v gody Katastrofy." *Vestnik Evreiskogo Universiteta v Moskve* 9 (1995): pp. 36-55.

Simonova, A. "Gery i subbotniki v opisanii anonimnogo rostovskogo sionista (osen' 1917 g.)." *Vestnik Evreiskogo Universiteta v Moskve* 1, no. 17 (1998): pp. 193-199.

Solonari, Vladimir. "Hating Soviets — Killing Jews: How Antisemitic Were Local Perpetrators in Southern Ukraine, 1941–42?" *Kritika: Explorations in Russian and Eurasian History* 15, no. 3 (Summer 2014): pp. 505-533.

Sorokina, Marina. "People and Procedures. Toward a History of the Investigation of Nazi Crimes in the USSR." *Kritika: Explorations in Russian and Eurasian History* 6, no. 4 (2005): pp. 797-831.

Spektor, Shmuel. Mass Flight and their Connection with the Jewish Uprising" (Hebrew), in Israel Gutman, ed. *Major Changes within the Jewish People in the Wake of the Holocaust: Proceedings of the Ninth Yad Vashem International Historical Conference held in Jerusalem in June 1993.* Jerusalem: Yad Vashem, 1996.

———. "The Holocaust of the Krymchak Jews during the Nazi Occupation" (Hebrew). *Peamim* 27 (1986): pp. 18-27.

———. "The Karaites in German-Dominated Europe in the Light of the German Documents" (Hebrew). *Peamim* 29 (1986): pp. 90-108.

Statiev, Aleksandr. "The Nature of Anti-Soviet Armed Resistance, 1942-44: The North Caucasus, the Kalmyk Autonomous Republic, and the Crimea." *Kritika: Explorations in Russian and Euroasian History* 6, no. 2 (Spring 2005): pp. 285-318.

Steinberg, Jonathan. "The Third Reich Reflected: German Civil Administration in the Occupied Soviet Union, 1941-4." *The English Historical Review* 110, no. 437 (June 1995): pp. 620-651.

Tatarov, Azamat. "Musul'manskie prazdniki v politike Tret'iego Reikha sredi gortsev Severnogo Kavkaza v 1942-1944 gg." *Nauchnyi zhyrnal KubGAU* 110 (2015): pp. 592-607.

———. "Sel'skokhoziaistvennye resursy Severnogo Kavkaza v ekonomicheskoi strategii Germanii v 1942-1944 gg." *Nauchnyi zhyrnal KubGAU* 107 (2015): pp. 484-907.

Tavanets, S. D. "Chislennost' zhertv Kholokosta na territorii Kalmykii". In Kalmytskii institut gumanitarnykh issledovanii Rossiiskoi akademii nauk et al., eds. *Velikaia Otechestvennaia voina: Sobytiia, liudi, istoriia.* Elista: Dzhangar, 2001.

Tiaglyi, Mikhail. "Antisemitic doctrine in the Tatar newspaper "Azat Kirim" (1942-1944)." *Dapim; Studies on the Shoah* 25, no. 1 (2011): pp. 161-182.

———. "Were the 'Chingené' Victims of the Holocaust? Nazi Policy toward the Crimean Roma, 1941-1944." *Holocaust and Genocide Studies* 23, no. 1 (2009): pp. 26-53.

———. "The Role of Antisemitic Doctrine in German Propaganda in the Crimea, 1941–1944." *Holocaust and Genocide Studies* 18, no. 3 (2004): pp. 421-459.

Tighe, Carl. "Six, Franz Alfred: A Career in the Shadows." *Journal of European Studies* 37, no. 1 (2007): pp. 5-50.

Torzecki, Ryszard. "Die Rolle der Zusammenarbeit mit der deutschen Besatzungsmacht in der Ukraine für der Okkupationspolitik," in Werner Röhr, ed. *Okkupation und Kollaboration (1938-1945): Beiträge zu Konzepten und Praxis der Kollaboration in der deutschen Okkupationspolitik*. Berlin and Heidelberg: Huethig Verlagsgemeischaft, 1994.

Veprintsev, V. B. and Mochalin, I. A. "Bandity stremilis'... sokhranit' fashistskii poriadok." *Voenno-Istoricheskii Zhurnal* 5 (1996): pp. 83-89.

Vershitskaia, Tamara. "Jewish Women Partisans in Belarus." *Journal of Ecumenical Studies* 46, no. 4 (2011): pp. 567-572.

Vikhnovich, Vsevolod. "Massovye etnicheskie deportatsii iz Kryma v 1944-1945 gg. i Krymskie karaimy." *Paralleli* 4-5 (2004): pp. 87-98.

Vol'fson, Bentsion. "Krovavye prestupleniia nemtsev v Kerchi." *Istoricheskii zhurnal* 8, 108 (1942): pp. 33-36.

Wegner, Bernd. "The War Against the Soviet Union, 1942-1943," in Horst Boog, et al. *The Global War, Germany and the Second World War*. Vol. 6, *The Global War: Widening the Conflict into a World War and the Shift of the Initiative 1941-1943*. Oxford: Clarendon, 2001.

Weinerman, Eli. "Racism, Racial Prejudice and Jews in Late Imperial Russia." *Ethnic and Racial Studies* 17, no. 3 (1994): pp. 442-495.

Wenzel, Mario. "Zwangasarbeiterslager für Juden in den besetzten polnischen und sowjetischen Gebieten," in Wolfgang Benz and Barbara Distel, eds. *Der Ort des Terrors: Geschichte der nationalsozialistischen Konzentrationslager*. Vol. 9. Munich: C. H. Beck, 2009.

Westerhoff, Christian. "'A Kind of Siberia': German Labour and Occupation Policies in Poland and Lithuania during the First World War." *First World War Studies* 4, no. 1 (2013): pp. 51-63.

Wilhelm, Hans-Heinrich. "Der SD und die Kirchen in den besetzten Ostgebieten 1941/42." *Militärgeschichtliche Mitteilungen* 29, no. 1 (1981): pp. 55-99.

Williams, Brian G. "The Hidden Cleansing of Muslims in the Soviet Union: The Exile and Repatriation of the Crimean Tatars." *Journal of Contemporary History* 37, no. 3 (2002): pp. 323-348.

Zand, Michael. "Notes on the Culture of the Non-Ashkenazi Jewish Communities under Soviet Rule," in Yaacov Ro'i and Avi Beker, eds. *Jewish Culture and Identity in the Soviet Union.* New York, London: New York University Press, 1991.

Zarubin, Viacheslav. "M. M. Vinaver i Krym." Viktoriia Mochalova, et al., eds. *Materialy 11 Ezhegodnoi Mezhdistsiplinarnoi konferentsii po iudaike.* Moscow: Sefer i Institut Slavianovedeniia RAN, 2004.

Zeidler, Manfred. "Das 'Kaukasische Experiment': Gab es seine Weisung Hitlers zur deutschen Besatzungspolitik im Kaukasus?" *Vierteljahre für Zeitgeschichte* 53, no. 3 (2005): pp. 475-500.

———. "Der Minsker Kriegsverbrechenerprozeß vom Januar 1946: Kritische Anmerkungen zu einem Sowjetischem Schauprozeß gegen Deutsche Kriegsgefangenen." *Vierteljahrshefte für Zeitgeschichte* 52, no. 2 (2004): pp. 211-244.

Zhuravlev, Evgenii. "Nemetskii okkupatsyonnyi rezhym i religioznyi vopros na yuge Rossii v gody Velikoi Otechestvennoi voiny." *Nauchnye problem gumanitarnykh issledovanii* 4 (2009): pp. 25-32.

Index

Names

Subject

Geographical